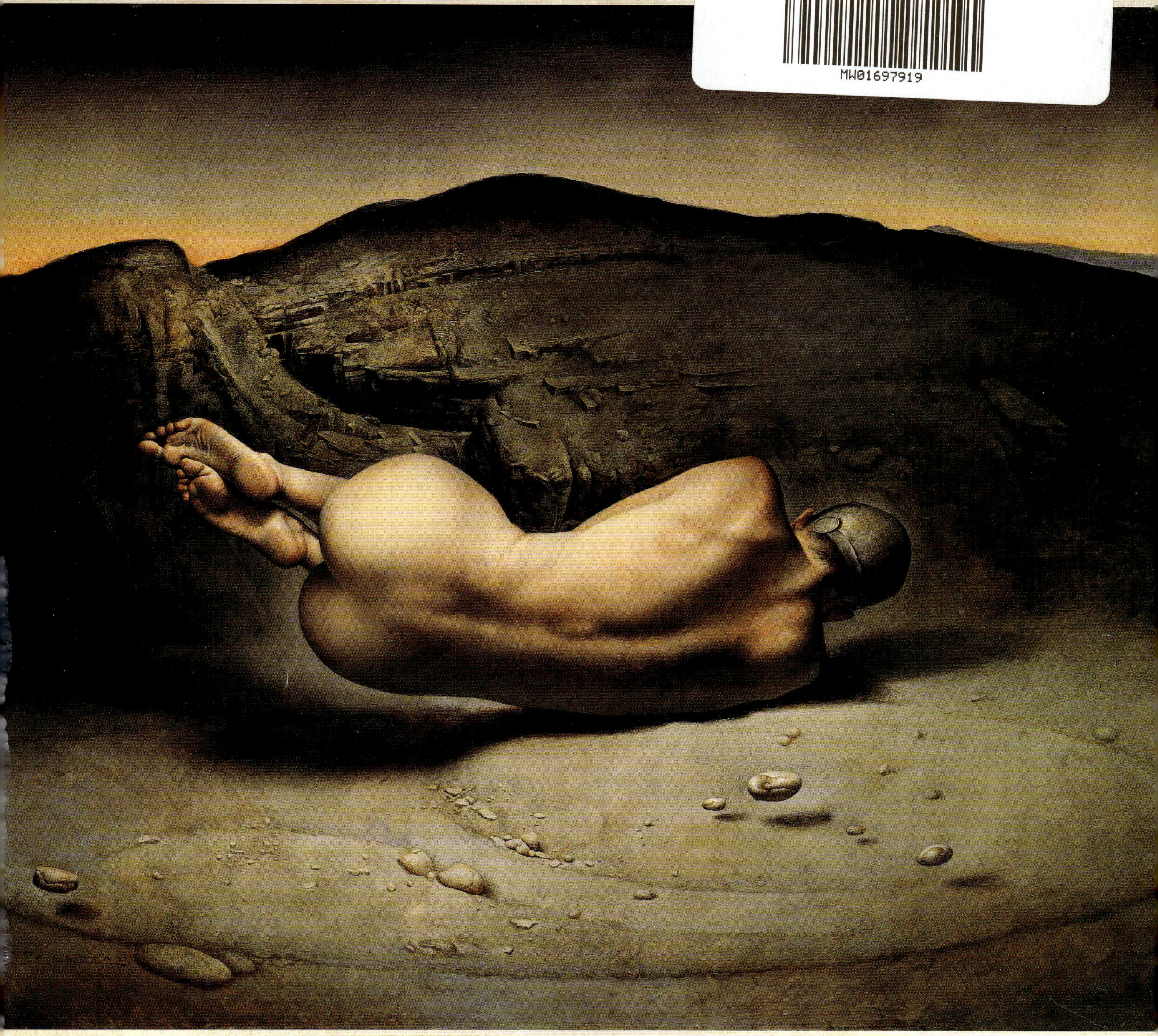

SPeCTRuM | 7

For information on limited edition fine art prints by James Christensen and Scott Gustafson call The Greenwich Workshop at 1-800-243-4246.

Trade Softcover Edition ISBN 1-887424-55-5
Hardcover Edition ISBN 1-887424-54-7
10 9 8 7 6 5 4 3 2 1

Special thanks to John Jude Palencar, Joe DeVito, Rick Berry, and Bud Plant for always being willing pitch in and get their hands dirty.

This edition of *Spectrum* is gratefully dedicated to
TIM UNDERWOOD
We had kicked around the idea of *Spectrum* for ten years before Tim, alone among all the other publishers we had approached, stepped up to the plate and said, "I'll do it."
His vision, and friendship, is the reason you've all been able to enjoy seven volumes in this series.
Thanks, Tim.

UNDER WOOD BOOKS

Published by UNDERWOOD BOOKS, P.O. BOX 1609, GRASS VALLEY, CA 95945
www.underwoodbooks.com
TIM UNDERWOOD / *Publisher*

Chairman's Message

This seventh addition to the *Spectrum* series wasn't intended to be the largest volume yet. At 200 pages and more than 200 artists it's a weighty tome. Our publisher, Tim Underwood, did the math, showed us the projected increase in production expenses, calculated the costs of shipping, figured all the variables. What could we do?

Blame the artists. It's all their fault for creating remarkable work throughout last year.

Spectrum is the result of an annual Call For Entries: each Fall we mail out posters to artists around the world inviting them to take part in the competition. Participation is open to everyone and is strictly voluntary. Structured similarly to other general art competitions and annuals (like those sponsored by the Society of Illustrators and *Communication Arts*), *Spectrum* is unique in its focus on works which embrace the themes of science fiction, fantasy, horror, the surreal, and the uncategorizable. The best in fantastic art. Though some in the fine arts community have questioned our use of the term "fantastic art" (they prefer it be applied to Magritte-inspired symbolists), we believe the subtitle applies. There is a world full of interpretations and sensibilities out there and *Spectrum* embraces them all.

The *Spectrum 7* jury convened in Kansas City in February, 2000 to make selections for this book from just under 3000 entries. Rough weather and flight delays created havoc with the travel of virtually every out-of-town judge; the difficulties may well have contributed to a bonding among the jury that resulted in an enjoyable, if frenzied, weekend for all involved. They laughed, they bumped heads, they argued and joked: an unwitting symbol of the creative community that annually puts aside its differences and pulls together to make this book possible. One variation this year from past judging events was the selection of award-winners in each category: instead of a straight vote, majority wins, we allowed the jury to debate the merits of each work under consideration. Judges were excluded from any discussions revolving around the consideration of their own works.

The final results you'll find in the pages ahead.

Our thanks to the jurors, the artistic community, and the readers for once again making *Spectrum* possible.

Cathy Fenner & Arnie Fenner

The Jury

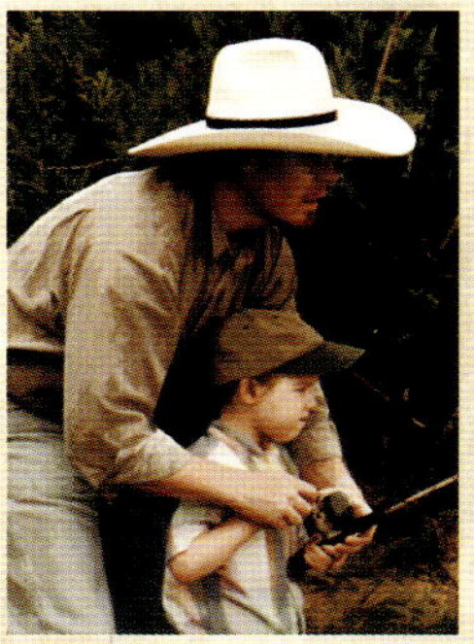

Rick Berry/artist
with daughter Nora

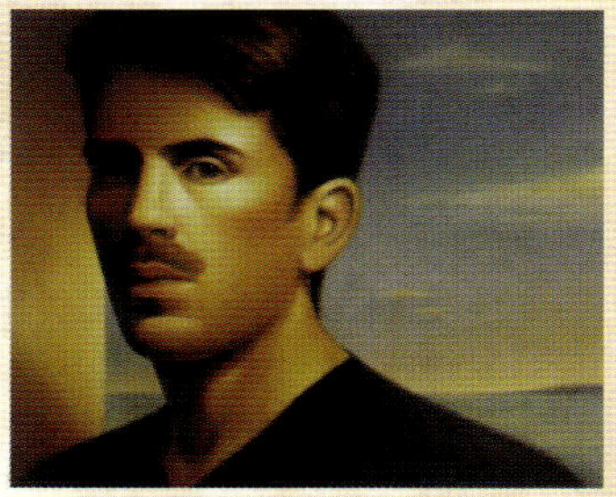

Vern Dufford/artist

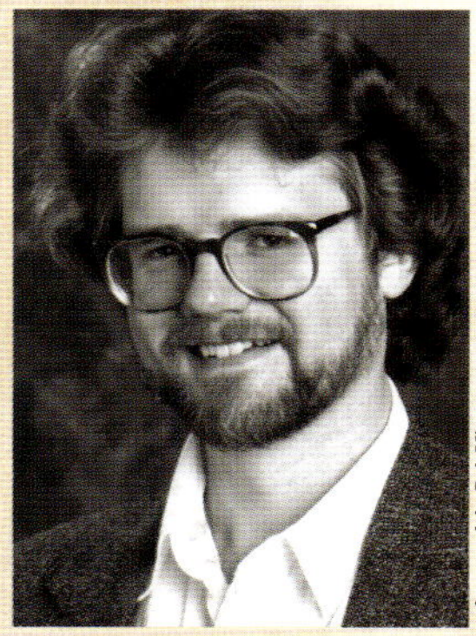

photograph by Bob Hixon

Scott Gustafson/artist

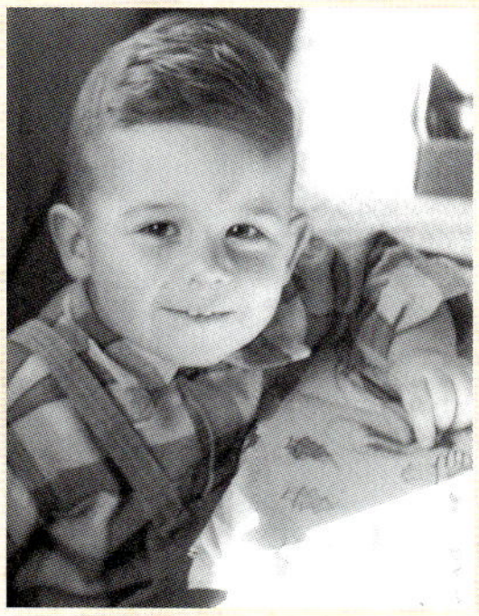

Bob Haas/artist

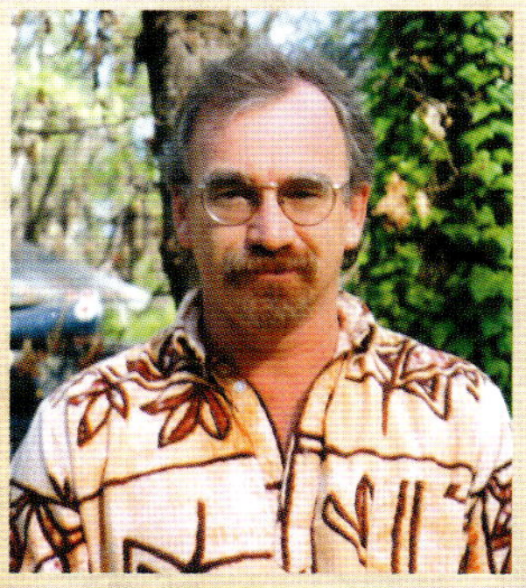

Bud Plant/illustration historian

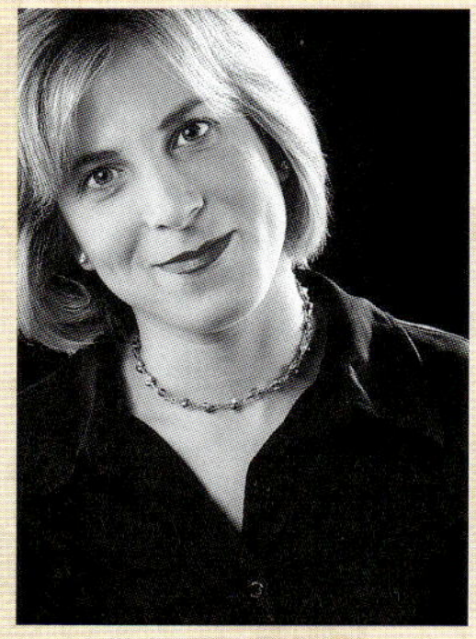

Toby Schwartz/art director
Doubleday Direct

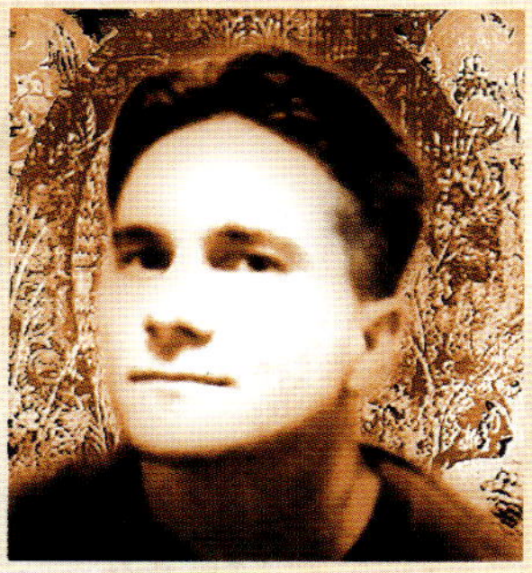

Greg Spalenka/artist

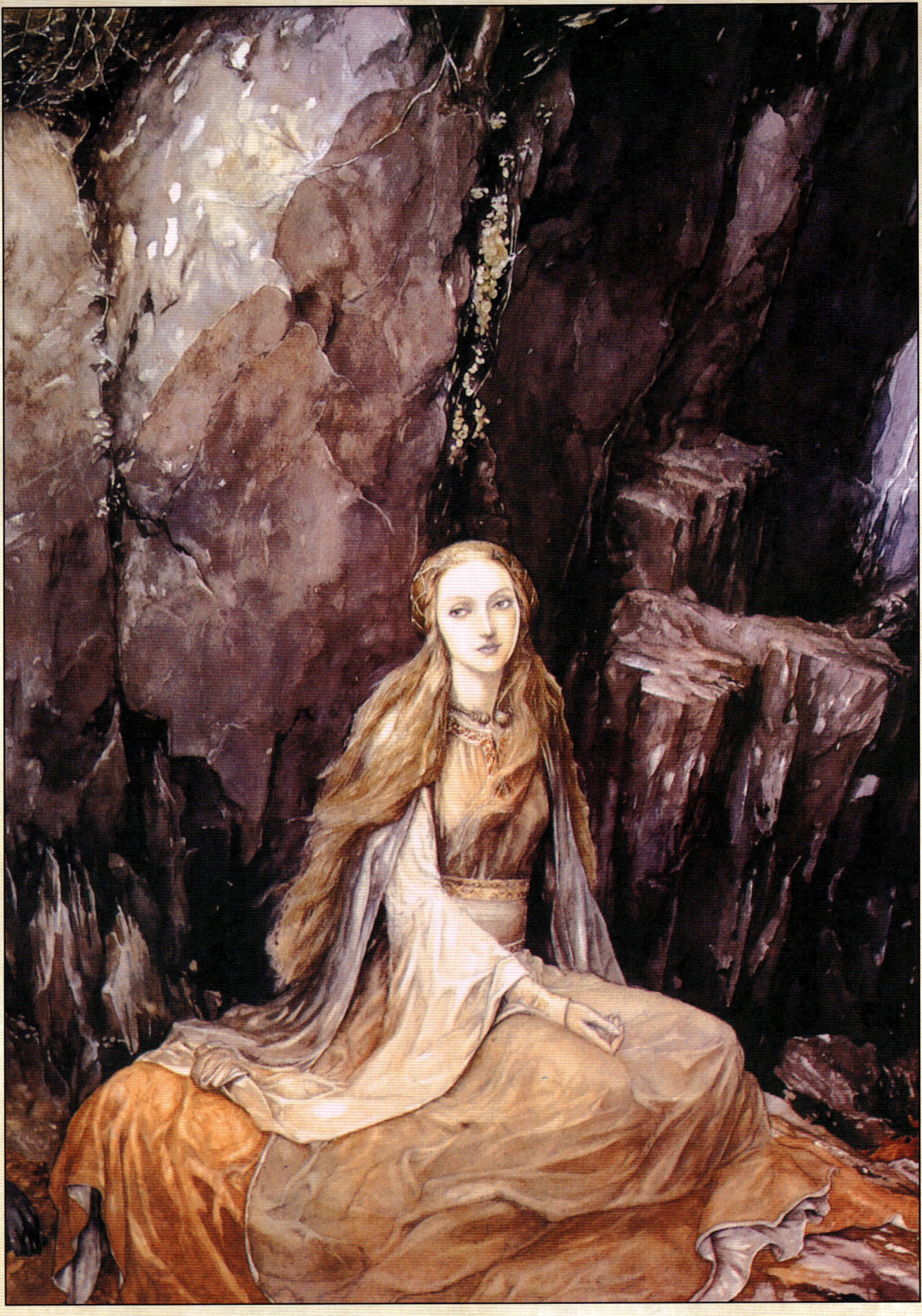

Alan LEE

G R A N D   M A S T E R   A W A R D

"The first books I remember reading were fairy stories," Alan Lee reveals, "and visits to the local library soon became focused on the myths and legends section—but my fate was really sealed when I was allowed to stay up late one night to watch Alexander Korda's wonderful fantasy film, *The Thief of Baghdad.* As a child I built castles from earth, stone, or cardboard, creating stories with plastic knights and imaginary monsters. However, I soon discovered that it was just as satisfying to play out these dramas and romances with pencil and paper and when I found that one piece of paper was not enough for all the convolutions of a story, my drawings started to take the form of comic strips."

Born in Harrow, Middlesex, Alan Lee cultivated an interest in Celtic and Norse mythology throughout his childhood. From 1966 to 1969 he studied at the Ealing School of Art in London, where he filled several portfolios which reflected his passion and ultimately the direction his career would take. David Larkin of Panther Books gave him his first professional assignments—covers for a series of comic novels by Colin Spencer—and Lee was quickly enmeshed in the hectic world of commercial art.

In 1975 he moved to Devon and began sharing studio space with Brian Froud. "I spent a year or so producing 125 color illustrations for a poorly paid book on 'the mysterious', which mysteriously disappeared, but then had the great good fortune to meet Ian and Betty Ballantine," Lee remembers. "I did some work for them on a book called *Once Upon a Time,* which was edited and designed by David Larkin, and shortly afterward they invited Brian and myself to collaborate on a book about fairies to follow their successful publication of *Gnomes* by Rien Poortrliet."

Still in print nearly 25 years later, *Faeires* introduced Lee and Froud to an international audience and the royalties afforded Alan the time to illustrate *The Mabinogion*, the collection of Welsh legends for Dragon's Dream. Working on the book was a life-long ambition and Lee's meticulous art exhibit his love for his subject matter. From there he proceeded to provide the art for a wide variety books (including exceptional work for Rosemary Suttcliff's retelling of *The Iliad* and *The Odyssey: Black Ships Before Troy* and *The Wanderings of Odysseus*) and contributed to the design of such films as *Legend*, *Eric the Viking*, and the TV movie *Merlin.*

Since the success of *Faeries*, however, Alan Lee has become best known in recent years for his watercolor illustrations for *The Hobbit* and *The Lord of the Rings.* Though many artists have produced memorable interpretations of the denizens of Middle Earth, Lee's name has arguably become synonymous with Tolkien's: his almost monochromatic panels capture a dignity and, at the same time, a sense of melancholy that sets him apart from other *Rings* painters. His definitive interpretations were also recognized by the director of the forthcoming film adaptations, Peter Jackson: he flew Alan to New Zealand for the better part of a year to help design the movie. "I read *The Lord of the Rings* as a teenager and felt that Tolkien had taken every element of all the myths and legends I'd read to that date and woven them into a seamless narrative," Lee says. "More importantly, he had created a vast, beautiful landscape that dwarfed its inhabitants and would endure long after they had departed."

In the commercial art world everything is a compromise, everything is due yesterday, everything is reliant on the whims of the client: that Alan Lee has been able pursue his passions without deviating from his course and with a clarity of vision is a tribute to his talent, patience, and perseverance. That his reputation among artists and readers continues to grow with each new work proves that his choices were and are correct.

As the creator of a body of work which challenges our perceptions, which delights our imaginations and which reawakens our sense of wonder, Alan Lee is an artist who will, like Tolkien's landscapes, endure in our memories.

born 1947 | Middlesex, England

The Year In Review

When people look back on 1999, in all likelihood it will be considered the year of frenzied hype and promotion; twelve months in which form was often more important than substance, when glitz and surface gloss *were* the substance. Regis kept asking, "Who wants to be a millionaire?" and as a nation we raised our hands and shouted in unison, "Me!" in the vain hope of being rewarded for remembering the answers to Trivial Pursuit® questions. Bigger, bolder, wilder, newer: the close of the century seemed to be an adjective waiting to happen. In the film adaptation of *Inherit the Wind* Spencer Tracy relates to Frederic March the story of a rocking horse named Golden Dancer on display in a store window which he coveted as a boy. On Christmas morning he finds Golden Dancer under the tree, thanks to the sacrifices of his parents; Tracy tells how he joyfully hopped on the horse...and it instantly broke into pieces. It was made of rotten wood and sawdust, all held together with a veneer of spit and varnish.

1999 witnessed a lot of hucksters hawking glittering wares or spouting lofty ideals just as an equal number of spin doctors worked overtime at damage control as their own "Golden Dancers" collapsed under the weight of their own breathless promotions or pretentious pronouncements. *Star Wars: The Phantom Menace* employed a healthy number of talented artists and, despite the shadow of hyped-expectations, was able to satisfy fans of the franchise. On the other hand, Warners' superb *The Iron Giant* undeservedly played to empty houses and was quickly relegated to the video rental shelves. *Pokémon* pandemonium grew to such proportions that it was parodied on the irreverent *South Park* while the low-budget, documentary-style conceit of *The Blair Witch Project*, combined with savvy web promotion, overwhelmed the outsider-cynicism of the GenX target audience. Geof Darrow's designs for *The Matrix* created the look and uniform of choice for cyberpunk wannabes everywhere almost at the same time that his and Frank Miller's *Big Guy & Rusty the Boy Robot* animated series (based on their Dark Horse comic) for Fox Kids TV crashed and burned. The wonderful and unique Words and Pictures Museum in Northampton, Massachussetts closed its doors for the last time, selling some of its collection through Sotheby's—and was promptly resurrected as a virtual museum on the web. (Unfortunately, it's sort of like "new" Coke™: it's just not the same.) We were swamped with e-commerce technobabble as Internet stock prices soared almost as high as Internet business debt. We watched multinational, multimedia companies merge, morph, and roll over the competition while the independent mom&pop entrepreneur helplessly cried foul (then ran around the corner and eroded the corporations' profitability by offering similar goods and services faster, better, and cheaper). We became furious as the number of copyright infringements by cretinous thieves on the Internet increased almost unabated, were reservedly optimistic as the Graphic Artists Guild joined the UAW/AFL/CIO union, chortled as NY's Mayor Giuliani became apoplectic over the "Sensations" art exhibition, and shook our heads as parent groups attacked the Harry Potter books for their "promotion" of witchcraft. Everything out of Hollywood was a "blockbuster," everything out of New York was a "break-out bestseller," and everything offered on eBay, the online auction site, was "rare" or "sexy" or both. We shuddered at the ceaseless apocalyptic predictions of a global computer meltdown and the repercussions of same come the mythic Y2K—and observed the calendar rollover without much of a hitch at midnight on New Year's Eve.

Certainly, every year has its share of people and products and events that are repeatedly pushed and promoted to the point of over-saturation and burn-out. But throughout 1999 it seemed that the hype machine was jammed in overdrive as everyone tried to stretch Andy Warhol's proverbial fifteen minutes of fame (and ostensibly a shot at your wallet) to the bursting point. Equally certain, however, was that quality ultimately wins out; that the work of creators with skill and originality will remain fresh in our minds for years to come just as the allegorical "Golden Dancers" are discarded and quickly forgotten.

That's the theory, anyway.

---

opposite: Don Maitz's cover painting for *Sorcerer's Gun* by Peter Garrison for Berkley Publishing (oil on masonite, 18"x27": Judy Murello, art director).

Arnie Fenner

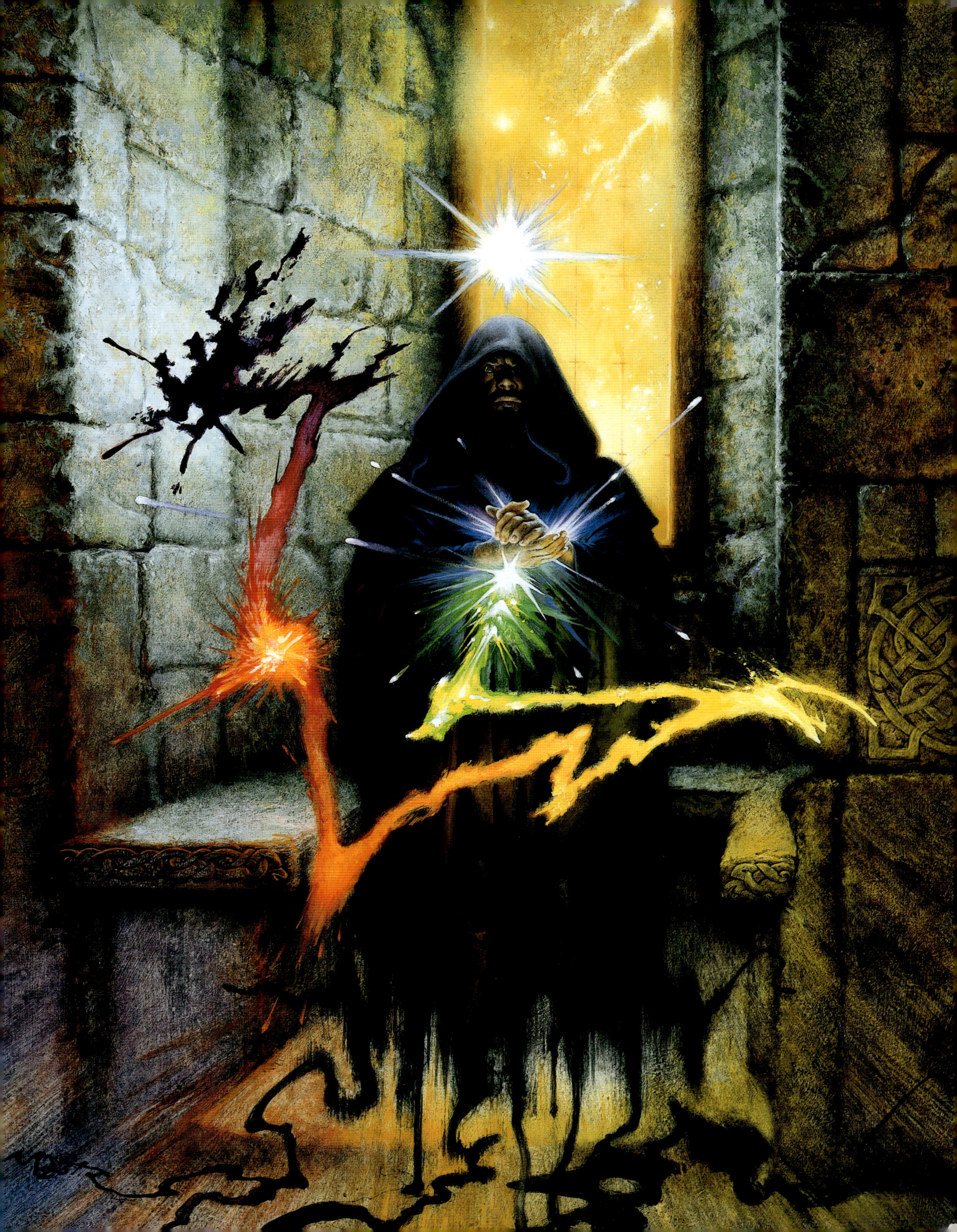

A D V E R T I S I N G

In the "good old days" of Madison Avenue, if a client wanted an unlikely and complicated situation for their product the ad agency would turn to an illustrator to make the idea "real." Dancing animals, Martian consumers, even the idealized American family, all were brought to life by a talented artist with a pencil and a paintbrush. Subsequently advertising accounts were the most lucrative for illustrators.

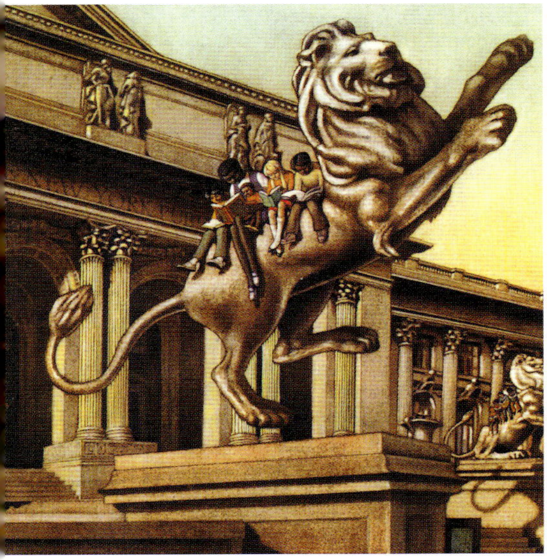

This excellent promotional poster by Grand Masters Leo and Diane Dillon was created for the 21st "New York is Book Country" fair.

Now days, with the widespread use of the computer and CGI, with the ability to make the illusion indistinguishable from reality, designers and photographers rule the ad biz. Illustrators count themselves fortunate when they're called in for work on retro-chic or cartoon-flavor campaigns.

Oh for the days of yore.

The nature of the advertising business make crediting notable efforts extremely difficult, if not impossible. Spotted were Joe Sorren's ad for Morrow Snowboards and Jody Hewgill's poster for the Arena Stage production of "How I learned to Drive"; I recognized some admirable work by Mark Summers, Bill Mayer, Brad Holland, and Rafal Olbinski, but only because their styles are readily identifiable.

B O O K S

Okay, when it comes to e-books I'm a Luddite. Old fashioned. Crusty. A poop.

Because I don't give a tinker's damn about all the buzz surrounding the future of electronic books. Regardless of NY's investments and ultimate pronouncements, I *don't want* books that are printed on-site (doesn't *that* concept show a huge amount of confidence by the publisher in their authors!), down-loaded from a server, or can only be perused when powered by a battery or plugged into an outlet. Don't give me all the stuff about dead trees: I *want* the tactile feel of paper, the smell of ink, the sound of rustling pages. So sue me.

Of course, lately the publishing industry as a whole rarely seems to be as interested in *books* as they are in the *perceptions* of books. The race to embrace electronic product certainly stems from envy of the hi-tech zillionaire boys' club rather than market savvy or perceived need: e-stuff is sexy and creates a media buzz. All of which is preferable to thinking about, oh, worrisome things like HarperCollins' purchase of Morrow/Avon. Or the downsizing and reorganization of Random House. Or the purchase by the British bookstore chain W.H. Smith of the U.K.'s Hodder Headline, the third largest publishing company in England. Or DK's disastrous overly-optimistic gamble on their *Star Wars: The Phantom Menace* tie-in books, which resulted in over $40 million in losses and culminated in the sale of the company. Or the bankruptcy and liquidation of the General Publishing Group. Yeah, come to think of it, it's lots more fun to think about the latest gimmick. At least until that sexy gimmick comes back to bite you on the financial ass.

Thankfully there were tons of memorable, traditionally produced compilations and covers published throughout 1999 that didn't require electricity, a monitor, or a gig of ram to view.

The worldwide success of R.K. Rowling's three Harry Potter novels made Mary GranPré *the* jacket artist of the hour. Her charming interpretations for the books and the covers of *Time* and *Nickelodeon* established a look that will be hard to match for the army of licensers ready to unleash a mountain of product in 2000. The really nice thing about Harry Potter fever and the associated art is that it reinforces what we've always known: there's an appreciative audience for illustration. And some of the *best* narrative artists are working in the f&sf fields. Examples? How about Donato Giancola's cover for *Dragon Shadow* by Barbara Hambly (Del Rey), or Michael Deas' for *Hell House* by Richard Matheson (Tor), or Manuel Sanjulian's for *Imperium Without End* by Lisa Mason (Bantam), or George Pratt's for *Walk In Hell* by Harry Turtledove (Del Rey)? Want more proof? Look no further than the paintings by John Berkey (*The Rift* by Walter Jon Williams/Harper Prizm), John Jude Palencar (*The Wild Swans* by Peg Kerr/Warner-Aspect), Alan Lee (*Prospero's Children* by Jan Siegel/ Voyager), Yvonne Gilbert (*The Winter Queen* by Devin Cary/Ace), and Thomas Canty (*Silver Birch, Blood Moon* edited by Ellen Datlow and Terri Windling/Avon). Other covers of merit were created by Bruce Jenson, Harry O. Morris, Doug Beekman, Jody Lee, Rick Berry, Geoff Taylor, Bob Eggleton, Michael Whelan, Kamil Vojnar, Rowena Morrill, and Gary Ruddell, among a host of others.

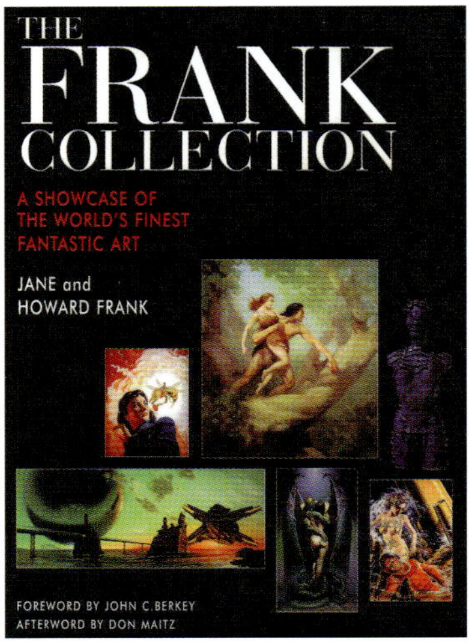

Collectors eat your hearts out! Paper Tiger chronicled Jane and Howard Frank's enviable collection.

Some of the illustrated volumes of note included James Gurney's long-awaited sequel, *Dinotopia: First Flight* (Harper Collins), *Women Warriors* by Marianna Mayer (Morrow) with paintings by Julek Heller, and *We Goddesses* by Doris Orgel (DK) with art by Marilee Heyer. The Dillons provided typically wonderful illustrations for *Wind Child* by Shirley Murphy (HarperCollins) and Kinuko Y. Craft's enchanting paintings enhanced daughter Charlotte Craft's retelling of *King Midas and the Golden Touch* (Morrow). Also creating worthwhile work were Jon J Muth (*Come On, Rain* by Karen Hesse), Paul O. Zelinsky (*Five Children and It* by E. Nesbit), and Barry Moser (*The Holy Bible*, available in editions priced at a whopping $10K and $30K—Holy Moses!).

The year saw a welcome host of single artist collections, including *Transluminal* by Hugo-winner Jim Burns and *A Cosmic Cornucopia* by Josh Kirby (Paper Tiger), *Legacy* by Grand Master Frank Frazetta (Underwood Books), *Dreams* by Boris Vallejo and *Soft As Steel* by the underrated Julie Bell (both from Thunder's Mouth Press), and another *Dreams* by the always intriguing Luis Royo (NMB). Royo had a second book published by Heavy Metal entitled *Prohibited*. Fantagraphics released the delightfully perplexing *Barry Windsor-Smith: Opus,* the first in a projected series of Smith art books, Manuel Auad edited *Toth: Black & White*, a celebration of one of best damn designers in the history of the comics, period, and *Wizard* magazine branched out to publish the respectable *Alex Ross Millennium.* Heavy Metal produced a real gem with *Overload: The Art of Juan Giménez,* Vanguard produced *The Neal Adams Sketchbook,* Abrams' *Maxfield Parrish: 1870-1966* examined one of our most popular artists, Pomegranate offered *Charles Bragg: The Works* by Alan Bisbort, and Terry Gilliam was showcased in *Dark Knights and Holy Fools* by Bob McCabe (St. Martin's Press). Illustration Books spotlighted Izubuchi Yutaka in *Record of the LoDoss War Illustrations: Anam* and 3-D master Yasushi Nirasawa in *Niragram.*

Anthology art compilations in '99 were plentiful as always. Personal favorites included *The Art of the National Geographic* edited by Alice Carter (National Geographic), featuring paintings from Wyeth to Lovell to Gurney; *The Frank Collection* by Jane and Howard Frank (Paper Tiger), an eclectic mix of the wonderful with the not, but a memorable tour nonetheless; *Fantasy Art Masters* by Dick Jude (Watson Guptill), which included great selections by and profiles of Alan Lee, Brom, John Howe, and Rick Berry, among others; *The Art of Vampire: The Masquerade* (White Wolf), a Goth-lover's fantasy come true with effective work by Tim Bradstreet, John Bolton, and Bill Sienkiewicz; and *Devilman Illustrations* (Illustration Books), consisting of interpretations of Go Nagai's anime creation by such talents as Tadanori Yakoo and Yoshitaka Amano. SQP was probably the most active art monograph publisher with their growing line of fantasy pin-up collections: their latest additions were *Eternal Temptation* and *Crimson Embrace Vol. 5.* Both included drawings by Joe Chiodo, Rich Larson and Steve Fastner, Mike Hoffman, and Esteban Maroto. A final trio of favorites that sort of fit in the anthology classification were *The Tarzan Chronicles* by Howard Green (Hyperion), a look at the creation of Disney's animated adaptation of Burroughs' Ape Man, with tons of wonderful conceptual art; *Science Fiction of the 20th Century* (Collector's Press), Frank Robinson's colorful follow-up to last year's *Pulp Culture;* and finally, *Superman Masterpiece Edition* (Chronicle) by Les Daniels was a fun salute to *the* comics icon, and even included a really nifty statue by Joe DeVito.

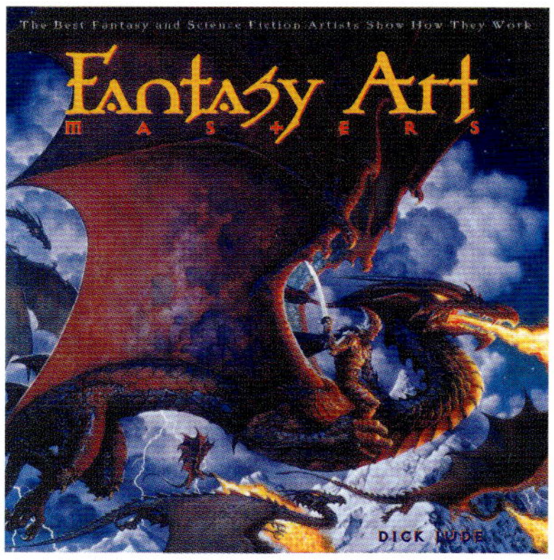

Alan Lee and Dave McKean were among the artists profiled in Dick Jude's book.

With all the superstores and all the web booksellers you might think it would be easy to track down virtually all of the illustrated books on your list: it just ain't so. That's why I continue to suggest Bud Plant Comic Art as the single best resource for people interested in all types of art-related products: I've yet to find anyone else that matches their inventory, variety, and customer service. Catalogs are available for $3 from Bud Plant Comic Art, P.O. Box 1689, Grass Valley, CA 95945/800-242-6642/www.budplant.com.

C O M I C S

I suppose the argument could be made that the comics are the Rodney Dangerfield of the entertainment industry: they don't get no respect. They're routinely dismissed as "kid stuff" at the same time children's books are lauded: when they've tackled adult subject matter they're attacked in turn by zealous parent groups and prosecutors. Hollywood routinely mines the field to make mediocre films which flop at the box office (*Mystery Men* is a recent example) and each failure seems to take the luster off of previous rare successes. At the same time many of the best creators were (and are) lured away to more profitable venues (like, hunh, film and TV) and were only heard or seen occasionally, if at all. Sales were easily half what they were seven years ago, prices appeared to be on a steadily upward spiral, and seemingly the most profitable item in your favorite funnybook store (brick & mortar or virtual) were superhero action figures. Toys for aging fanboys.

God, I love comics.

And what's *not* to love? There's high drama and bitter feuds and camaraderie and pretension and gut-wrenching battles—and that's just among the artists, fans, and publishers. How *anything* ever makes it into the shops (which are mostly run by Drew Friedman characters) is anyone's guess. And sure, Sturgeon's law certainly applies to the books that *are* released: 90% are crap. But if you recall the rest of the caveat you know that 90% of *everything* is crap. It's the hunt for that elusive 10% that makes comics fun: it's being able to *find* that 10% that is the ray of hope for an unappreciated wholly American art form.

DC Comics was once again the most diverse and interesting of the Big Boy publishers. Adult titles, children's comics, franchise characters, experimental concepts, and untraditional artists: they had it all throughout the year. Where else could readers find creators as diverse as Phil Hale and Sue Coe (covers for *Flinch*), Travis Charest (covers for the Wildstorm imprint's *Wildcats*) and Mike Kaluta (covers for *The Books of Magic*); as Alex Ross (*Batman: War On Crime*, written by Paul Dini) and Dan Bereton (who wrote and painted the *Giantkiller* mini-series)? Nowhere, I betcha. John Van Fleet turned in a bravura performance with *Batman: The Chalice* (written by Chuck Dixon), Dave McKean's new covers for *The Dreaming* reprints stopped browsers in their tracks, Ted McKeever produced the edgy and excellent *Faith* (which he also wrote) and *Batman: Nosferatu* (scripted by Randy and Jean-Marc Lofficier), and Adam Hughes' covers for *Wonder Woman* were eye-poppers that made me shell-out for a comic I normally don't buy. Other notable DC work was created by Scott Hampton (*Lucifer*), Tony Harris (*Starman*), John K. Syder II (*Dr. Mid-Nite*), Essad Ribic (*Four Horsemen*), Glen Fabry (*Preacher*), Charles Vess and Hermann Mejia (both for *The Books of Fairie*), and Tim Sale (*Batman: Dark Victory*). Of course the biggest buzz about DC, both within the industry and in the mainstream press, surrounded the heirs of Jerry Siegel (co-creator with Joe Shuster of Superman) move to reclaim half of the copyright to The Man of Steel. The debates over whether it could or should happen and what the financial implications might be kept magazines and Internet sites busy, but DC maintained a professional attitude and

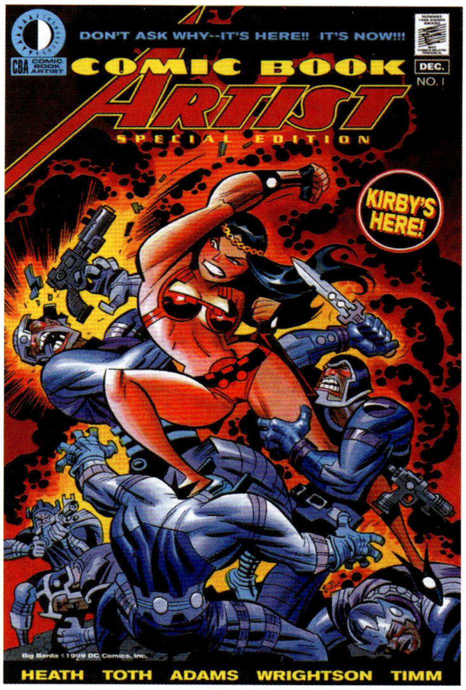

Bruce Timm provided this peachy cover for the special issue of Comic Book Artist.

conducted their private business... privately. Unusual in an industry notorious for public displays and pronouncements. But the likelihood of *Superman* disappearing from the shelves or moving to another company?

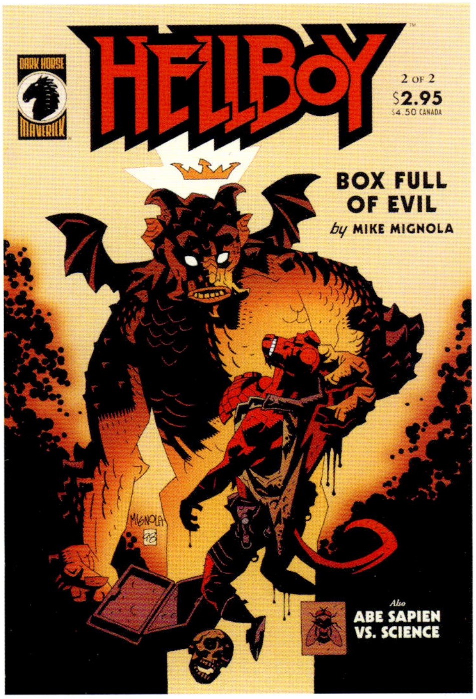

Fans of Mignola's Hellboy *could visit the official website for the latest news: www.hellboy.com*

Don't bet the house on it.

Anyone who has read my previous reviews will have tumbled to the fact that I think Mike Mignola's *Hellboy* is pretty hot stuff: impeccably designed and drawn, wonderfully (and often hilariously) written, Mignola's work is what comics are *all about.* His latest from Dark Horse, *Hellboy: Box Full of Evil,* was further proof. Even his two-page throw-away Hellboy Jr. joke, "Pancakes", in *DHP Jr.* was a royal hoot. Also from Dark Horse and certainly as irresistible was Gary Gianni's *The Monster Men,* which exhibited some of the most exciting brush and ink work wrapped around an original storyline one could hope for. Other works of merit included *The Ghost Handbook #1* (featuring Adam Hughes, Arthur Adams, and Chris Warren), *Shadow Lady* by Masakazu Katsura, various covers by Mark Schultz (including *Subhuman* and *Tarzan the Untamed*), and, if you want to stretch the definition a hair of "fantasy", Frank Miller's *Sin City* series. (C'mon, any story whose characters take the lickin's and keep on tickin' as Miller's do *has* to be a fantasy...)

Image published some intriguing work by David Mack (*Kabuki*), Liam McCormack-Sharp (*Spawn: The Dark Ages*), Ashley Wood (the gorgeously macabre *Spawn: Blood & Salvation* to name only one title), Andy Park and Jon Sibal (*Tomb Raider*), Hajime Sorayama (covers for the cyberpunk *Tsunami Girl*), and Kent Williams (just a *stunning* series of covers for *The Crow*).

The Sirius Entertainment line was strongly anchored by Joseph Michael Linsner's beautifully rendered *Dawn* series and produced some great work by Jill Thompson (*Scary Godmother*), Mark Smylie (the epic *Artesia*), and Jason Alexander (*Empty Zone*). New company Penny Farthing Press made a splash with their character *The Victorian*, moodily interpreted by Jim Steranko, Bernie Wrightson, Michael Kaluta, and Doug Beekman while Fantagraphics released Barry Windsor-Smith's *Adastra In Africa*, *Weasel* by Dave Cooper, Chris Ware's *Acme Novelty Library #13*, and the first volumes in their *Charles Burns Library*. NBM published the latest in Vincent Segrelles Mercenary series, *Giants,* as well as Miran Kim's *The Fallen*, Slave Labor unleashed *Gloom Cookie* by Ted Naifeh (written by Sernena Valentino) and *Lenore* by Roman Dirge (hmmmm), and Andrews McMeel offered Patrick McDonnell's charming Herrimanesque *Mutts: Sundays.*

Frank Frazetta Fantasy Illustrated folded its tent after a year's run (with some nice work by Daren Bader and Alex Horley) while *Forbidden Zone* apparently went belly-up after a raucous first issue, which featured stories by Richard Corben and Arthur Suydam. *Heavy Metal* seemed to be the only magazine-sized comic able to hold its own in the marketplace and was one of the few sources (along with NBM) for translations of European graphic novels.

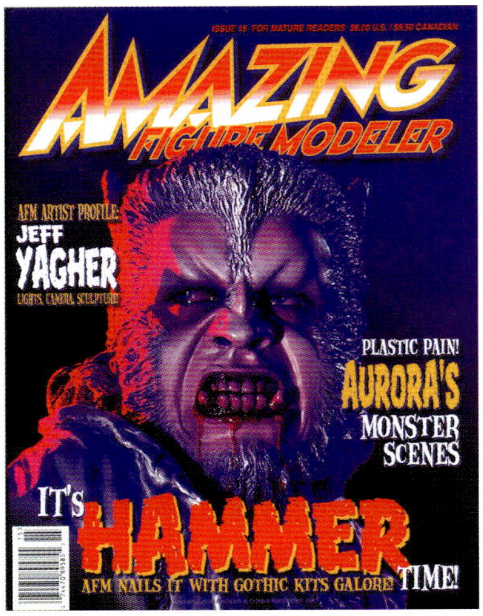

Amazing Figure Modeler *is easily the best resource for what's happening in the field of genre model kits and statues*

The Internet comics news sites pretty much scooped the field's traditional magazines for breaking developments, but if readers wanted something more than headlines and sound bites they still needed to look to the newstands. The closest thing the industry has to a trade publication is *The Comics Journal*; the caveat "closest thing" because *TCJ* has always worn their biases as badges of honor and only occasionally allow objectivity to override the prejudices of their writers and editors—there's almost always the perception, rightly or wrongly, that the slant of negative stories are the result of personal vendettas. That said, *The Journal* is still the most evenhanded (scary thought) of the various print magazines, unafraid to ruffle feathers or alienate publishers and artists, and produces well-researched articles and thorough interviews. (*The Comics Journal*, 7563 Lake City Way NE, Seattle WA 98115.) Fans with more of a nostalgic-bent were well-served by Jon B. Cooke's *Comic Book Artist* (TwoMorrows, 1812 Park Dr., Raleigh, NC 27605) and Diamond's *Comic Book Marketplace* (Gemstone Publishing, Inc., P.O. Box 180700, Coronado, CA 92178).

DIMENSIONAL

I remember that as a kid reading *Eerie* and *Creepy* and reprints of the old EC comics one of the things I always thought was neat was that artists like Frank Frazetta and Al Williamson and Wallace Wood included drawings of fanciful statues in panels otherwise consisting of talking heads: warriors battling monsters, stunning female figures, and animated wildlife scenes spiced up otherwise visually bland situations. Obviously some other readers were equally impressed, so much so that they grew up to create dimensional work that captured the same sensibility.

If anything, 1999 was almost *too much* of a good thing as a legion of sculptors unleashed a horde of statues, toys, and model kits on a relatively modest market. Let's face it, there aren't as many consumers and retail outlets for genre characters as there are for, oh, Precious Moments figures.

Randy Bowen's company produced a number of excellent pieces, including *Astro City*'s "The Samaritan" (sculpted by Randy and designed by Brent Anderson and Alex Ross), a bust of H.P. Lovecraft created by Stephen Hickman, "The Rocketeer" (designed by Dave Stevens/sculpted by Ken Melton), and "Grendel Prime" (created in collaboration with the talented Shiflett Bros.). Bowen also released a popular line of Marvel superhero mini-busts and his own action figure, "Bionica", a take-off on the False Maria from *Metropolis.*

Moore Creations created the impressive "The Barbarian" (sculpted by Clayburn Moore), the second of their Frazetta-based statues, as well as Susumu

Sugita's seductive take on comic's bad girl, "Vampirella". Moore Creations was also responsible for some very impressive and expressive additions to the action figure market, notably some dead-on likenesses of the cast of *Buffy the Vampire Slayer*.

DC Comics offered a number of first class pieces including "Darkseid", "Manhunter" (from a design by Walter Simonson), and a "Batman Snowglobe", all sculpted by William Paquet. Other tasty icons were "Kingdom Come: Shazam!" by Alex Ross and "Crisis on Infinite Earths" by Tim Bruckner.

Fewture Models was responsible for both Takayuki Takeya's excellent "Warrior Alien" and "Alien Pile", Shigeru Yamazaki's stunning "10th Anniversary Dawn" figure (designed by Joseph Michael Linsner) and whimsical "Chi-Chian" statue (designed by Voltaire), and Yasushi Nirasawa's "Devilman", "Guillotinna", and "Dokuro Nina" action figures. The Greenwich Workshop (thought to be at least partially, if not entirely, owned by conglomerate Hallmark Cards) produced fanciful bisques based on the art of James Christensen (including "Queen Mab"), Will Bullas, and Scott Gustafson; Tony McVey reinterpreted *Forbidden Planet*'s "Id Monster" for Menagerie Productions; Dark Horse unveiled Kent Melton's version of "The Big Guy & Rusty the Boy Robot" (designed by Geof Darrow) as well as Jean-Louis Crinon's humorous interpretations of Basil Wolverton's "Weirdos"; Sam Greenwell and Dan Horne collaborated on Tolkien's "Lord of the Nazgûl" for Toy Vault; solo, Horne created "Gron Elfslayer" for Flying Carpet Studio; X-O Facto offered "Deborah Dutch as the Warrior Goddess", sculpted by the Joy & Tom Studio; and Japan's Alpha released Yoshimasa Nakao's "Motoko Kusanagi", the principle character from the classic anime *Ghost In the Shell*.

Ok, and though I made the flip comment earlier about "toys for fanboys" (which really is as truthful as it is sarcastic), McFarlane Toys does some of the coolest figures (or "conversation starters") on the market. As I type these words Frank Miller's "Marv" menaces me from atop my computer monitor, Geof Darrow's severed head dangling from one hand; Joseph Linsner's "Dawn" stares over my shoulder. Their *Sleepy Hollow* figures will join them shortly and "The Crow" already guards Cathy's Mac. Dammit. McFarlane makes it pretty difficult for me to make smartass comments and not look like a hypocrite. But, wait: these *are* conversation starters, *not* toys, so I'm safe. Right.

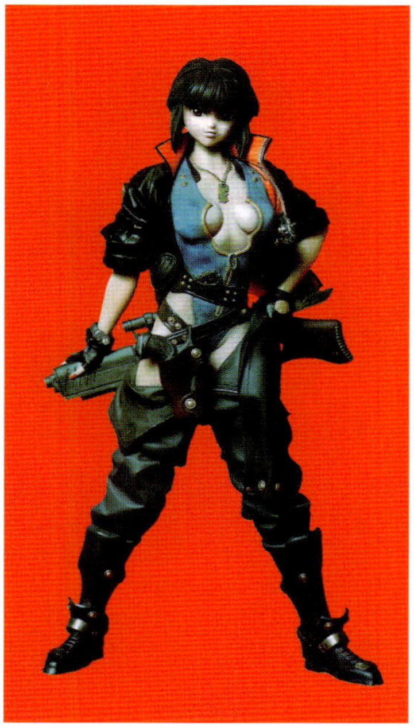

Some incredibly nice statuettes were produced in Japan, including the anime-inspired "Motoko Kusanagi".

EDITORIAL

Years ago I attended a conference that featured David Carson as a speaker. At the time Carson was art director for the short-lived *Beach Culture*, a hip flavor-of-the-month magazine both popular and notorious for its alternative typographic and design solutions. Trademarks were tiny run-on text and headlines that rivaled Rick Griffen for illegibility. David announced that he was more concerned with the "look" than with comprehension, explaining that when he was forced to break-up an article and continue it in another part of the magazine he would place the continuation wherever he wanted without providing the reader with directions to turn to another page: "I figured if you were 'with it', you'd find the rest sooner or later," he said. Designers tend to love Carson's style; readers tend not to.

So, if David Carson (or to a slightly lesser degree, Britain's Neville Brody) represent the "edge" of contemporary magazine design, many of the genre publications are examples of viewpoints stuck in the '50s. Though their conservative layouts, traditional artistic solutions, and middle-of-the-road editorial directions don't show contempt for their readers, neither do they challenge or excite them. And that's precisely what a magazine should do, without losing sight of the needs of their audience—and *has* to do if it hopes to maintain their customer base, attract advertisers, and ultimately survive.

That's one of the reasons I'm rooting for Wizards of the Coasts' *Amazing Stories*. Art Director Shauna Wolf Narciso has been pushing the genre envelope with tip-top design and exceptional art by the likes of John Jude Palencar, Anita Kunz, Cliff Nielson, and Greg Spalenka. Granted, the covers tended to be a little weak and played to the prejudices and expectations of the traditional sf audience (and/or media fans): marketing is, afterall, marketing. But I trust the outside will be as impressive as the

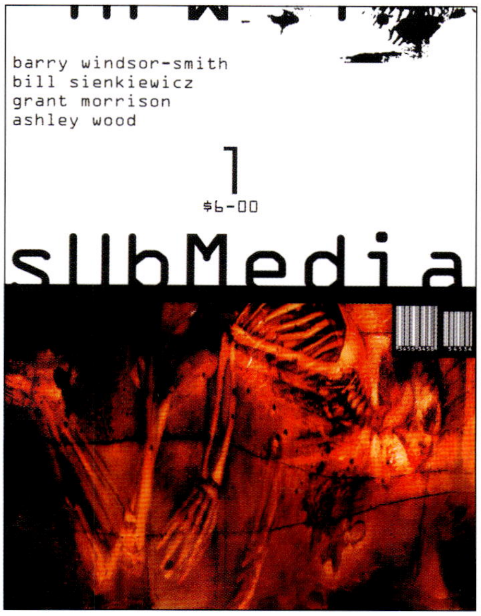

Publishing a magazine can be a frustrating venture as the folks at SubMedia *quickly discovered.*

inside in the near future. On a similar note, I had high hopes for Woodhaus Studios' *Submedia:* featuring strong, contemporary design, its first (and to my knowledge, only) issue included great art, interviews, and articles by and about Ashley Wood, Barry Windsor-Smith, and Bill Sienkiewicz. I hope it reemerges, but the odds don't look good. Suffering a similar fate was Coppervale's International Studio. Its single issue featured Bryn Barnard, Paul Chadwick, and Andrew Loomis. Publisher James Owen promises a relaunch; I'll keep my fingers crossed. Still perking along (if a little irregularly) was Vanguard's *Tales From the Edge*—their 15th issue was devoted to Sienkiewicz and was an instant sell-out.

Realms of Fantasy, though using almost exclusively reprint covers, included some original interiors by John Hanley, Broeck Steadman, John Berkey, and Steven Adler. Jim Burns, Nicholas Jainschigg, and Jon Foster provided the covers for *Asimov's SF Magazine*, *Analog* sported work by George Krauter and Ron Miller, and the *Magazine of Fantasy & Science Fiction* boasted covers by Bob Eggleton, Barclay Shaw, and Jill Bauman. Still the best way to track the changes in our ever-evolving genre is to read *Locus*, f&sf's trade journal." Sample copies are available from Locus , P.O. Box 13305, Oakland, CA 94661/$5 sample.

Of course, exemplary fantastic art appeared in magazines outside of the traditional venues. I stumbled across some wonderful pieces by Charles Burns in

Esquire, Roberto Parada in *Entertainment Weekly,* C.F. Payne in *Rolling Stone*, and David Seeley in *The Village Voice.* Robert Williams' *Juxtapoz* provided a forum for contemporary "outsider" art, i.e. gallery work that flirts with underground comics, pop symbols, horror, and biker philosophy. Meanwhile, Aussie Damien Michael's *Art Visionary* focused on the equally jarring European-inspired school of fantastic surrealism: both publications showcased challenging painters worthy of further exposure. But you know, at the end of the day I'm *always* rewarded by the diversity of the work published in *Playboy,* art directed by Tom Staebler. Featuring simply tremendous illustrations by Kent Williams, Guy Billout, and Dave McKean to name only a few, *Playboy* remains the last exciting link to the golden age of magazine illustration. Time to renew my subscription!

INSTITUTIONAL

Standing before a daunting expanse of entries to be judged, Juror Toby Schwartz asked me, "What exactly *is* the 'Institutional' category?" My response was a shrug, a wave, and a brief, "Everything else."

Packaging, greeting cards, posters, promotions, pro-bono assignments: anything that doesn't easily fit within the other categories winds up in Institutional. As such, it's virtually impossible to track any trends or artists with any real accuracy. Just as an example, the print market ain't what it used to be and...the print market is better than ever. Hunting for works in the galleries (or frame shops) by anyone other than Dali or Michael Parkes might prove frustrating. But dropping by ASFA's Print Shop at various conventions or checking out individual artists' websites would reveal that the choices, sizes, and prices for frameable reproductions has become almost endless. Similarly, specialty shops have never done great business with posters and portfolios of comics character despite modest prices and the focus of their clientele, but visiting the Internet auction sites would reveal the same dead inventory selling rather briskly. Or, better, walk into a Warner Studios store at you favorite mall and you'd see limited edition *Batman* or *Justice League* prints at $400 and up being sold as soon as they were offered. Obviously there's an eager audience "out there": finding them efficiently seems to be the challenge.

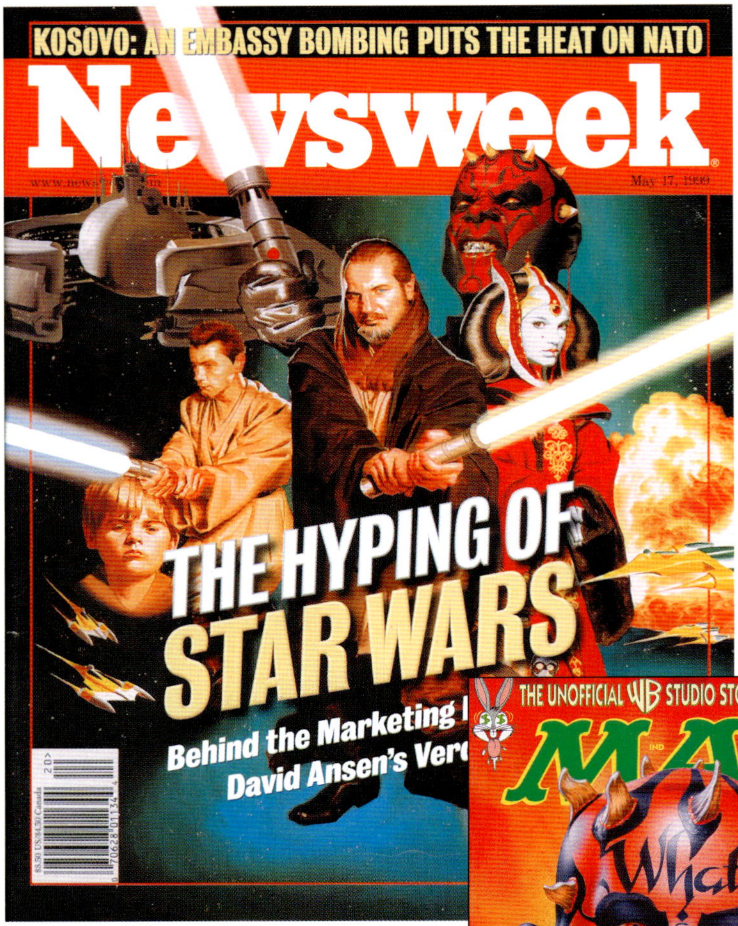

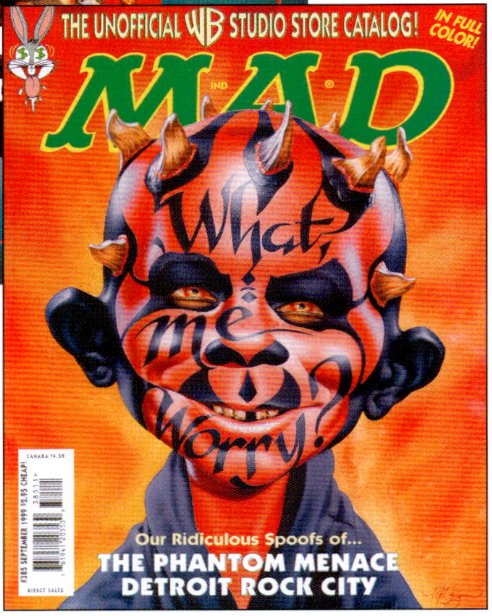

Star Wars: The Phantom Menace *dominated the media in the first half of 1999, making the covers of both* Newsweek *(by Drew Struzan) and* Mad *(by Mark Stutzman).*

Anyway, some of the art I noticed this past year (in no particular order) included prints by Glenn Barr ("Bad Betty/Poor Barney"), Mark Ryden ("Pele"), Coop ("Major Hard-On"), and Alex Ross ("The Joker & Harley Quinn"); portfolios by Bill Stout ("World of Oz"/Art Works Fine Arts), Doug Chiang ("Star Wars: Episode 1"/ Chronicle), and Travis Charest ("New Horizon"/Wildstorm Productions); and a nice selection of calendars by Joseph Michael Linsner (*Dawn*/Sirius), Ted Nasmith (*Lord of the Rings*/HarperCollins), Gil Bruvel, Boris Vallejo (Workman), Julie Bell (Golden Turtle), and Daniel Merriam (Ronnie Sellers), to name only a handful.

Artist trading cards have rapidly become the Edsels of the field: another once-hot venue killed by over-saturation, ridiculous pricing, and speculation. However, the role-playing game industry still seems to be the largest visible market for fantastic artists—and is as difficult to keep track of as advertising and the film industries. Who drew all those damn *Pokémon* critters? You've got me. I know if you search you can find some great game images by Brom and R.K. Post and Ron Spears and Tim Bradstreet and Mark Zug and probably anyone else you can imagine, but where to start the search? Again, you've got me. The one bit of news (beyond the phenomenal success of the aforementioned *Pokémon* and the sure-to-be-equally-hot 2000 release of the *Harry Potter* game) that sent a ripple through the market was Hasbro Toys purchase of Wizards of the Coast for $325 million (which in-turn had previously bought out TSR). Still operating independently, the general consensus seems to be that the consolidation of companies will strengthen the industry and help avoid repetition in products and sales declines. Time will tell.

IN PASSING

In 1999 we said farewell to these members of the creative community:
David Allen (b. 1945), artist and popular stop-motion movie animator.
Joel Beck (b. 1943), under-ground comix artist.
Edvin Biukovic (b. 1969). comics artist.
Lee Falk (b. 1912), creator and writer of *The Phantom* and *Mandrake the Magician* newspaper strips.
Eddie Jones (b. 1935), British sf artist.
Ludek Pesek (b. 1919), astronomical artist.
John Prentice (b. 1920), artist for the *Rip Kirby* newspaper strip.
Shel Silverstein (b. 1932), artist and writer, best known for *Where The Sidewalk Ends.*
Eric Stanton (b. 1927), cartoonist and fetish artist.
Saul Steinberg (b. 1914), cartoonist primarily remembered for his work for *The New Yorker.*
Vincent Sullivan (b. 1911), cartoonist, editor, and publisher of ME Comics. †

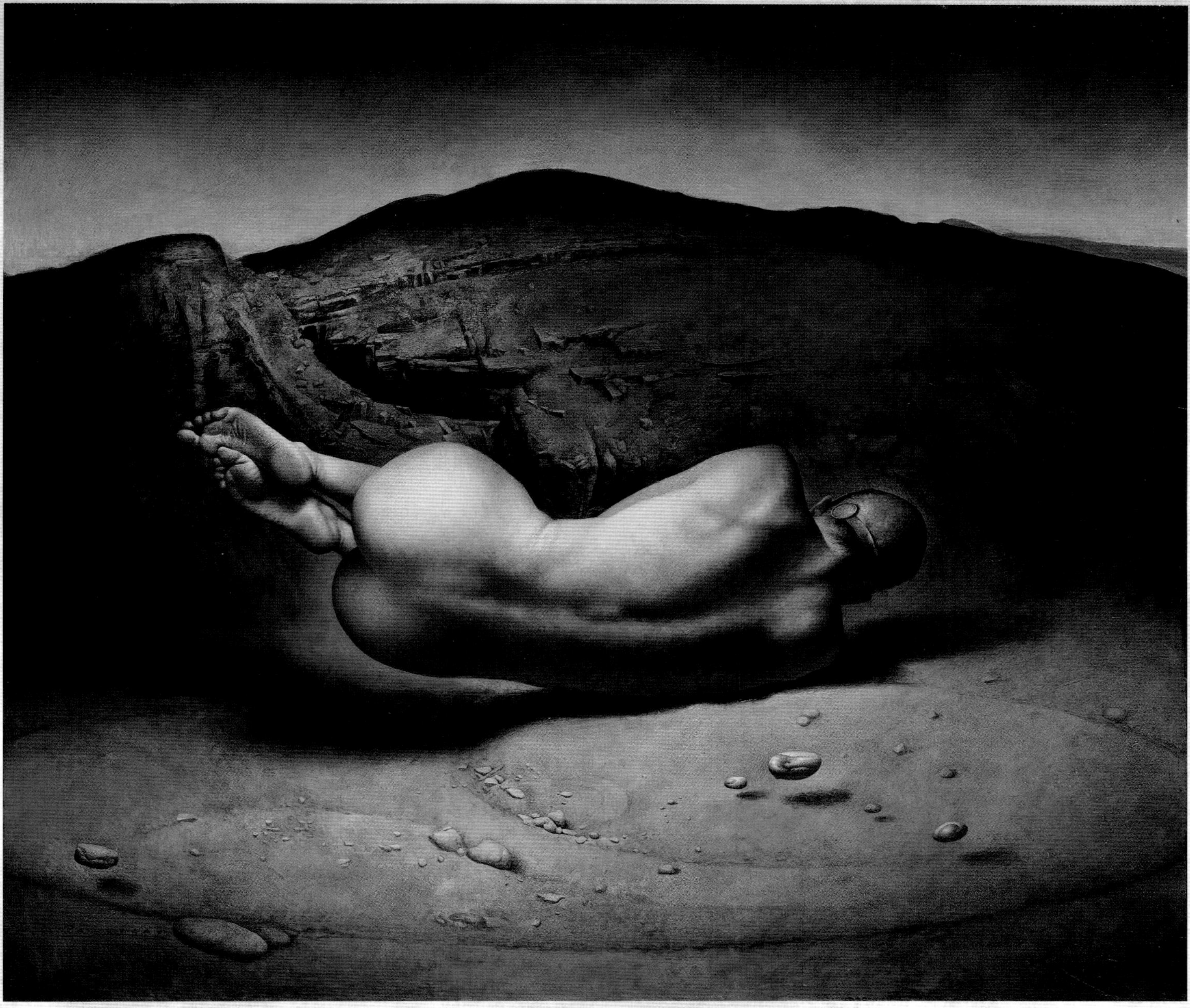

ThE | SHoW

Spectrum 7 Call For Entries Poster
by John Jude Palencar

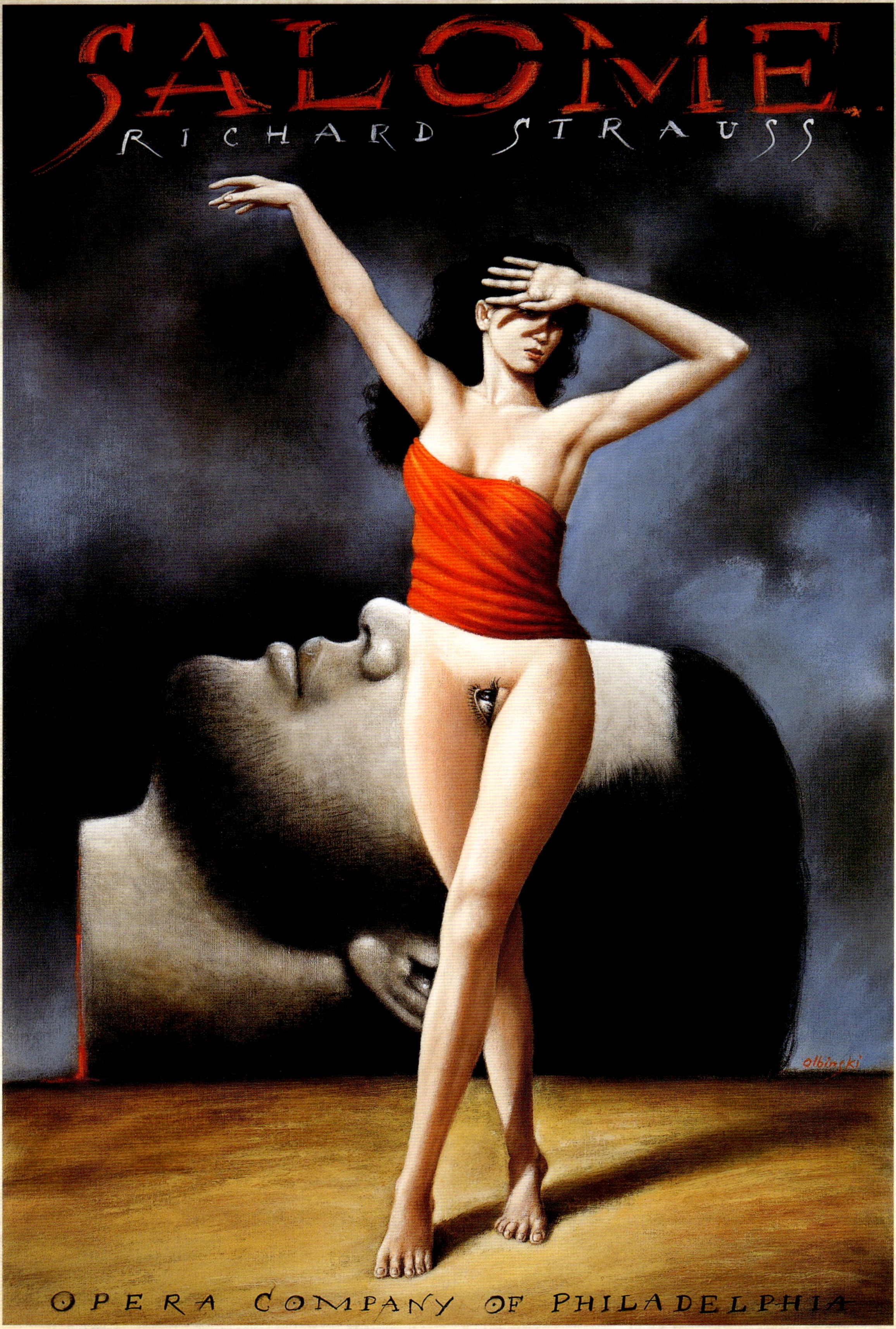

artist: RAFAL OLBINSKI
client: The Philadelphia Opera *title:* Salomé *size:* 20"x30" *medium:* Acrylic

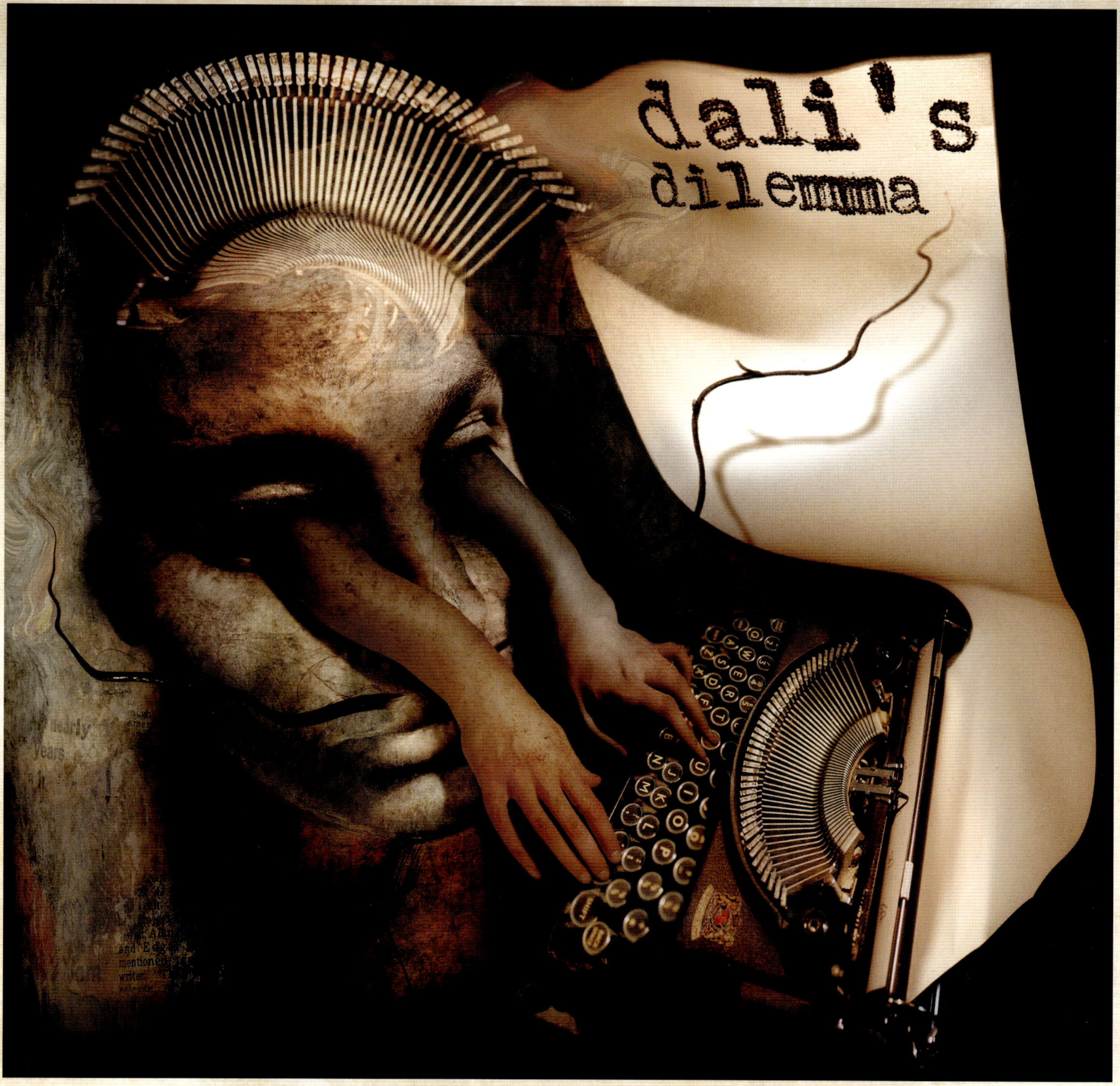

artist: DAVE McKEAN
designer: Dave McKean *client:* Magna Carta Records/Dali's Dilemma
title: Manifesto for Futurism *size:* 14"x14" *medium:* Mixed/digital

1
artist: BEN VERKAAIK
art director: David Bartels
designer: David Bartels
client: Interadnet
title: We're In Touch
medium: Oil
size: 27 1/2"x13 3/4"

2
artist: GARY L. FREEMAN
art director: Victoria Hart
client: Westwood Studios
medium: Digital painting
size: 16"x11 1/2"

3
artist: PETER BOLLINGER
art director: Tamara Shannon
client: MindSlap Studios
title: Demon Chick
medium: 3-D digital

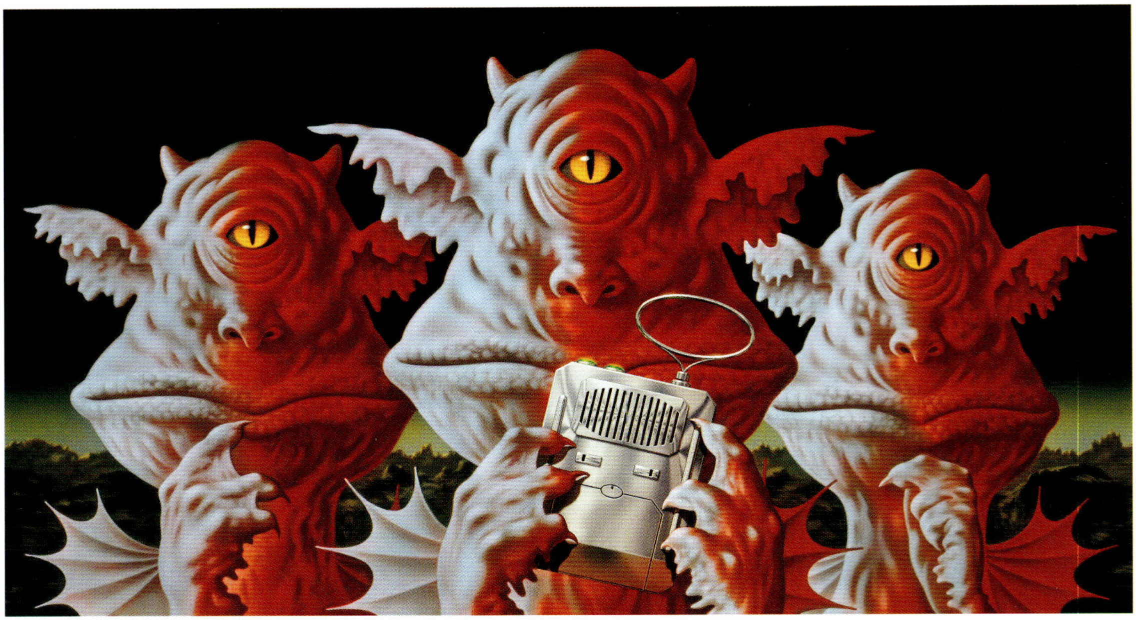

1

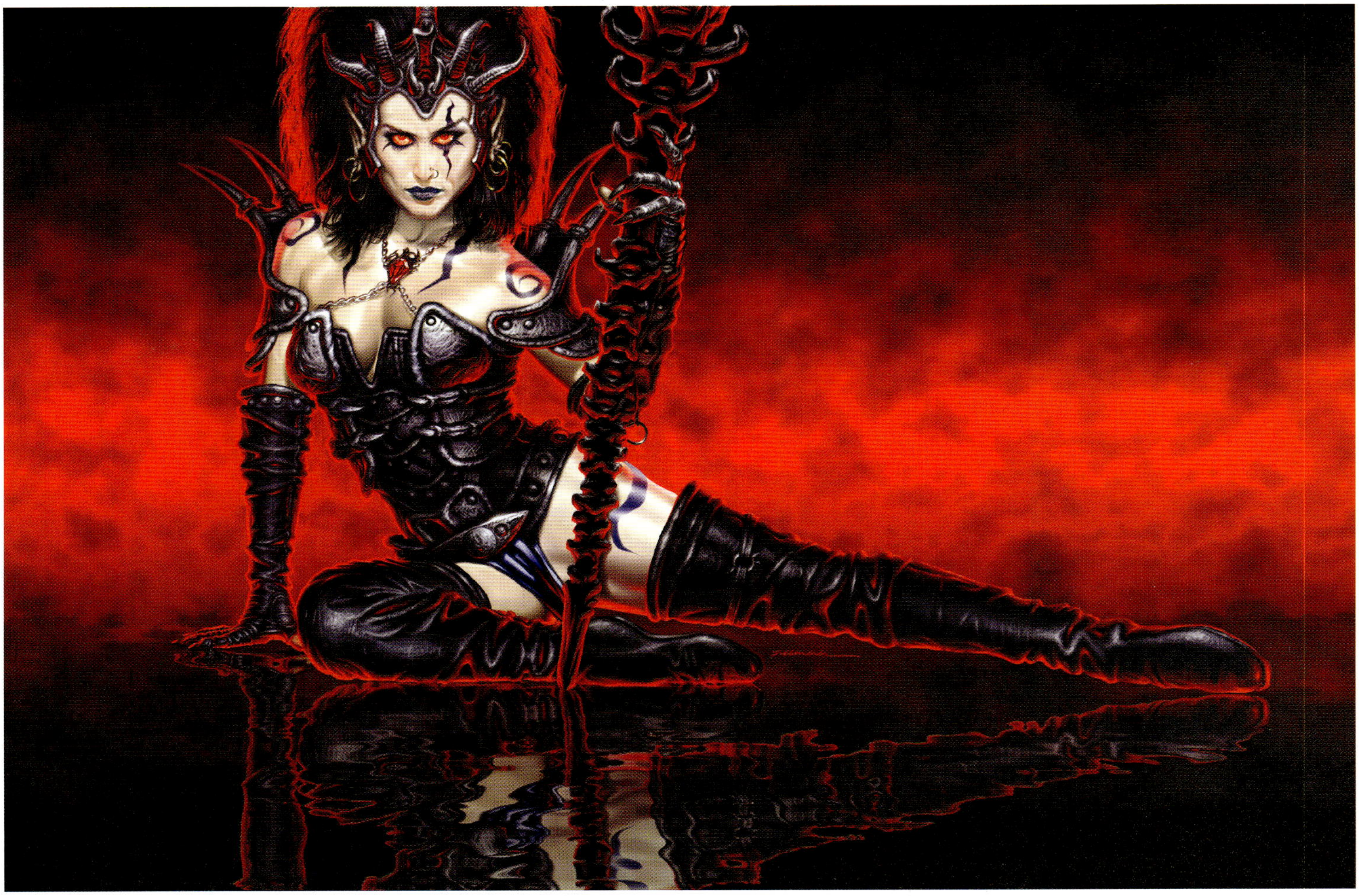

2

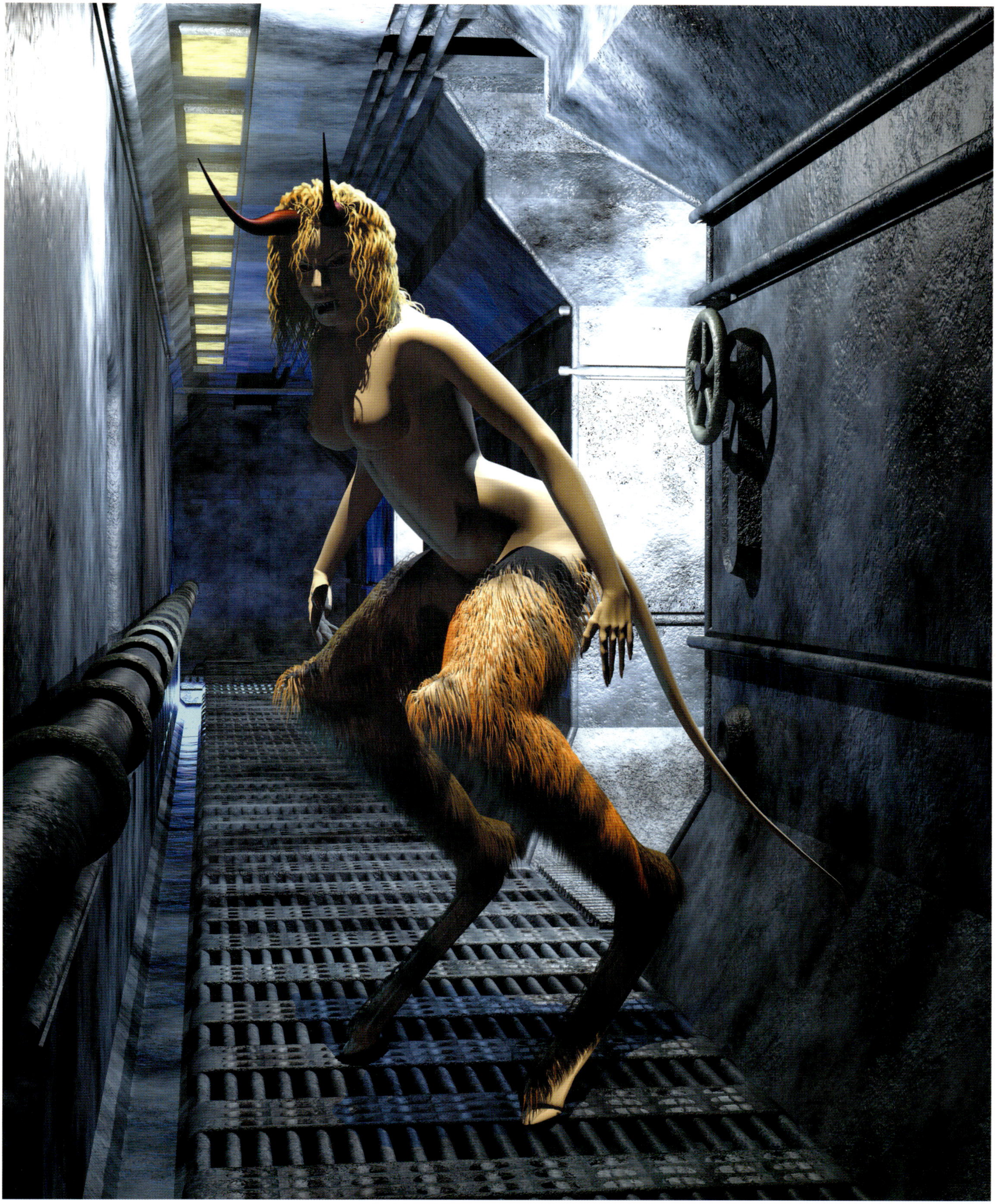

3

1
artist: RYAN WOOD
art director: Brian Moose
client: Metacreations
title: Canhead
medium: Digital
size: 6"x4 1/2"

2
artist: GREG CALL
art director: Clayton Kauzlaric
designer: Greg Call
client: Cauedog Entertainment
title: Wind
medium: Acrylic
size: 17 1/2"x24"

3
artist: GREG CALL
art director: Clayton Kauzlaric
designer: Greg Call
client: Cauedog Entertainment
title: Fire
medium: Acrylic
size: 17 1/2"x24"

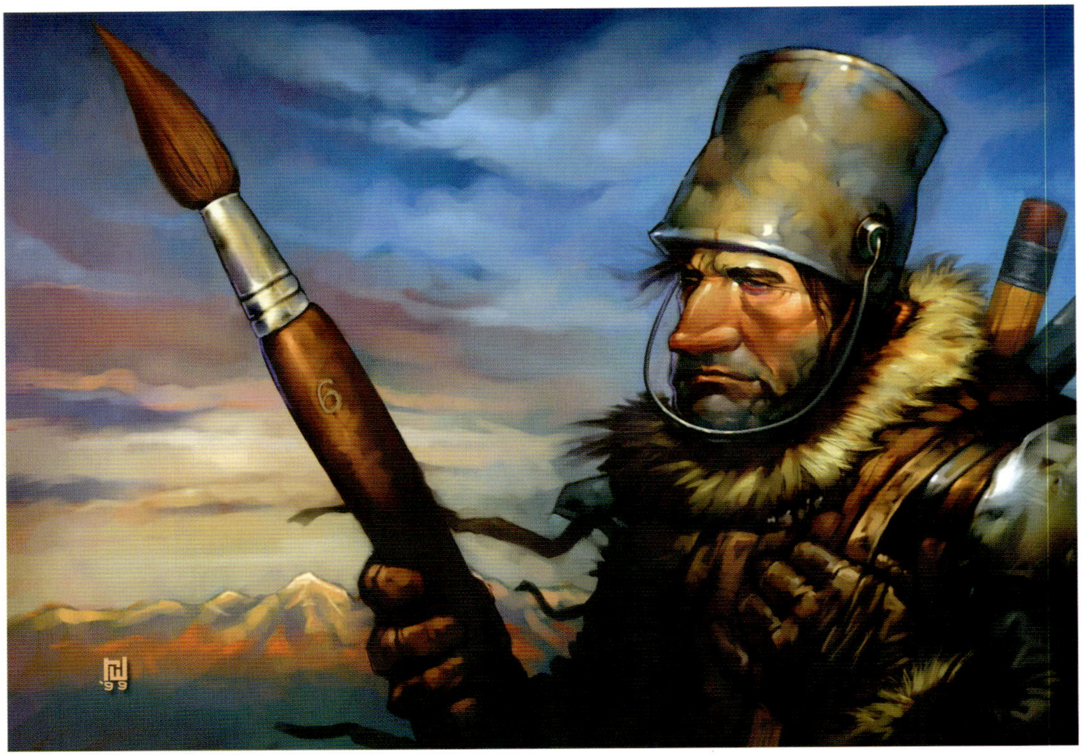

1

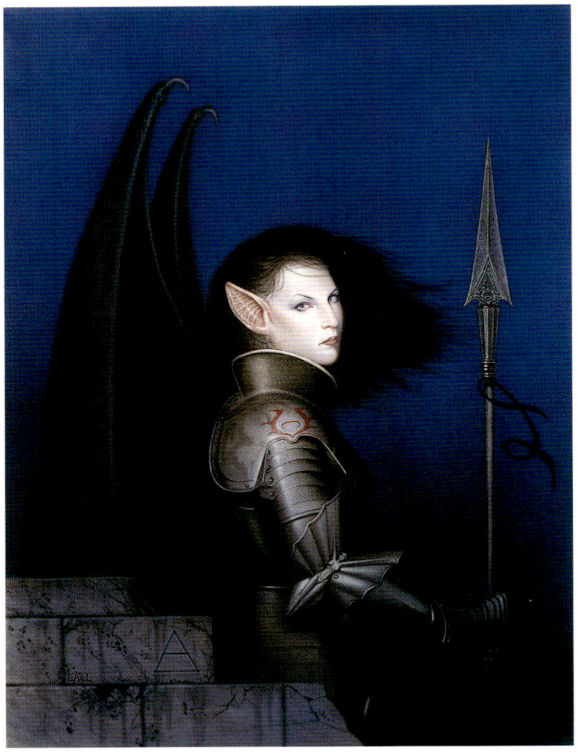

2

4
artist: GREG CALL
art director: Clayton Kauzlaric
designer: Greg Call
client: Cauedog Entertainment
title: Water
medium: Acrylic
size: 17 1/2"x24"

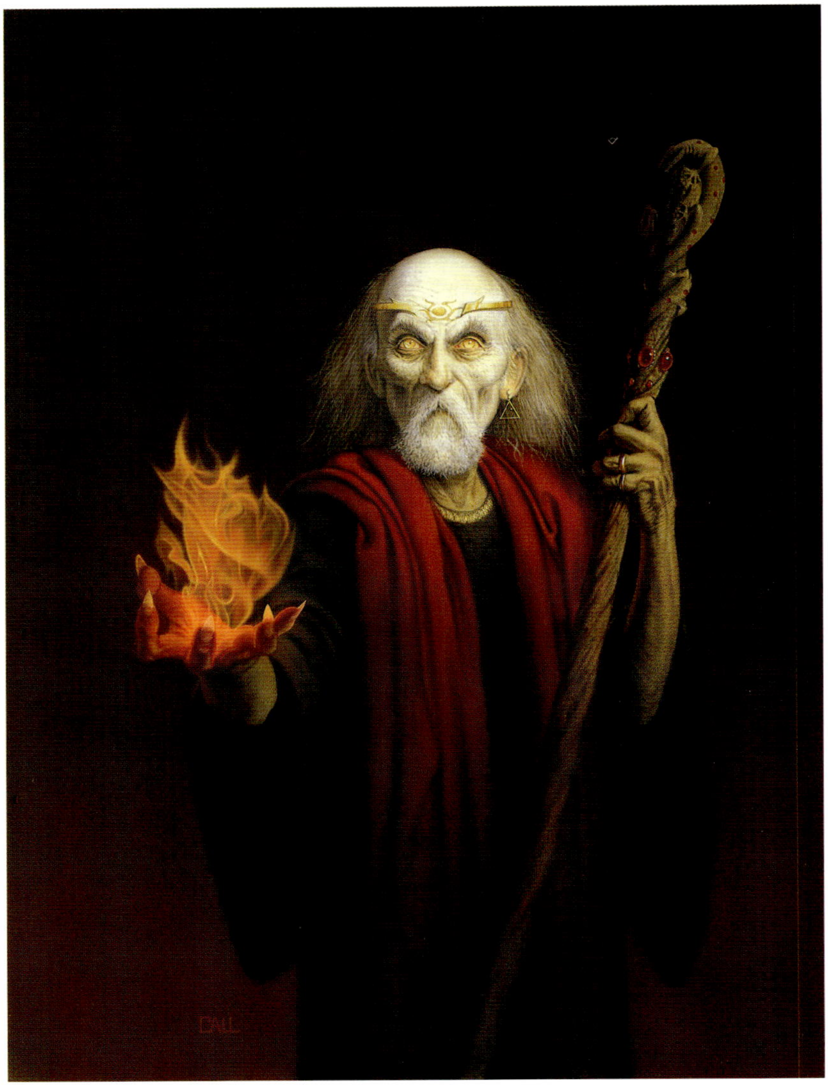

3

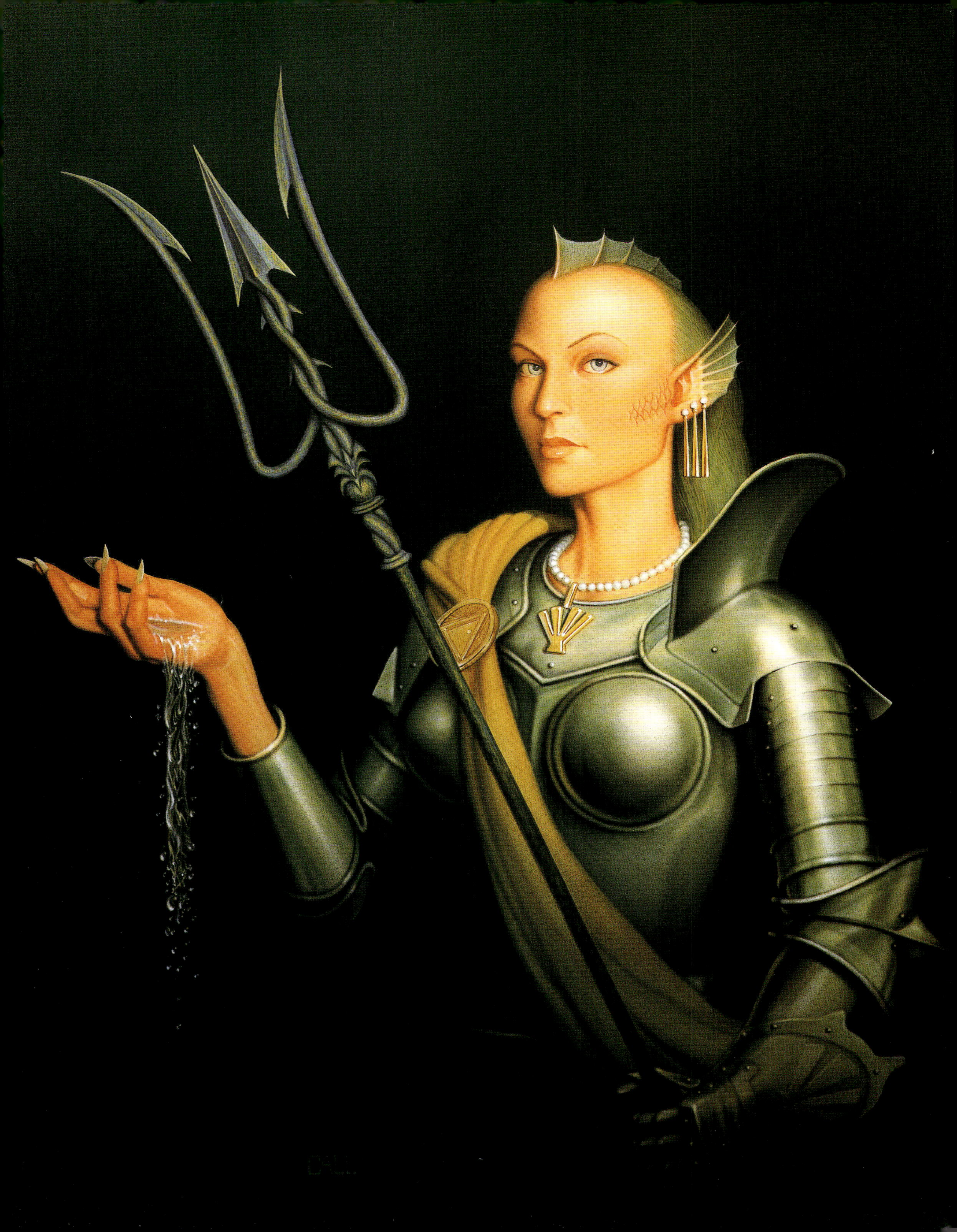

1
artist: SLAWEK WOJTOWICZ
art director: Slawek Wojtowicz
client: FGL—Verlag GbR
title: Robots Like to Swim, Too
medium: Digital
size: 10"x7"

2
artist: NEIL BLEVINS
client: CoproFago
title: Fallen Angel
medium: Digital

3
artist: NORIAKI KANEKO
art director: Noriaki Kaneko
designer: Noriaki Kaneko
client: Tappan Gala/Mitsubishi
title: Flying Sitting
medium: Digital
size: 18"x36"

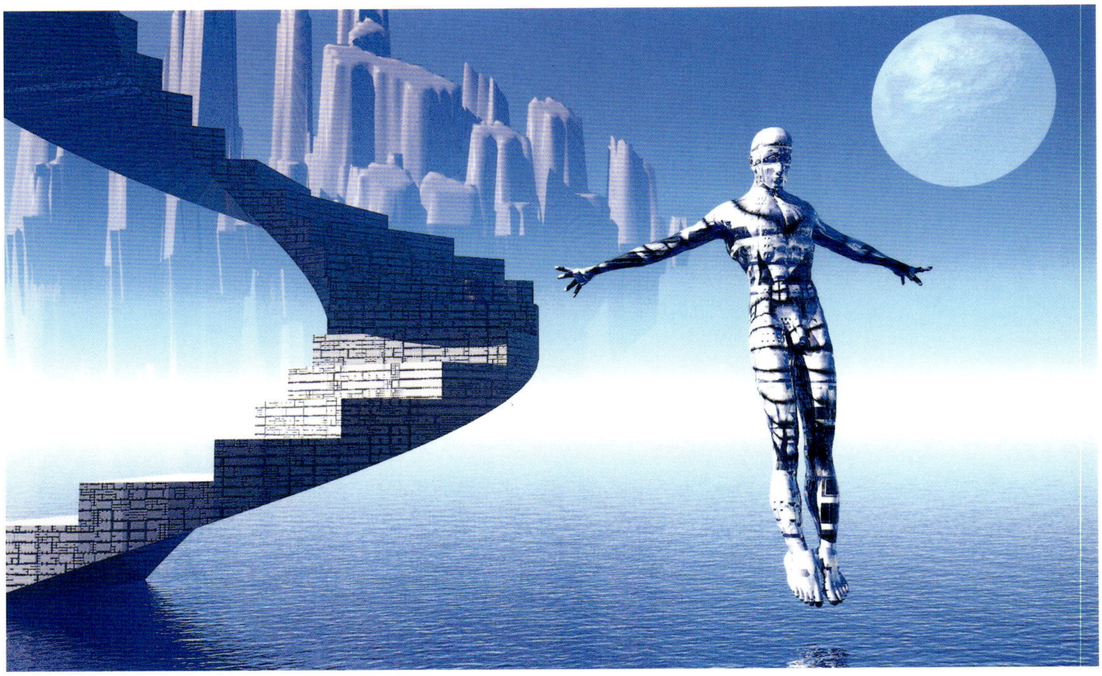

1

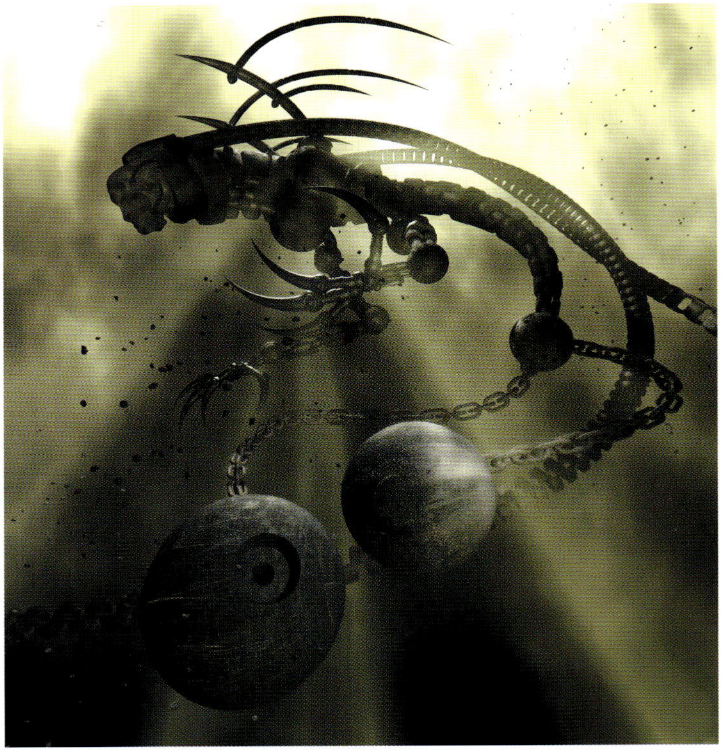

2

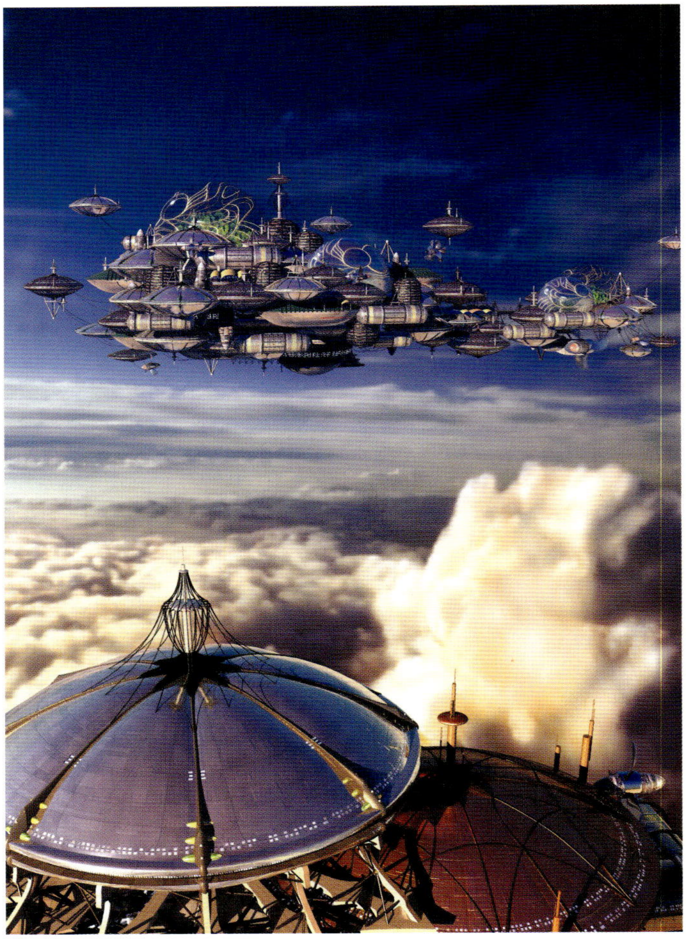

3

4
artist: ODDWORLD INHABITANTS REALTIME CG TEAM
art director: Lorne Lanning
designer: Raymond Swanland, Silvio Aebischer, Gautam Babbar
client: Oddworld Inhabitants
medium: Digital

4

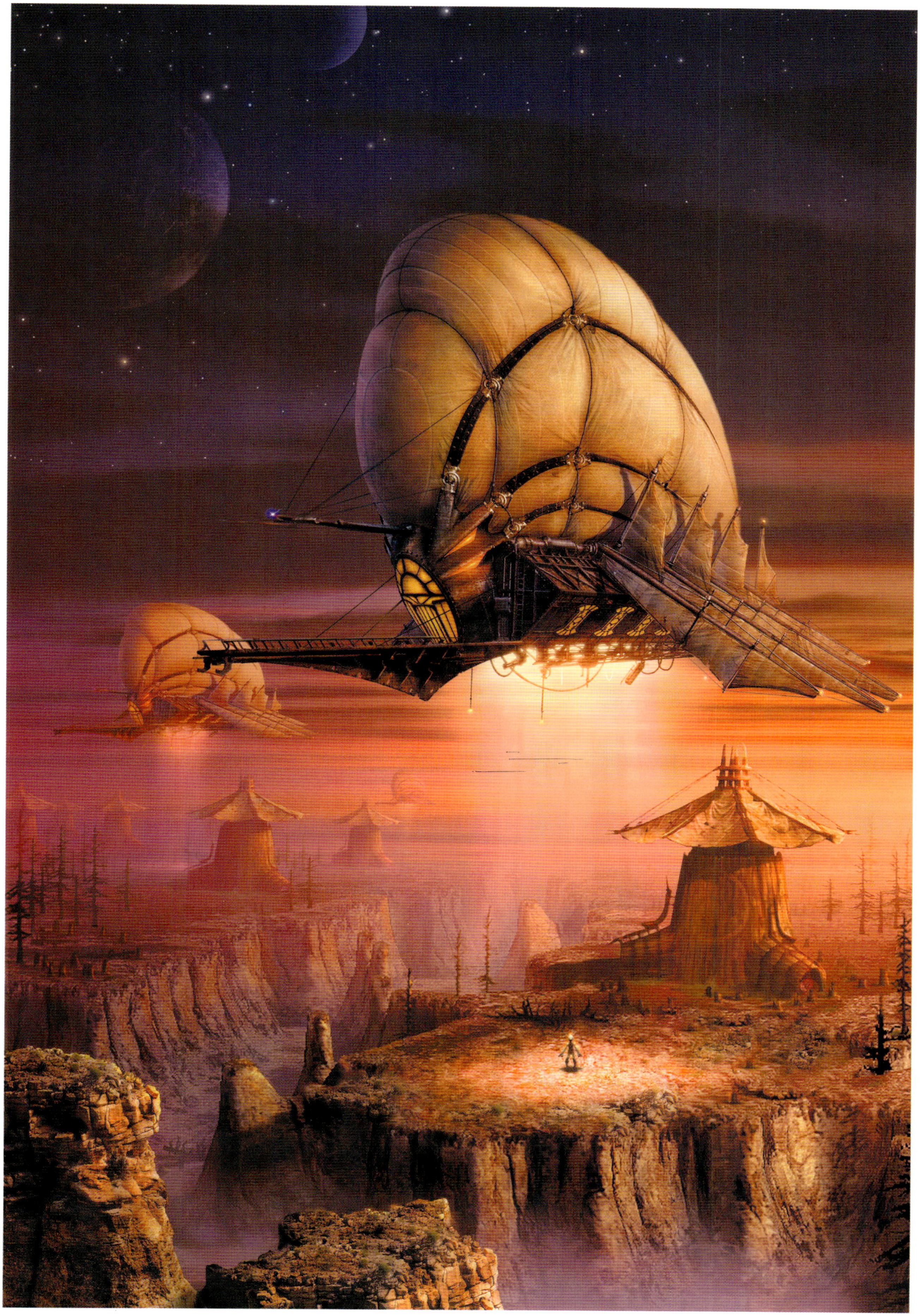

1
artist: DON SEEGMILLER
art director: Brian Moose
client: Metacreations
title: Close To the Edge
medium: Digital
size: 6"x4"

2
artist: BLEU TURRELL
art director: Mary Jo Brown
designer: Mary Jo Brown
client: Rivertree Productions
title: Little ProtoEither.
medium: Mixed
size: 15"x20"

3
artist: DONATO GIANCOLA
art director: Toby Schwartz
client: Doubleday Direct
title: Dragonsight
medium: Oil
size: 20"x27"

4
artist: BROM
art director: Dawn Murin
client: TSR
title: Heaven

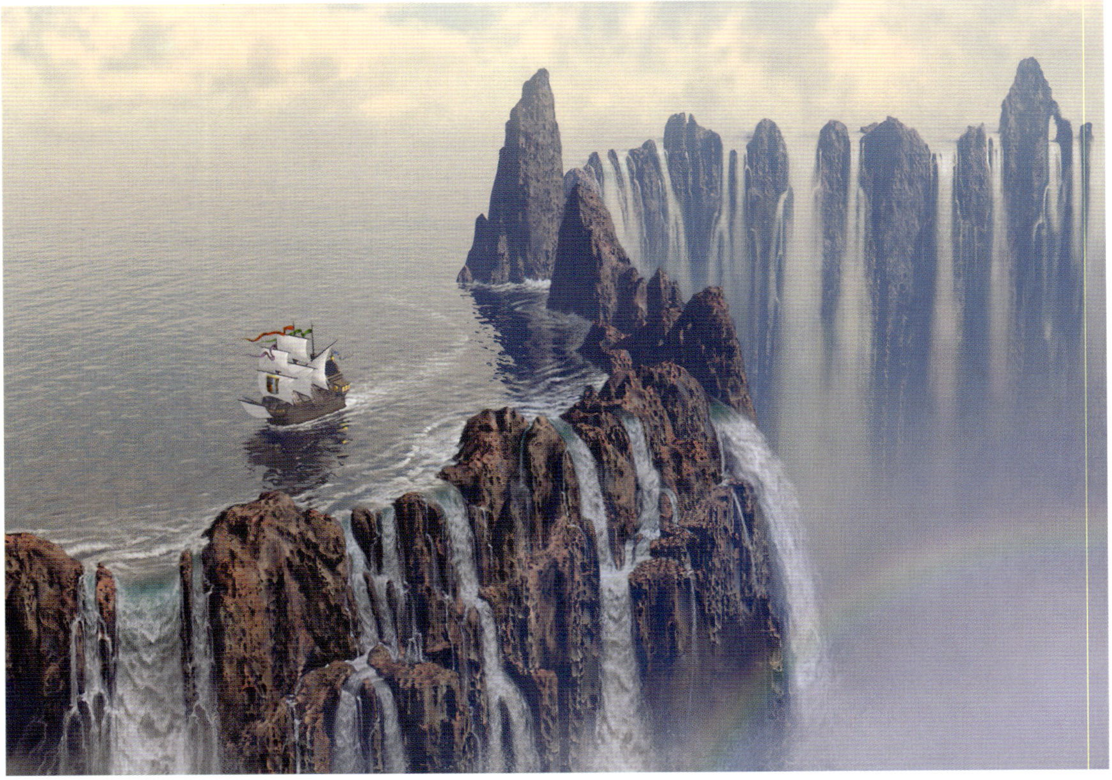

1

3

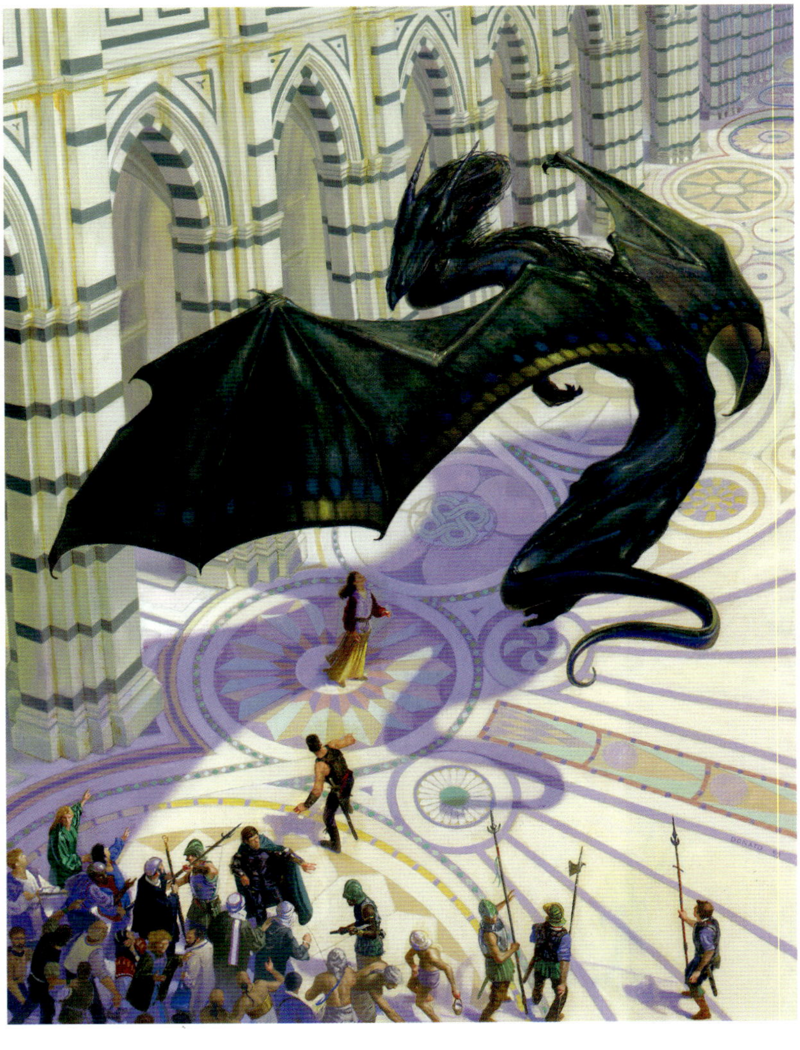

2

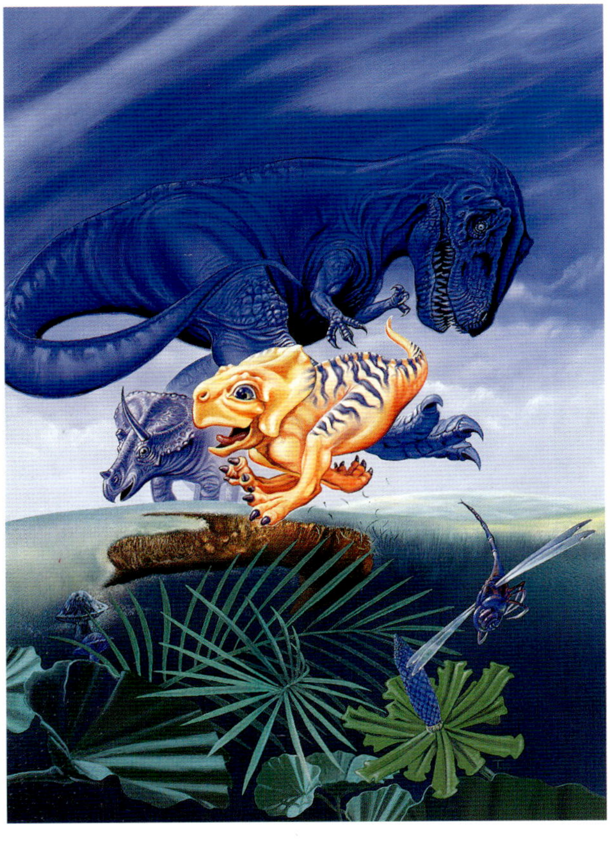

4

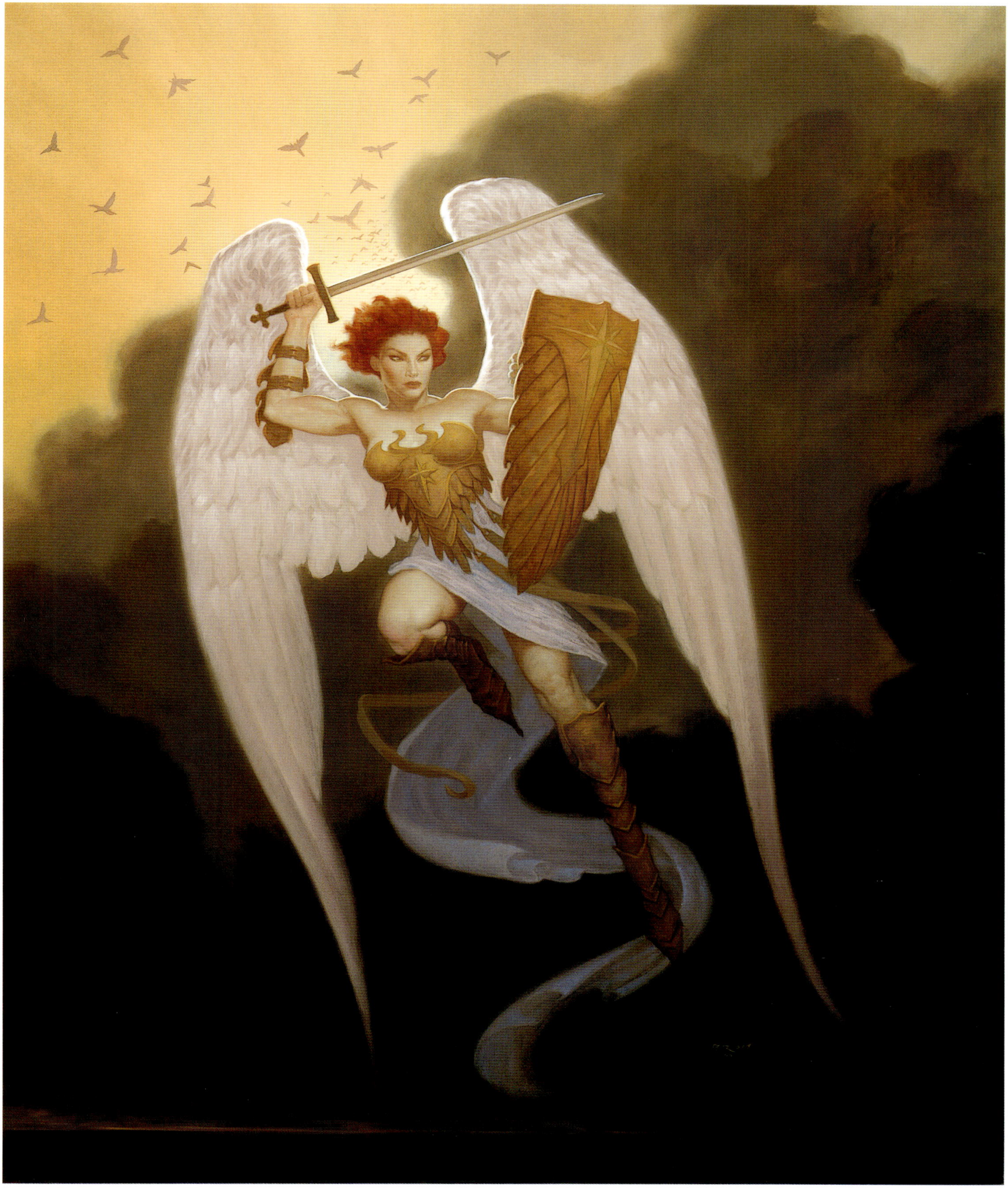

1
artist: DAVE McKEAN
designer: Dave McKean
client: Shrapnel Records
title: James Murphey Feeding the Machine
medium: Mixed/digital *size:* 14"x14 1/2"

2
artist: TERESE NIELSEN
art director: Larry Smith
designer: Larry Smith
client: Dragon Magazine
title: Swanmay
medium: Acrylic/oil size: 9"x12"

3
artist: EZRA TUCKER
art director: David Kudja
designer: Ezra Tucker
client: Sony Development
title: Moebius Airtight Garage
medium: Acrylic *size:* 30"x40"

4
artist: ROBH RUPPEL
art director: Garrett Burke
designer: Chris Reardon
client: B.D. Fox
medium: Digital

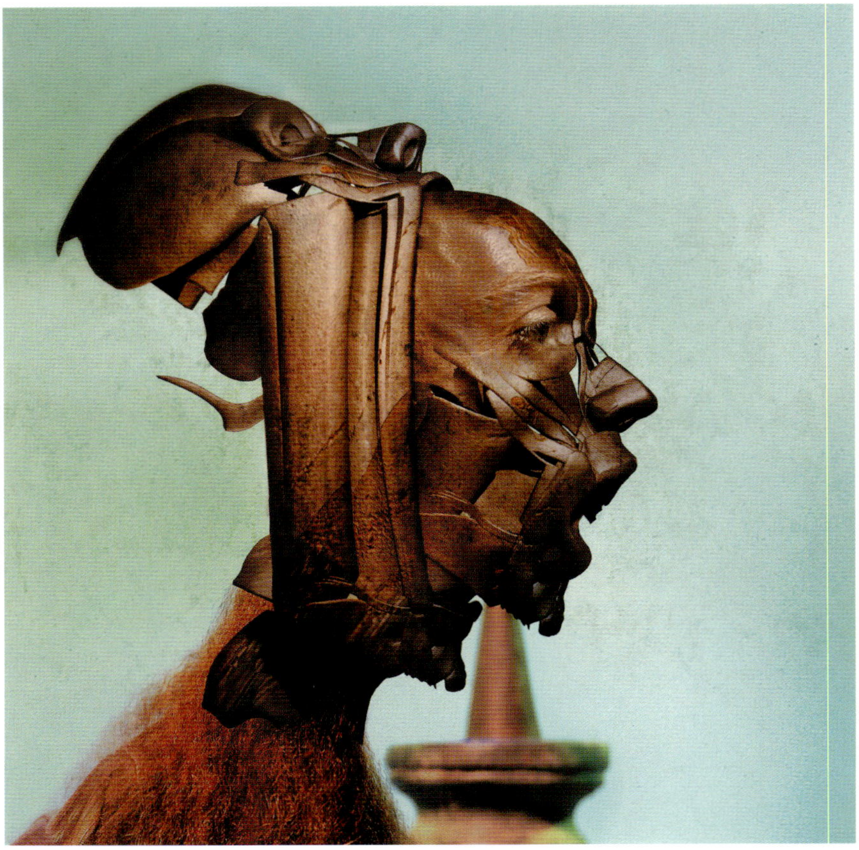
1

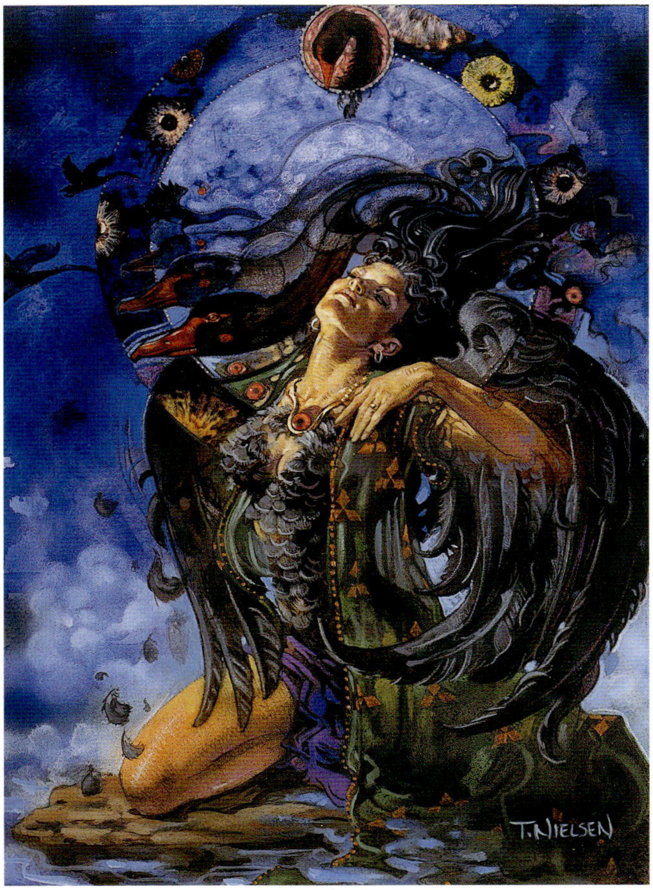

2

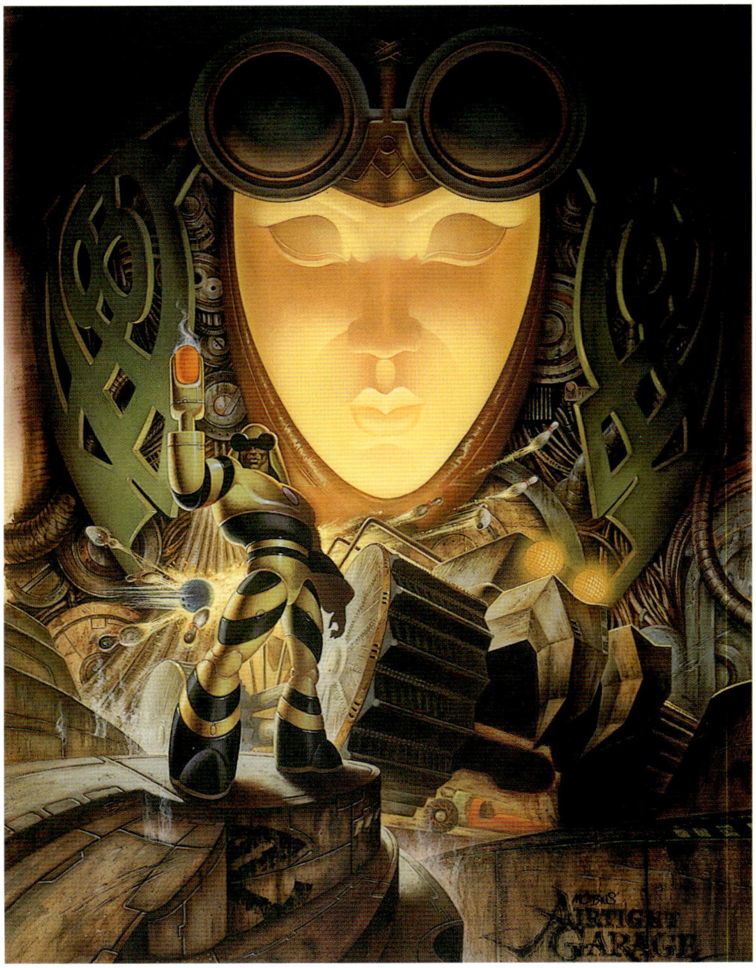

3

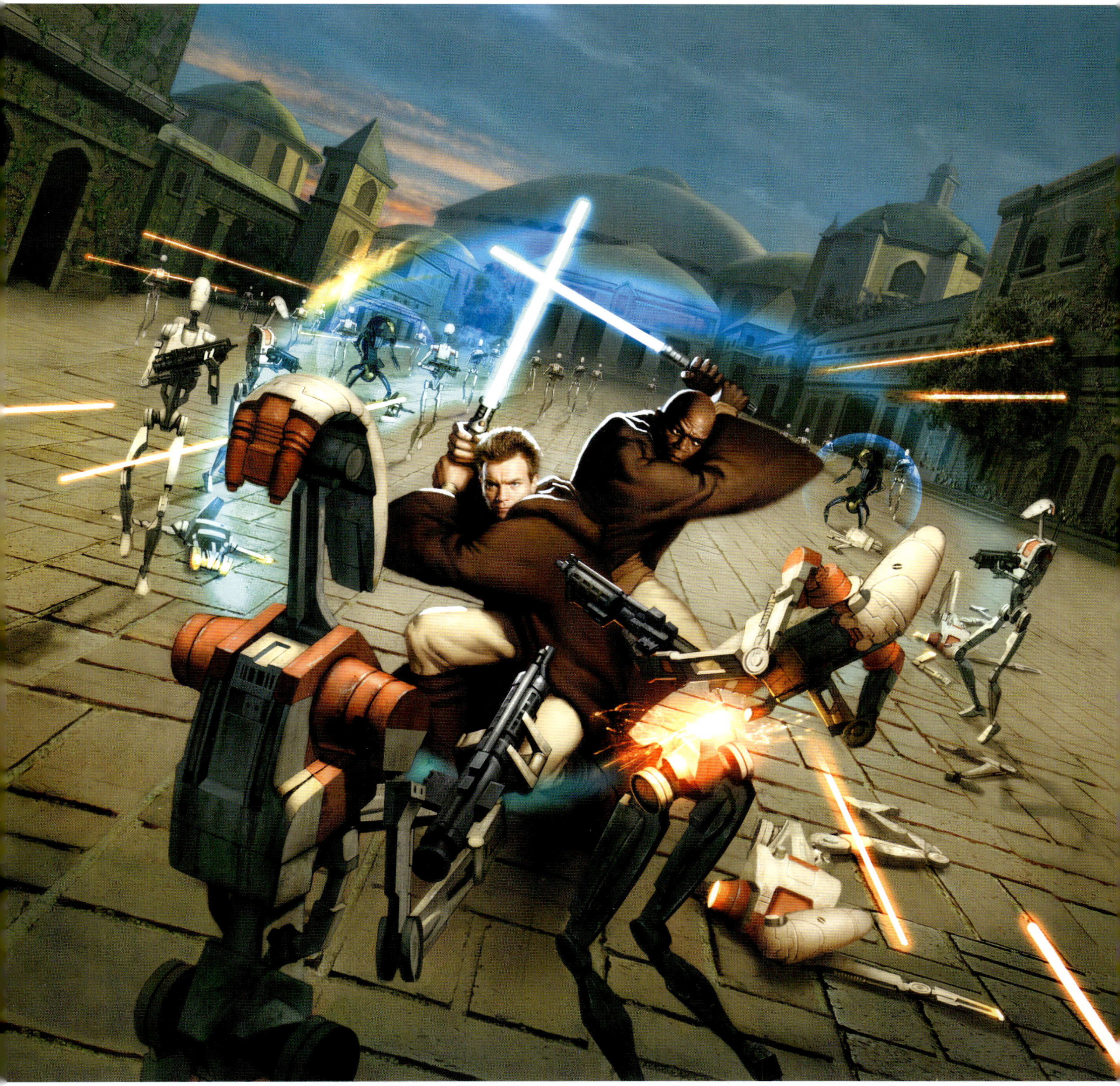

4

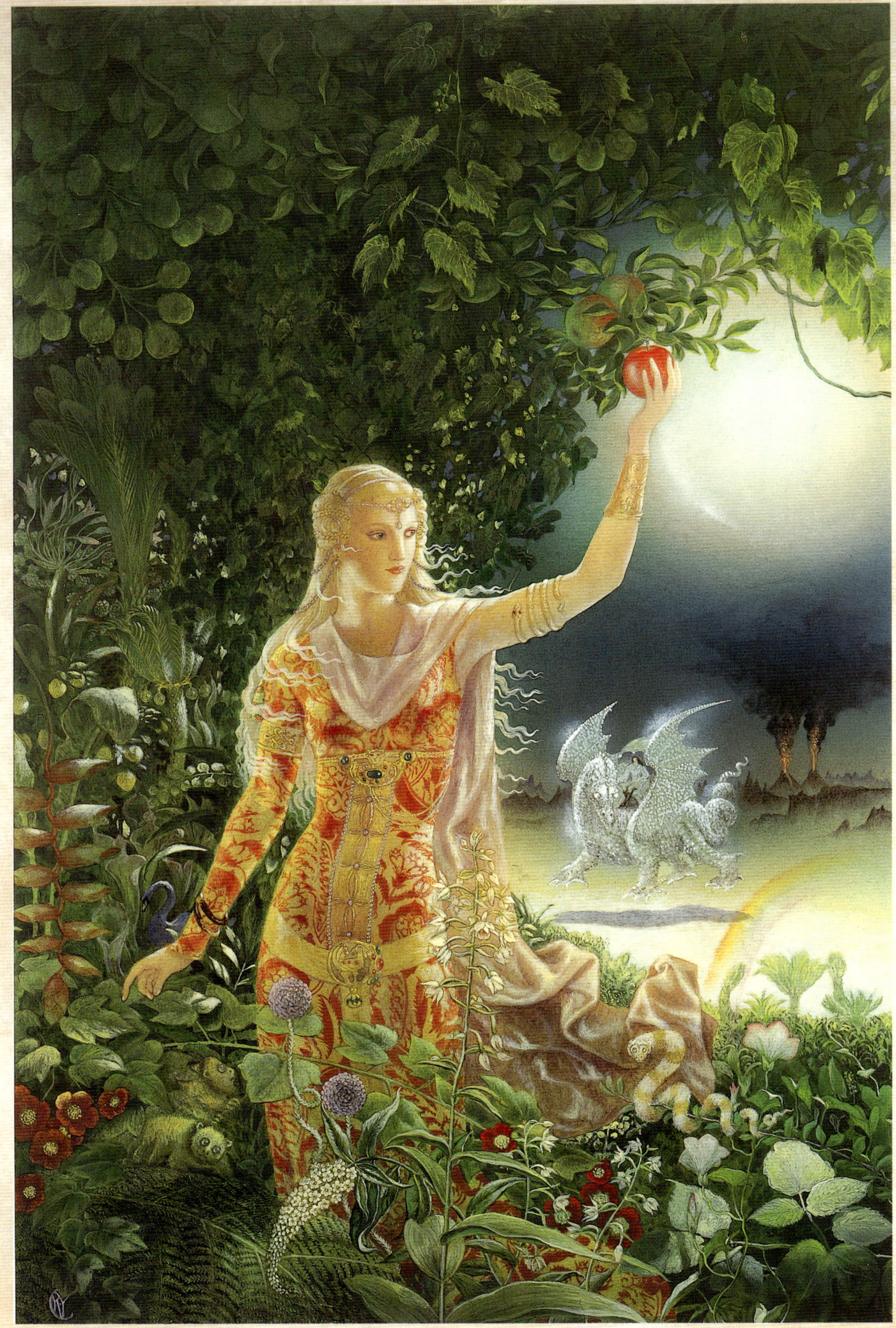

artist: KINUKO Y. CRAFT
art director: Jamie Warren Youll *client:* Bantam Books
title: Biting the Sun *size:* 16"x24" *medium:* Mixed

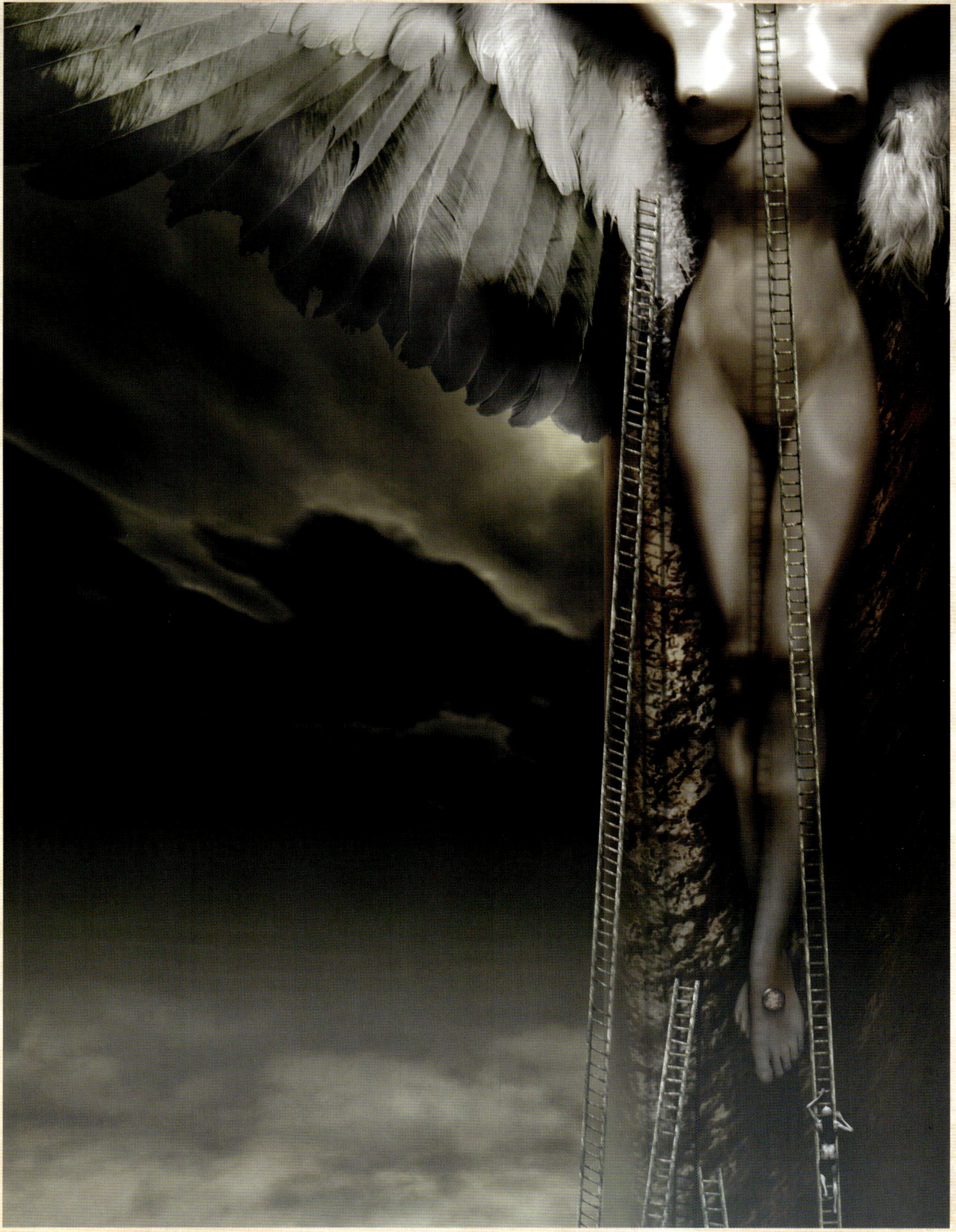

artist: DAVID HO
art director: David Ho   *client:* Sungood Books
title: The Chosen Few   *size:* 16"x20"   *medium:* Mixed/digital

1
artist: GREG NEWBOLD
art director: Anne Diebel
client: Hyperion Books
title: Songs of Power
medium: Acrylic
size: 13"x9"

2
artist: JEAN PIERRE TARGETE
art director: Judith Murello
client: Ace Books
title: Wrapt In Crystal
medium: Oil
size: 20"x30"

3
artist: VINCE NATALE
art director: Nick Krenitsky
client: Harper Collins
title: Starbright
And The Dream Eater
medium: Oil
size: 15"x20"

4
artist: JEAN PIERRE TARGETE
art director: Judith Murello
client: Ace Books
title: Circle At Center
medium: Oil
size: 20"x30"

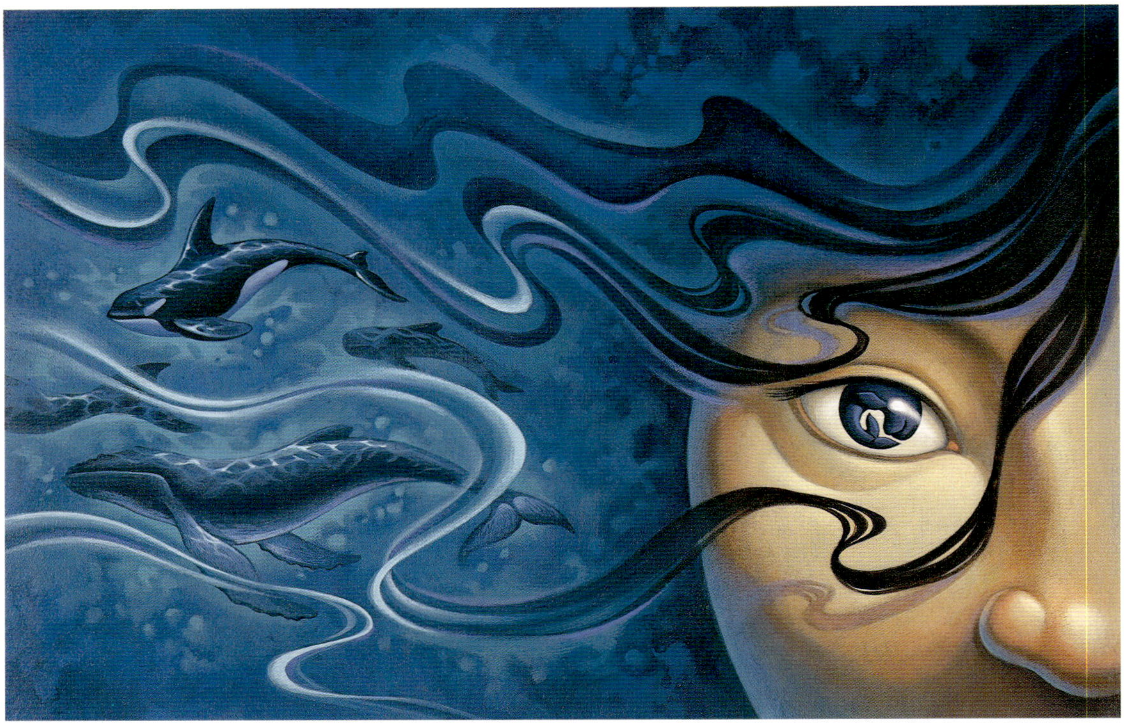

1

3

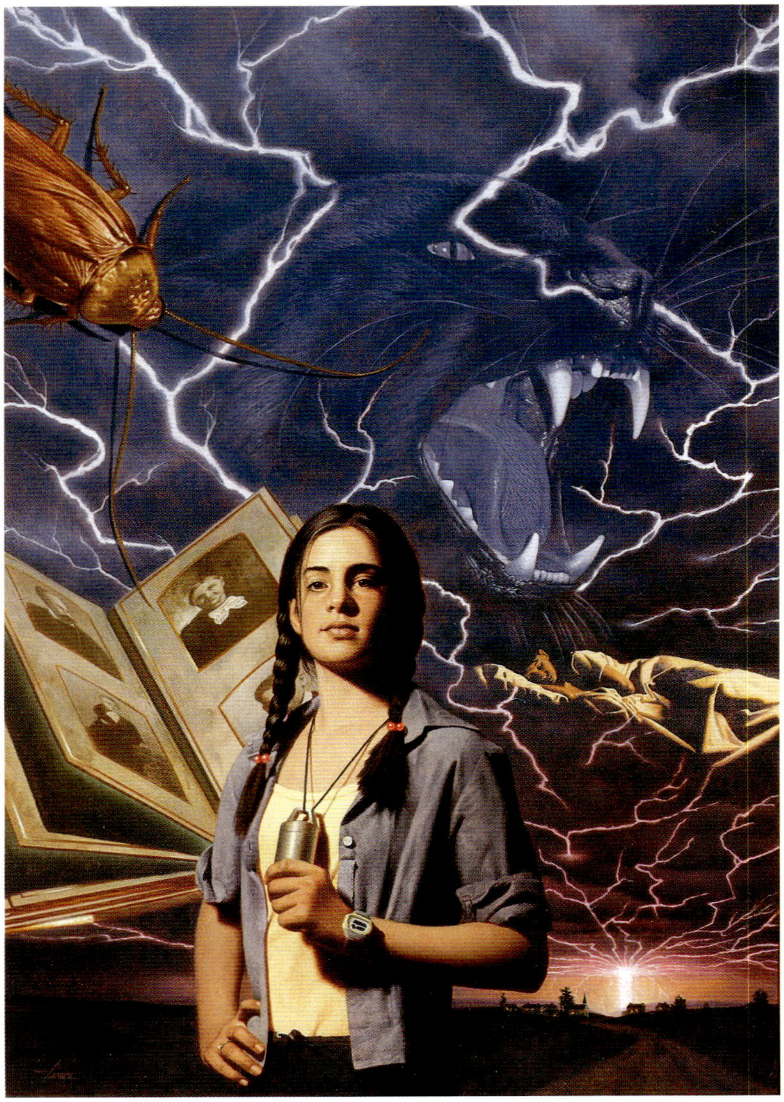

2

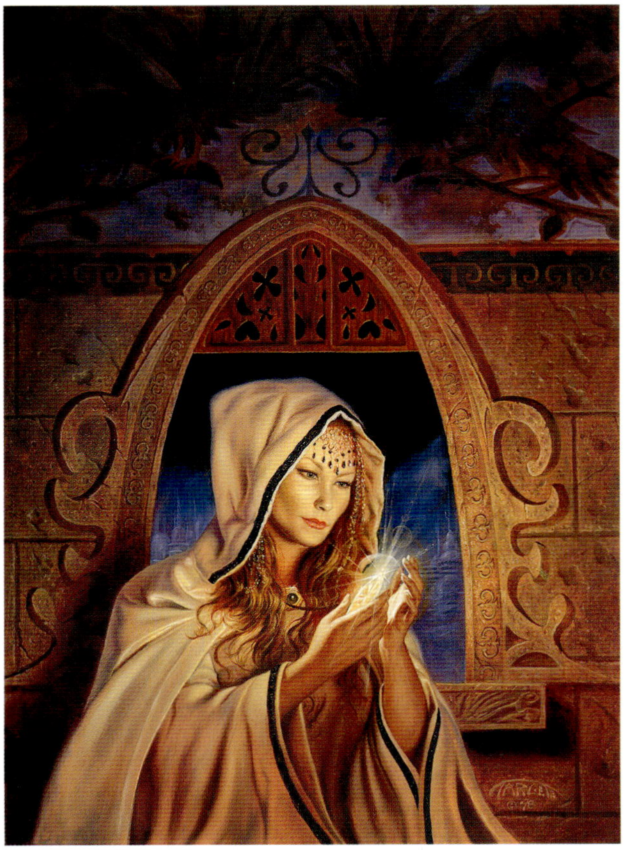

4

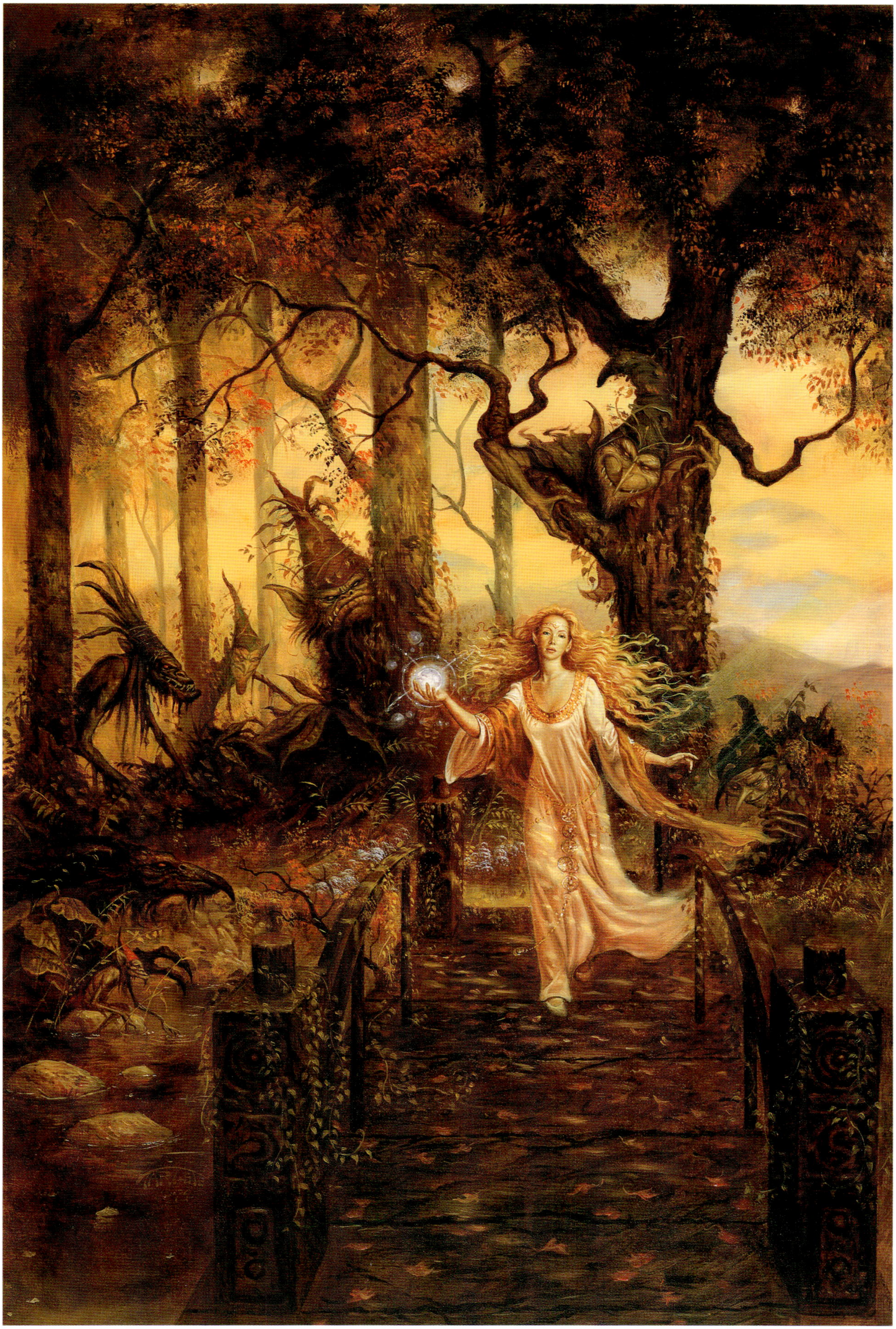

1
artist: JAMES NELSON
art director: James Nelson
client: FASA Corporation
title: Golems
medium: Watercolor
size: 8 1/4"x6 5/8"

2
artist: LES EDWARDS
designer: Lucie Straicker
client: Orion Publishing
title: Star Maker
medium: Oil

3
artist: JOHN PICACIO
art director: David Stevenson
client: DelRey
title: Millennium Rising
medium: Digital

4
artist: PAUL YOULL
art director: Toby Schwartz
client: Doubleday Direct
title: Rogue Moon
medium: Oil & acrylic
size: 18"x24"

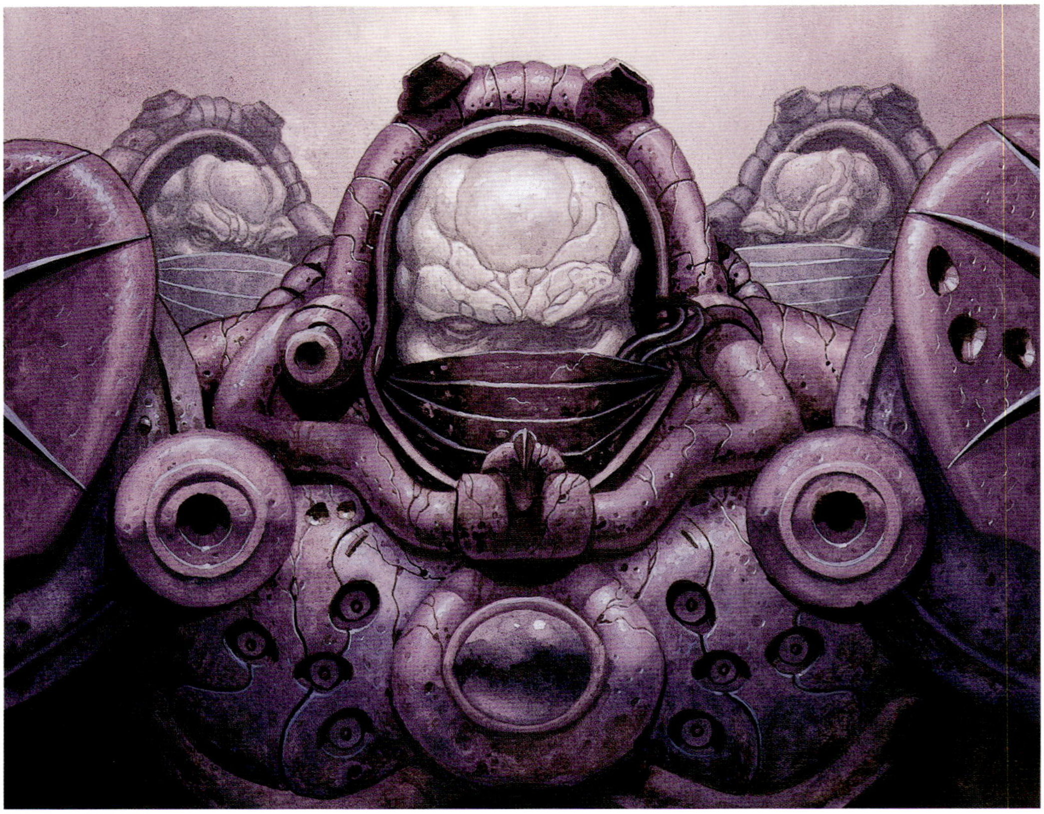

1

2

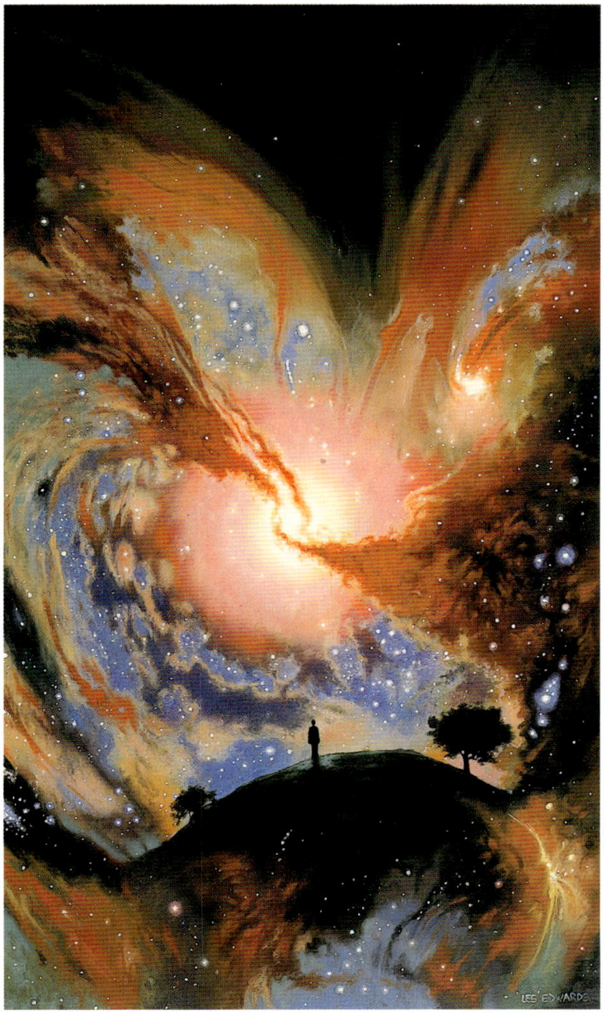

3

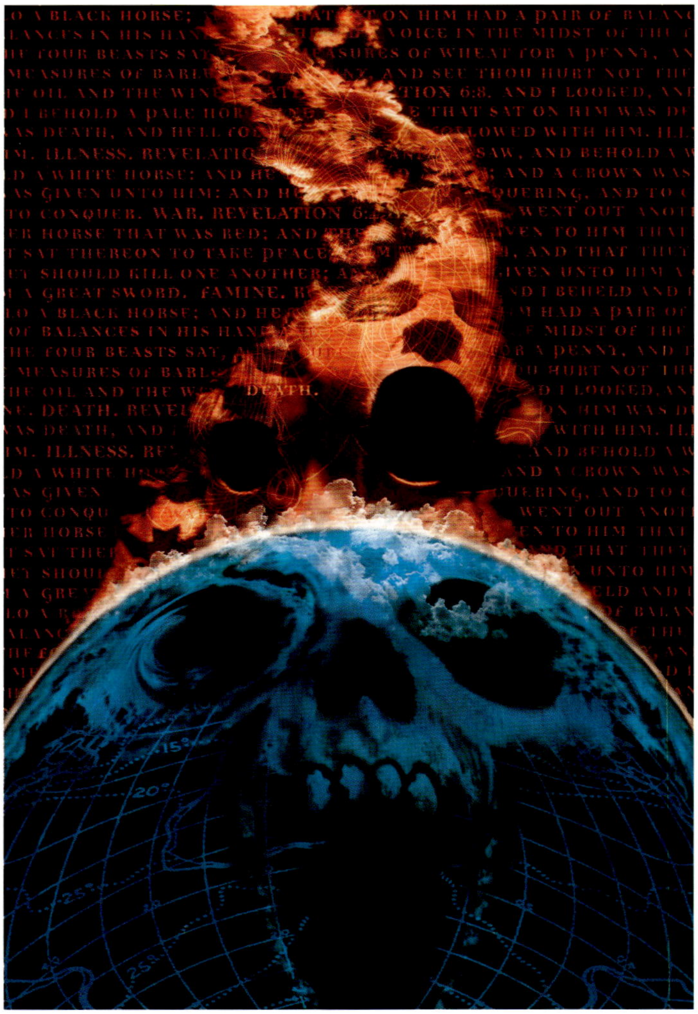

4

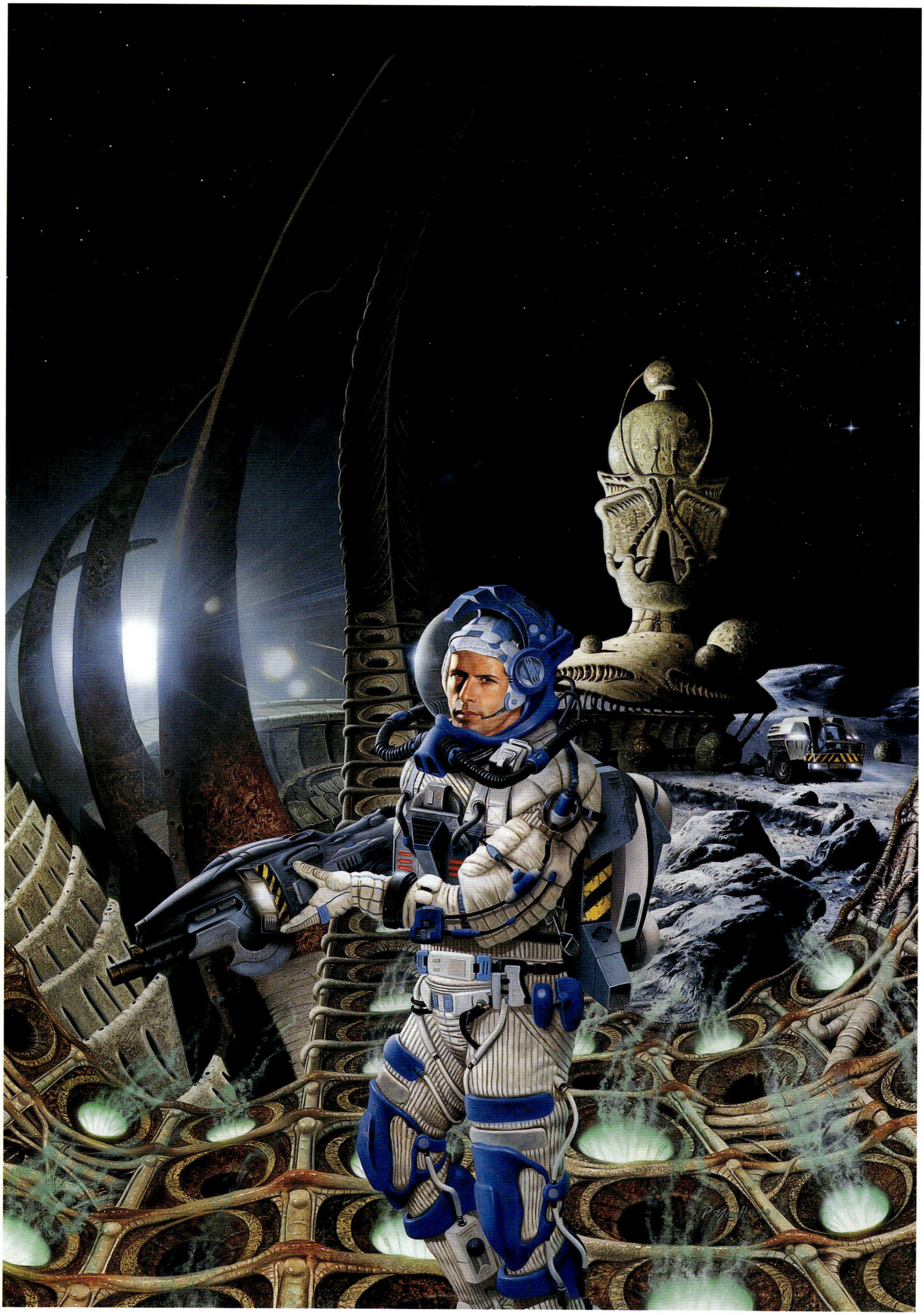

1
artist: HOWARD LYON
art director: Don Seegmiller
client: David Farland
title: The Fourth Giant
medium: Digital

2
artist: PETER DESEVE
art director: Rosanne Serra
client: Penguin
title: The Sooterkin
medium: Watercolor

3
artist: MARK ELLIOTT
art director: Isabel Warren-Lynch
client: Knoph Books
title: Robin's Country
medium: Acrylic
size: each 12"x18"

4
artist: SCOTT GUSTAFSON
art director: Susan Meyers
designer: Scott Gustafson
client: Harcourt Brace
title: Jester & King
medium: Oil
size: 11"x14"

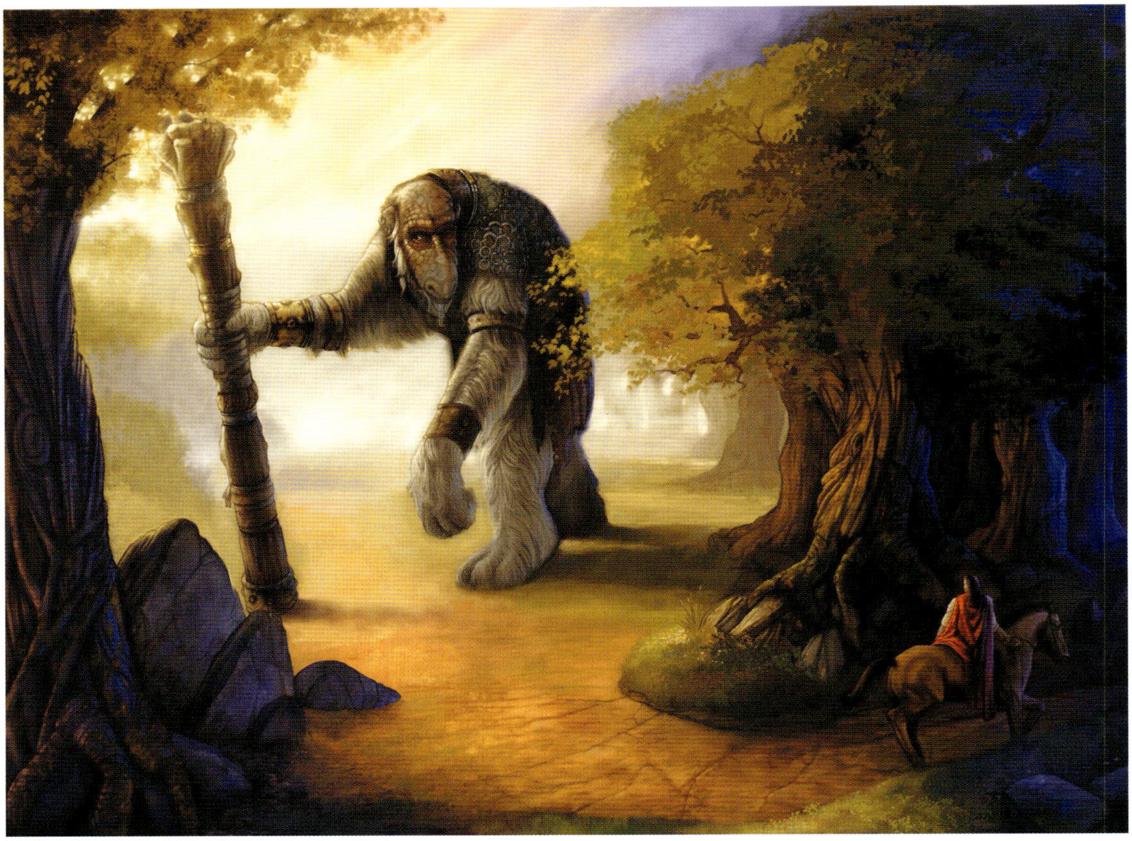

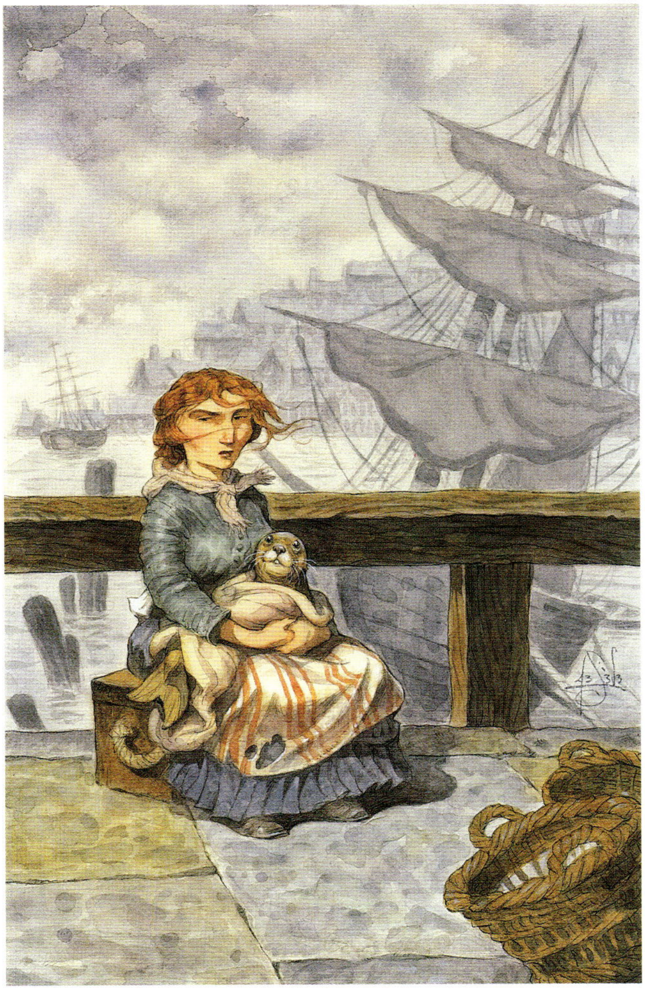

2

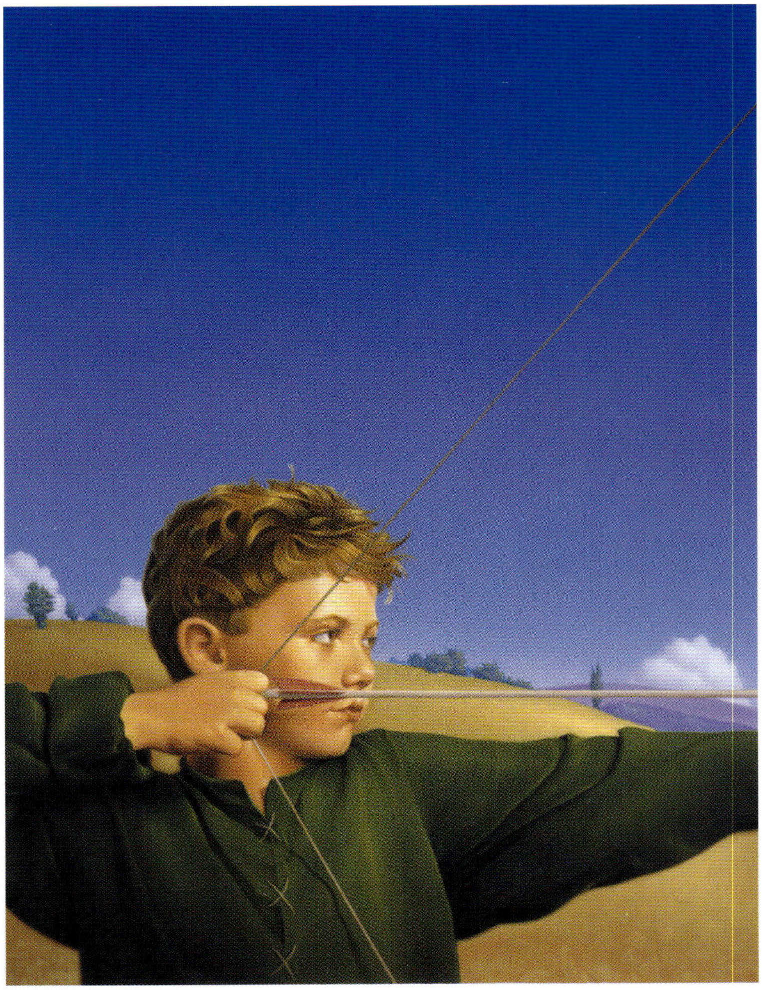

3

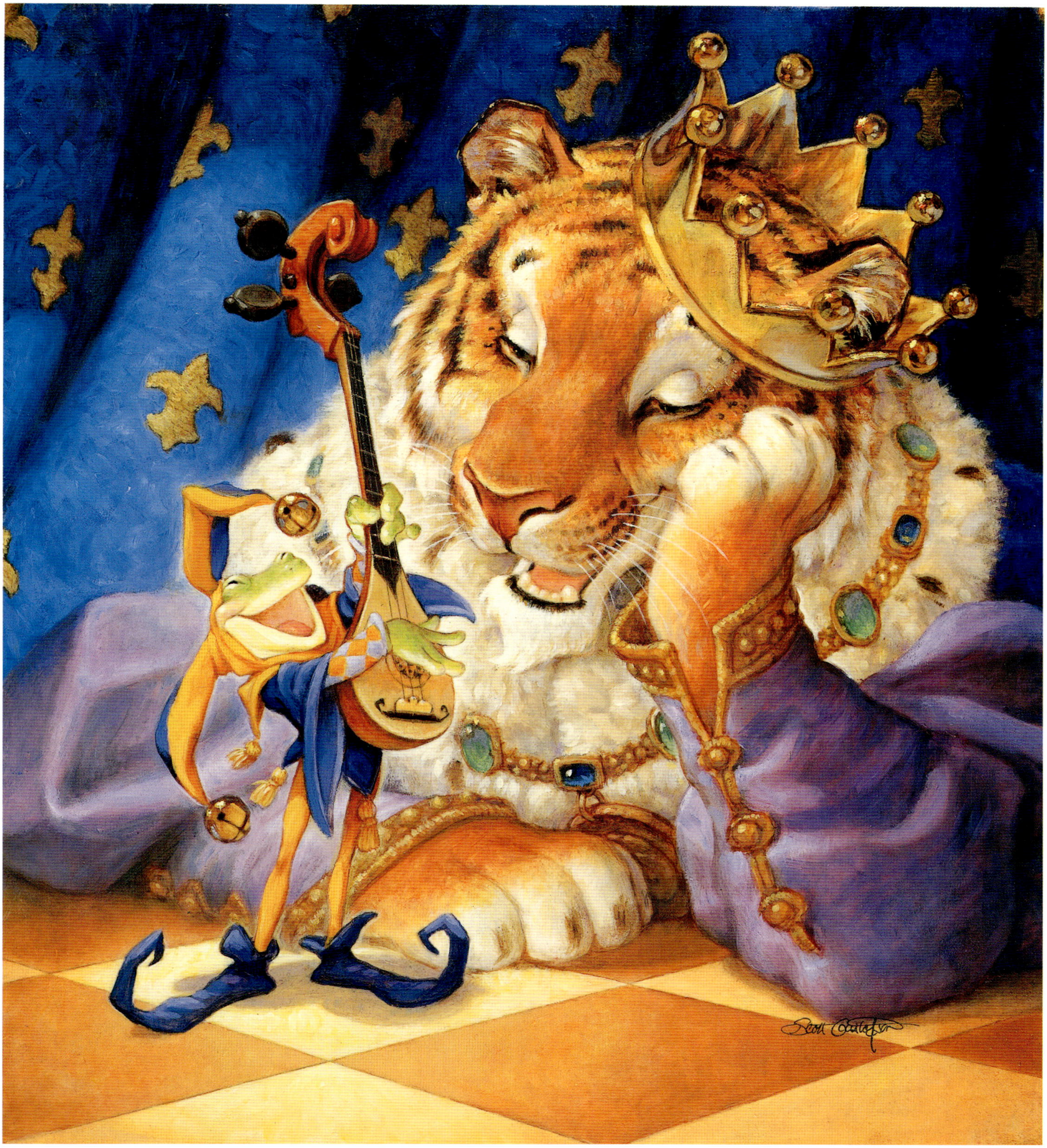

4

b o o k

1
artist: JAMES GURNEY
art director: James Gurney
client: HarperCollins
title: First Flight
medium: Oil
size: 39"x12"

2
artist: KINUKO Y. CRAFT
art director: Judith Murello
client: Ace Books
title: The Tower
At Stony Wood
medium: Mixed
size: 24"x16"

3
artist: MICHAEL WHELAN
art director: Sheila Gilbert
client: DAW Books
title: Otherland III
medium: Acrylic
size: 22"x30"

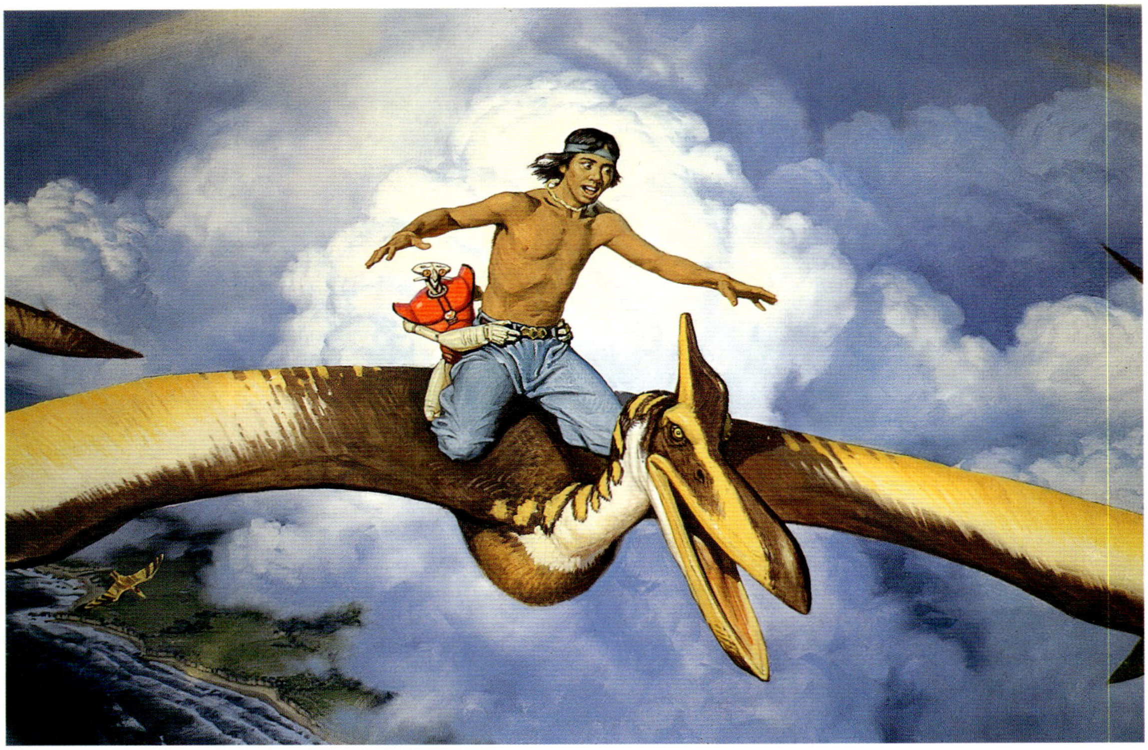

1

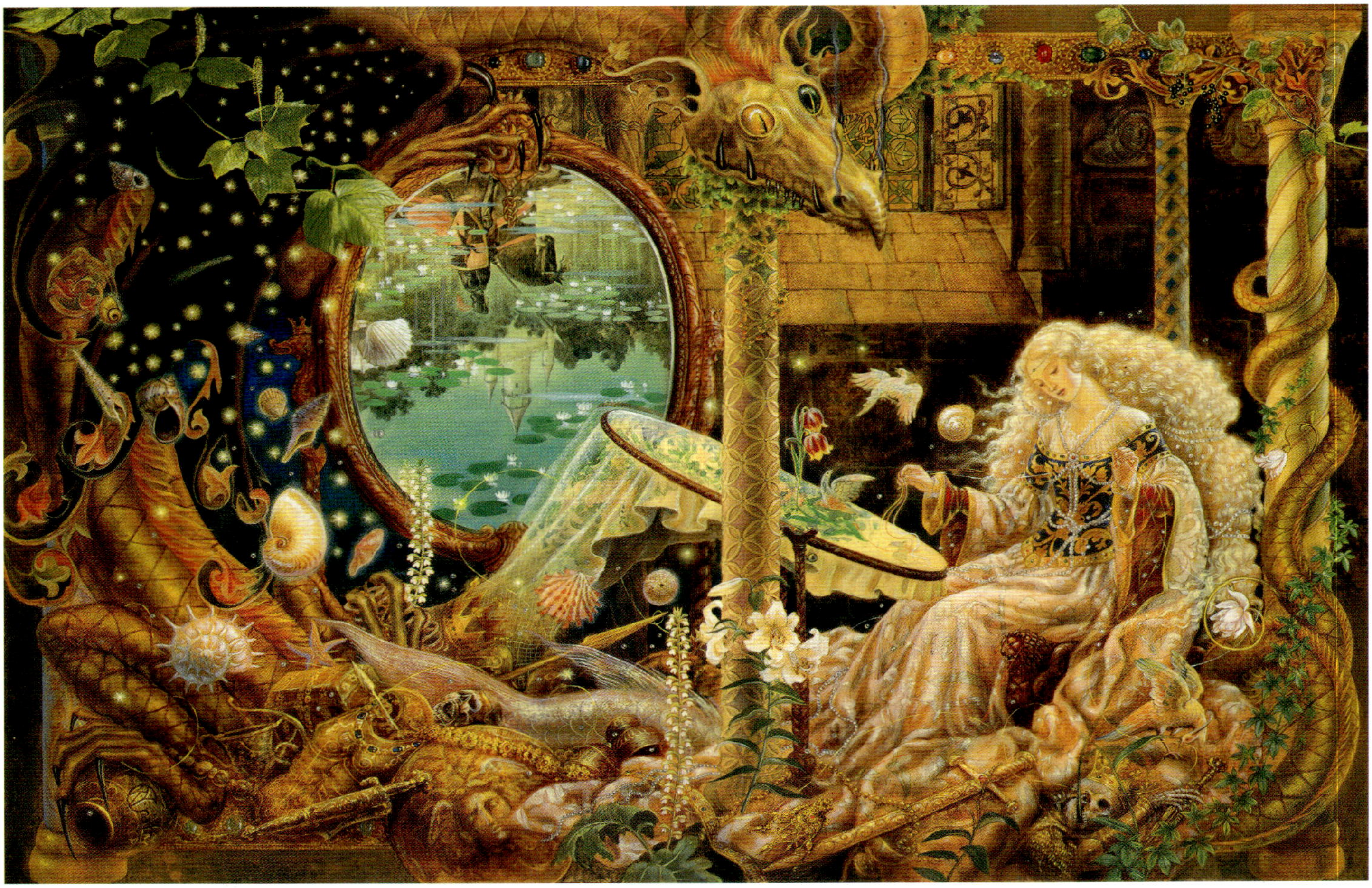

2

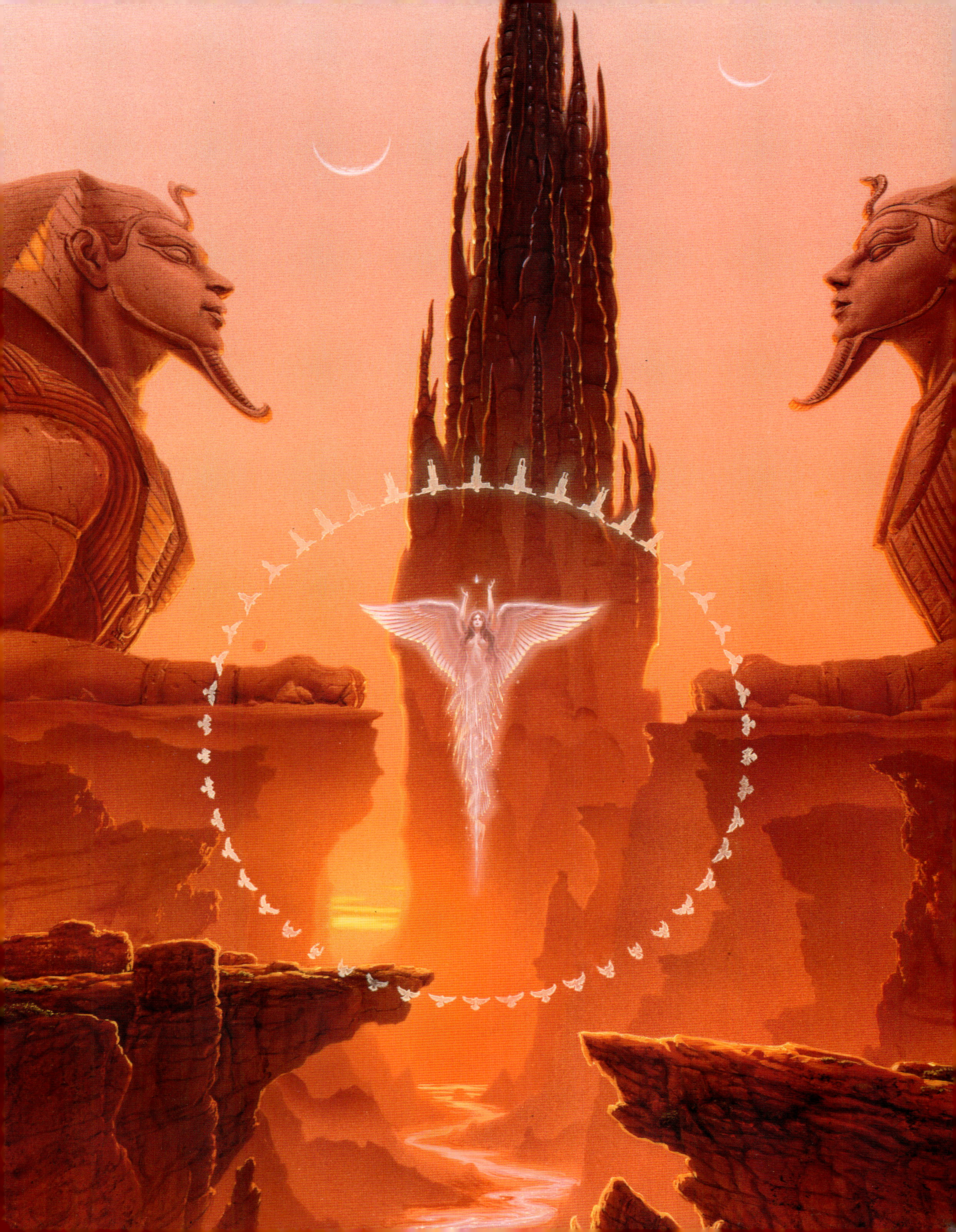

1
artist: JIM BURNS
art director: Liz Laczynska
lient: Transworld
title: Paradox
medium: Oil

2
artist: BRUCE JENSON
art director: Toby Schwartz
client: Doubleday Direst
title: On Company Time
medium: Acrylic
size: 14"x20"

3
artist: PETER SCANLON
art director: Jim Nelson
client: FASA
title: Behind the Crimson Veil
medium: Digital
size: 11"x13 1/2"

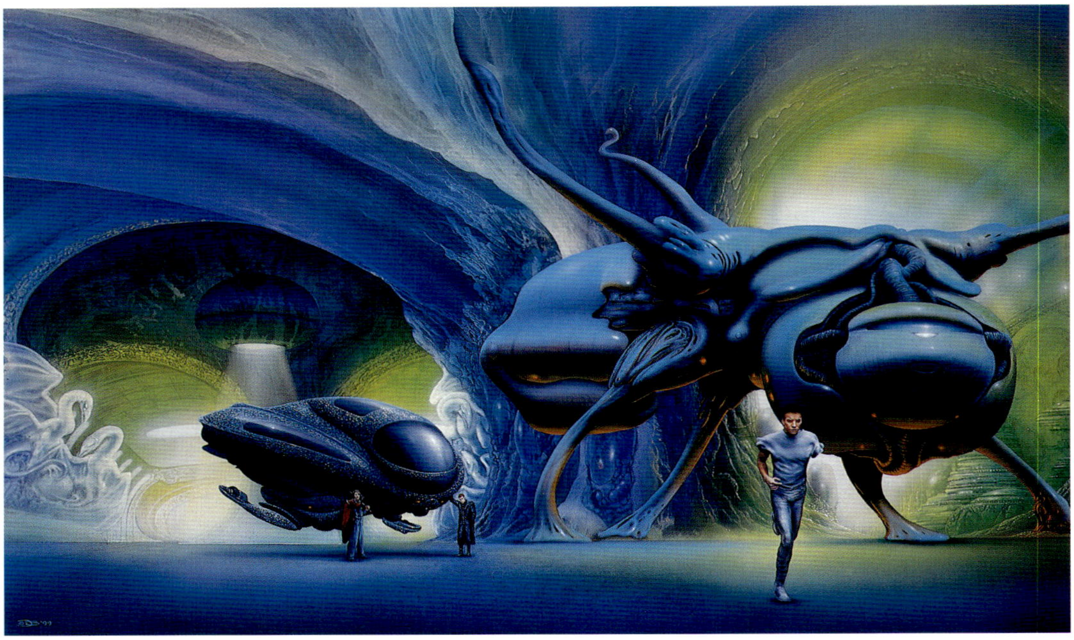

1

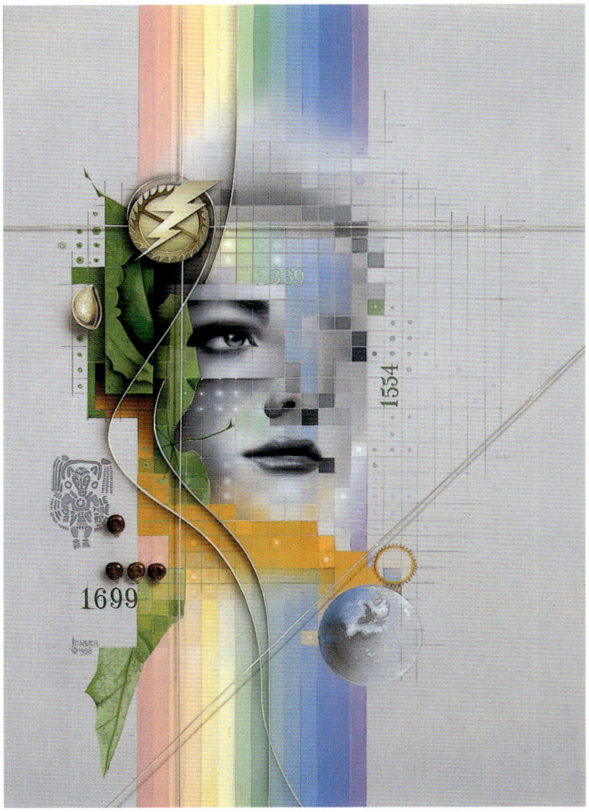

2

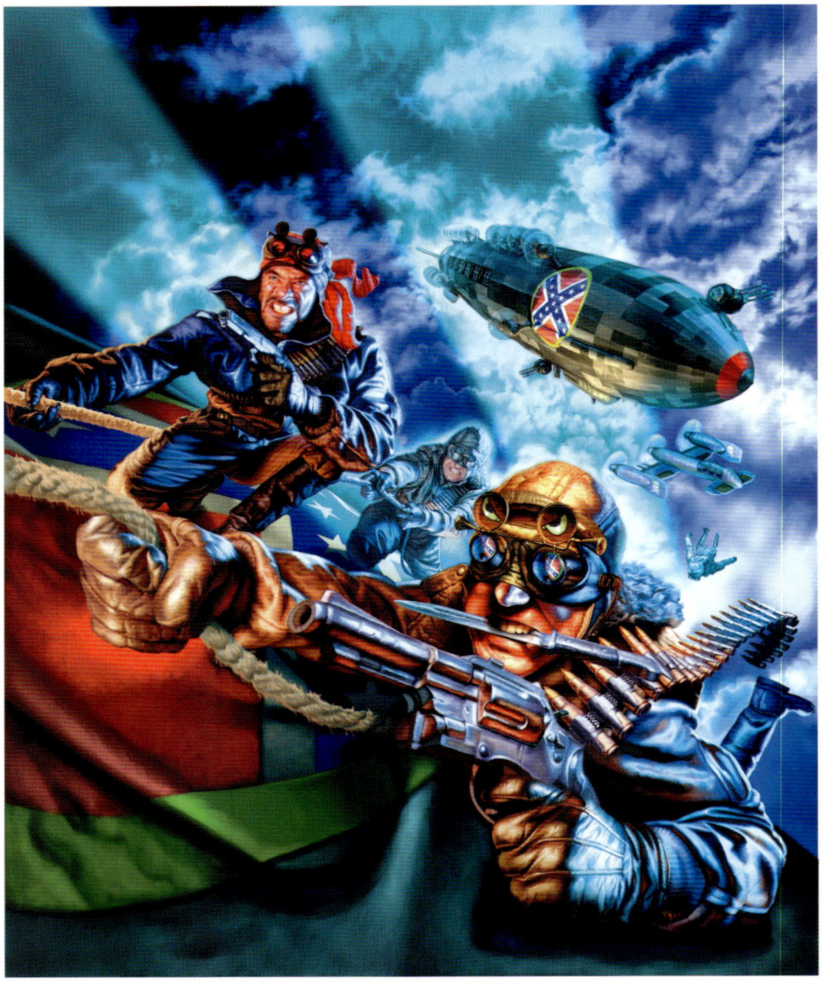

3

4
artist: BRUCE JENSON
art director: Irene Gallo
client: Tor Books
title: Starfish
medium: Acrylic
size: 14"x20"

4

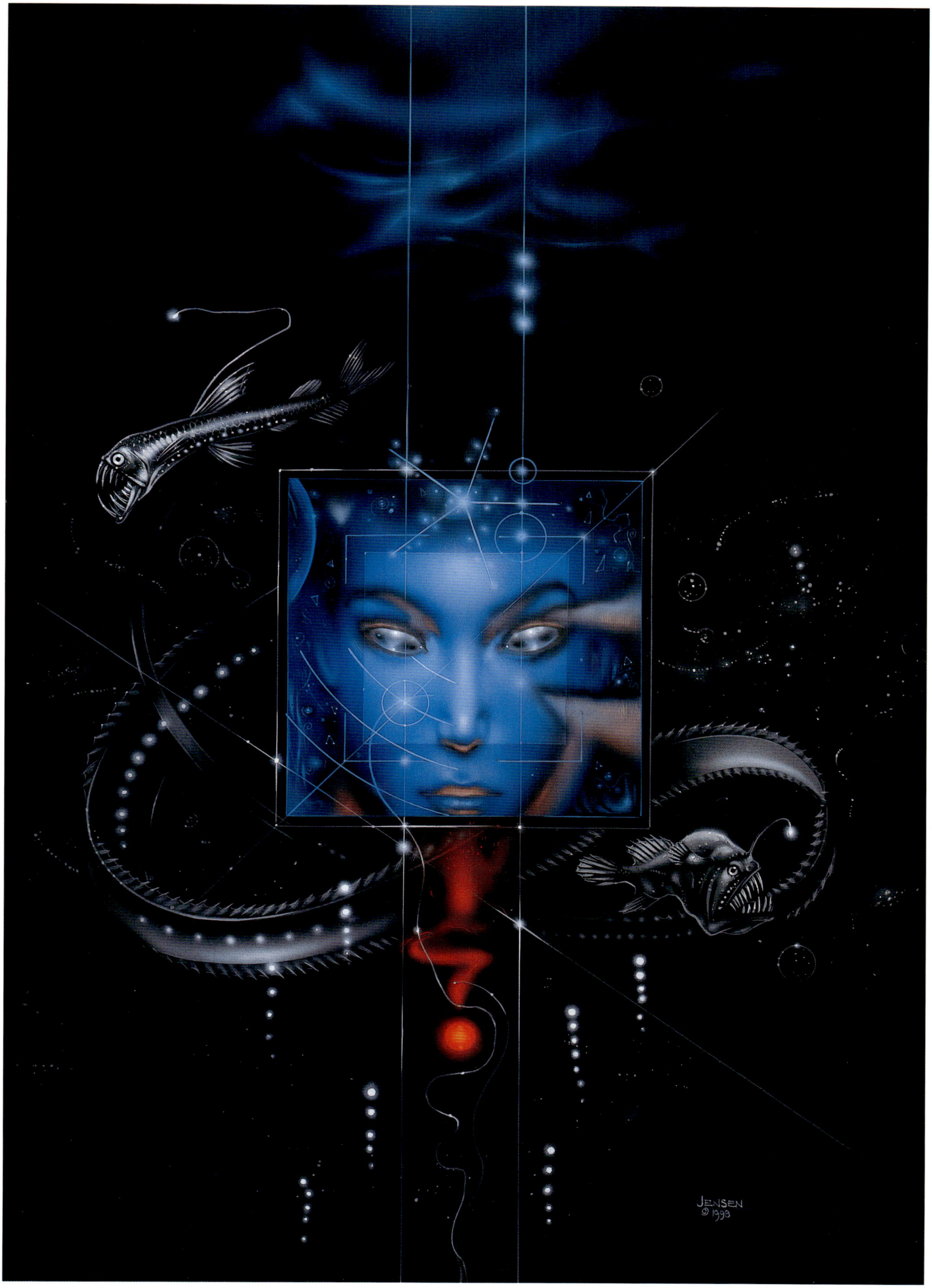

1
artist: ROB ALEXANDER
art director: Rob Alexander
client: Shadowlands Press
title: At the End of It All
medium: Watercolor *size:* 19"x12"

2
artist: GARY GIANNI
art director: Marcelo Anciano
client: Wandering Star
title: "...into the bowels of the earth!"
medium: Oil *size:* 30"x40"

3
artist: RICK BERRY
art director: Kevin Murphy
designer: Rick Berry
client: Meisha/Merlin
title: Ishtar
medium: Mixed

4
artist: GARY GIANNI
art director: Marcelo Anciano
client: Wandering Star
title: "...strokes of death"

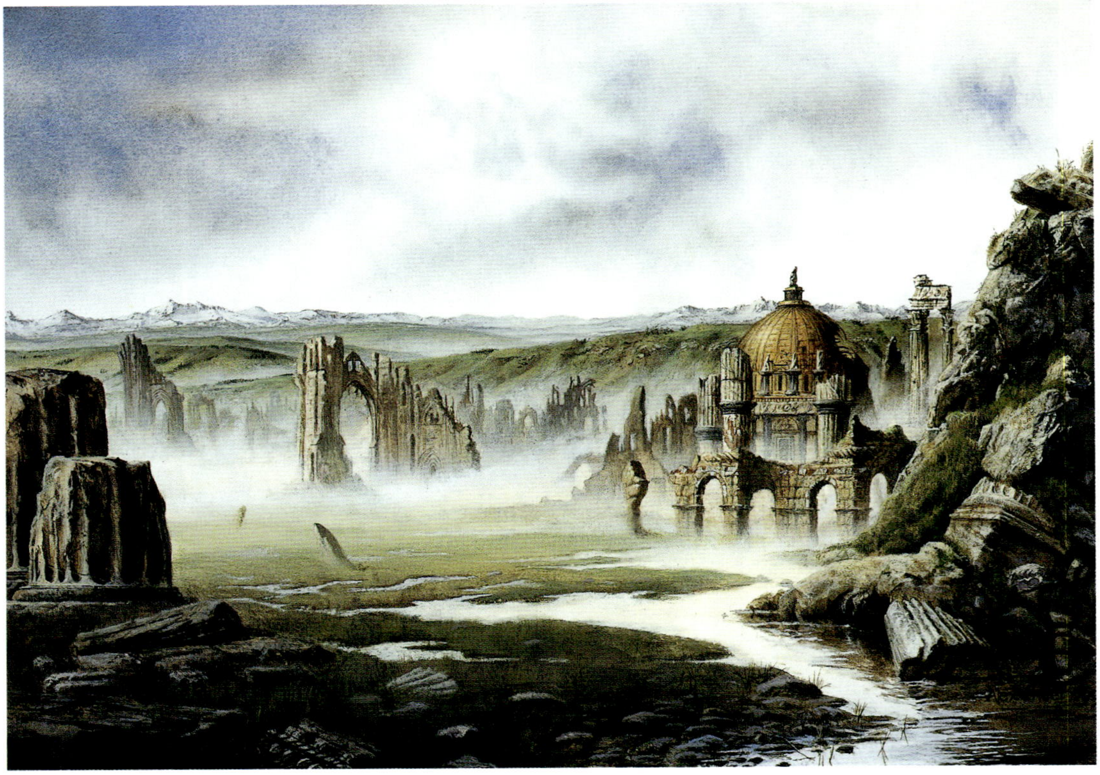

1

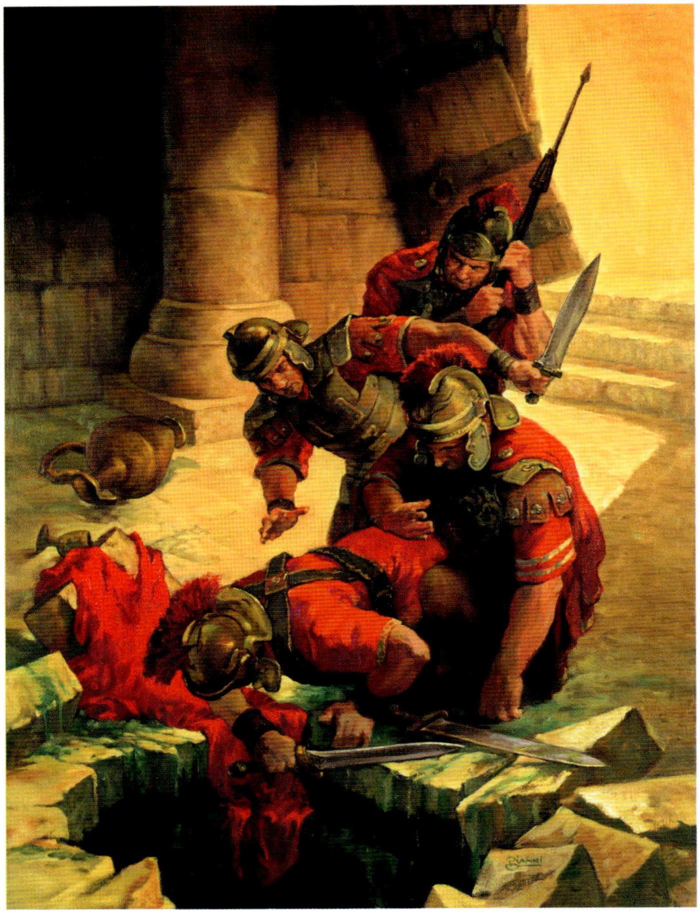

2

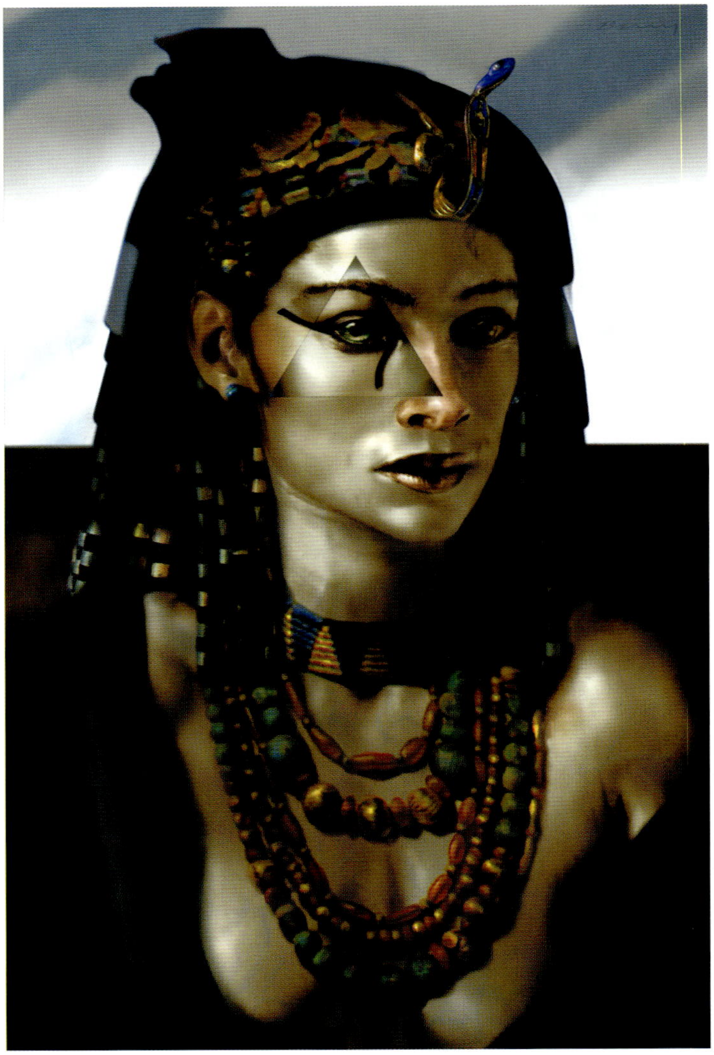

3

4

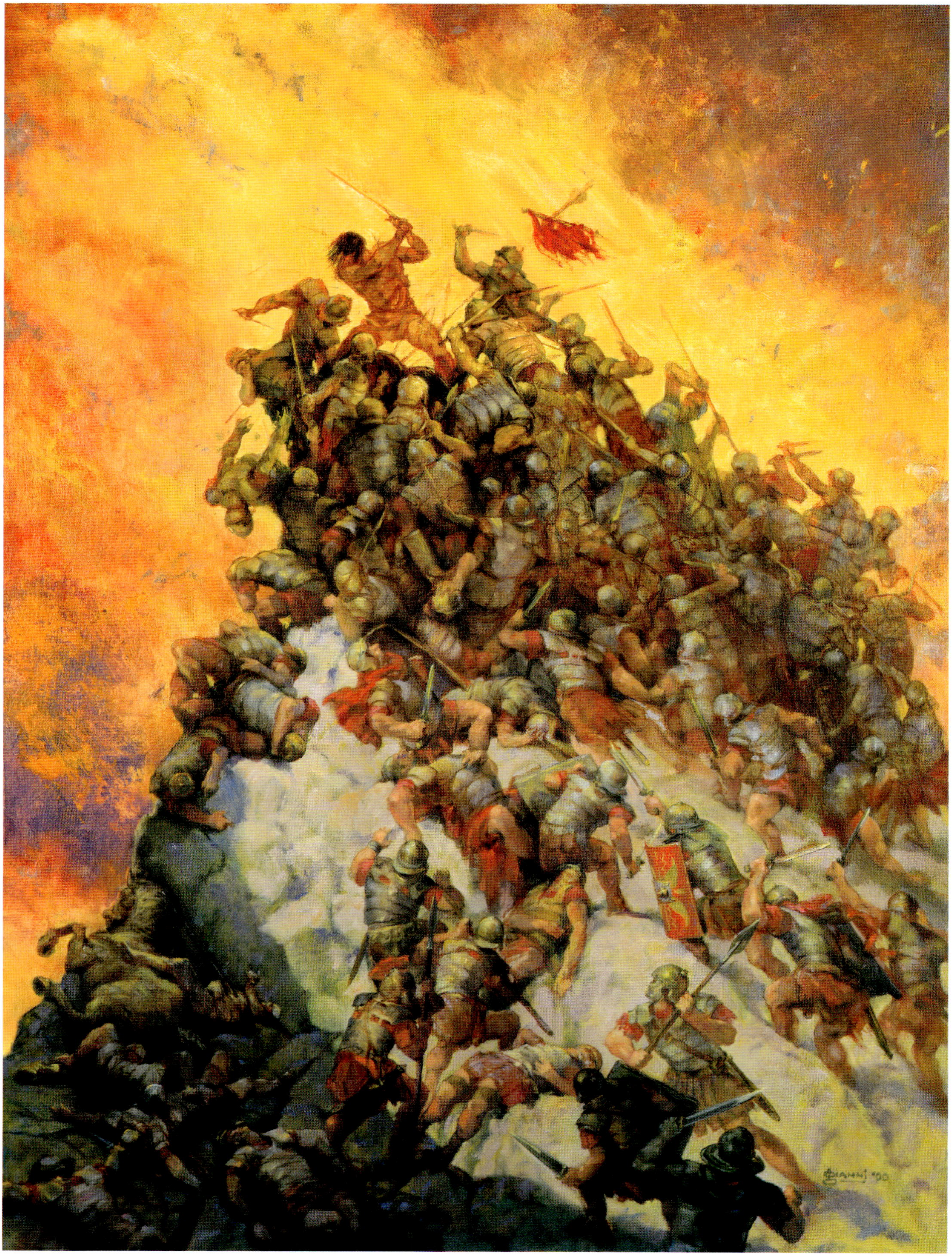

1
artist: DAVID BOWERS
art director: Lisa Peters
client: Harcourt Brace
title: The Pearl of the Soul of the World
medium: Oil *size:* 10 3/4"x18"

2
artist: GARY RUDDELL
art director: Jim Baen
client: Baen Books
title: The Unlikely Ones
medium: Oil *size:* 16"x20"

3
artist: JODY LEE
art director: Sheila Gilbert & Betsy Wollheim
client: DAW Books
title: The Black Swan
medium: Mixed *size:* 30"x20"

4
artist: DAVID BOWERS
art director: Tom Egner
designer: Mark Stringer
client: Avon Books
title: The Annunciate
medium: Oil *size:* 14 1/2"x20 1/2"

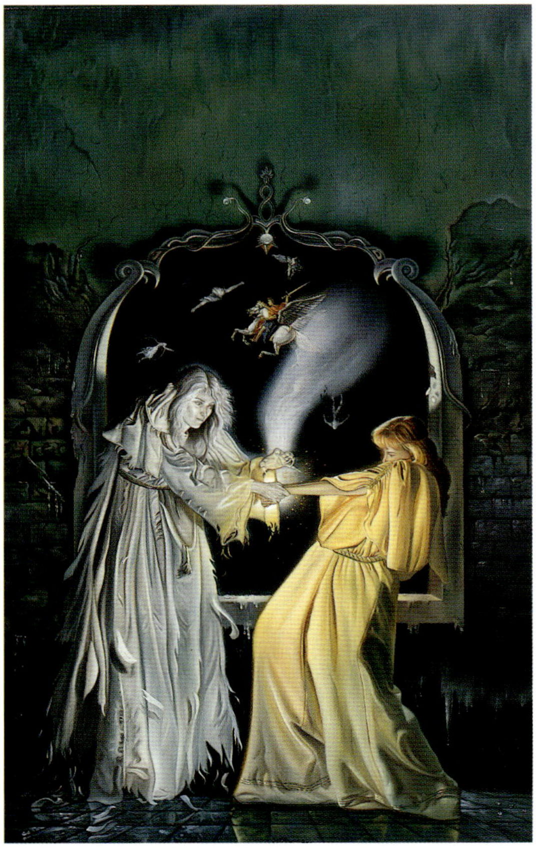

1

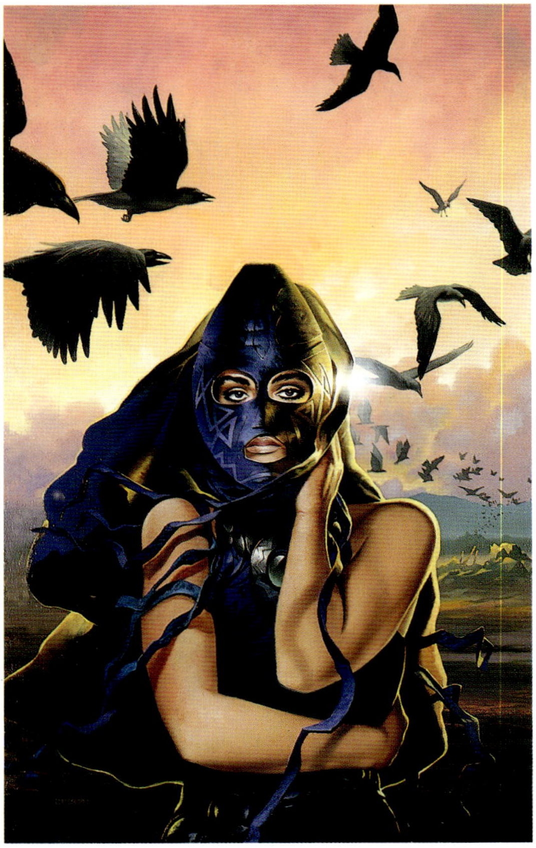

2

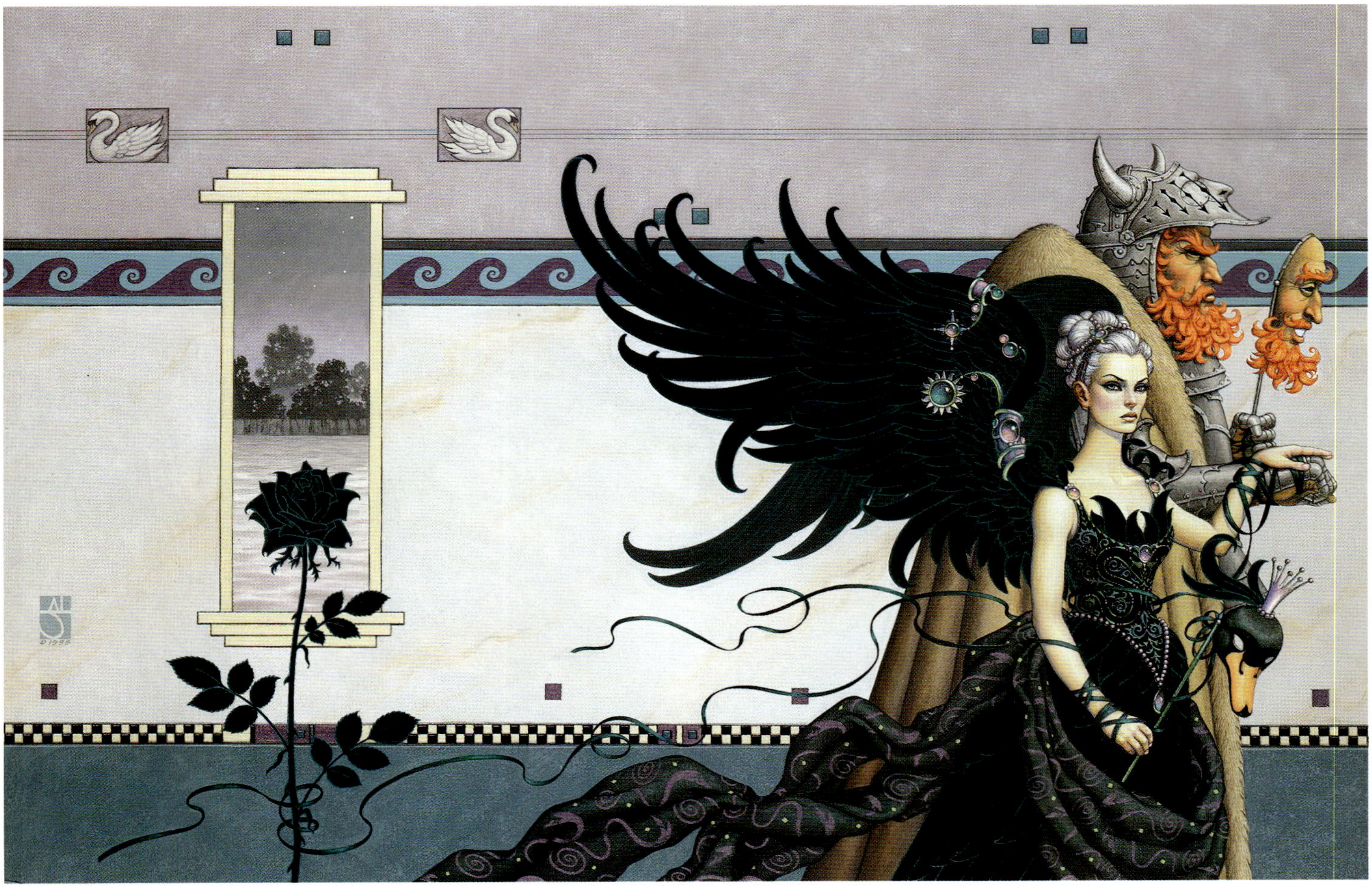

3

4

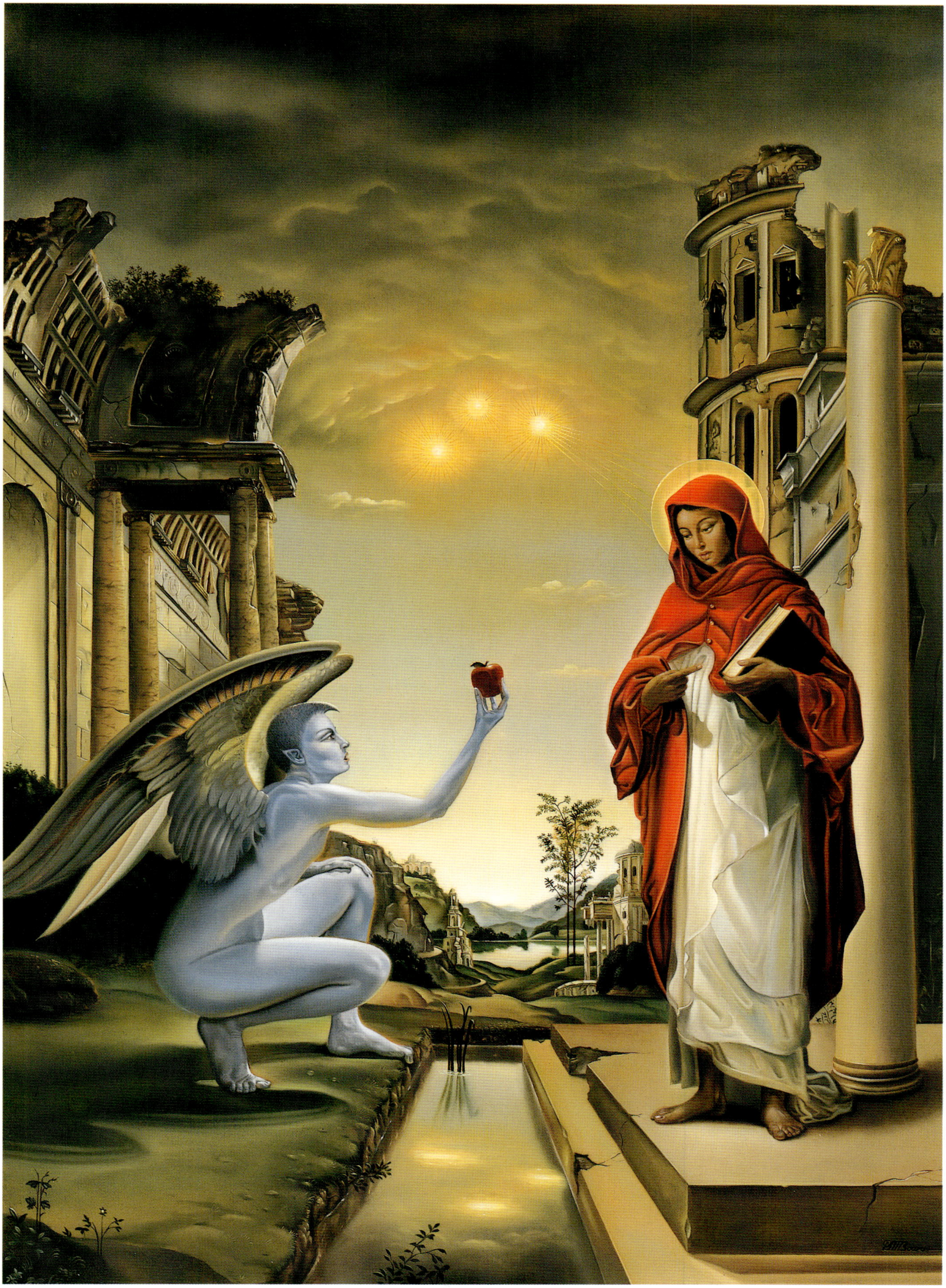

1
artist: TOM ANG
art director: Richard Thomas
client: White Wolf Publishing
title: Sunglasses After Dark
medium: Digital

2
artist: THOM ANG
art director: Margaret Clark
client: Pocket Books
title: Paradox of Virtue
medium: Digital

3
artist: CHRIS MOORE
art director: Lucie Stericker
client: Orion Books
title: The Rediscovery of Man
medium: Acrylic
size: 11"x17"

4
artist: JOHN C. BERKEY
art director: Toby Schwartz
client: Doubleday Direct
title: Chronicles of the Lensman
medium: Casein acrylic
size: 14"x22"

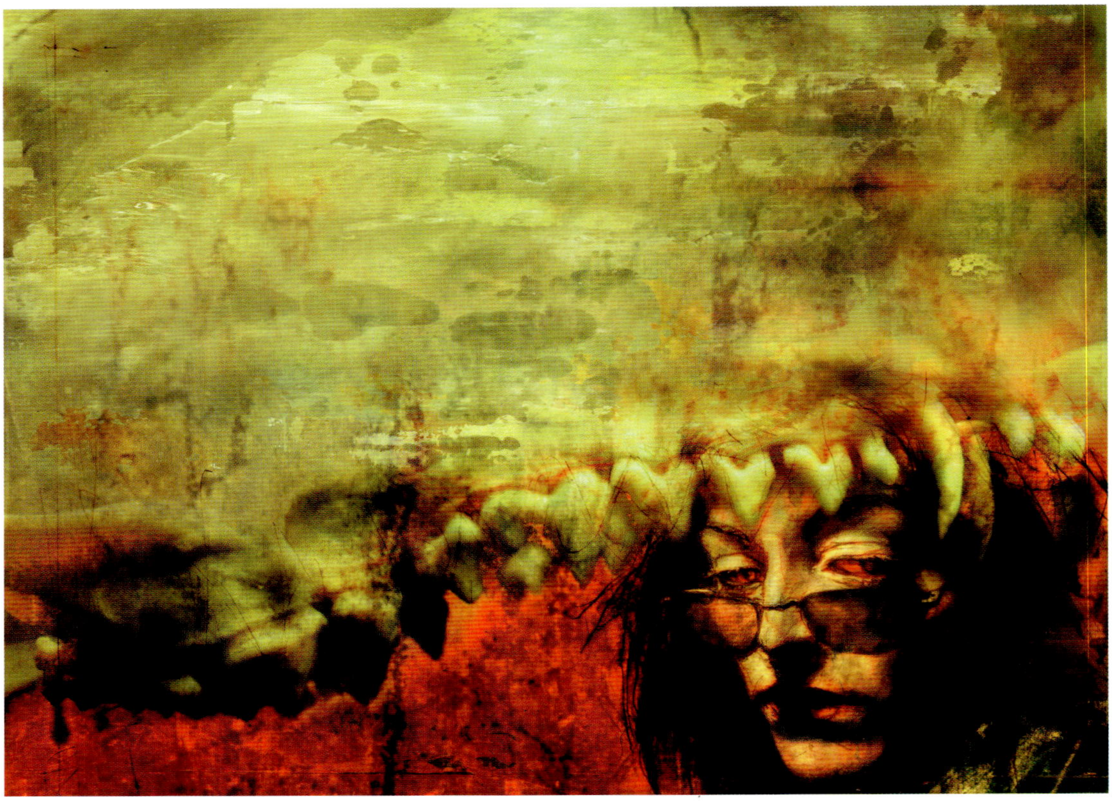
1

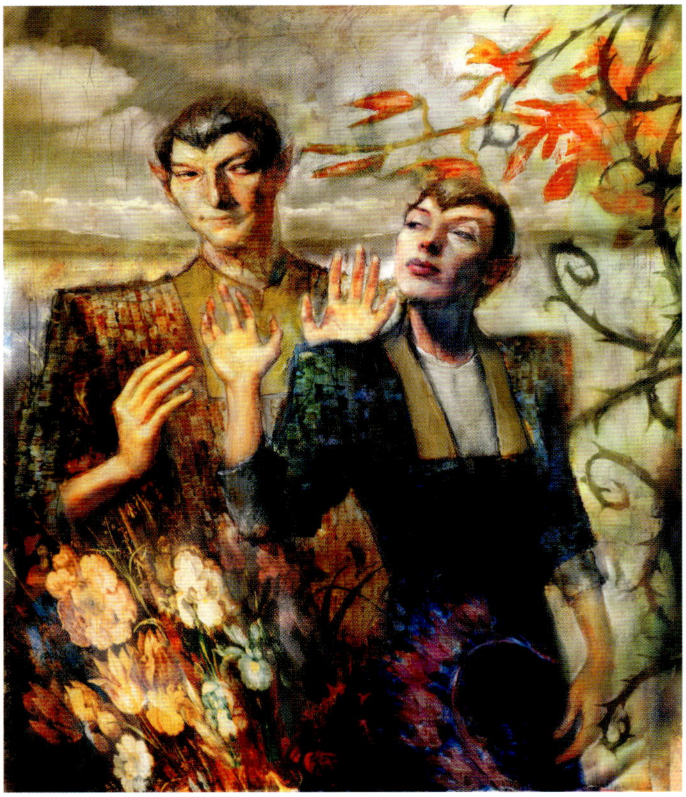

2

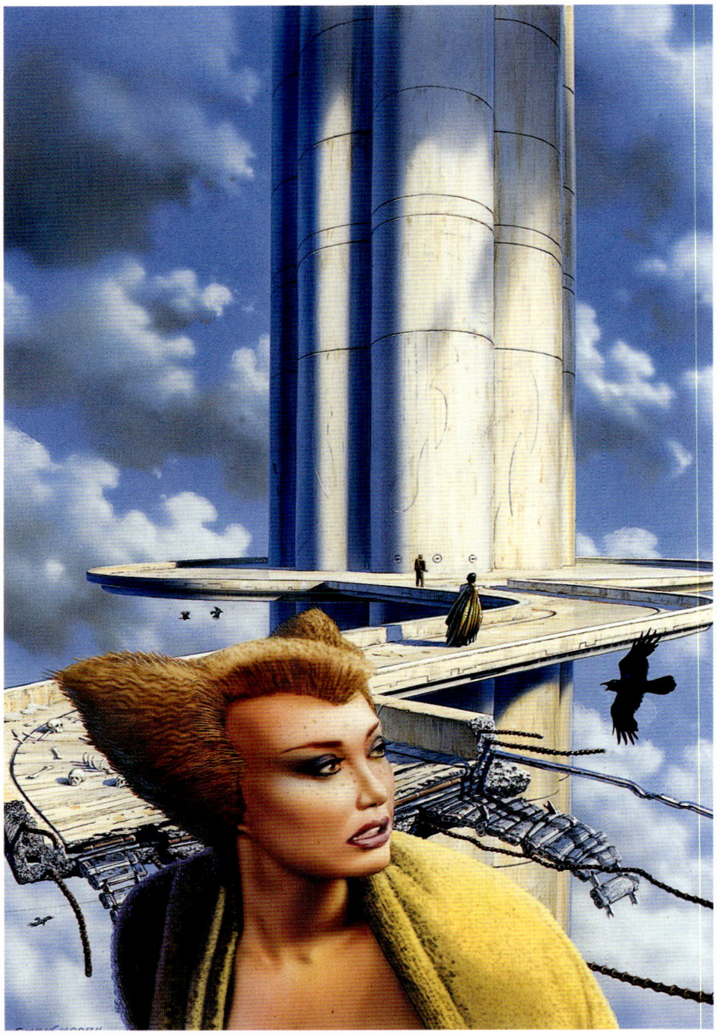
3

4

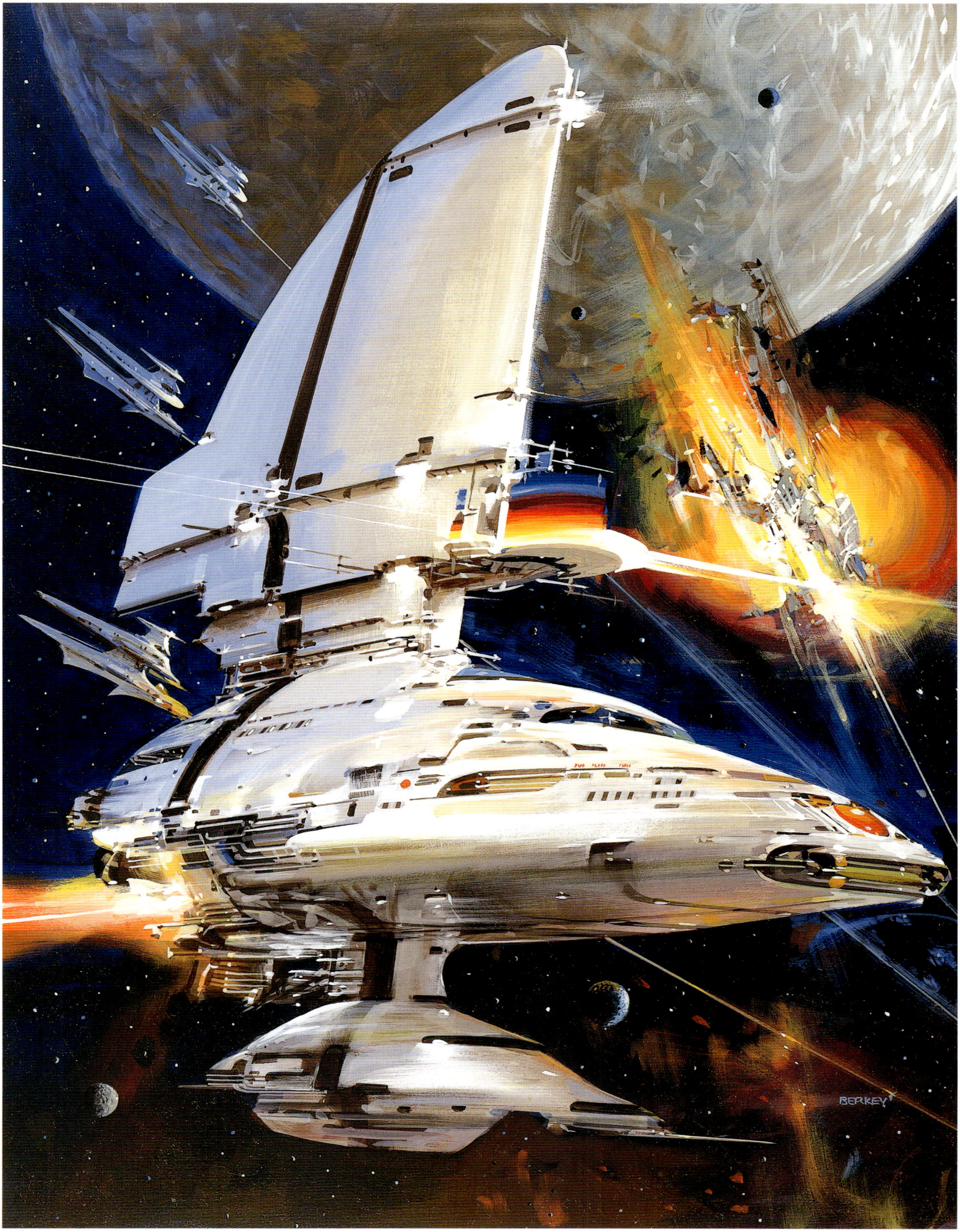

1
artist: CIRUELO
art director: Jamie Warren Youll
client: Bantam Books
title: Shadow Star
medium: Acrylic
size: 28"x20"

2
artist: JON SULLIVAN
art director: Lucy Stericker
client: Orion PLC
title: Black Swan
medium: Oil
size: 24"x13"

3
artist: CIRUELO
art director: Ciruelo
client: SQP, Inc.
title: Magia:
The Ciruelo Sketchbook
medium: Oil/digital
size: 20"x28"

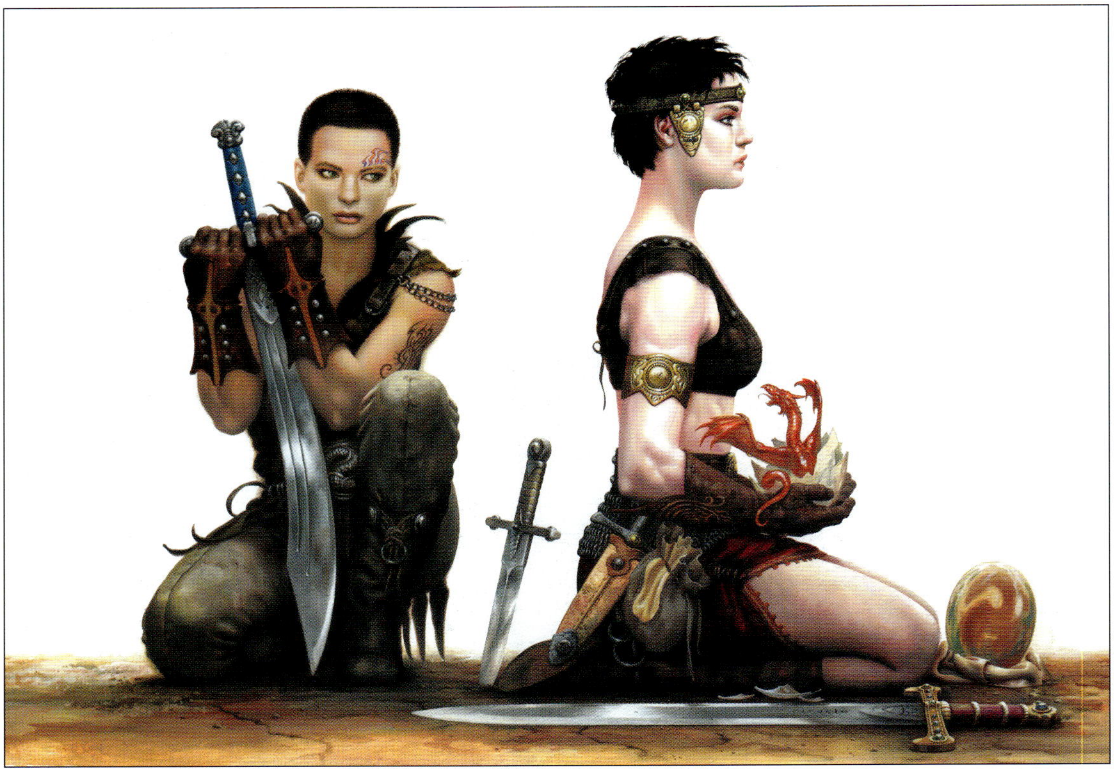

1

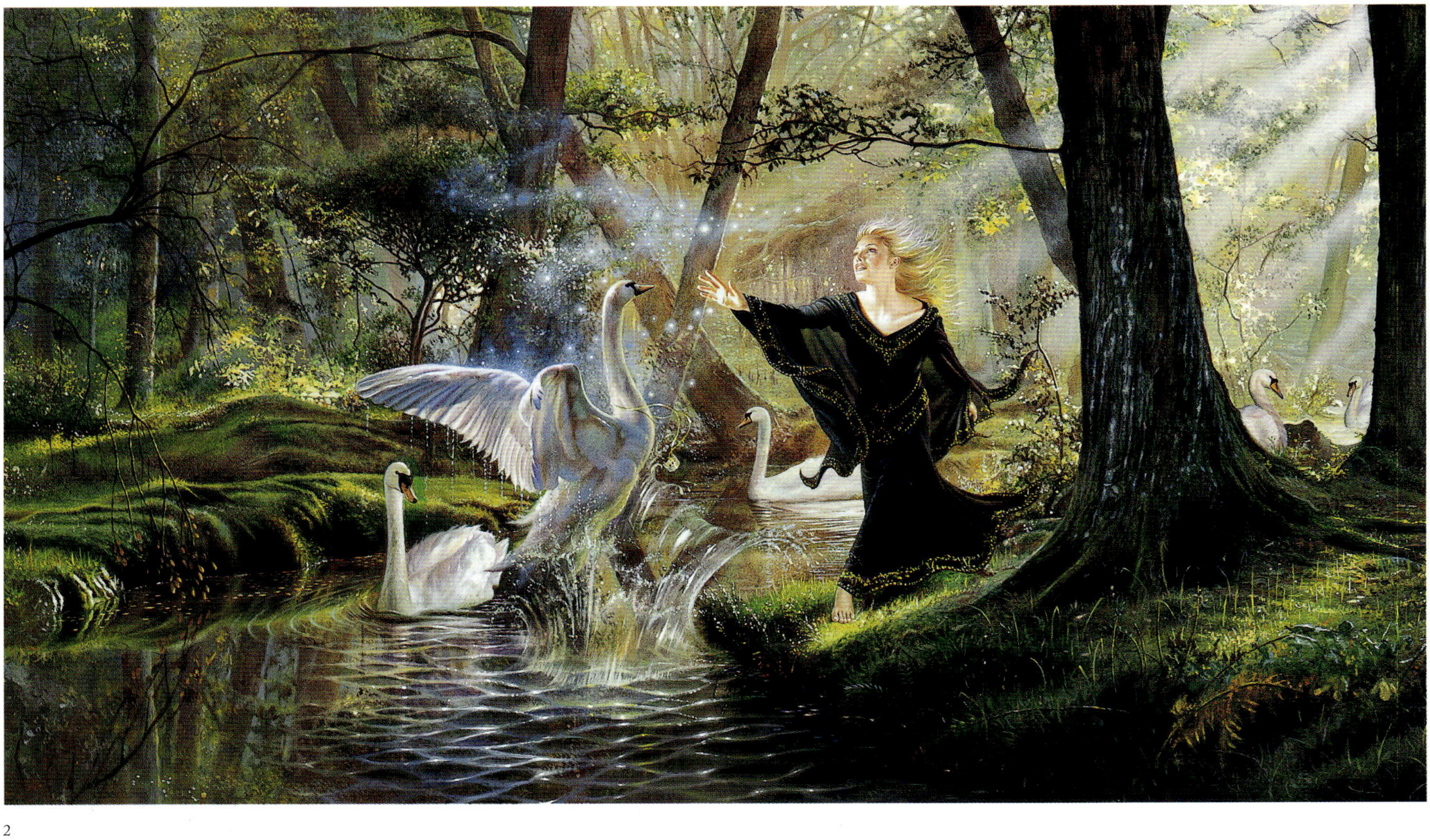

2

3

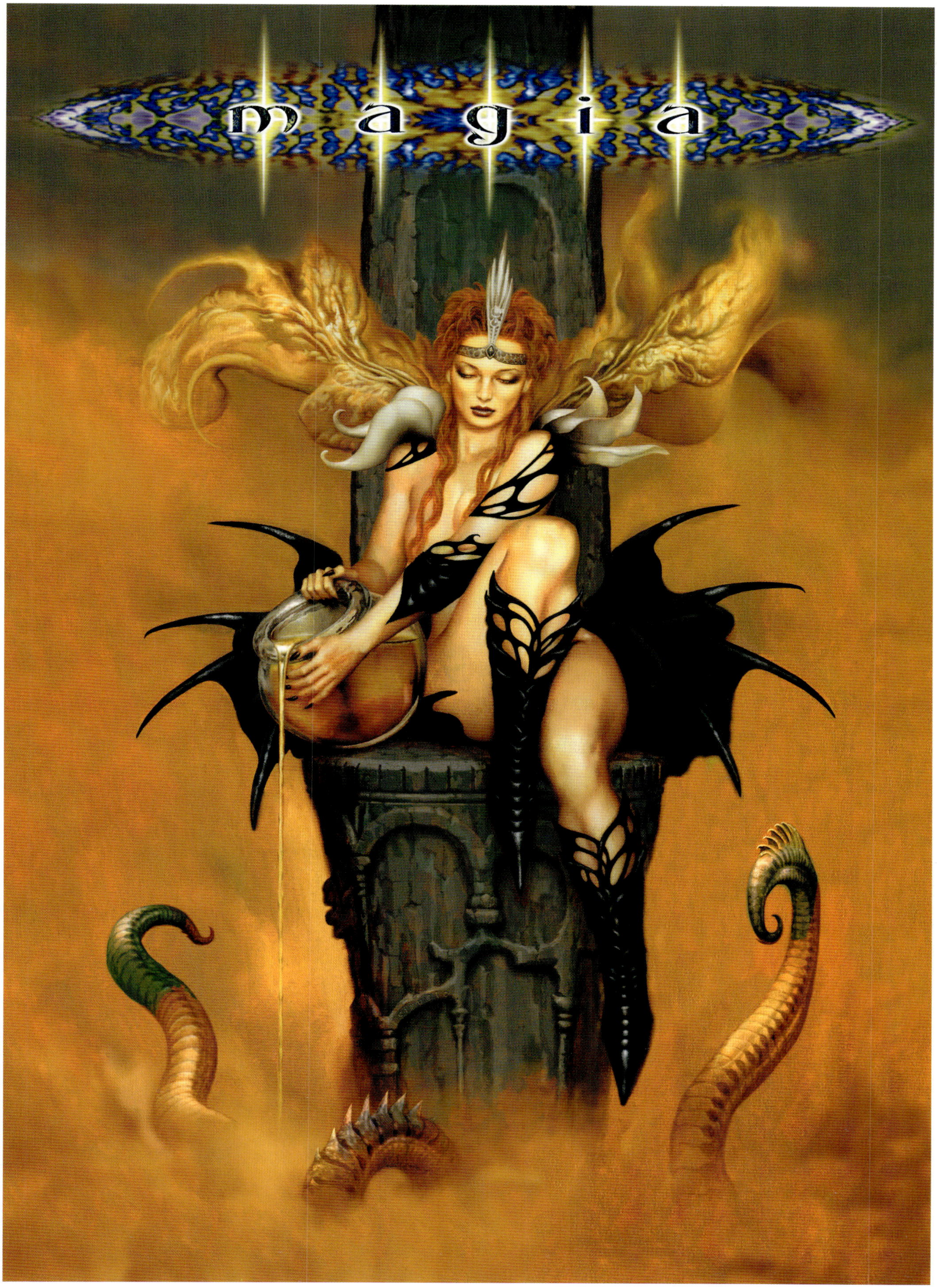

1
artist: JUDY YORK
art director: Sheila Gilbert
client: DAW Books
title: Flightless Falcon
medium: Digital

2
artist: JUDY YORK
art director: Joni Friedman
client: Berkley Books
title: Love Potion #9
medium: Digital

3
artist: MARK HARRISON
art director: Nadina Gray
client: Hodder Headline
title: Sweet Dreams Are Made of This
medium: Digital

4
artist: OSCAR CHICHONI
client: Norma Editorial S.A.
title: Mekanika
medium: Oil

1

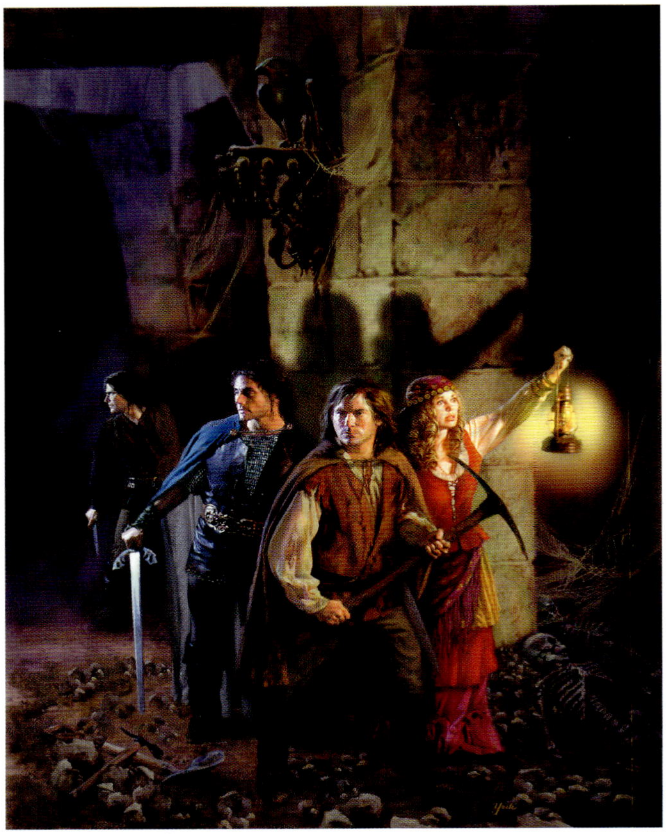

2

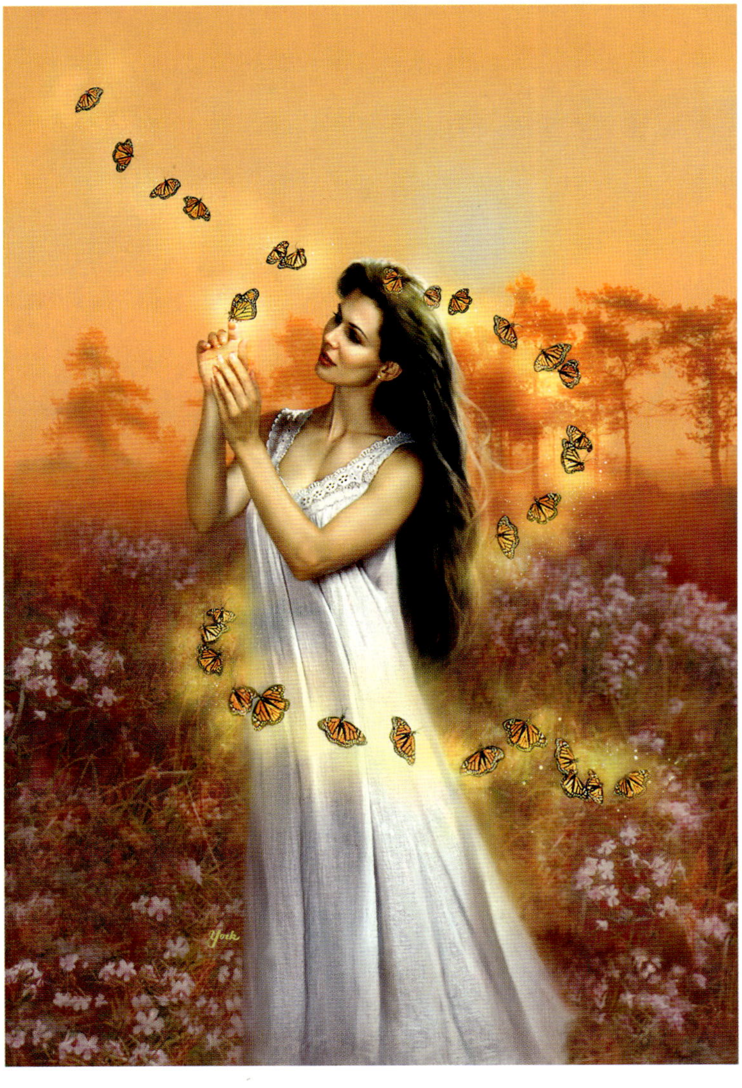

3

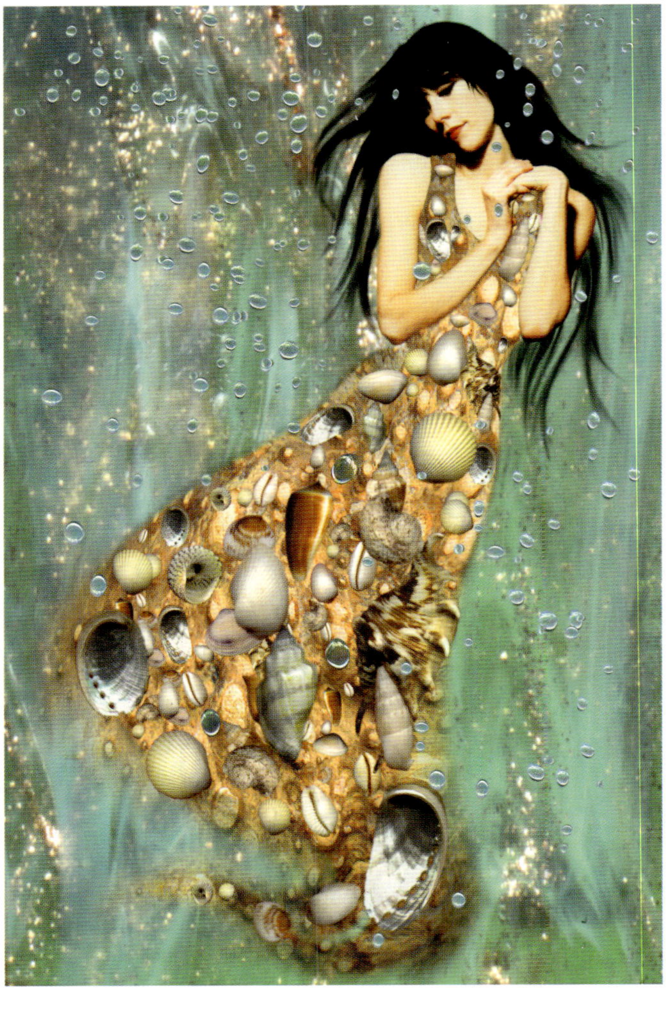

4

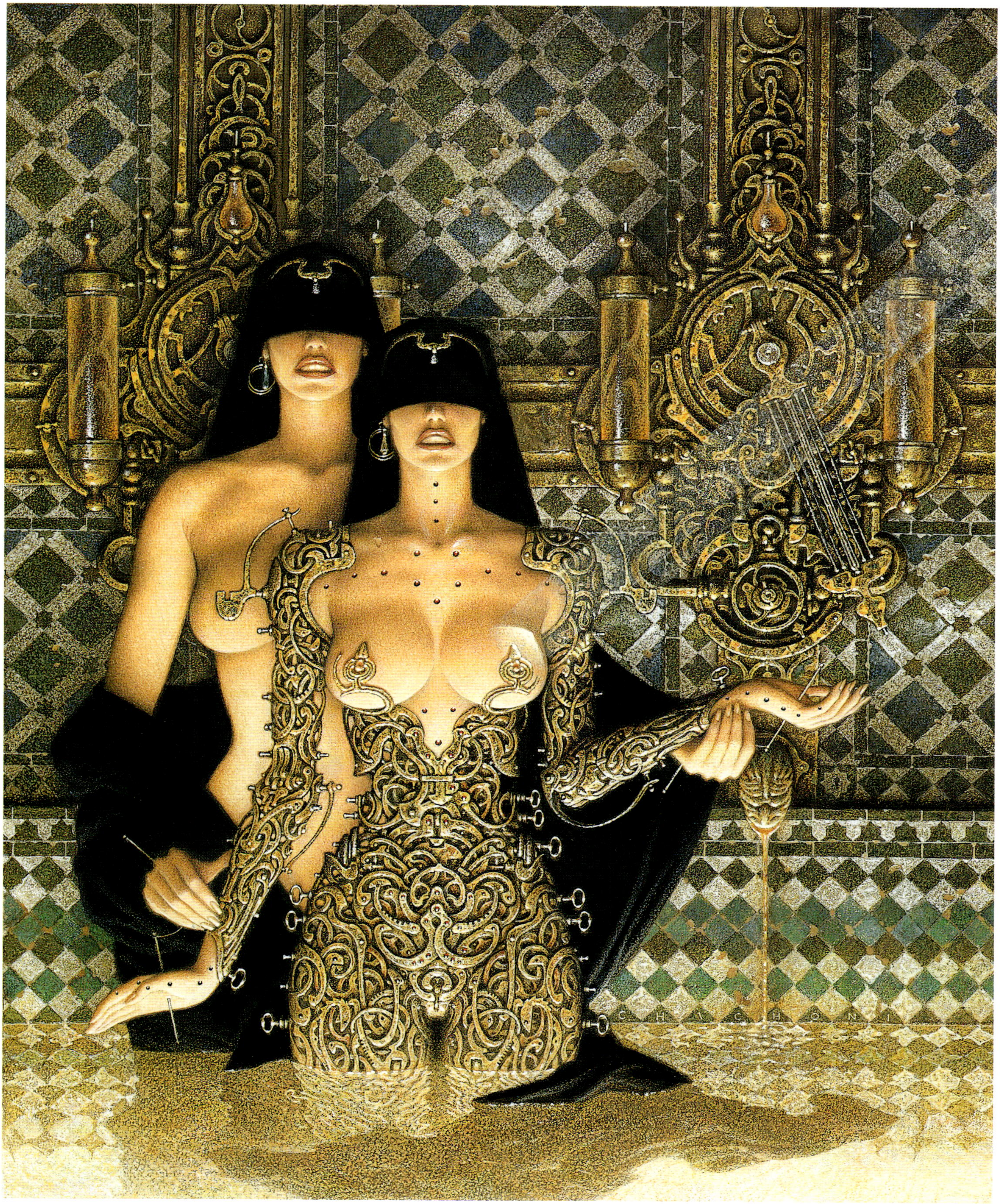

b o o k

1
artist: JOHN JUDE PALENCAR
art director: Irene Gallo
designer: Irene Gallo/Peter Lutsen
client: Tor Books
title: Forest of the Heart
medium: Acrylic
size: 33"x18"

2
artist: EDWARD BINKLEY
art director: Edward Binkley
client: University of Wisconsin Press
title: Of Men and Monsters
medium: Digital

3
artist: DAVID HO
art director: David Ho
client: Sungood Books
title: Temptation
medium: Mixed/digital
size: 16"x20"

4
artist: JOHN JUDE PALENCAR
art director: Irene Gallo
designer: Irene Gallo
client: Tor Books
title: Daughter of the Forest
medium: Acrylic
size: 32"x20"

1

2

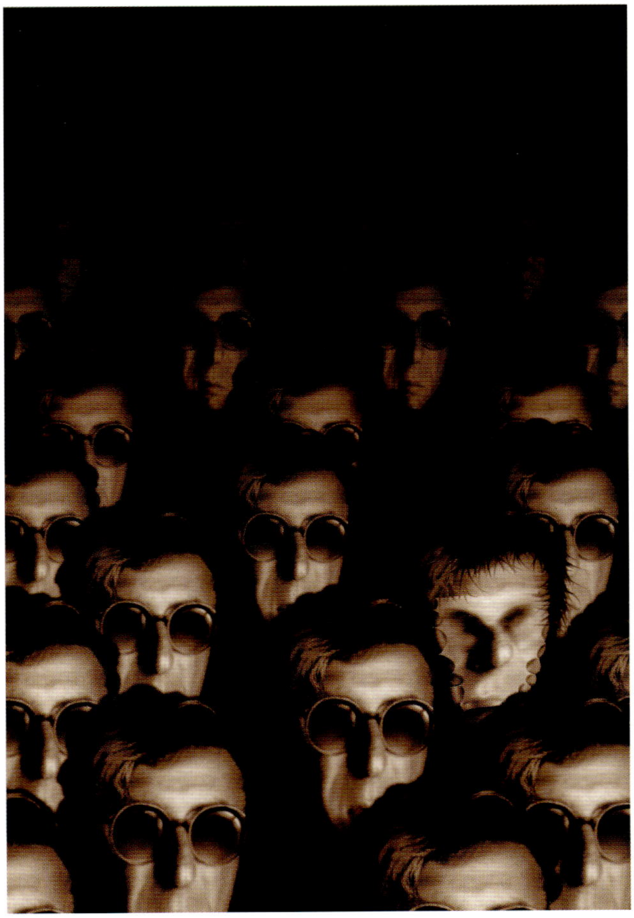

3

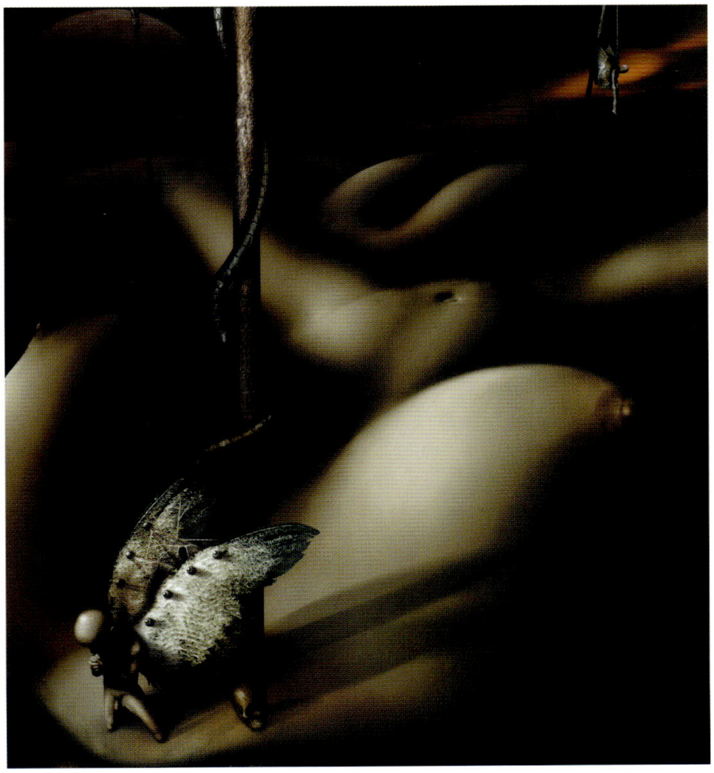

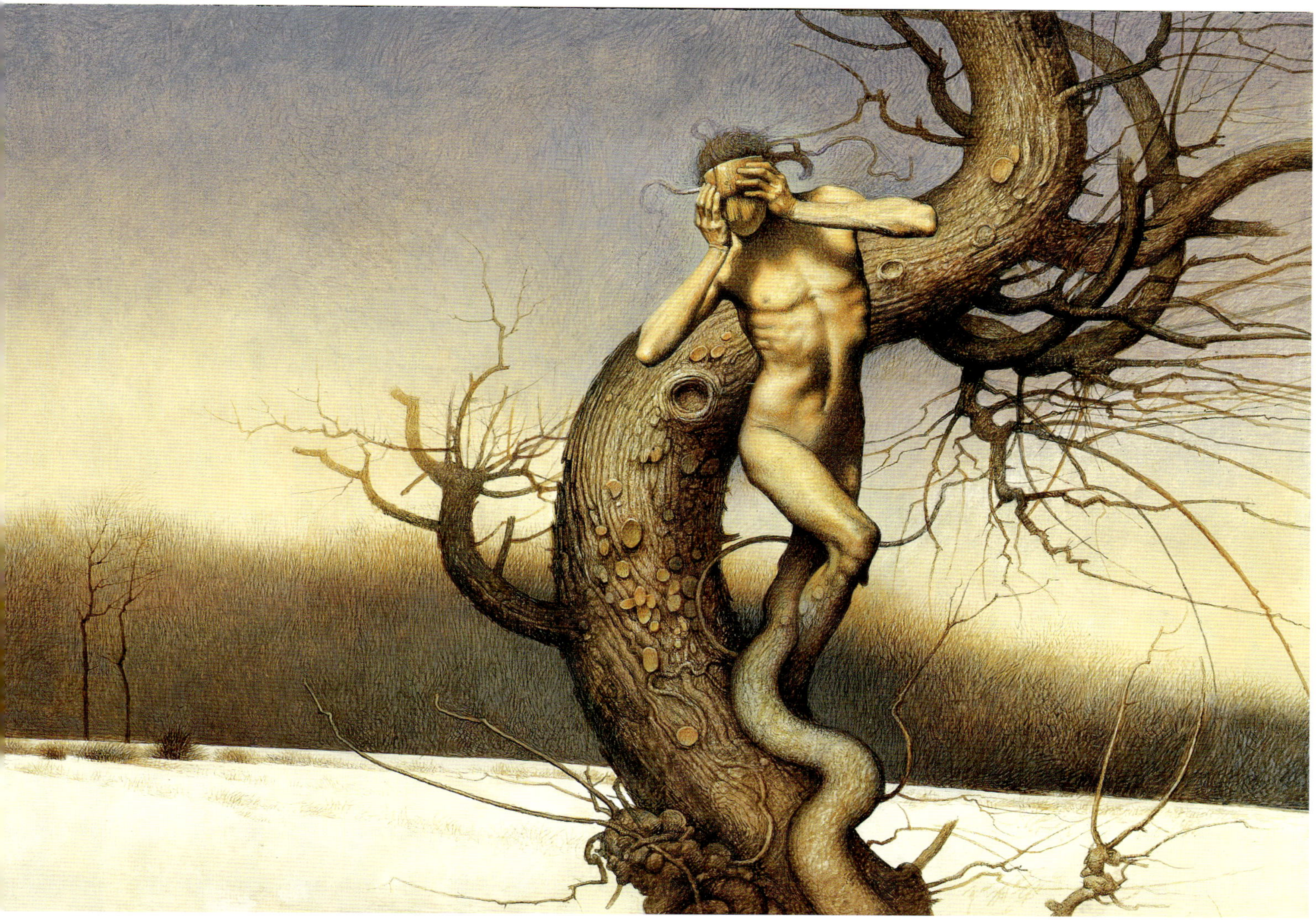

4

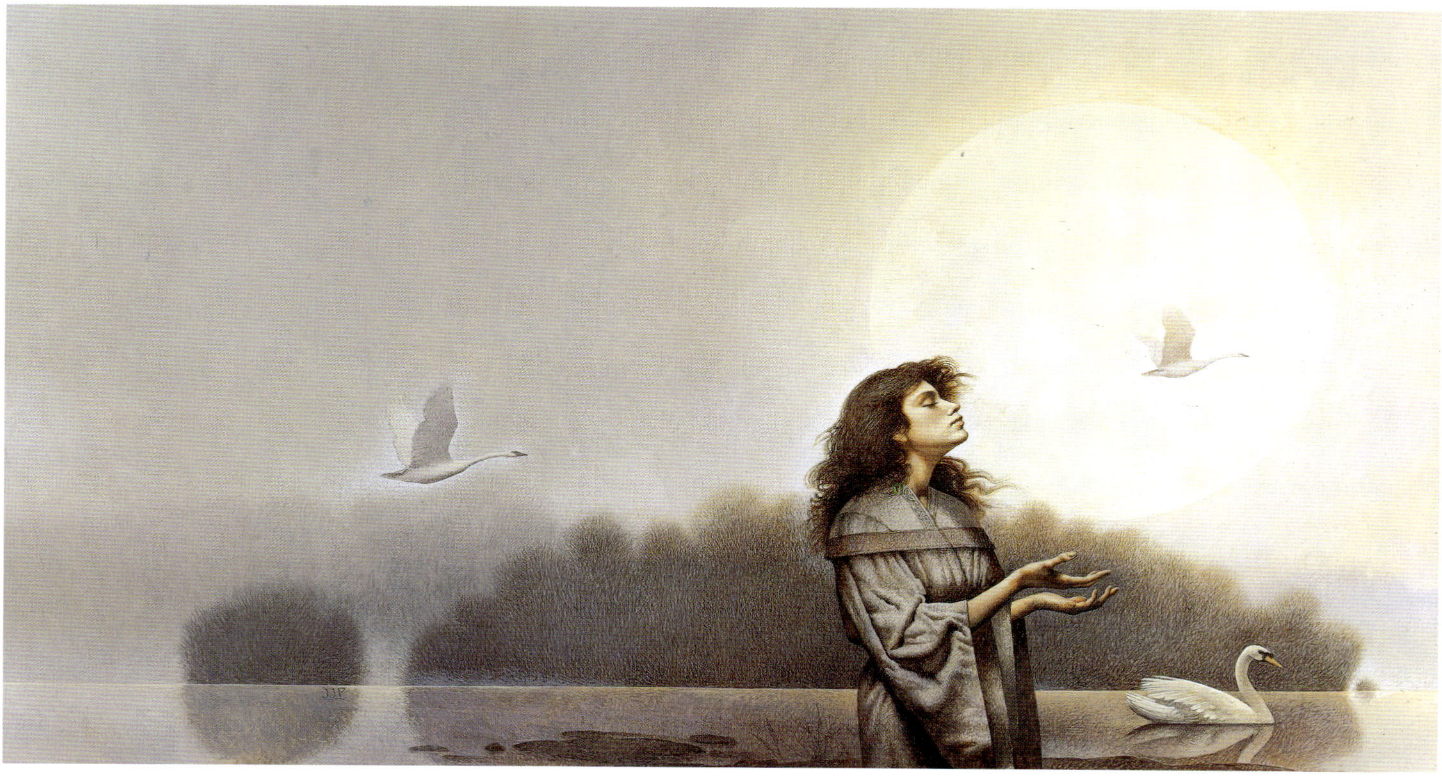

1
artist: JON FOSTER
art director: Jon Schindehette
client: Wizards of the Coast
title: The Magehound
medium: Mixed

2
artist: DONATO GIANCOLA
art director: Heather Kern
client: Ballantine Books
title: Dragonflight
medium: Oil
size: 18"x27"

3
artist: GRIESBACH/MARTUCCI
art director: Sheila Gilbert
designer: George Long
client: DAW Books
title: Jerlayne
medium: Oil
size: 18"x24"

4
artist: DONATO GIANCOLA
art director: Irene Gallo
client: Tor Books
title: Obernewtyn
medium: Oil
size: 16"x27"

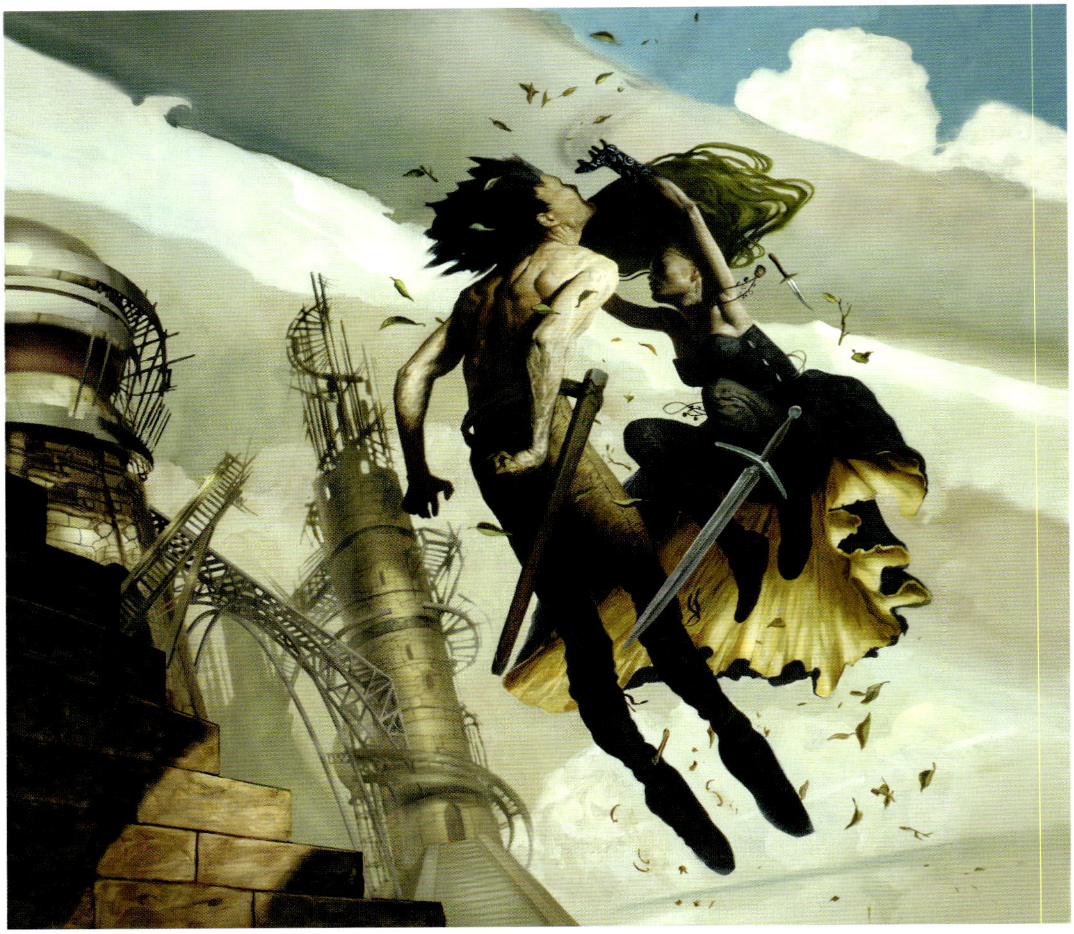

1

2

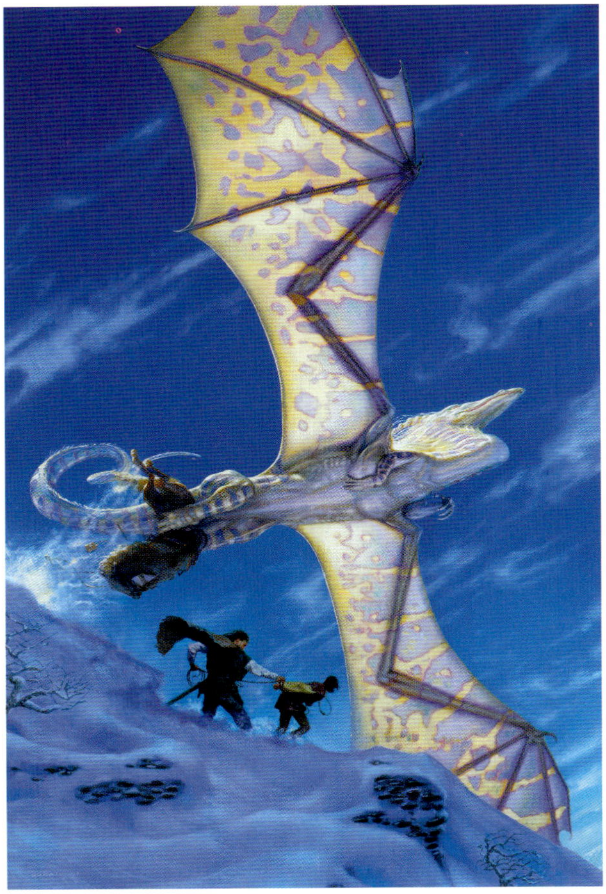

3

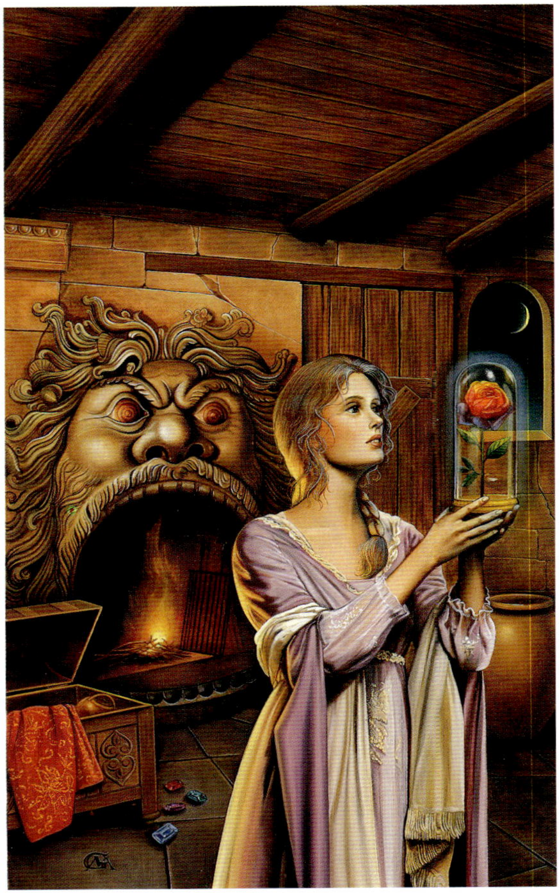

4

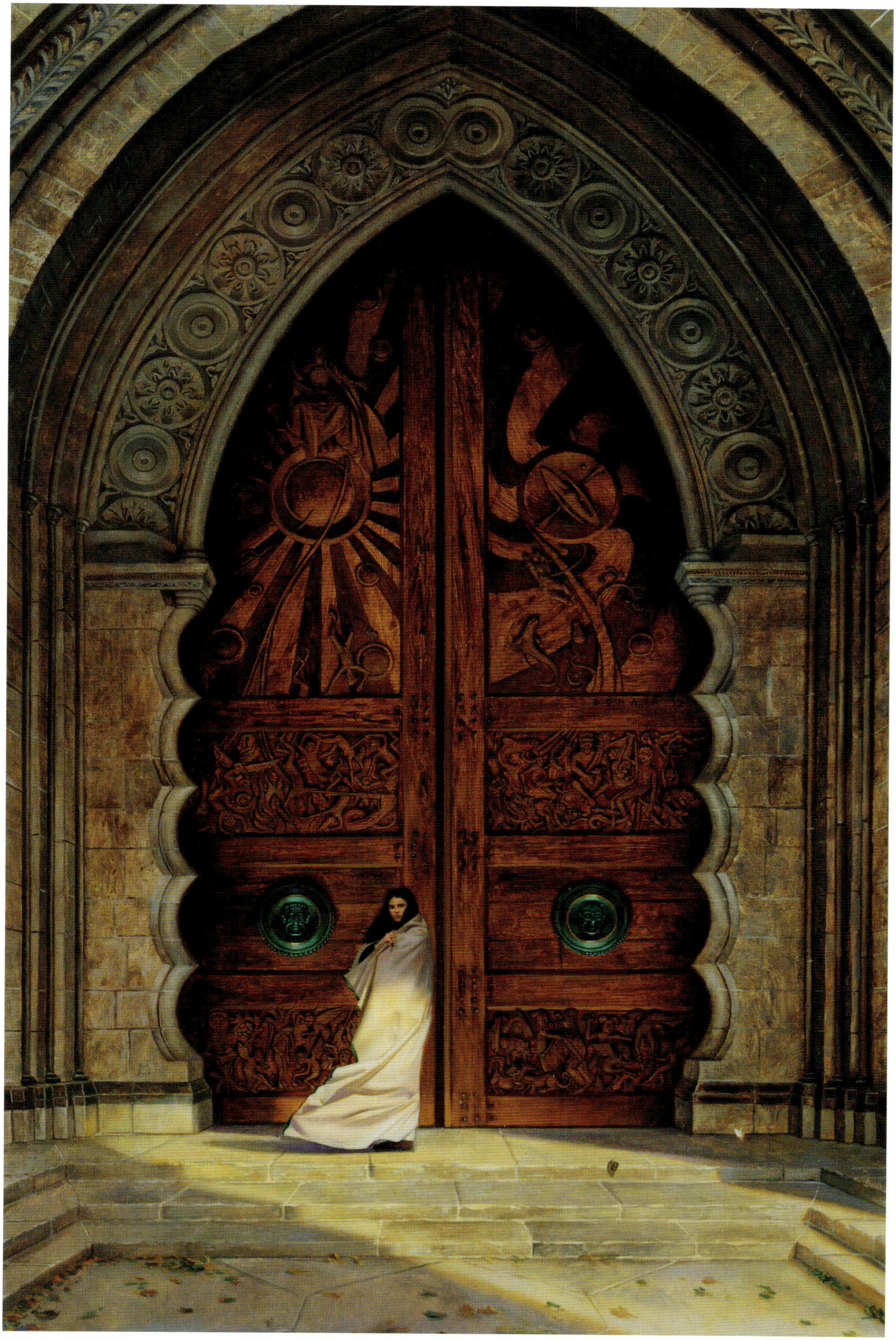

b o o k

1
artist: DONATO GIANCOLA
art director: Irene Gallo
client: Tor Books
title: Psychohistorical Crisis
medium: Oil
size: 36"x22"

2
artist: MARK ZUG
art director: Jon Schindehette
client: Wizards of the Coast
title: Sanction

3
artist: MATT STAWICKI
art director: Matt Adelsperger
client: Wizards of the Coast
title: Dragons of Spring Dawning
medium: Digital

4
artist: MARK ELLIOT
art director: Alix Reid
client: HarperCollins
title: Cinderellis & the Glass Hill
medium: Acrylic
size: 14"x18"

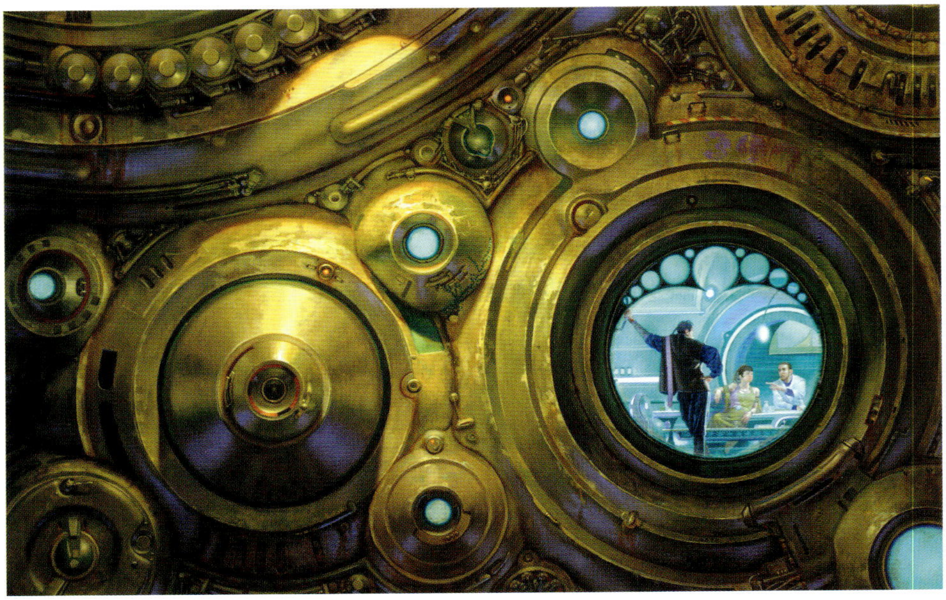

1

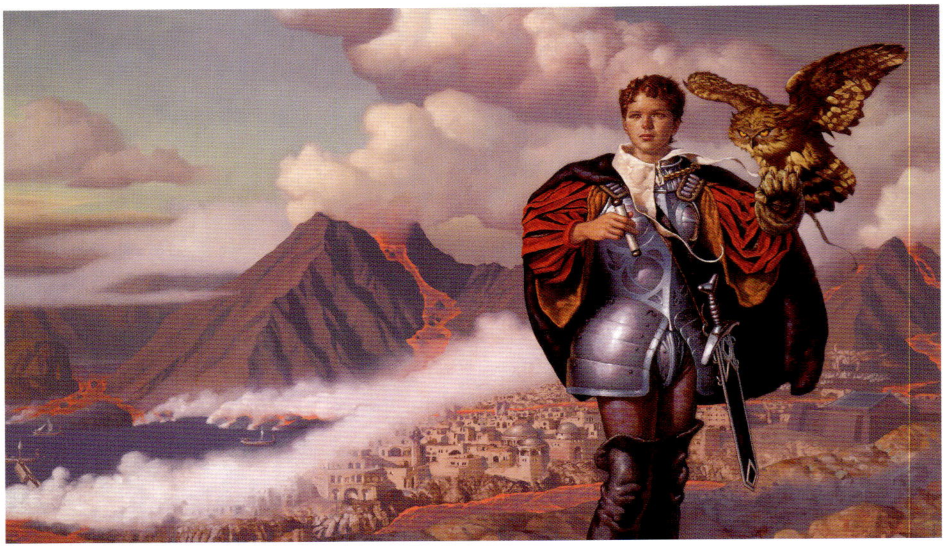

2

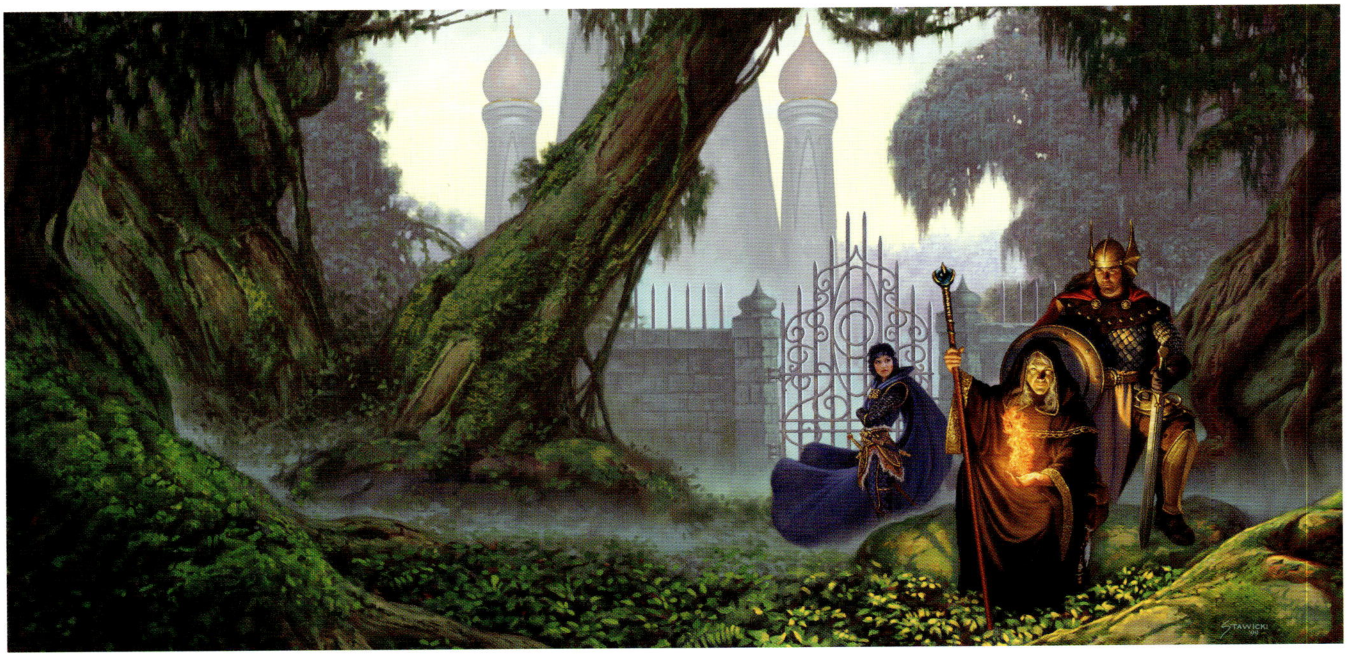

3

4

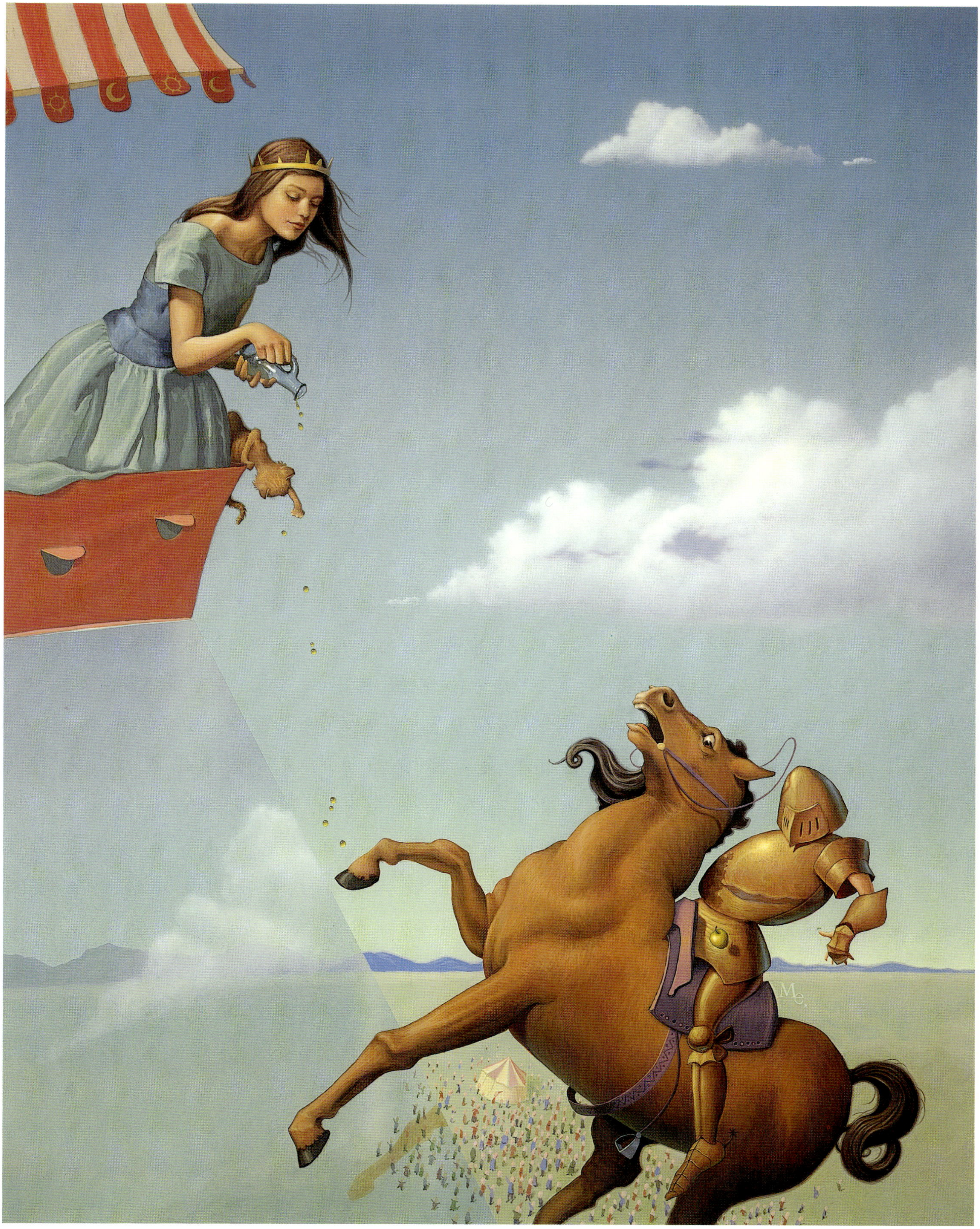

1
artist: JOHN ZELEZNIK
art director: Kevin Siembieda
client: Palladium Books
title: Splyun Dimensional Market
medium: Acrylic
size: 26"x17"

2
artist: TOM KIDD
art director: Barbara Fitzsimmons
designer: Al Getty
client: Morrow Jr. Books
title: Master Race
medium: Oil
size: 21"x27"

3
artist: TOM KIDD
art director: Barbara Fitzsimmons
designer: Al Getty
client: Morrow Jr. Books
title: Martian Raises Tube
medium: Oil
size: 21"x27"

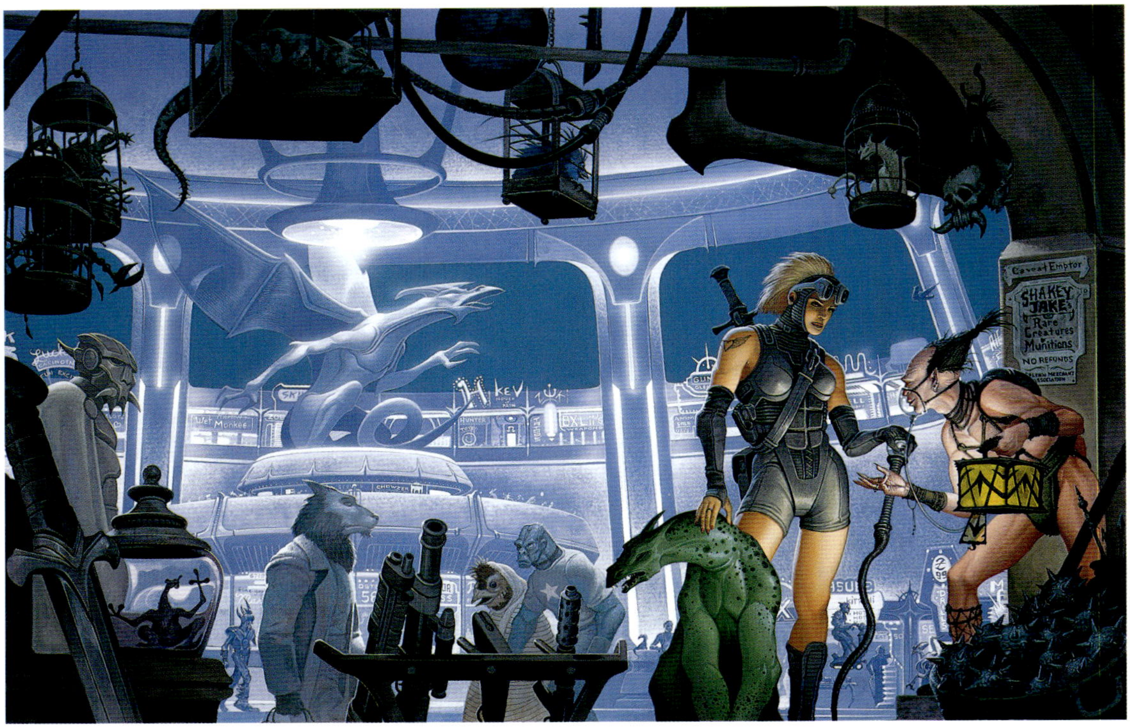

1

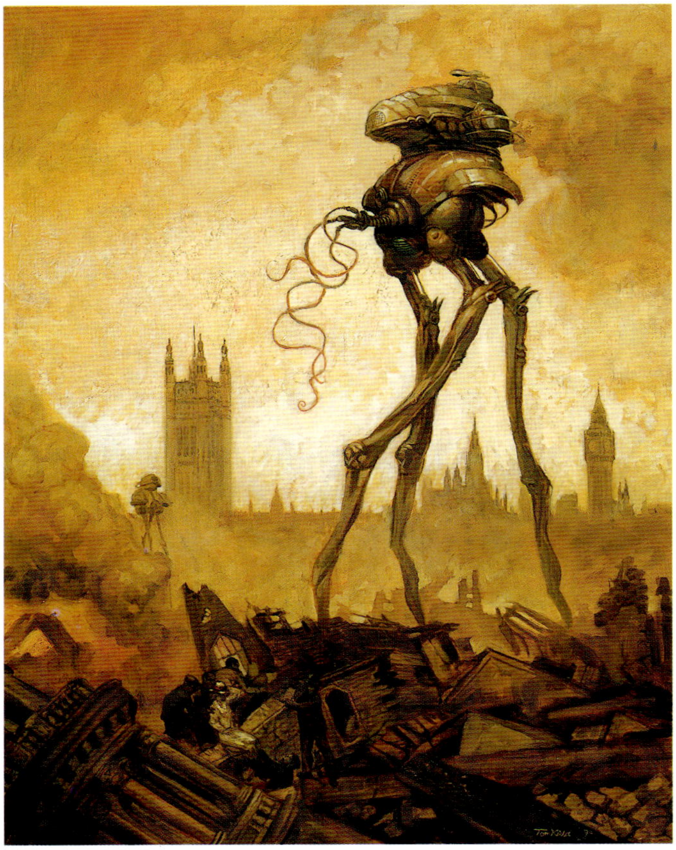

2

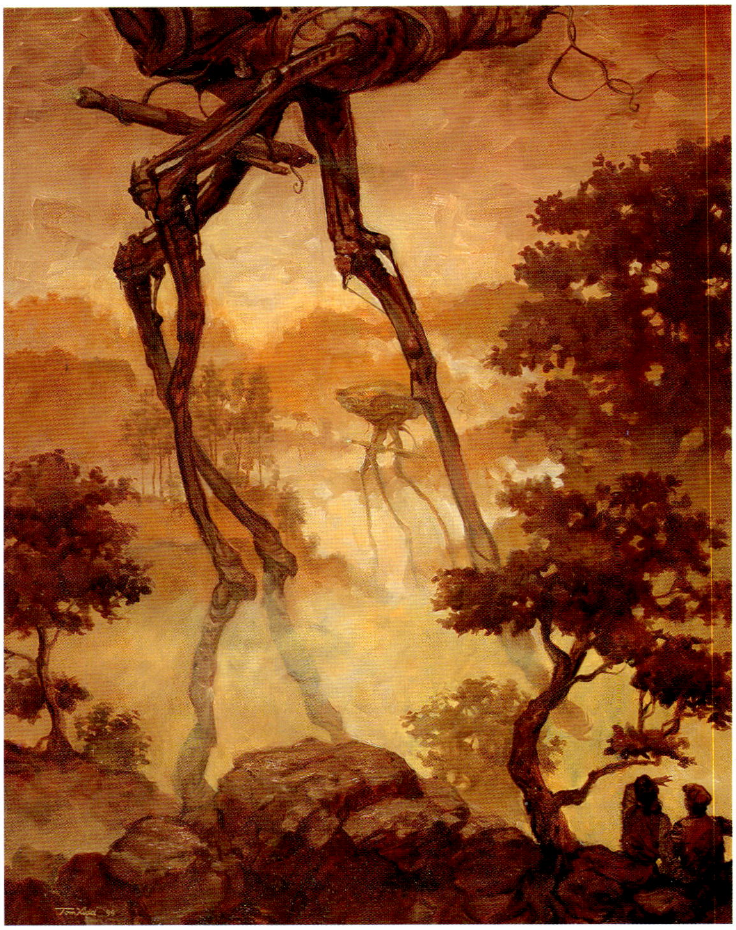

3

4
artist: MICHAEL KOELSCH
art director: Vaughn Andrews
client: Harcourt Brace
title: Women of Wonder
medium: Acrylic/pencil
size: 16"x20"

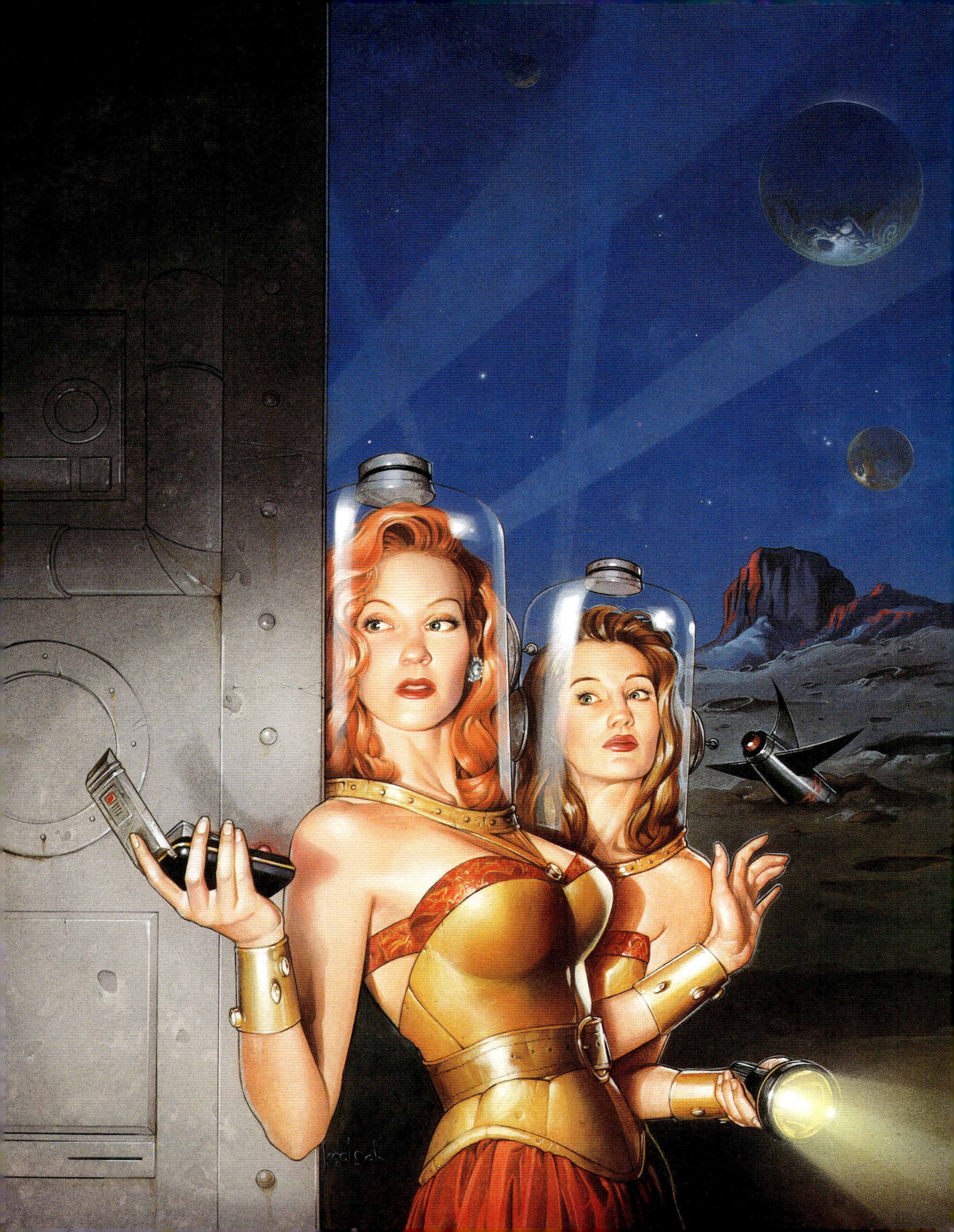

1
artist: JOHN ZELEZNIK
art director: Rich Thomas
client: White Wolf
title: Stardance
medium: Acrylic/digital *size:* 15"x20"

2
artist: DAVID BOWERS
art director: Larry Laukhuf
designer: Larry Laukhuf
client: Angels on Earth
title: Angel With Bubble
medium: Oil *size:* 13"x21"

3
artist: MILES TEVES
art director: Miles Teves
client: Skyrealms Publishing
title: Burdoth
medium: Graphite *size:* 13"x17"

4
artist: TERESE NIELSEN
art director: Min Choi
client: DelRey Books
title: Age of Unreason
medium: Acrylic/oil *size:* 10"x15"

1

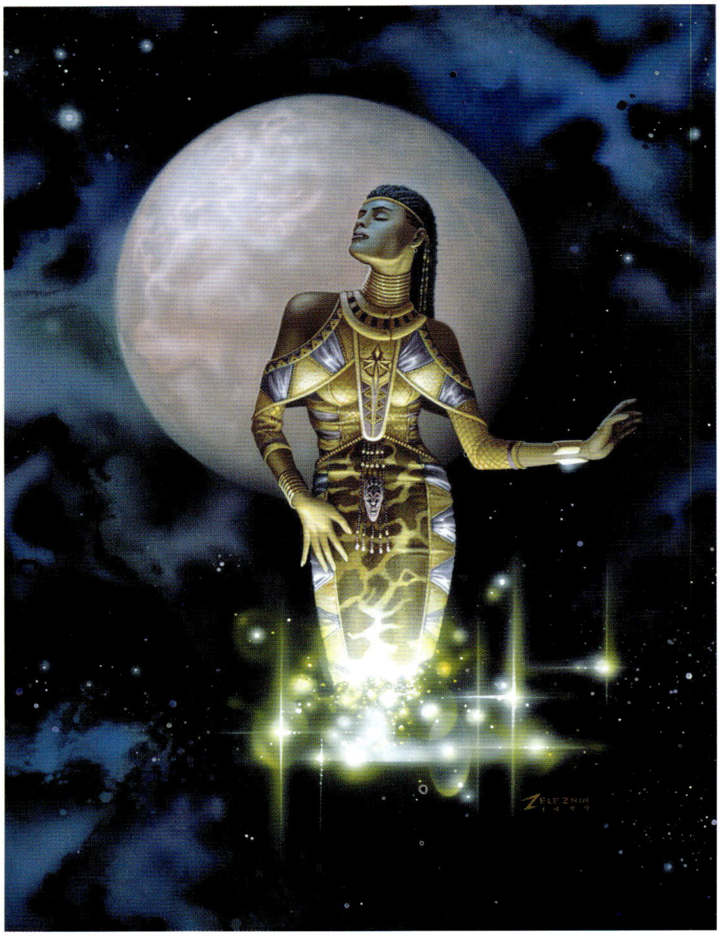

2

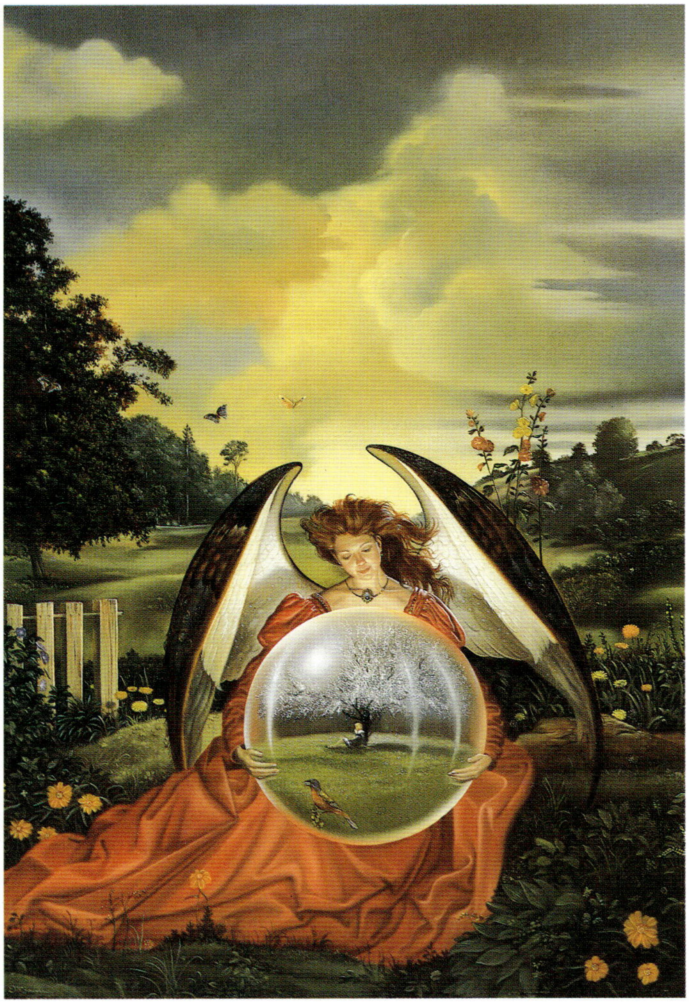

3

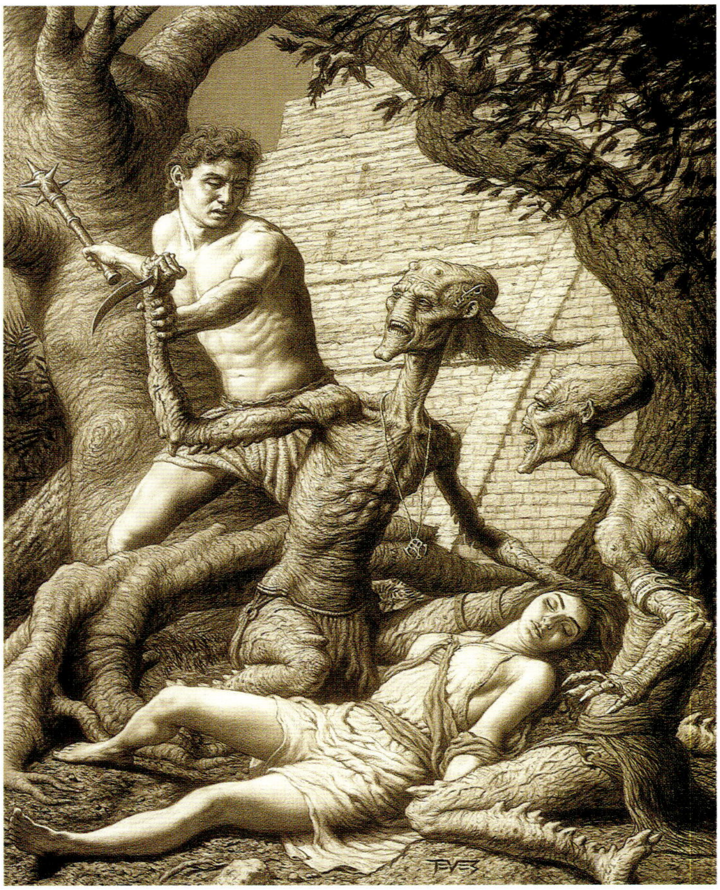

4

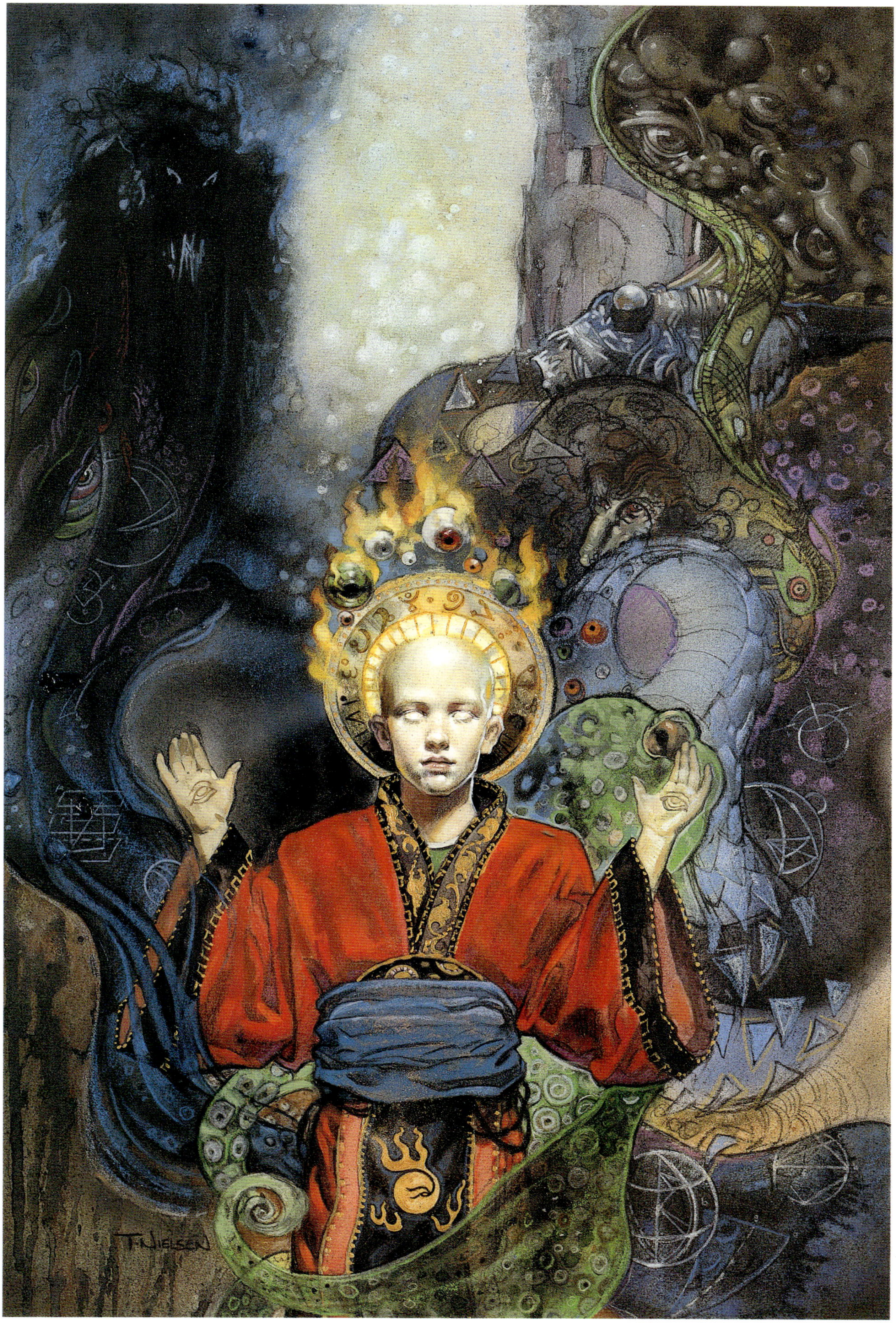

1
artist: LUIS ROYO
client: Norma Editorial/NBM
title: Dreams
medium: Acrylic
size: 10"x16"

2
artist: ANDREJ DUGIN & OLGA DUGINA
art director: Mathias Berg
designer: Andrej Dugin
client: Esslinger Verlag J.F. Schreiber
title: Brothers Grimm: A Little Brave Tailor
medium: Watercolor
size: 37.5cmx16.2cm

3
artist: ANDREJ DUGIN & OLGA DUGINA
art director: Mathias Berg
designer: Andrej Dugin
client: Esslinger Verlag J.F. Schreiber
title: Brothers Grimm: A Little Brave Tailor
medium: Watercolor
size: 38cmx21.5cm

4
artist: ANDREJ DUGIN & OLGA DUGINA
art director: Mathias Berg
designer: Andrej Dugin
client: Esslinger Verlag J.F. Schreiber
title: Brothers Grimm: A Little Brave Tailor
medium: Watercolor
size: 37.5cmx16.2cm

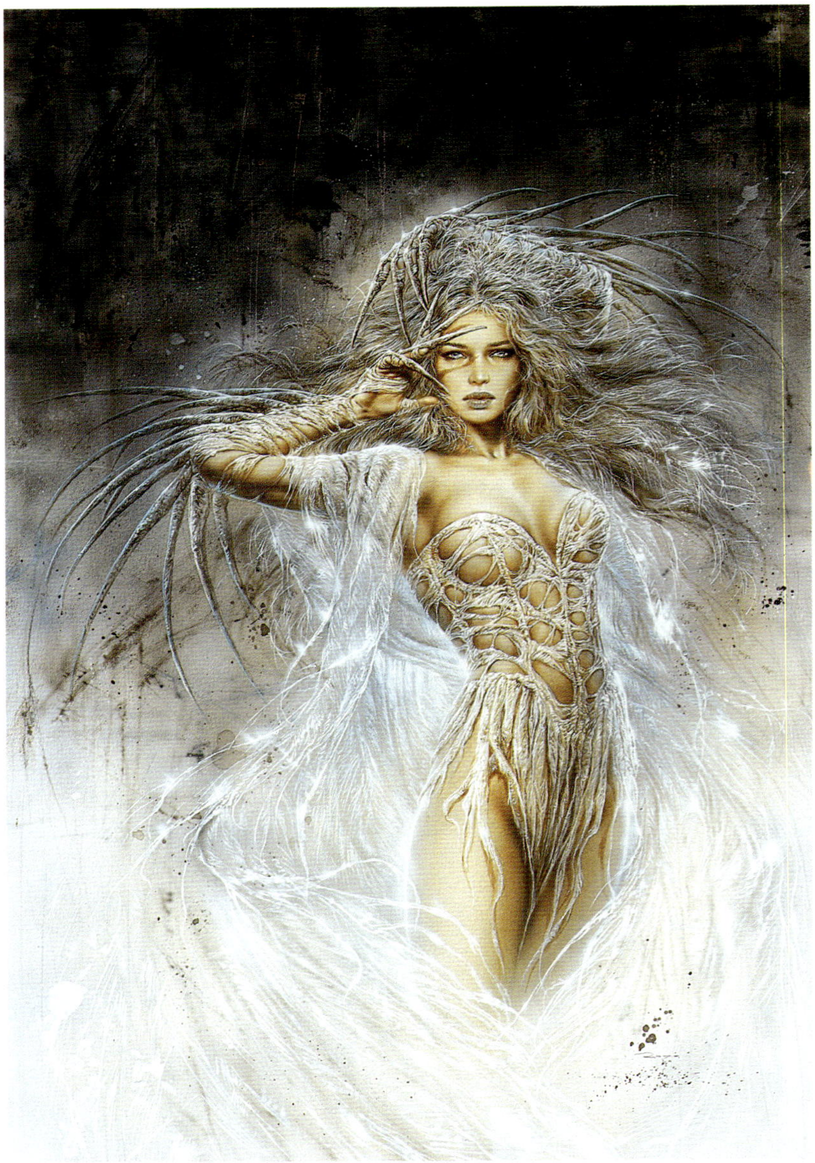

1

2

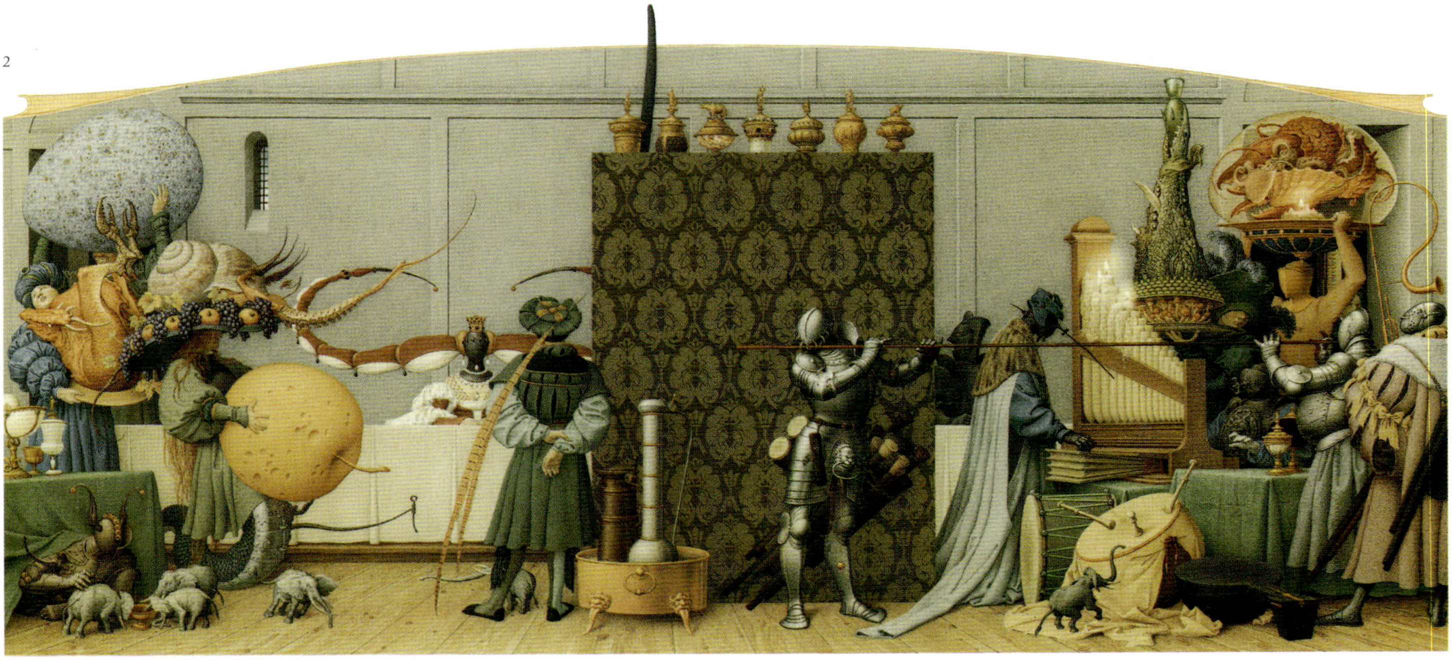

3

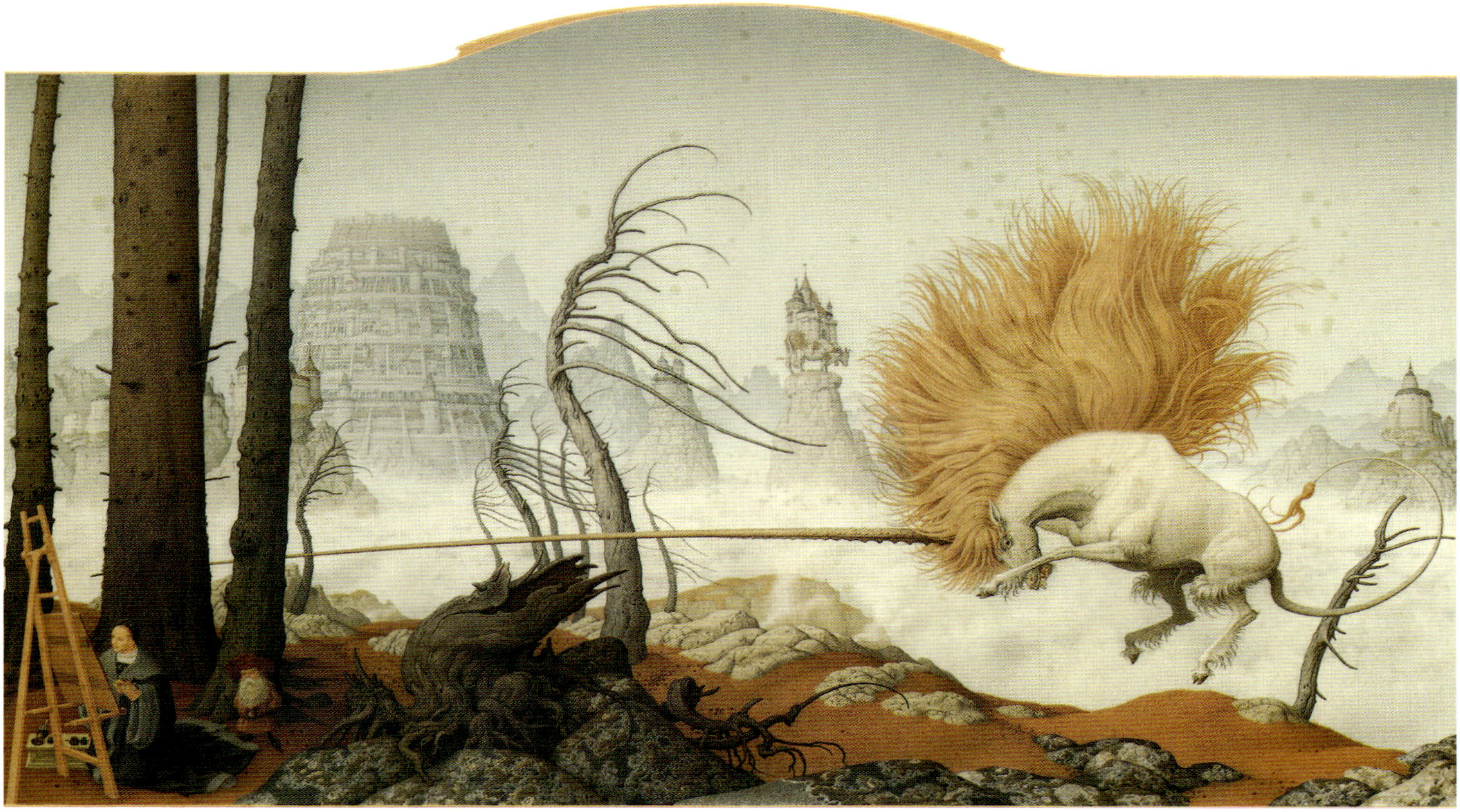

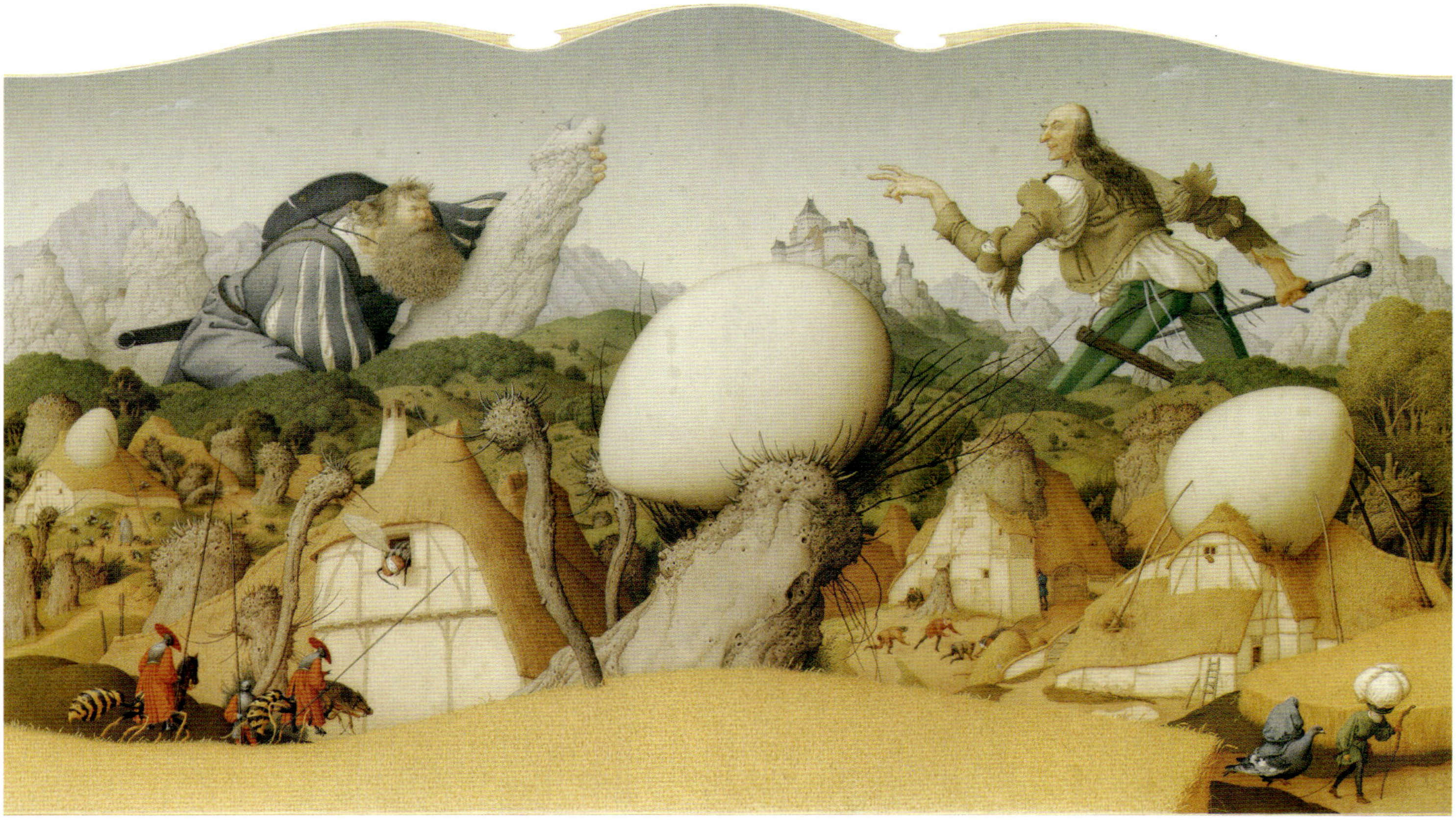

4

1
artist: GREG LOUDON
client: SQProductions
title: Crimson Embrace 4
medium: Acrylic
size: 15"x20"

2
artist: BROM
art director: Dave Stevenson
client: DelRey Books
title: Witch Storm
medium: Oil

3
artist: LARRY ELMORE
art director: Jim Baen
client: Baen Books
title: Ravenstone
medium: Oil *size:* 20"x30"

4
artist: JOHN VAN FLEET
art director: Rich Thomas
client: White Wolf Publications
title: 1/2 Damned
medium: Acrylic/mixed
size: 10 1/2"x14 1/4"

1

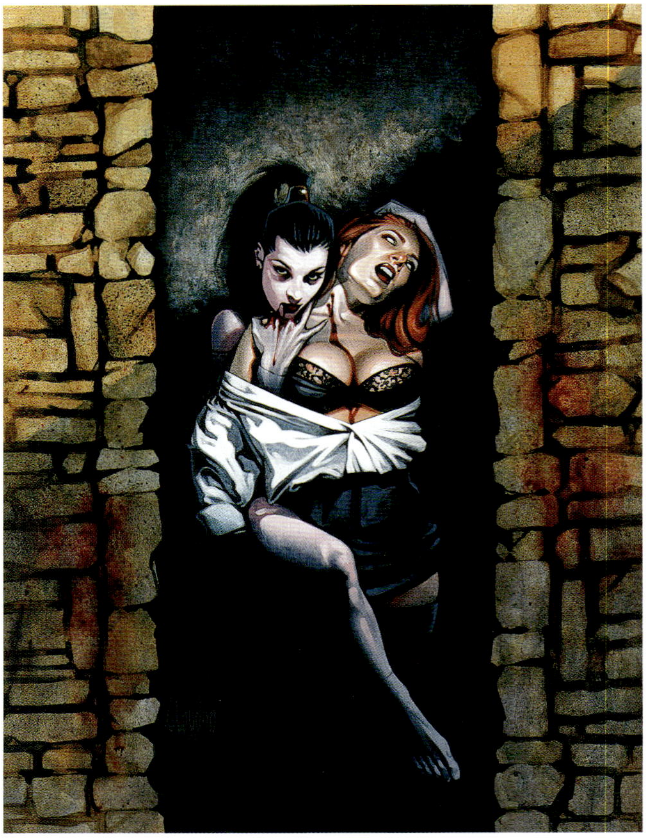

2

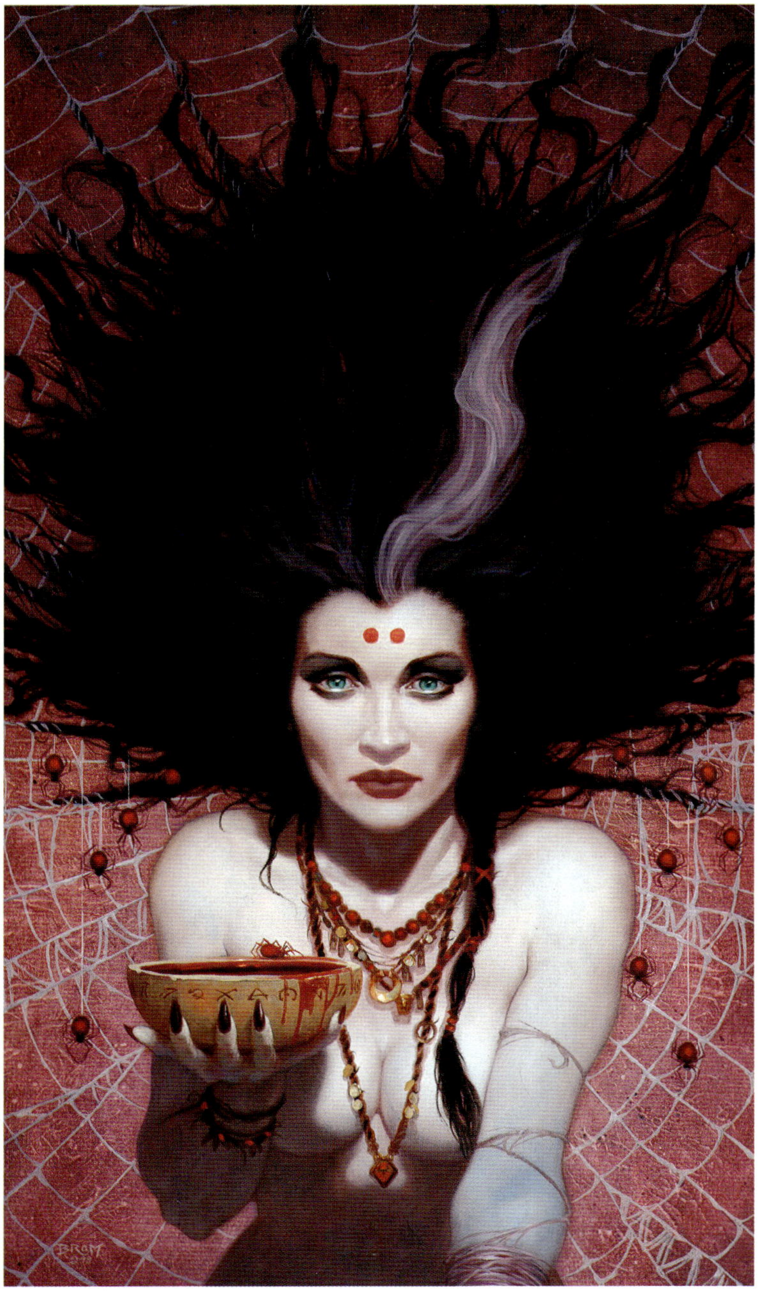

3

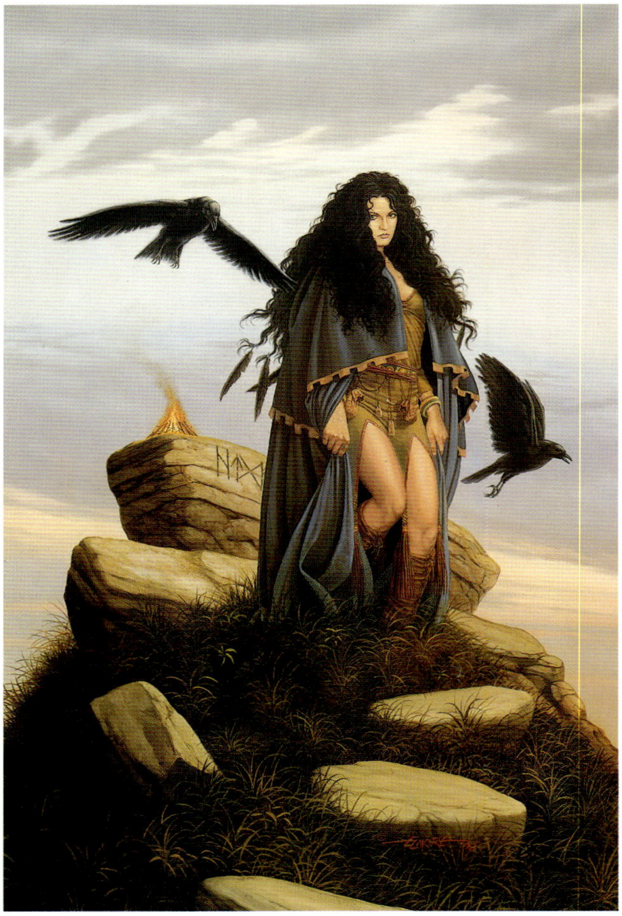

4

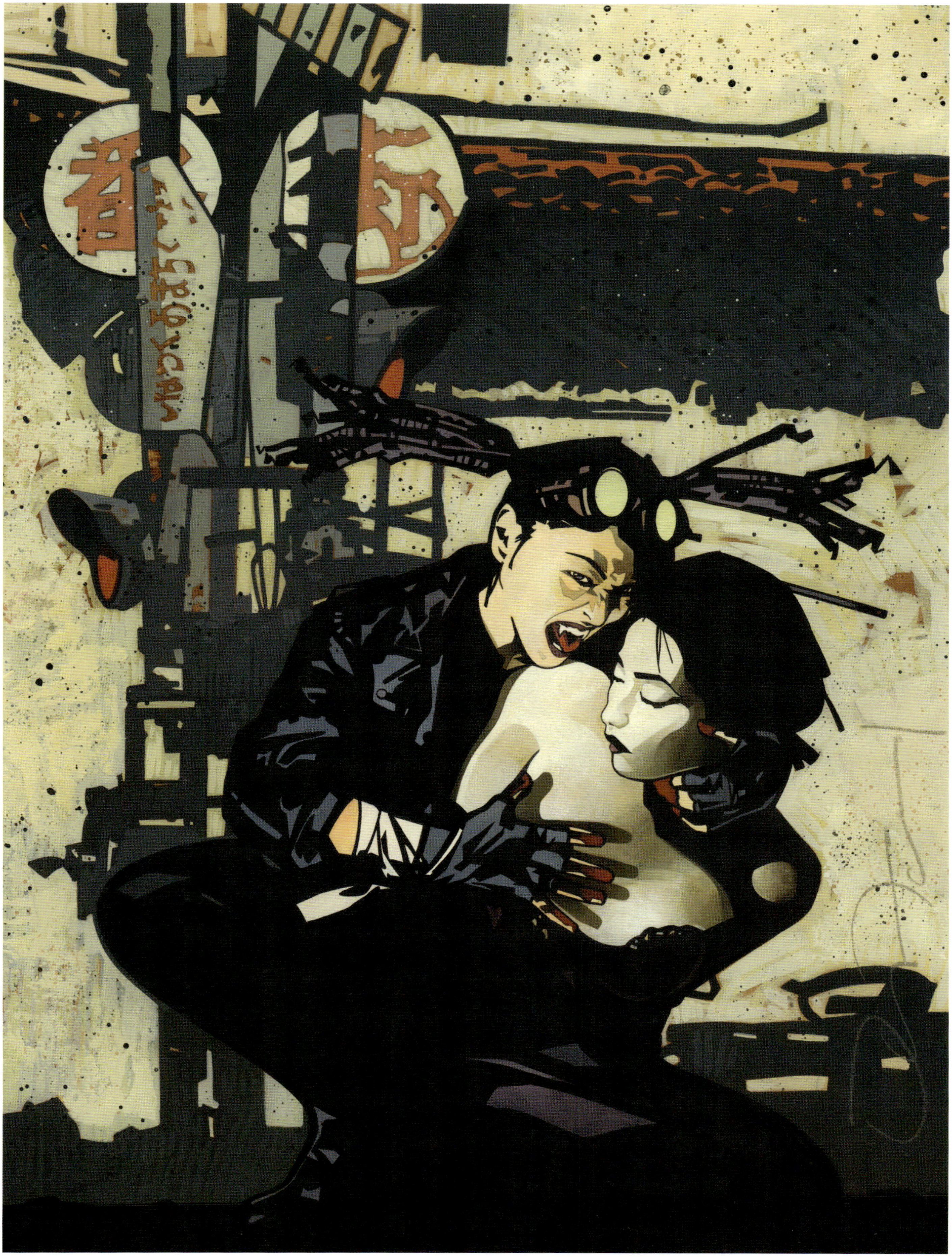

1
artist: STEPHEN YOULL
art director: Jamie Warren
art director: Stephen Youll
client: Bantam Books
title: Ship of Destiny
medium: Oil
size: 19"x28"

2
artist: CHRIS MOORE
art director: Lucie Stericker
client: Orion Books
title: The Collapsium
medium: Acrylic
size: 16"x22"

3
artist: TODD LOCKWOOD
art director: Dawn Murin
client: Wizards of the Coast
title: The Dragonlance
size: 20"x30"

4
artist: GNEMO
art director: Tom Kidd
designer: Shadoe Stevens
client: Rhythm Radio
title: Friedrich Ruins (Gnemo)
medium: Oil
size: 22"x36"

1

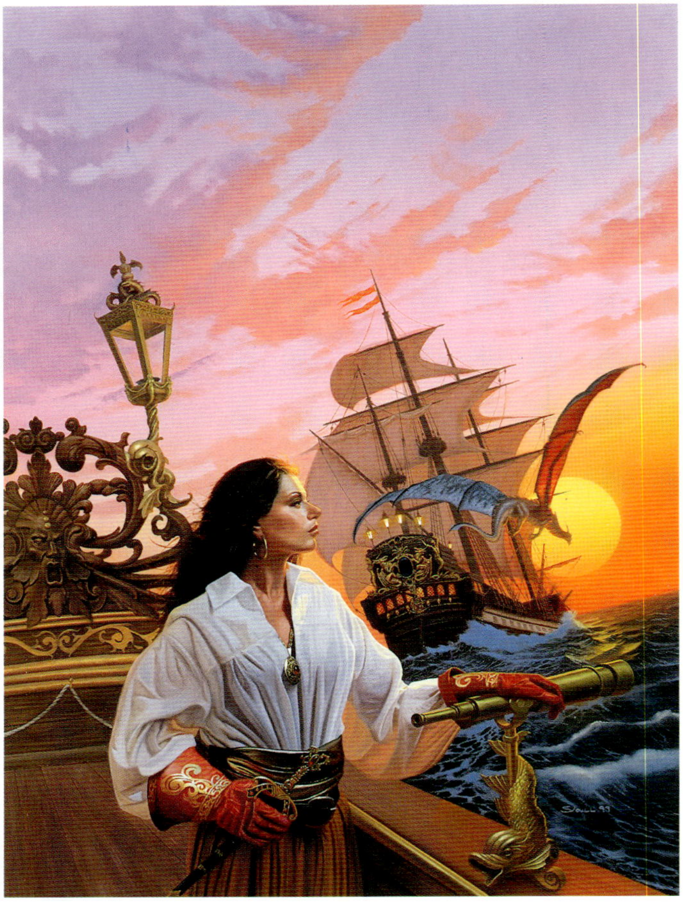

2

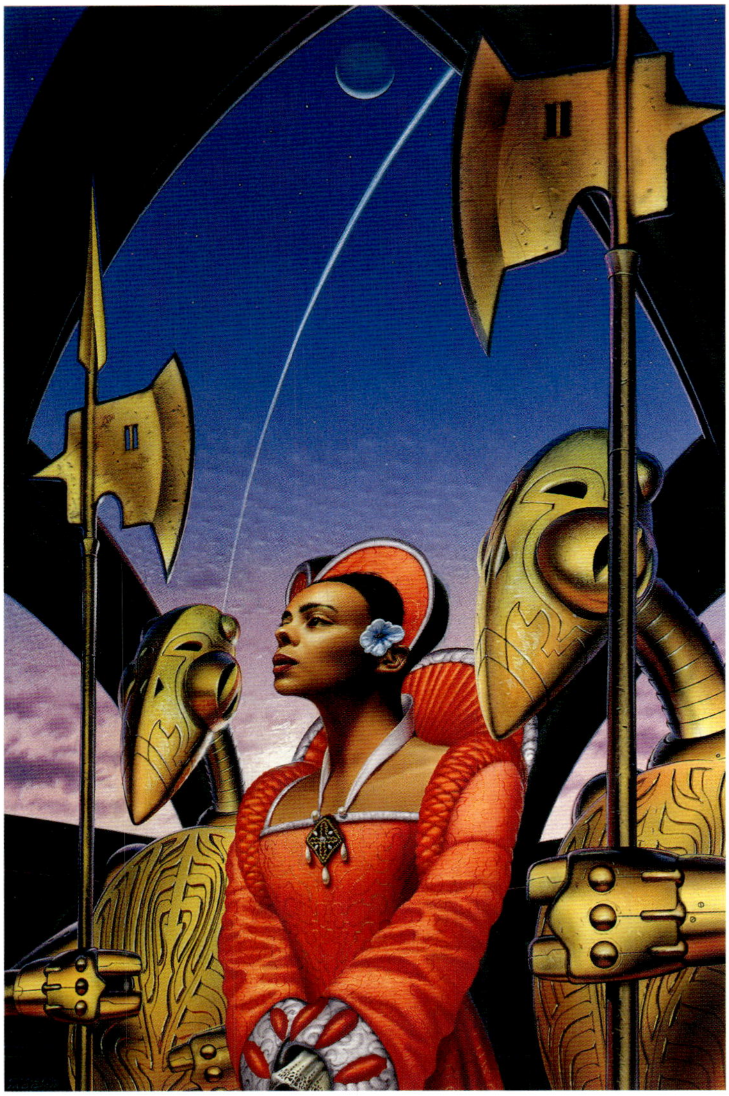

3

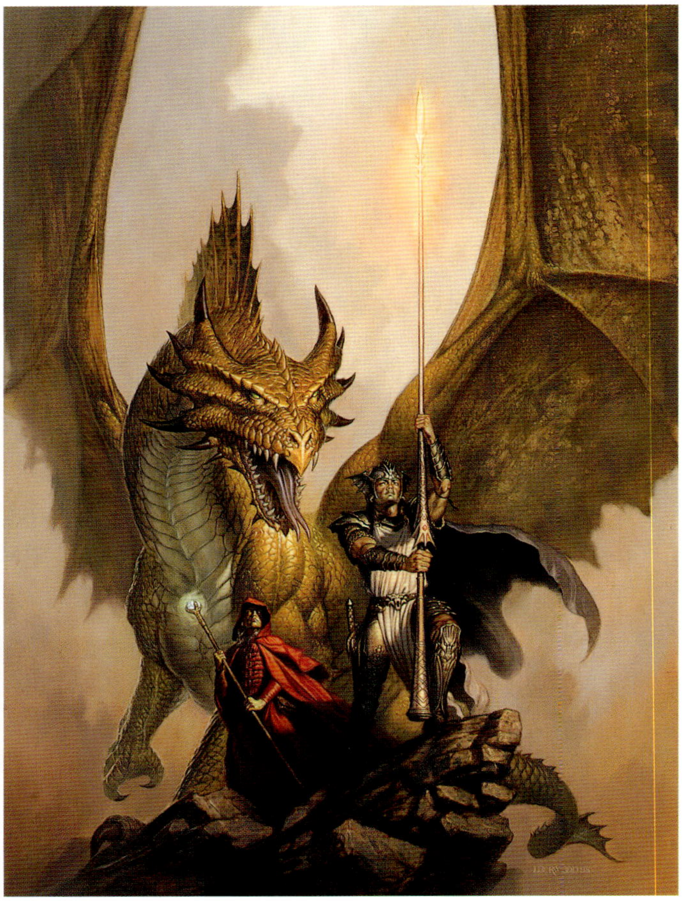

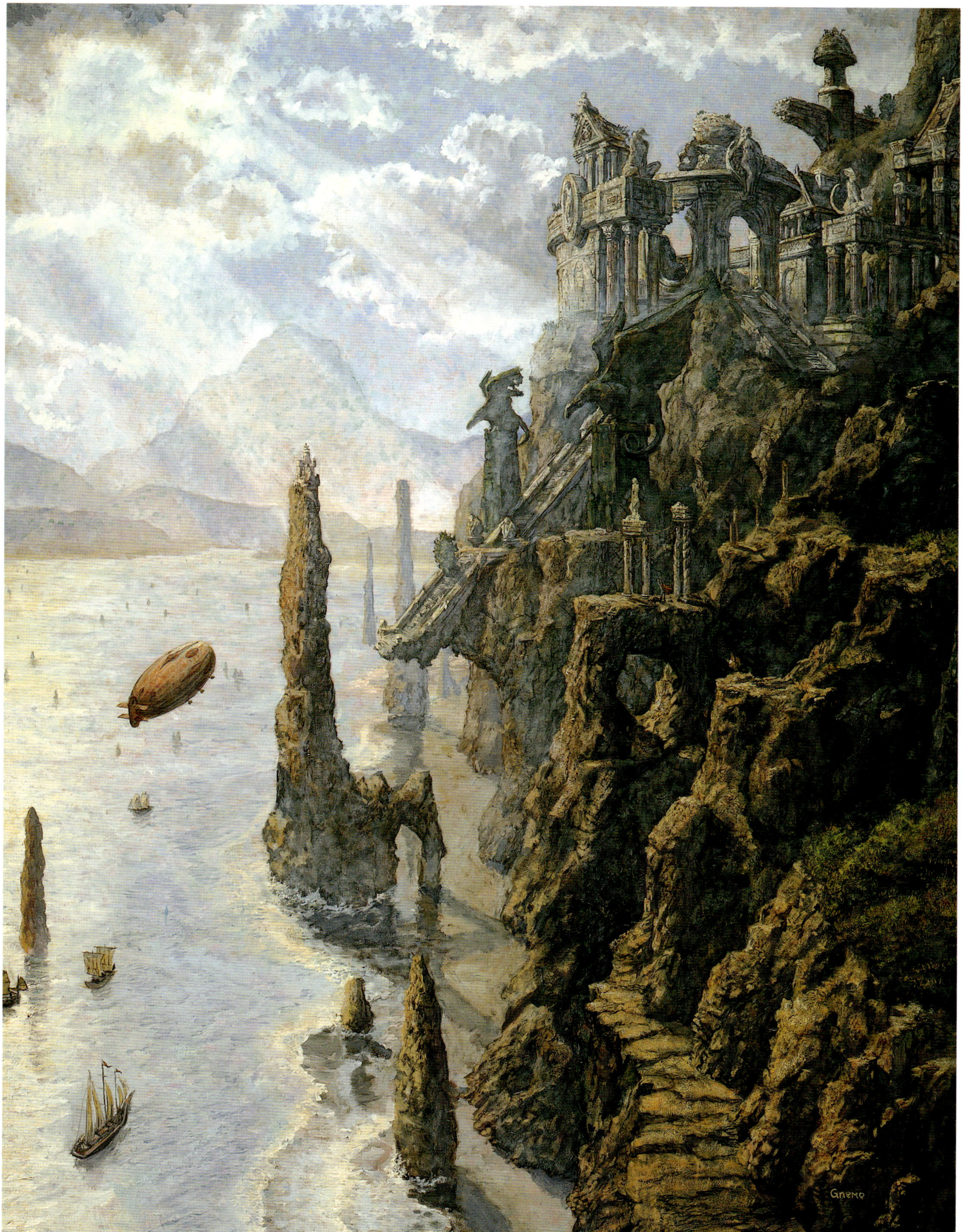
GNEMO

1
artist: DAVE McKEAN
art director: Margaret Clark
designer: Red Herring Design
client: Pocket Books
title: Q-4 Scarecrow
medium: Mixed/digital
size: 9"x10 3/4"

2
artist: CLIFF NIELSEN
art director: Carl Galian
client: HarperCollins
title: The Crow
medium: Mixed/digital
size: 8"x10"

3
artist: TOMMY LEE EDWARDS
art director: Rich Thomas
client: White Wolf Publishing
title: Redeemer
medium: Ink/digital
size: 10"x13"

4
artist: CLIFF NIELSEN
art director: Irene Gallo
client: Tor Books
title: Dawn Song
medium: Mixed/digital
size: 8"x10"

1

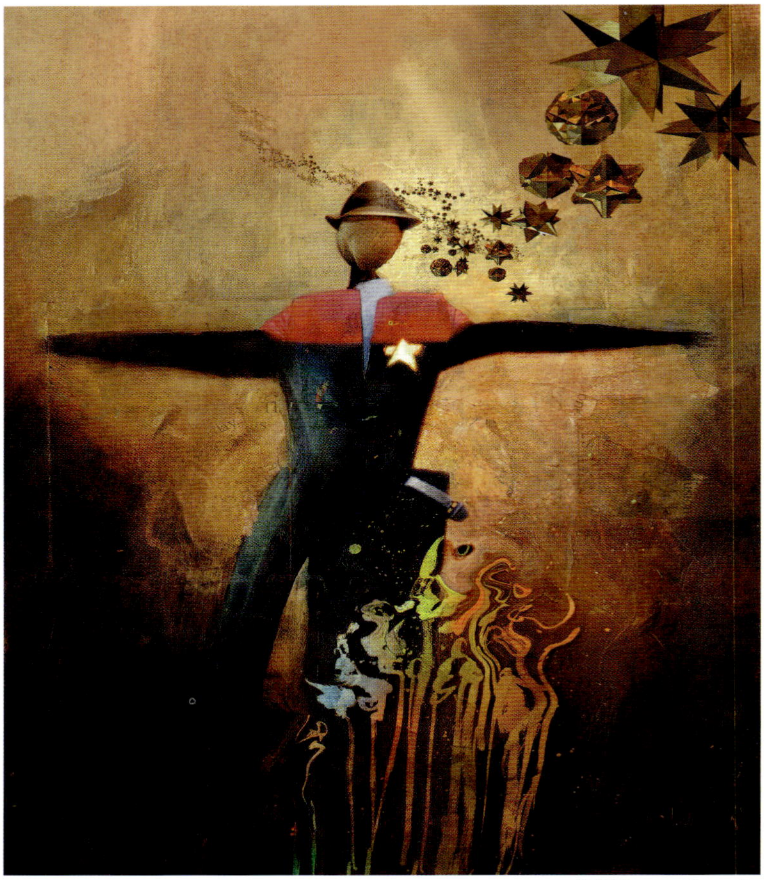

2

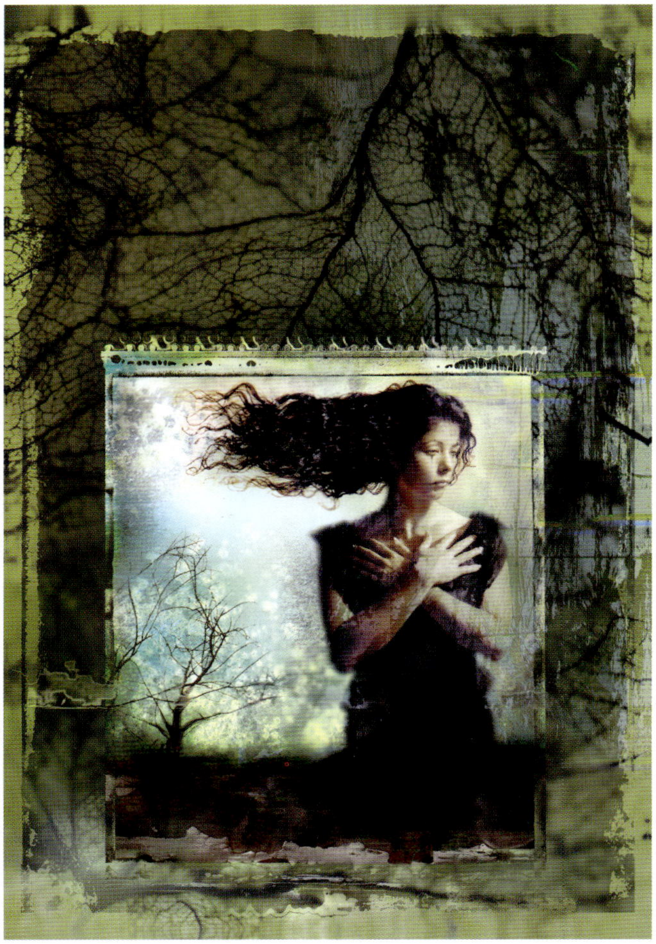

3

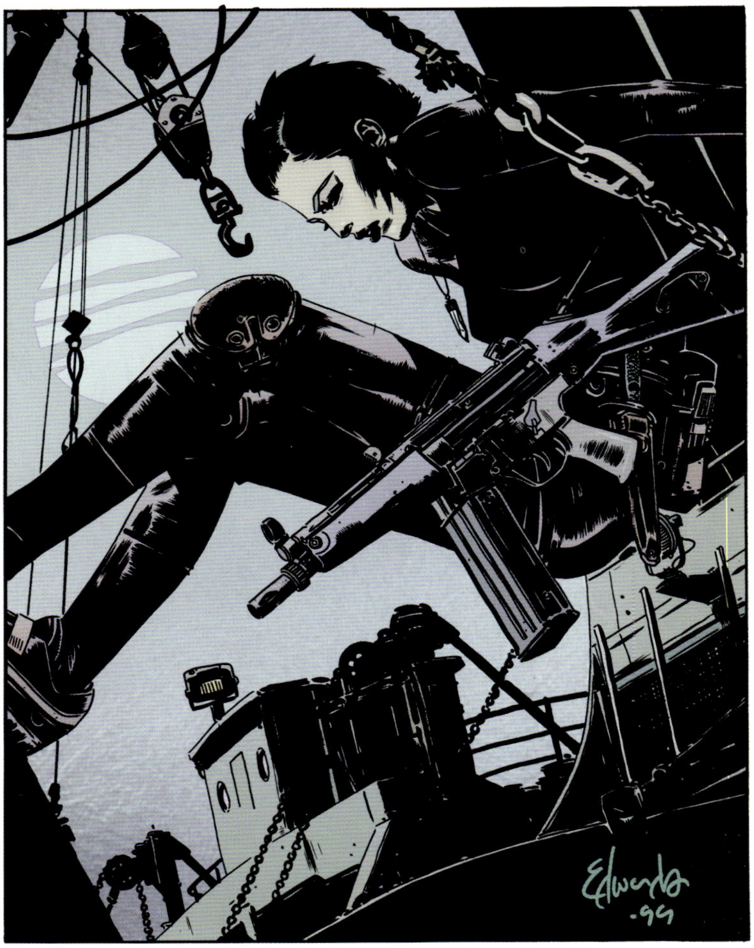

4

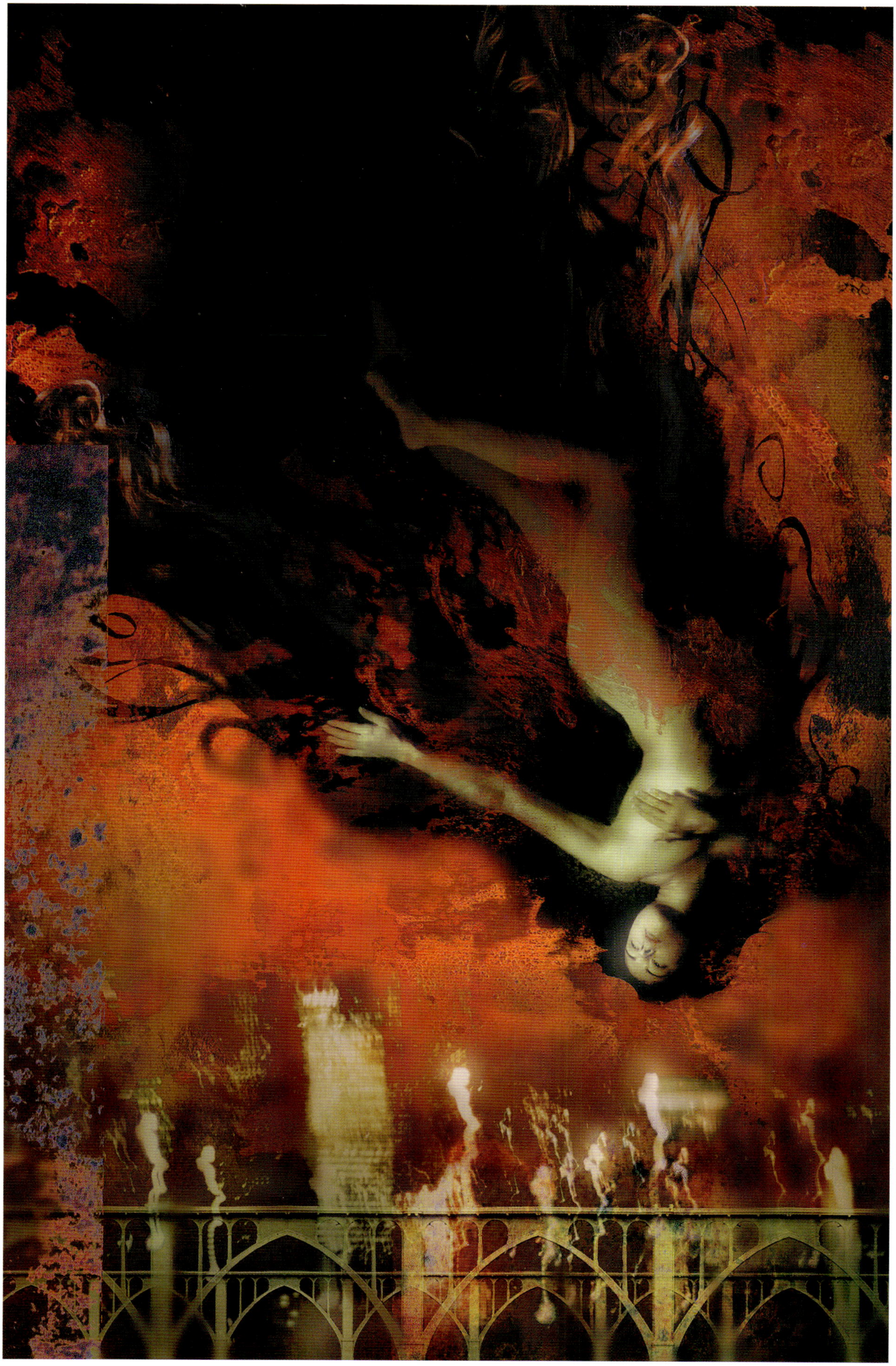

1
artist: ENI OKEN
designer: Eni Oken
title: Resident Alien
medium: Digital

2
artist: JON J MUTH
art director: Margaret Clark
designer: Red Herring Design
client: Pocket Books
title: Borg Queen 1
medium: Mixed
size: 18"x10 3/4"

3
artist: YVONNE GILBERT
art director: Carl Gallian
client: HarperCollins/Avon
title: King Maker's Sword
medium: Colored pencil
size: 10"x16"

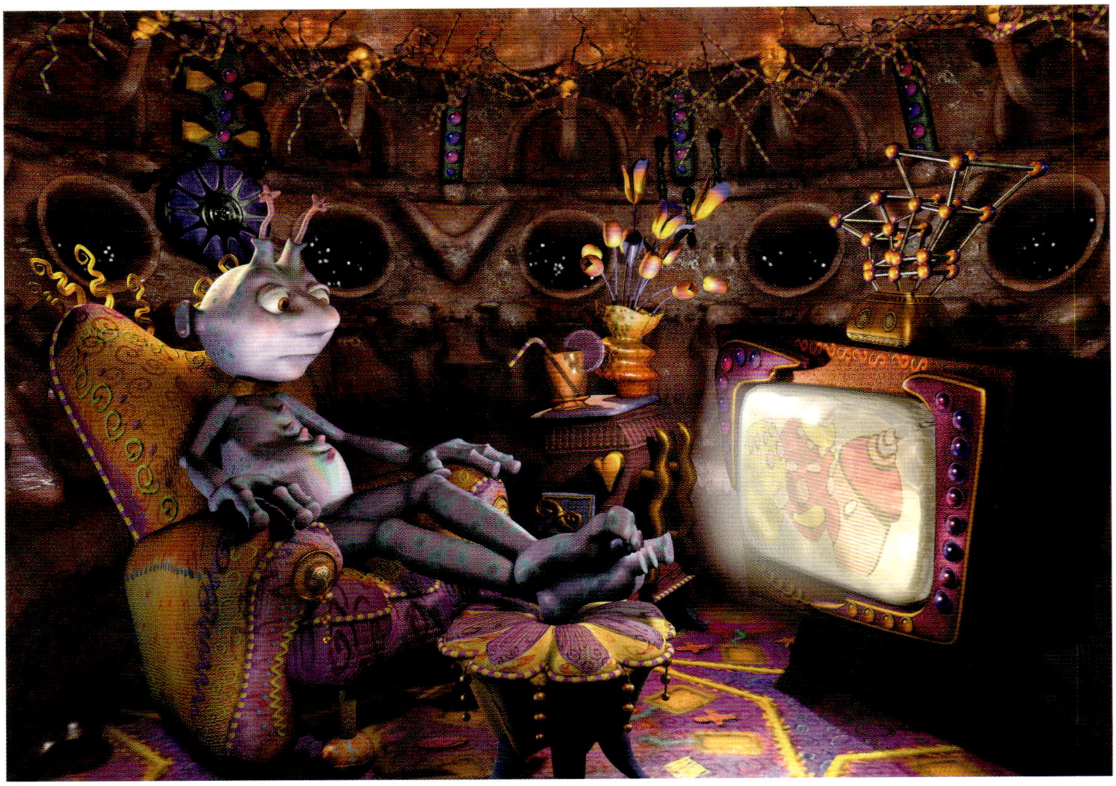

1

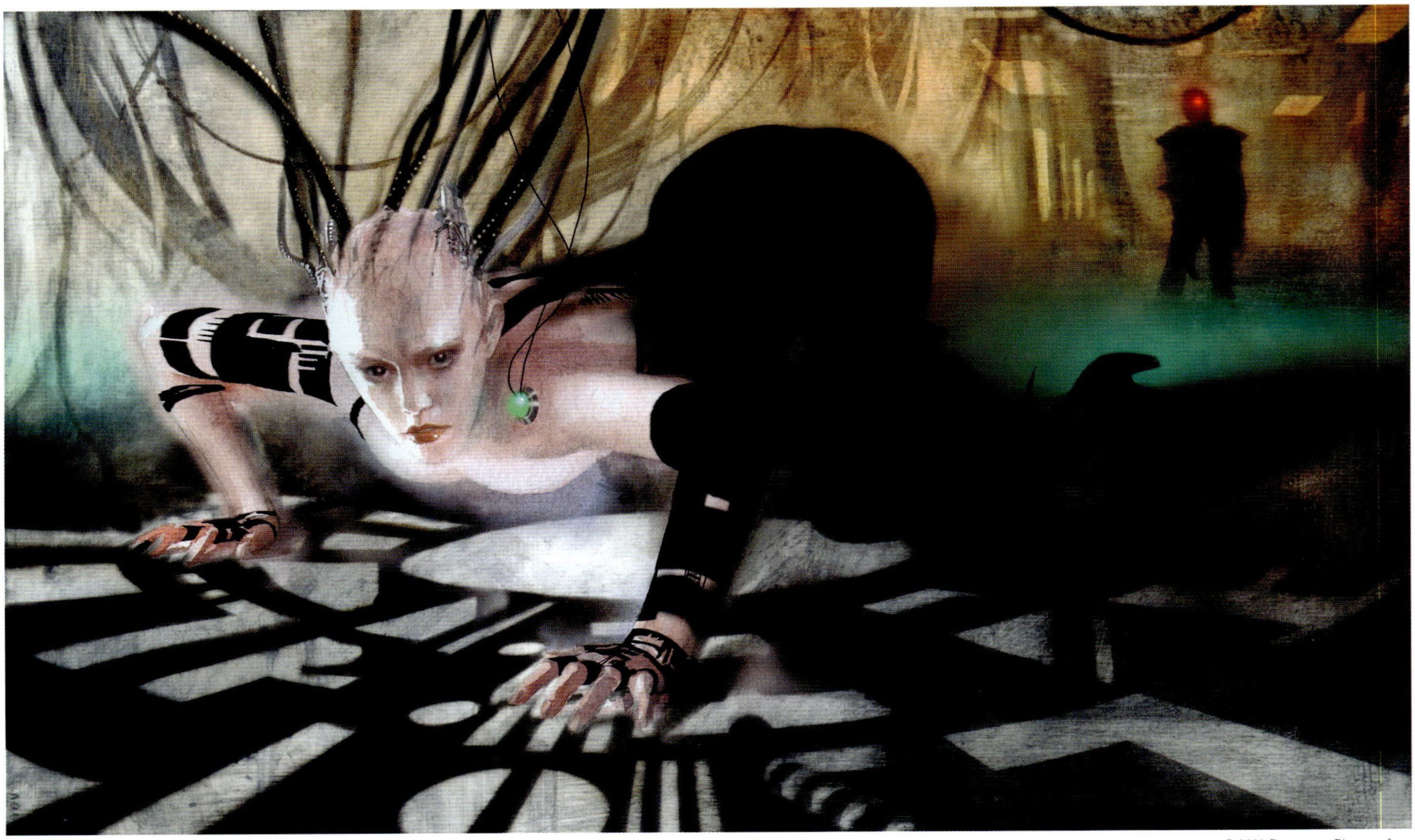

2

3

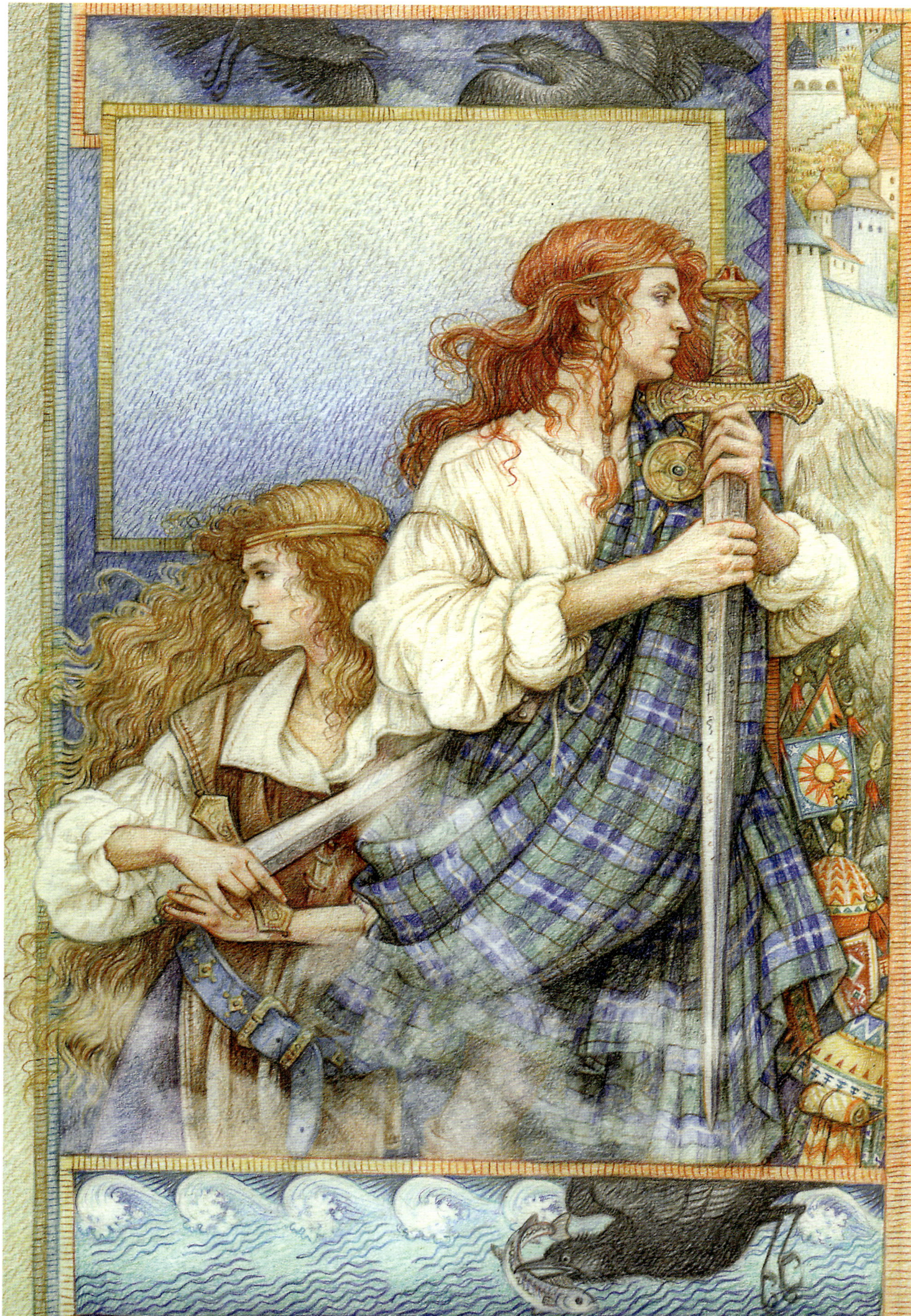

1
artist: GREGORY MANCHESS
art director: Nancy Leo Kelly
client: Dial Books
title: Nanuki: Lord of the Ice
medium: Oil
size: 15"x20"

2
artist: TONY DiTERLIZZI
editor: Kevin Lewis
designer: Anahid Hamparian
client: Simon&Schuster
title: Jimmy Zangwow
medium: Watercolor/gouache
size: 28"x18"

3
artist: TONY DiTERLIZZI
editor: Kevin Lewis
designer: Anahid Hamparian
client: Simon&Schuster
title: Jimmy Zangwow
medium: Watercolor/gouache
size: 28"x18"

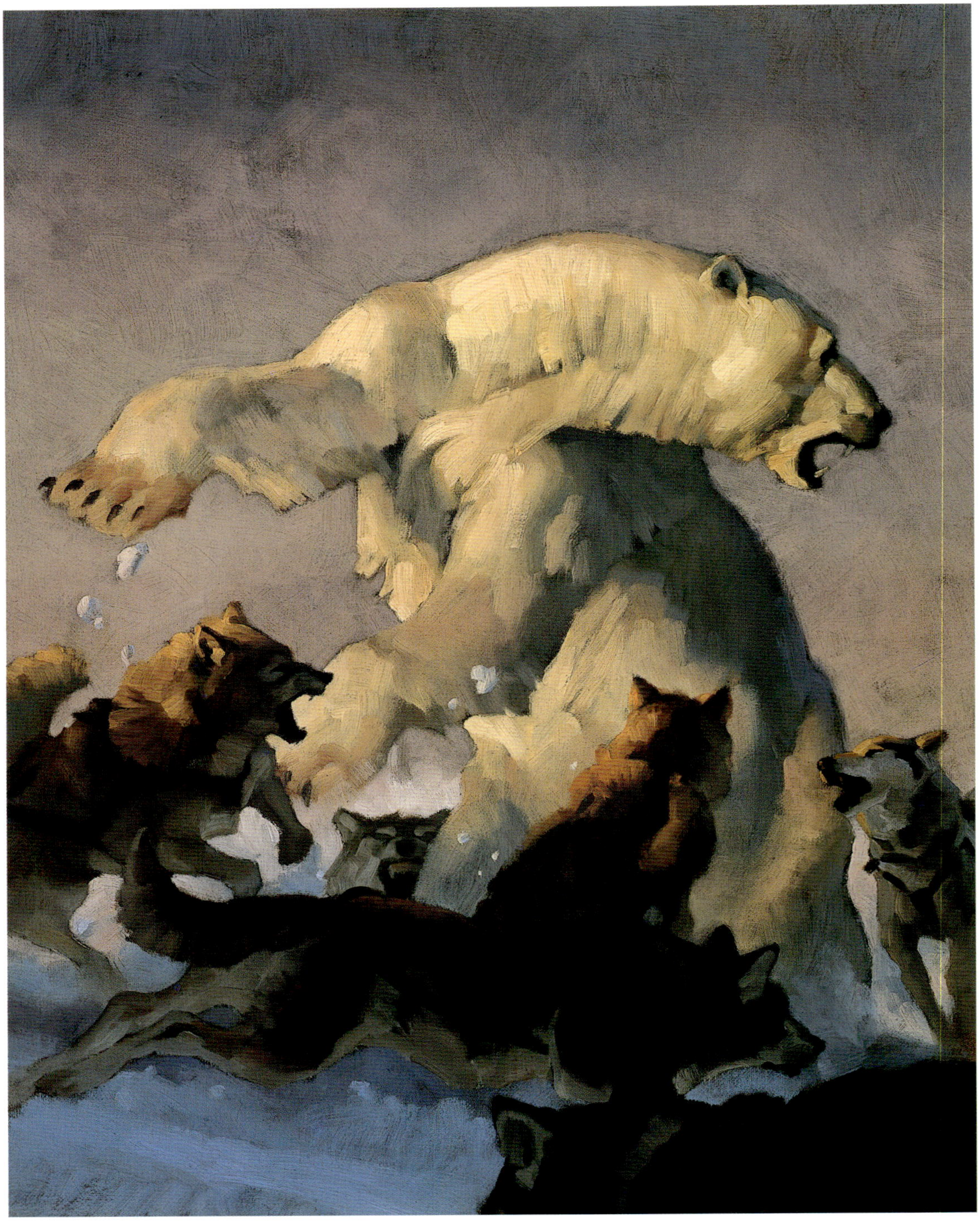

1

2

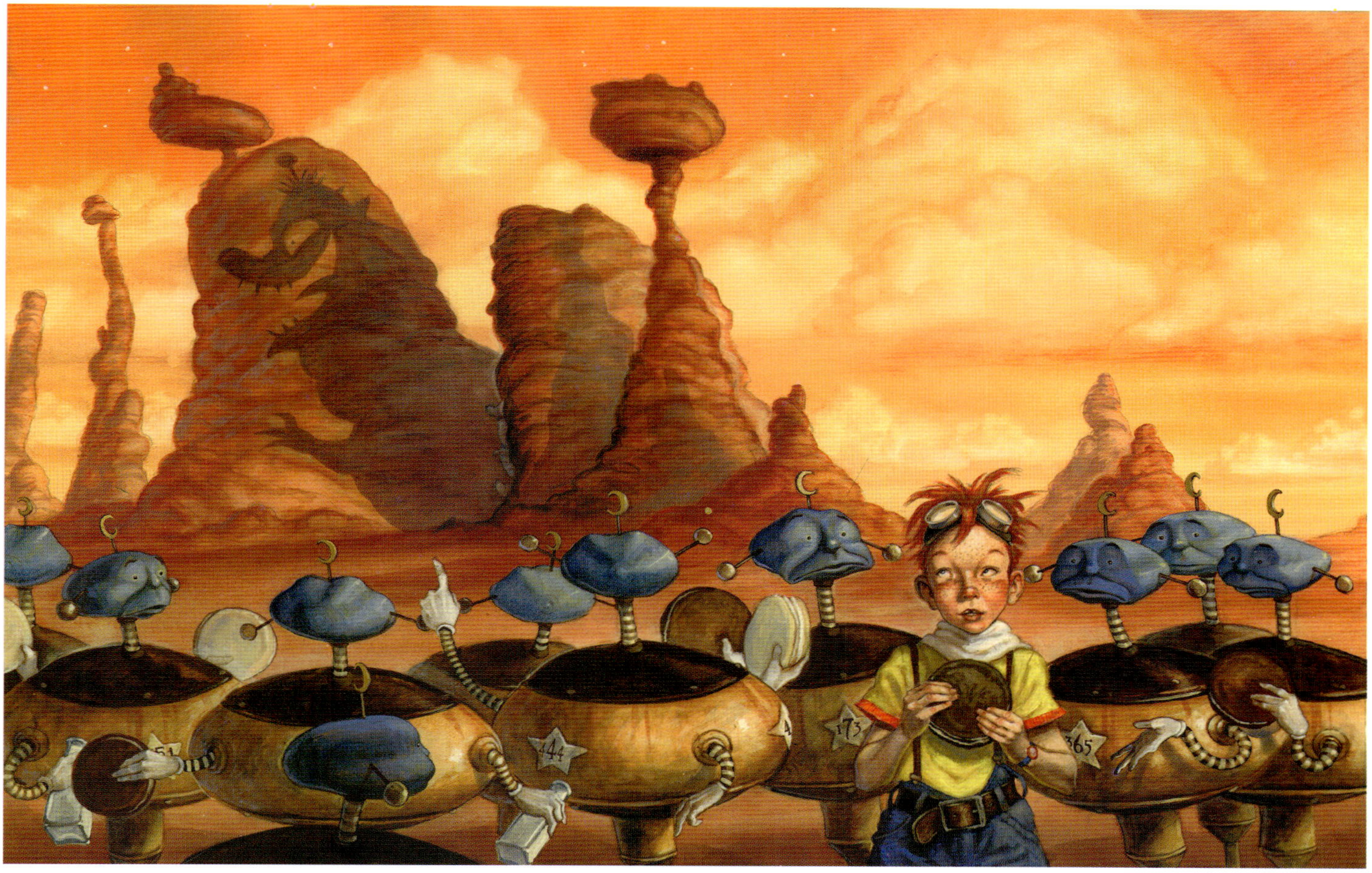

3

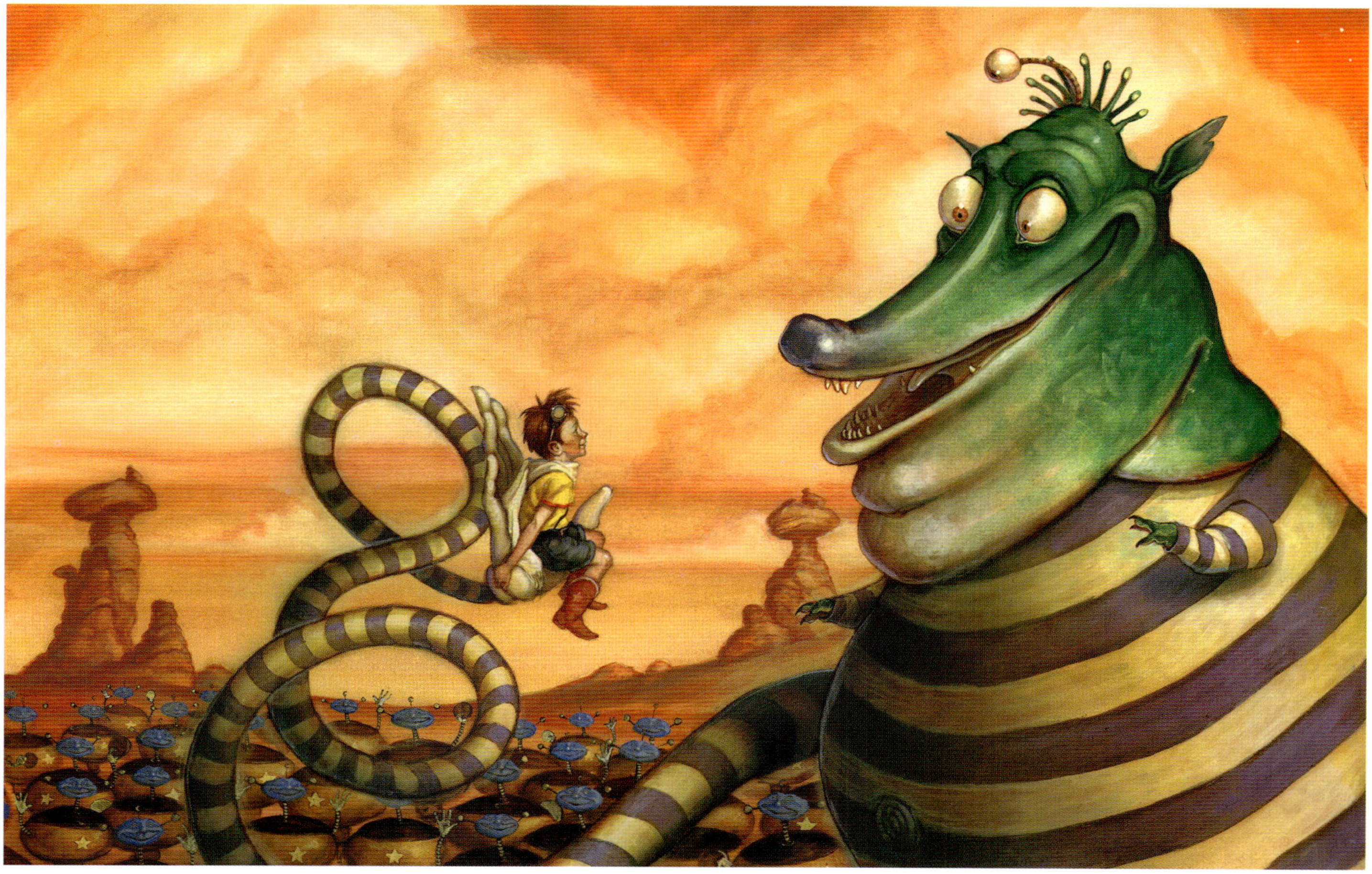

GOLD AWARD
[*comics*]

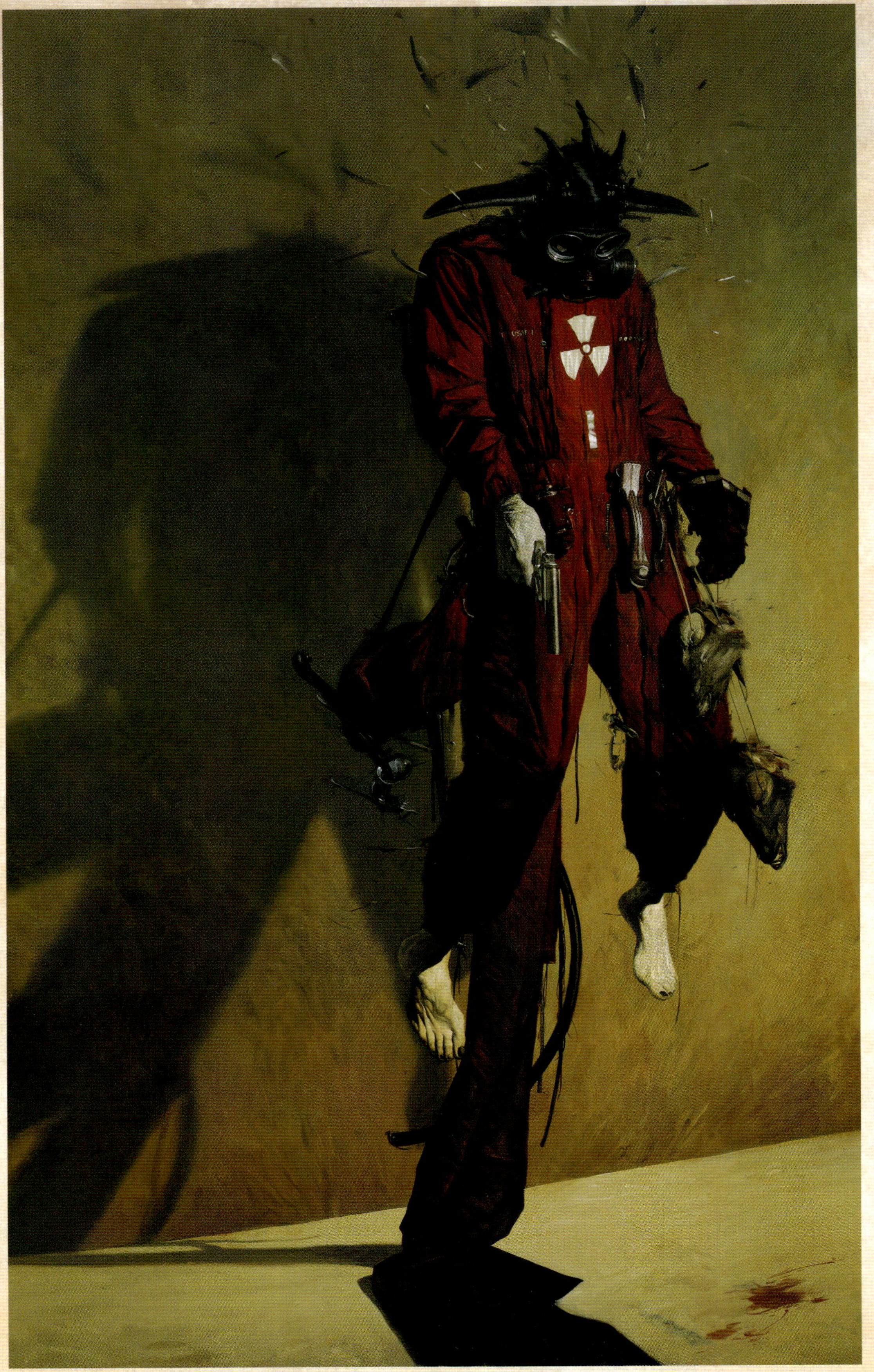

artist: PHIL HALE
client: DC Comics *title:* Beat the Meatles [Weird War Tales Special #1] *size:* 4'x7' *medium:* Oil

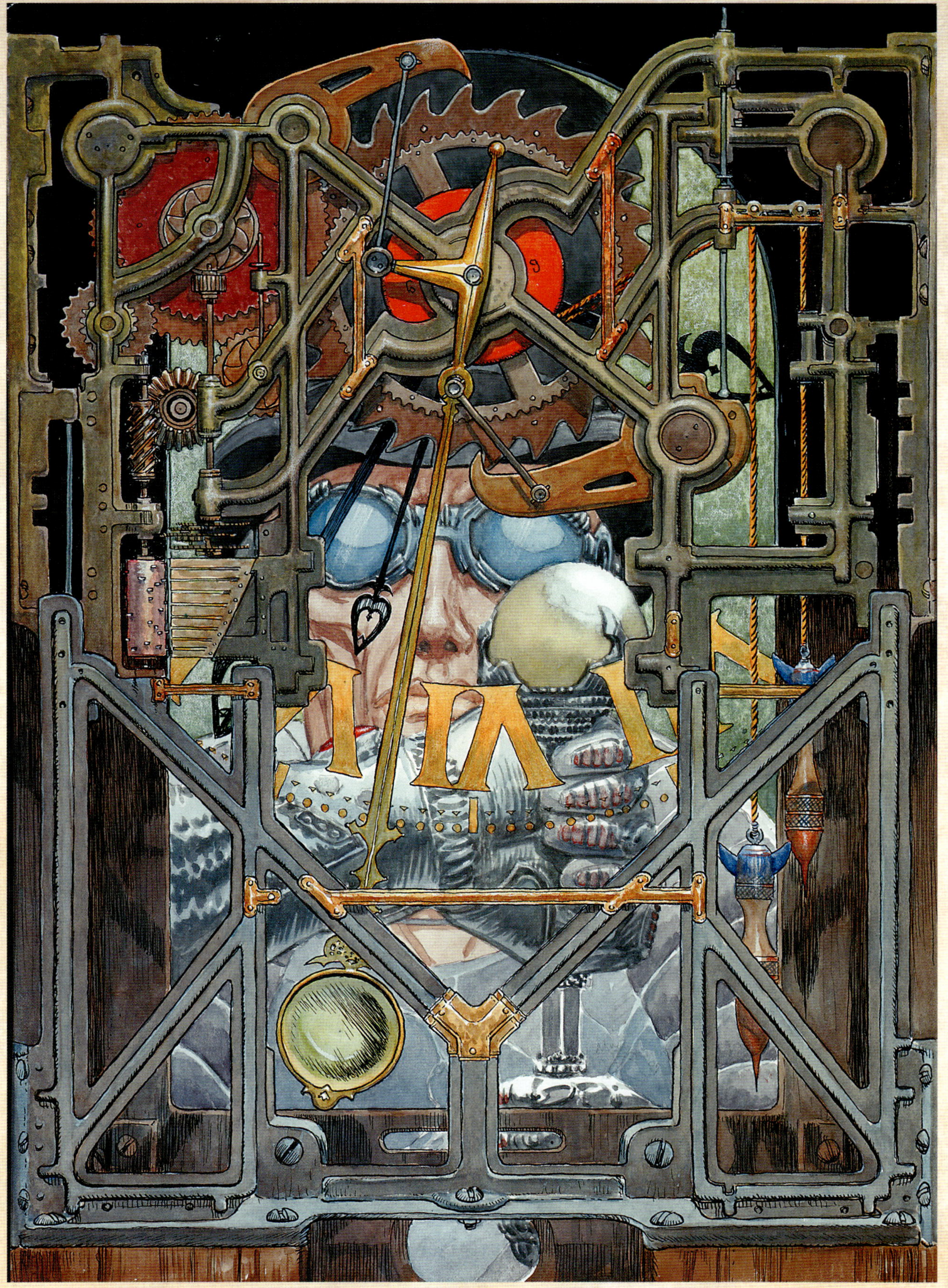

artist: MICHAEL WM. KALUTA
client: Penny-Farthing Press *title:* The Victorian #8 *size:* 12"x17" *medium:* Ink/watercolor

1
artist: KENT WILLIAMS
art director: Todd McFarlane
designer: Brent Ashe
client: Todd McFarlane Productions
title: The Crow #2 Cover
medium: Mixed/digital

2
artist: KENT WILLIAMS
art director: Todd McFarlane
designer: Brent Ashe
client: Todd McFarlane Productions
title: The Crow #6 Cover
medium: Mixed/digital

3
artist: KENT WILLIAMS
art director: Todd McFarlane
designer: Brent Ashe
client: Todd McFarlane Productions
title: The Crow #4 Cover
medium: Mixed/digital

4
artist: KENT WILLIAMS
art director: Todd McFarlane
designer: Brent Ashe
client: Todd McFarlane Productions
title: The Crow #3 Cover
medium: Mixed/digital

1

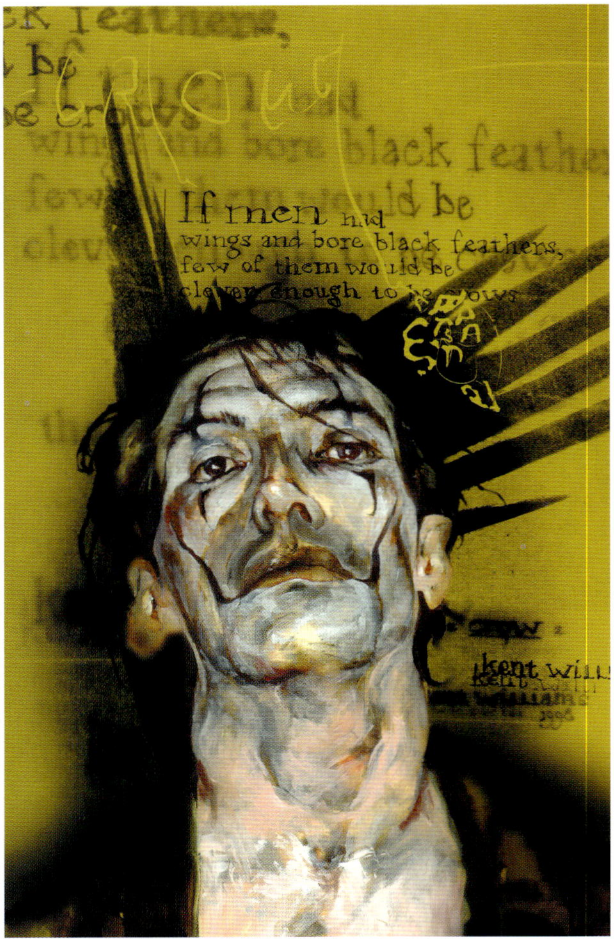

2

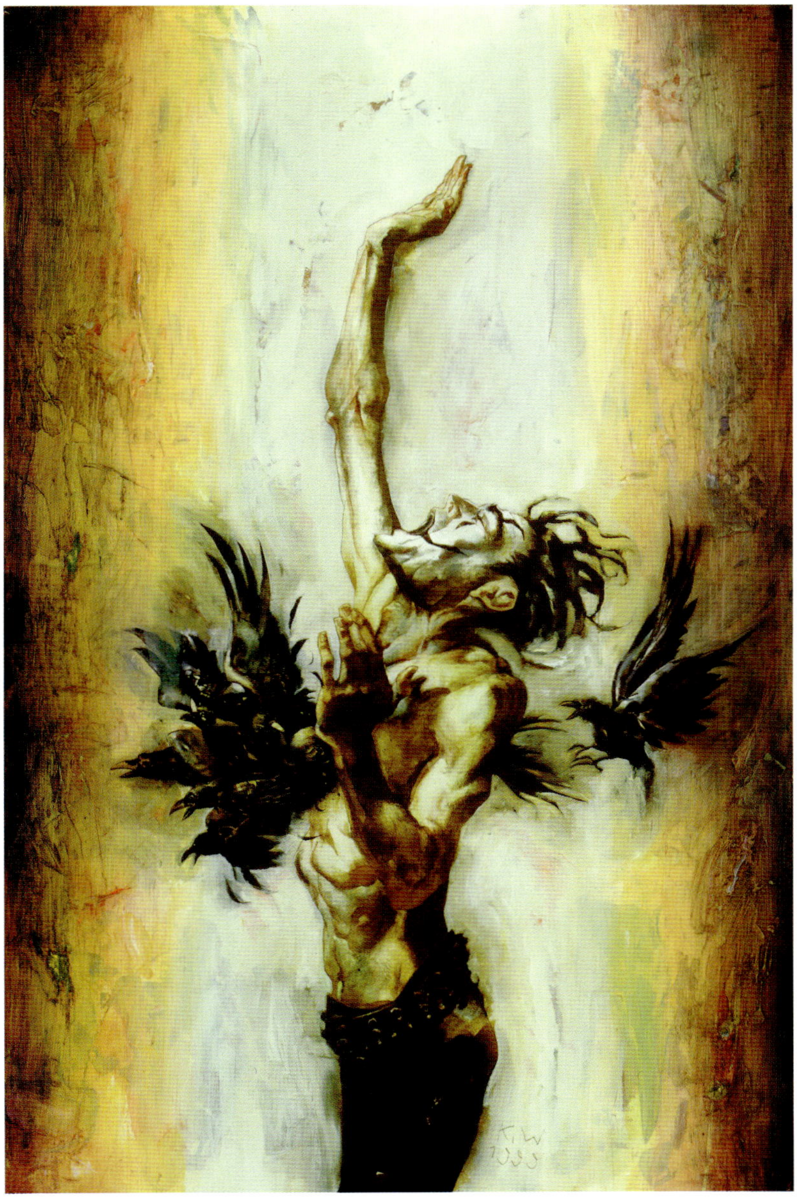

3

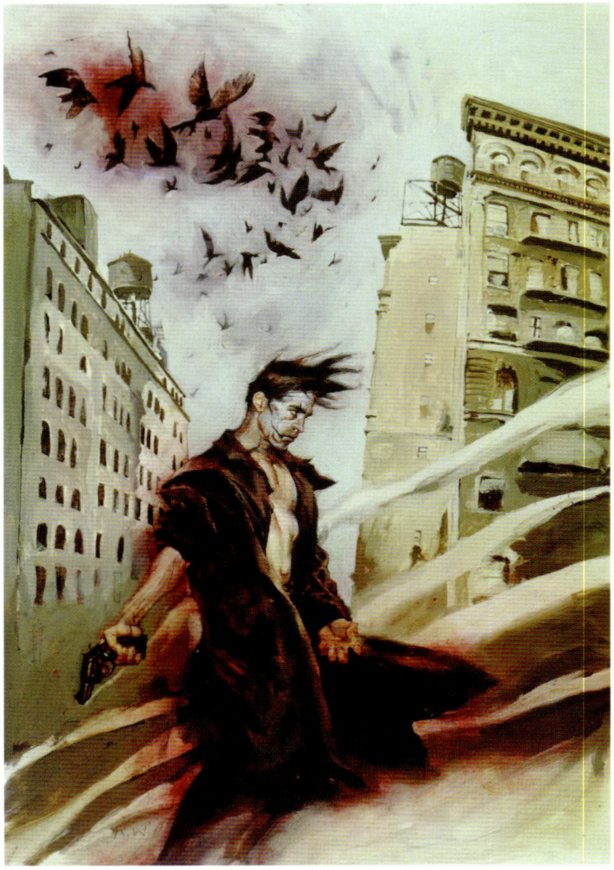

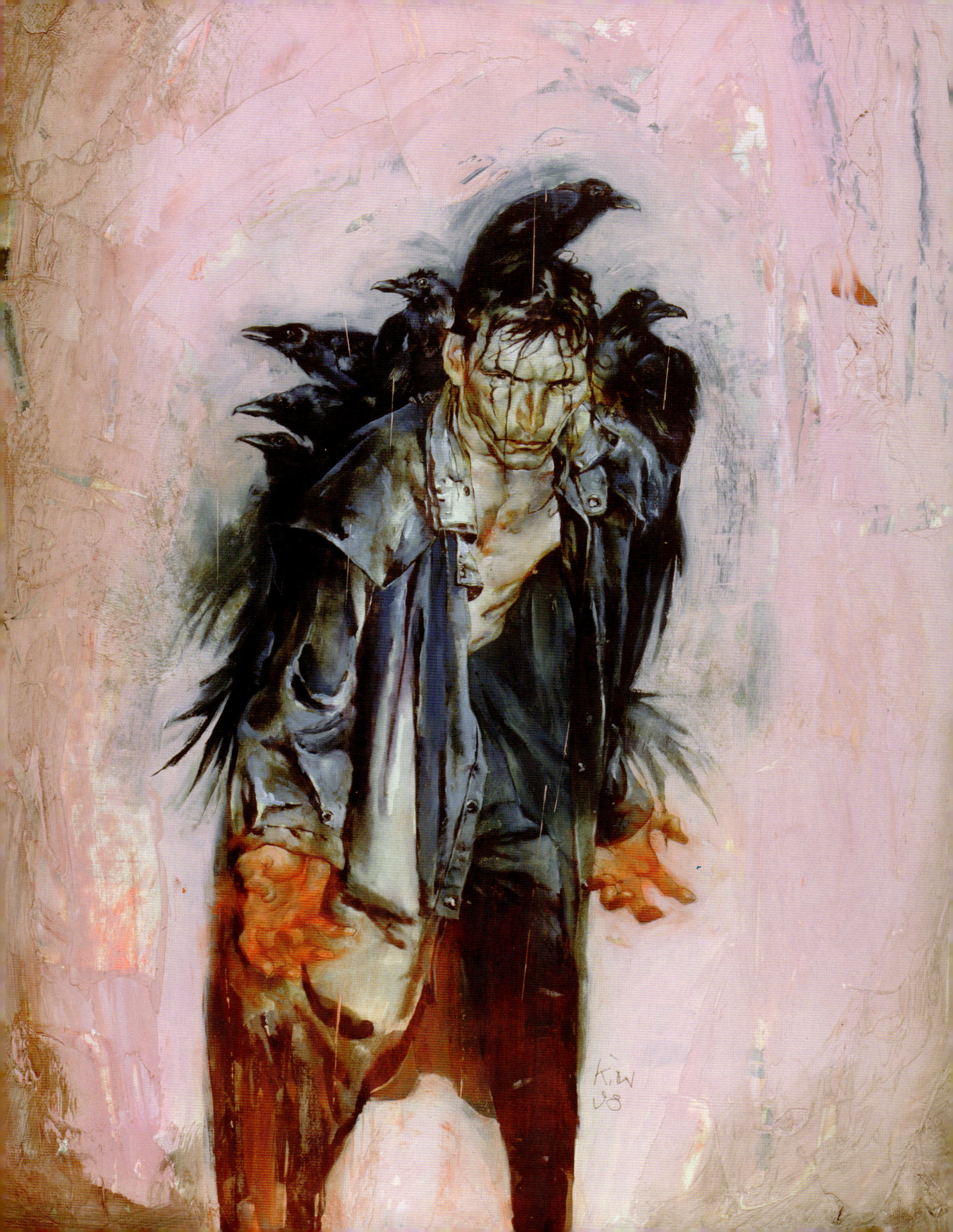

1
artist: DREW PIECE
medium: Digital

2
artist: WILLIAM STOUT
art director: William Stout
designer: William Stout
client: Big Apple Conventions/ Alexander Gallery
title: "Oh, sh--!"
medium: Ink/watercolor
size: 13¼"x21"

3
artist: BRIAN HORTON
art director: Scott Allie
client: Dark Horse Comics
title: Angel: Love;y, Dark & Deep #2
medium: Digital
size: 6.8"x10.5"

4
artist: ADAM HUGHES
art director: Rachel Penn
client: Dark Horse Comics
title: Dirty Pair
medium: Mixed/digital
size: 16"x28"

1

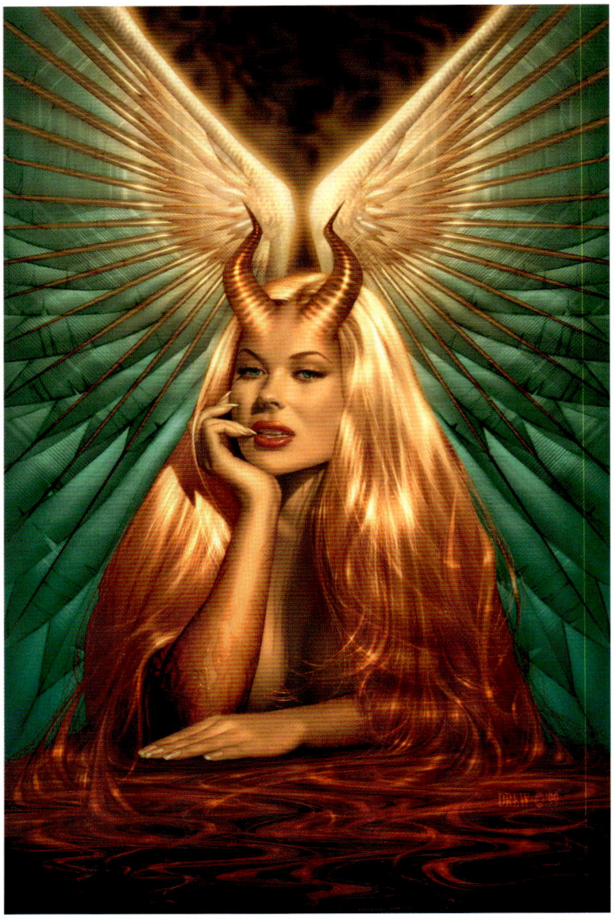

2

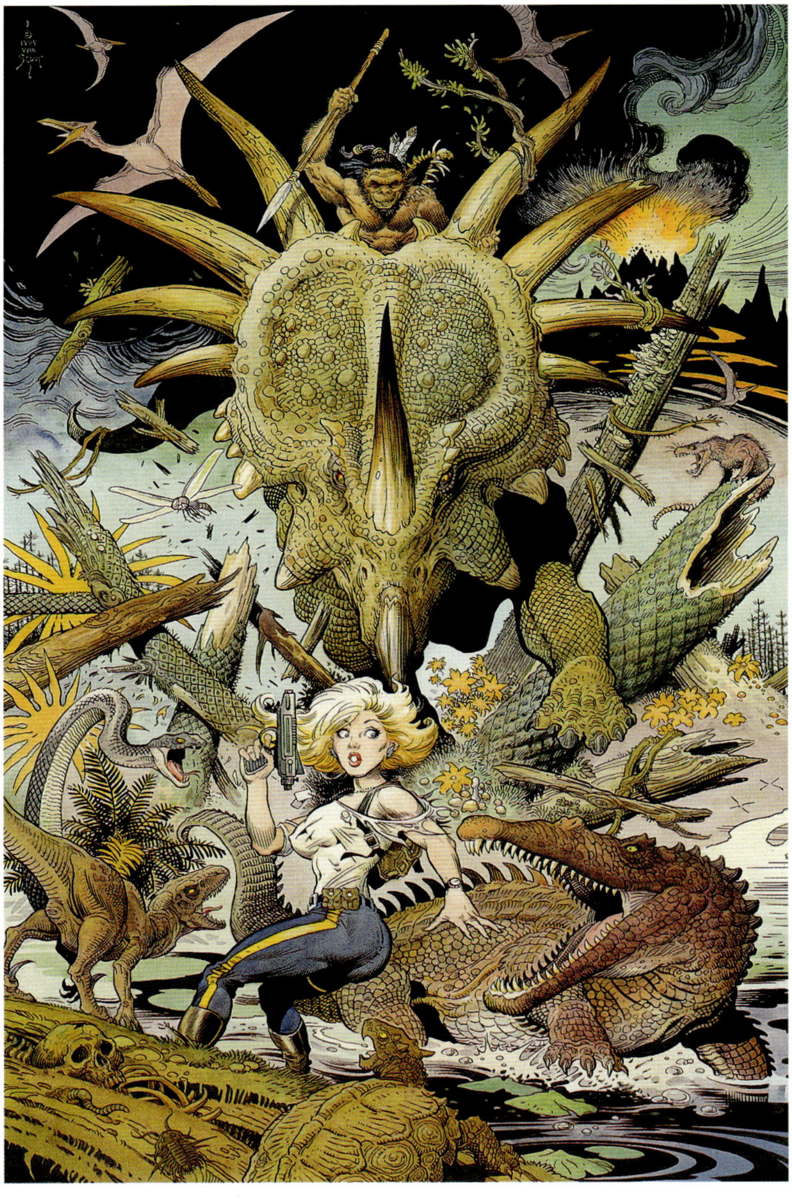

3

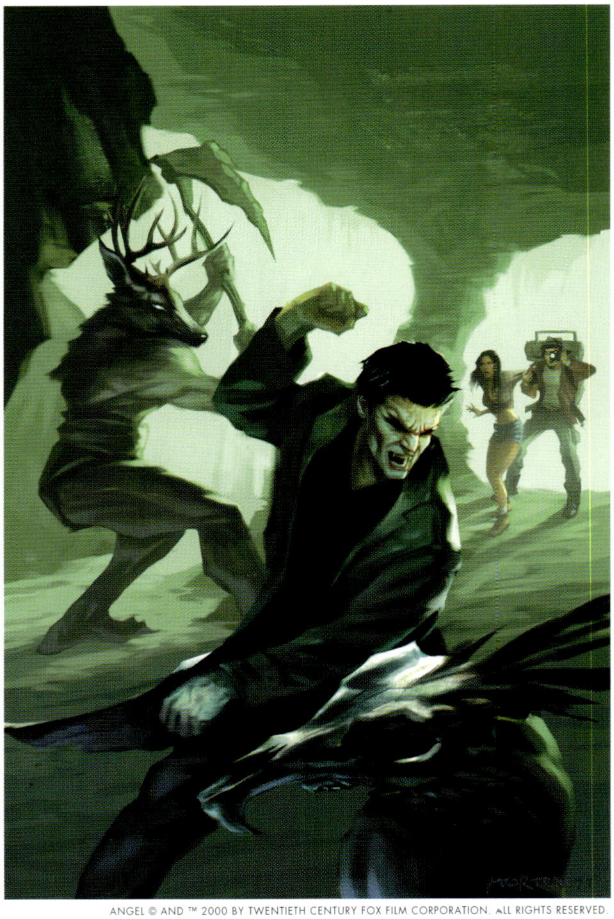

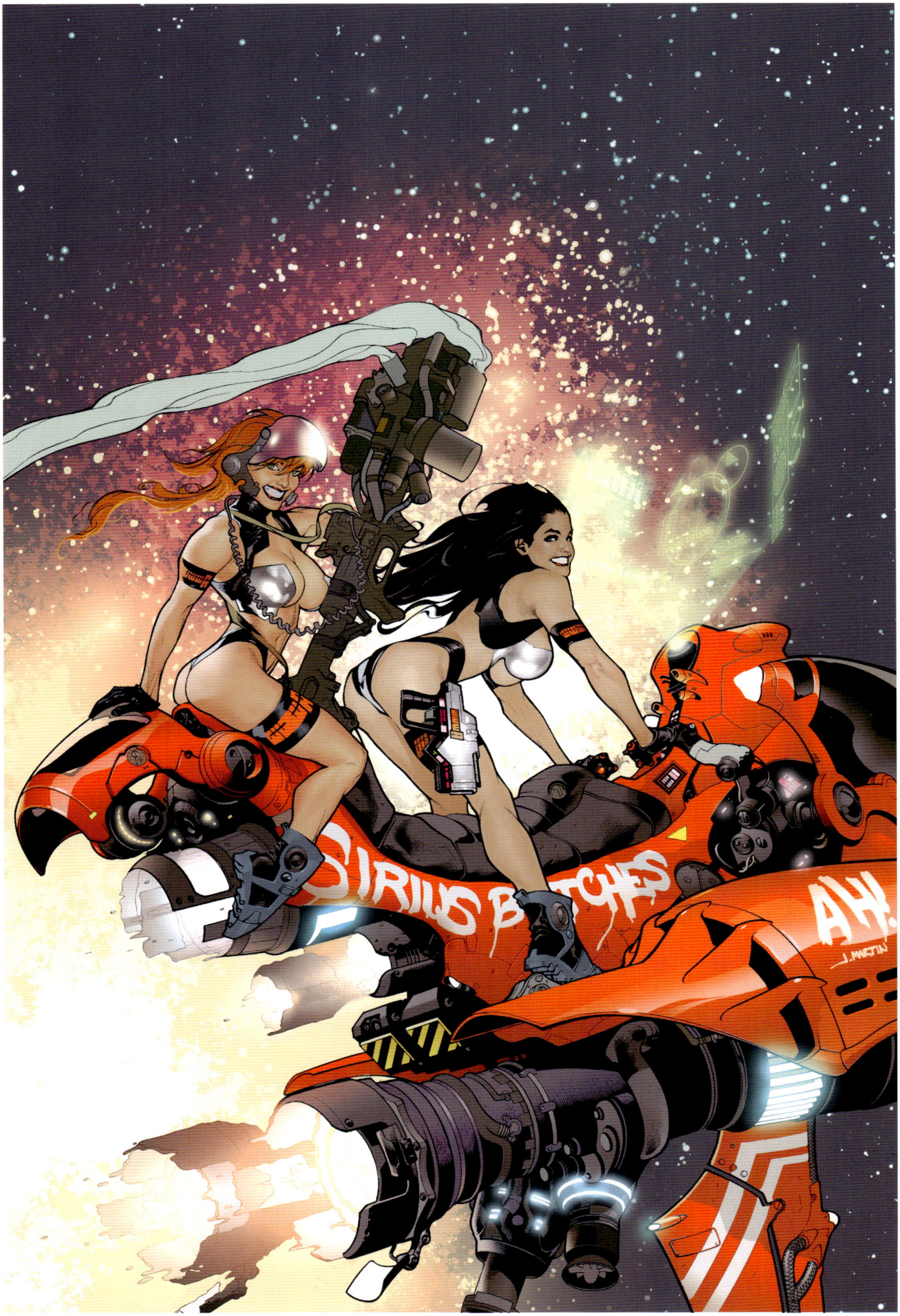
SIRIUS BITCHES
AH!
J. MARTIN

1
artist: PHIL HALE
client: DC/Vertigo Comics
title: Name of Bender
[*Strange Adventures #2*]
medium: Oil

2
artist: DOUG BEEKMAN
art director: K. White
client: Penny-Farthing Press
title: Mirage in the Mist
medium: Mixed
size: 17"x24 1/2"

3
artist: TIM BRADSTREET
art director: Bruce Ingram
client: Penny-Farthing Press
title: Societas Clandestina Aeterna
medium: Ink/watercolor
size: 11"x17"

4
artist: JIM STERANKO
client: Penny-Farthing Press
title: The Synchronometry of Paranoia
medium: Acrylic
size: 16"x24"

1

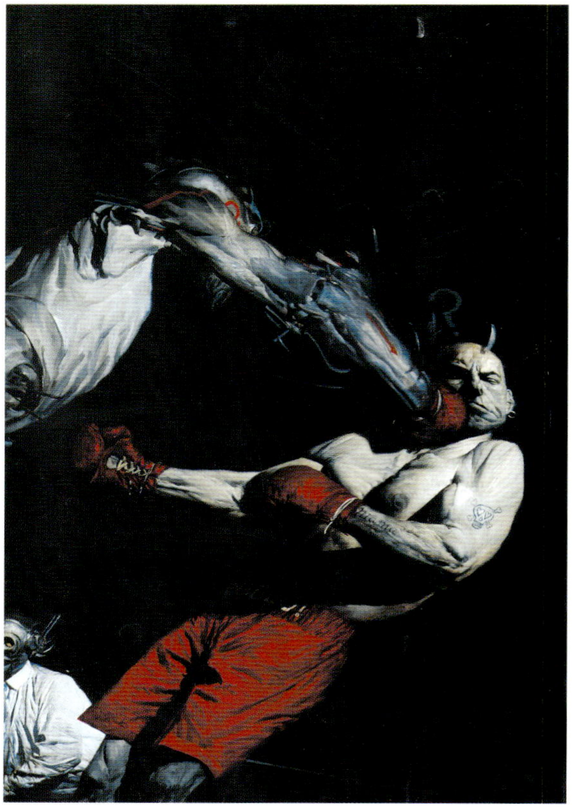

2

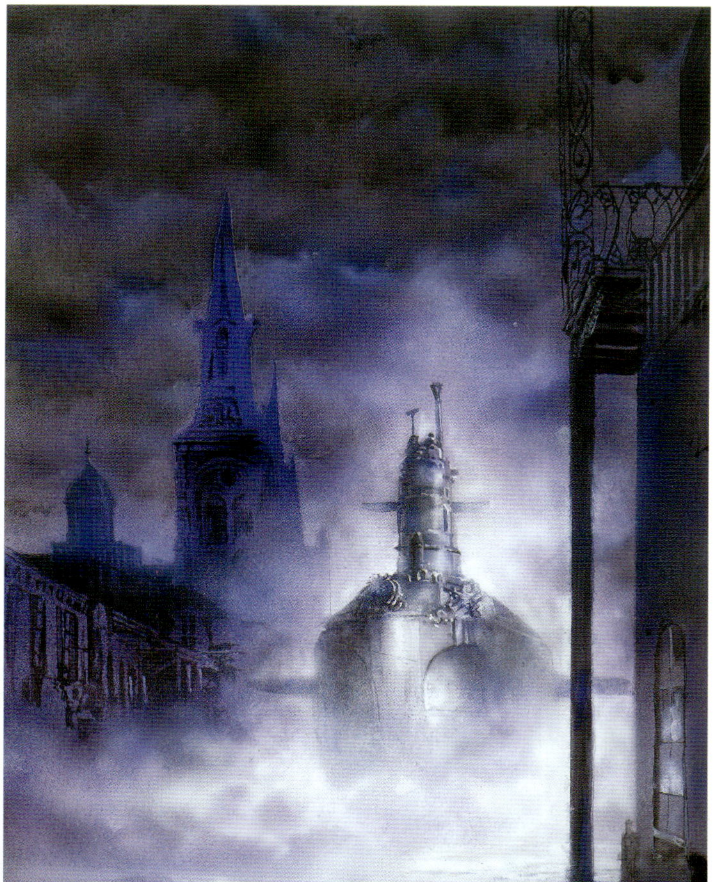

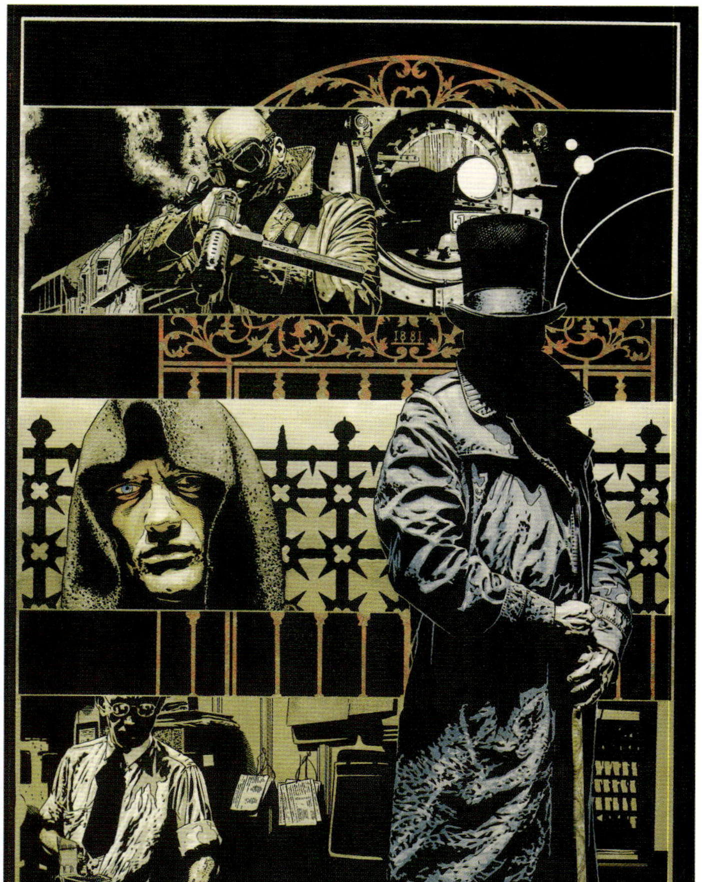

3

4

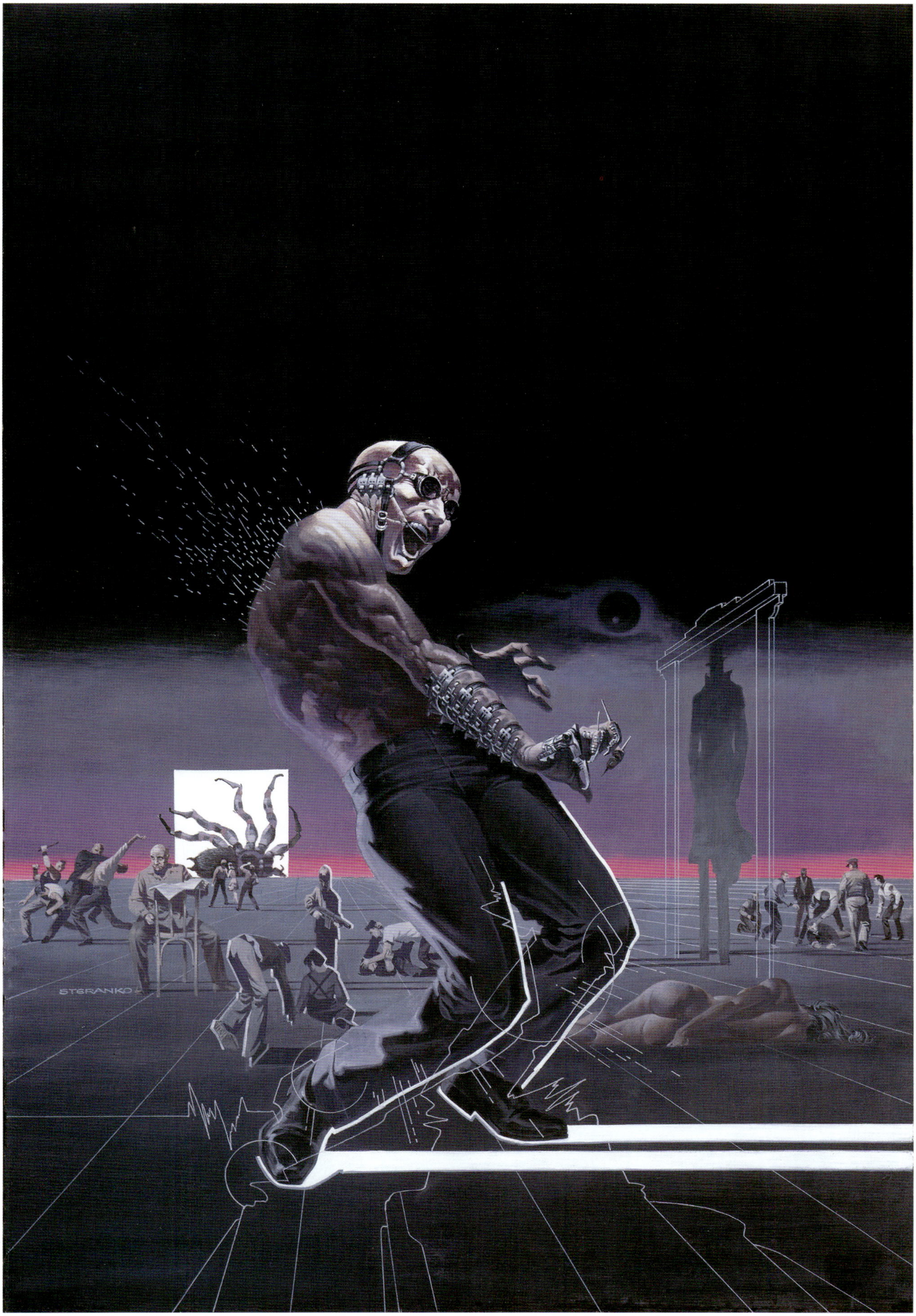

1
artist: CHRISTOPHER SHY
art director: Joseph Linsner
designer: Christopher Shy
client: Sirius Entertainment
title: Empty Zone #5
medium: Digital

2
artist: PHIL HALE
client: DC Comics/Vertigo
title: Hellblazer
medium: Oil

3
artist: RAVENWOOD
art director: Dave Land
client: Lucasfilm, Ltd.
title: Phantom Menace
medium: Oil
size: 25"x34"

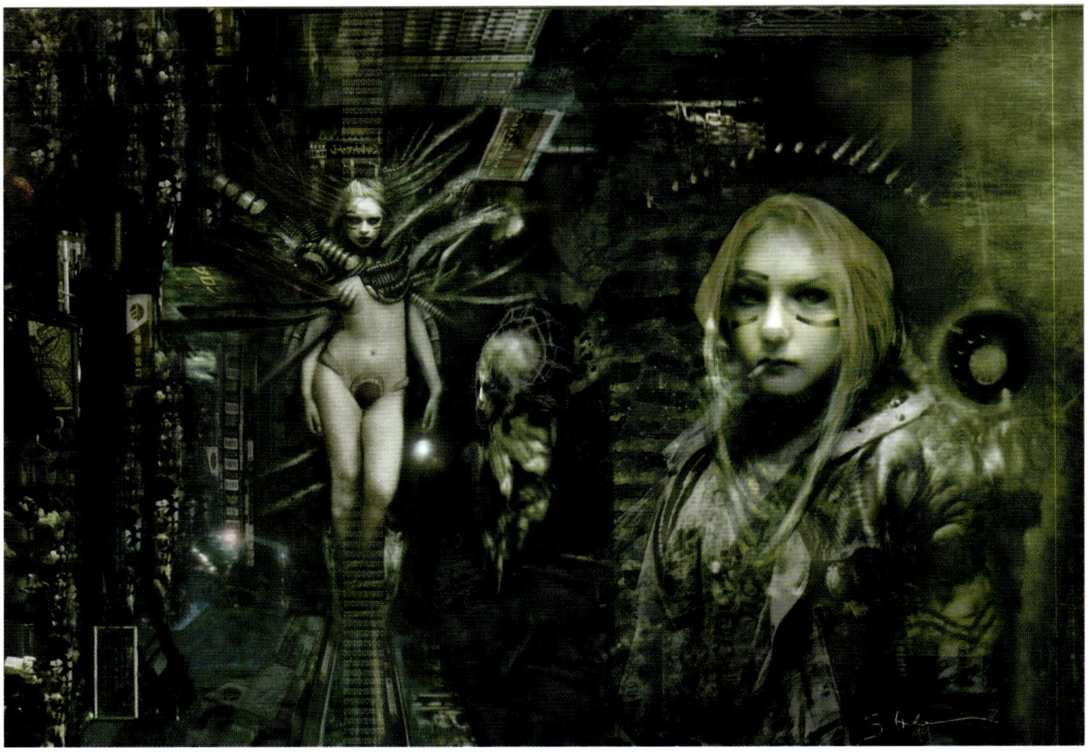

1

2

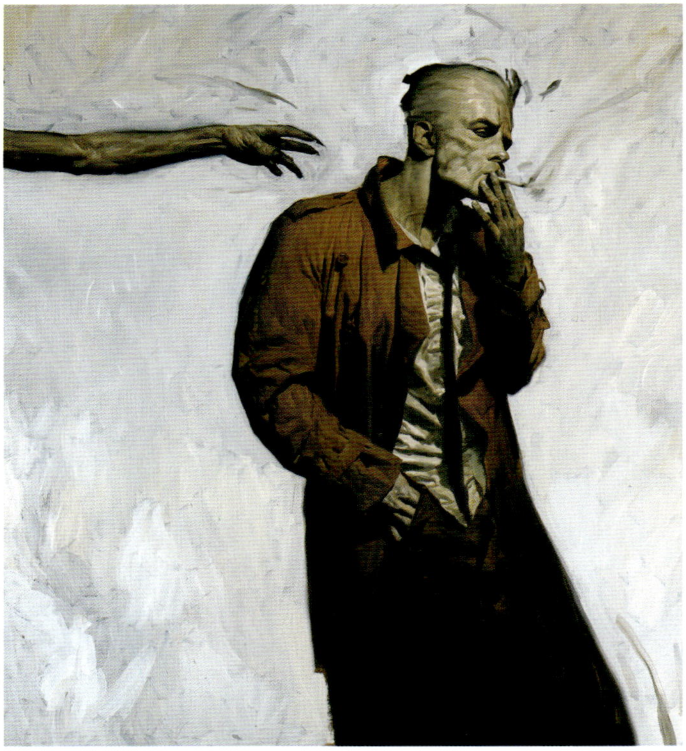

3

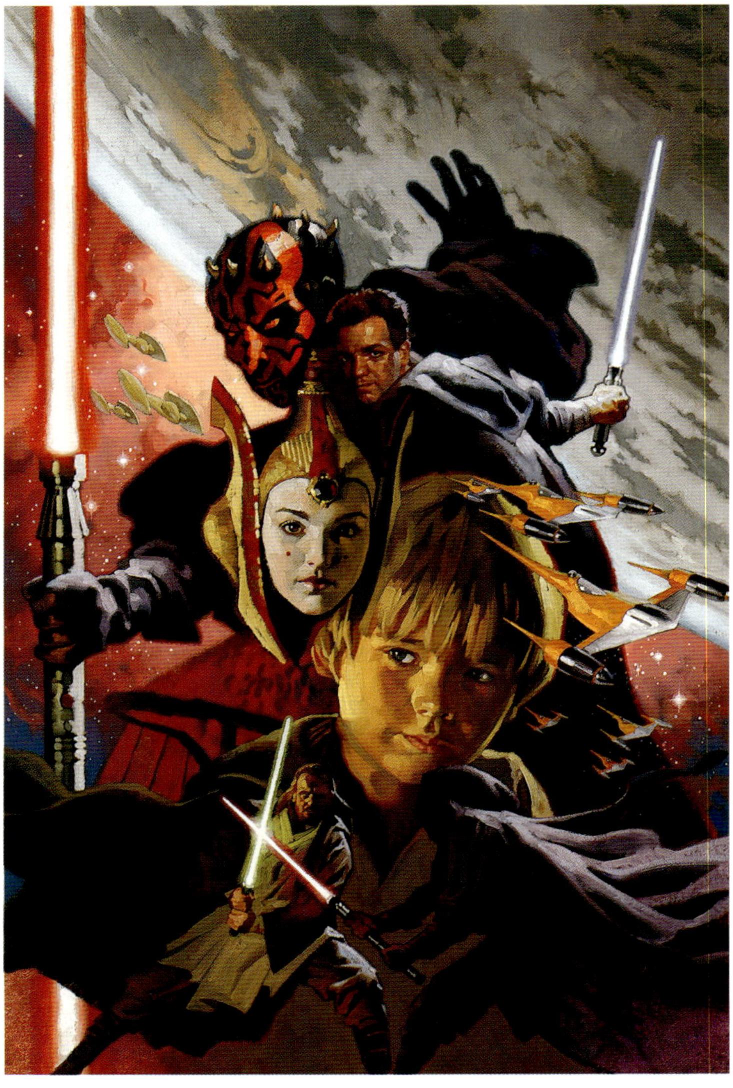

4
artist: JOHN VAN FLEET
art director: Matt Idelson
designer: Ammie Brockway
client: DC Comics
title: The Chalice [cover]
medium: Mixed/acrylic
size: 10 1/2"x14"

4

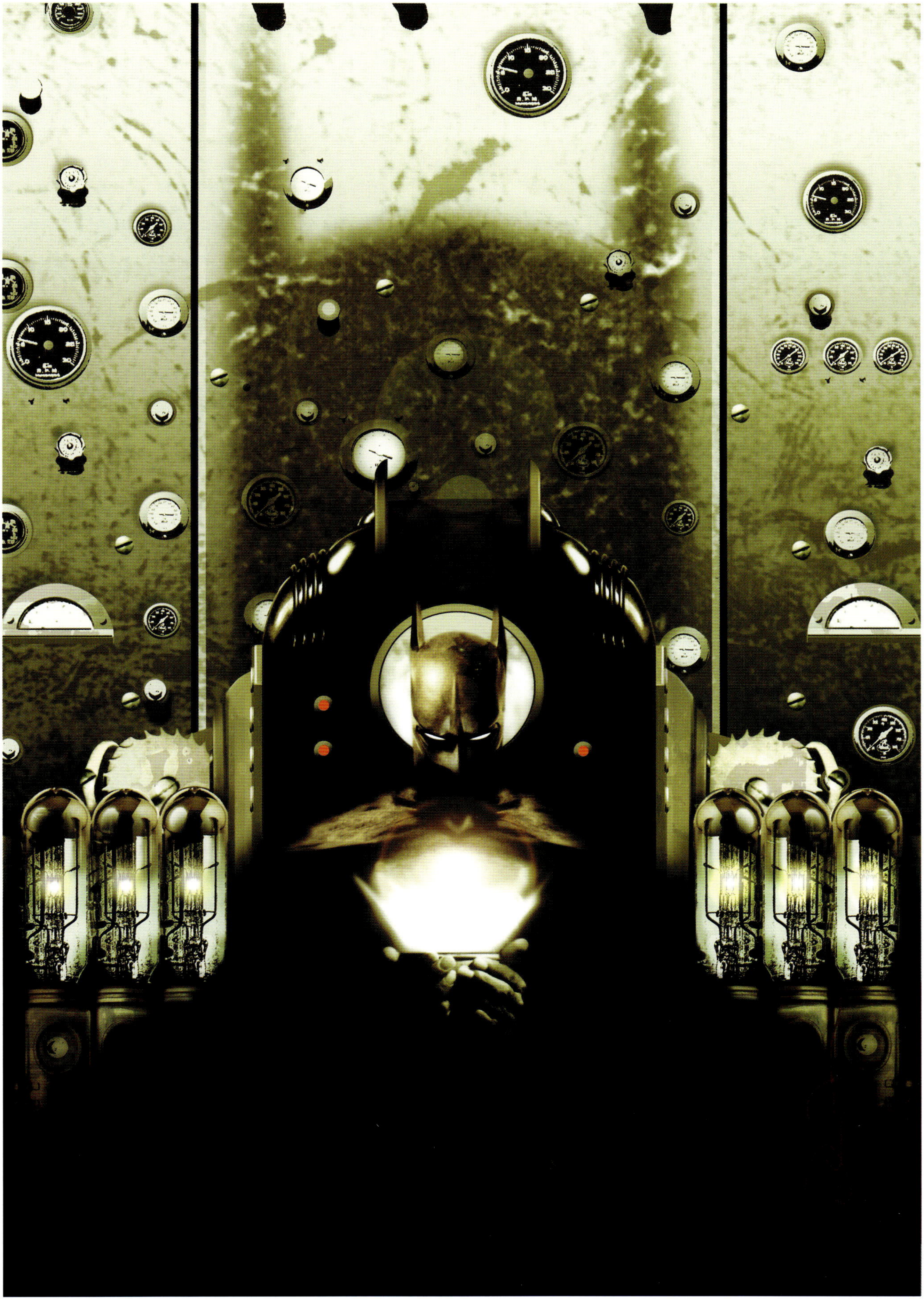

1
artist: JOSEPH MICHAEL LINSNER
art director: Joseph Linsner
designer: Joseph Michael Linsner
client: Sirius Entertainment
title: Crypt of Dawn 6
medium: Mixed/digital

2
artist: GLEN ORBIK
art director: Joseph Illidge
client: DC Comics
title: Batman: No Man's Land #0
medium: Oil
size: 13"x22"

3
artist: GARY GIANNI
client: Dark Horse Comics
title: The Monster Men
medium: Oil
size: 20"x30"

4
artist: JOE JUSKO
client: Top Cow Productions
title: Tomb Raider
medium: Acrylic
size: 11"x17"

1

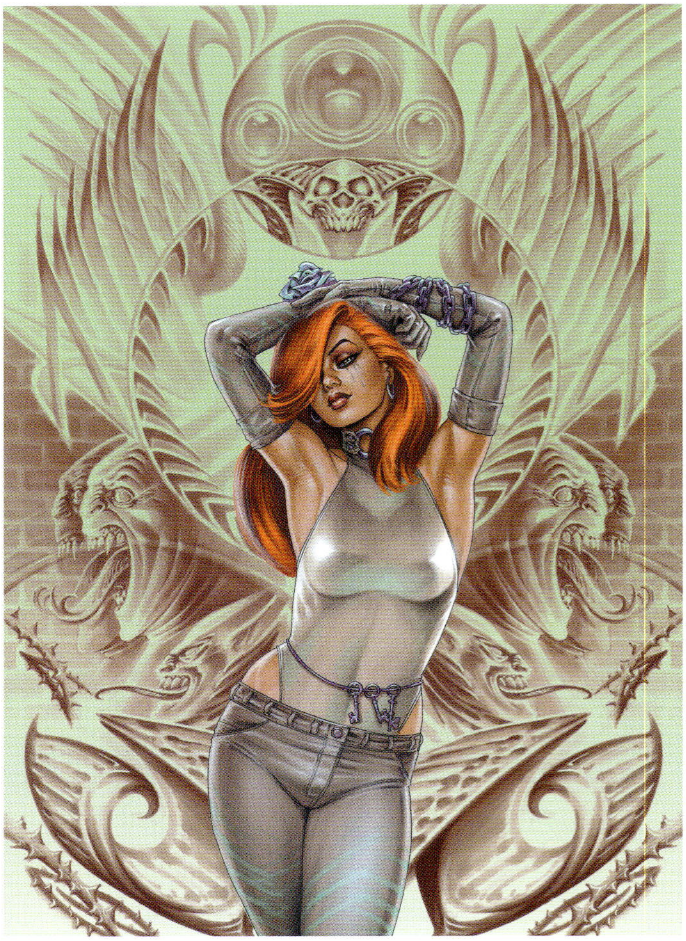

2

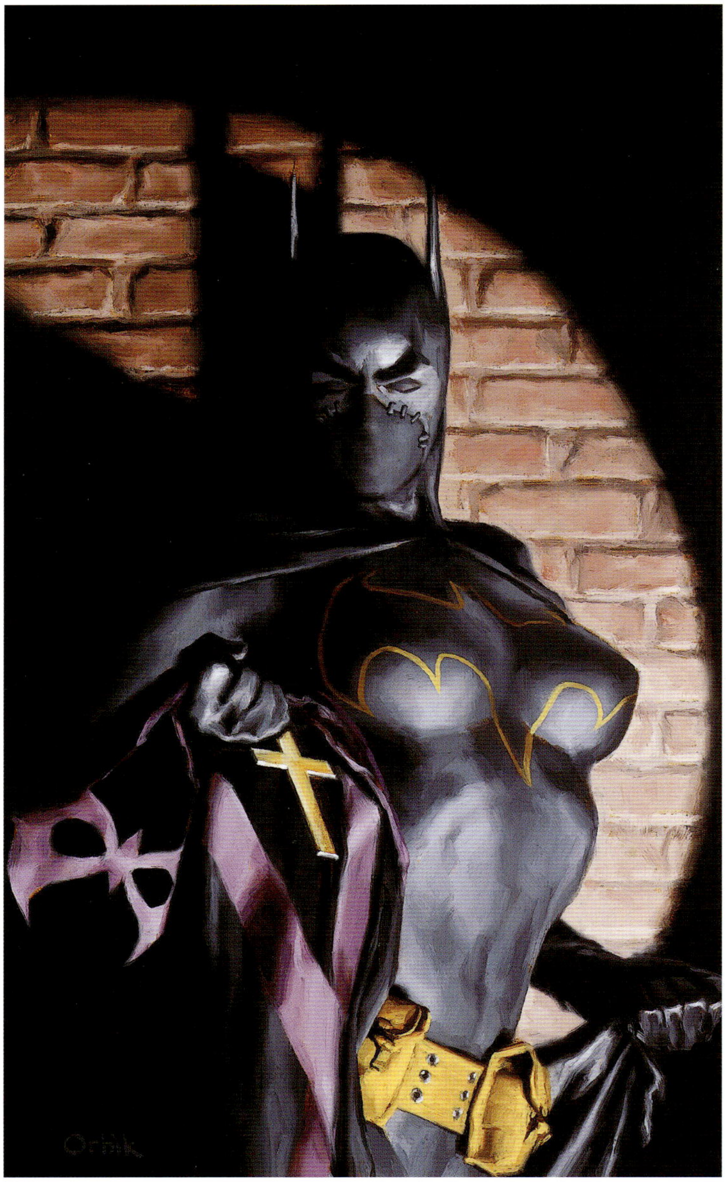

3

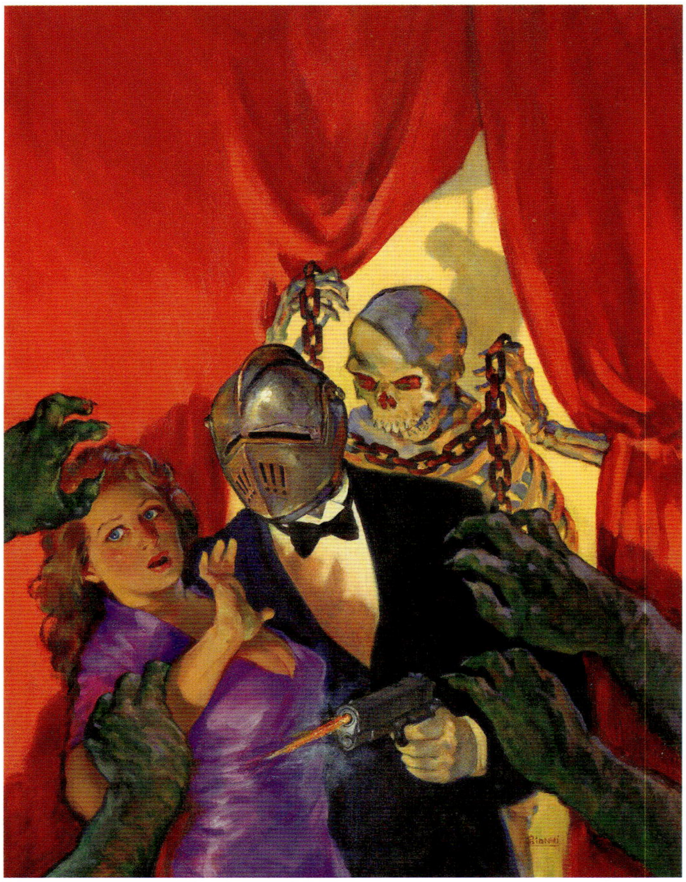

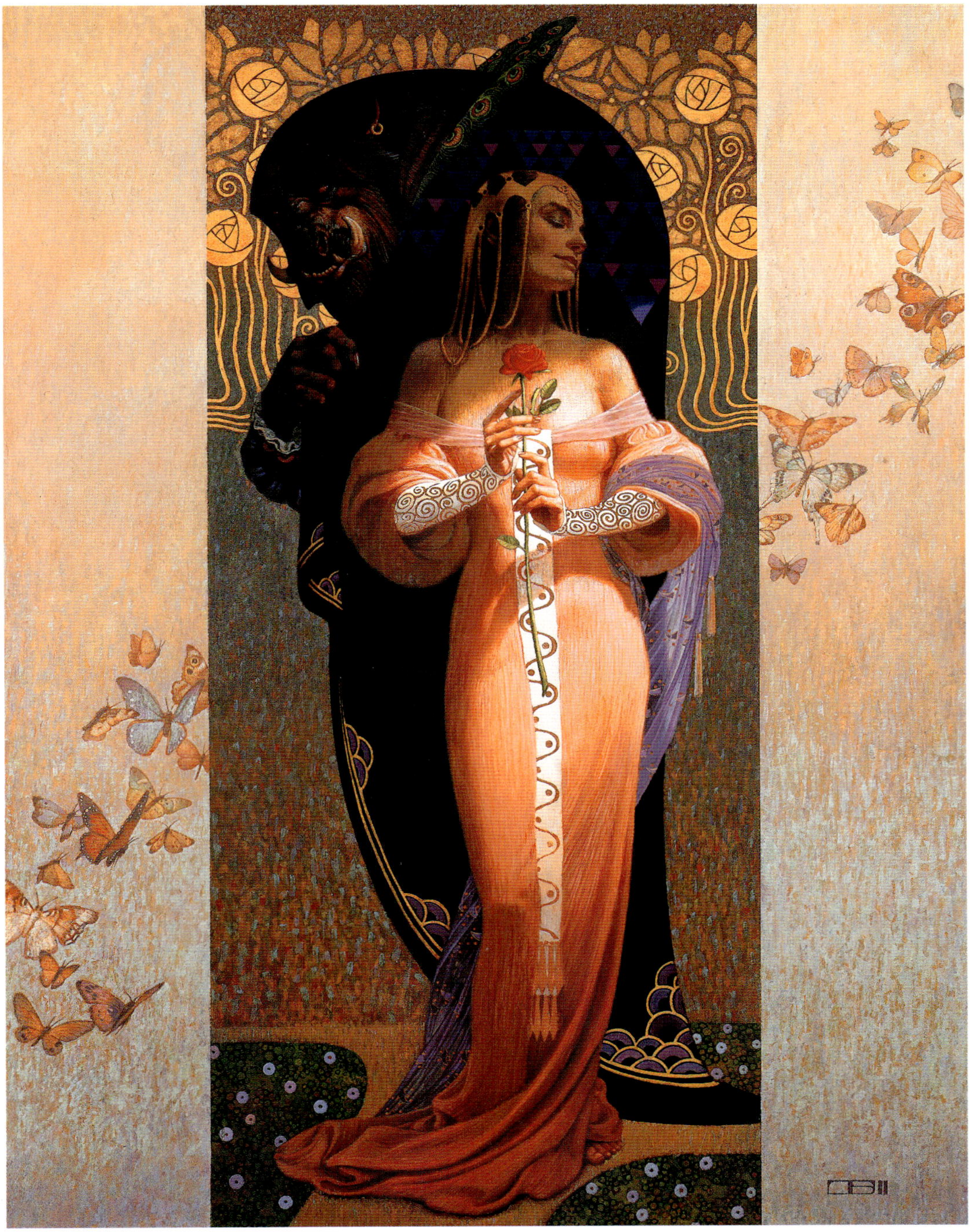

136
artist: **THOMAS BLACKSHEAR II**
art director: Thomas Blackshear II
designer: Thomas Blackshear II
client: The Greenwich Workshop
title: Beauty and the Beast
medium: Oil and gold leaf
size: 26x34

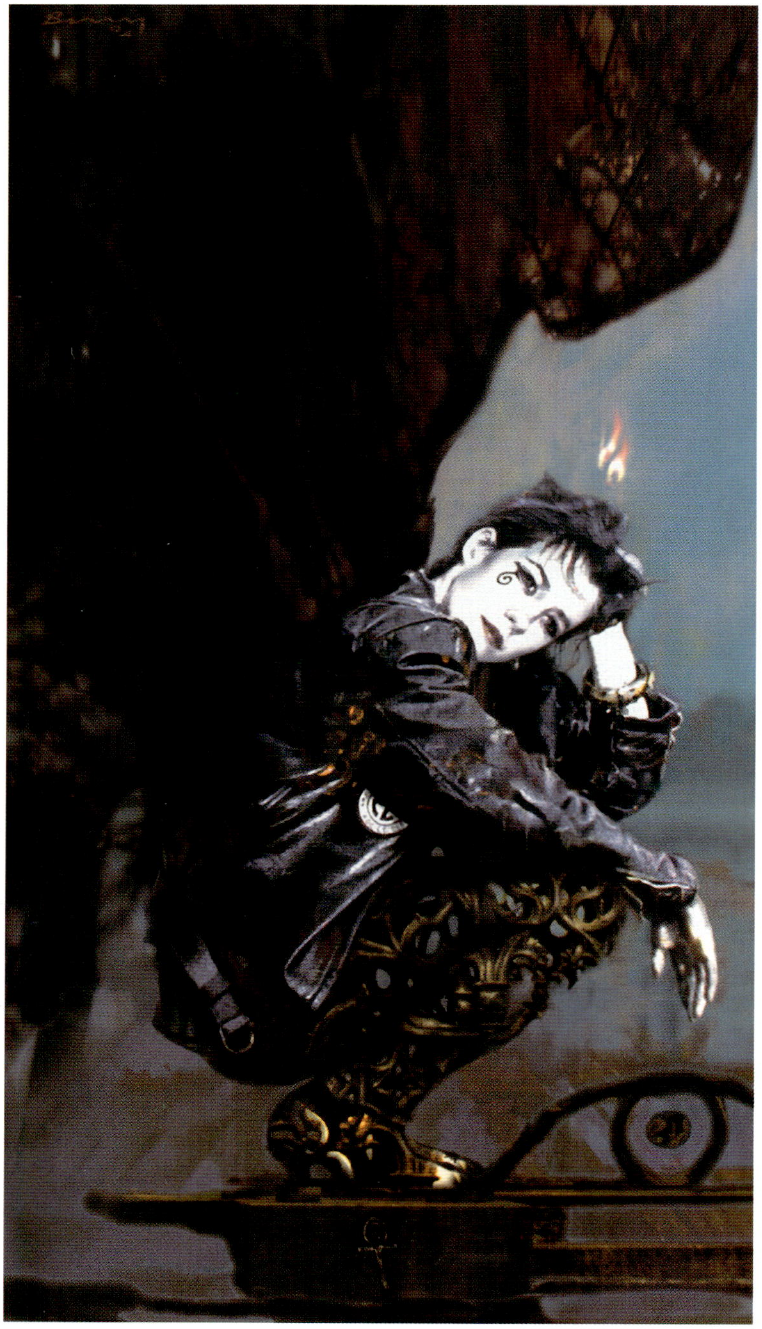

137
artist: **RICK BERRY**
art director: Sean Taggart
designer: Rick Berry
client: DC Comics/Vertigo
title: Death
medium: Digital
size: 6x9

4

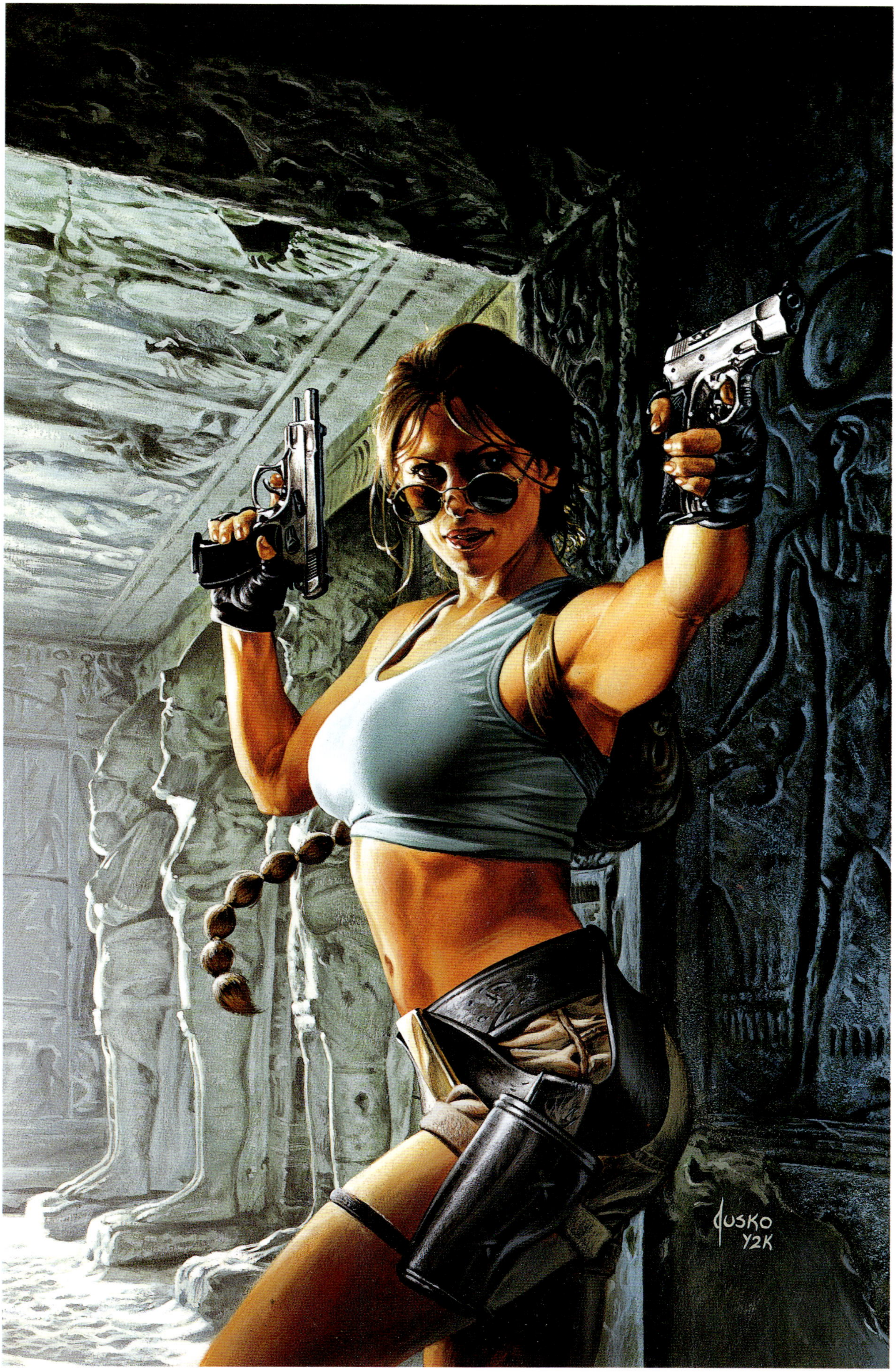

1
artist: STEPHEN JOHN PHILLIPS
JOSE VILLARRUBIA
art director: Amie Brockway
designer: Stephen John Phillips
client: DC Comics/Vertigo
title: Veils: Sultan's Chamber
medium: Mixed/digital

2
artist: STEPHEN JOHN PHILLIPS
JOSE VILLARRUBIA
art director: Amie Brockway
designer: Stephen John Phillips
client: DC Comics/Vertigo
title: Veils [cover]
medium: Mixed/digital

3
artist: GLEN ORBIK/LAUREL BLECHMAN
art director: Darren Vincenzo
client: DC Comics
title: Batman: Shadow of the Bat #88
medium: Oil *size:* 13"x22"

4
artist: GLEN ORBIK/LAUREL BLECHMAN
art director: Darren Vincenzo
client: DC Comics
title: Batman #568
medium: Oil *size:* 13"x22"

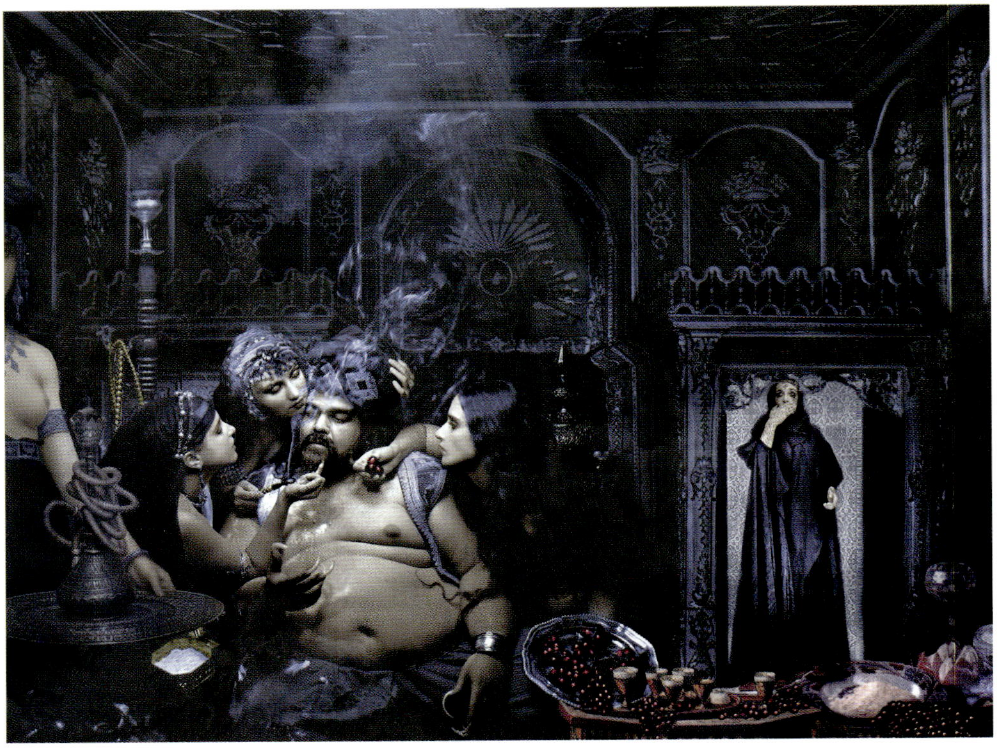

1

3

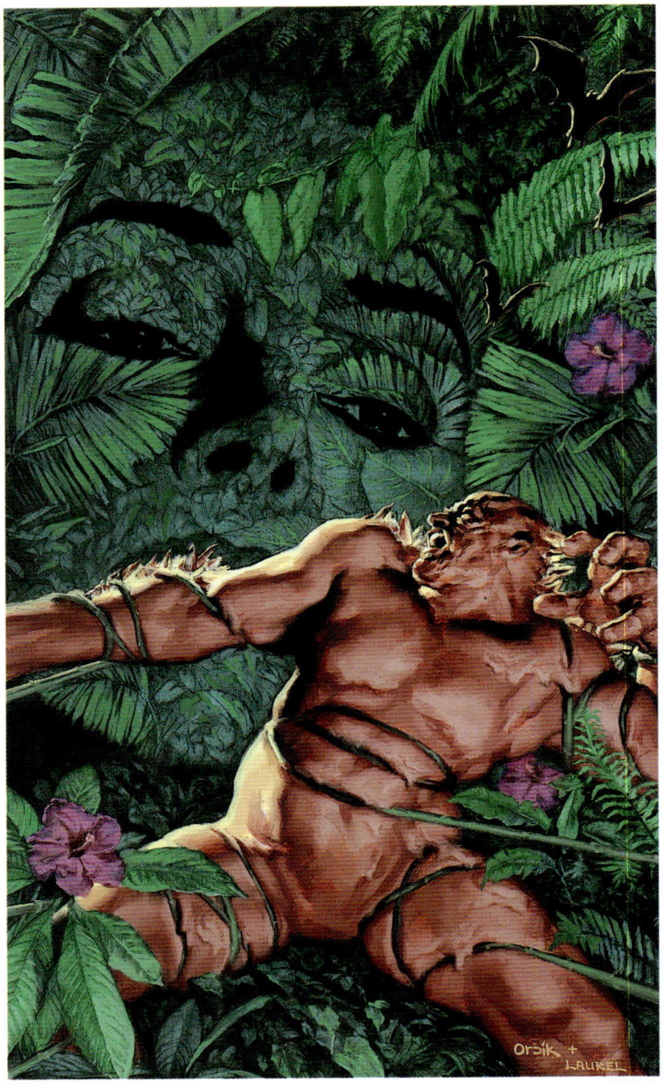

2

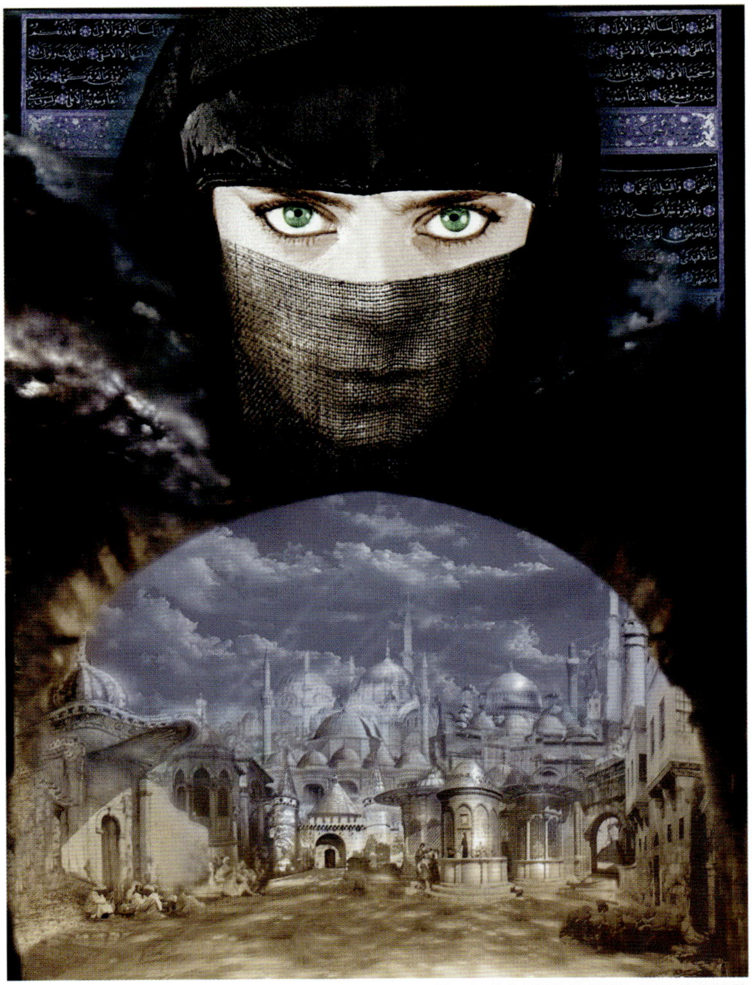

4

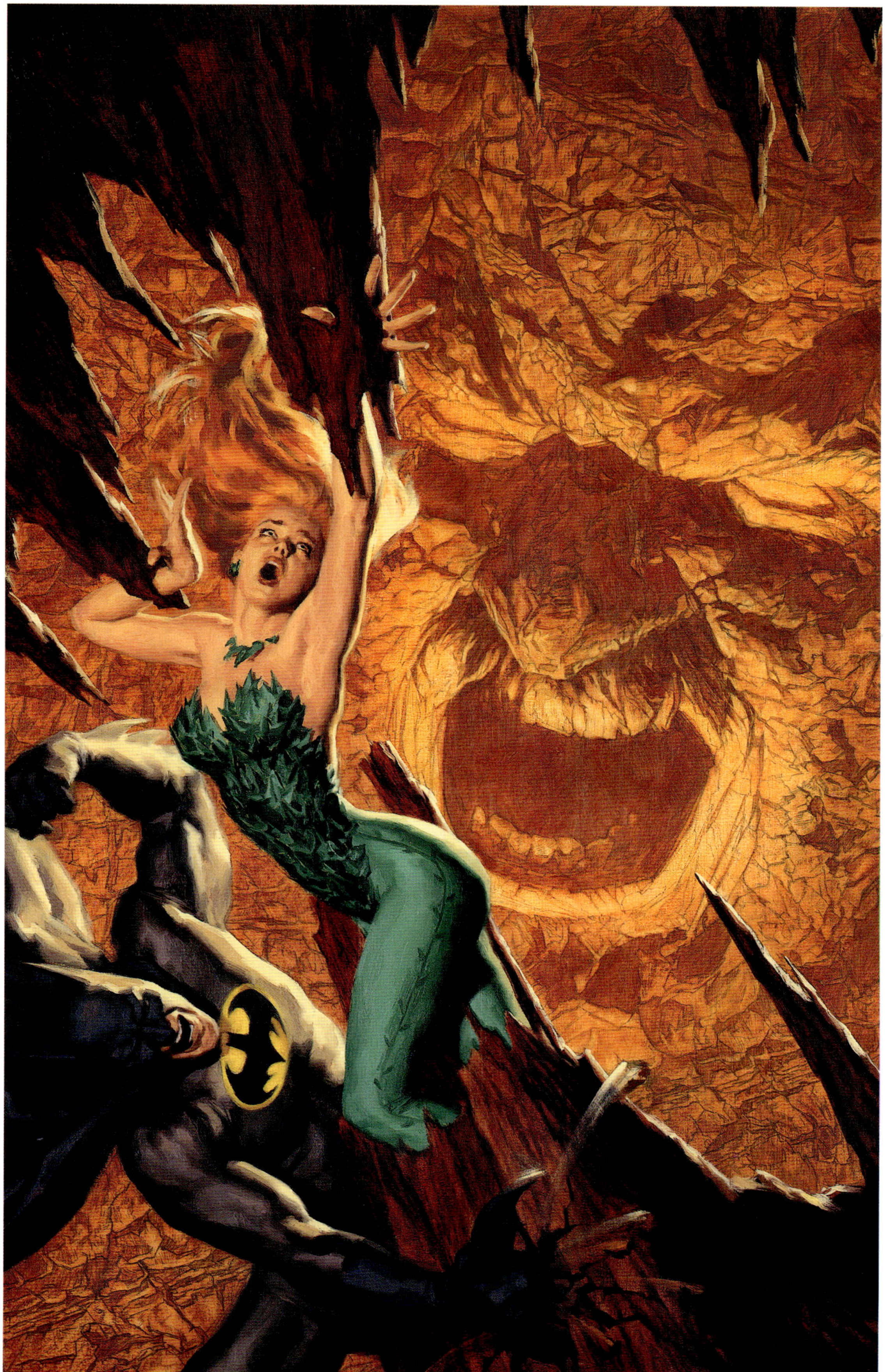

1
artist: JILL THOMPSON
art director: Joseph Linsner
designer: Jill Thompson
client: Sirius Entertainment
title: Scary Godmother: The Mystery Date
medium: Mixed
size: 20"x15"

2
artist: JOHN K. SNYDER III
art director: Aime Brockway
editor: Archie Goodwin/Dan Raspler
client: DC Comics
title: Dr. Mid-Nite #1
medium: Mixed

3
artist: MARK CRILLEY
art director: Joseph Linsner
designer: Mark Crilley
client: Sirius Entertainment
title: Akiko in Slumberland
medium: Mixed
size: 8"x13"

4
artist: JOSEPH MICHAEL LINSNER
art director: Joseph Linsner
designer: Joseph Michael Linsner
client: Sirius Entertainment
title: Dawn: Return of the Goddess#1 (ltd.)
medium: Mixed

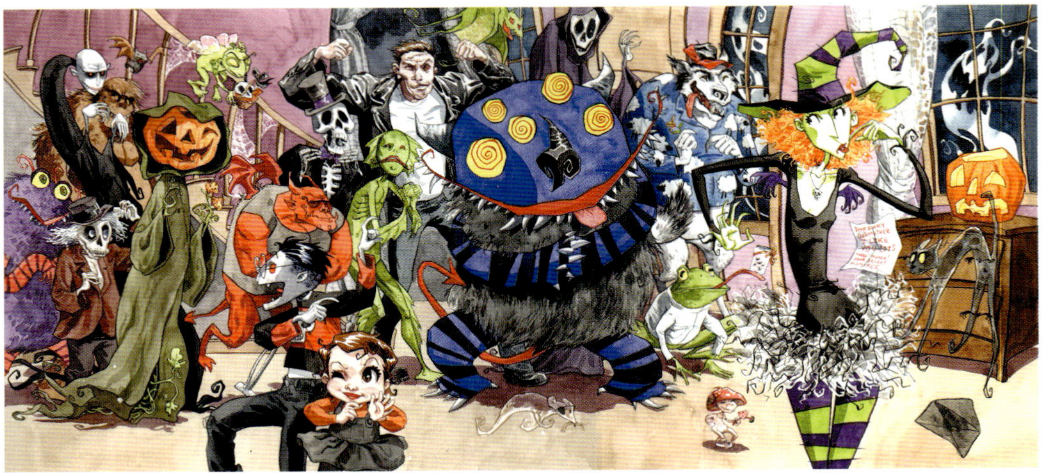

1

3

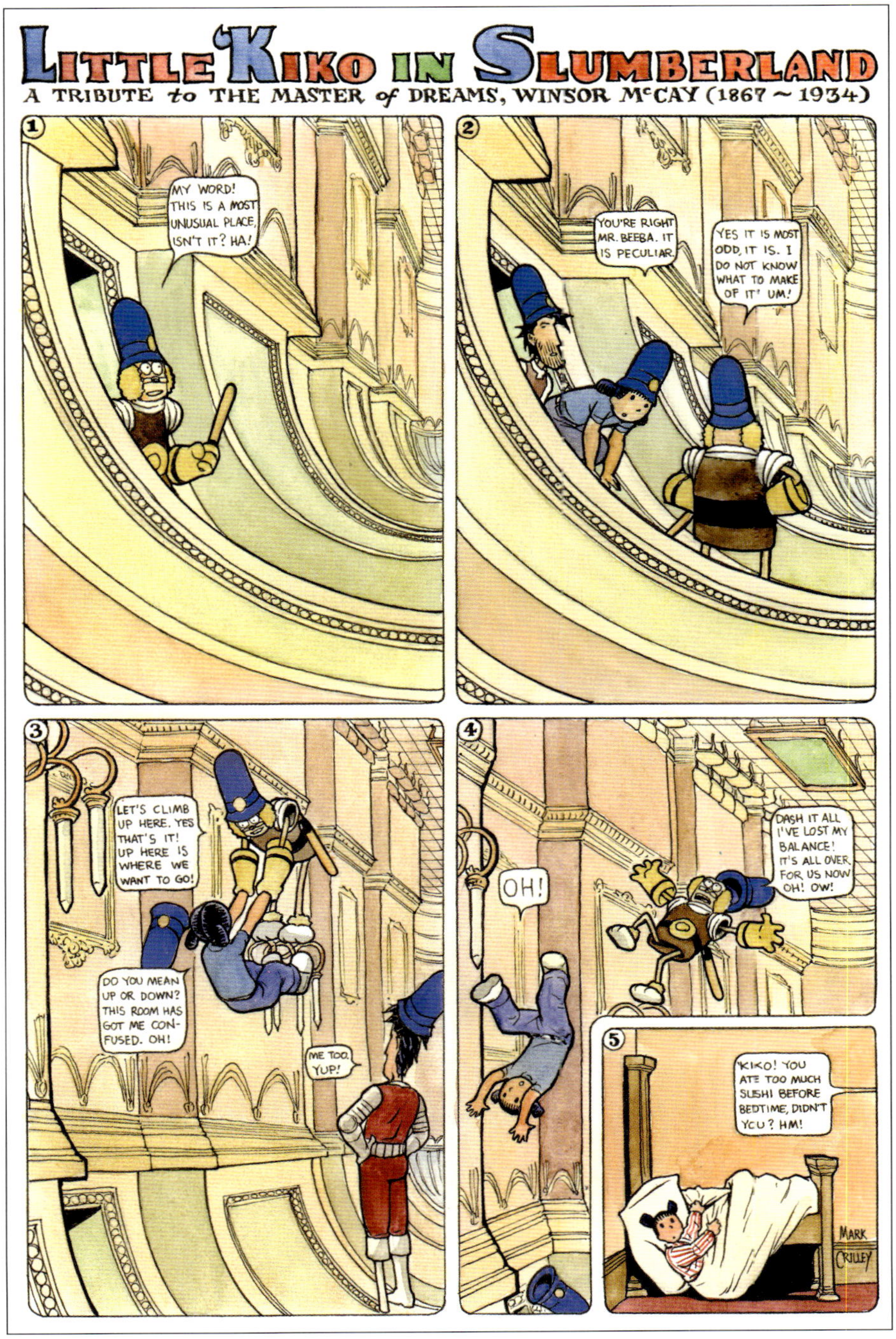

2

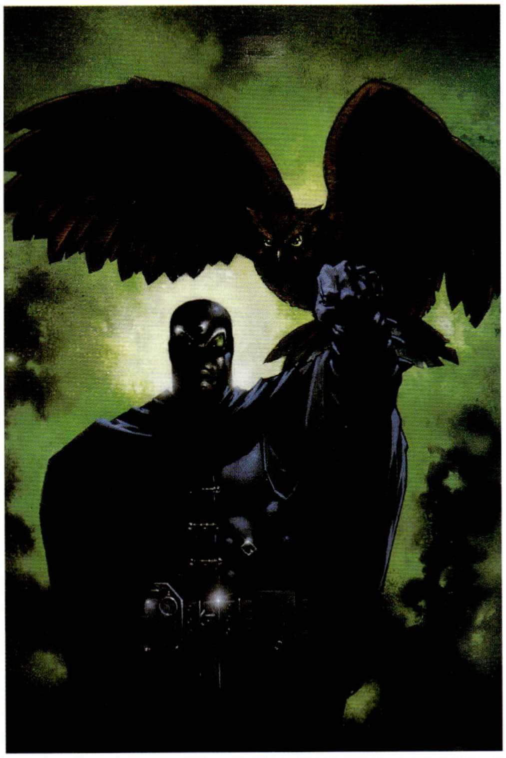

4

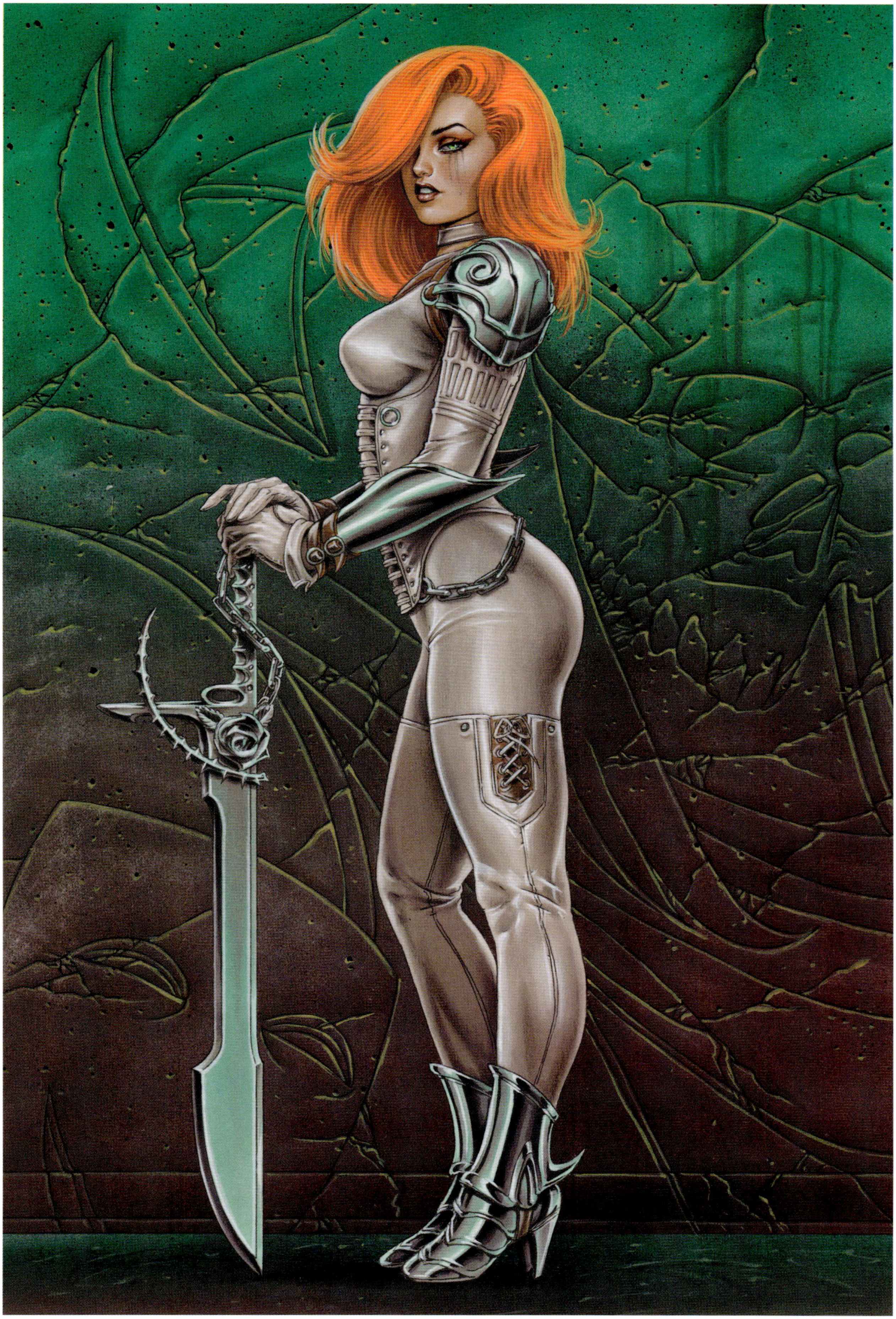

1
artist: BILL WRAY
designer: Darcy Hockett
client: Dark Horse Comics
title: Hellboy Jr.

2
artist: MIKE HUDDLESTON
client: Oni Press
title: The Coffin #1 [cover]
medium: Mixed
size: 10"x15"

3
artist: MARK CRILLEY
art director: Joseph Linsner
designer: Mark Crilley
client: Sirius Entertainment
title: ToonWarz: *Primear*
medium: Mixed
size: 8"x13"

4
artist: PATRICK ARRASMITH
art director: Rhode Montijo
designer: Patrick Arrasmith
client: Abismo
title: The Old Fire God
medium: Scratchboard
size: 12"x18"

1

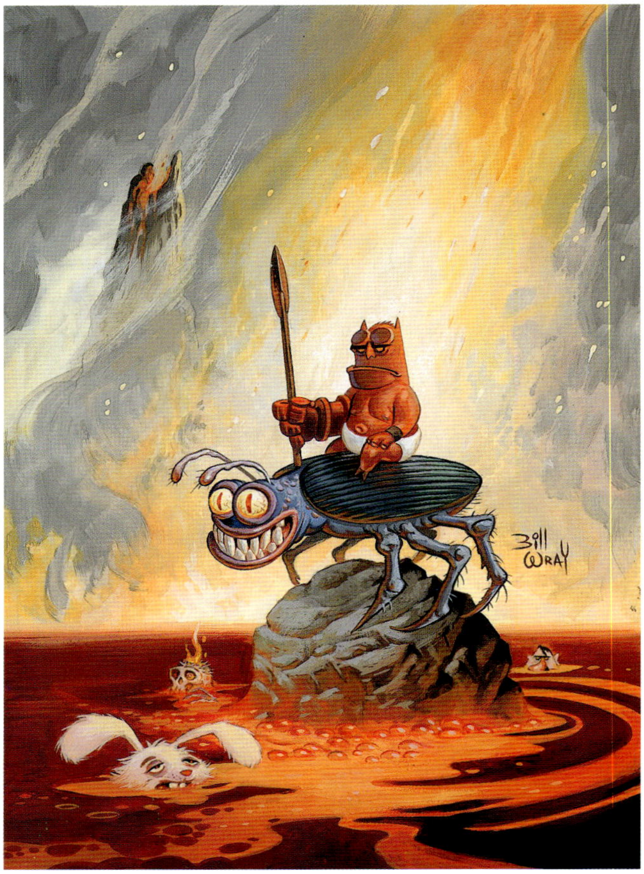

2

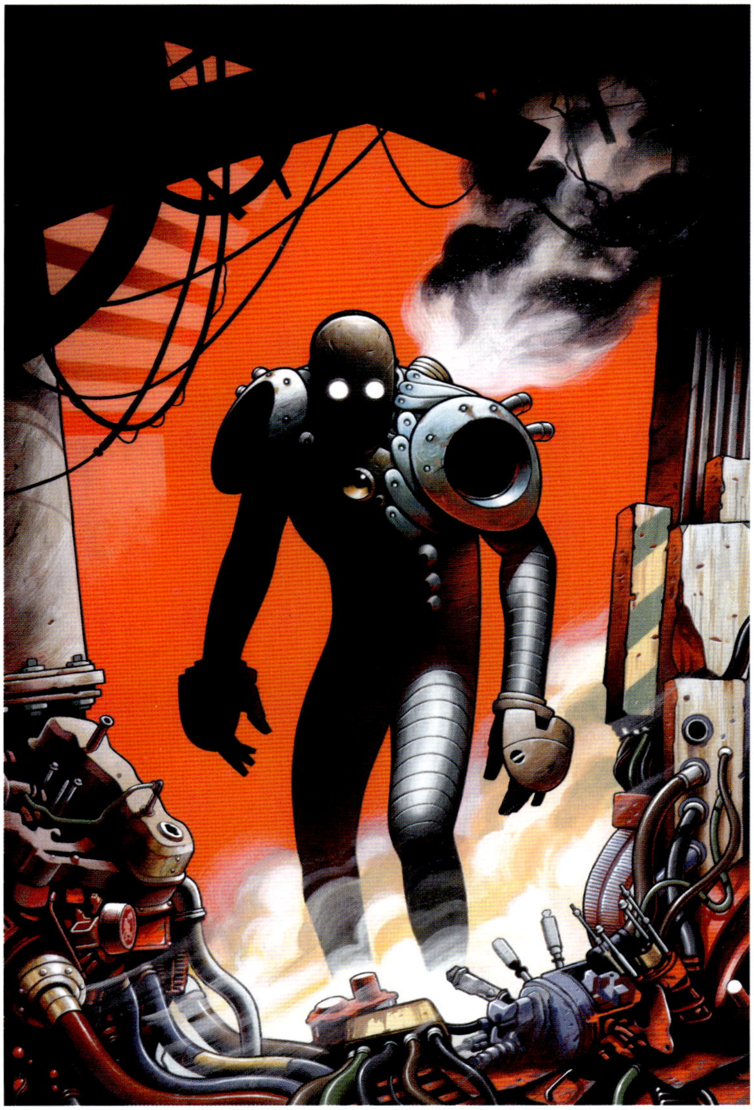

3

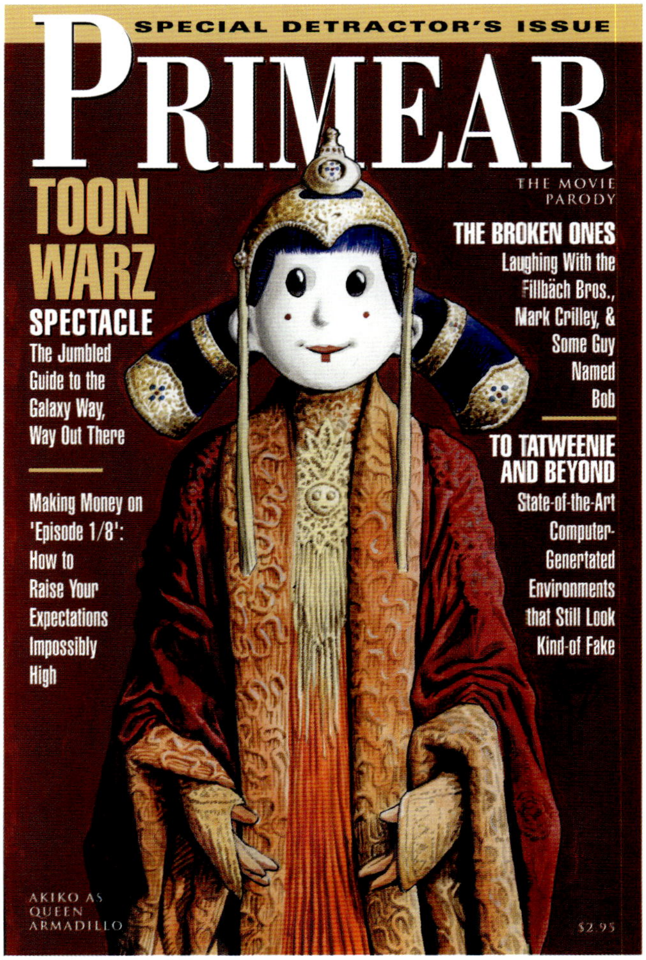

4

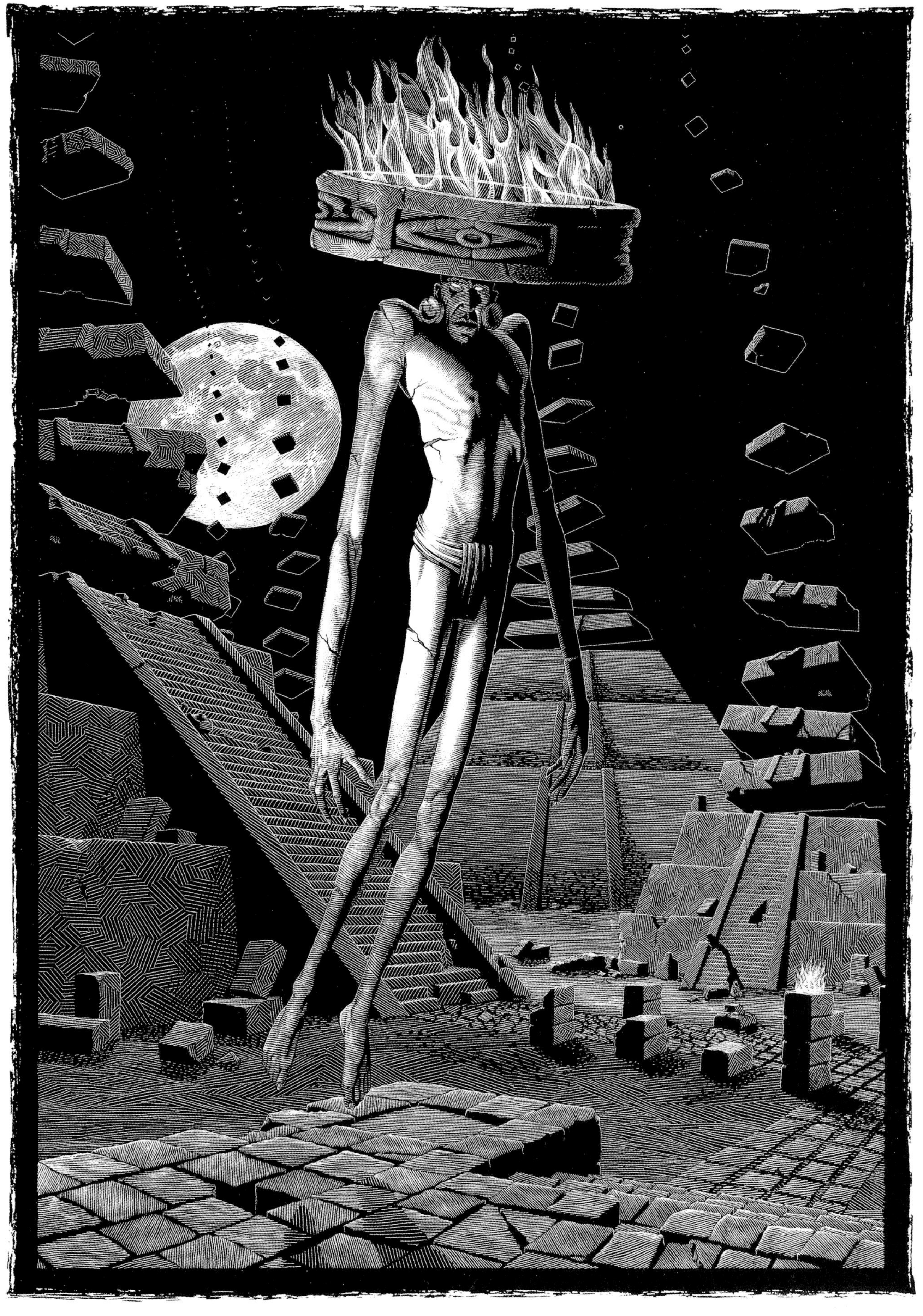

1
artist: STEVE RUDE
client: DC Comics
title: Transilvane #1
medium: Acrylic
size: 17"x24"

2
artist: ASHLEY WOOD
art director: Brent Ashe
client: Todd McFarlane Prod.
title: Blood and Salvation
medium: Mixed
size: 11"x17"

3
artist: JILL THOMPSON
art director: Joseph Linsner
designer: Jill Thompson
client: Sirius Entertainment
title: Scary Godmother #23
medium: Mixed
size: 10"x14"

4
artist: STEVE RUDE
client: DC Comics
title: Transilvane #2
medium: Acrylic
size: 17"x24"

1

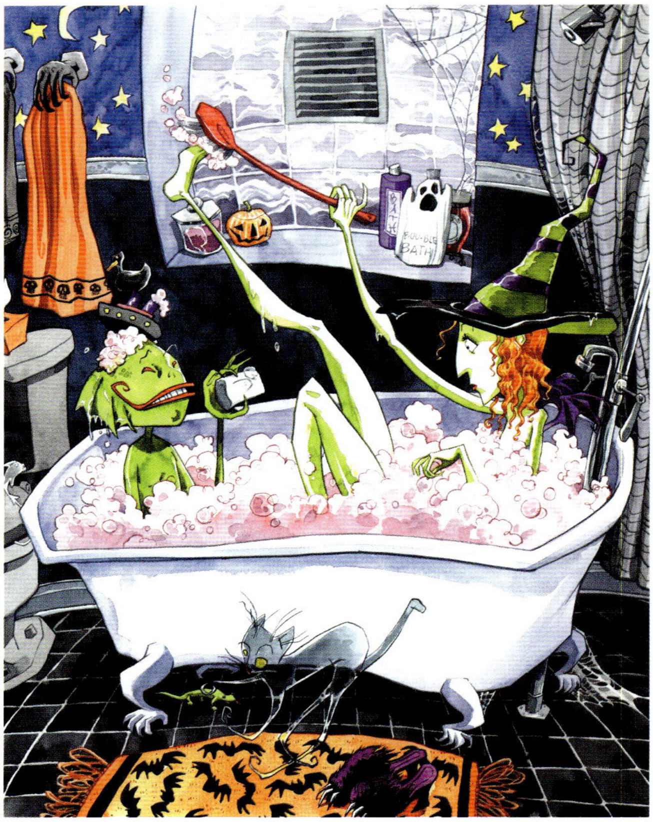

2

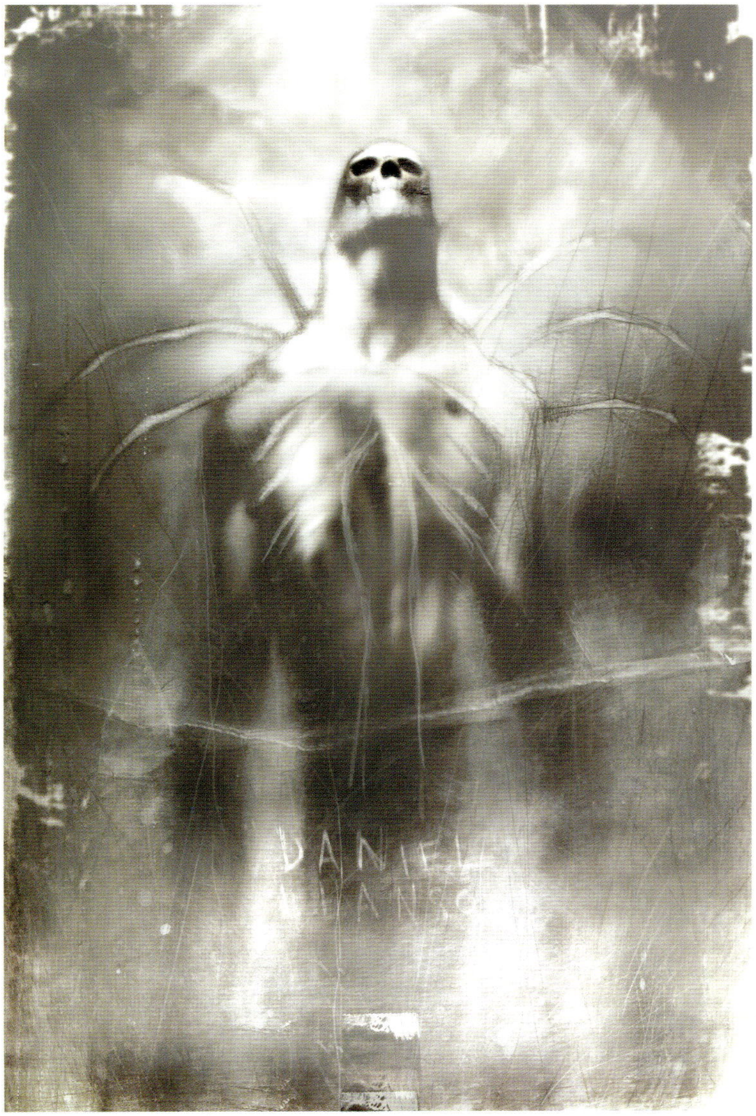

3

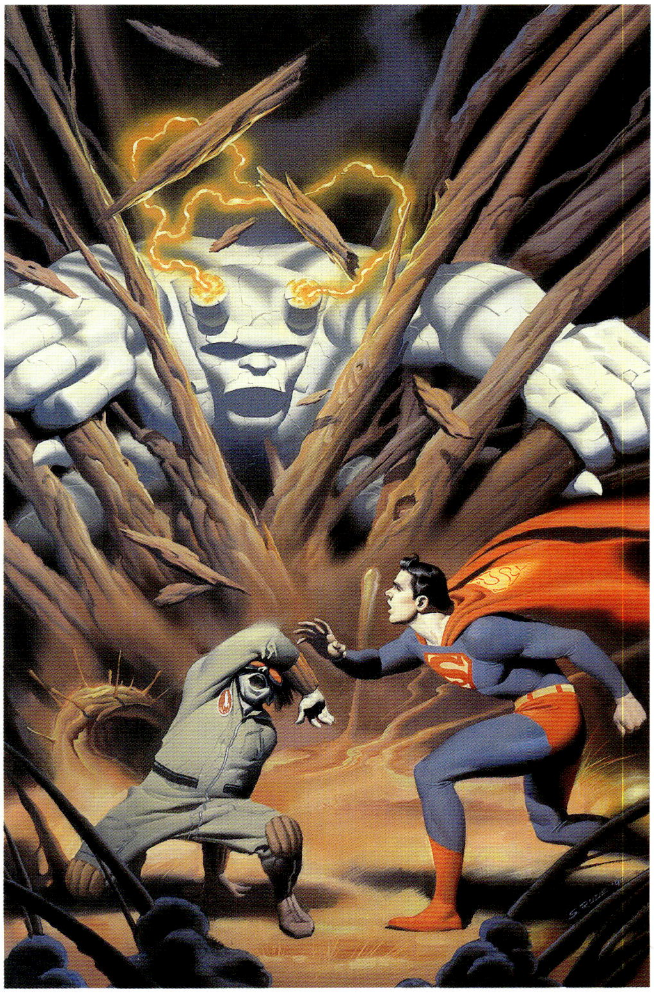

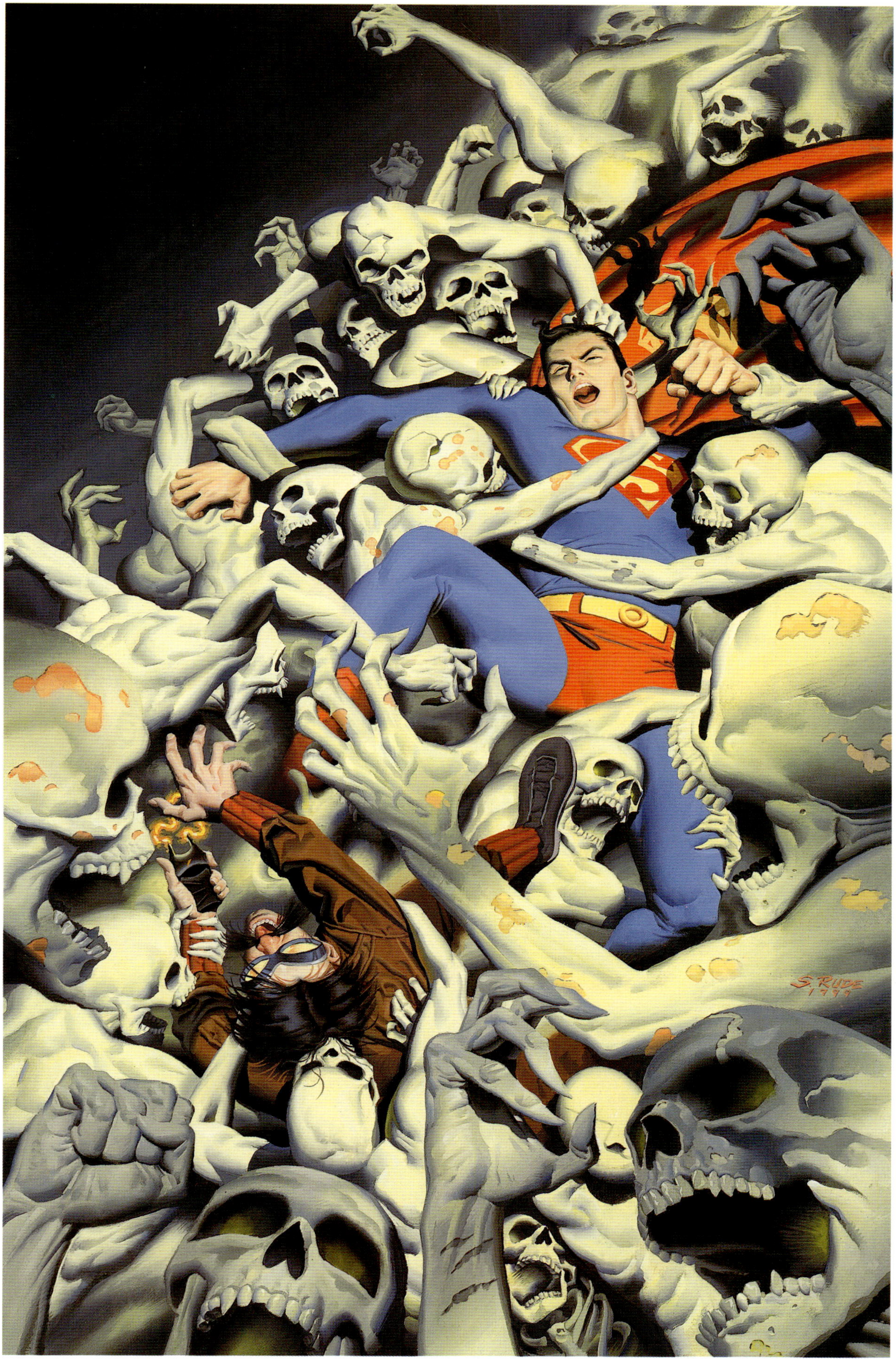
S. RUDE
1999

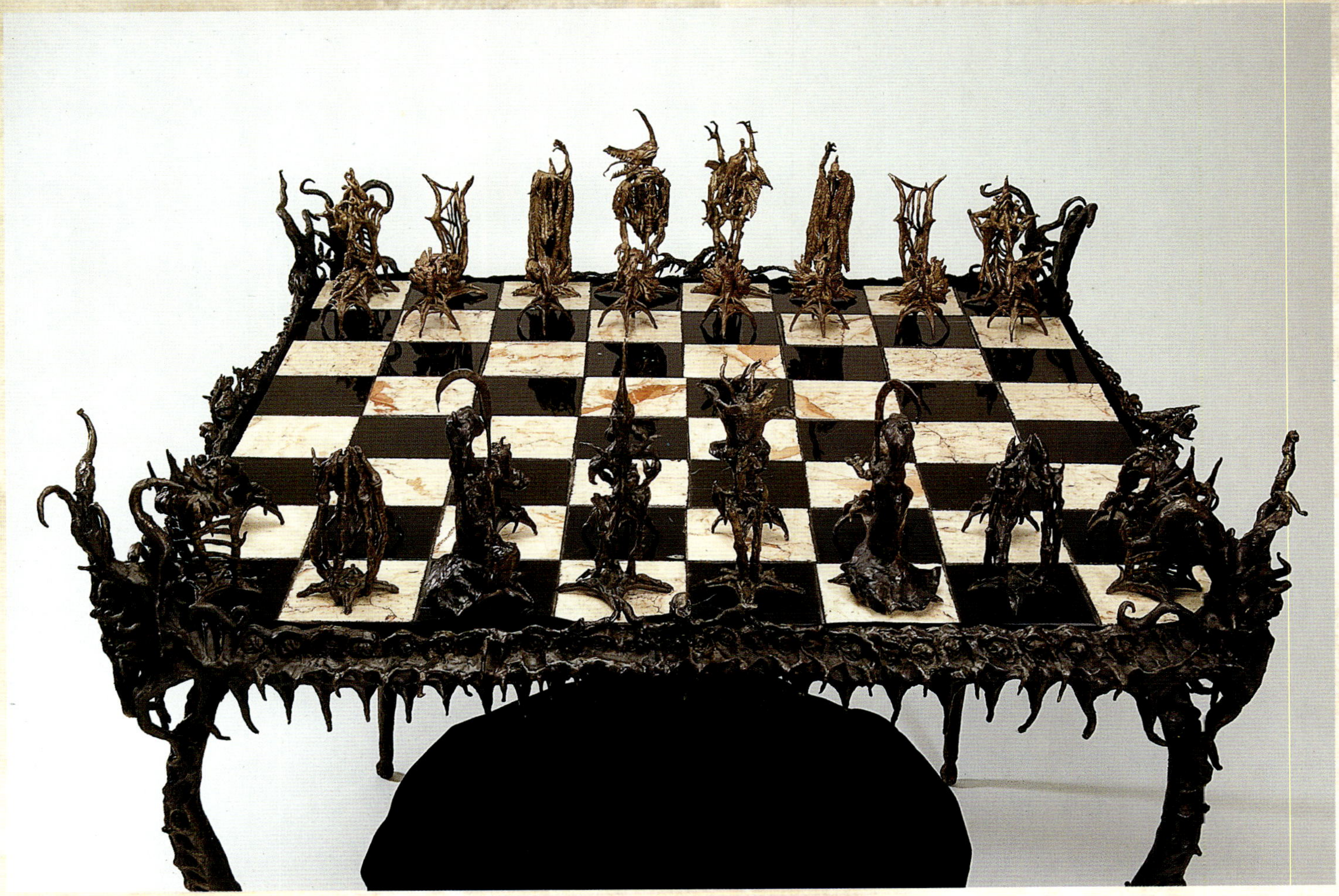

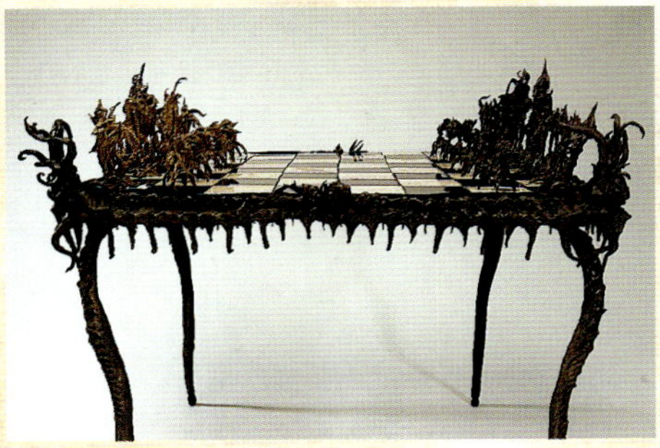

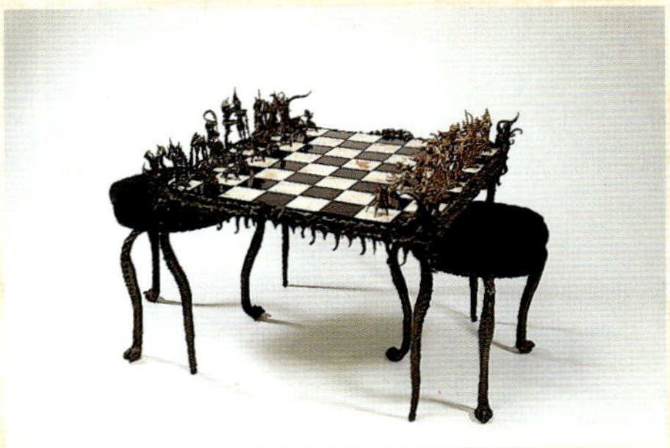

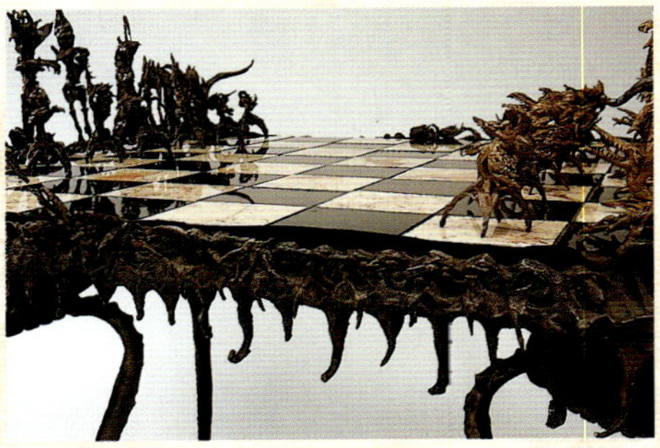

artist: SHARON MATSUMOTO
art director: Sharon Matsumoto   *client:* Hawaiian Reflections Gallery   *title:* Chess Set
size: 36"x36"x17"   *medium:* Bronze/steel/marble

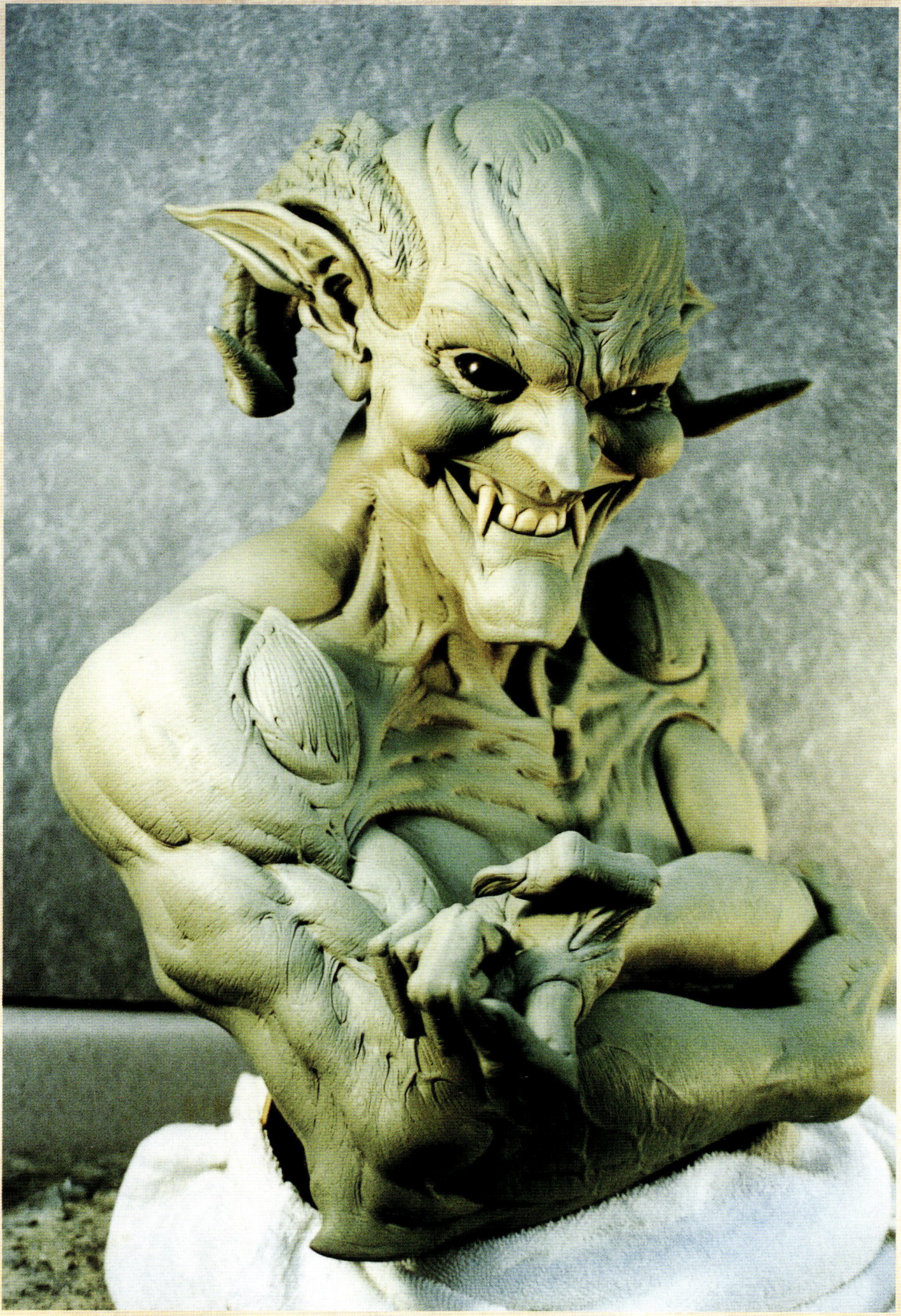

artist: **GREG POLUTANOVICH**
designer: Greg Polutanovich *title:* The Dark One *size:* 17 1/2"x19" *medium:* Roma clay

1
artist: STEPHEN HICKMAN
art director: Stephen Hickman
client: Bowen Designs
title: H.P. Lovecraft
medium: Cold-cast porcelain
size: 8" tall

2
artist: GREGORY S. SMITH
title: Boris Karloff's Monster
medium: Bonded marble
size: 16"x10"x6"

3
artist: JOEL HARLOW
client: Matt Viman
title: Legion
medium: Bronze
size: 9" tall

4
artist: HENRY ALVAREZ
art director: Henry Alvarez
designer: Wolf's Head Productions, Inc.
client: Universal Studios & Lugosi Enterprises
title: Dracula
medium: Bronze
size: 15" tall

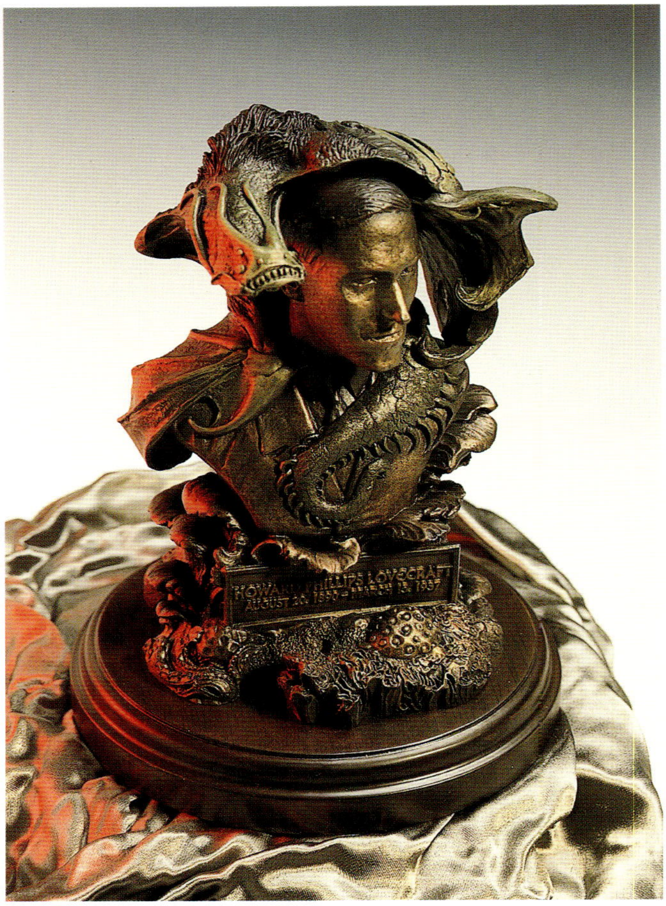

1

2

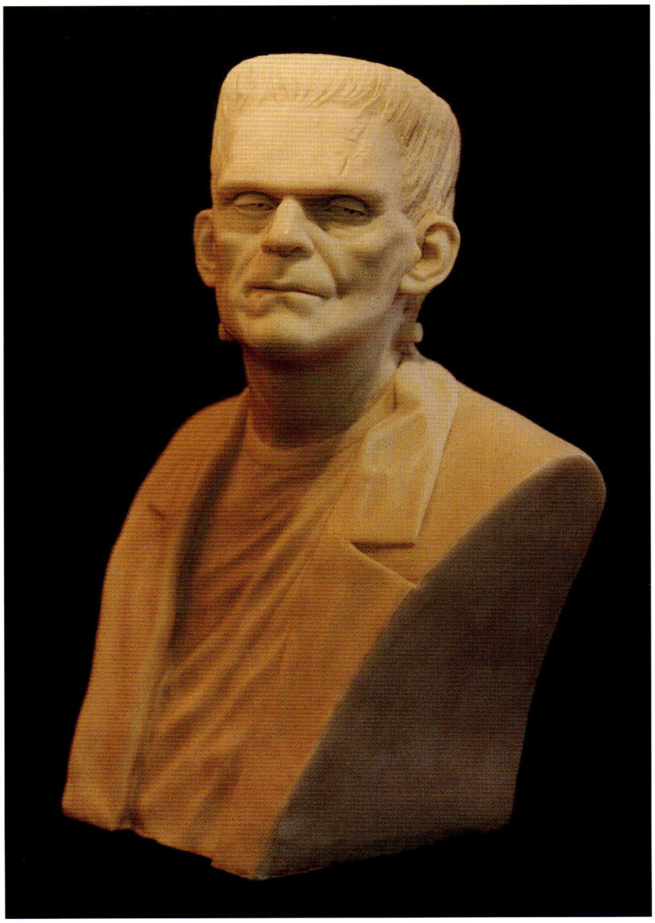

3

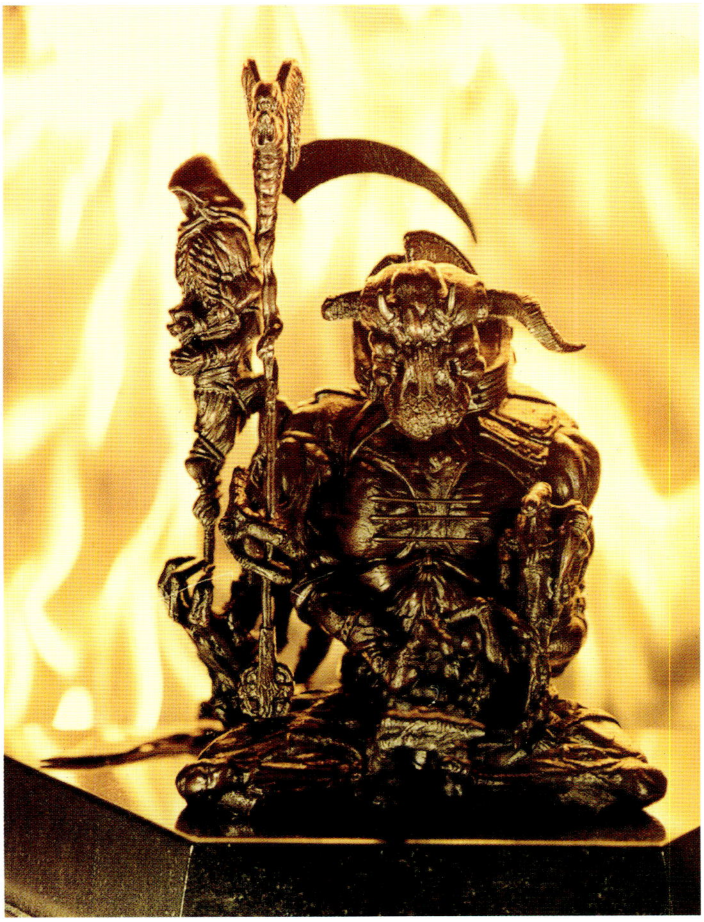

4

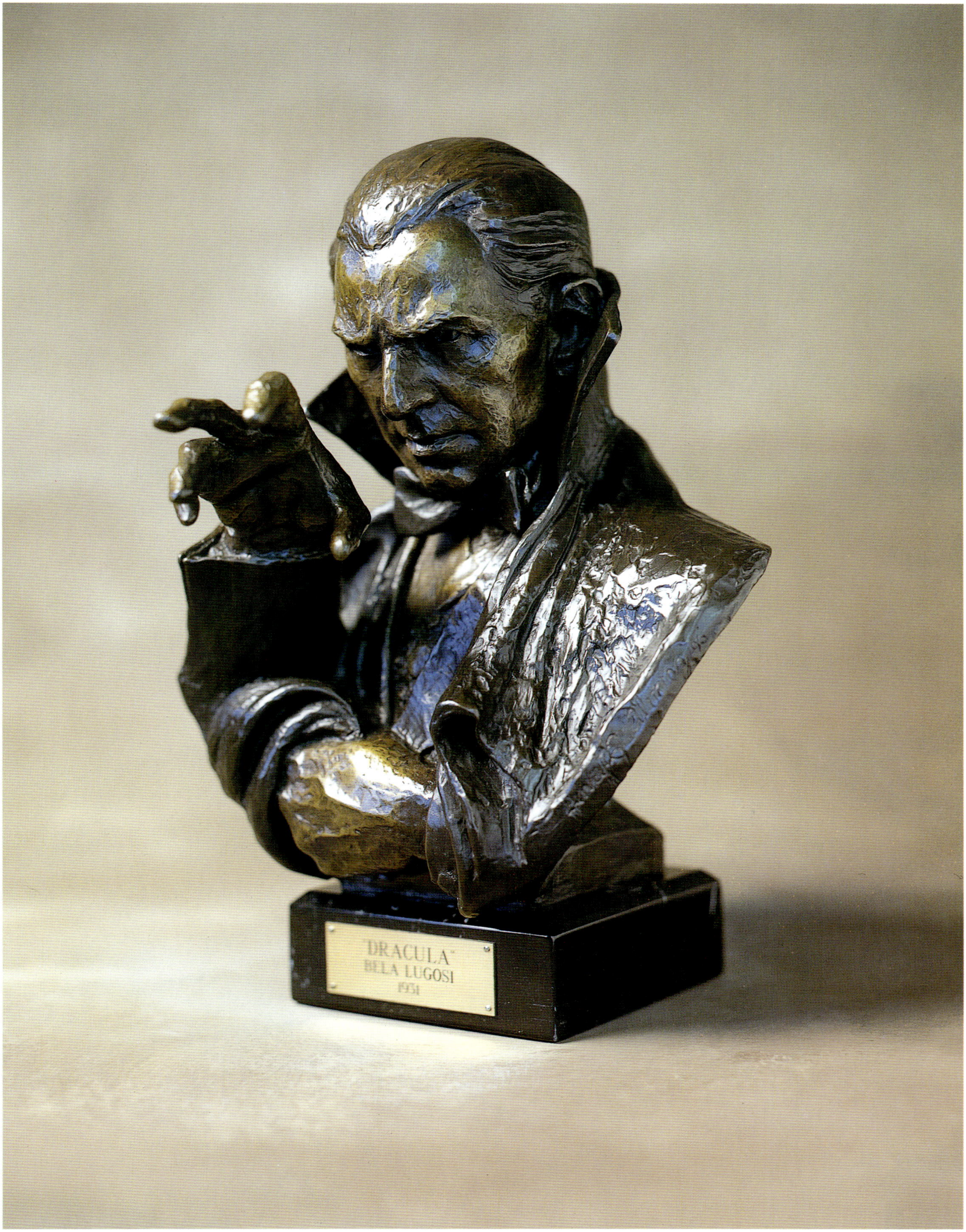

1
artist: CLAYBURN MOORE
art director: Clayburn Moore & David Mack
client: David Mack
title: Kabuki
medium: Resin
size: 6" tall

2
artist: CLAYBURN MOORE
art director: Clayburn Moore
designer: Clayburn Moore
client: Kevin Eastman Studios, Inc.
title: F.A.K.K.^{2} Julie
medium: Resin
size: 6" tall

3
artist: JOY SNYDER
art director: Tom Snyder
desugner: George Pérez
client: George Pérez
title: Crimson Plague
medium: Resin/metal/plastic
size: 12" tall

4
artist: CLAYBURN MOORE
art director: Clayburn Moore
designer: Clayburn Moore
client: Frank Frazetta
title: Frazetta's Barbarian
medium: Cold-cast porcelain
size: 15" tall

1

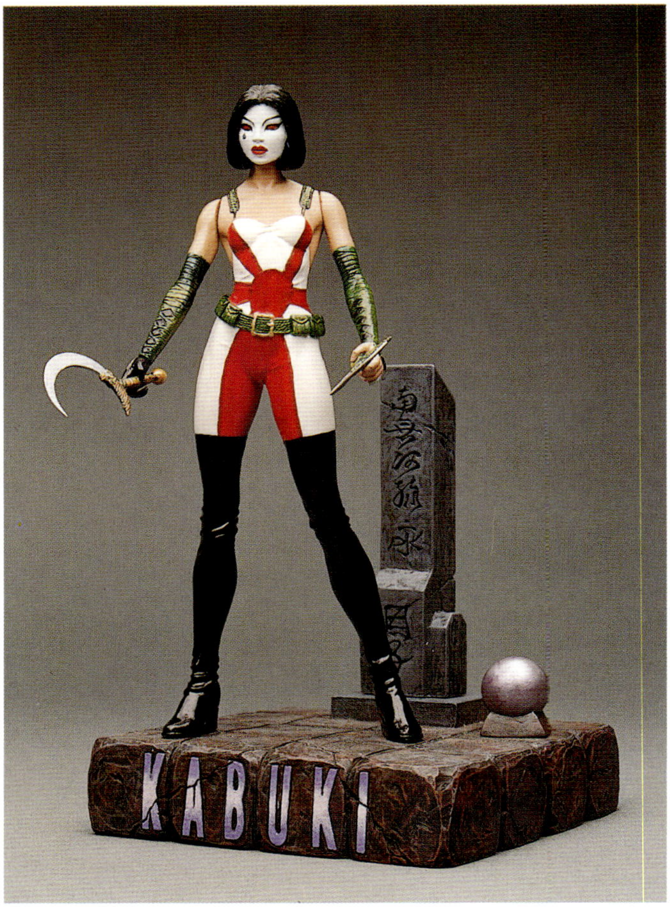

2

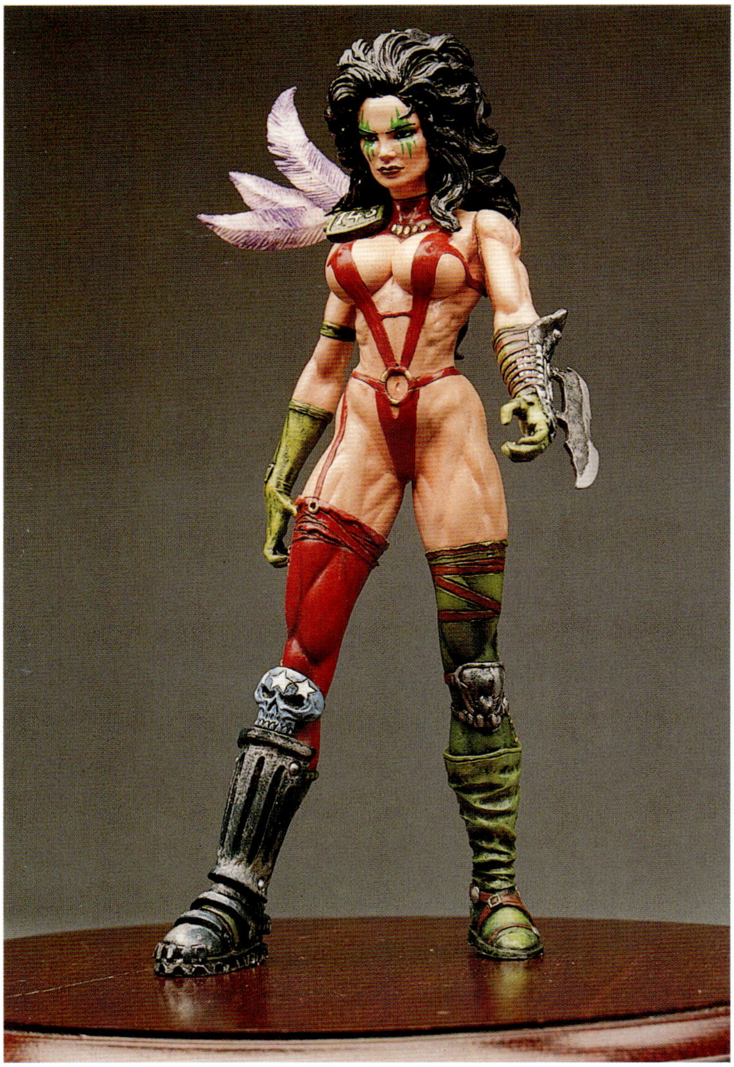

3

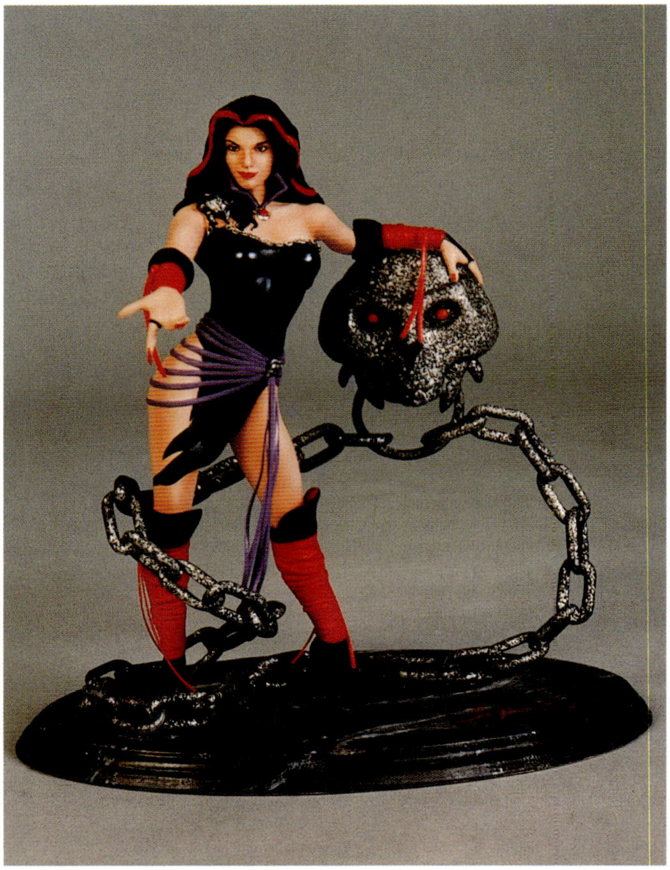

4

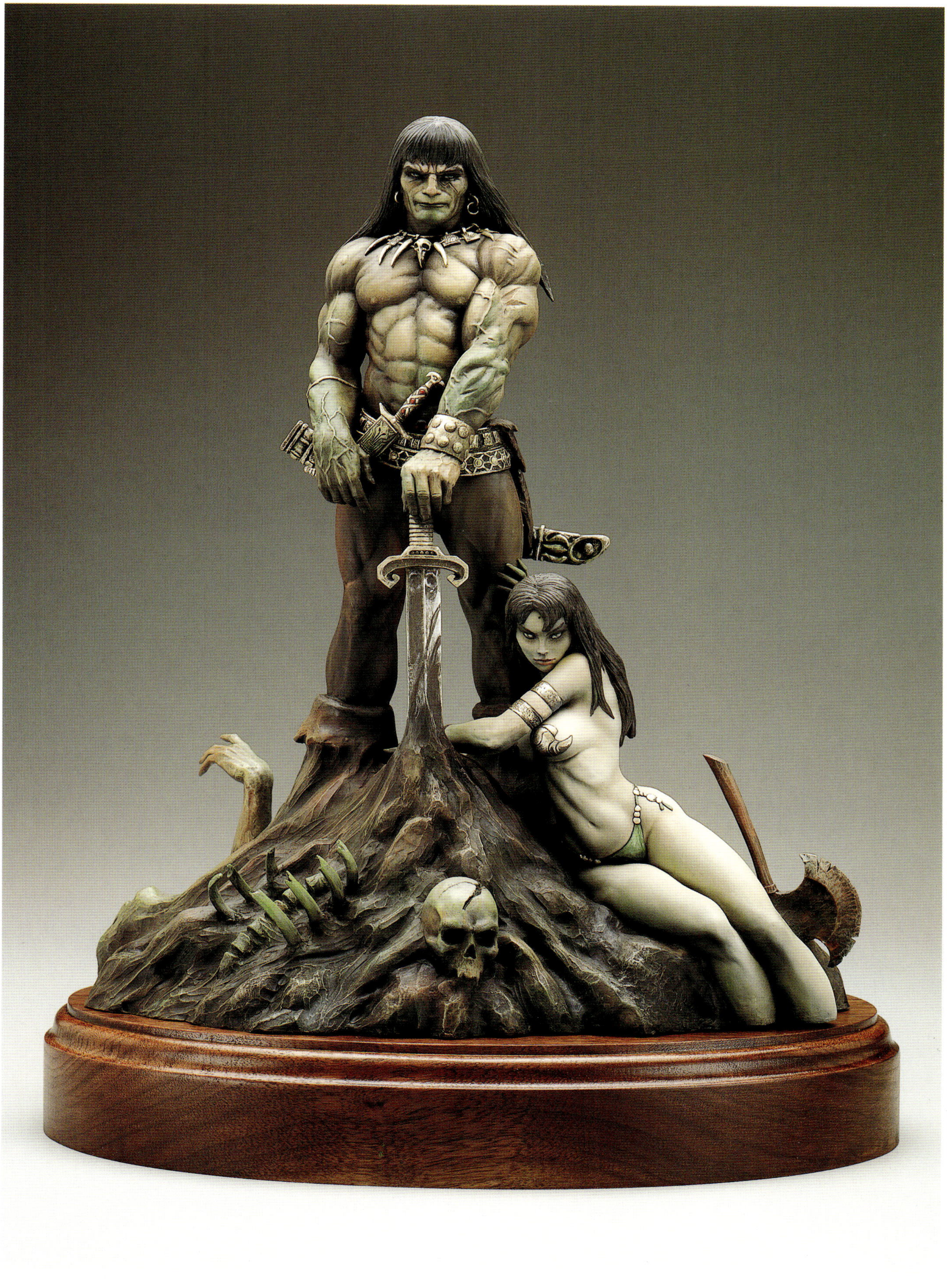

1
artist: LAWRENCE NORTHEY
designer: Lawrence Northey
client: Mark Parker
title: The Queen's Entourage
medium: Mixed *size:* 30"-36" tall

2
artist: JEAN-MARC LAROCHE
client: Private collection
title: Space Daggers
medium: Mixed
size: 16" and 6" in length

3
artist: DANIEL L. HAWKINS
art director: Daniel L. Hawkins
client: Hawkins Design Studio
title: Ancestor Mask
medium: Mixed *size:* 16"x12"

4
artist: JAMES C. CHRISTENSEN
art director: Scott Usher
client: The Greenwich Workshop
title: Queen Mab and her Faeries
medium: Pearl Bisque

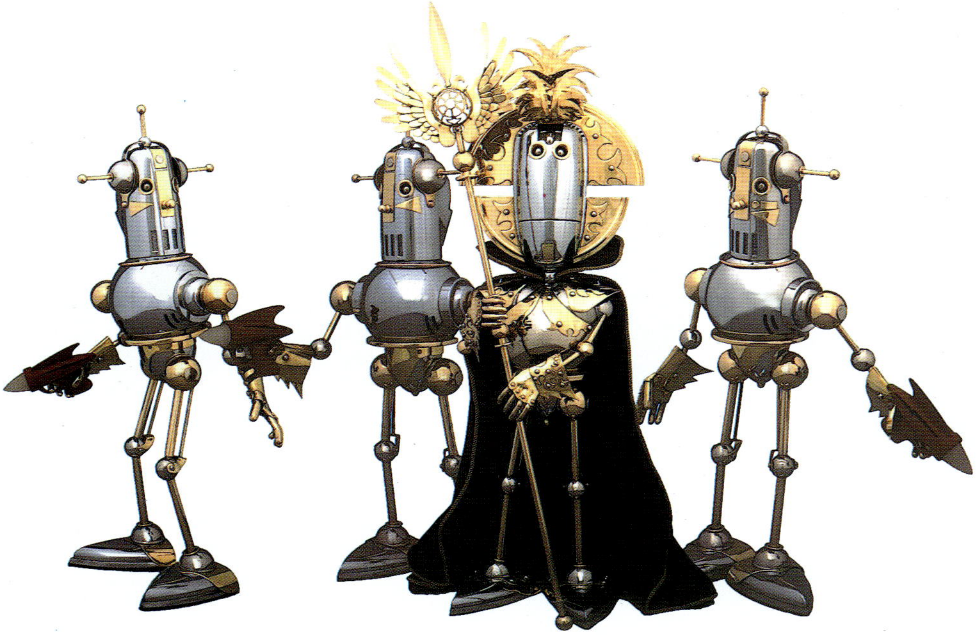

1

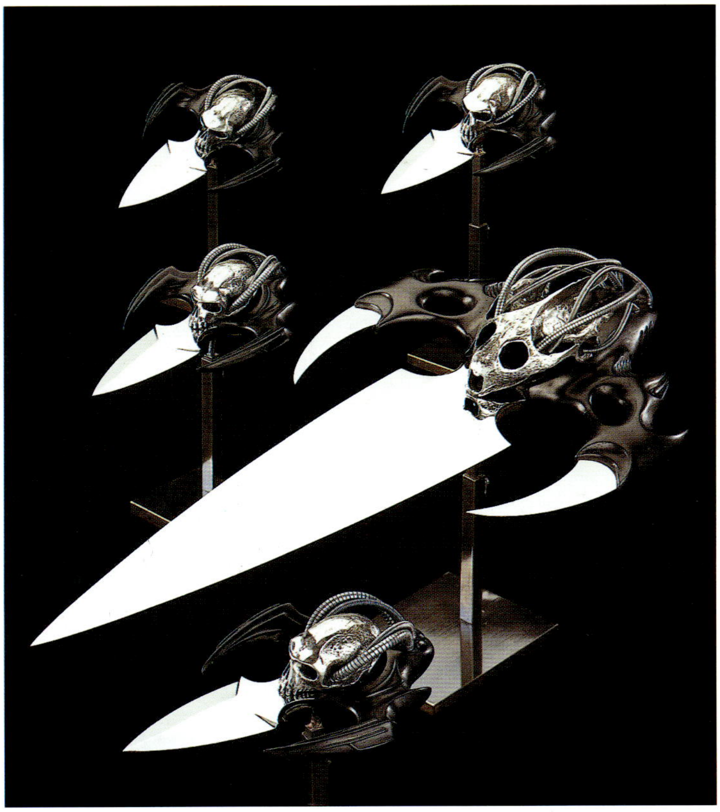

2

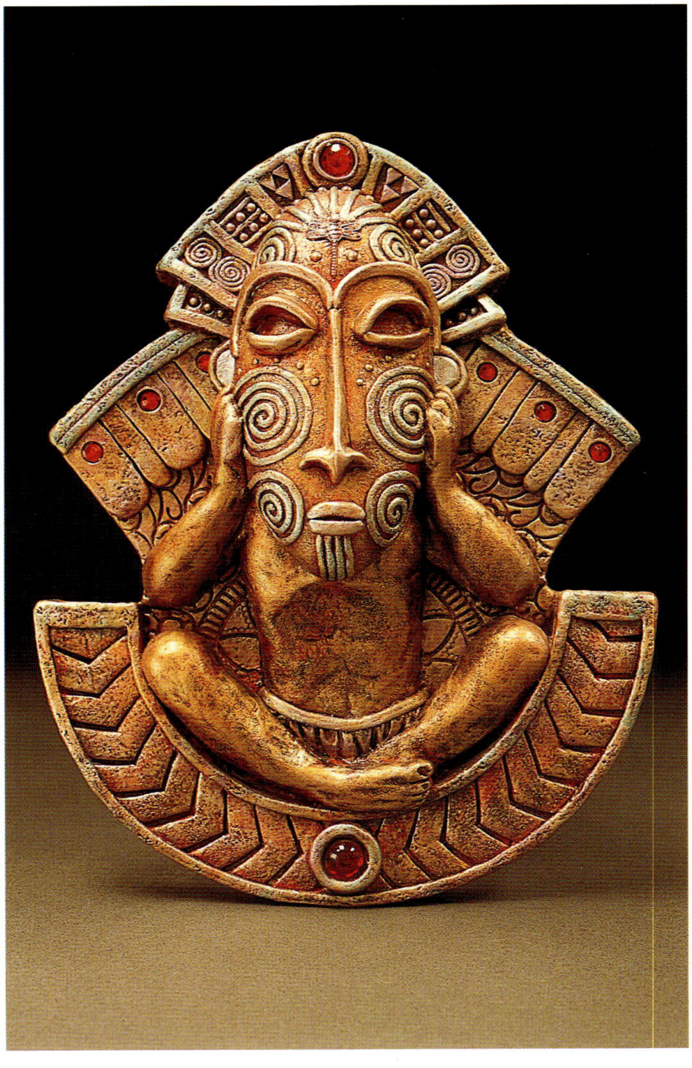

3

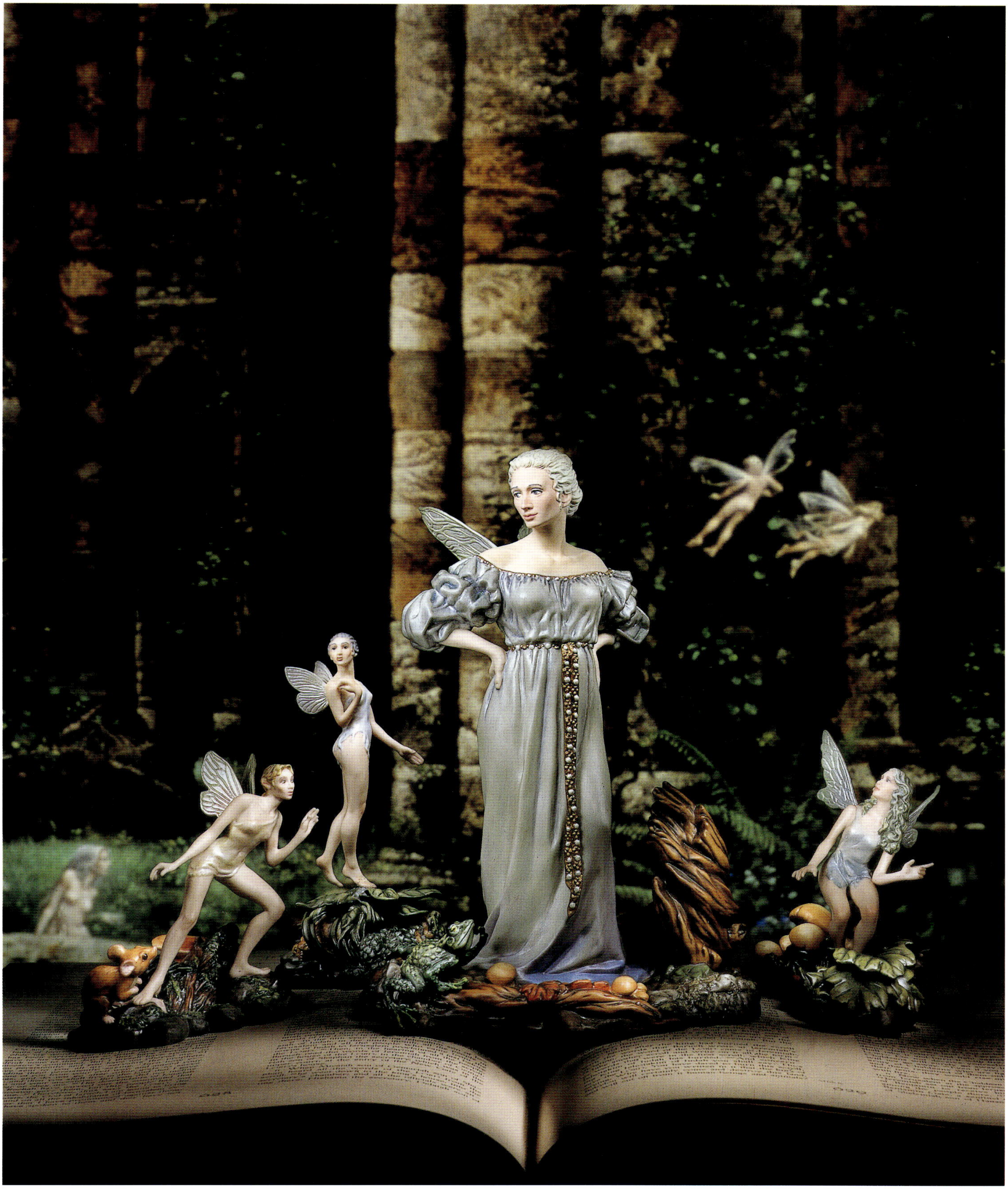

4

1
artist: STEVEN LAWRENCE
art director: Steven Lawrence
client: Proteus Designs
title: Rhinoman
medium: Painted resin
size: 4" tall by 5" wide

2
artist: TIM HOLTER BRUCKNER
art director: Georg Brewer
client: DC Direct
title: Crisis on Infinite Earth
medium: Resin *size:* 7 1/2" tall

3
artist: WILLIAM PAQUET
art director: Georg Brewer
designer: Simon Bisley
client: DC Direct
title: Batman
medium: Cold-cast porcelain

4
artist: TIM HOLTER BRUCKNER
art director: Tim Holter Bruckner
client: The Art Farm
title: Major Marjorie
medium: Resin *size:* 6 1/4" tall

1
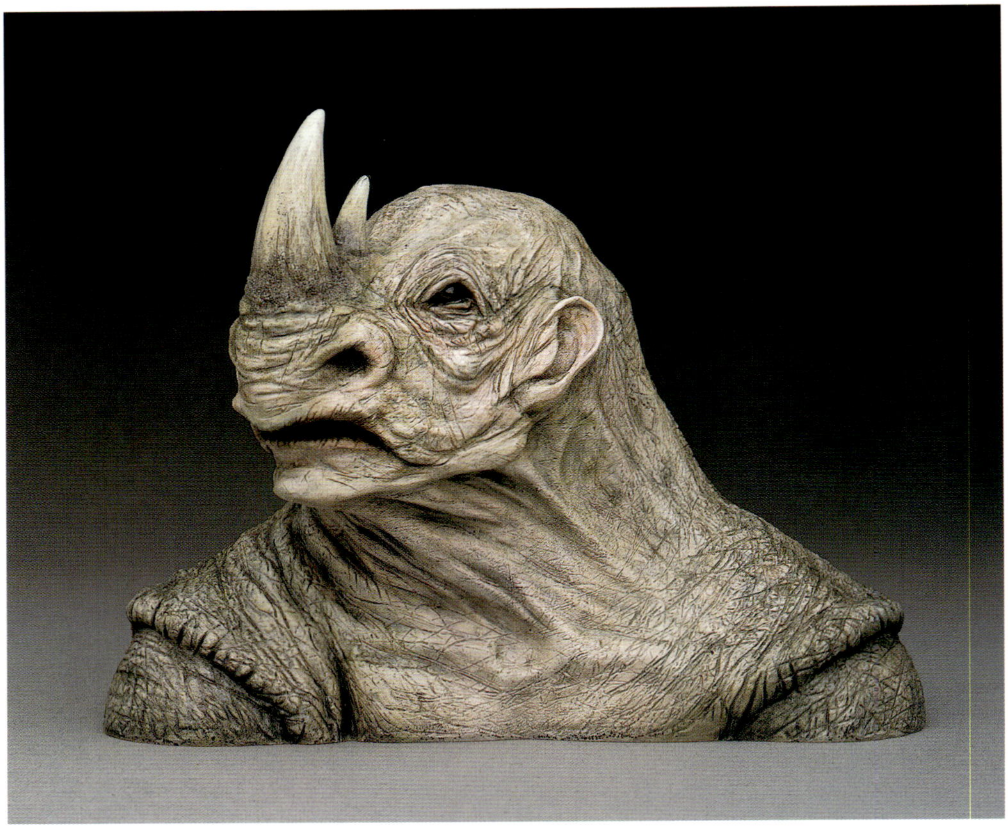

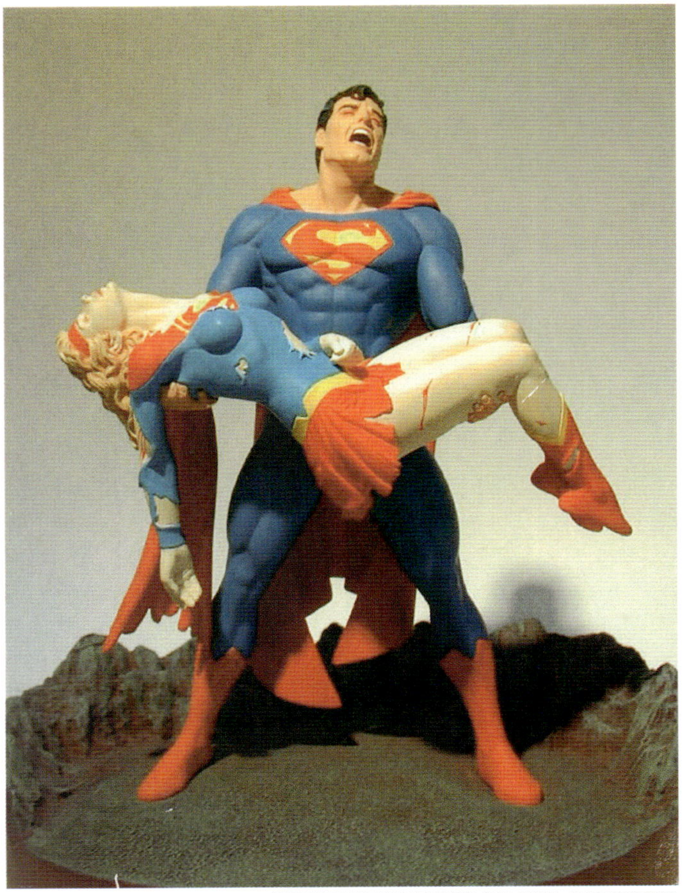

2

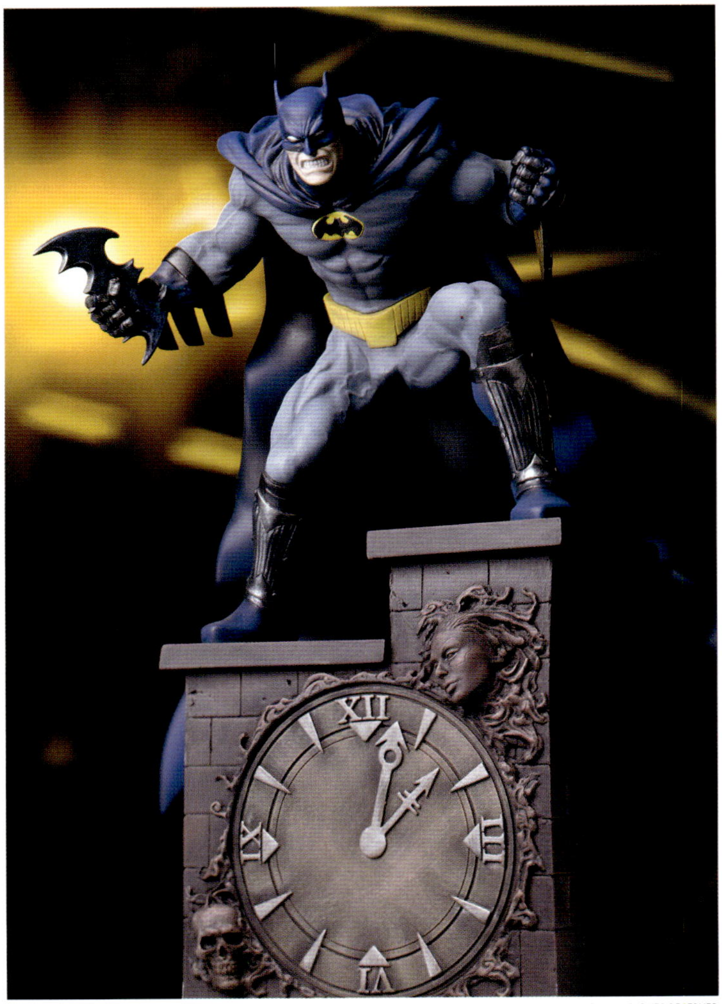

3

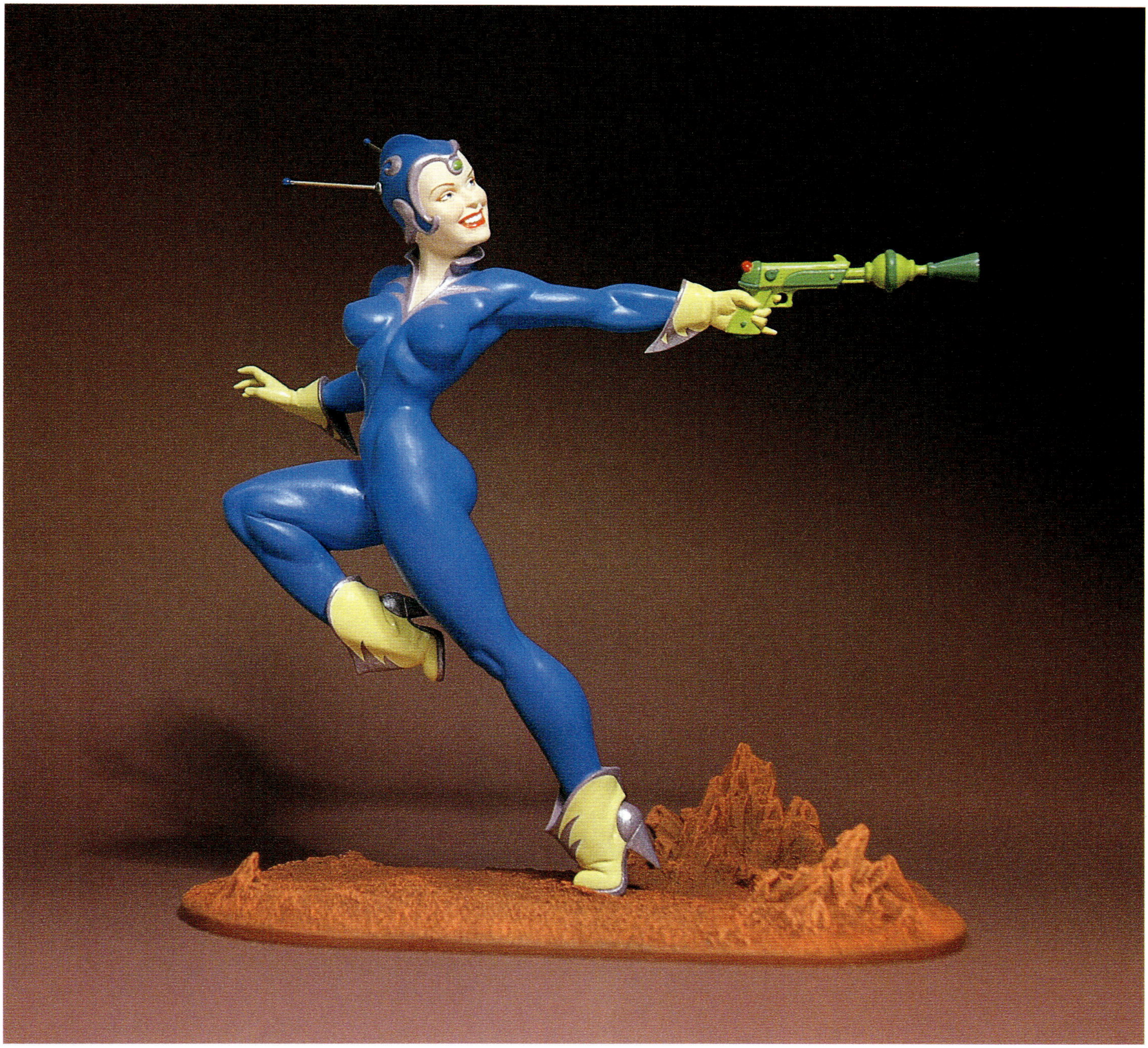

4

1
artist: JEFF PETERSON
designer: Jeff Peterson
title: The Wizard of Dragons
medium: Sculpey clay
size: 15" tall by 22" wide

2
artist: FERNANDO FAVILA
art director: Henry Alvarez
designer: Wolf's Head Productions/ Delbert Winans
client: Disney
title: Captain Hook
medium: Bronze *size:* 20" tall

3
artist: GREG POLUTANOVICH
designer: Greg Polutanovich
title: Draq
medium: Roma clay
size: 14"x16"

4
artist: JACK HOOD
art director: Henry Alvarez
designer: Wolf's Head Productions
client: Disney
title: Captain Nemo
medium: Bronze *size:* 20" tall

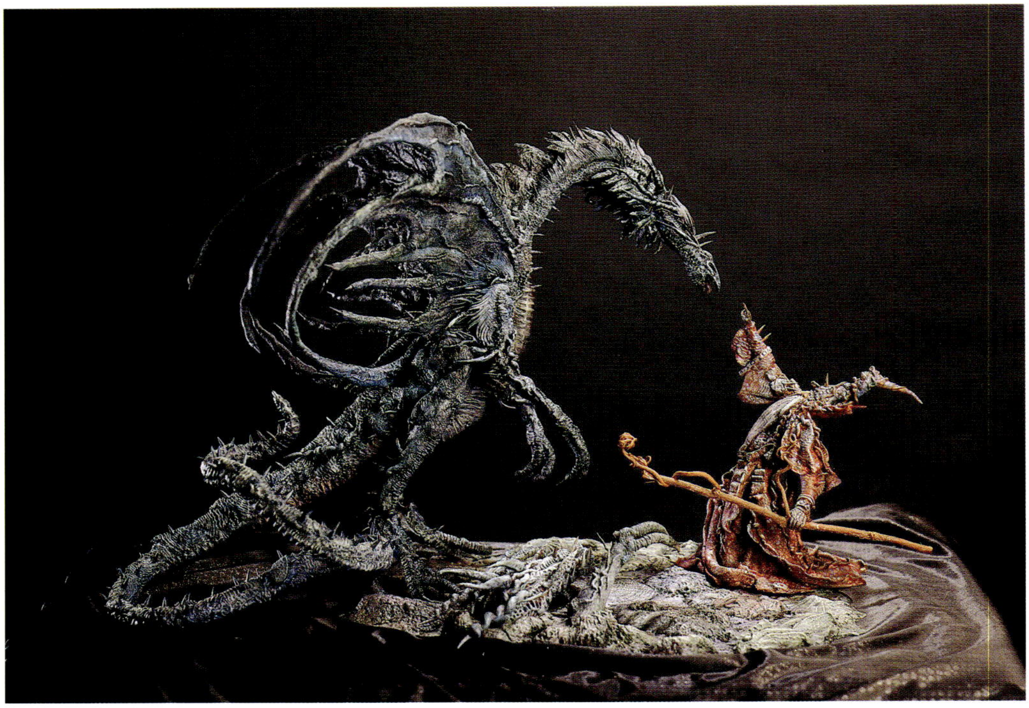

1

3

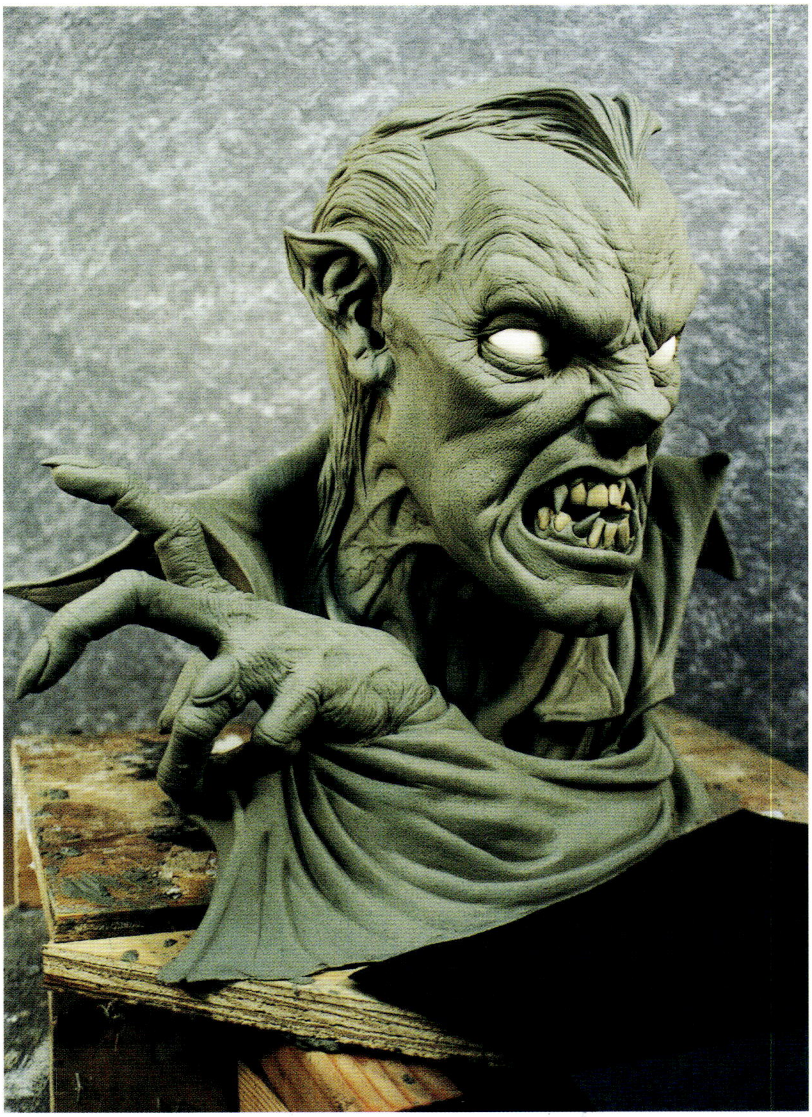

2

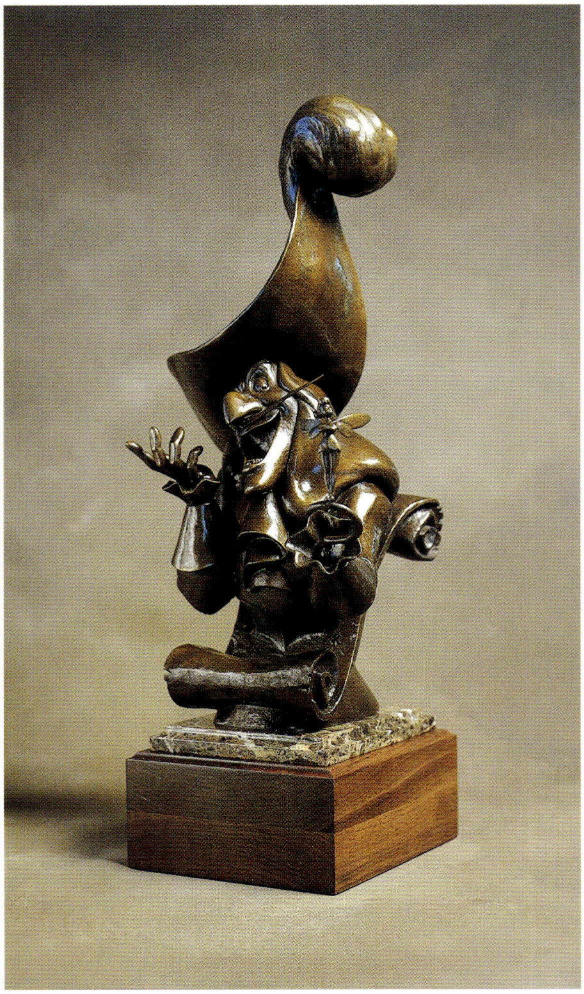

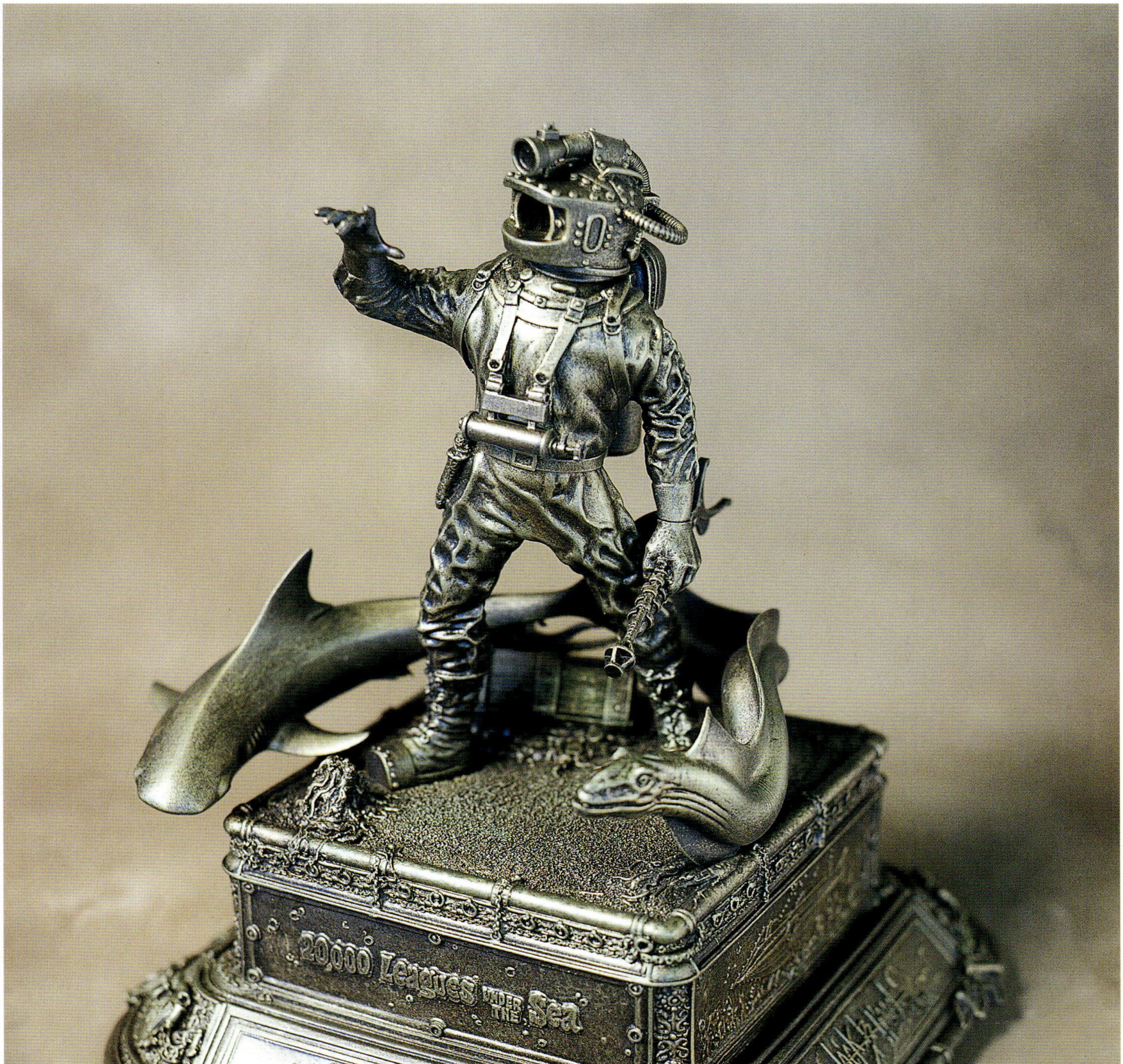
20,000 Leagues under the Sea
capt. Nemo

1
artist: JOSEPH DEVITO
art director: Gerg Brewer
designer: Alex Ross
client: DC Direct/Chronicle Books
title: Golden Age Superman
medium: Super sculpy
size: 8" tall

2
artist: WILLAIM PAQUET
art director: Georg Brewer
designer: Darick Robertson
client: DC Direct
title: Transmetropolitan
medium: Cold-cast porcelain

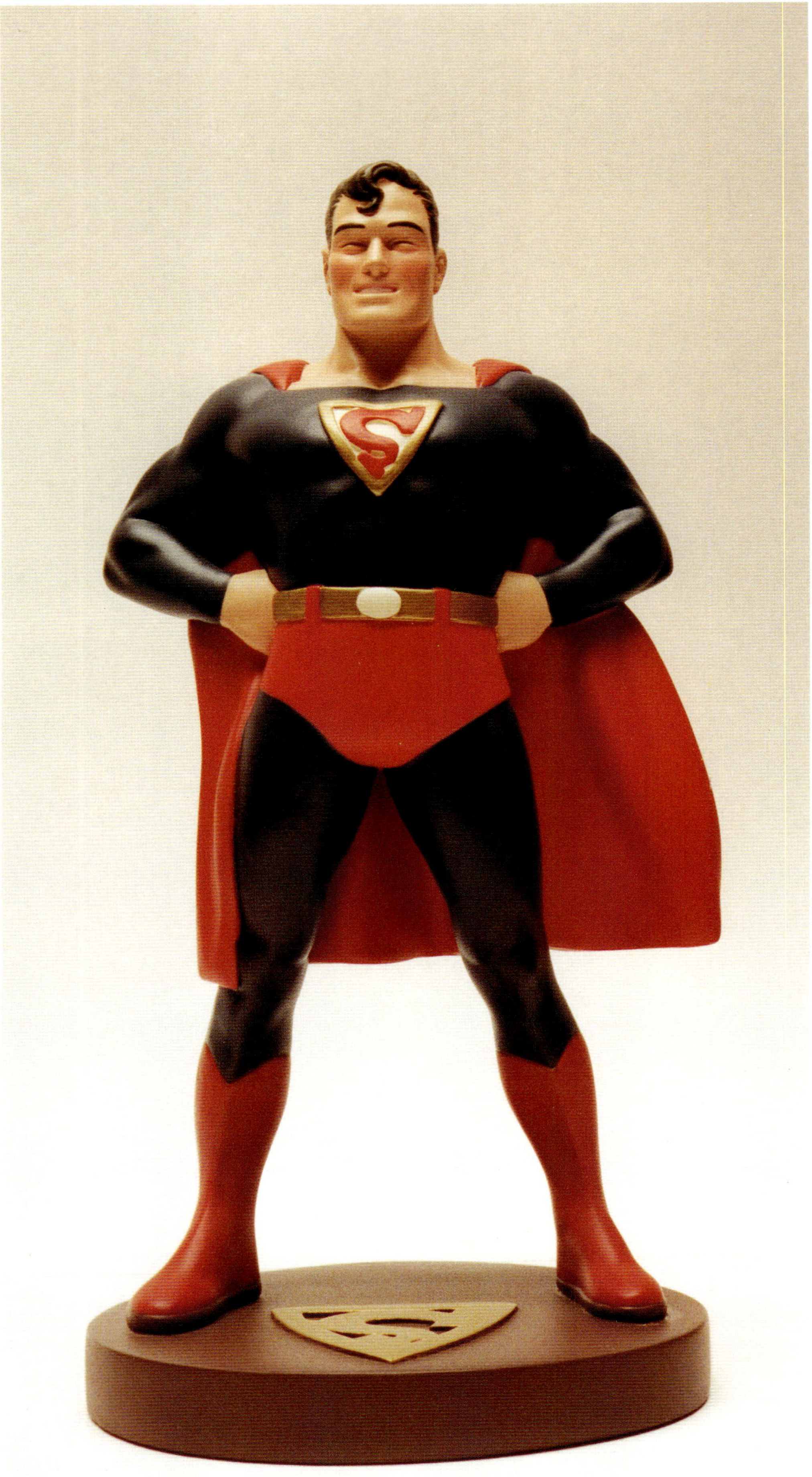

1

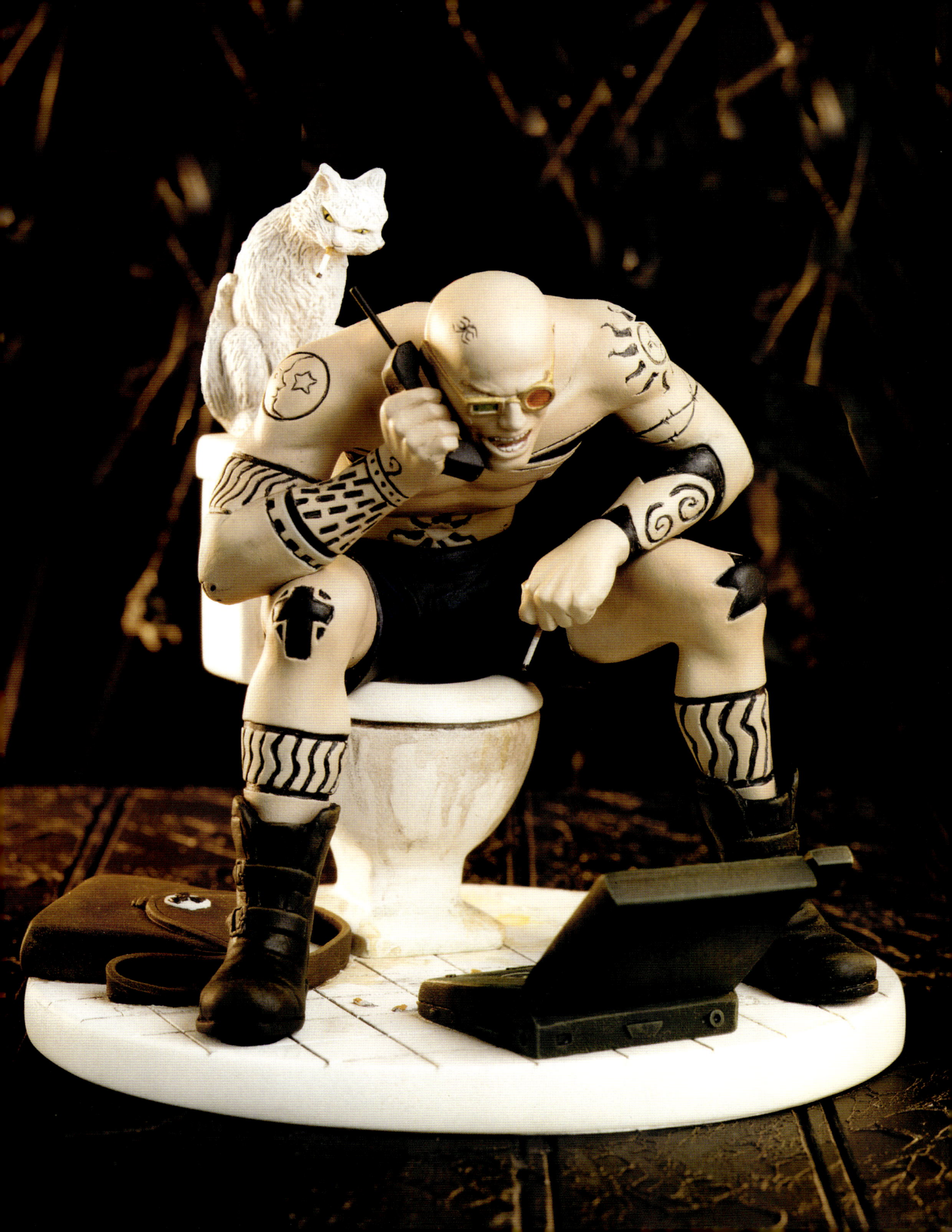

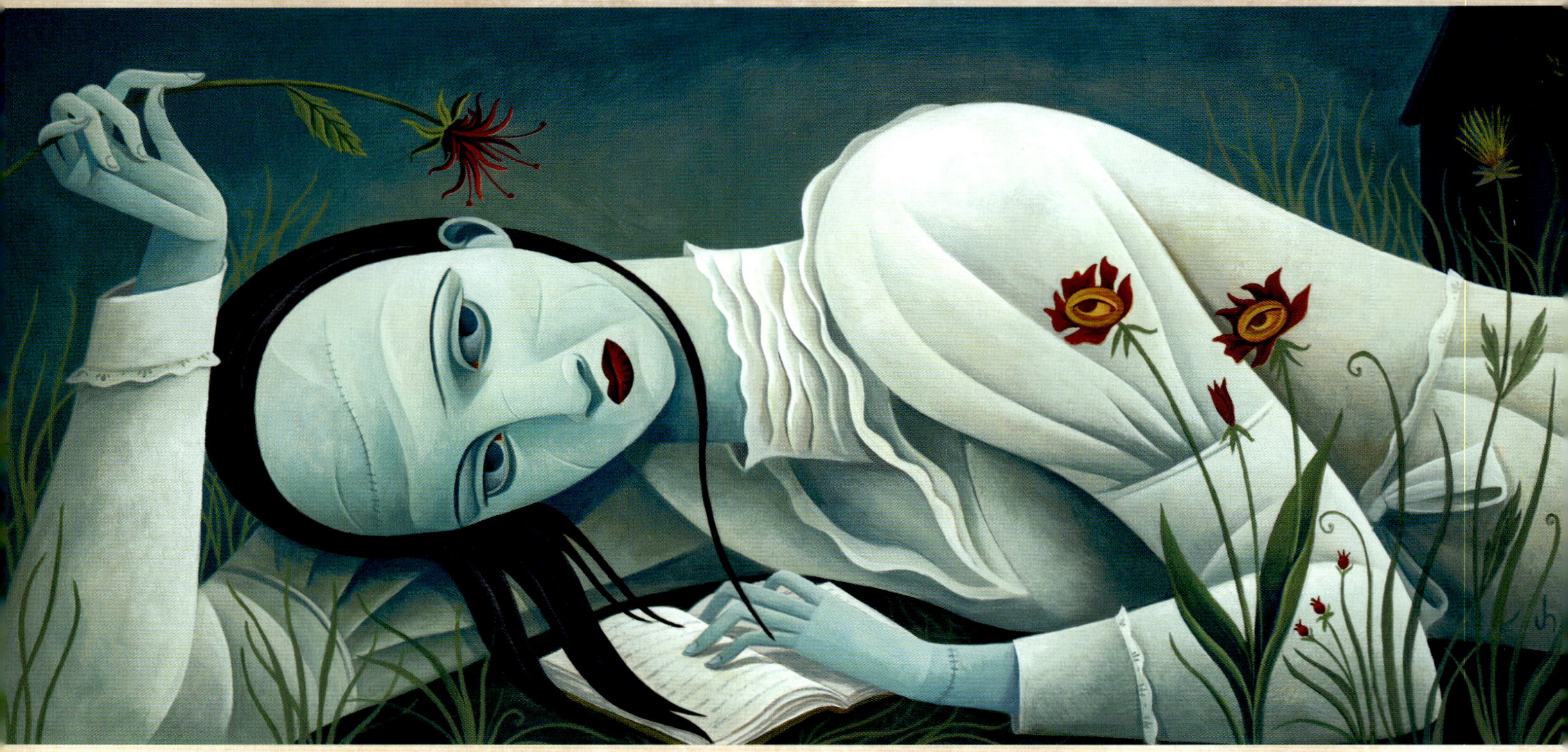

artist: JODY HEWGILL
art director: Shauna Wolf Narciso *client:* Amazing Stories *title:* The Bride

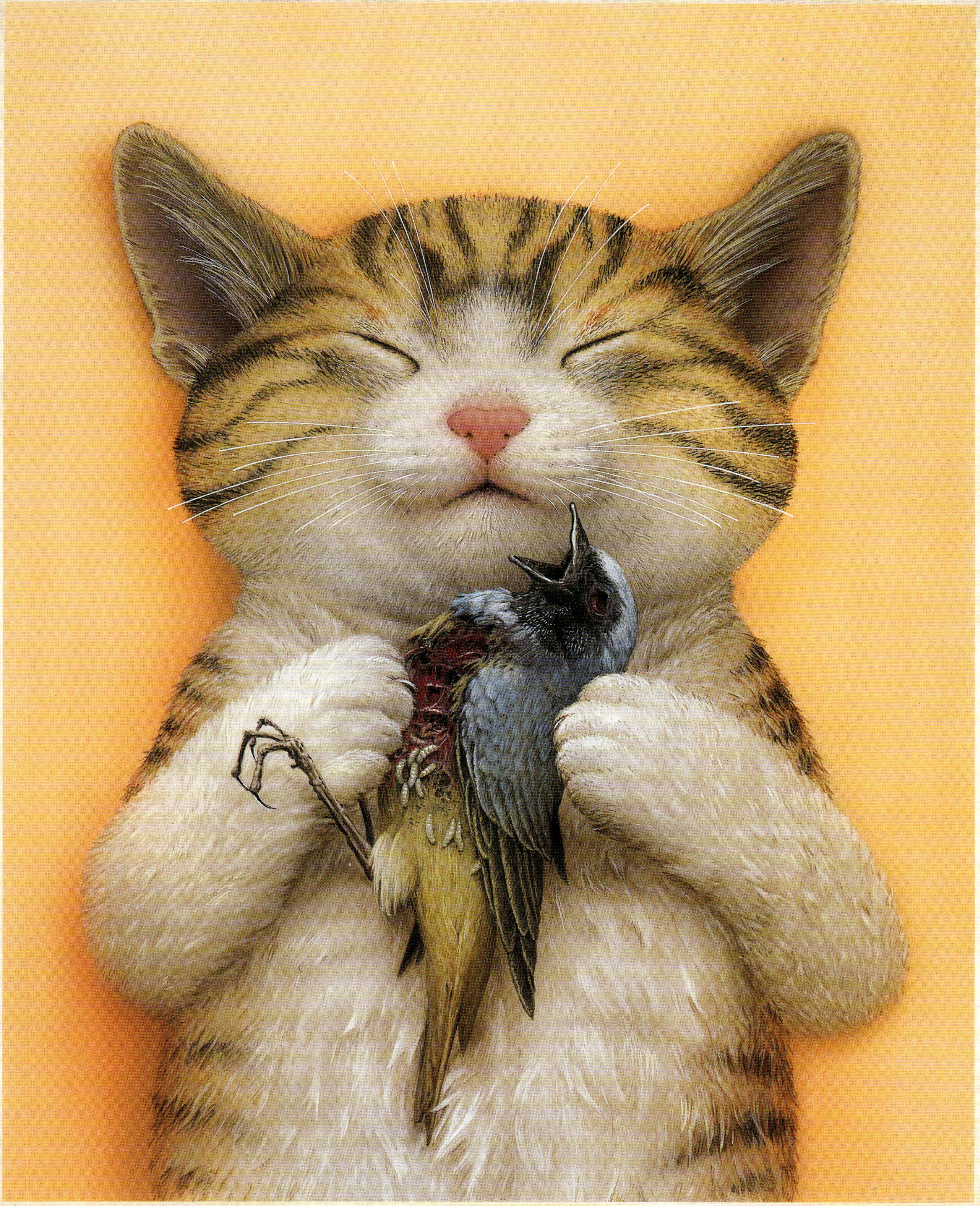

artist: WES BENSCOTER
client: Your Flesh Quarterly *title:* Contentment *size:* 30cmx38cm *medium:* Acrylic

1
artist: ANITA KUNZ
art director: Traci Churchill
client: Your Company
title: Snowball In Hell
medium: Mixed
size: 10"x10"

2
artist: PETER MAX
art director: Tom Staebler
designer: Peter Max
client: Playboy Magazine
title: Playboy 2000 [cover]

3
artist: DAVE DeVRIES
art director: Shauna Wolf Narciso
client: Amazing Stories
title: Travelers
medium: Mixed

4
artist: ANITA KUNZ
art director: Brandon Kavulla
designer: Brandon Kavulla
client: Vibe Company
title: Gun Man
medium: Mixed
size: 11"x14"

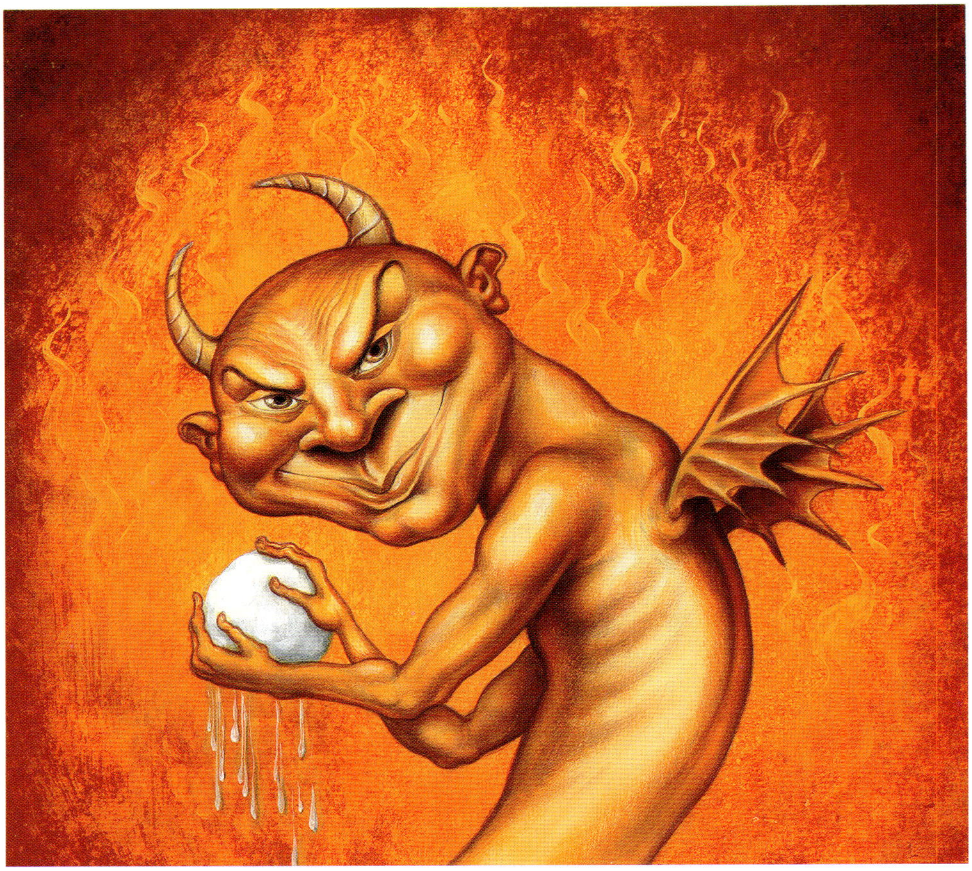

1

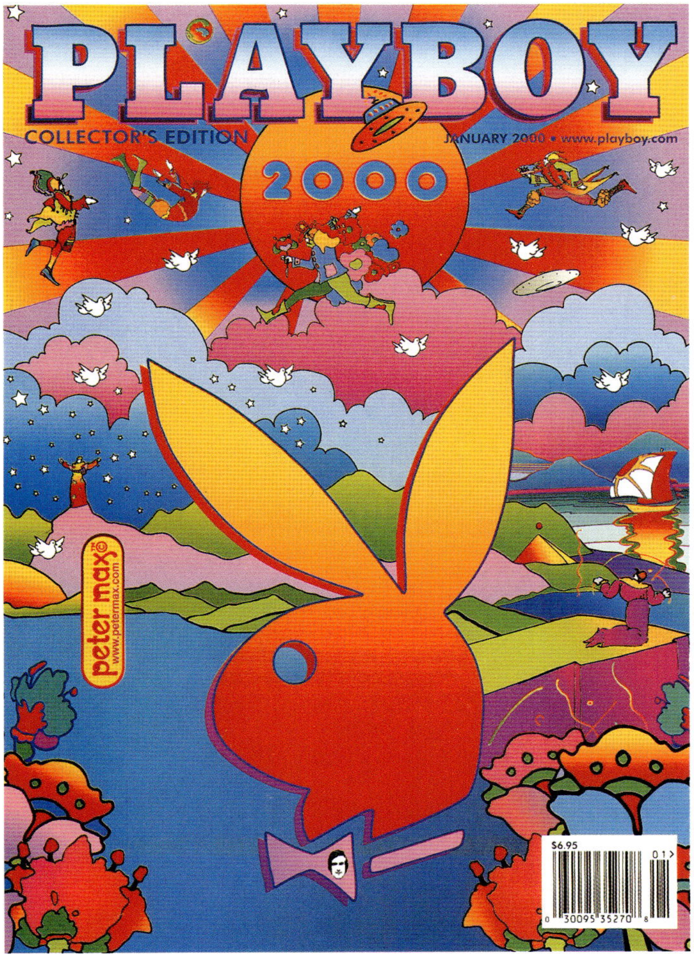

2

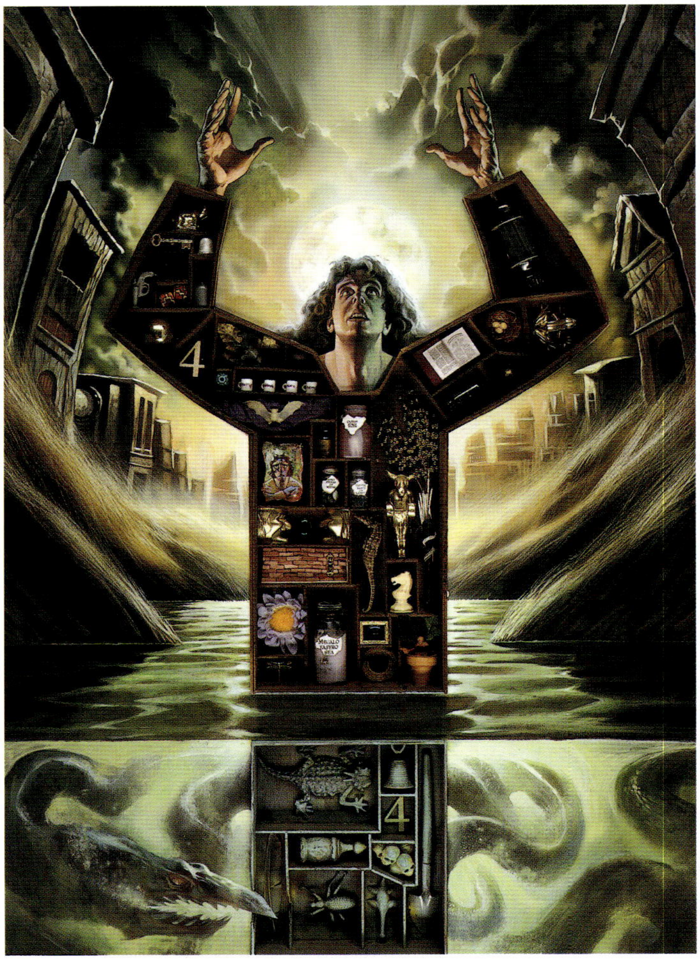

3

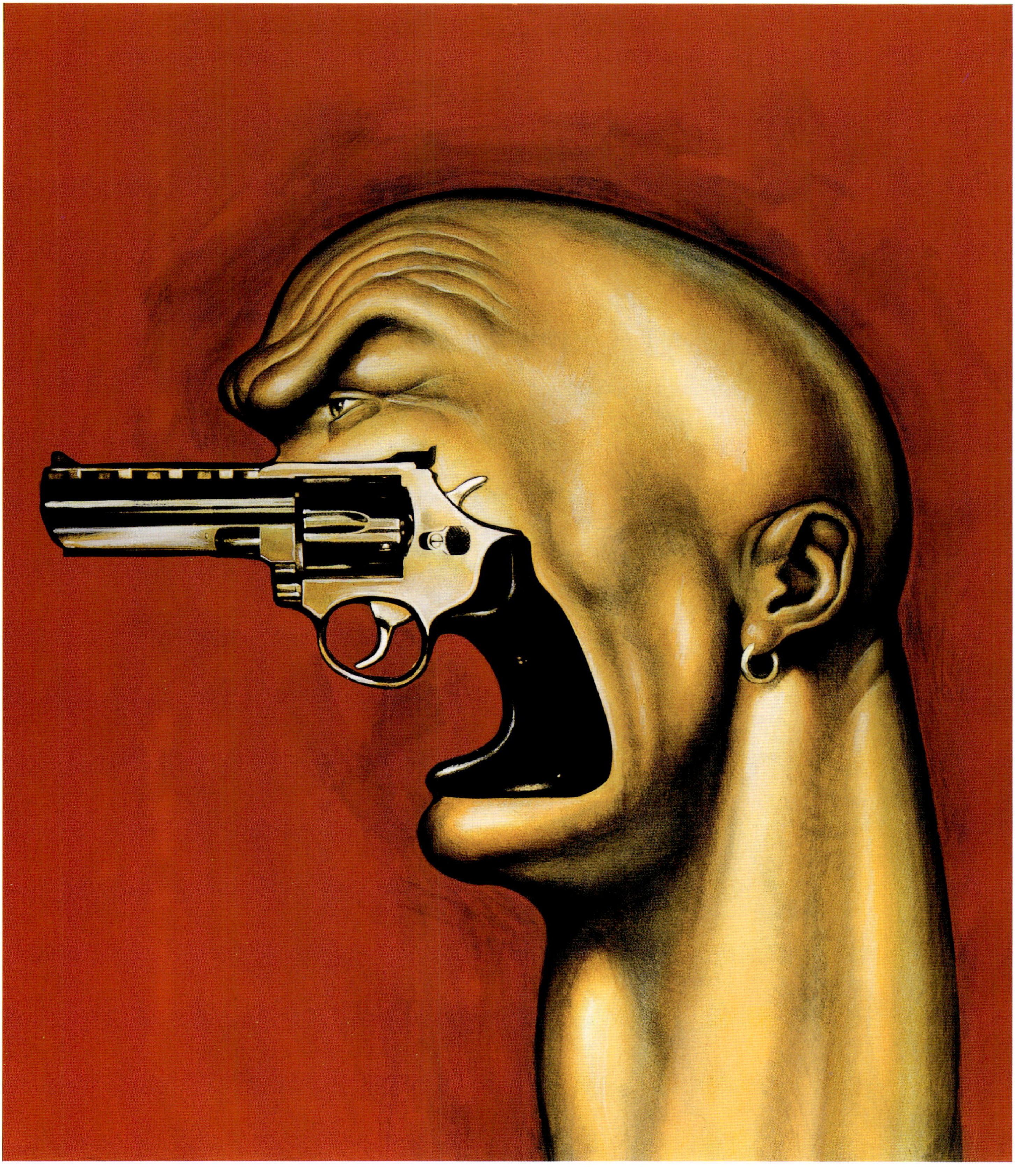

4

1
artist: JOHN JUDE PALENCAR
art director: Ed Rich
client: Smithsonian Magazine
title: Terror In A.D. 1000
medium: Acrylic
size: 30"x37"

2
artist: JEFF FAERBER
art director: Kevin Boyd
designer: David Frasier
client: San Jose Mercury News
medium: Acrylic/pencil
size: 12 1/2"x17"

3
artist: WES BENSCOTER
client: Carbon 14 Magazine
title: Geishaphobic
medium: Acrylic
size: 31cmx42cm

4
artist: TRISTAN ELWELL
art director: J. Porter
client: Yankee Magazine
title: Devil's Advocate (Benedict Arnold)
medium: Oil/acrylic
size: 11 3/4"x17"

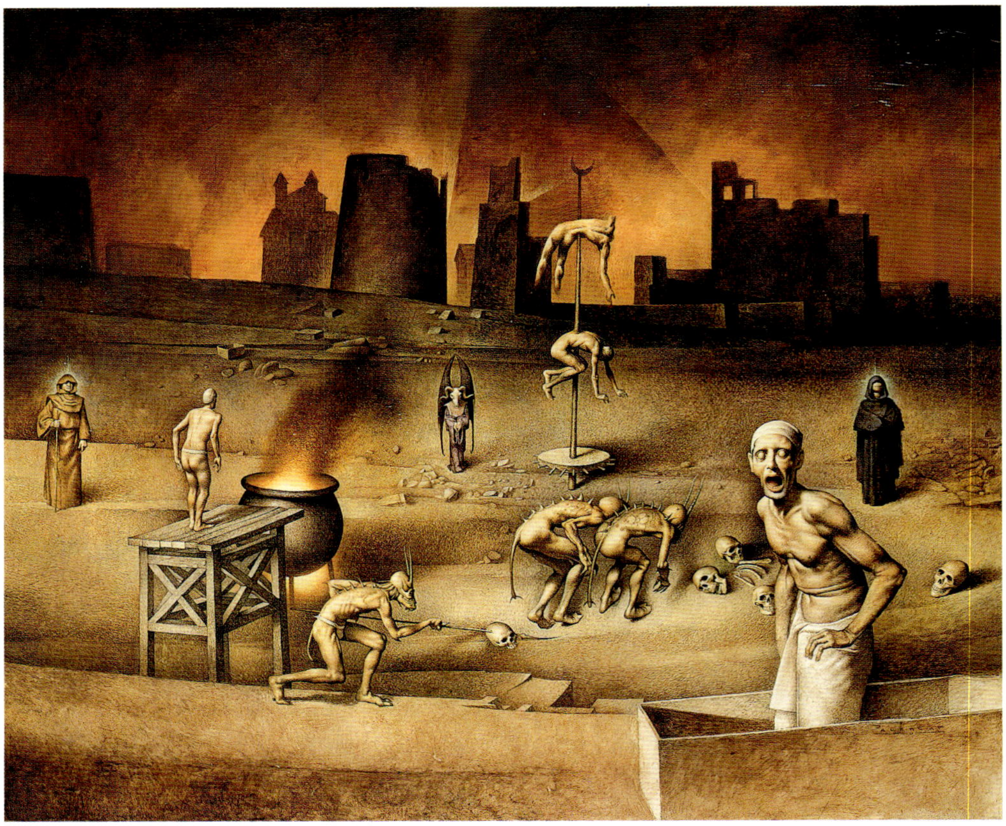

1

3

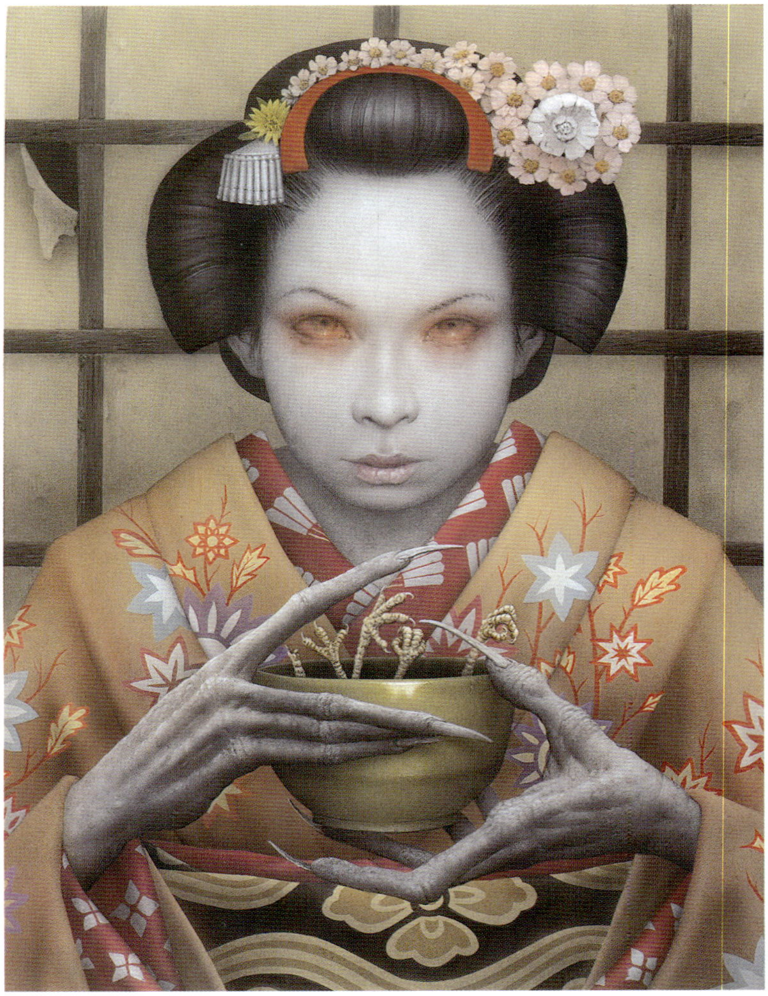

2

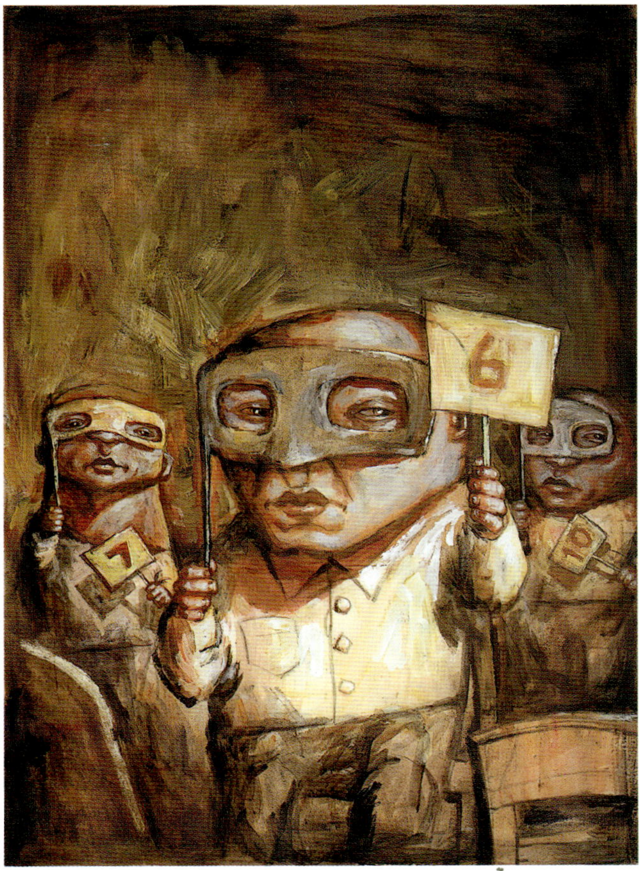

4

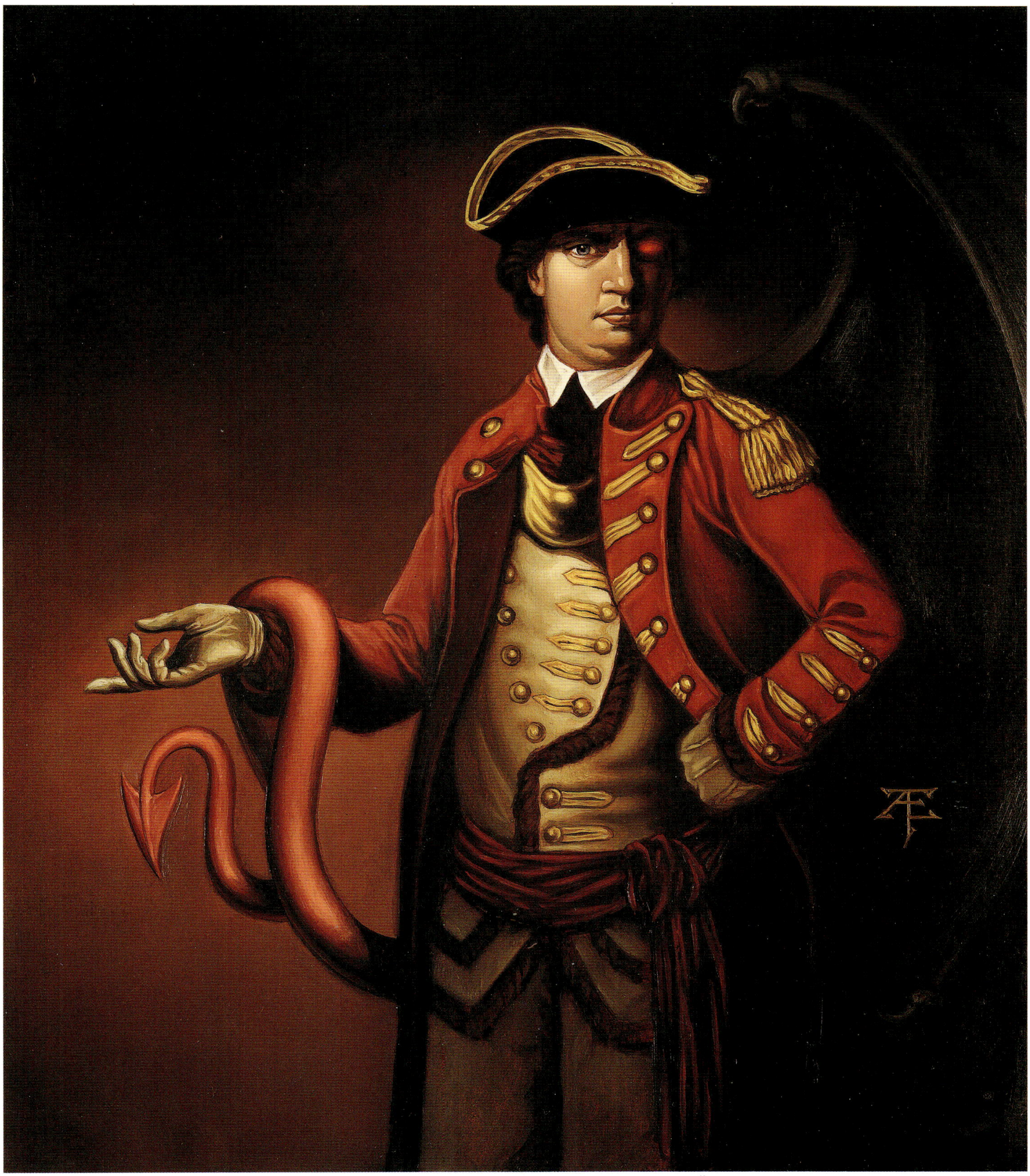

1
artist: JACQUES BREDY
art director: Carl Gnam
designer: Daniel Belknap
client: Realms of Fantasy
title: Highland People
medium: Oil

2
artist: OSCAR CHICHONI
title: The Bath
medium: Oil
size: 12"x18"

3
artist: THOMAS CHRISTIAN WOLFE
art director: Thomas Christian Wolfe
client: Masterworks & Best of Maui
title: Maui, The Hawaiian Demigod
medium: Oil
size: 36"x48"

4
artist: NICHOLAS JAINSCHIGG
art director: Rachel Holmen
designer: Rachel Holmen
client: Marion Zimmer Bradley's Fantasy Magazine
title: Wild Swan
medium: Oil/acrylic
size: 20"x28"

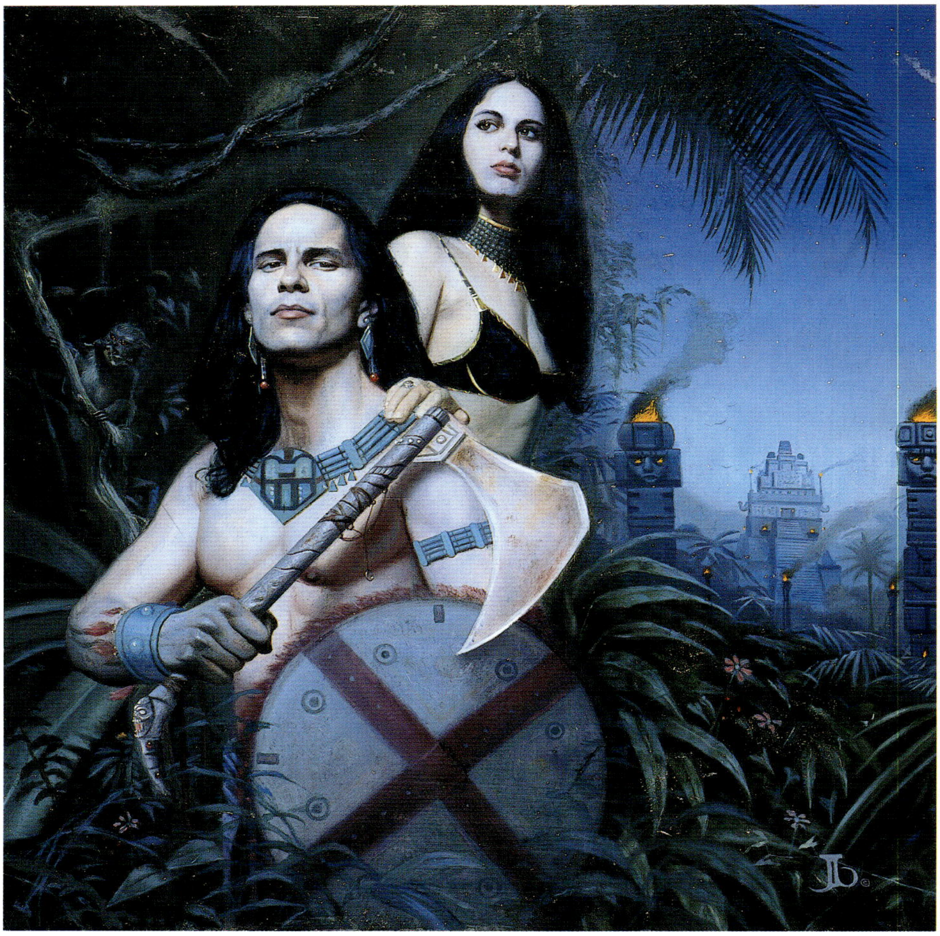

1

2

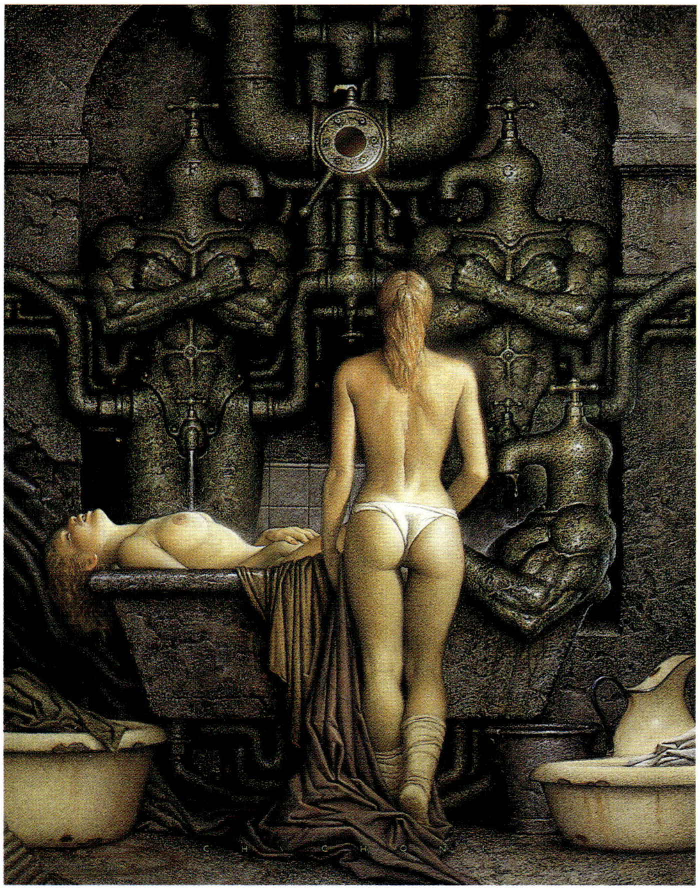

3

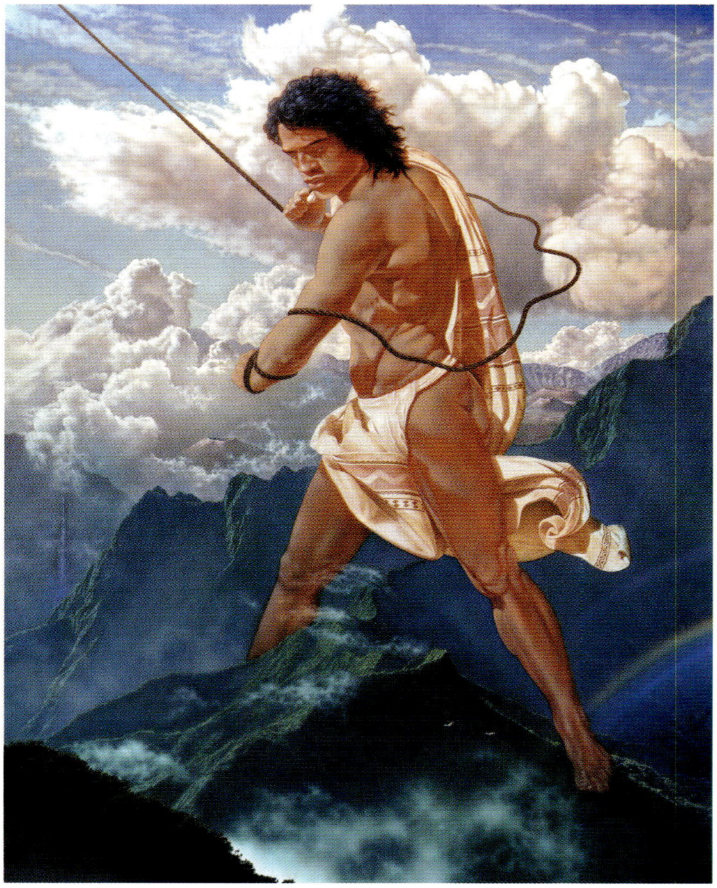

4

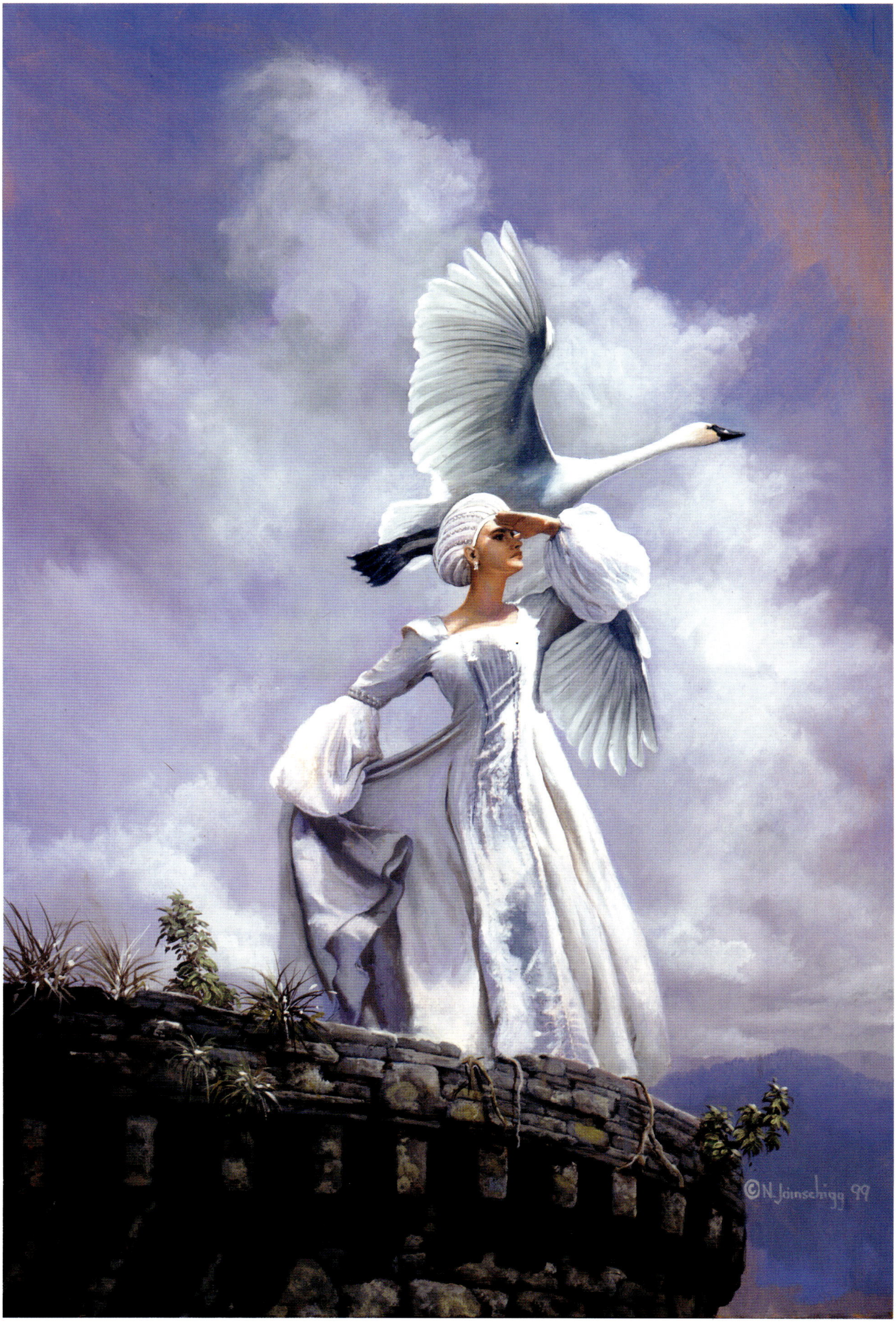

1
artist: JOHN JUDE PALENCAR
art director: Shauna Wolf Narciso
client: Amazing Stories
title: Instant Labor

2
artist: ROXANA VILLA
art director: Ronn Campisi
designer: Ronn Campisi
client: Smith Alumni Magazine
title: New Beginnings
medium: Acrylic/mixed
size: 8 1/2"x11"

3
artist: H.P. JANSEN
art director: G. Gladow
designer: H.P. Jansen
client: Spirit Magazine
title: Ship of the Soul: Stardust
medium: Oil
size: 130cmx90cm

4
artist: JOHN JUDE PALENCAR
art director: Shauna Wolf Narciso
client: Amazing Stories
title: Common Mind

1

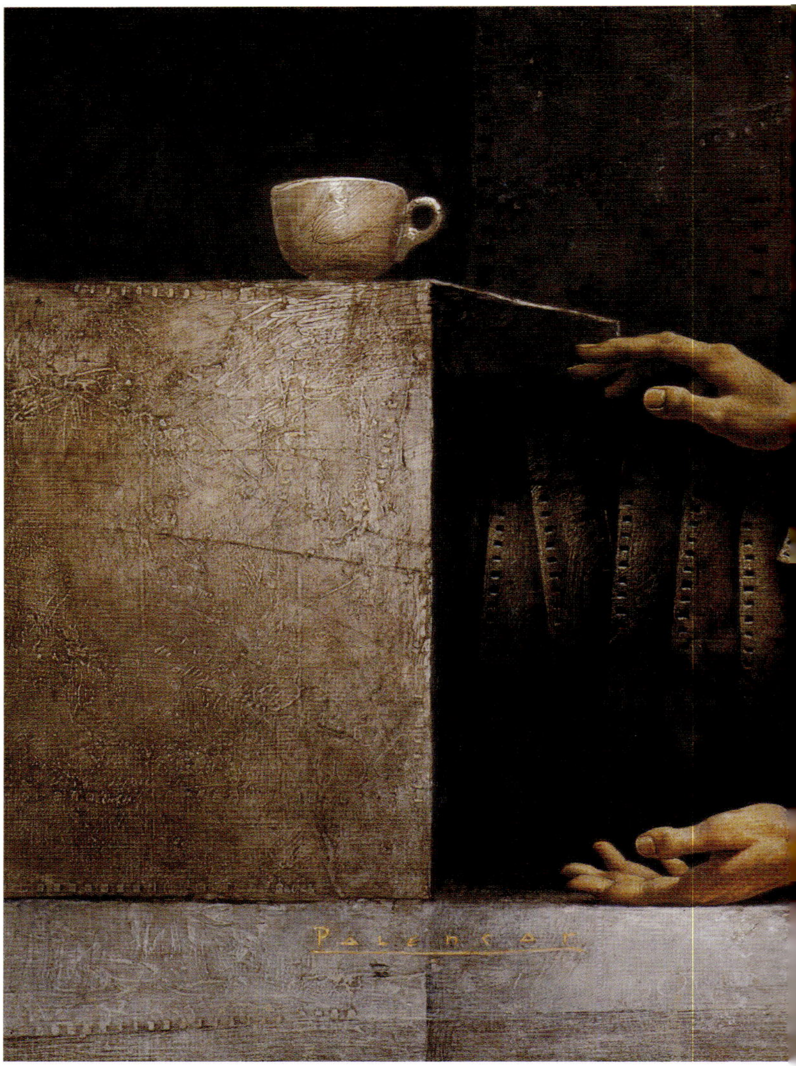

2

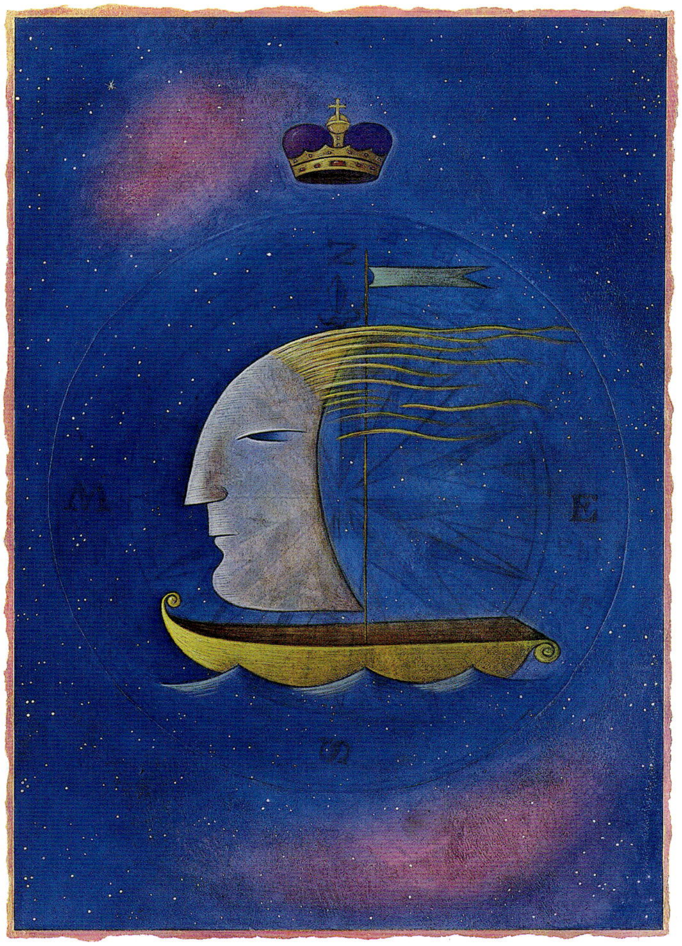

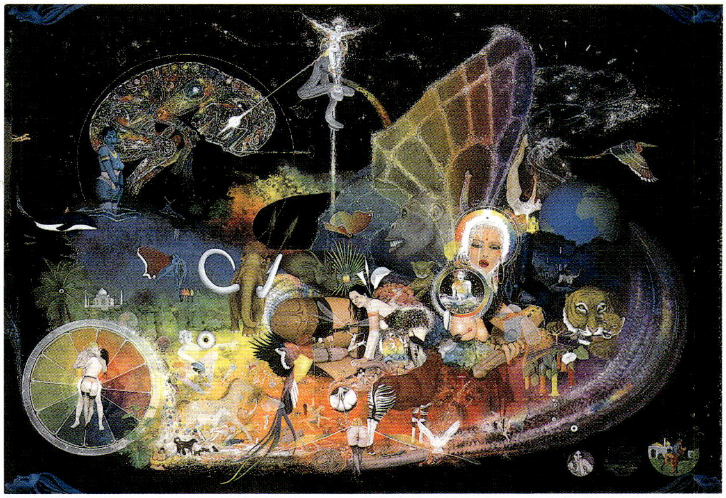

3

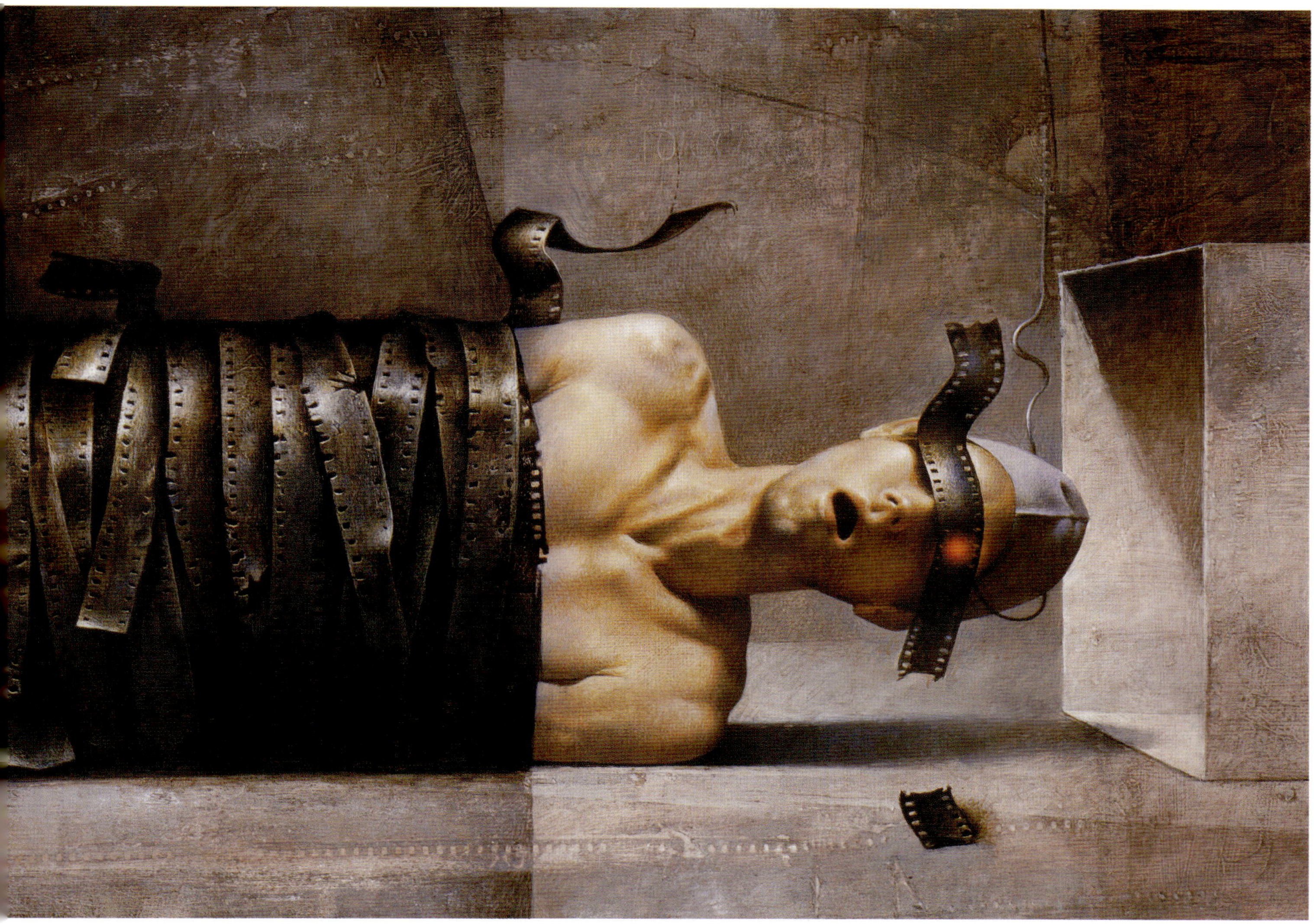

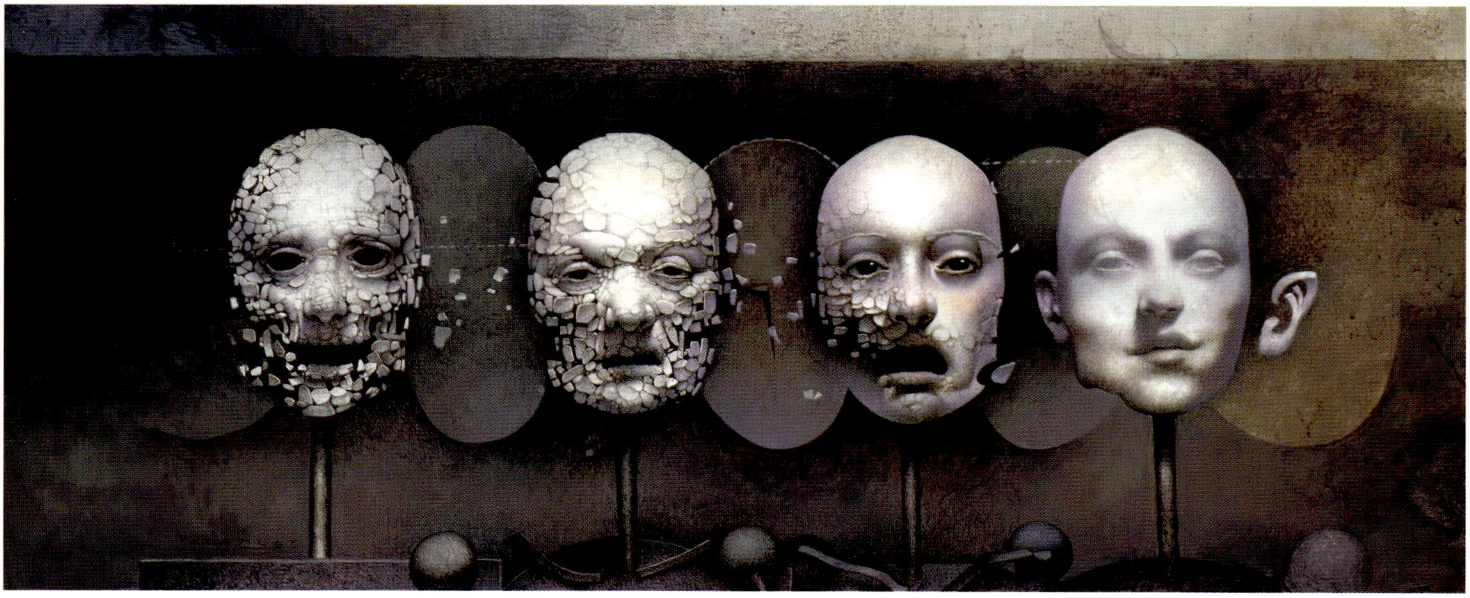

4

1
artist: STU SUCHIT
art director: Shauna Wolf Narciso
client: Amazing Stories
title: London, Paris, Banana
medium: Mixed
size: 8 1/2"x3 3/4"

2
artist: JOSEPH DeVITO
art director: Jonathan Schneider
client: Mad Magazine
title: Cyclops Alfred
medium: Oil
size: 15"x25"

3
artist: PETER DESÈVE
art director: Ken Newbaker
client: U.S. News & World Report
title: Hell
medium: Watercolor

4
artist: PETER DESÈVE
art director: Chris Curry
client: The New Yorker
title: The Man Who Was Eaten Alive
medium: Watercolor

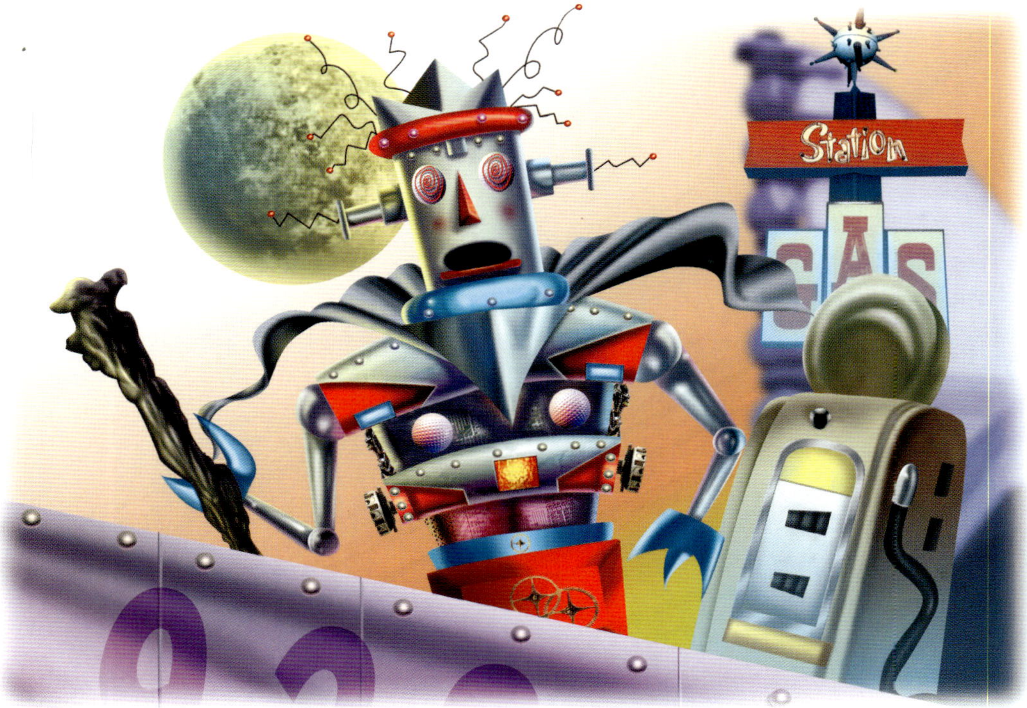

1

3

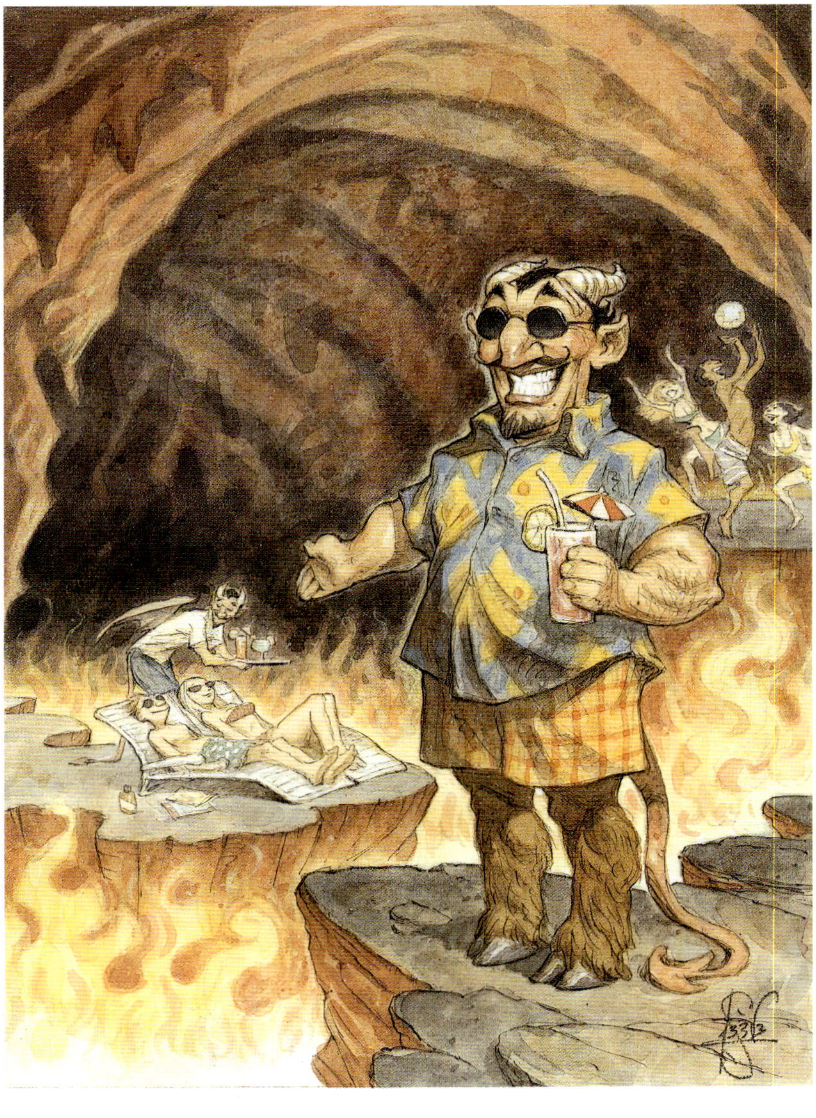

2

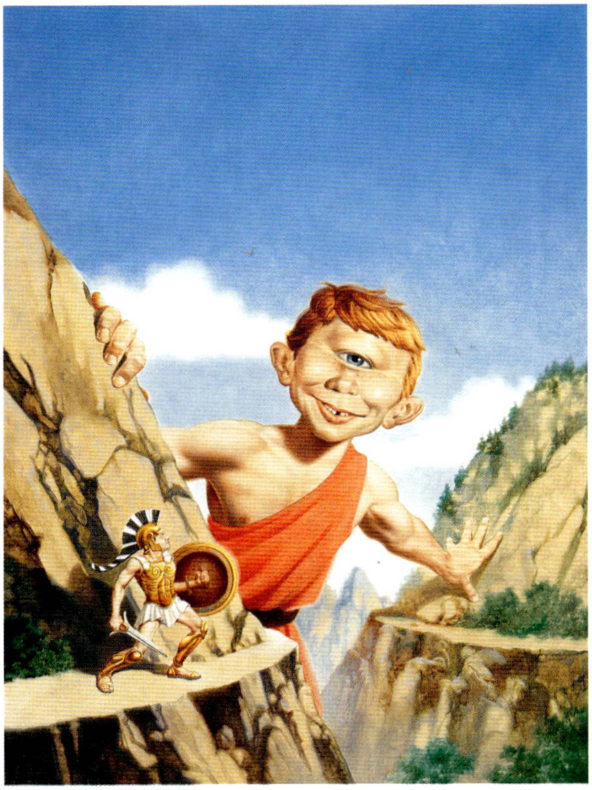

4

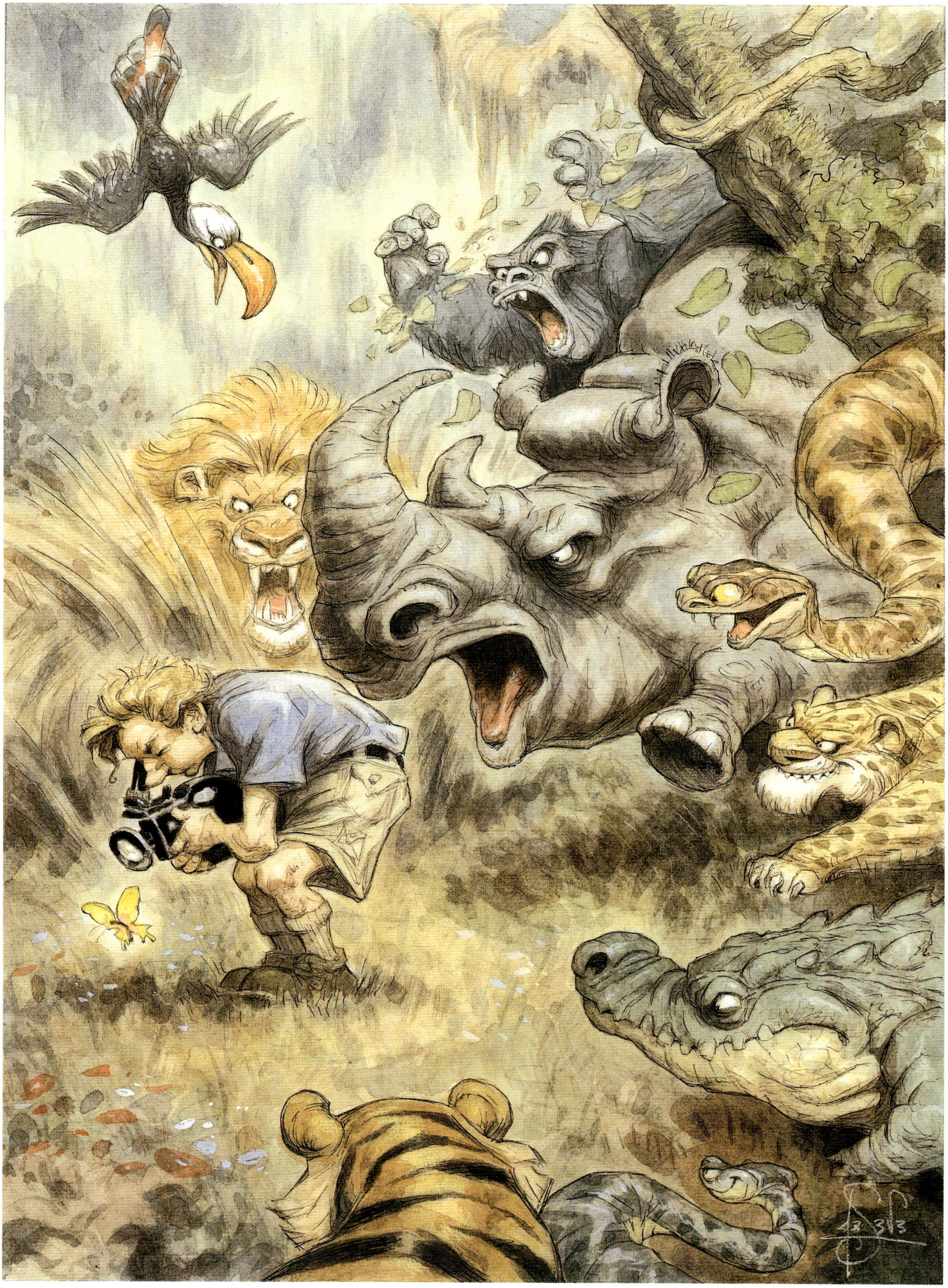

1
artist: ISTVAN BANYAI
art director: Tom Staebler
designer: Kerig Pope
client: Playboy Magazine
title: Webcamorama
medium: Mixed

2
artist: KENT WILLIAMS
art director: Tom Staebler
designer: Kerig Pope
client: Playboy Magazine
title: The Shadow Trees
medium: Mixed

3
artist: THOM ANG
art director: Shauna Wolf Narciso
client: Amazing Stories
title: Moondance
medium: Mixed
size: 9"x12"

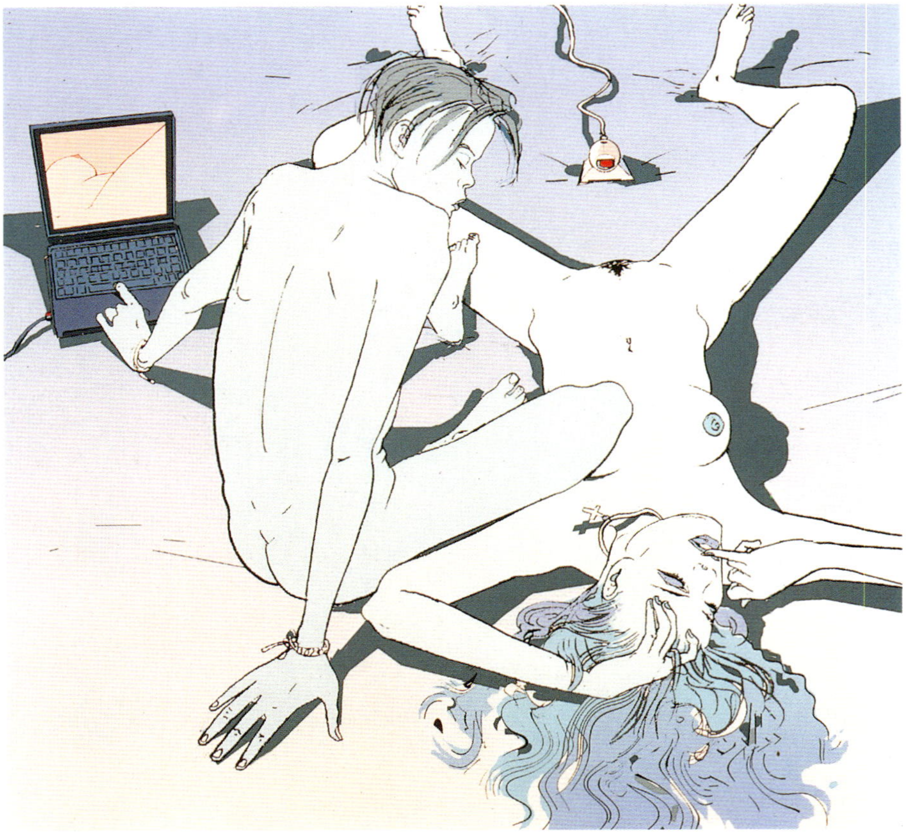

1

2

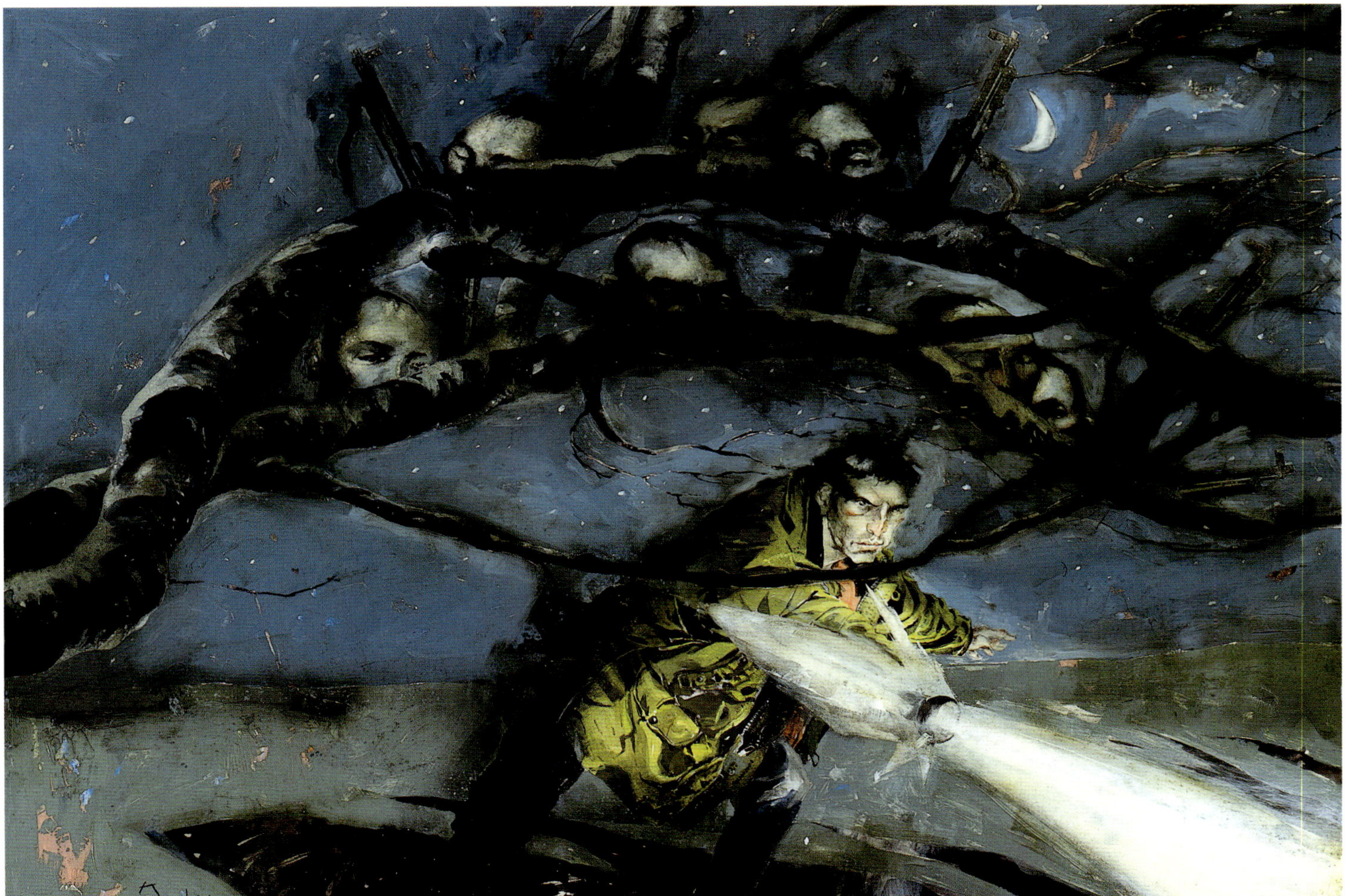

3

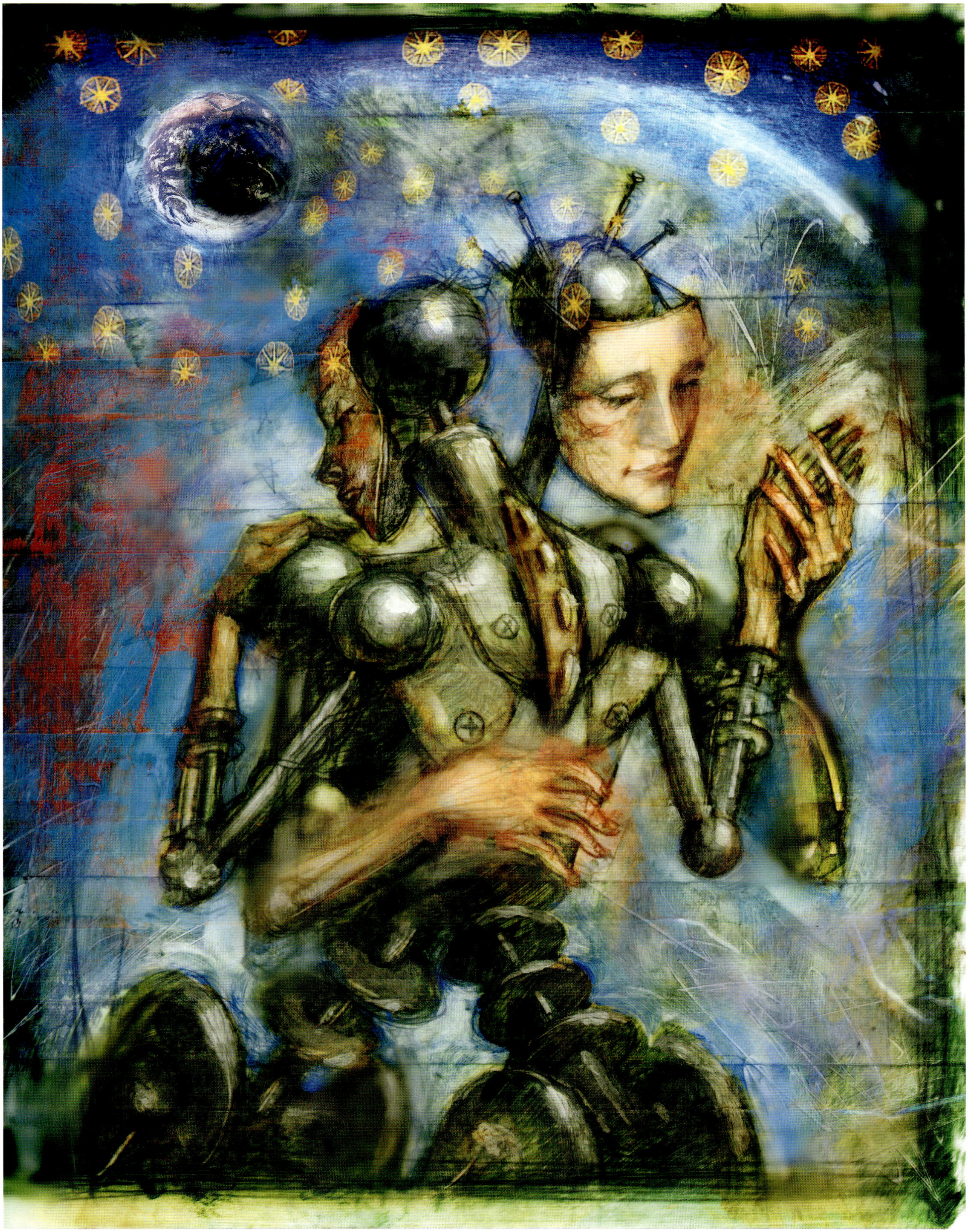

1
artist: JAMES WARHOLA
art director: Tom Staebler
designer: Kerig Pope
client: Playboy Magazine
title: Smut Talk

2
artist: DONATO GIANCOLA
art director: Tom Staebler
designer: Len Willis
client: Playboy Magazine
title: Grooming 2000
medium: Oil

3
artist: DONATO GIANCOLA
art director: Tom Staebler
designer: Kerig Pope
client: Playboy Magazine
title: Cities On the Moon
medium: Oil

4
artist: SYD MEAD
art director: Tom Staebler
designer: Syd Mead
client: Playboy Magazine
title: There's No Space Like Home

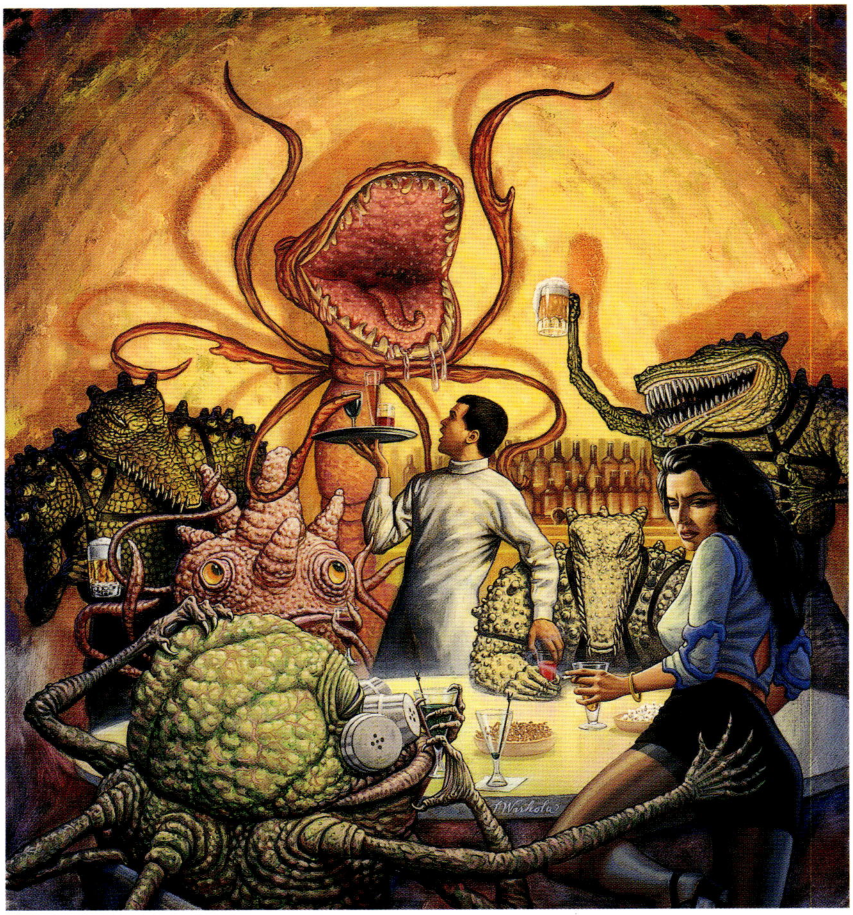

1

2
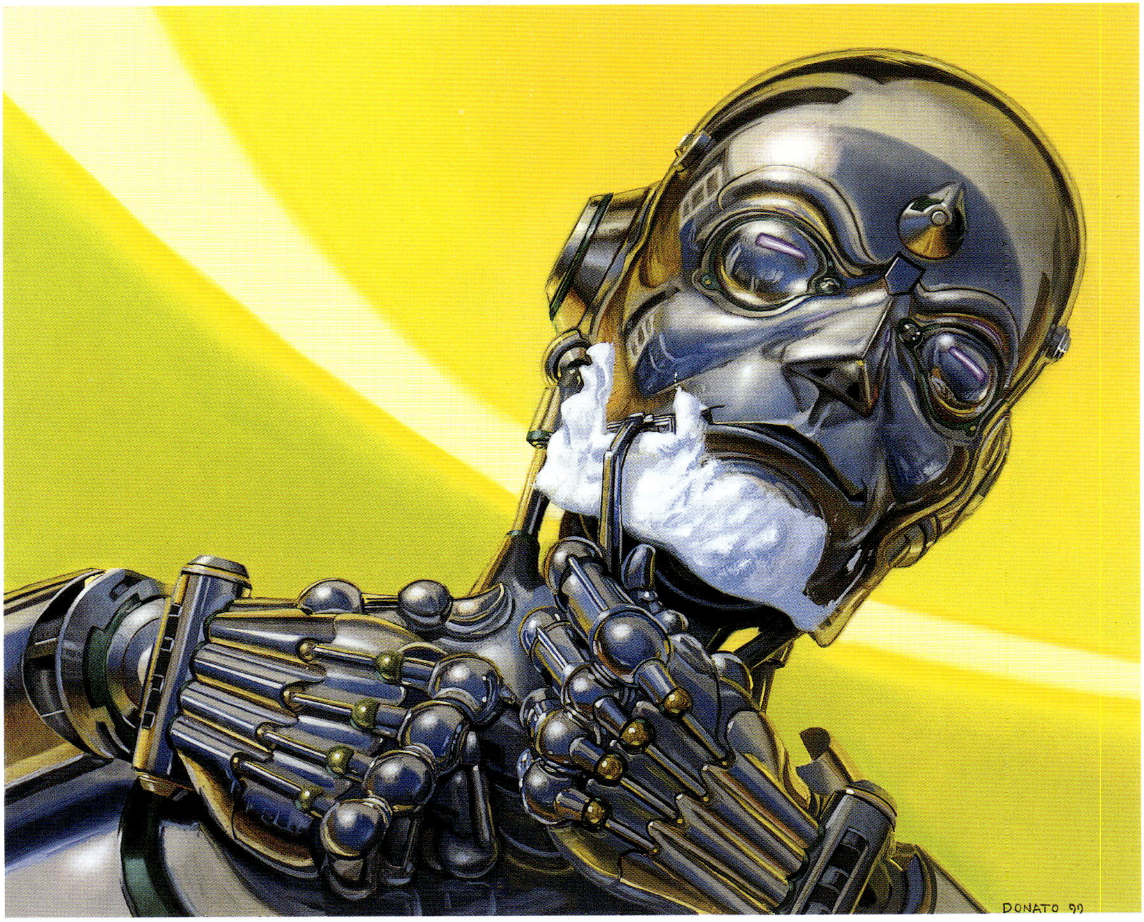

3

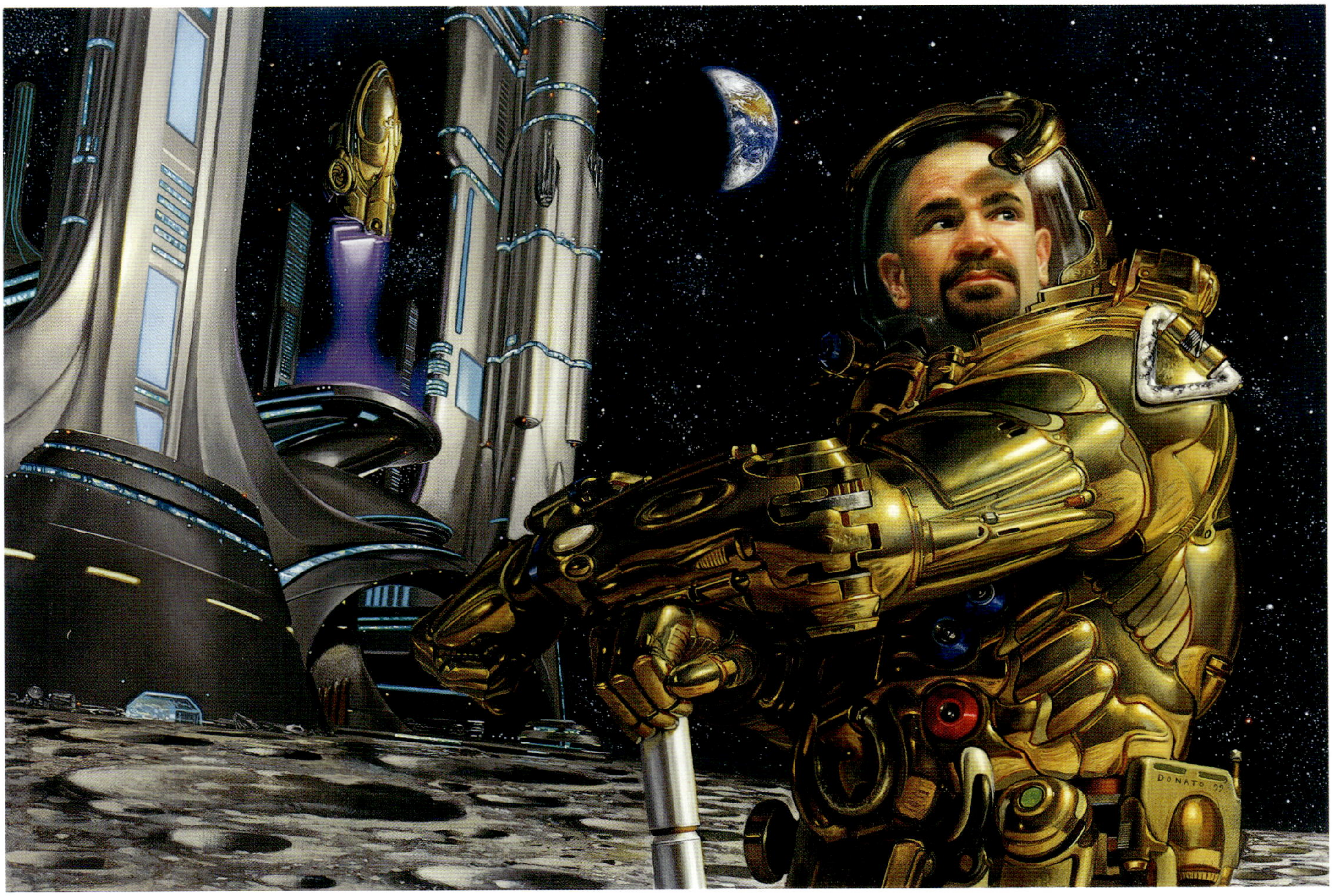

4

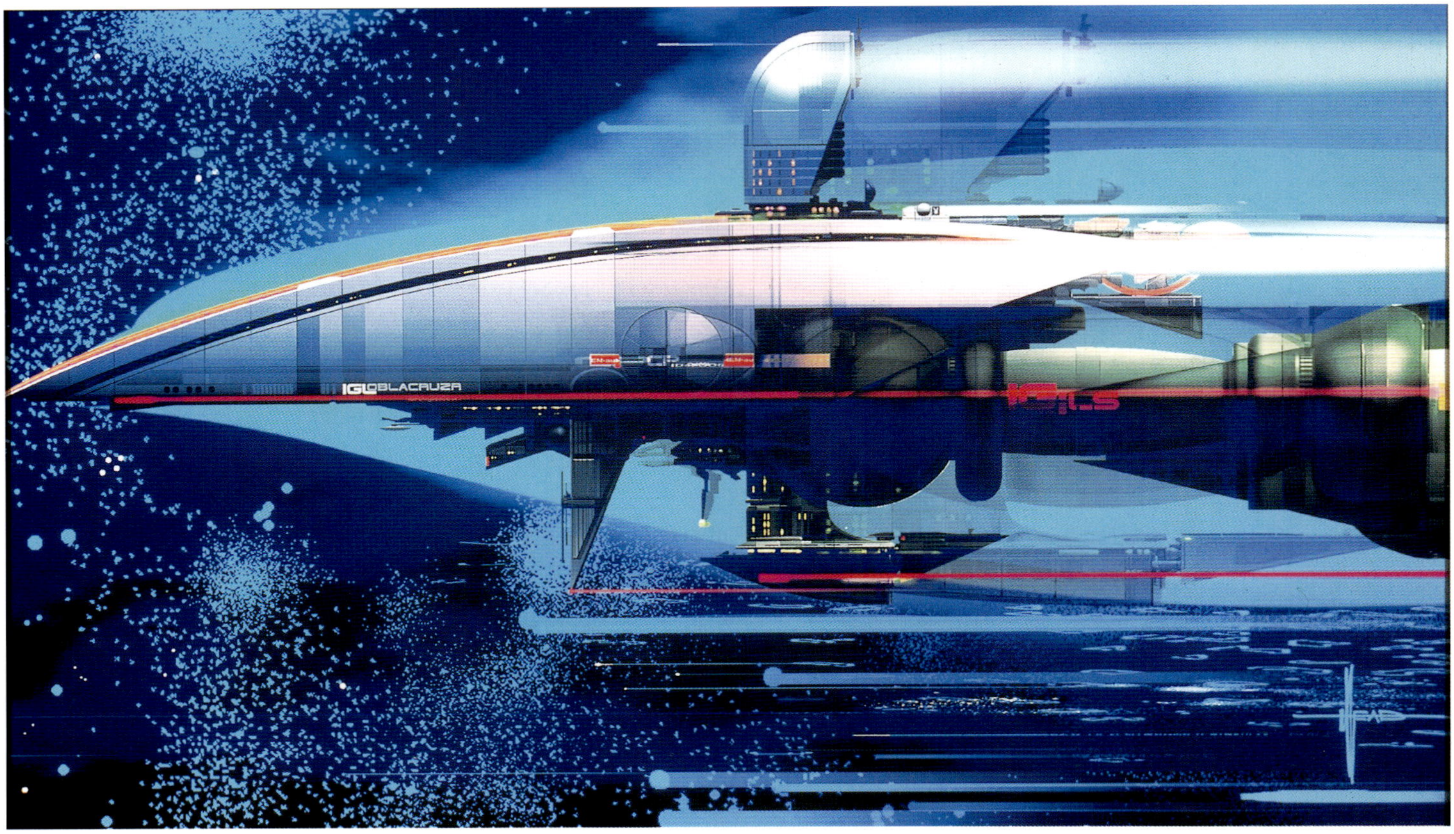

1
artist: DAVE McKEAN
art director: Tom Staebler
designer: Kerig Pope
client: Playboy Magazine
title: The Fan Man Returns
medium: Mixed

2
artist: DAVE SEELEY
art director: Ted Leller/Minh Uong
photographer: Portrait of Stephen Merritt by Raphael Fuchs
client: The Village Voice
title: The Magnetic Fields
medium: Photo/digital

3
artist: MARC SASSO
art director: Larry Smith
client: Dragon Magazine
title: The Treatment
medium: Digital

4
artist: GREG SWEARINGEN
art director: Gary Sluzewski
client: Cleveland Magazine
title: Artful Considerations
medium: Mixed
size: 13"x17"

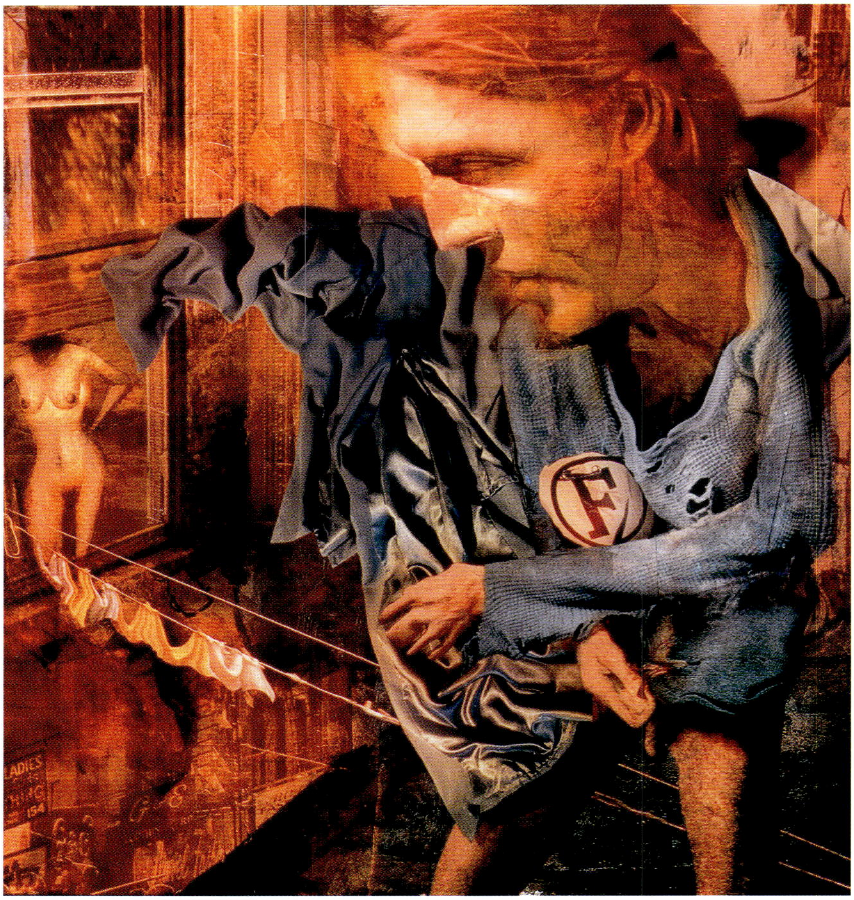

1

2

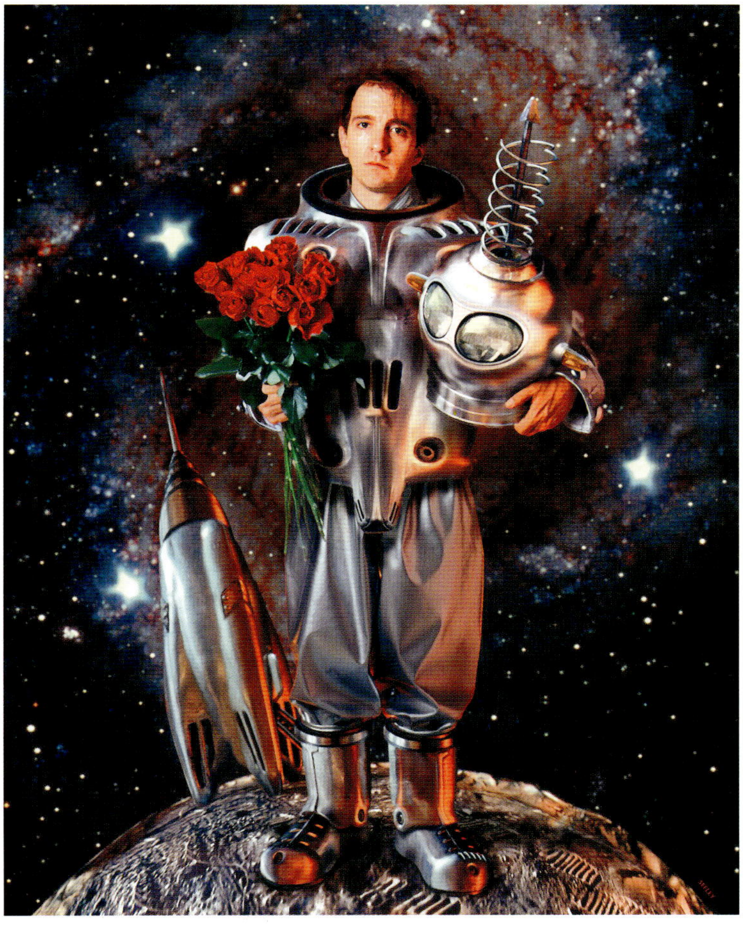

3

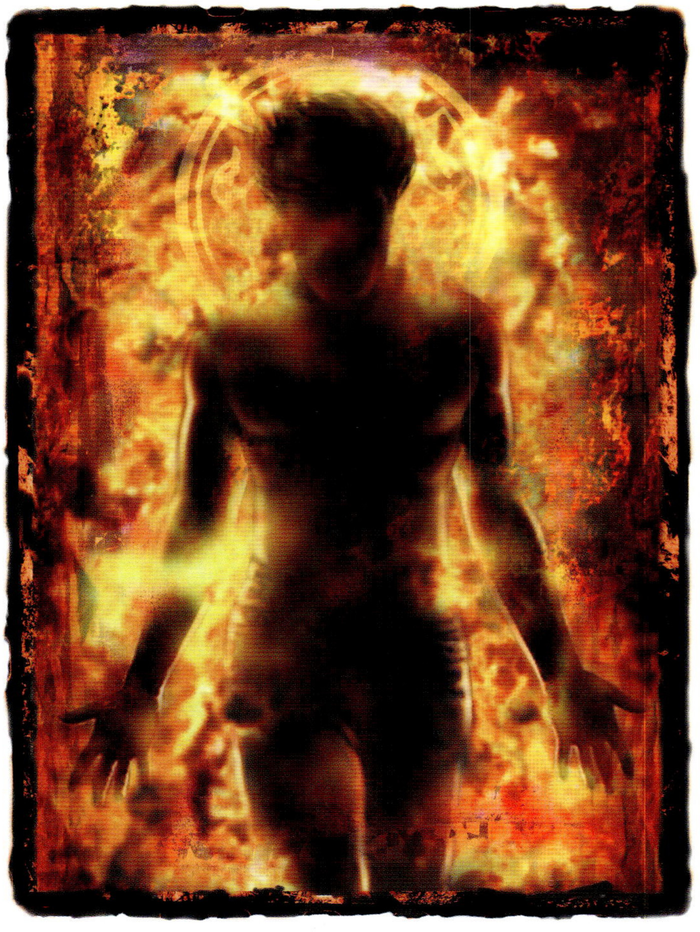

4

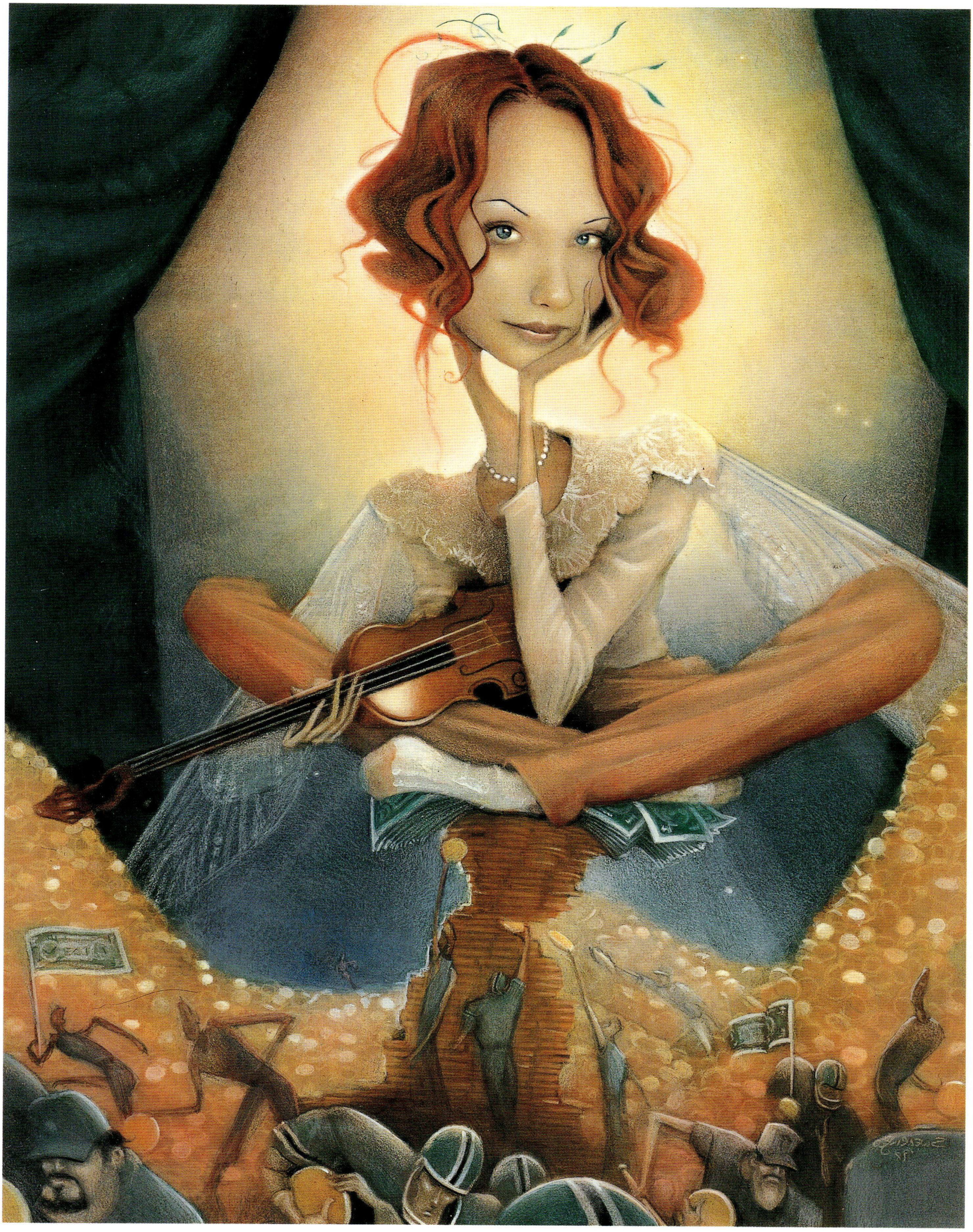

1
artist: GREG COUCH
art director: Shauna Wolf Narciso
client: Amazing Story
title: The Fourth Branch

2
artist: MARK ZUG
art director: Larry Smith
designer: Scott Ricker
client: Dragon Magazine
title: Draconic Design
medium: Oil
size: 24"x32"

3
artist: MARK ZUG
art director: Shauna Wolf Narciso
client: Amazing Story
title: A Whisper of Caladan Seas

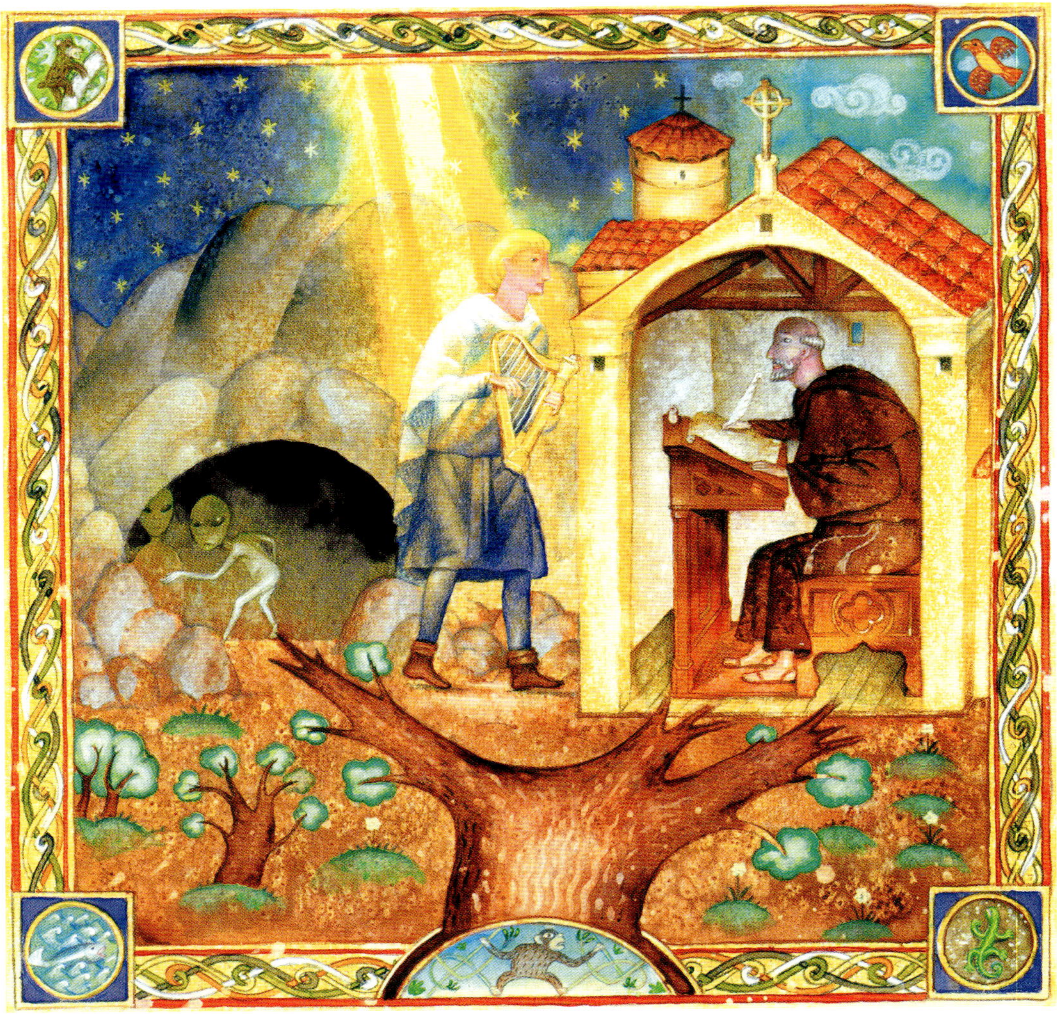

1

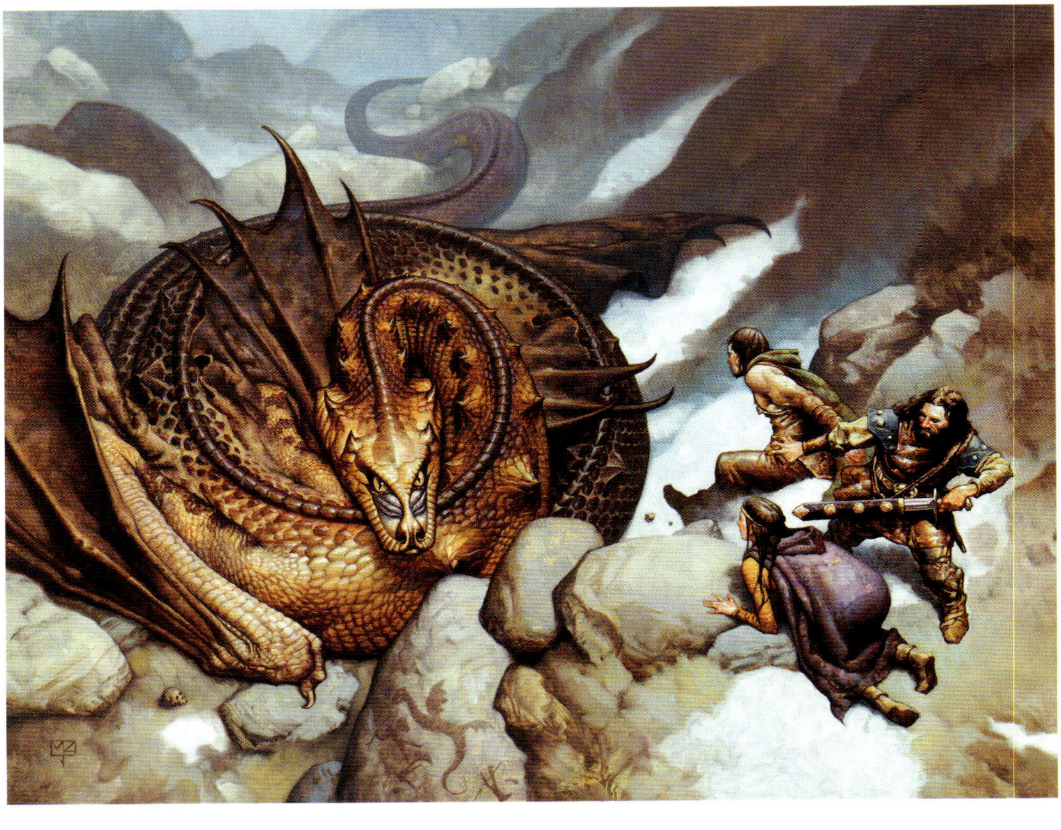

2

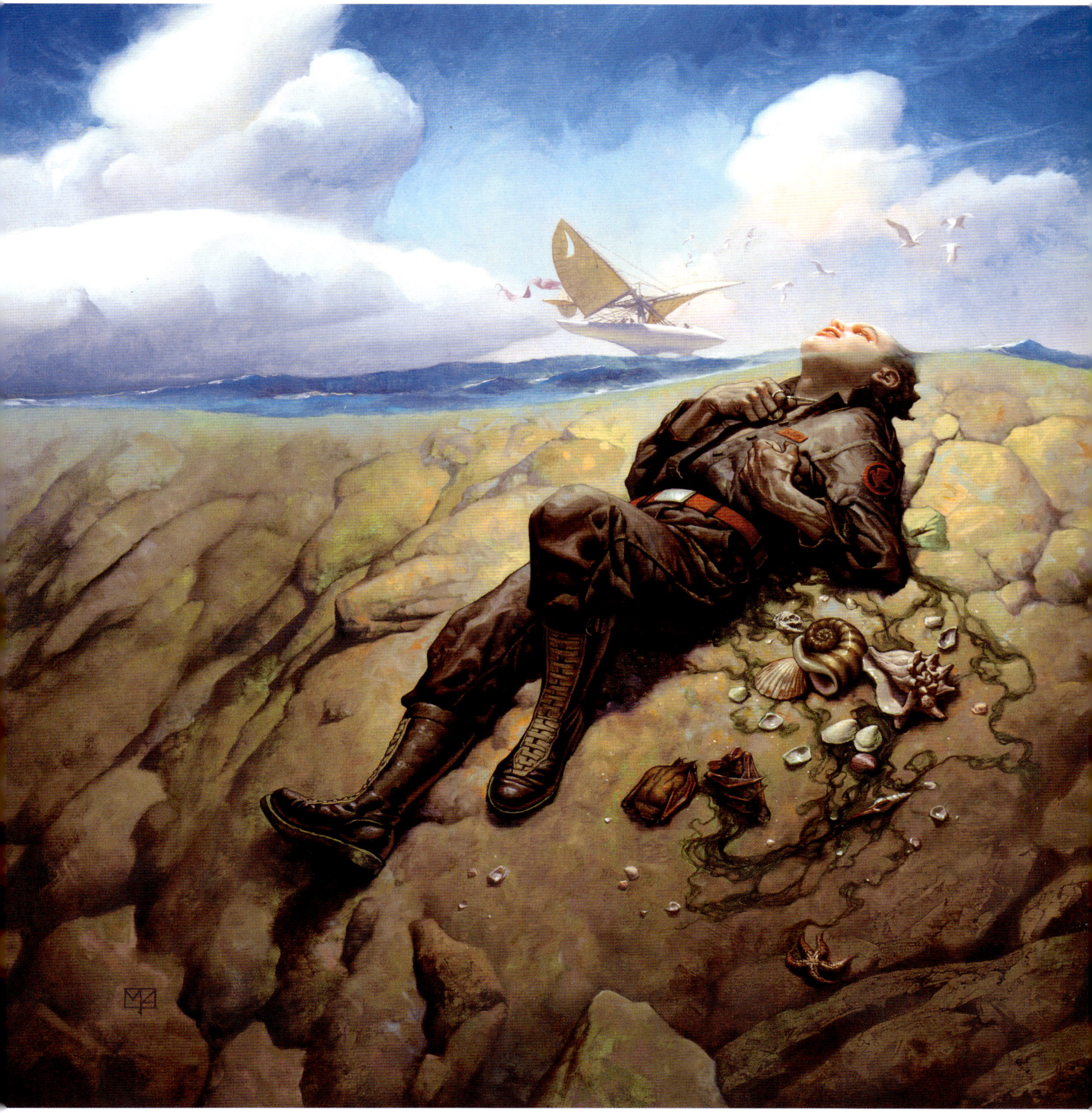

3

1
artist: OMAR RAYYAN
art director: Tony Jacobson
client: Spider Magazine
title: The Music Critic
medium: Watercolor
size: 8"x10"

2
artist: DON MAITZ
art director: Christopher Sloan
client: National Geographic Magazine
title: Taking The Whydah
medium: Oil
size: 28"x28"

3
artist: CHRISTOPHER MOELLER
art director: Shauna Wolf Narciso
client: Amazing Stories
title: Yearning For the Future
medium: Acrylic
size: 20"x30"

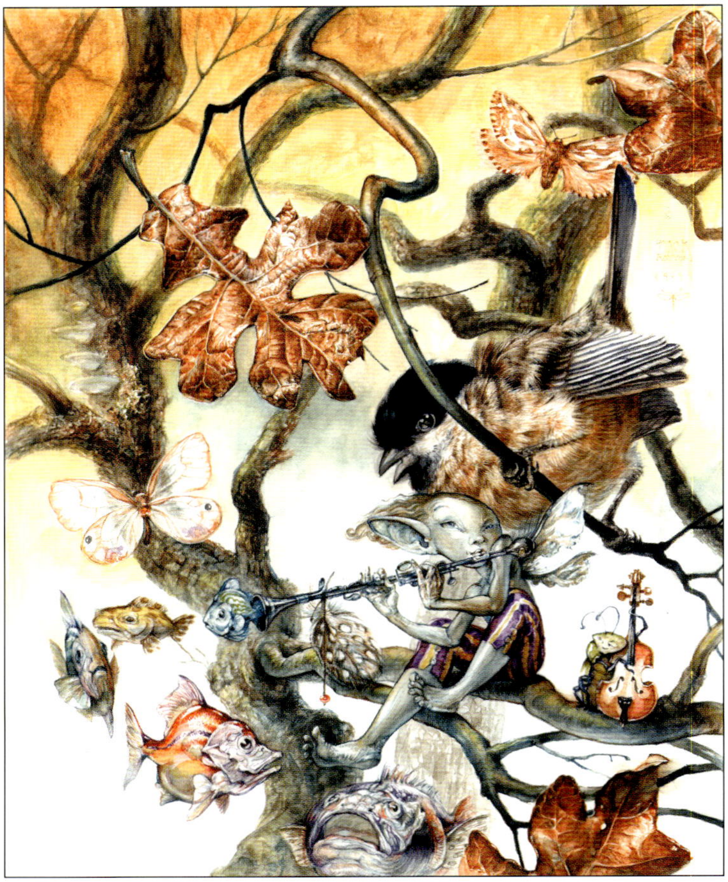

1

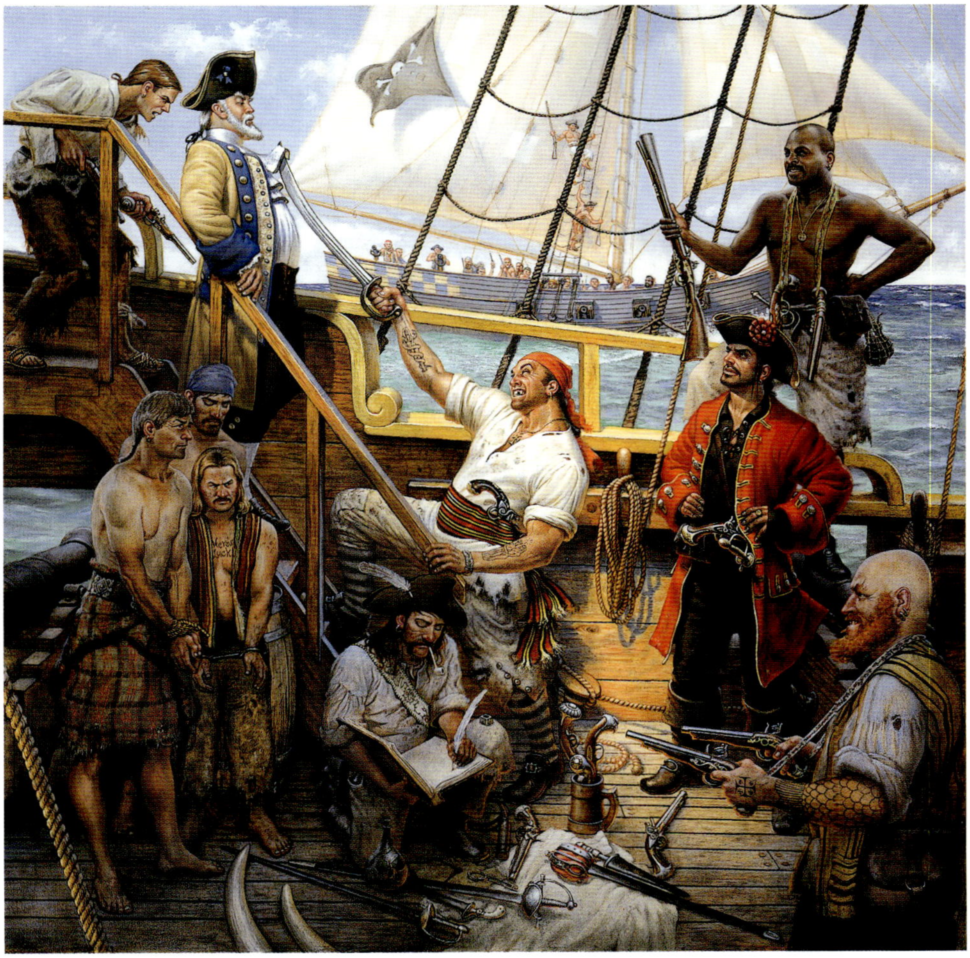

2

3

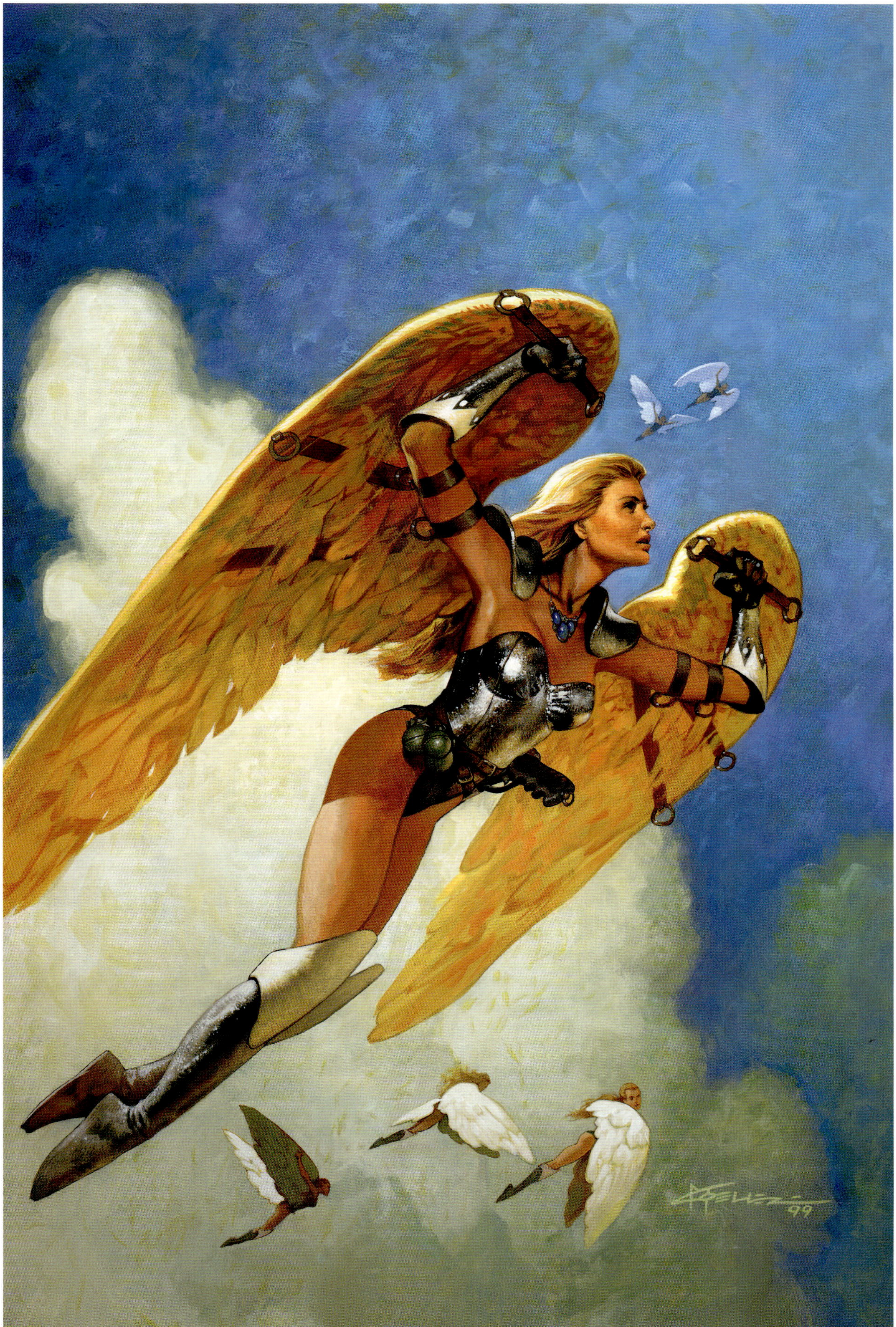

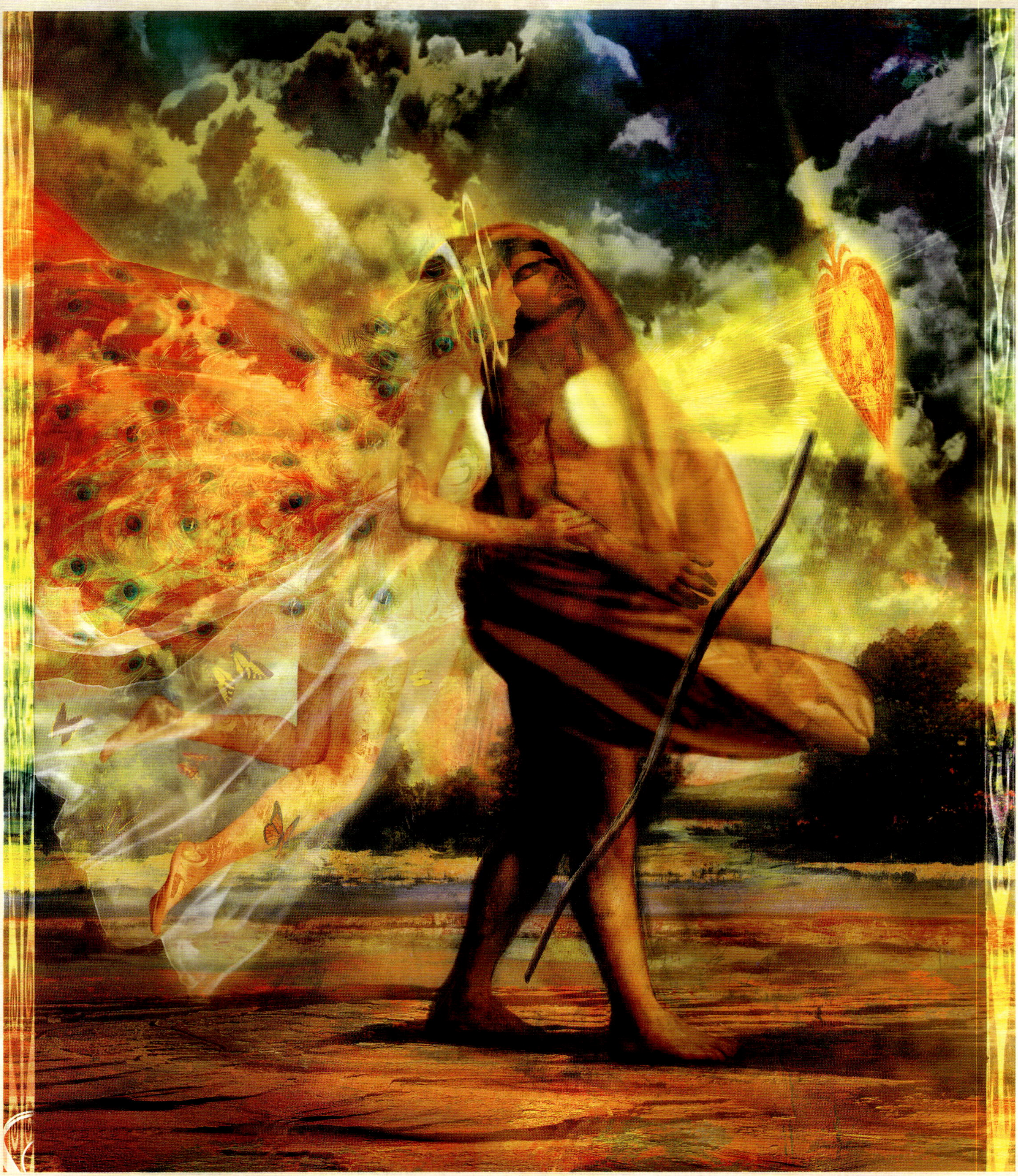

artist: GREG SPALENKA
art director: Anthony Padilla *designer:* Jeff Burne *client:* Art Insitute of Southern California
title: Ignite Thy Passion *size:* 24"x36" *medium:* Mixed/digital

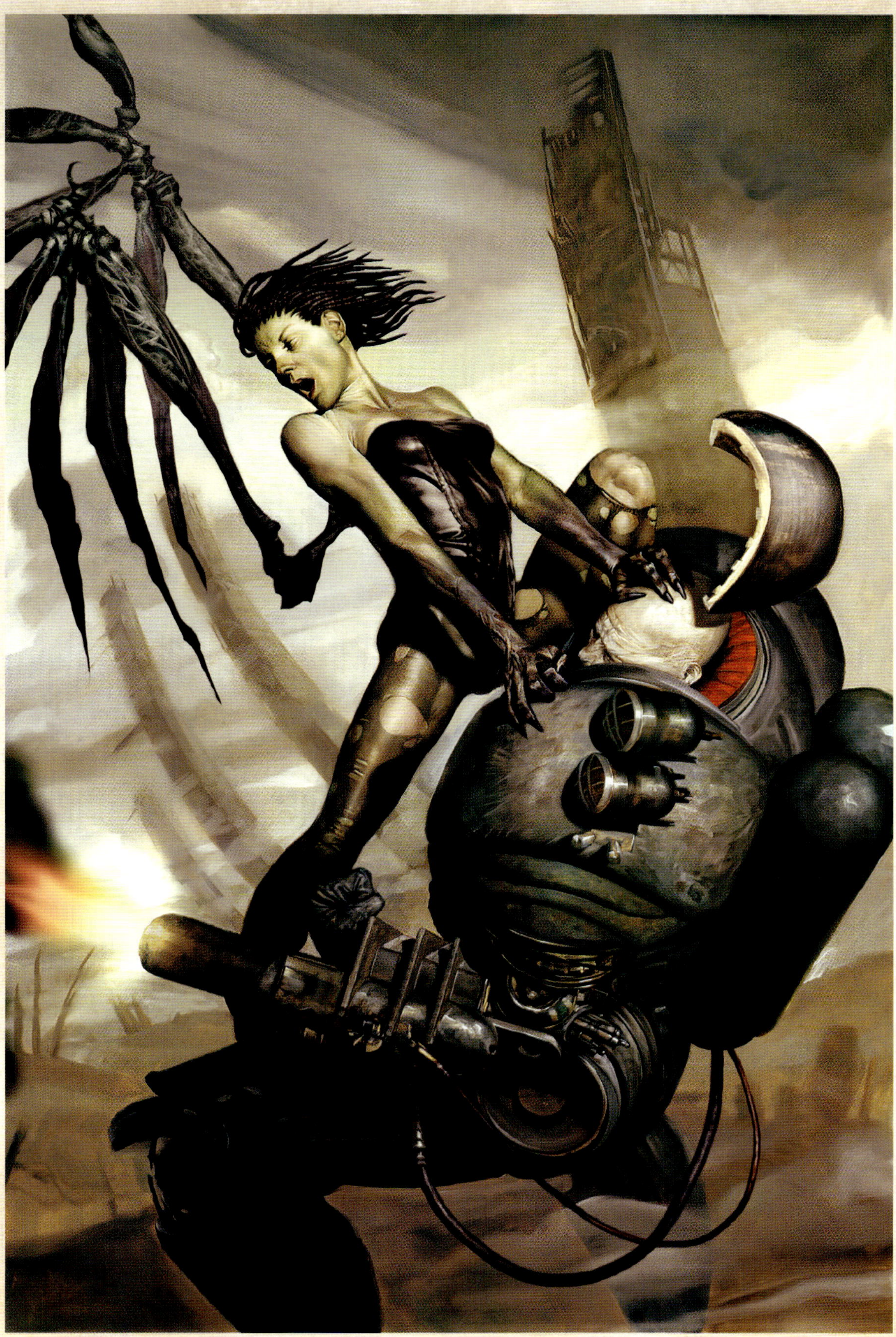

artist: JON FOSTER
art director: Paul Hanchette *client:* TSR *title:* Kerrigan
size: 32"x48" *medium:* Oil/digital

1
artist: MICHAEL MORGENSTERN
art director: Paul Hiscock
client: Adobe
title: Millennium
medium: Mixed/digital
size: 14 1/2"x15"

2
artist: DARREL ANDERSON
client: Braid Media Arts
title: Moon Vault
medium: Digital
size: 12"x30"

3
artist: ASHLEY WOOD
art director: Dawn K. Murin
client: Wizards of the Coast
title: Dark Matter
medium: Digital

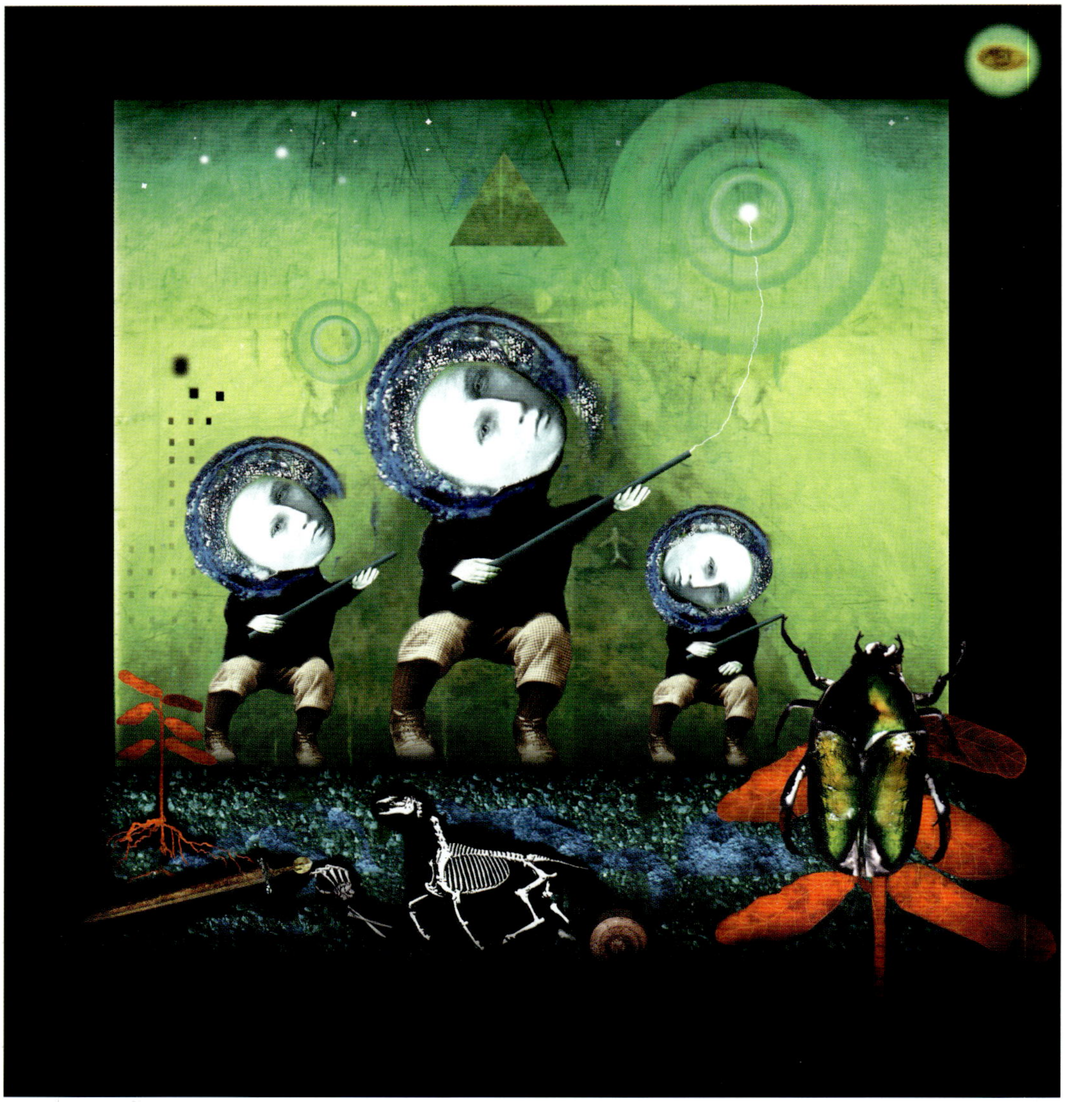

1

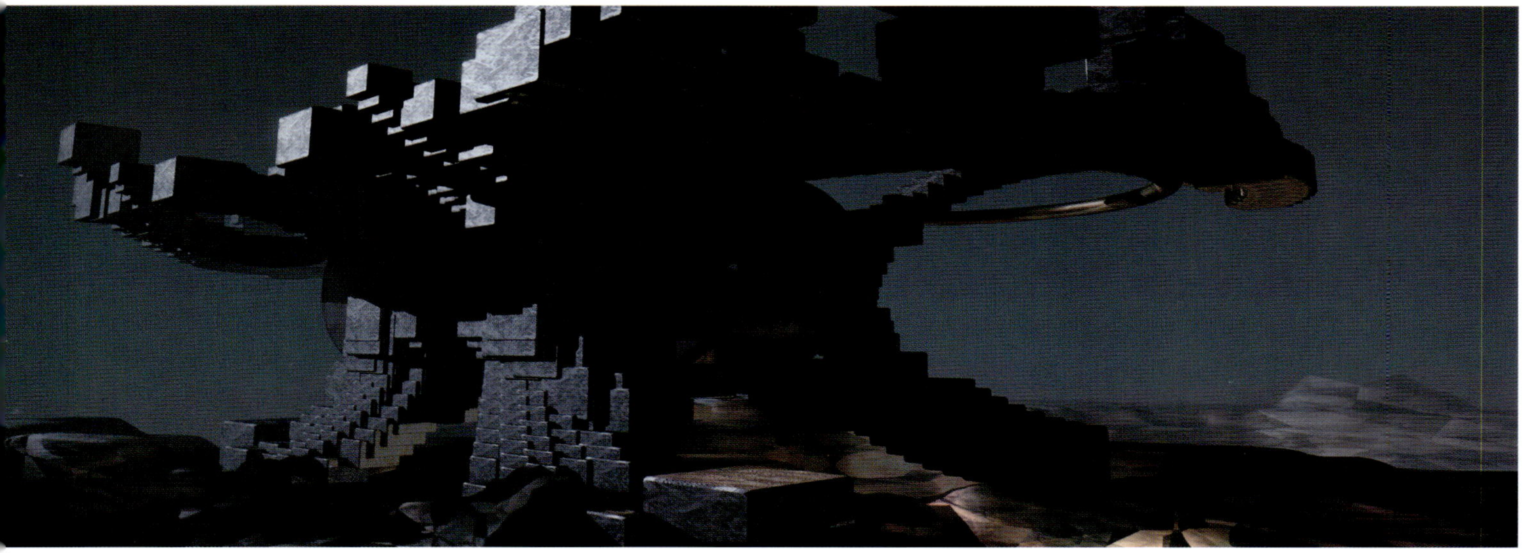

2

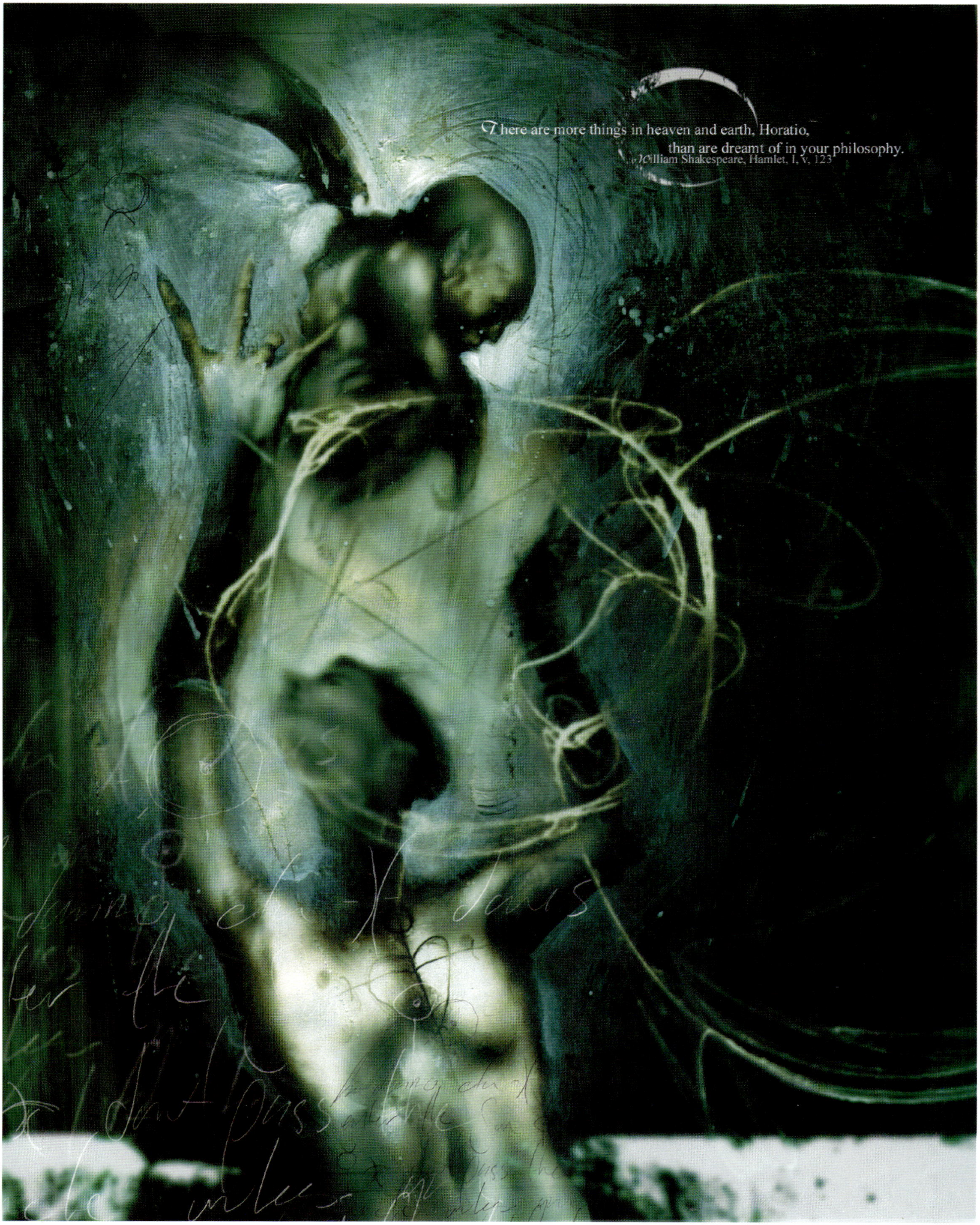
There are more things in heaven and earth, Horatio,
than are dreamt of in your philosophy.
William Shakespeare, Hamlet, I, v, 123

3

1
artist: WILLIAM STOUT &
DAVE STEVENS
art director: Lamar Waldron
designer: William Stout
client: Dragon Con
title: Saurian Sweetie
medium: Ink/watercolor
size: 11"x10"

2
artist: BRADLEY WILLIAMS
designer: Bradley Williams
title: Decieved
medium: Acrylic/oil
size: 11 1/2"x15"

3
artist: WILLIAM STOUT
art director: Richard Trimarchi &
William Stout
designer: William Stout
client: Art Works Fine Art Publishing
title: Wicked Witch of the East
medium: Ink/watercolor
size: 9"x13"

3
artist: WILLIAM STOUT
art director: William Stout
designer: William Stout
client: William Stout, Inc.
title: Winter
medium: Ink/watercolor
size: 7 1/2"x11"

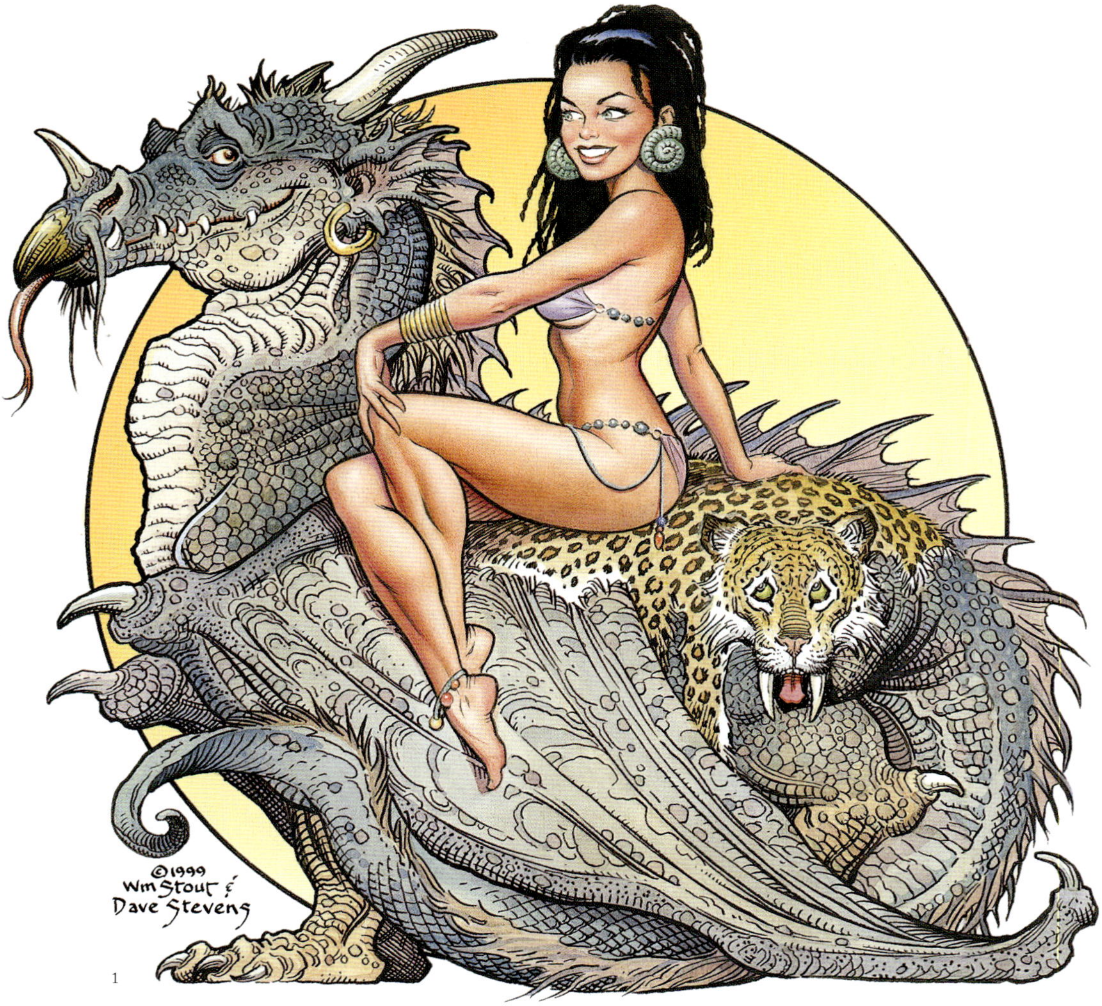

1

2

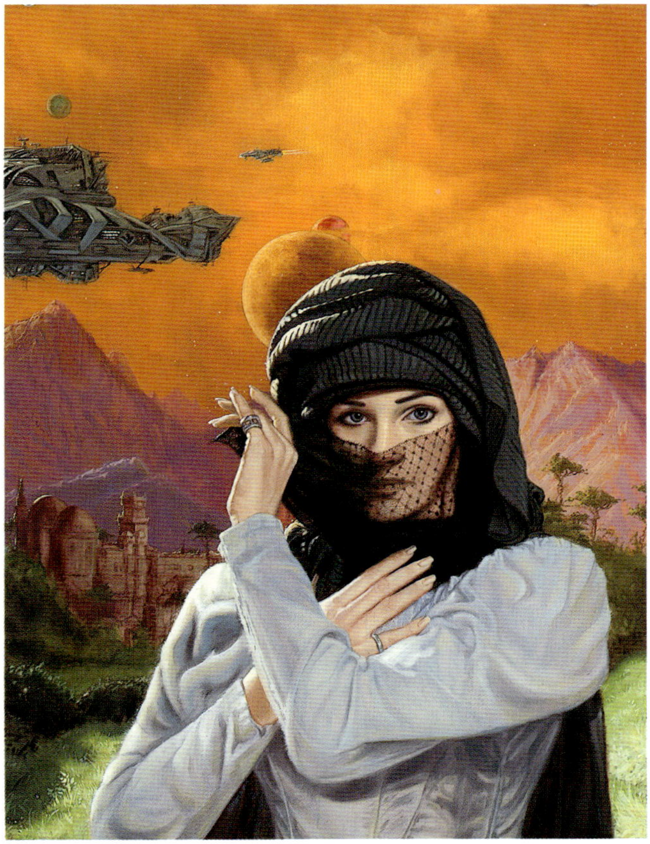

3

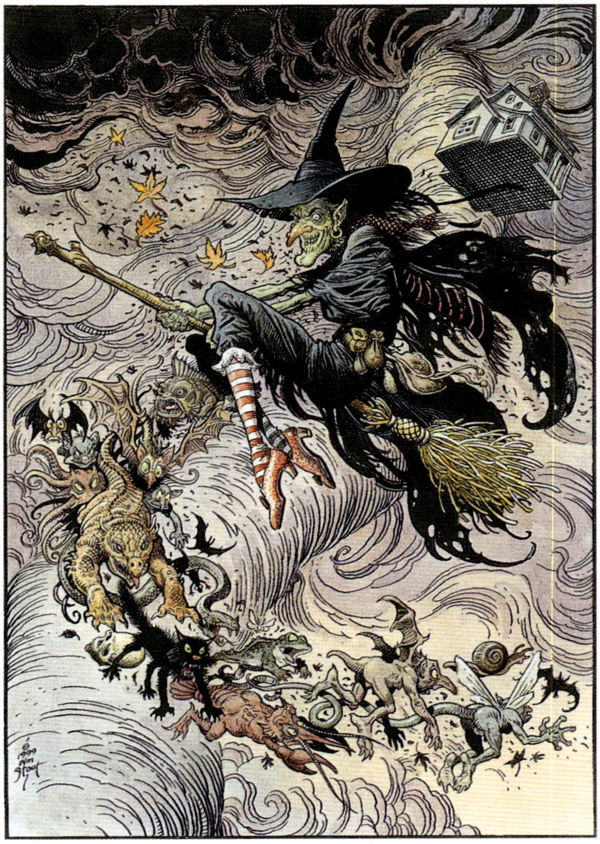

4

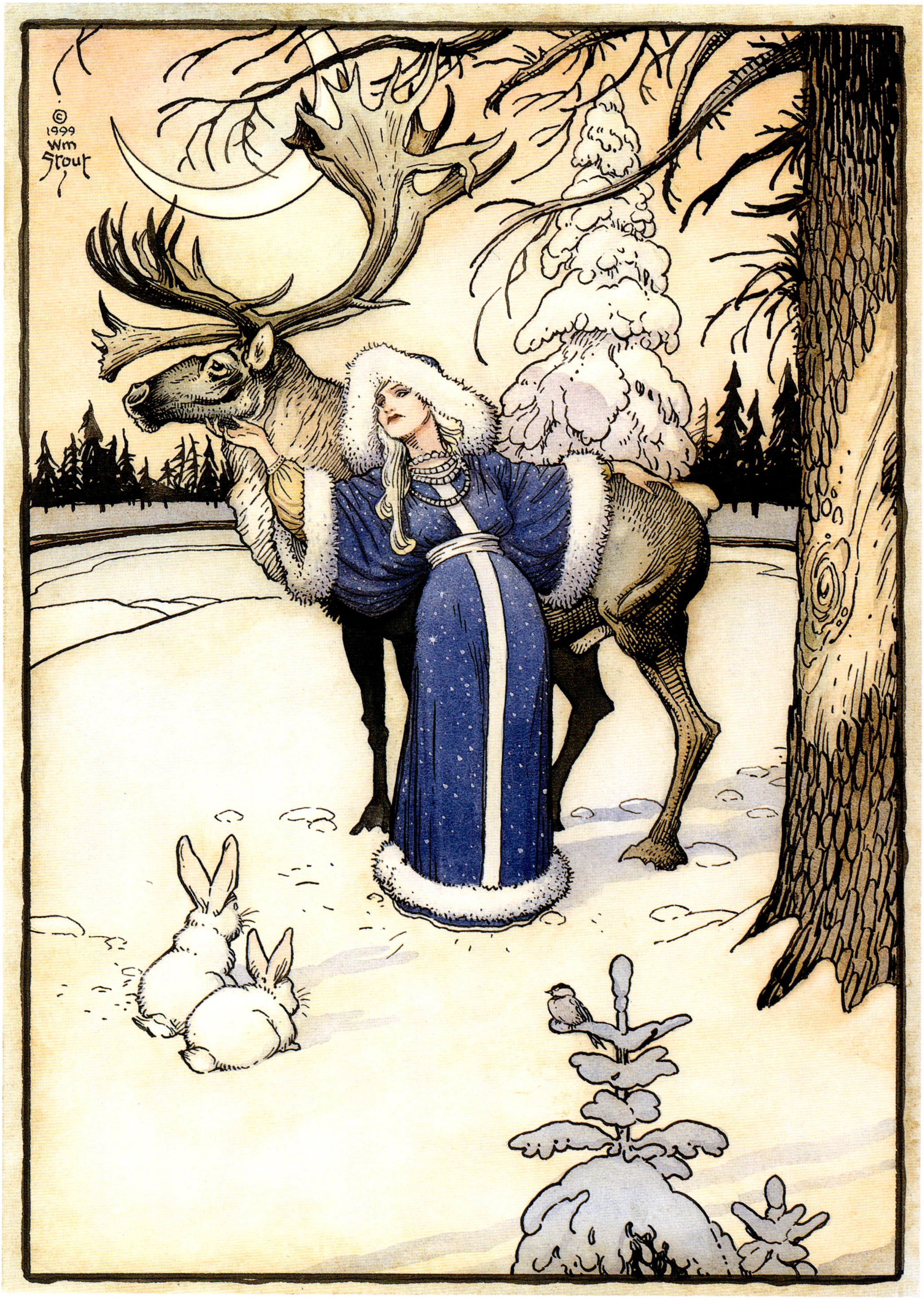

1
artist: MICHAEL SUTFIN
art director: Ron Spears
client: Wizards of the Coast
title: Myths of Magic
medium: Oil

2
artist: TERESE NIELSEN
art director: Larry Snelly
client: White Wolf
title: Changling:
The Enchanted
medium: Acrylic
size: 11"x12"

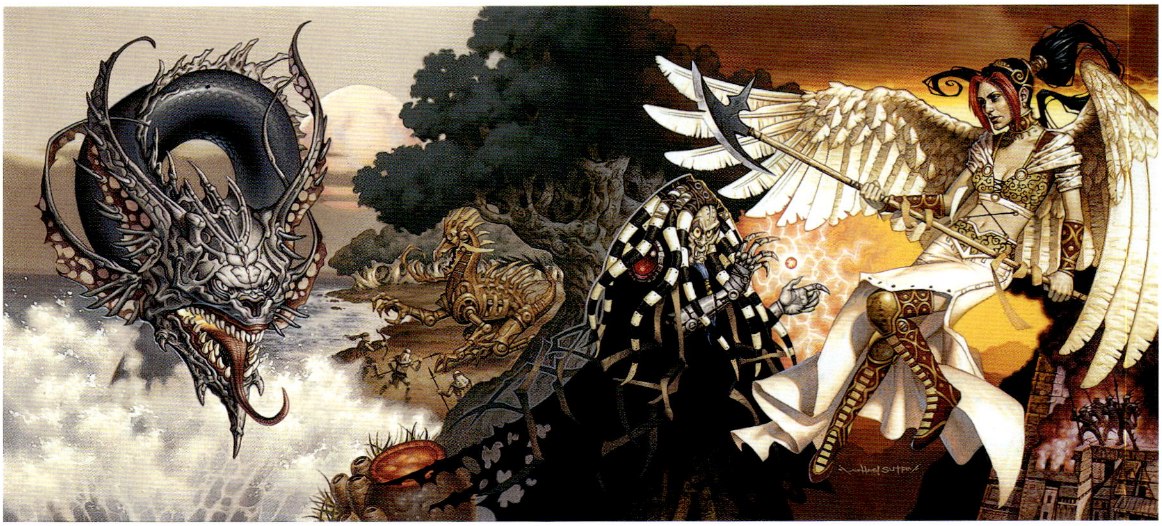

1

2

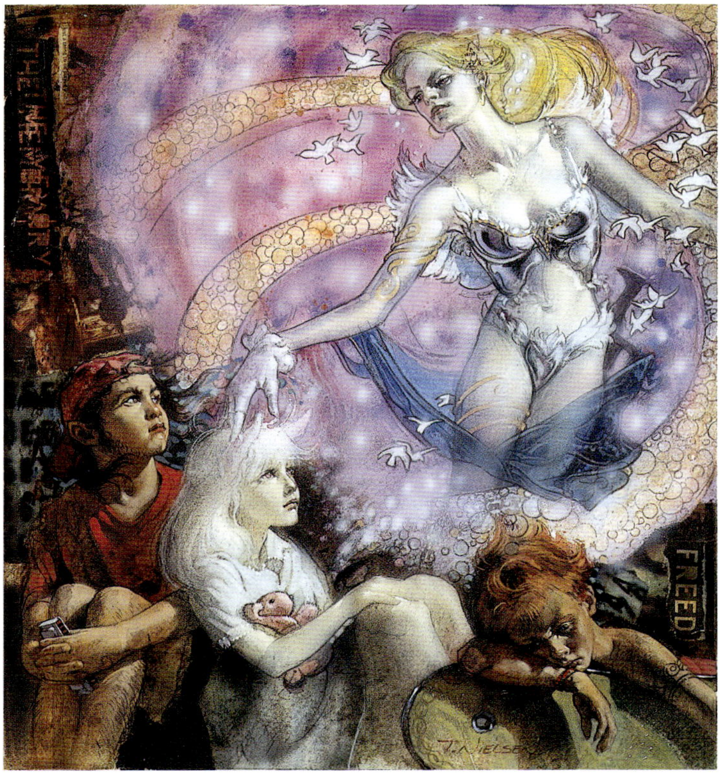

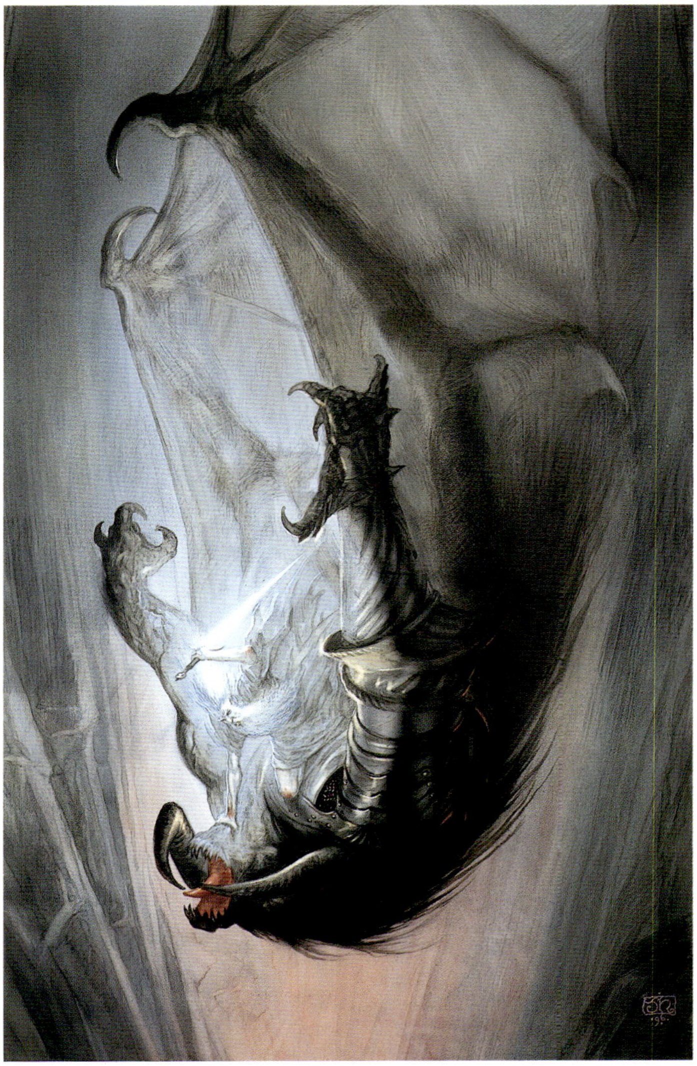

3

3
artist: JOHN HOWE
art director: James Annal
client: HarperCollins
title: Gandalf Falls with the Balrog
medium: Ink/watercolor

4
artist: JOHN HOWE
art director: James Annal
client: HarperCollins
title: Gandalf Fights with the Balrog
medium: Ink/watercolor

4

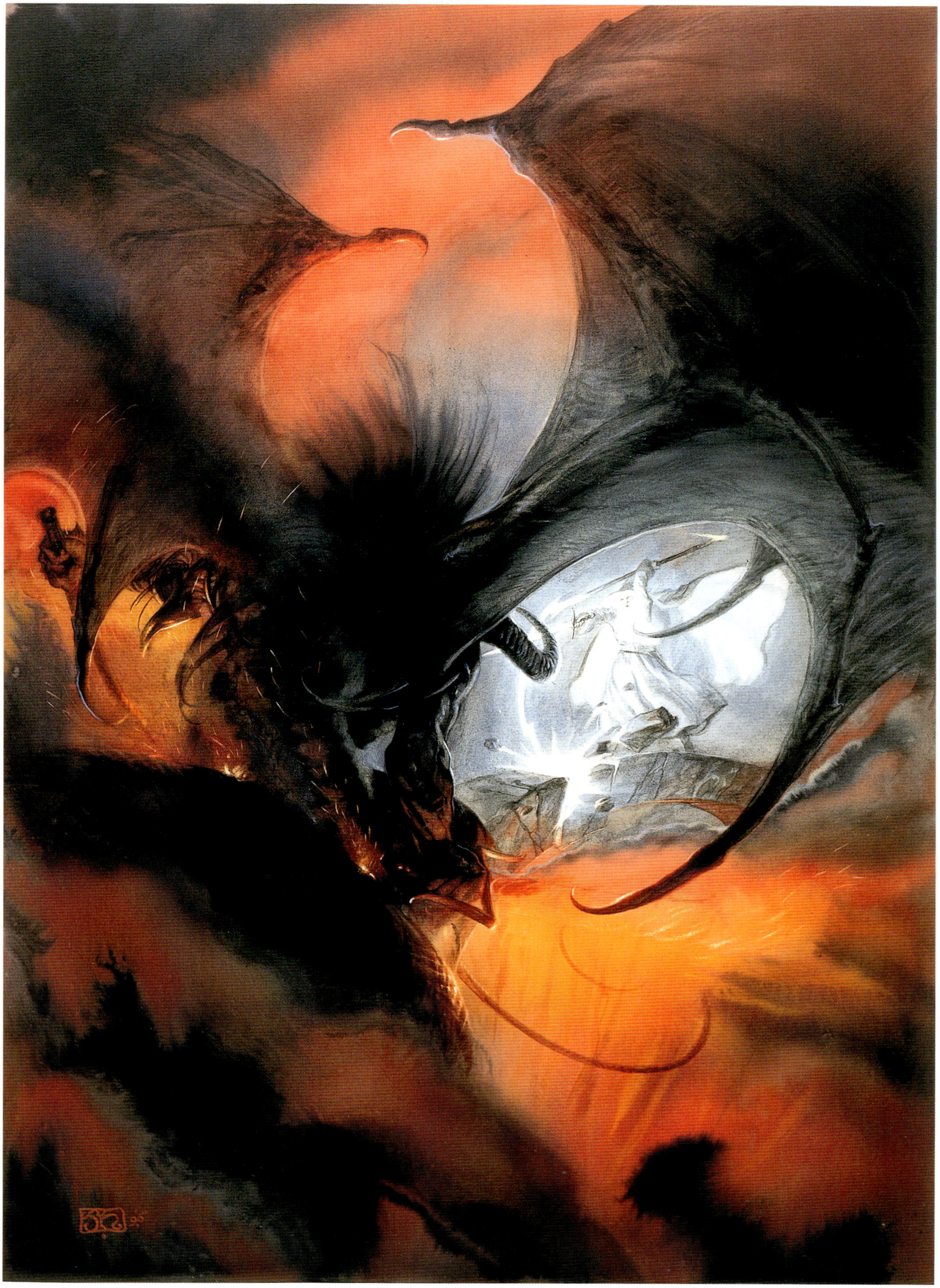

1
artist: ANDY LACKOW
art director: Andy Lackow
title: Island of Yorum
medium: DIGITAL
size: 14"x11"

2
artist: COREY D. MACOUREK
title: Faith
medium: Digital
size: 20"x20"

3
artist: RAYMOND SWANLAND
art director: Lorne Lanning
client: Oddworld Inhabitants
title: Oddworld: Hand of Odd logo
medium: Digital

4
artist: RICK BERRY
art director: Rick Berry
client: Braid Media Arts
title: Tardigrade
medium: Mixed/digital

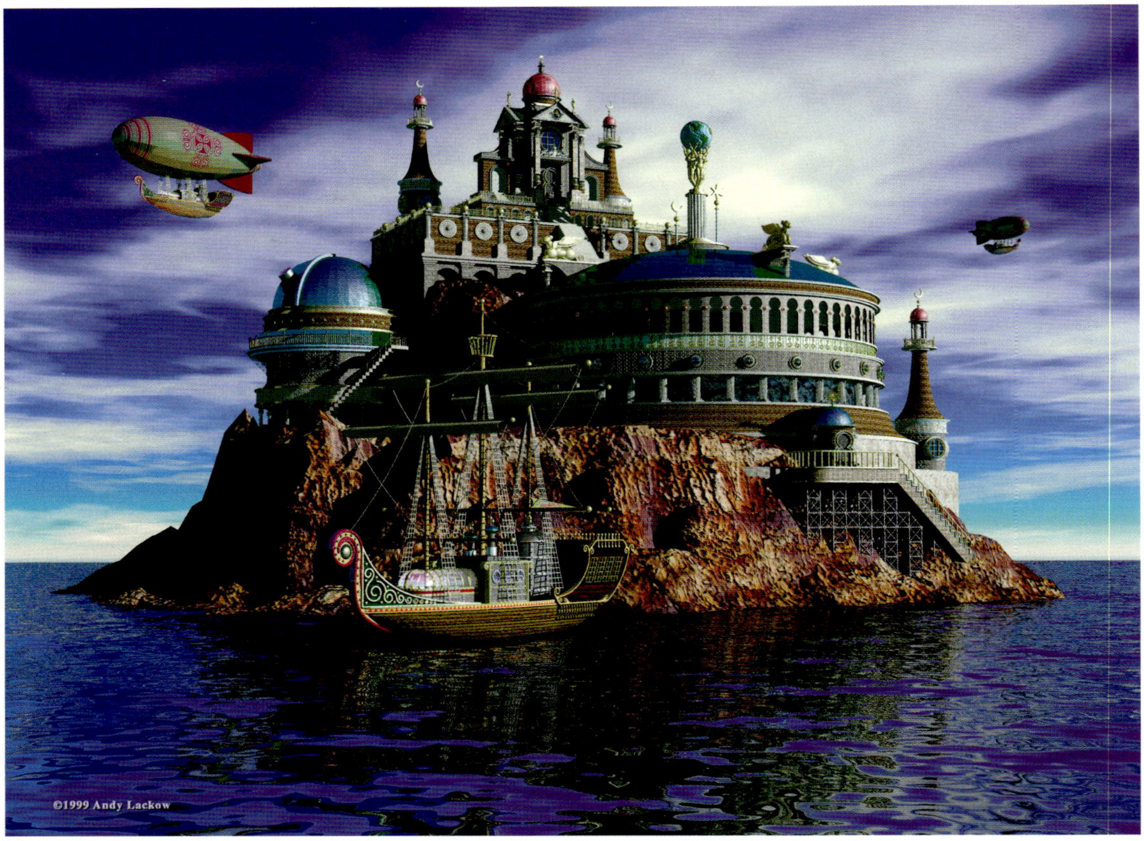

1

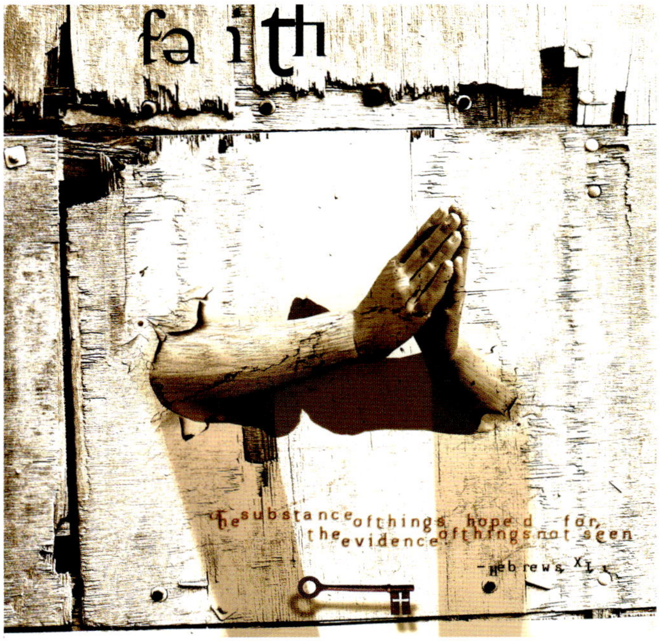

2

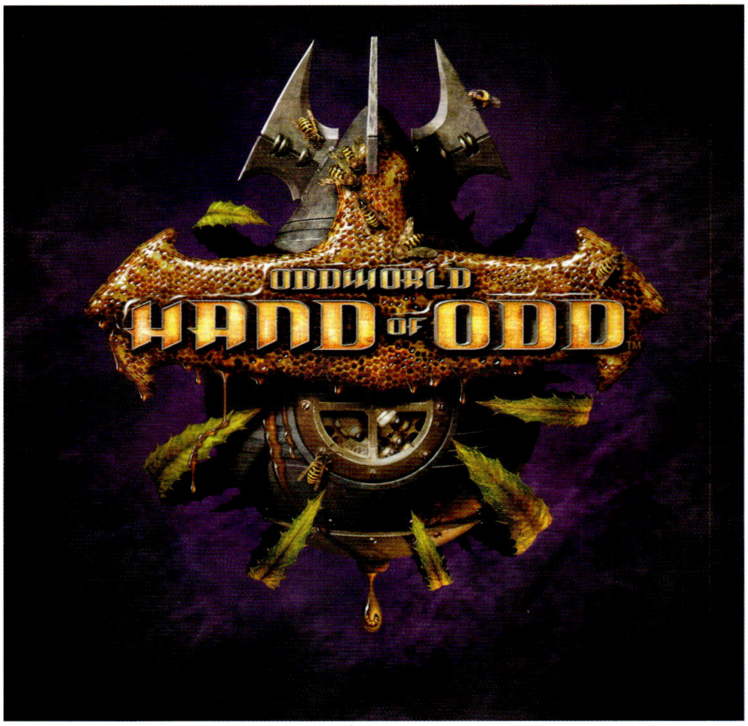

3

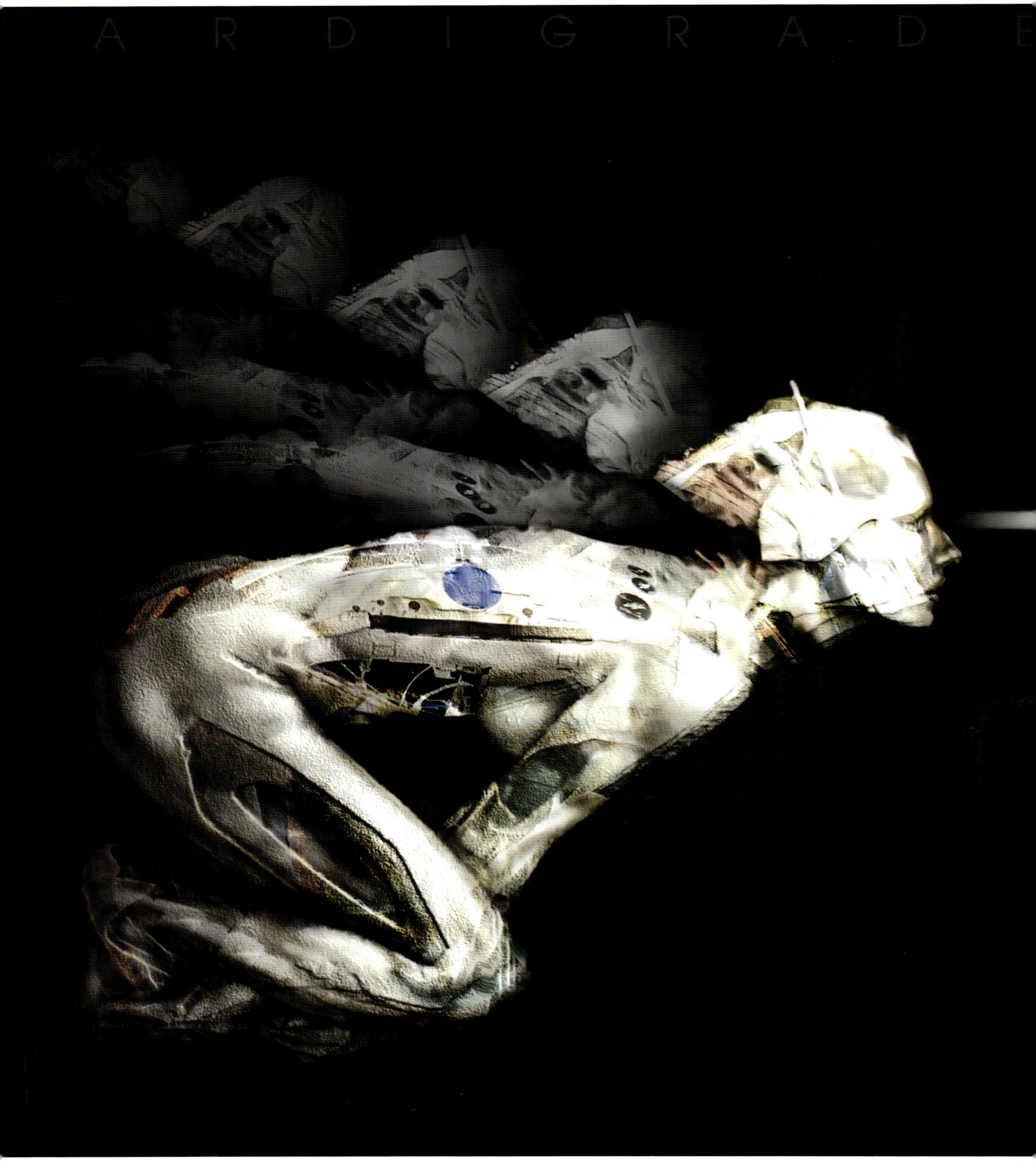

4

1
artist: CHRIS GALL
art director: Mark Murphy
client: Mark Murphy Design
title: Jeb's Surprise
medium: Scratchboard/digital
size: 12"x12"

2
artist: JOSEPH PAGE KOVACH
art director: Joseph Page Kovach
designer: Joseph Page Kovach
client: American Showcase
title: Where There's Smoke...
medium: Mixed
size: 9"x12"

3
artist: BRIAN DESPAIN
client: Eli 5 Stone
title: My Oal Enigma
medium: Pencil
size: 7"x9"

4
artist: OWEN RICHARDSON
art director: Kellan Hatch
client: GT Interactive
title: Ratman
medium: Mixed/digital

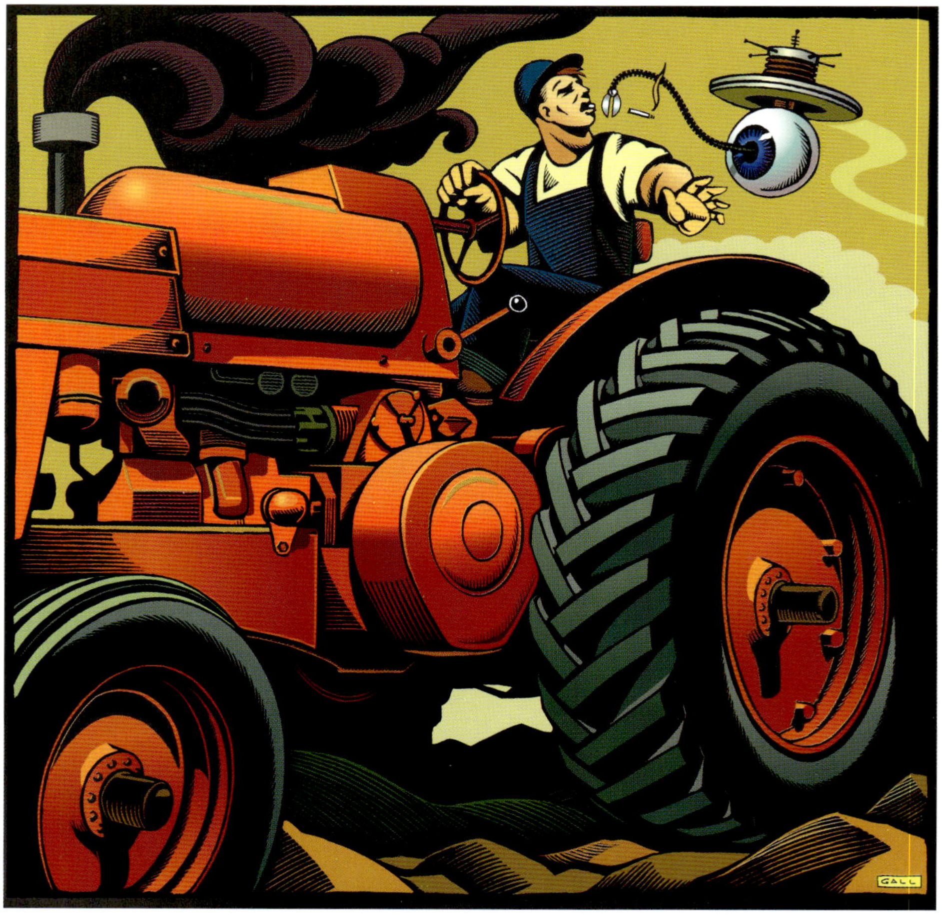

1

2

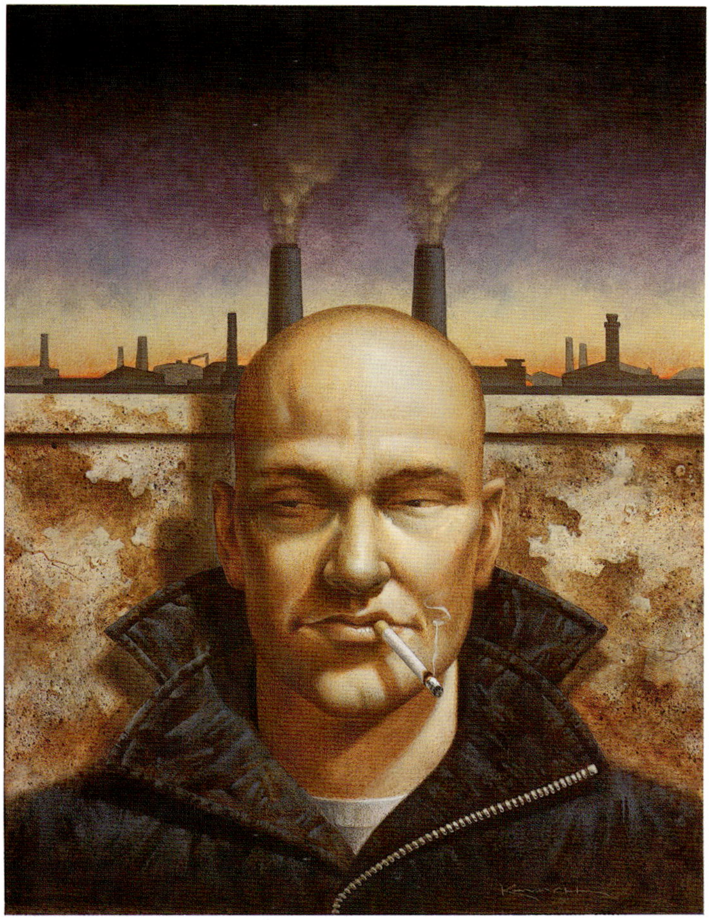

3

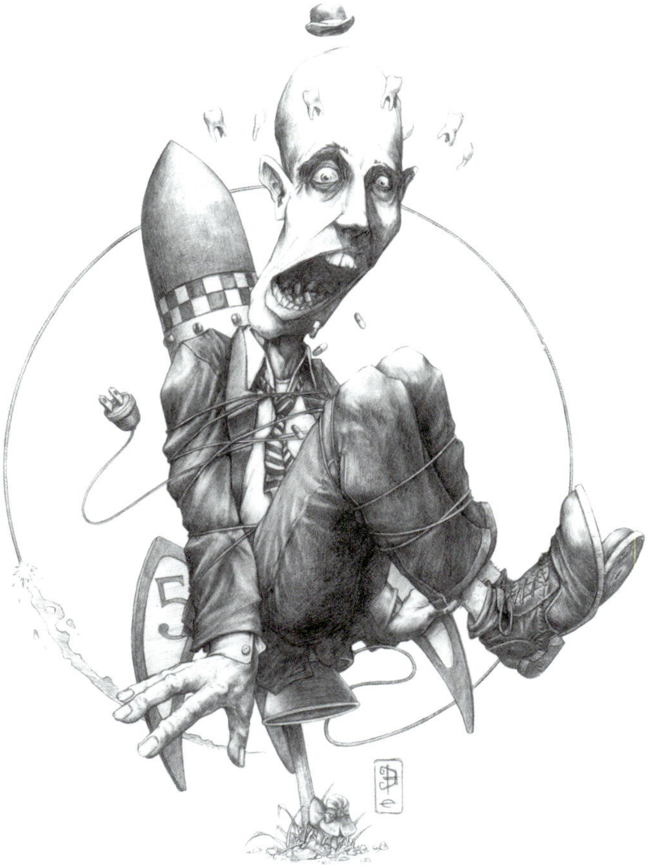

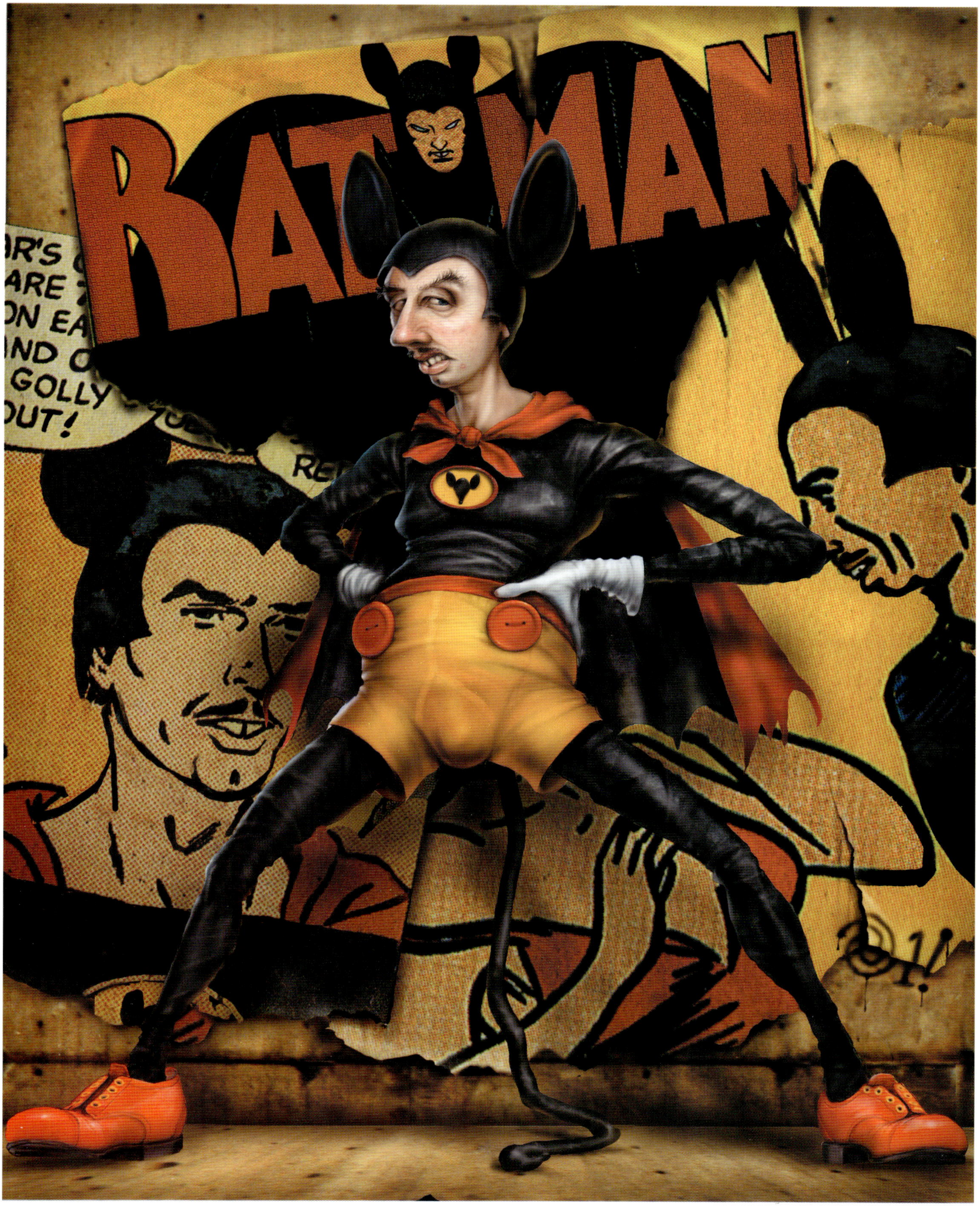

4

1
artist: DOUGLAS KLAUBA
title: Mercury Jack
medium: Acrylic
size: 20"x13"

2
artist: RK POST
art director: Ron Spears
client: Magic the Gathering
title: Unmask
medium: Oil
size: 18"x24"

3
artist: ERIC BOWMAN
title: Free At last,
Free At Last
medium: Oil
size: 18"x22"

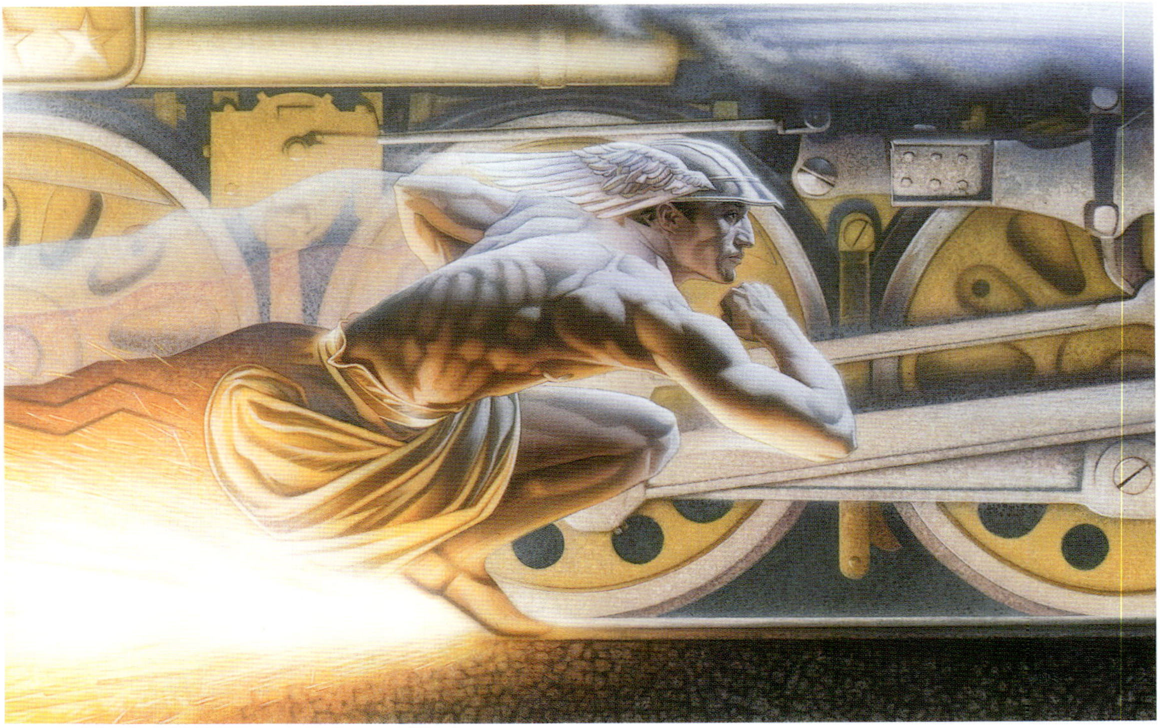

1

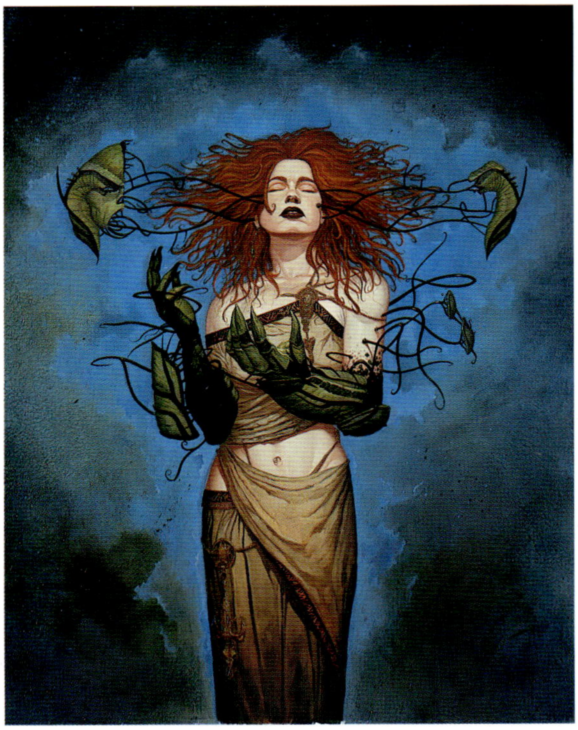

2

4
artist: MICHAEL BOHBOT
art director: Michael Bohbot
designer: Michael Bohbot
client: San Francisco Society of Illustrators
title: The Seer
medium: Acrylic/digital
size: 9"x12"

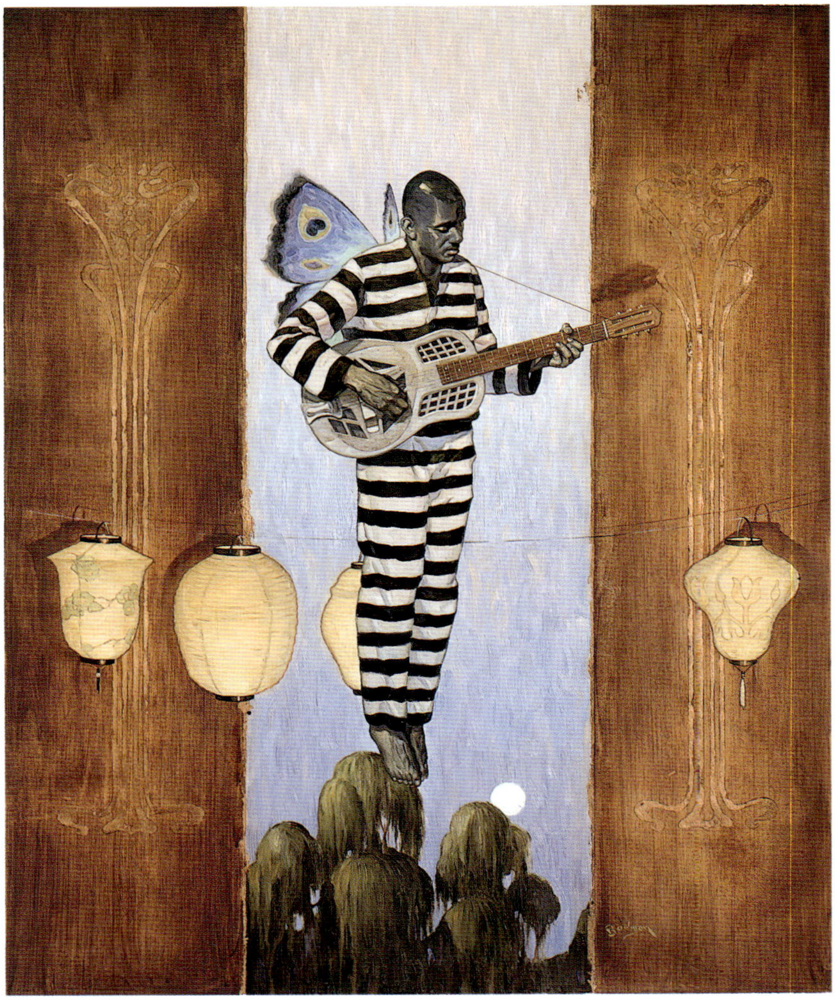

3

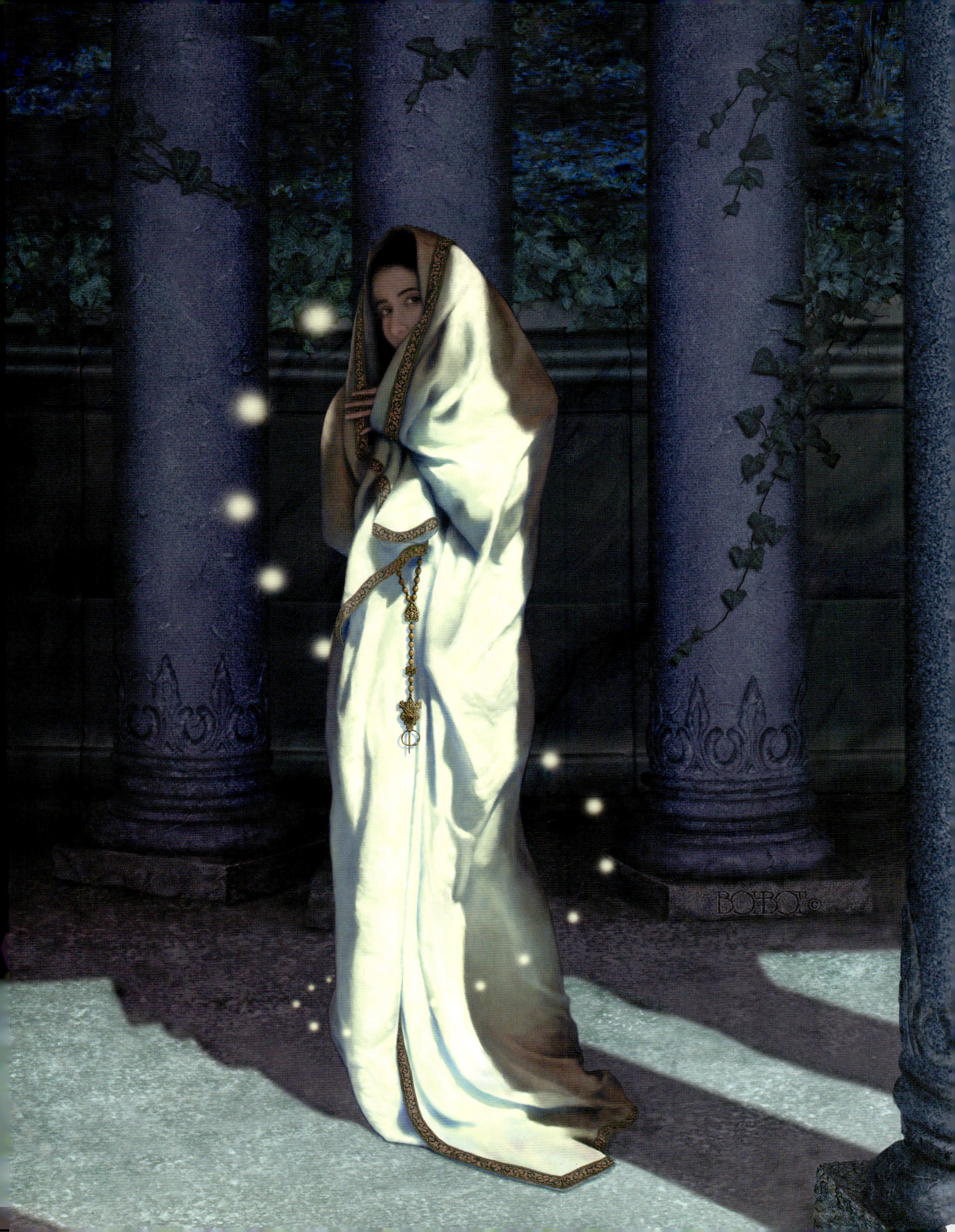
BOYBOT©

1
artist: CHARLES FRIZZELL
designer: Helstrom Studios
client: Visionary Publishing
title: Arrival of the Messenger
medium: Mixed *size:* 18"x14"

2
artist: MARC GABBANA
title: Battebots
medium: Acrylic *size:* 36"x19"

3
artist: RICK BERRY
title: Silver Tongue
medium: Mixed/digital

4
artist: JON FOSTER
art director: Paul Hanchette
client: TSR
title: To the Rescue
medium: Oil/digital *size:* 32"x48"

5
artist: OWEN RICHARDSON
art director: Kellan Hatch
client: GT Interactive
title: Necrobot
medium: Mixed/digital

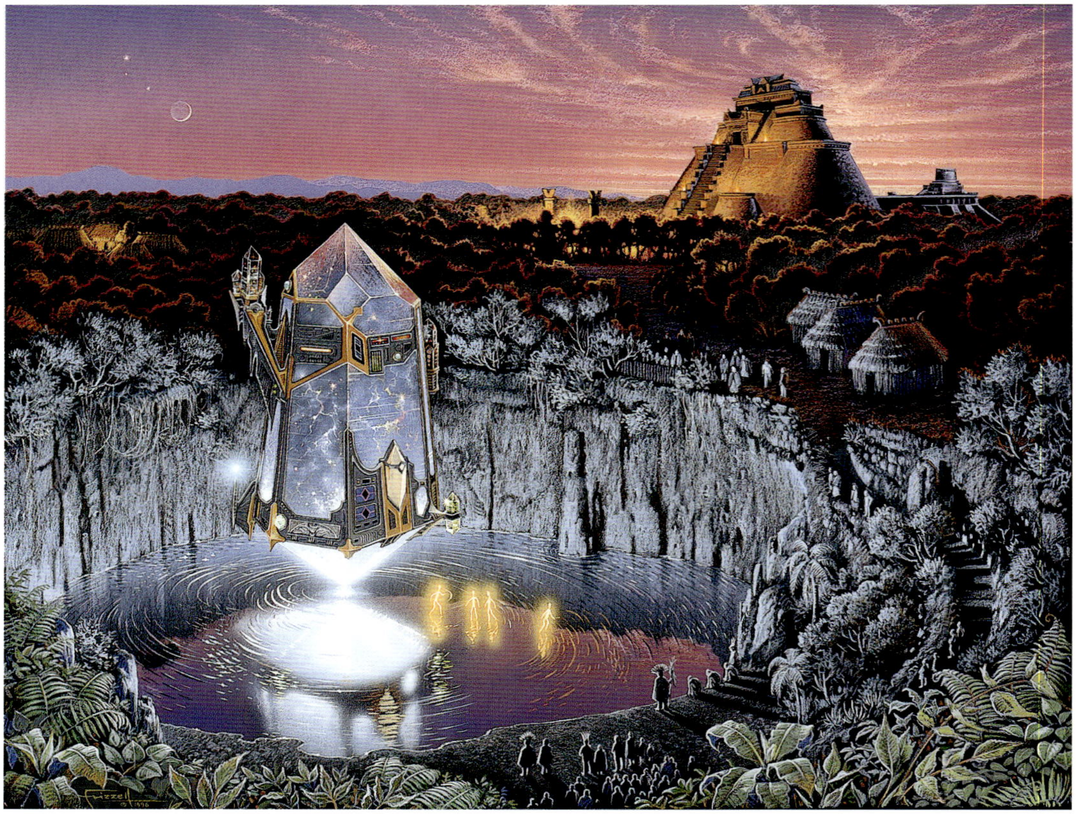

1

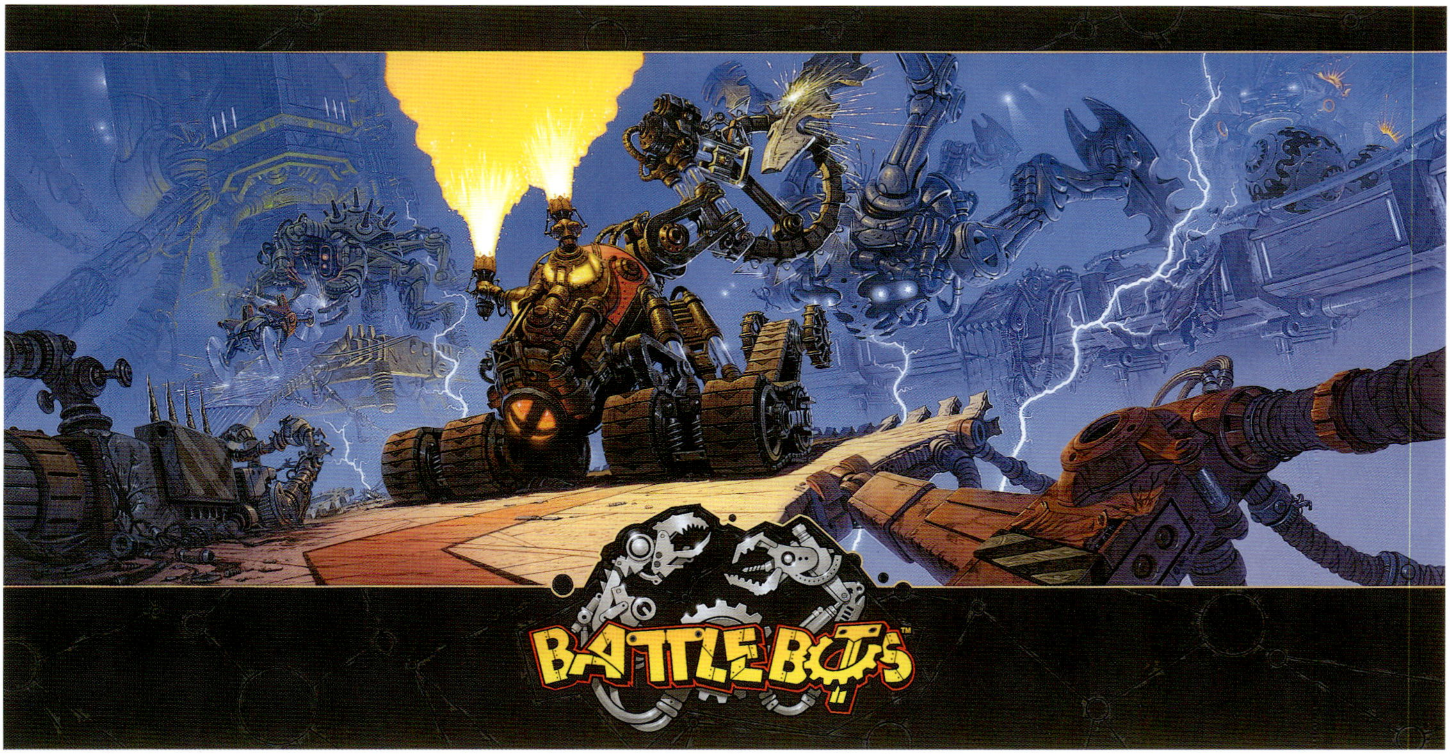

2

6
artist: RICK BERRY
art director: Rick Berry
designer: Ron Spears
client: Wizards of the Coast
title: Jump
medium: Oil
size: 30"x40"

3

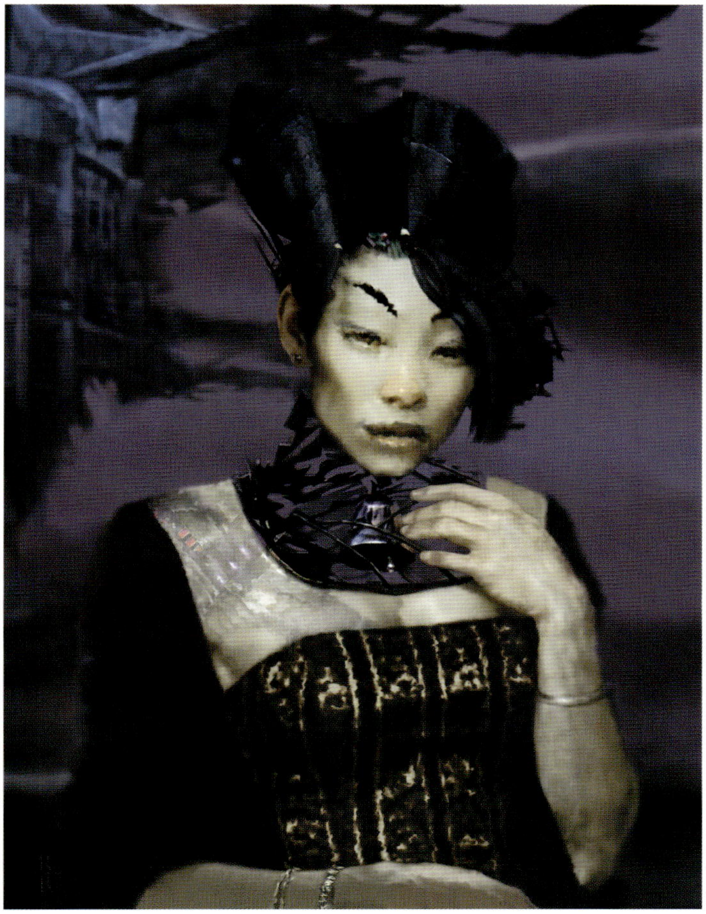

4

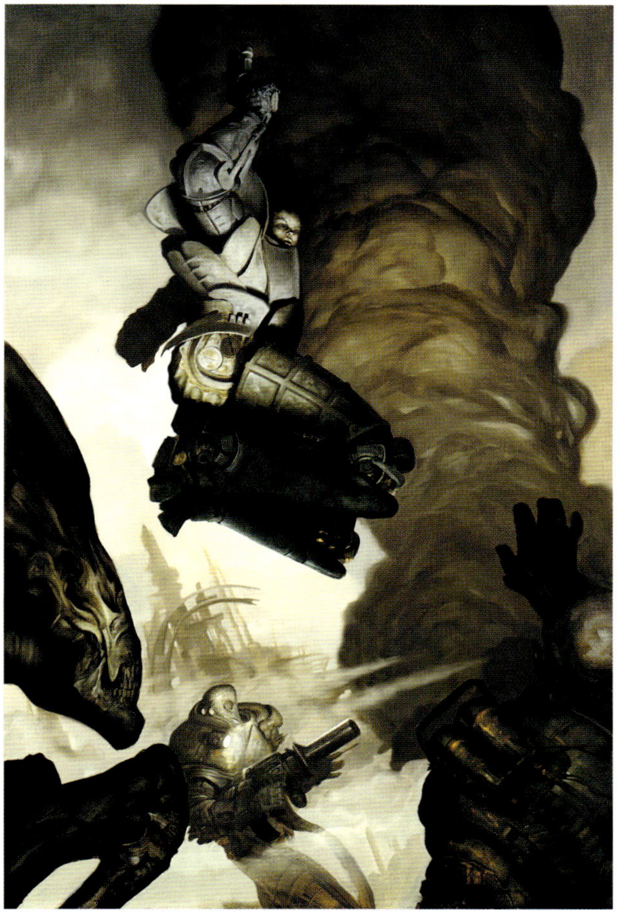

5

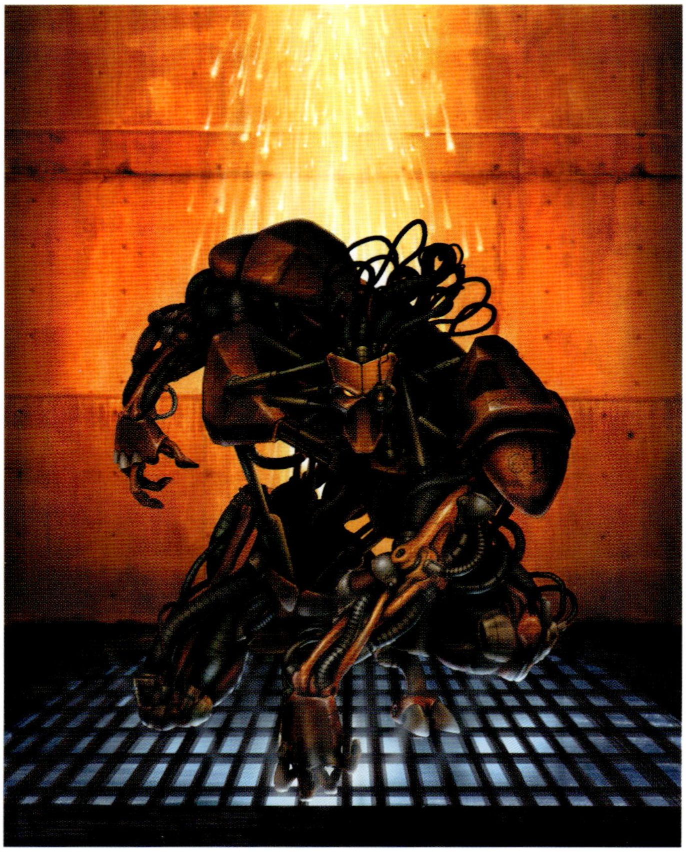

6

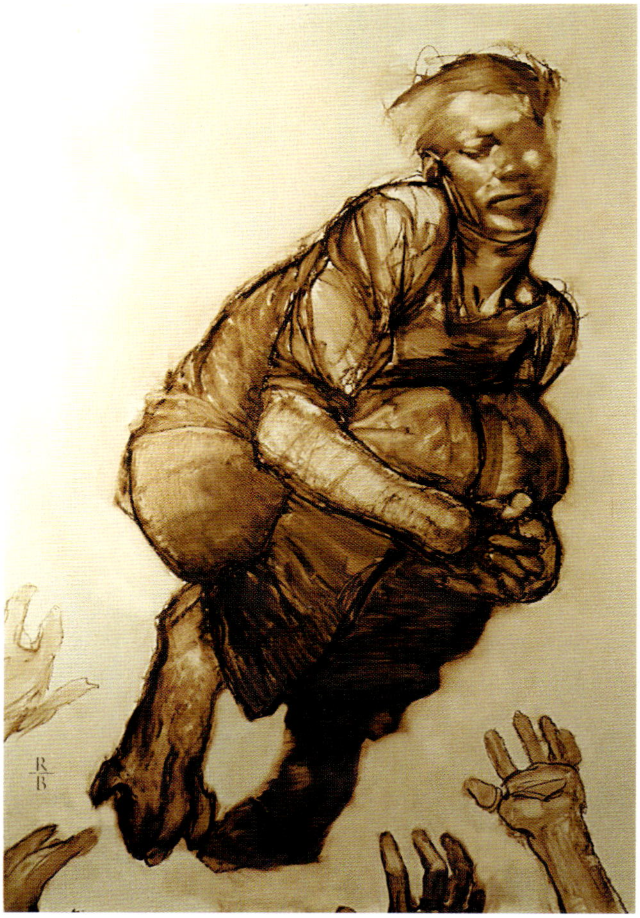

1
artist: DOUG GRAY
designer: Doug Gray
title: Succubus 2
medium: Mixed
size: 9 1/2" diameter

2
artist: CARL LUNDGREN
client: Carl Lundgren Studios
title: Autumn
medium: Oil
size: 32"x32"

3
artist: GRIESBACH/MARTUCCI
art director: Joni Friedmen
designer: Stanley Martucci
client: Bernstein & Andriulli
medium: Oil
size: 18"x24"

4
artist: RK POST
art director: Paul Hanchette
client: Wizards of the Coast
title: Klick Klack
medium: Oil
size: 11"x14"

1

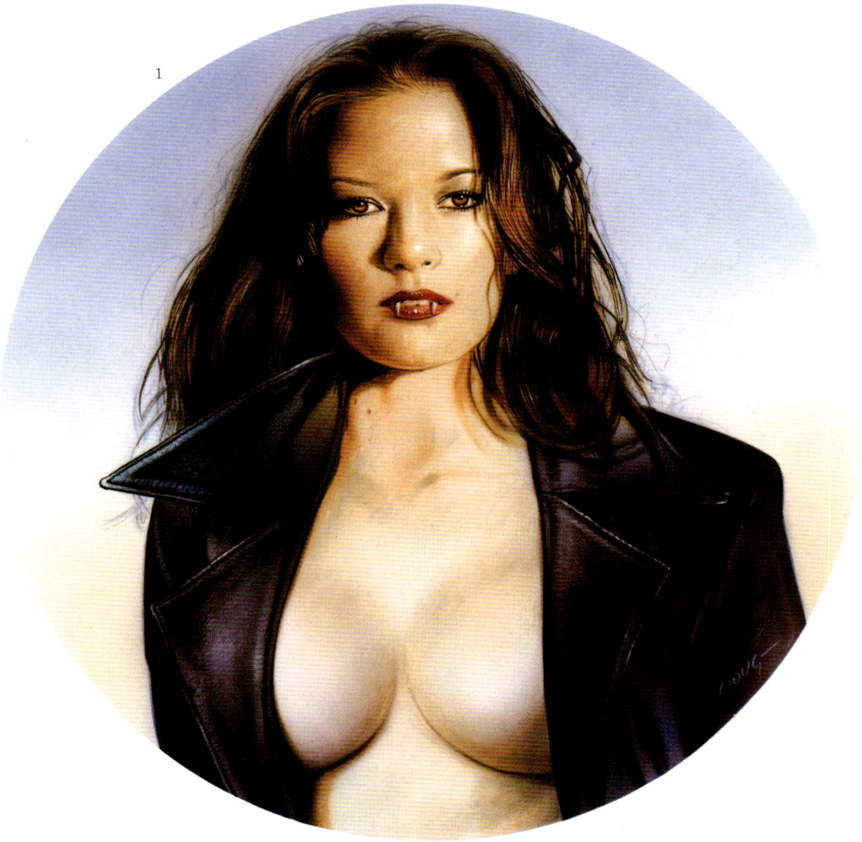

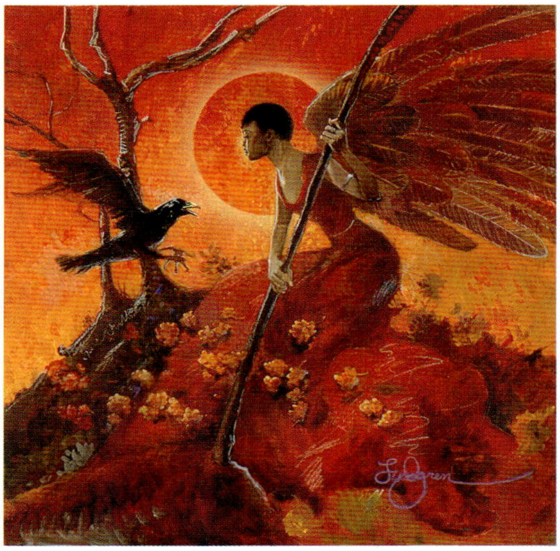

2

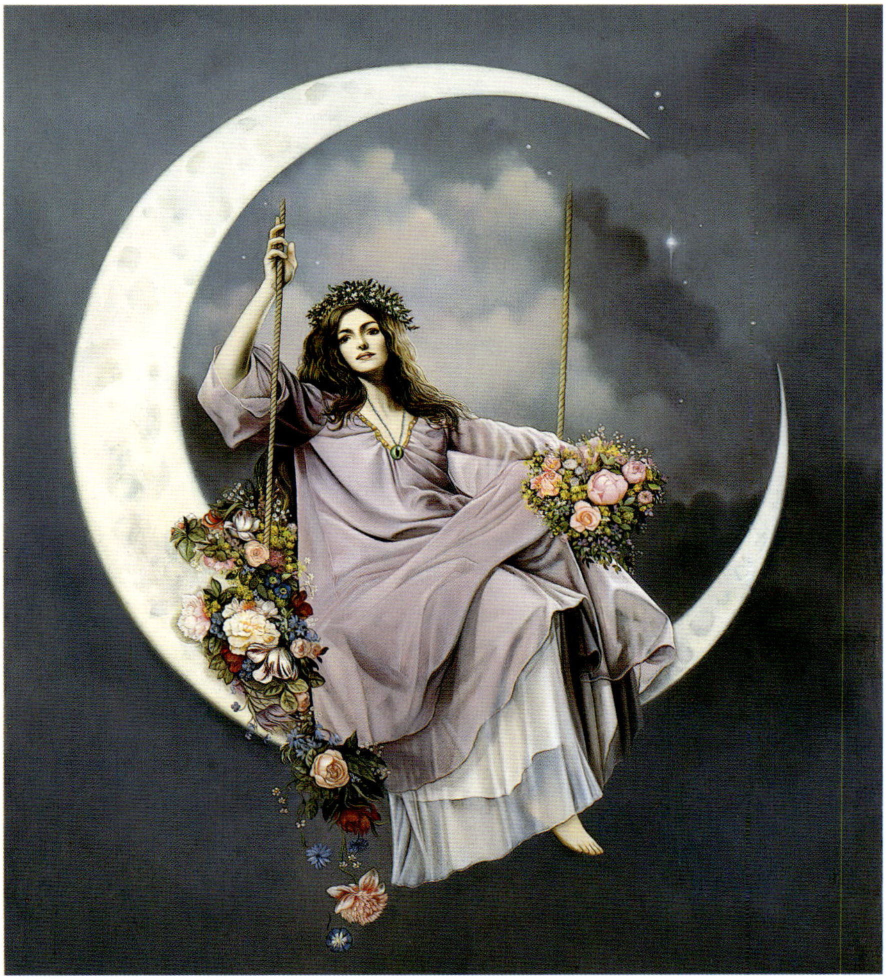

3

4

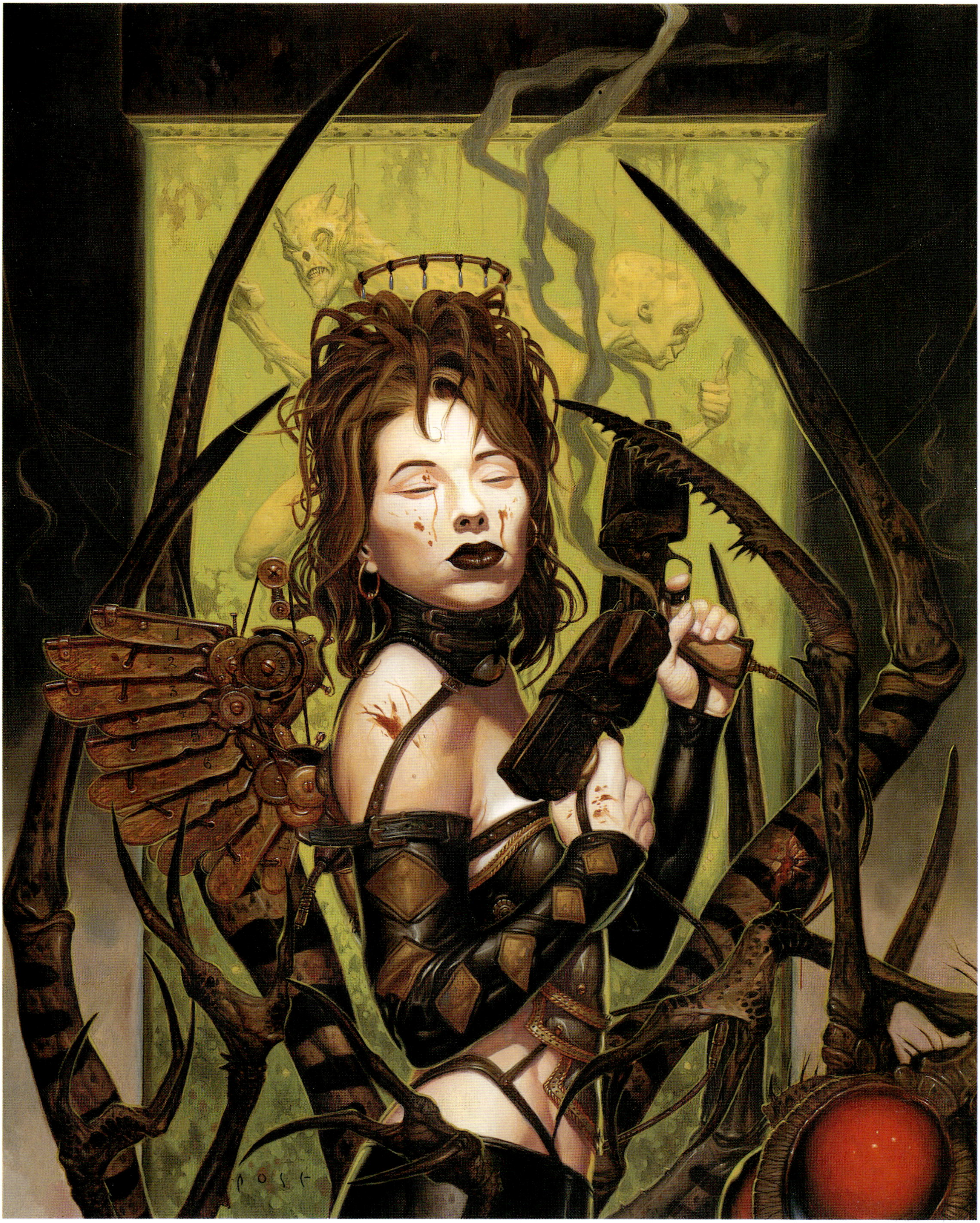

1
artist: RON SPEARS
art director: Ron Spears
client: Wizards of the Coast
title: Rags
medium: Oil
size: 10"x8"

2
artist: KEN WESTPHAL
art director: Ken Westphal
designer: Jason Hungate
client: Heartland Community Church
title: Mask of the Great Deceiver
medium: Acrylic
size: 8 1/2"x10 1/2"

3
artist: RAY-MEL CORNELIUS
client: Those 3 Reps
title: She May Be A Mermaid
medium: Acrylic

4
artist: TRAVIS A. LOUIE
art director: Travis A. Louie
title: Chester's 4:00 Repose
medium: Acrylic/ink
size: 30"x40"

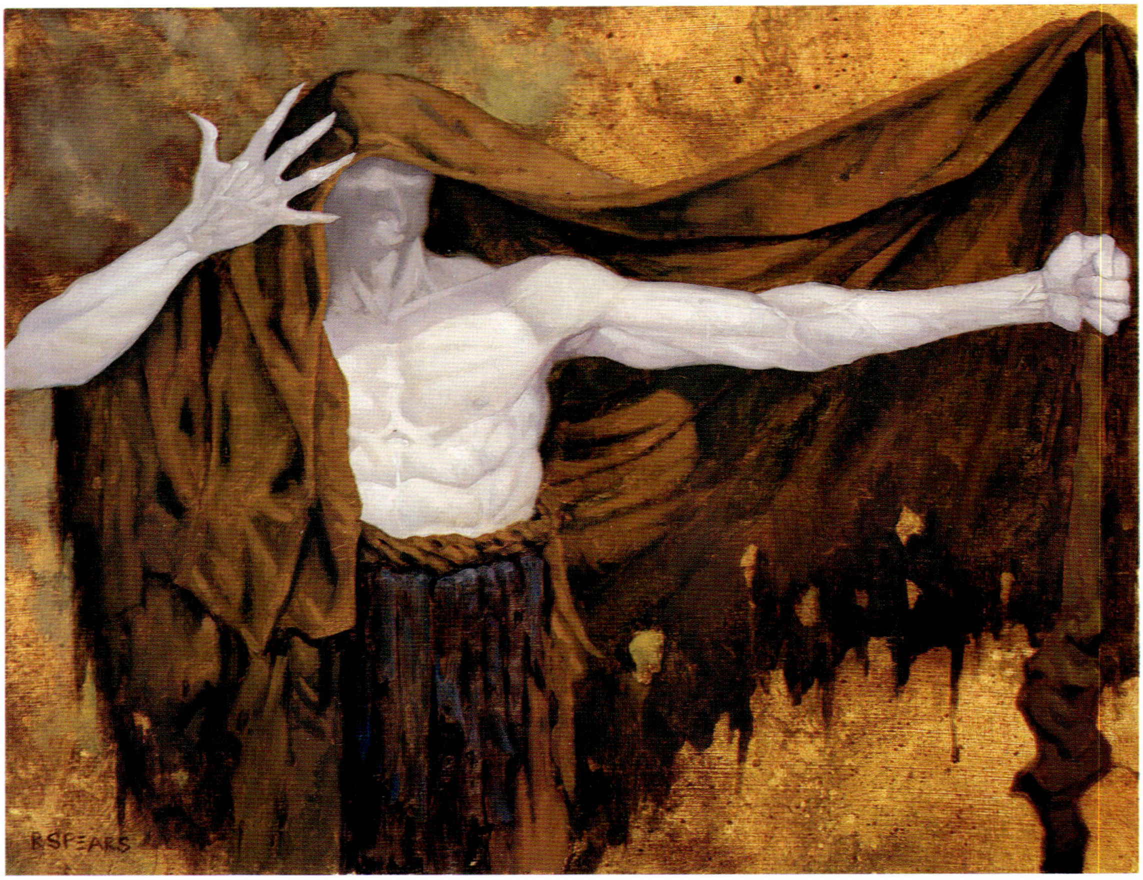

1

2

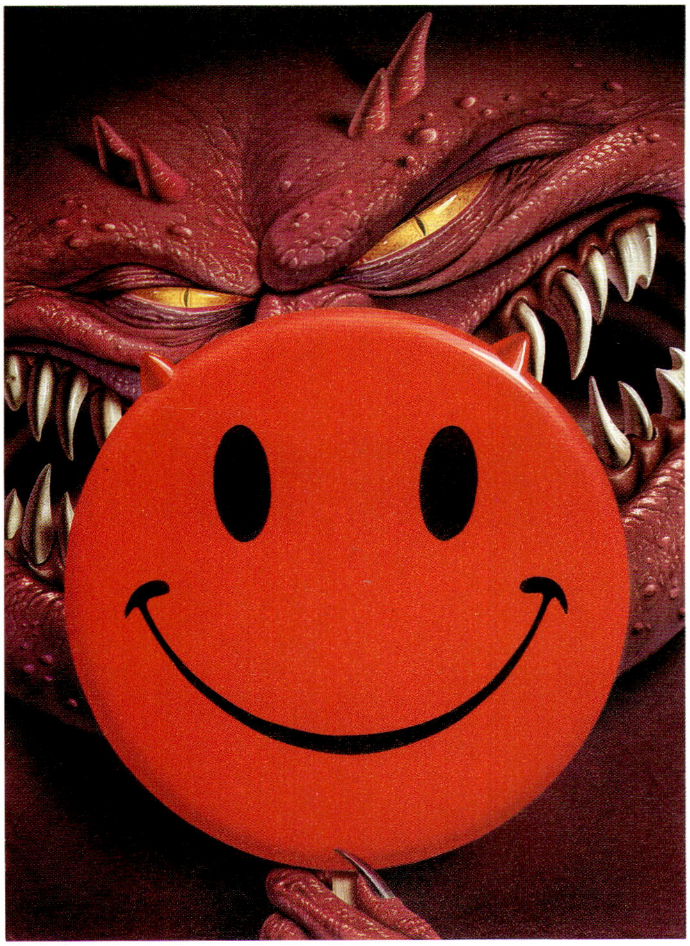

3

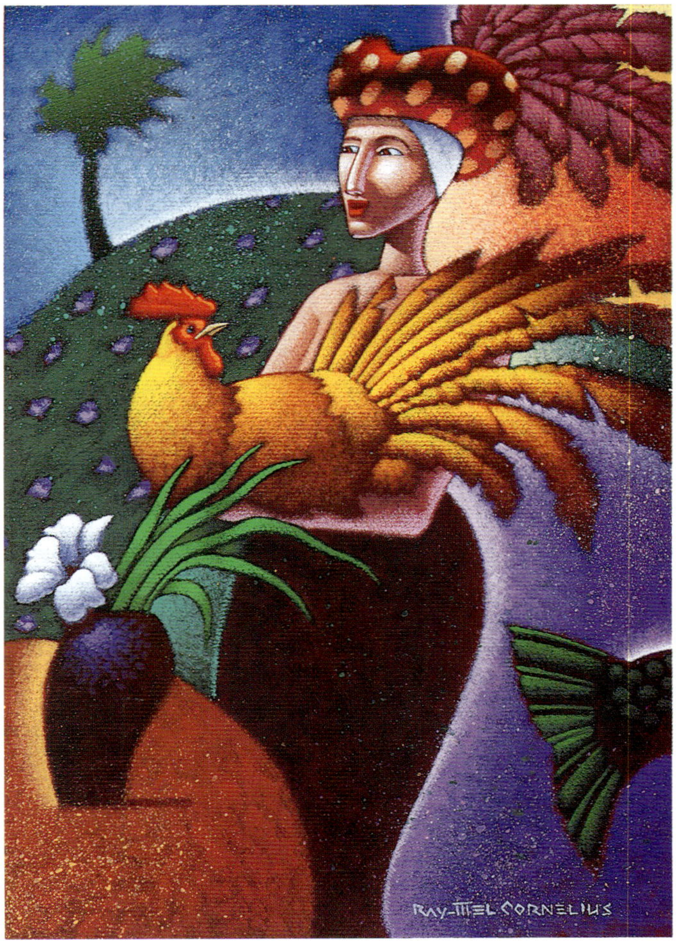

4

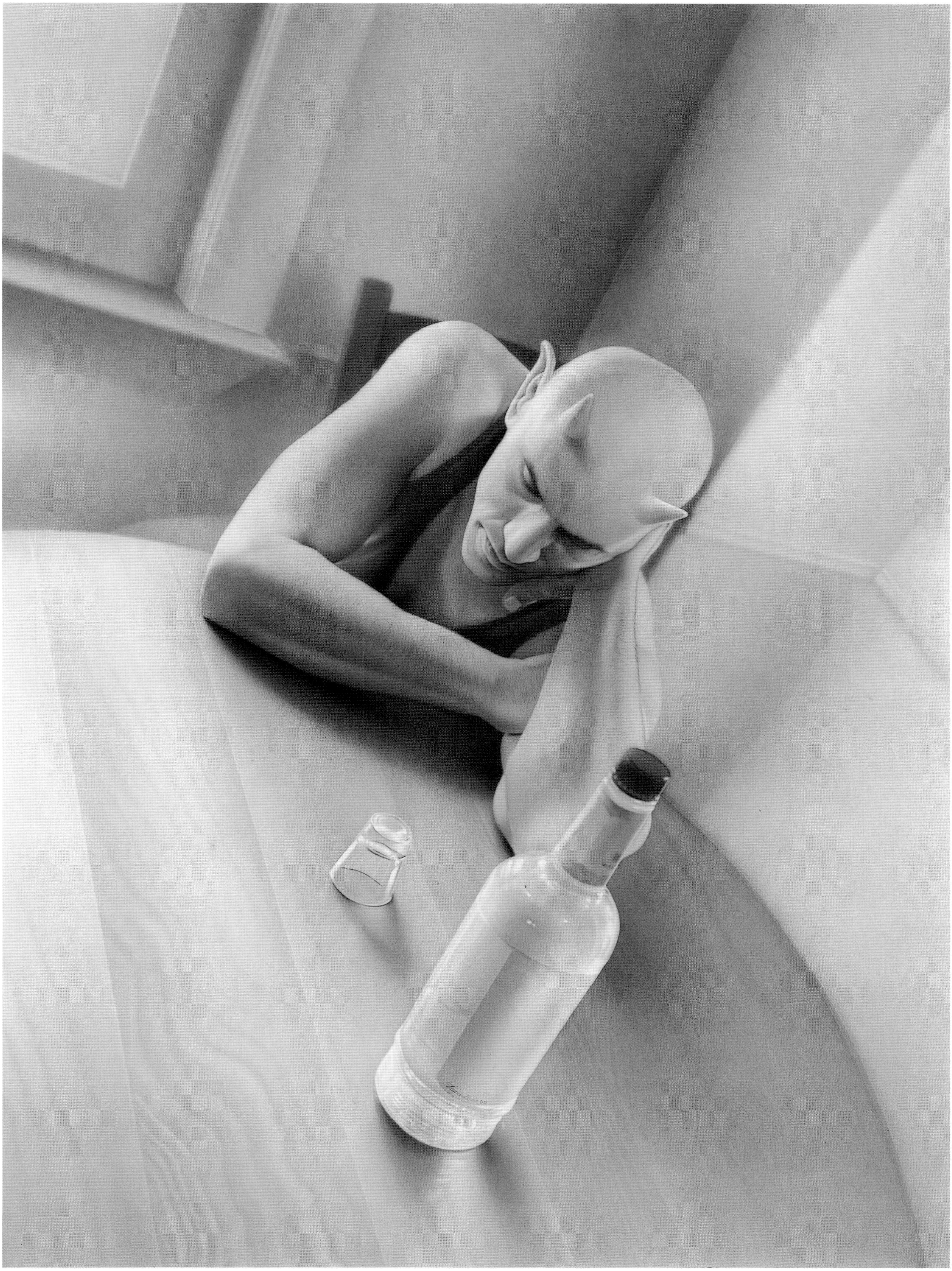

1
artist: JERRY LoFARO
art director: Woody Litwhiler
title: Sometimes Reserved.
Sometimes Twisted.
Occasionally a Bit of a Ham.
medium: Acrylic
size: 14"x18"

2
artist: JAMES CUKR
client: Lightspeed Fine Arts
title: Godzilla: Hail to the King
medium: Mixed
size: 30"x40"

3
artist: PAUL BONNER
art director: Jim Nelson
client: FASA Corporation
title: Vor: The Maelstrom
medium: Watercolor
size: 590cmx403cm

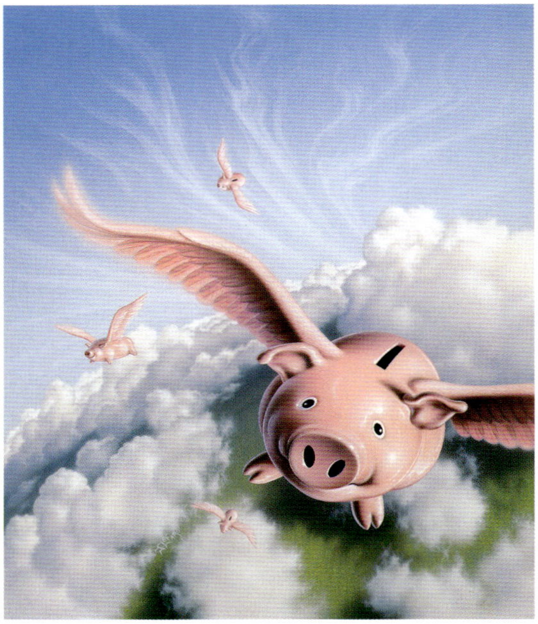

1

2

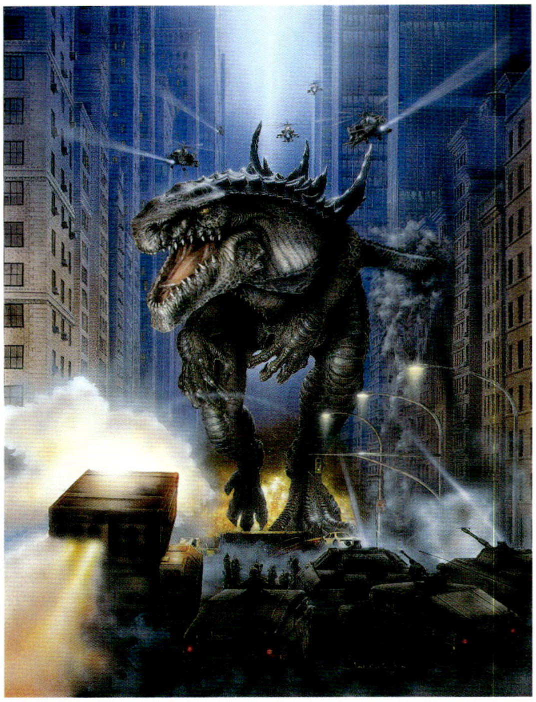

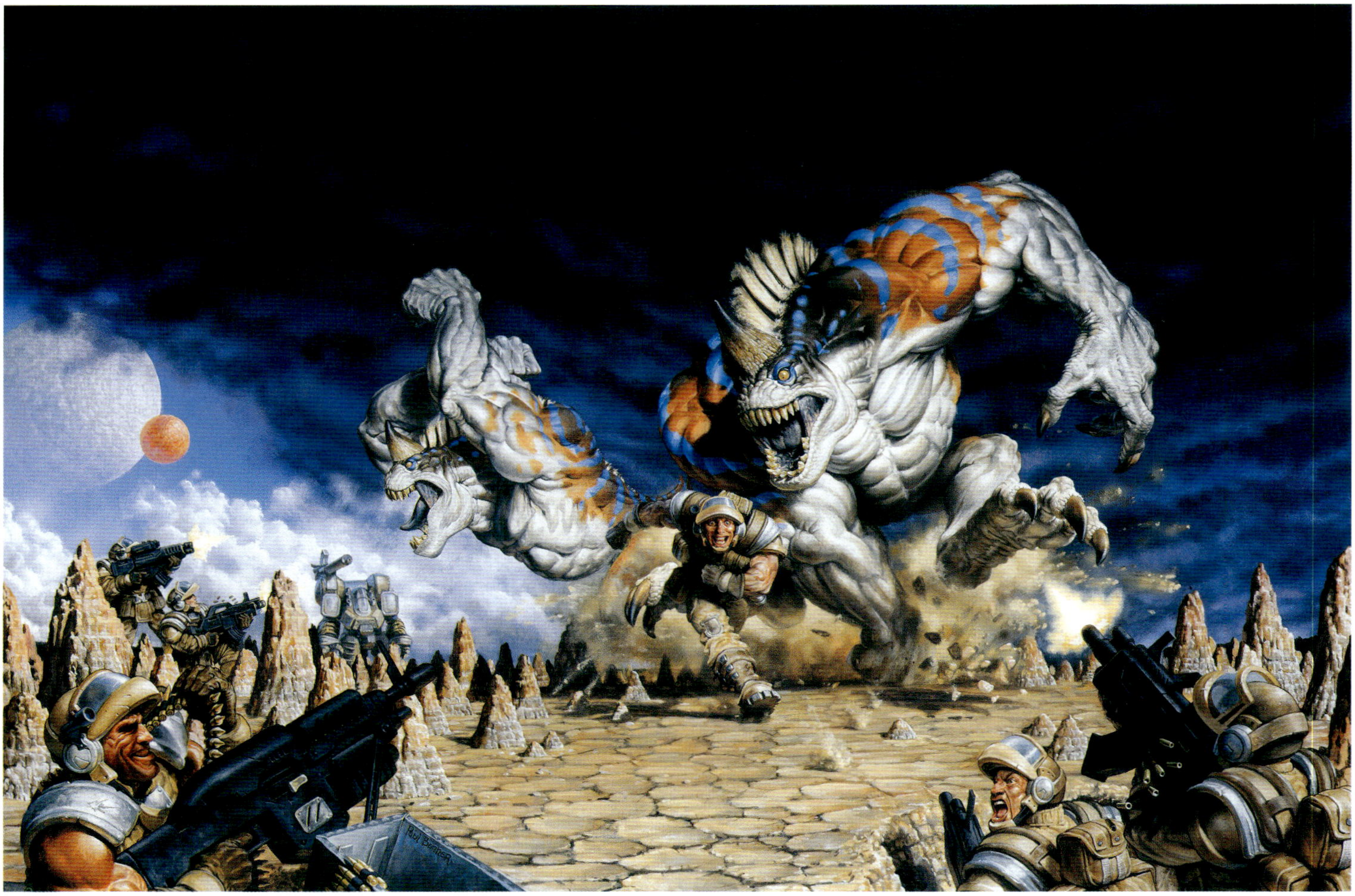

3

4
artist: DAVE DORMAN
art director: Dana Knutson *client:* Wizards of the Coast
title: The Cow Thief *medium:* Oil *size:* 11"x1s"

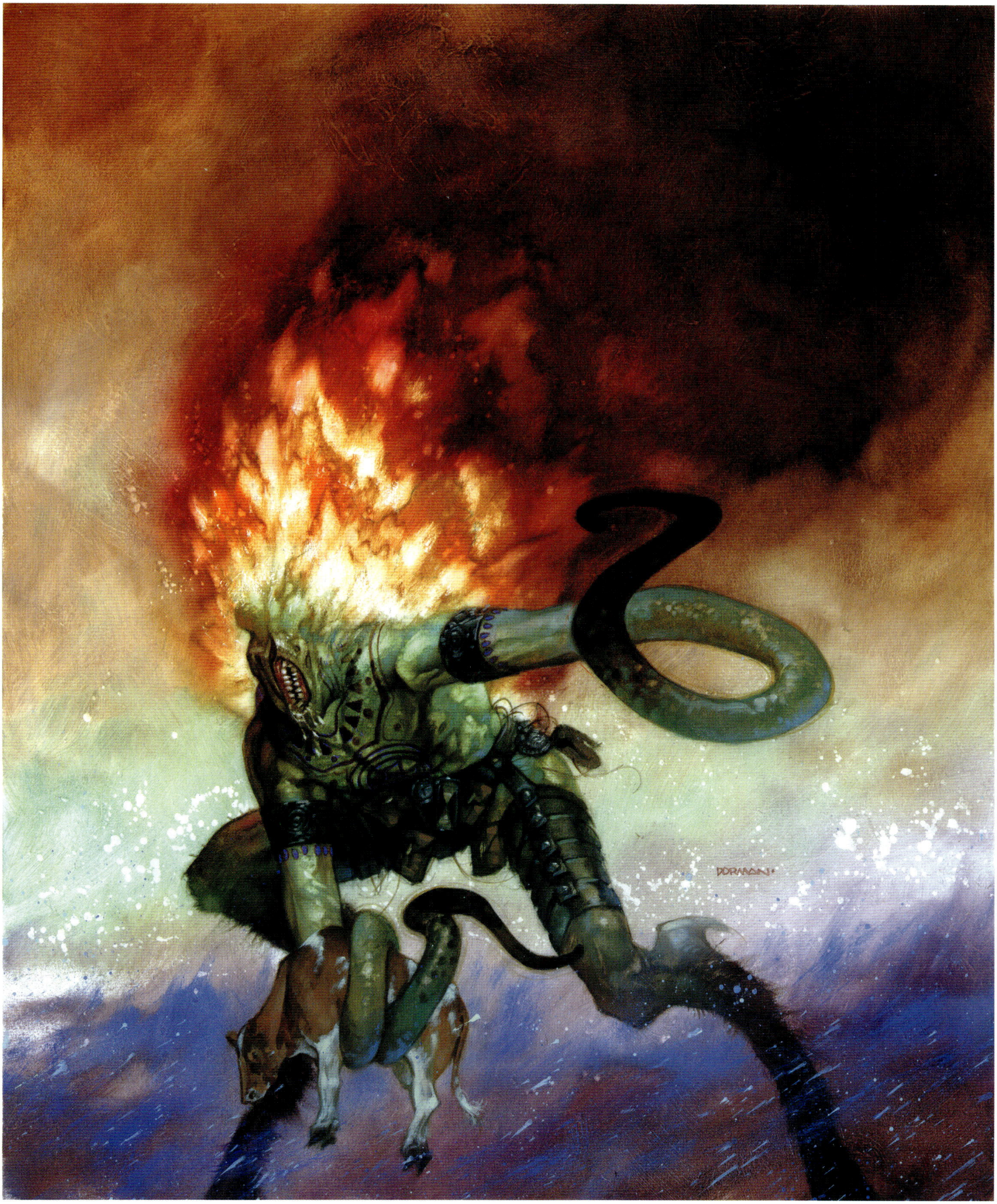
DORMAN

1
artist: PAOLO PARENTE
art director: David Bishop
client: 2000 AD
title: Slaine
medium: Acrylic

2
artist: KEITH PARKINSON
art director: Brad McQuaid
client: Sony—989 Studio
title: Everquest: The Ruins of Kunark
medium: Oil
size: 54"x20"

3
artist: TONY MAURO
art director: Tony Mauro
client: Glass House Graphics
title: Jade Warriors 3
medium: Digital
size: 7 1/2"x11 1/4"

4
artist: BOB EGGLETON
art director: Bob Eggleton
client: Self-promotion
title: Ceratosaurs
medium: Acrylic
size: 18"x36"

5
artist: STEPHEN DANIELE
art director: Jim Ward
client: Precedence Entertainment
title: Armed & Dangerous
medium: Oil
size: 18"x26"

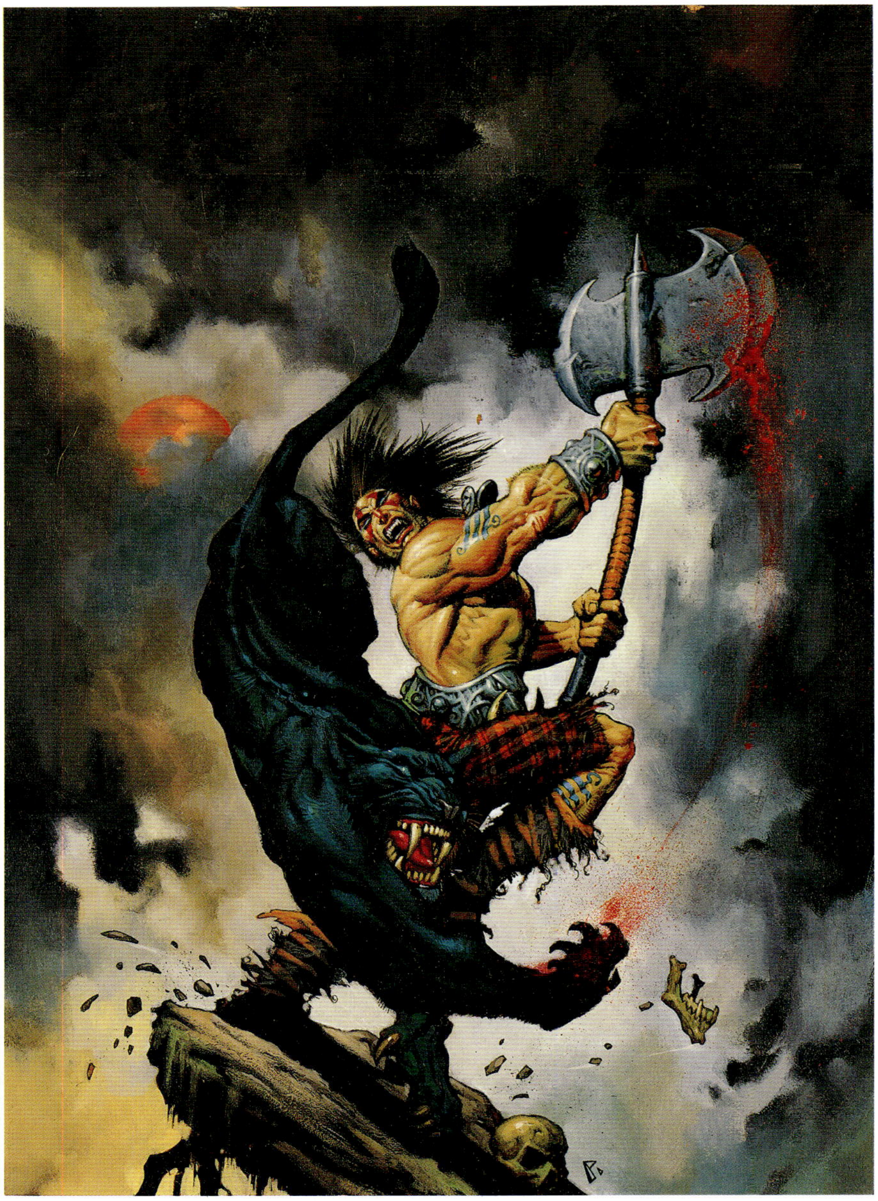

1

2

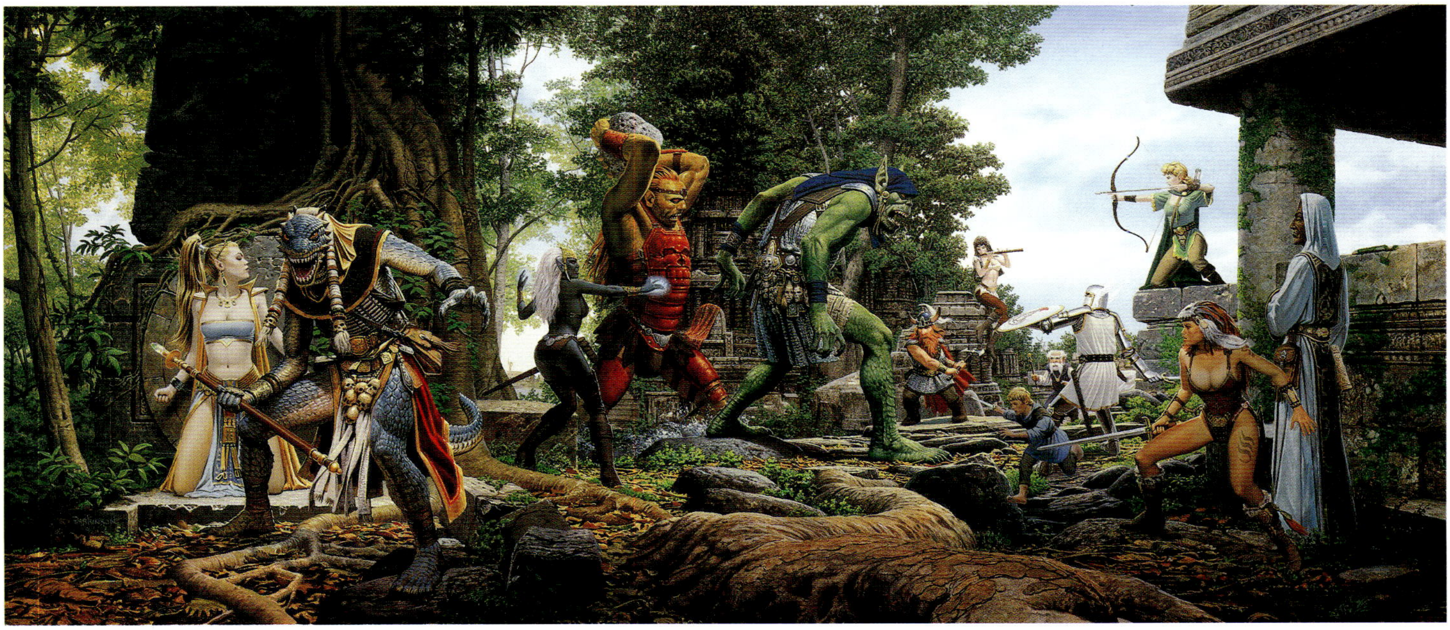

3

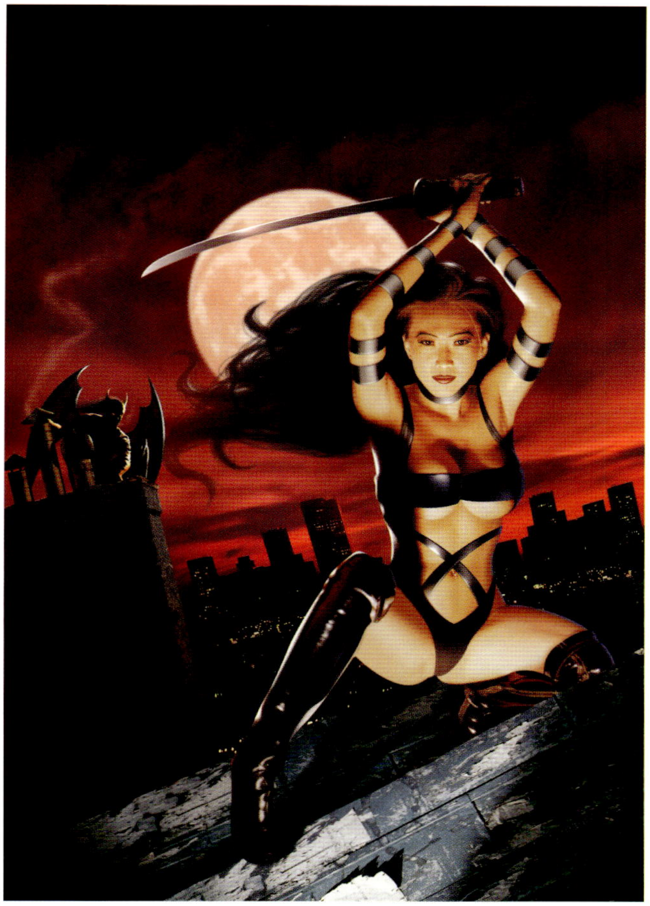

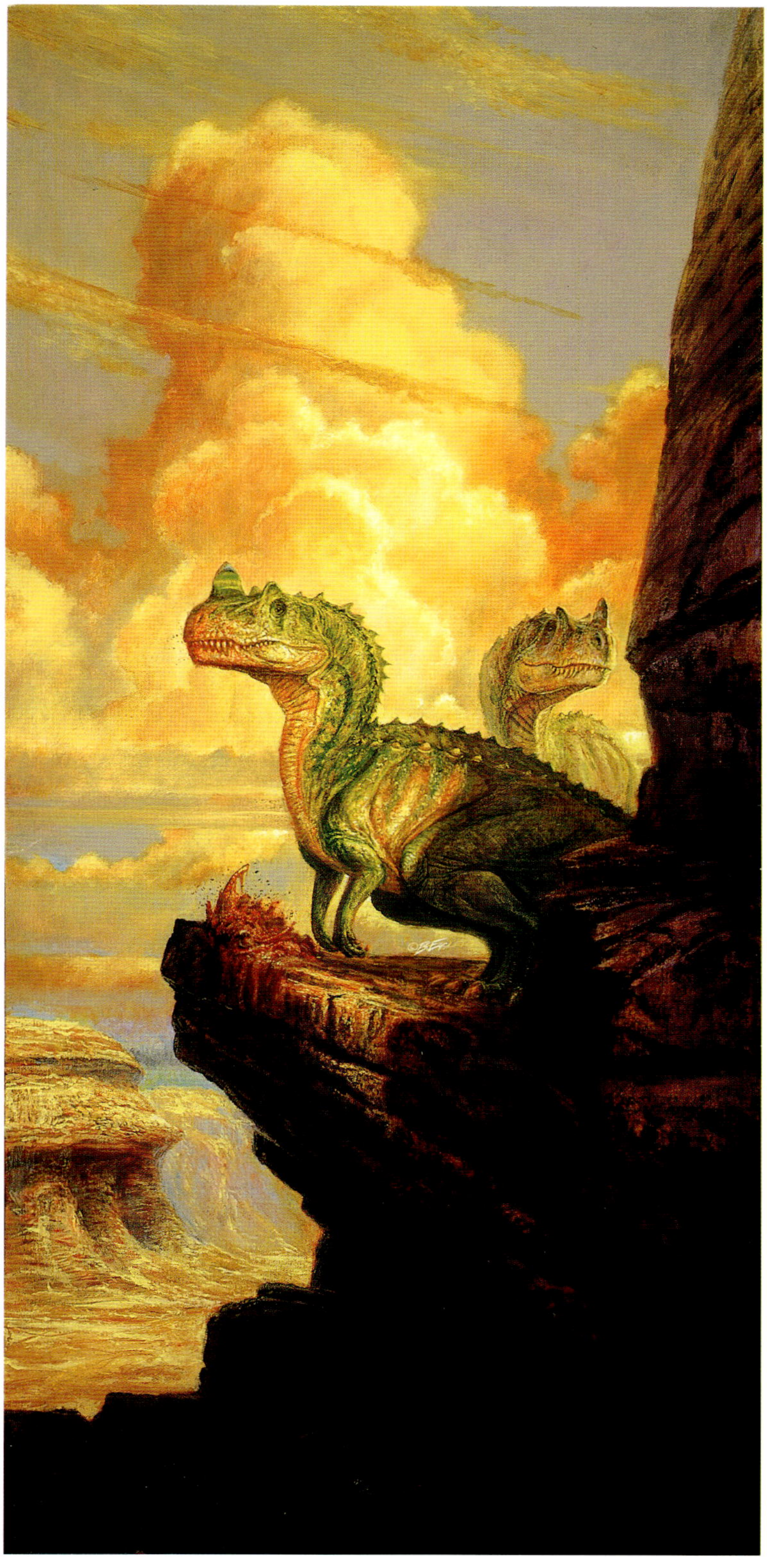

4

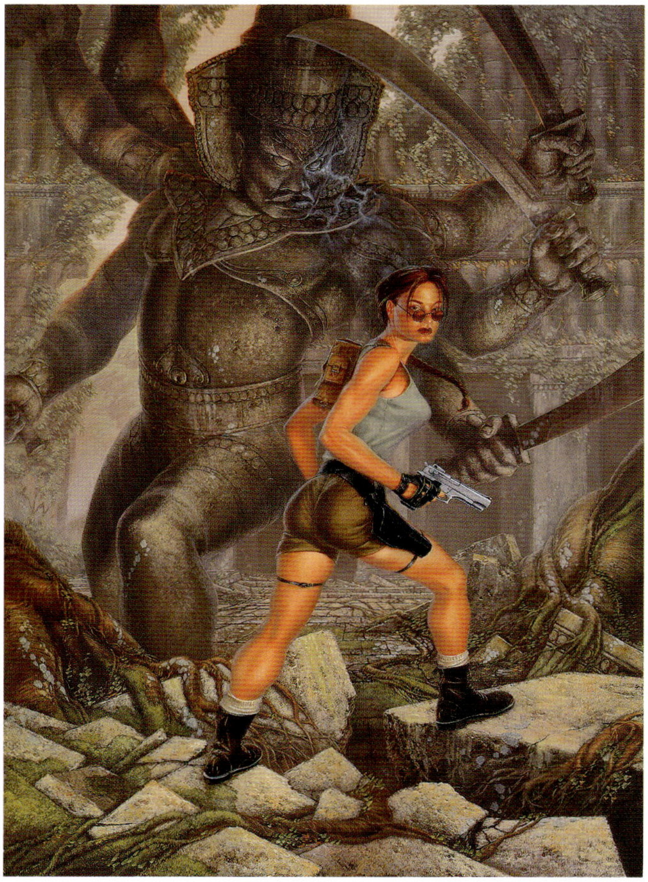

5

1
artist: LARRY MACDOUGALL
art director: Patricia Lewis
client: Underhill Studio
title: Storm Warning
medium: Mixed *size:* 12"x9"

2
artist: BRIAN HORTON
art director: Brian Horton
client: DreamWorks Interactive
title: Clara—Siog
medium: Digital *size:* 11"x17"

3
artist: BRIAN HORTON
art director: Brian Horton
client: DreamWorks Interactive
title: Lizbeth—Siog
medium: Digital *size:* 11"x17"

4
artist: JON J MUTH
art director: Todd McFarlane
designer: Brent Ashe
client: Todd McFarlane Productions
title: Angela: Prey for the Hunter
medium: Watercolor
size: 22"x34"

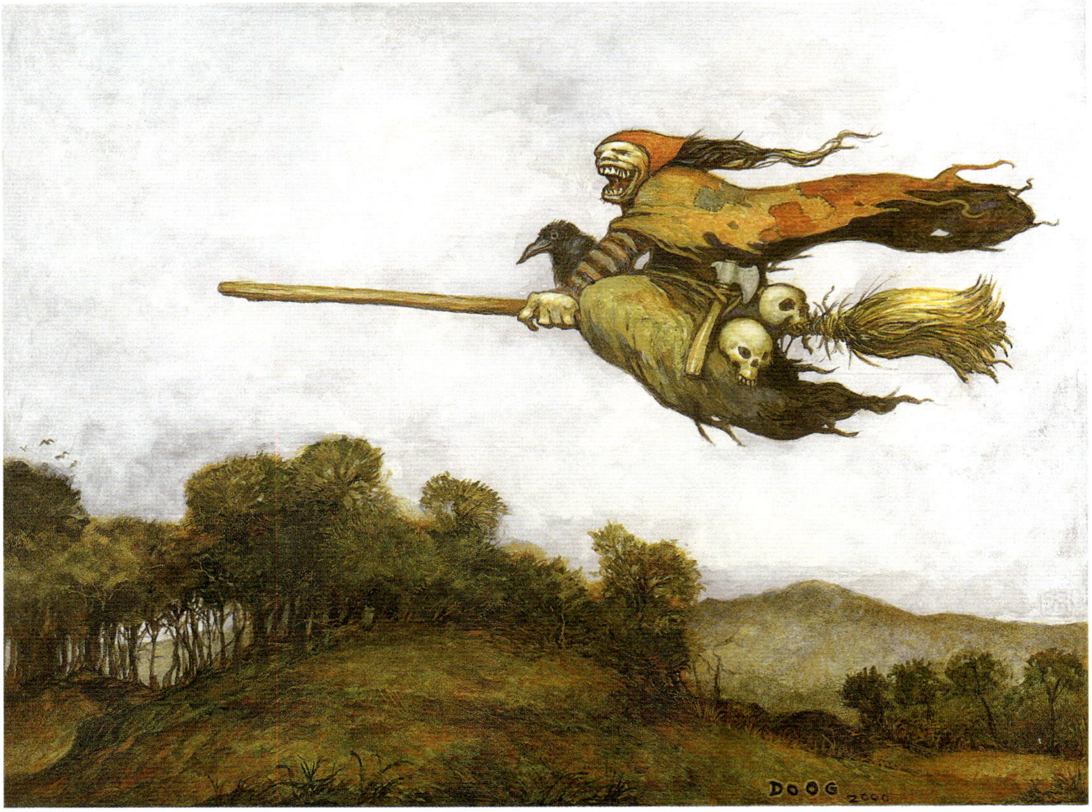

1

2
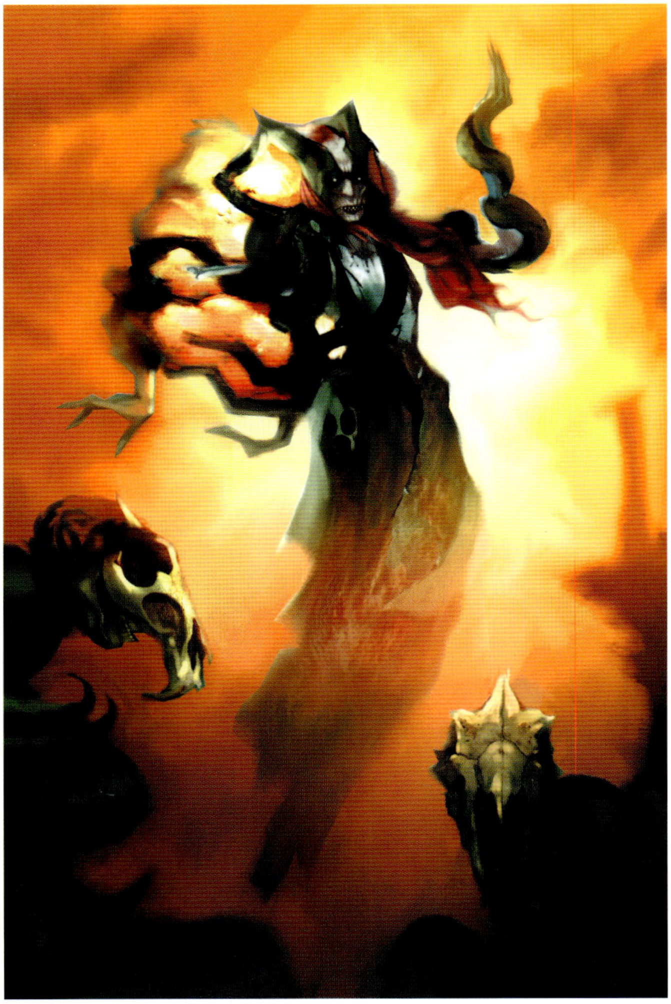

3
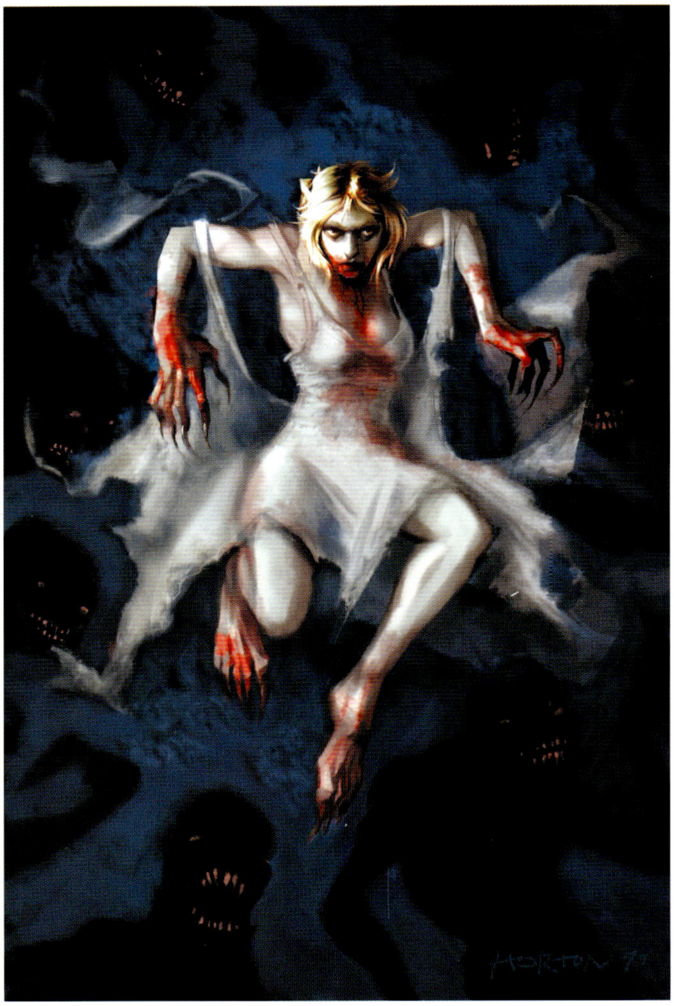

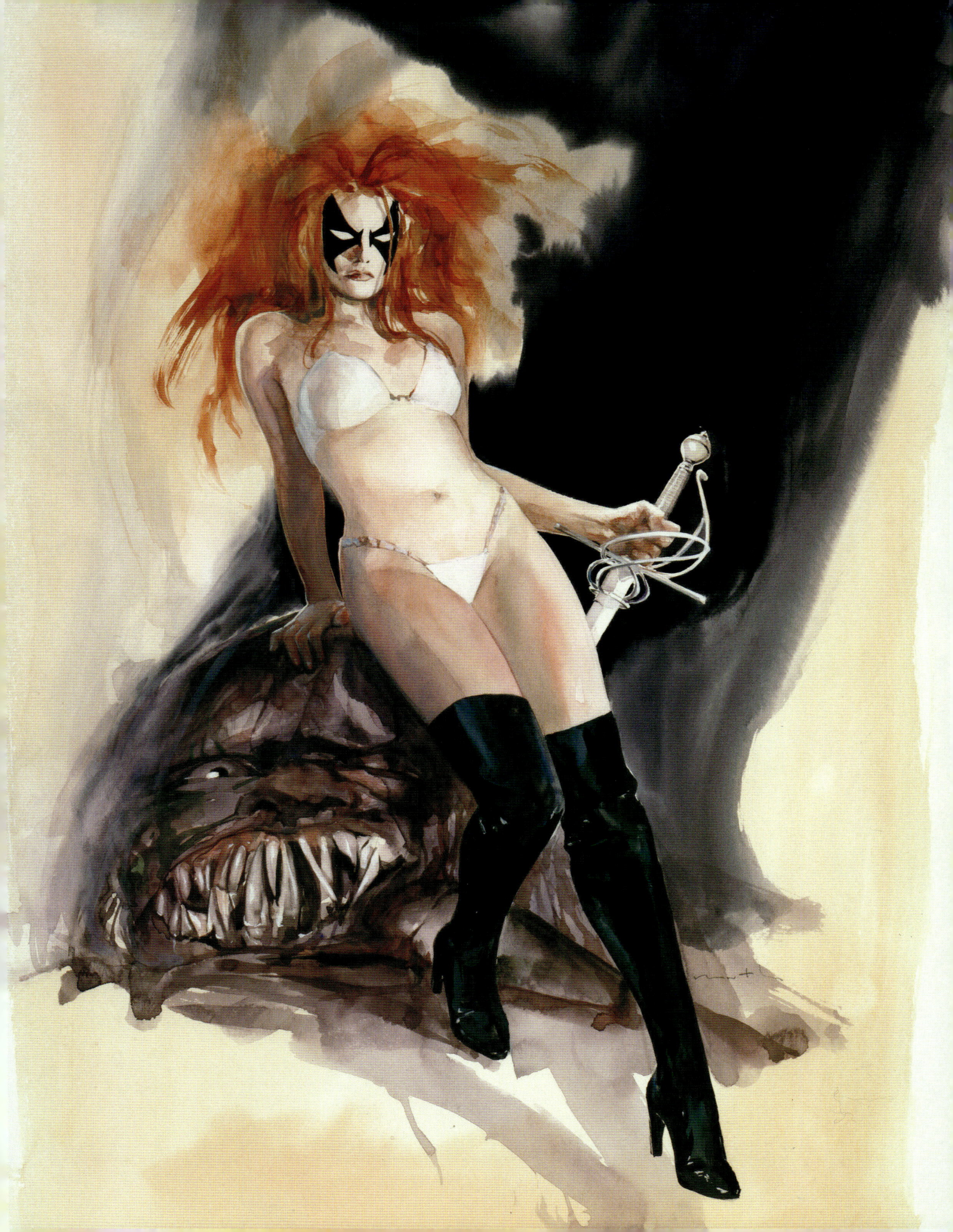

1
artist: CHRISTOPHER MOELLER
art director: Dan Raspler
client: DC Comics
title: Mars
medium: Acrylic
size: 20"x30"

2
artist: SCOTT GUSTAFSON
art director: Scott Usher
designer: Scott Gustafson
client: The Greenwich Workshop
title: The Wizard of Oz
medium: Oil
size: 40"x26"

3
artist: SCOTT GUSTAFSON
art director: Scott Usher
designer: Scott Gustafson
client: The Greenwich Workshop
title: Don Quixote
medium: Oil
size: 21"x27"

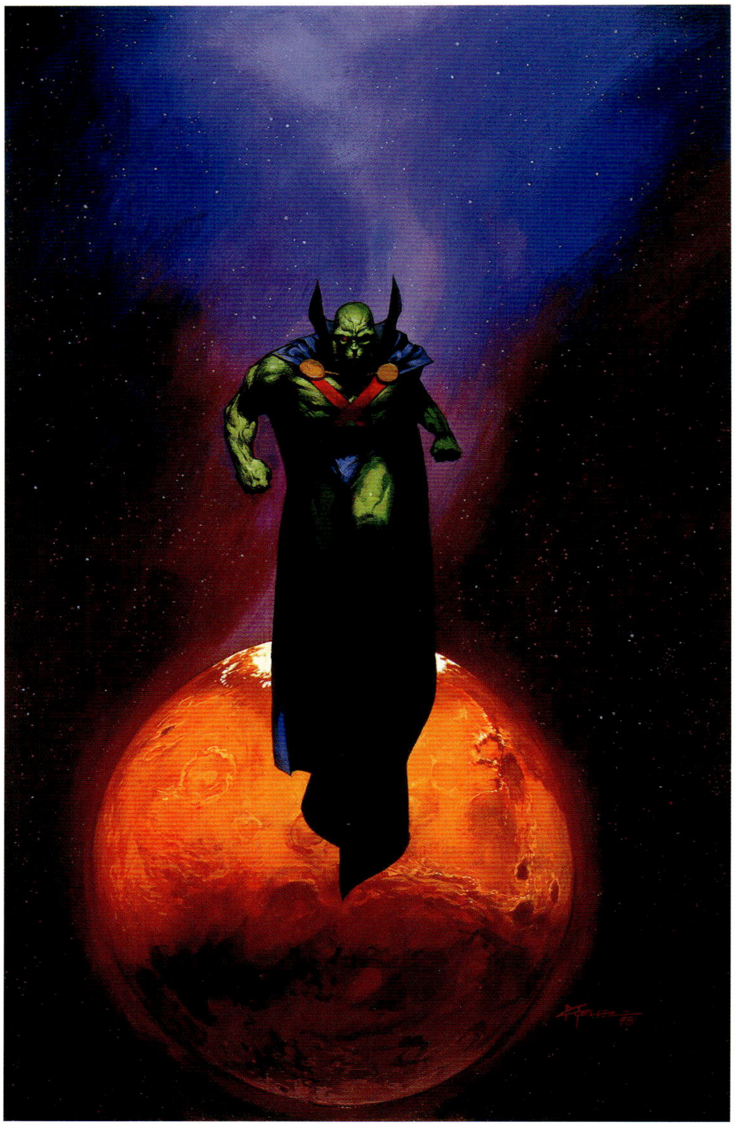

1

2

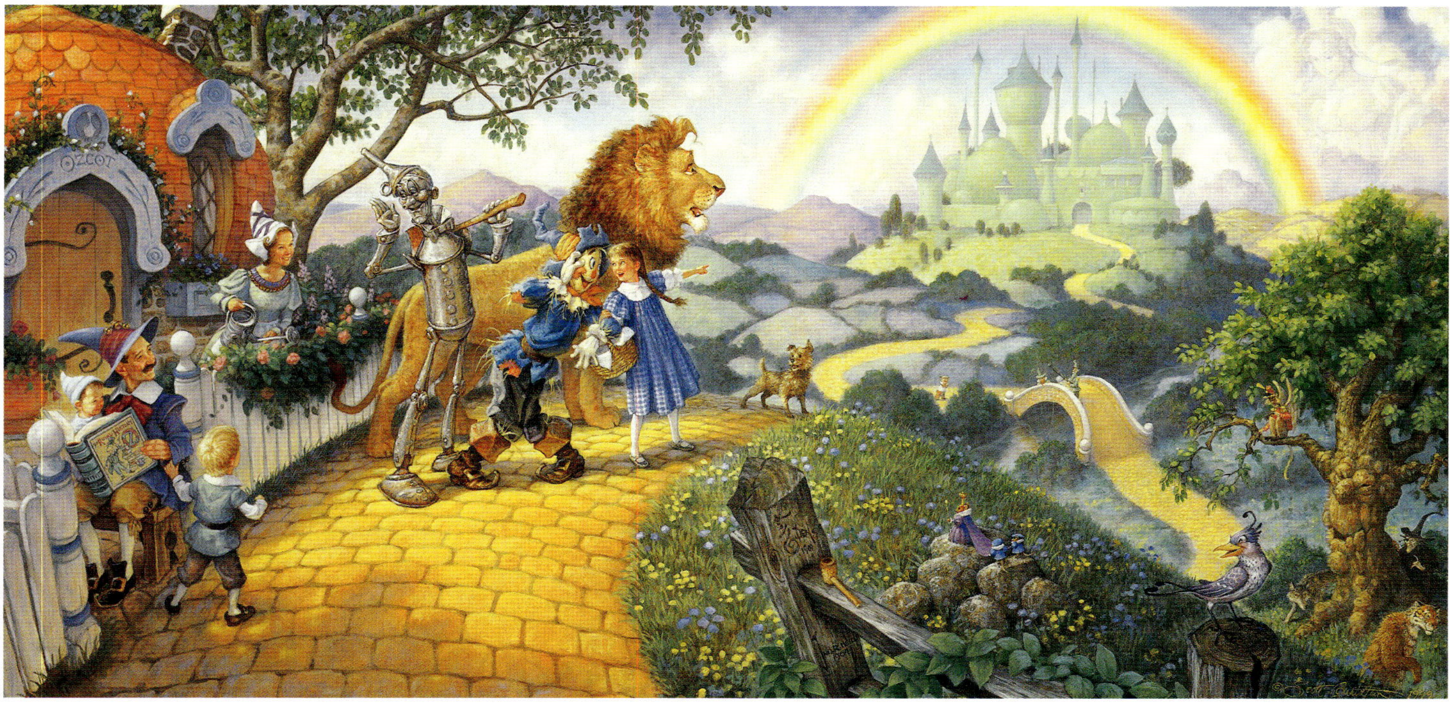

3

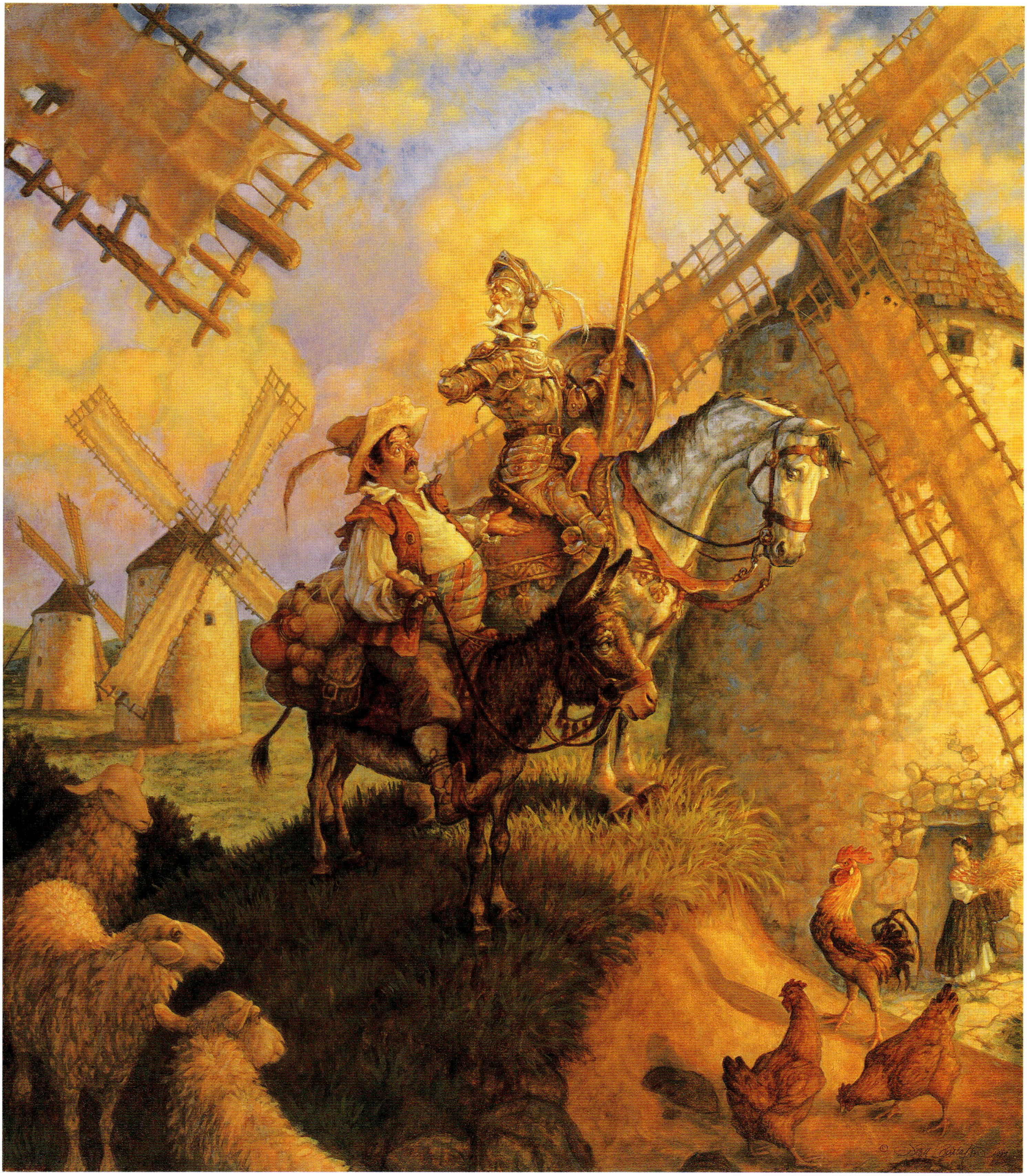

1
artist: GREGORY MANCHESS
art director: Bob Zeidler
client: John Deere & Co.
title: Above Crater Alphonsus
medium: Oil
size: 24"x16"

2
artist: JOHN MONTELEONE
designer: John Monteleone
client: Kaliedescope Gallery
title: Eternal Love
medium: Oil
size: 43"x16 1/2"

3
artist: RICHARD BOBER
art director: Richard Bober
designer: Richard Bober
client: Tamar.
title: Glorantha
medium: Oil/acrylic
size: 22"x30"

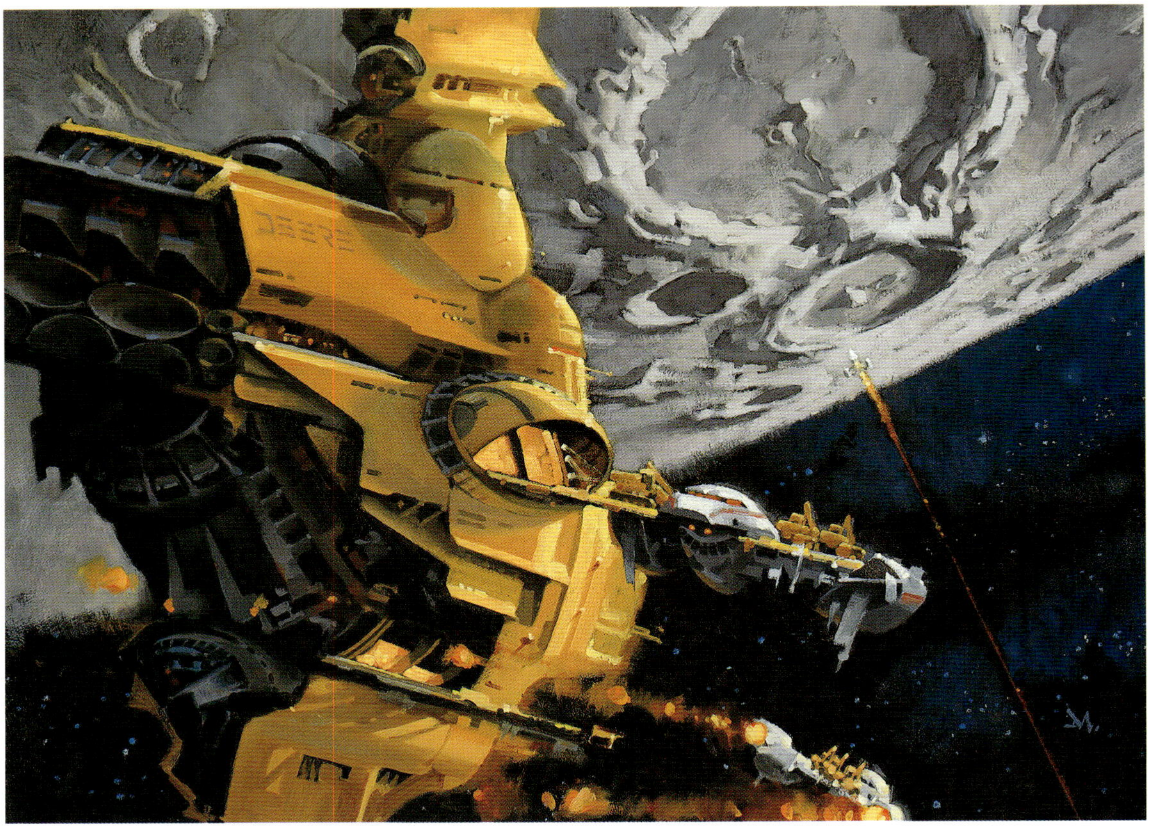

1

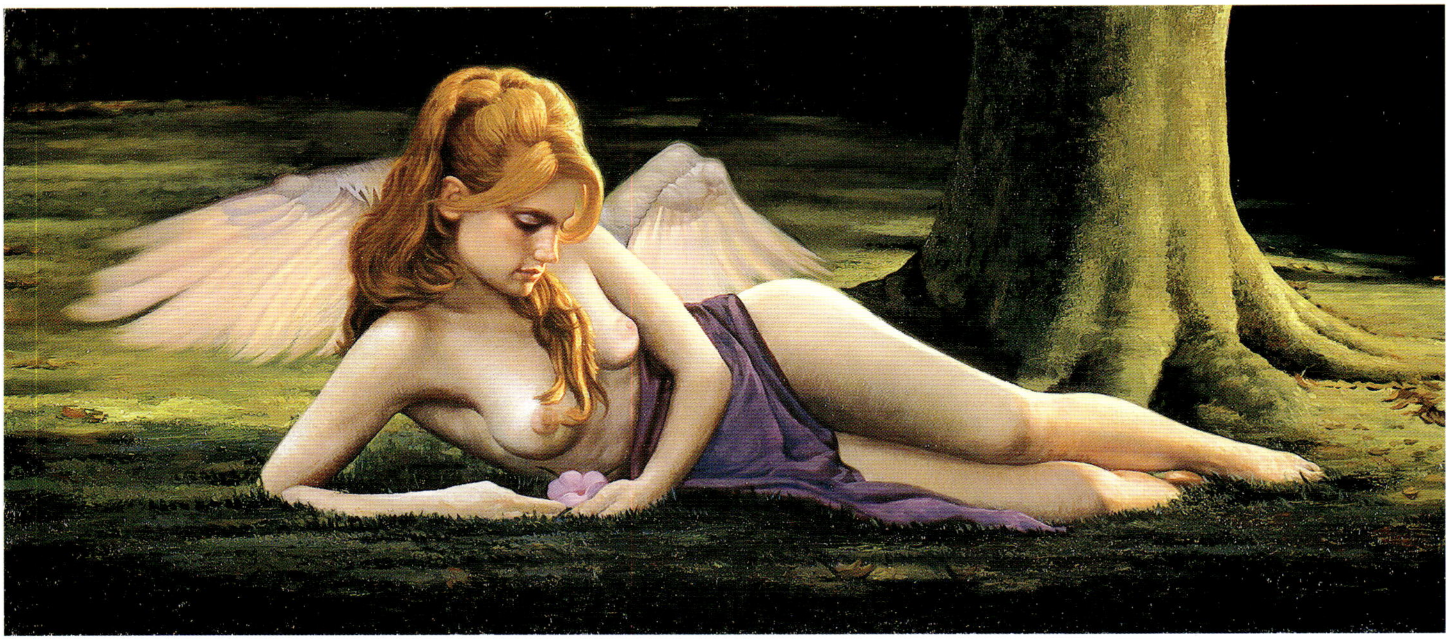

2

3

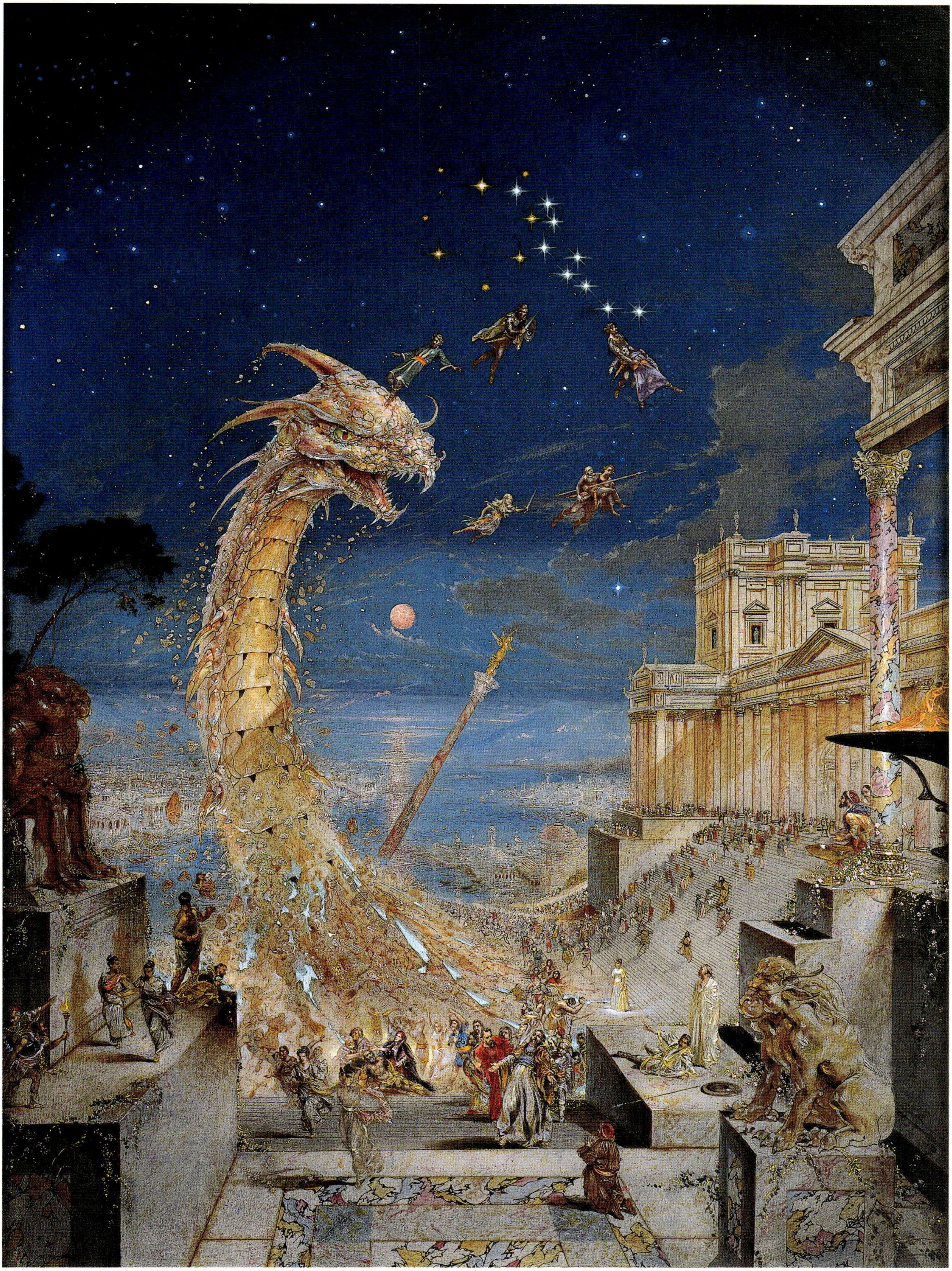

1
artist: JAMES C. CHRISTENSEN
art director: Scott Usher
client: Greenwich Workshop
title: Flight of the Fablemaker
medium: Oil *size:* 48”x36”

2
artist: RICHARD HESCOX
art director: Richard Hescox
client: NorwesCon
title: The Twilight Gate
medium: Oil *size:* 33”x22”

3
artist: DAVID BOWERS
art director: James Frederick
client: James Gallery
title: Breaking Ties
medium: Oil *size:* 10”x19 1/2”

4
artist: RAFAL OLBINSKI
art director: Rafal Olbinski
client: Patinae, Inc.
title: Uverture
medium: Acrylic *size:* 20”x30”

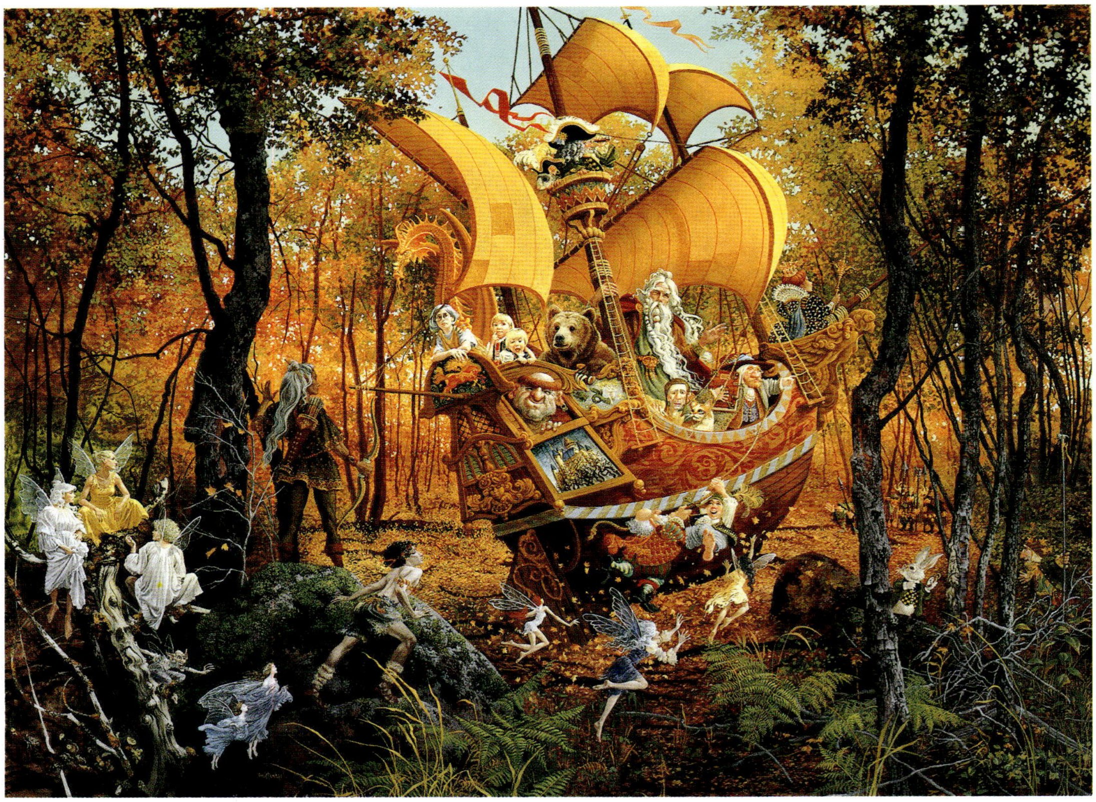

1

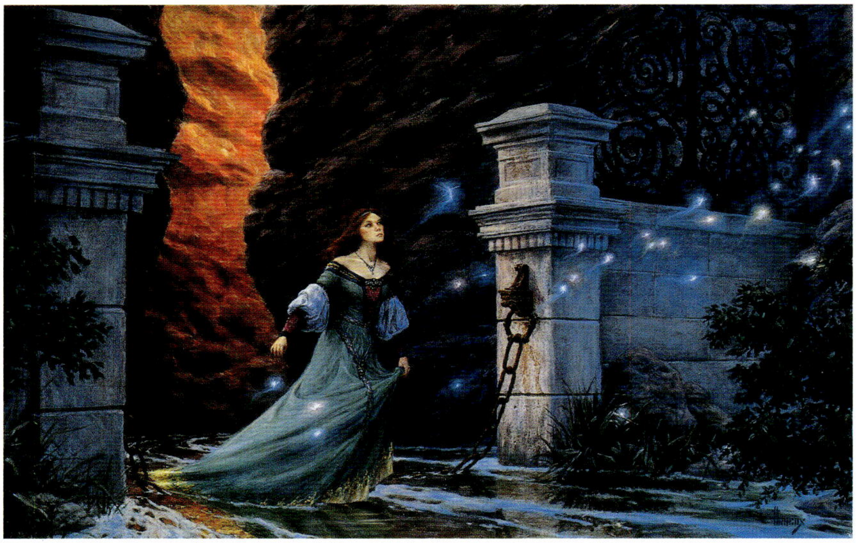

2

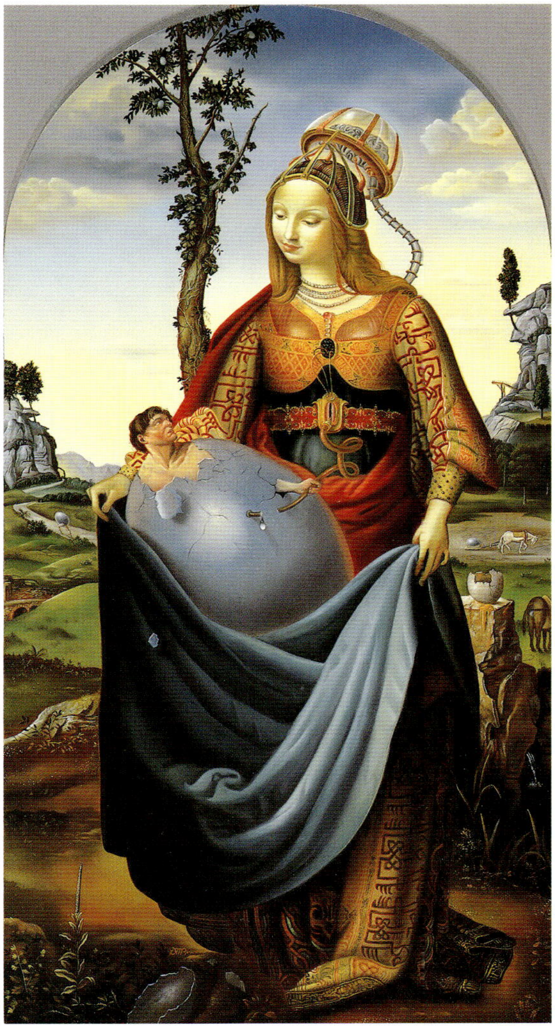

3

4

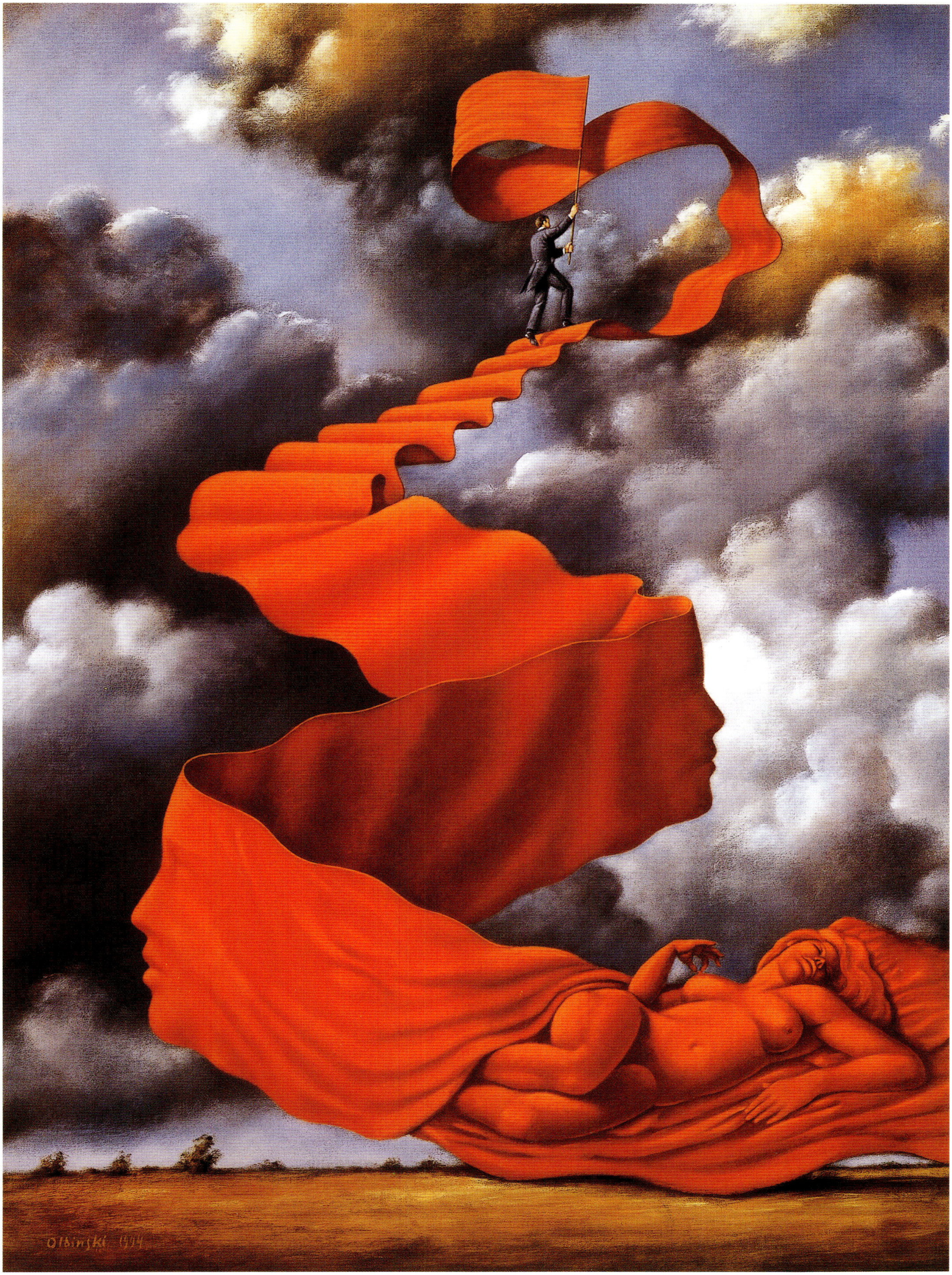

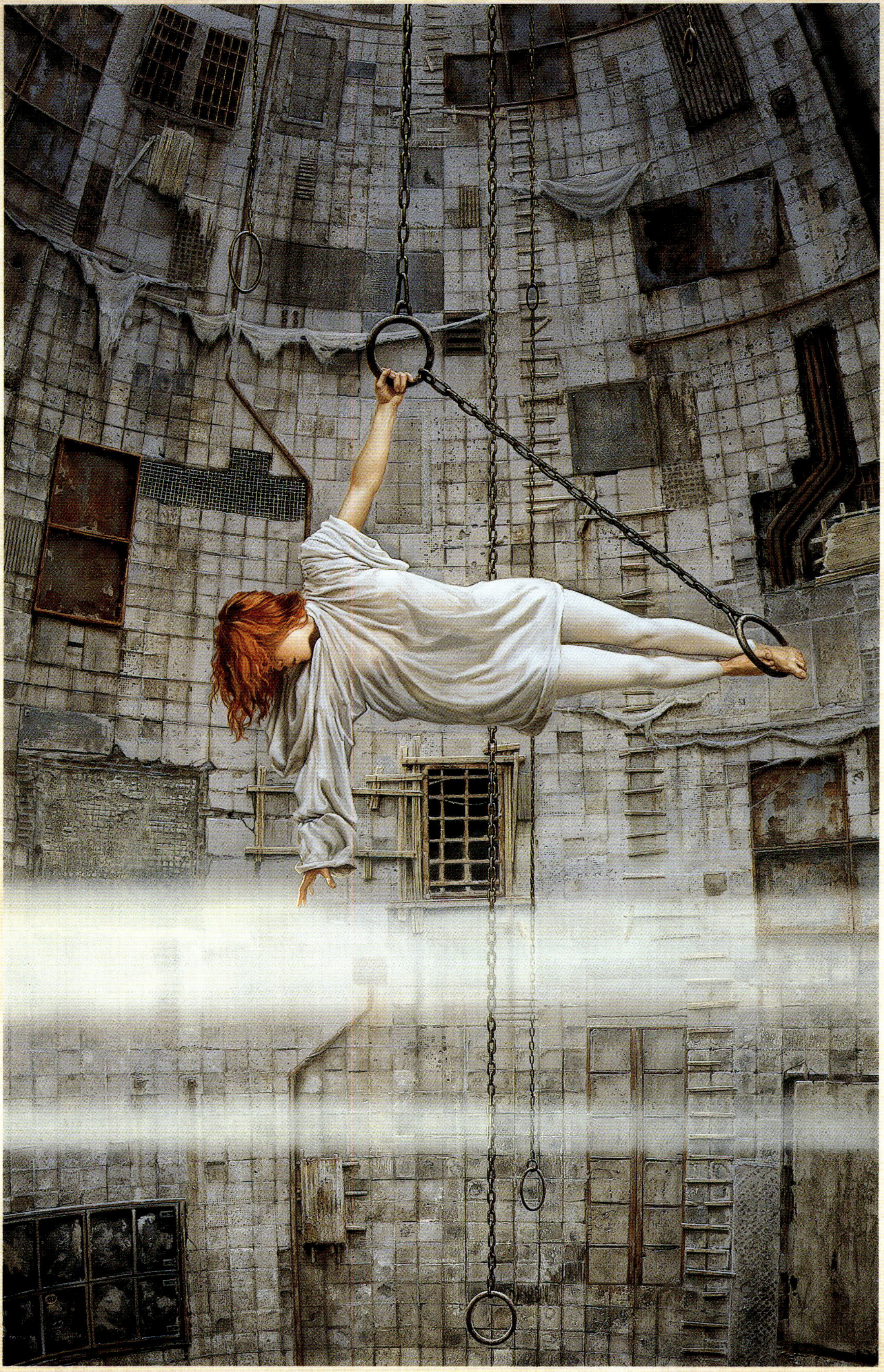

artist: MICHAEL WHELAN
title: Reach *size:* 36"x48" *medium:* Acrylic

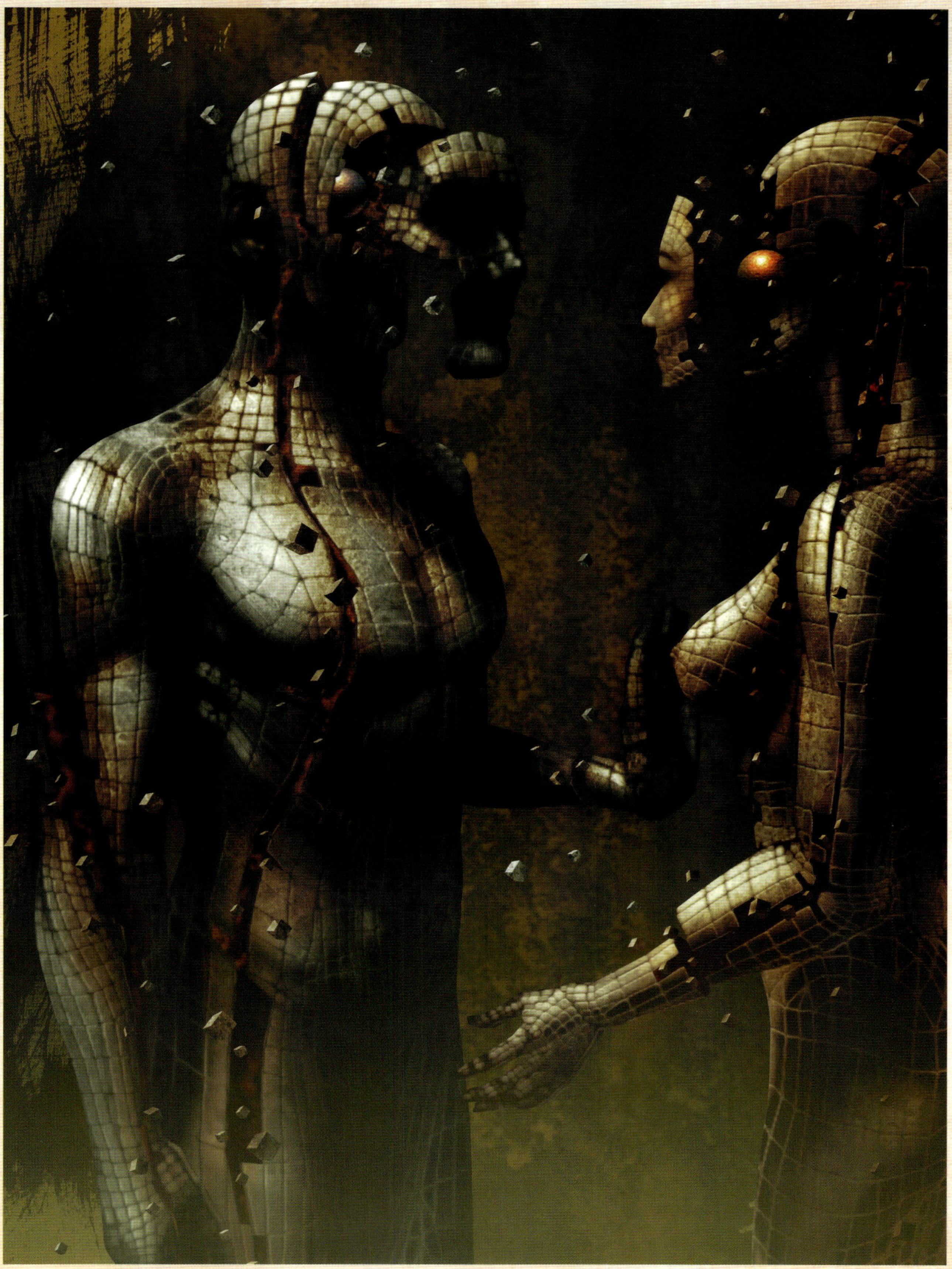

artist: DAVID HO
art director: David Ho *title:* The Union
size: 16"x20" *medium:* Mixed/digital

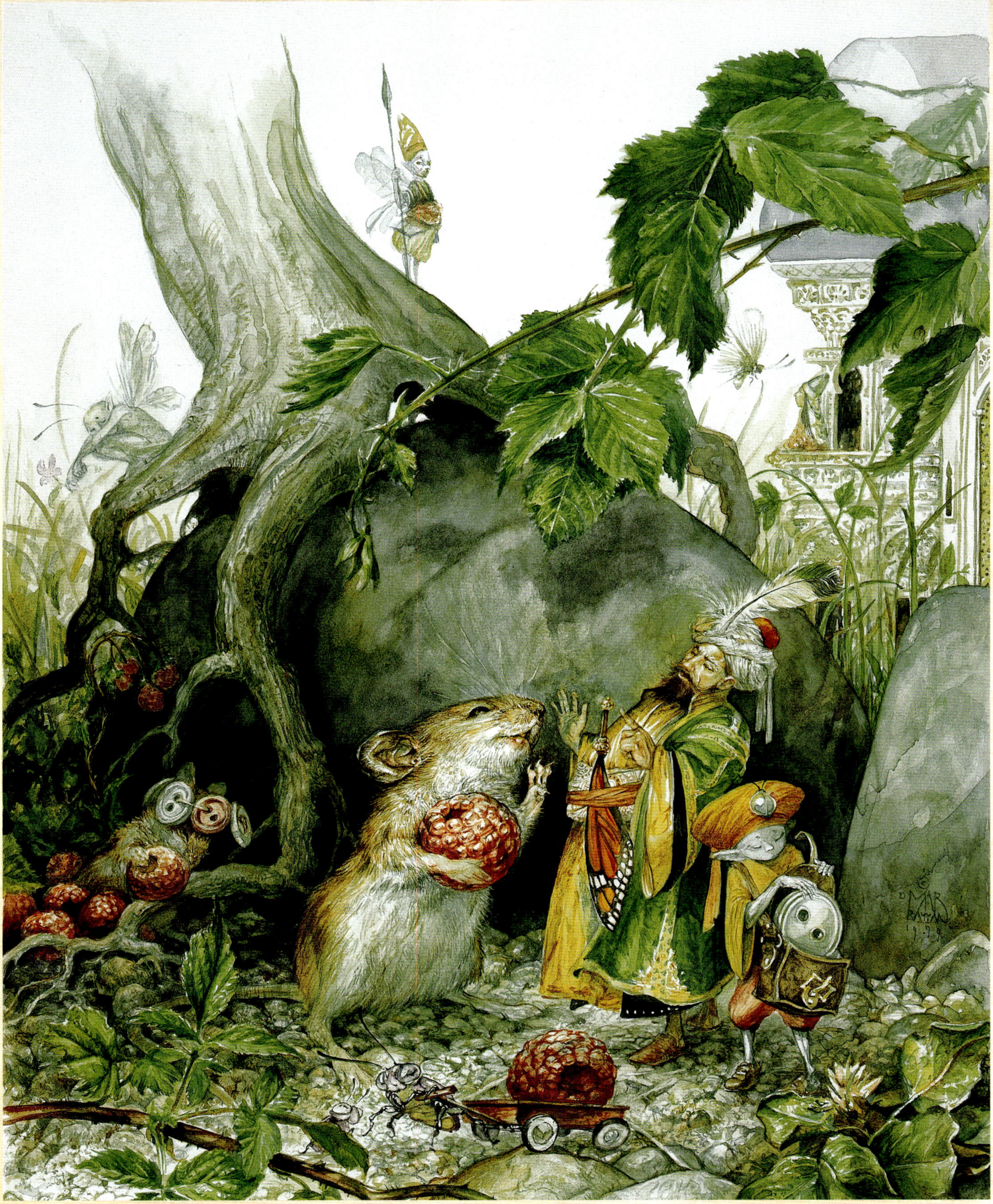

artist: OMAR RAYYAN
title: The Berry Market *size:* 8"x10" *medium:* Watercolor

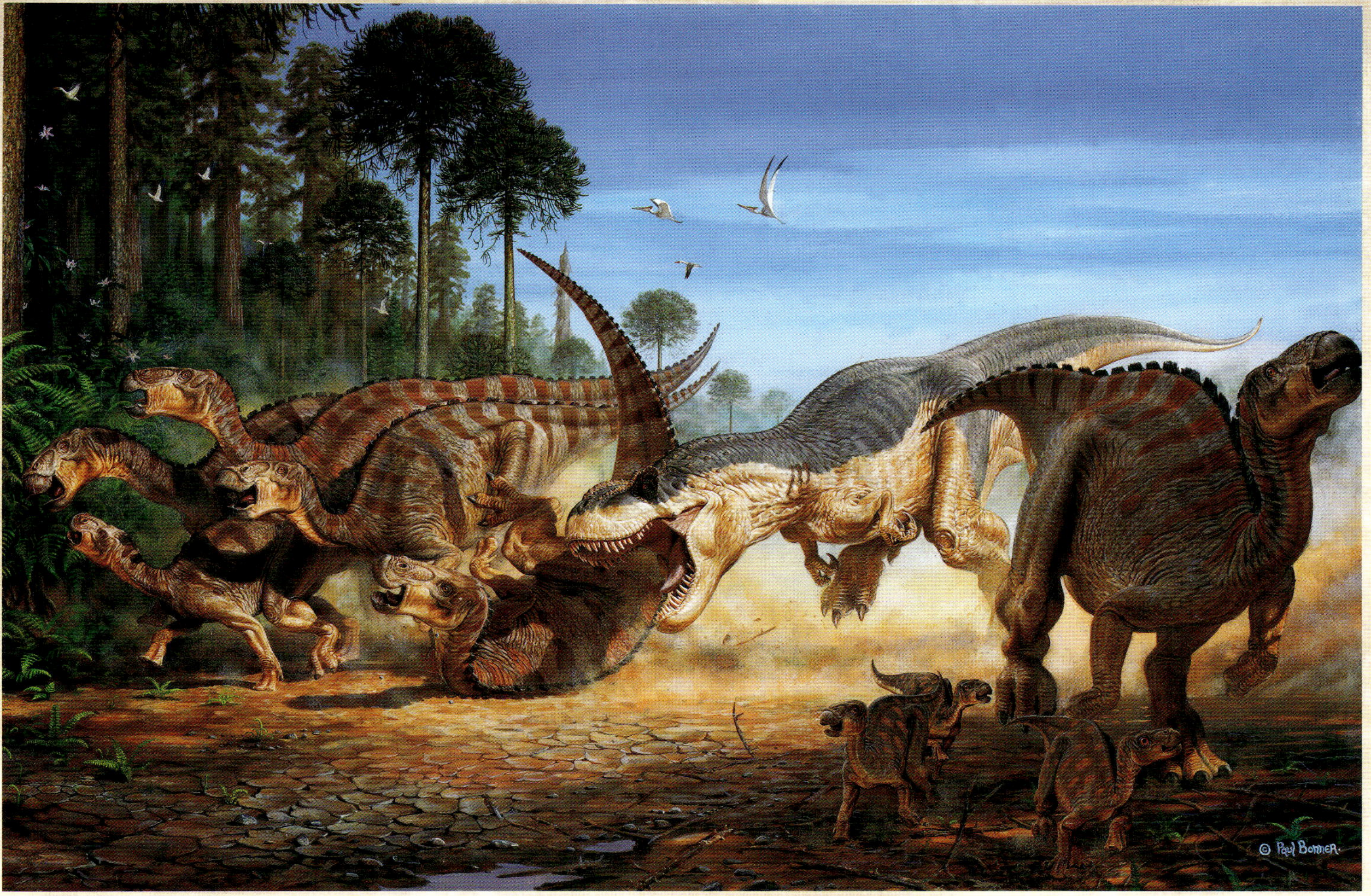

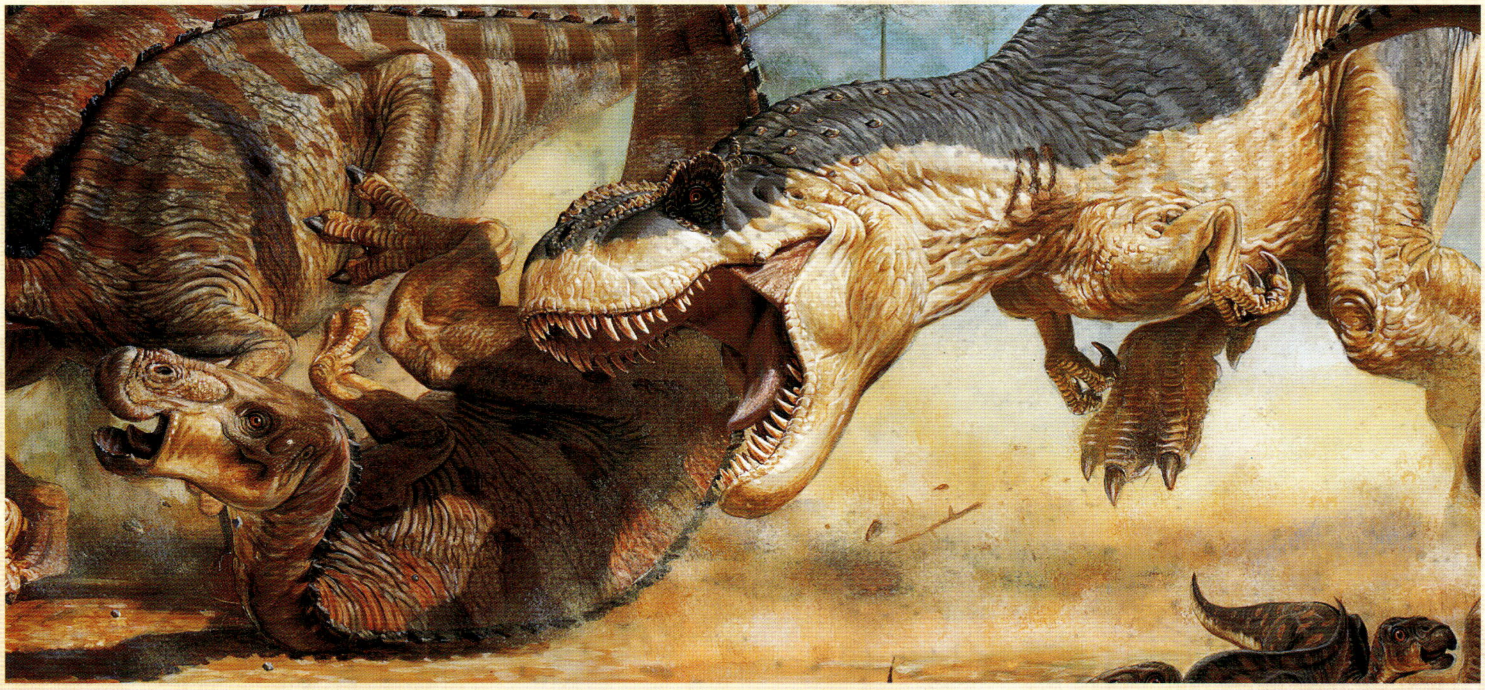

artist: PAUL BONNER
art director: Paul Bonner *designer:* Paul Bonner *client:* Self-promotion *title:* Edmontasaurs & T-Rex
size: 610mmx410mm *medium:* Watercolor

1
artist: ALLEN G. DOUGLAS
title: Through the Dragon Glass
medium: Oil *size:* 13"x18"

2
artist: JOEL HAFFNER
title: The Mountain Queen
medium: Oil *size:* 13 1/2"x22"

3
artist: COREY WOLFE
title: The Oracle
medium: Oil *size:* 32"x48"

4
artist: RICHARD HESCOX
title: Moonstone
medium: Oil *size:* 16"x18"

1

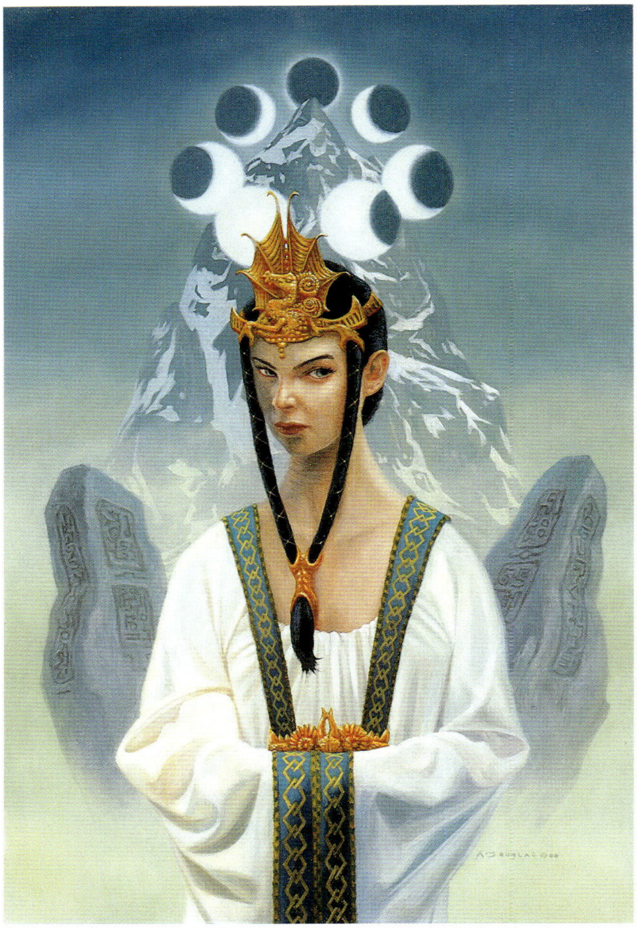

2

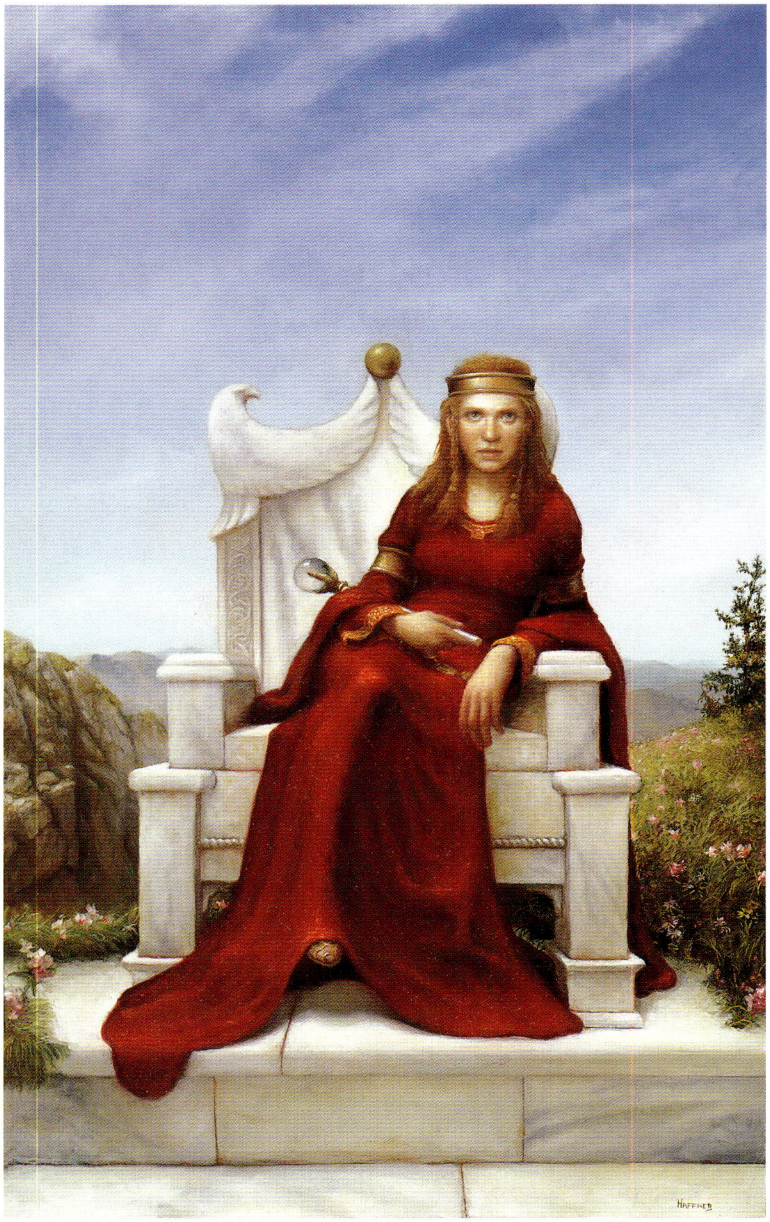

3

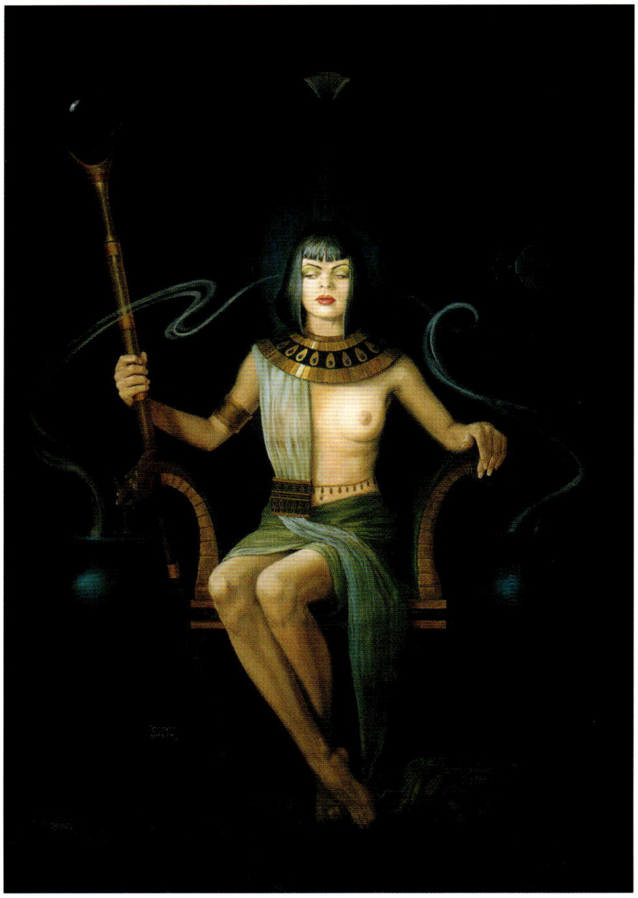

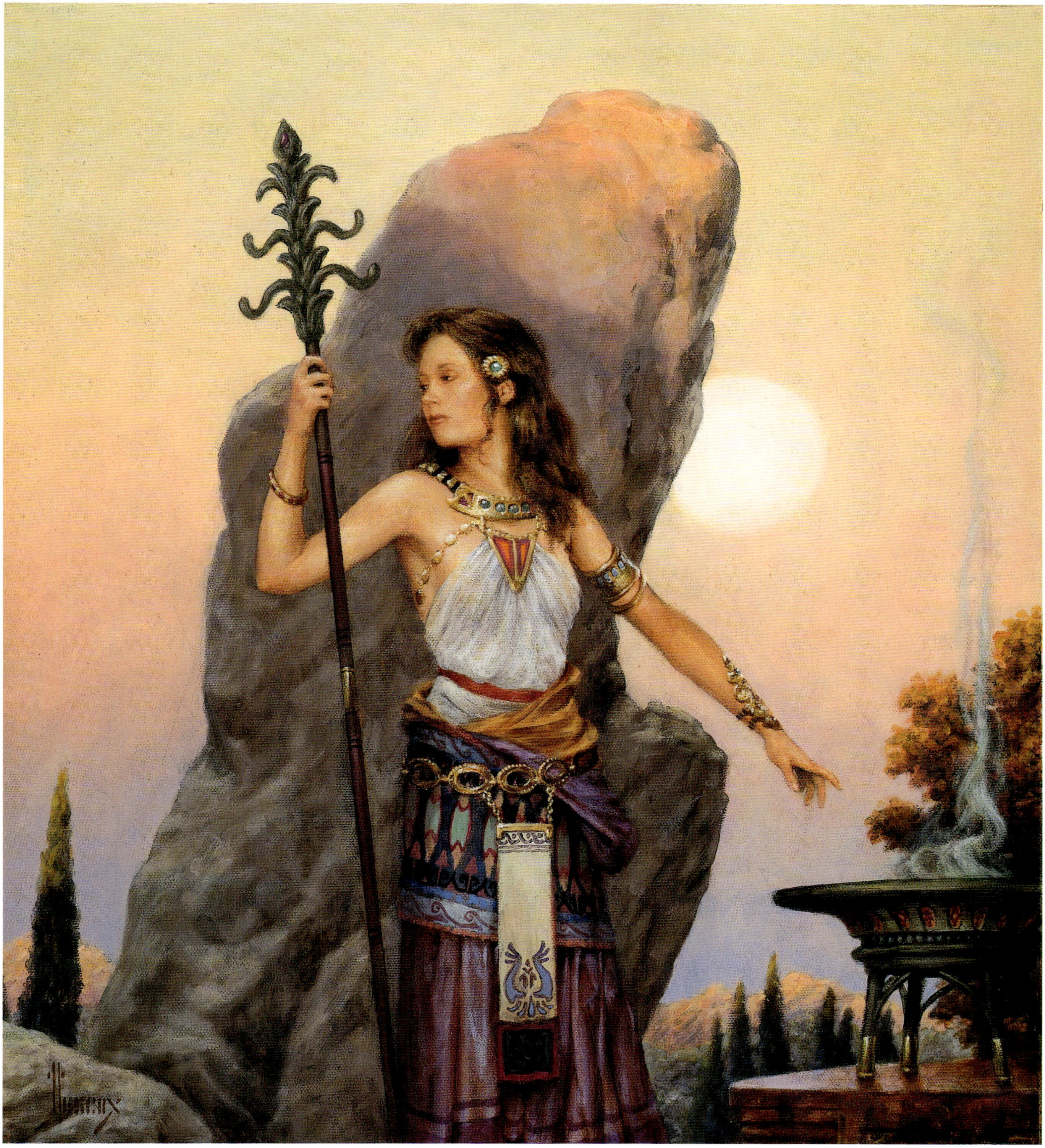

4

1
artist: JOSEPH KRESOJA
title: Suck Nectar
medium: Gouache
size: 13"x12"

2
artist: CHRISTOPHER WOOD
art director: Richard Lyon
designer: Christopher Wood
title: One Minute Late
medium: Digital

3
artist: DOMINICK SAPONARO
title: Blue Elephant

4
artist: SHAWN ALAN PETERS
title: Vampire
medium: Acrylic
size: 10"x14"

5
artist: JERAL TIDWELL
designer: Jeral Tidwell
title: Exit Mouse Trap
medium: Acrylic
size: 30"x24"

1

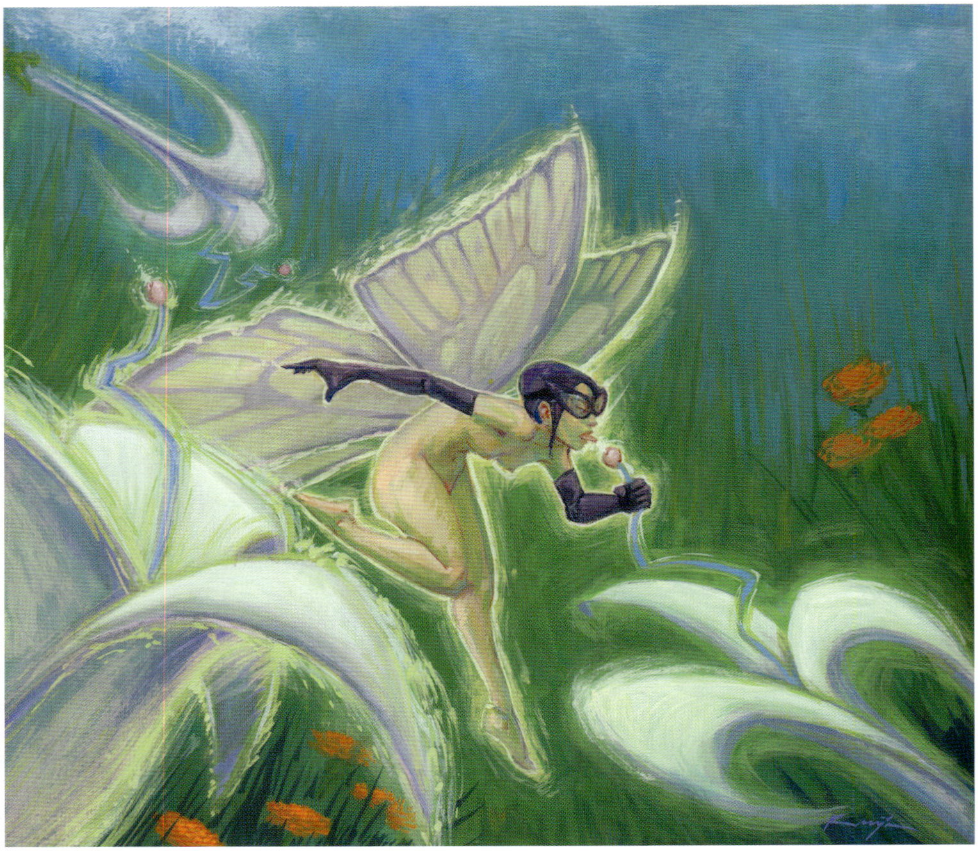

2

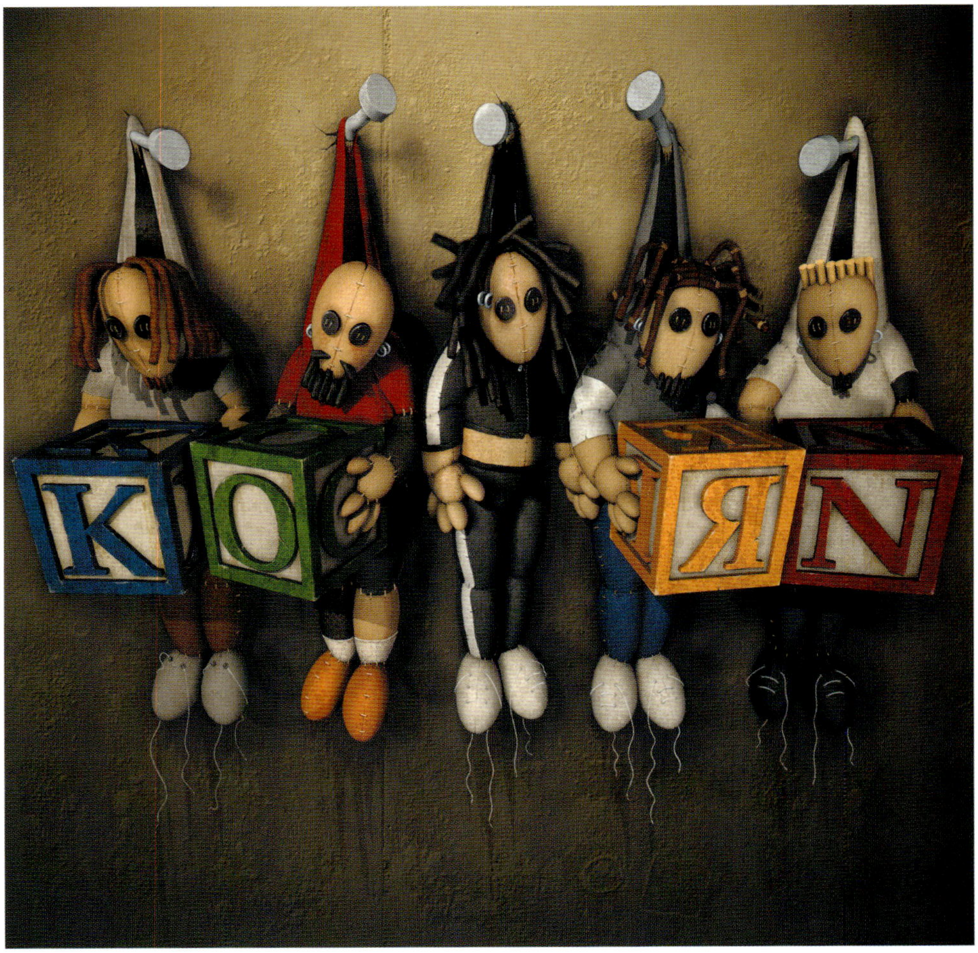

3

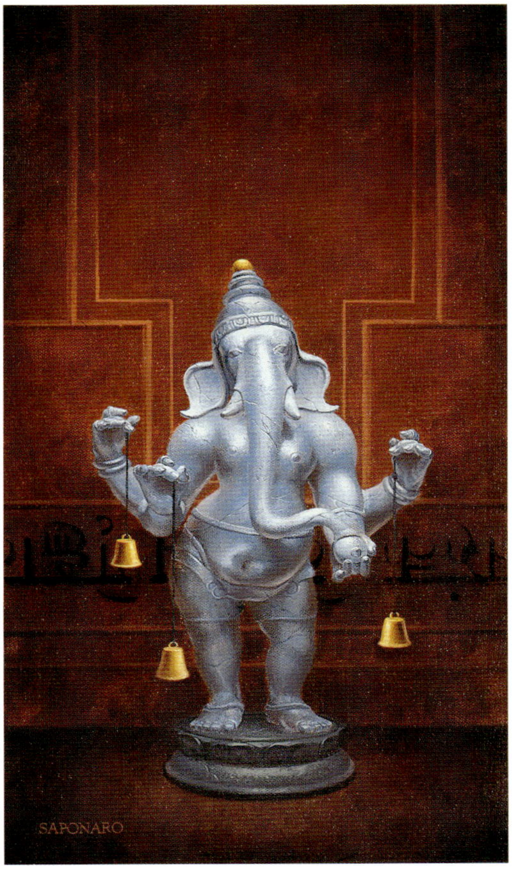

4

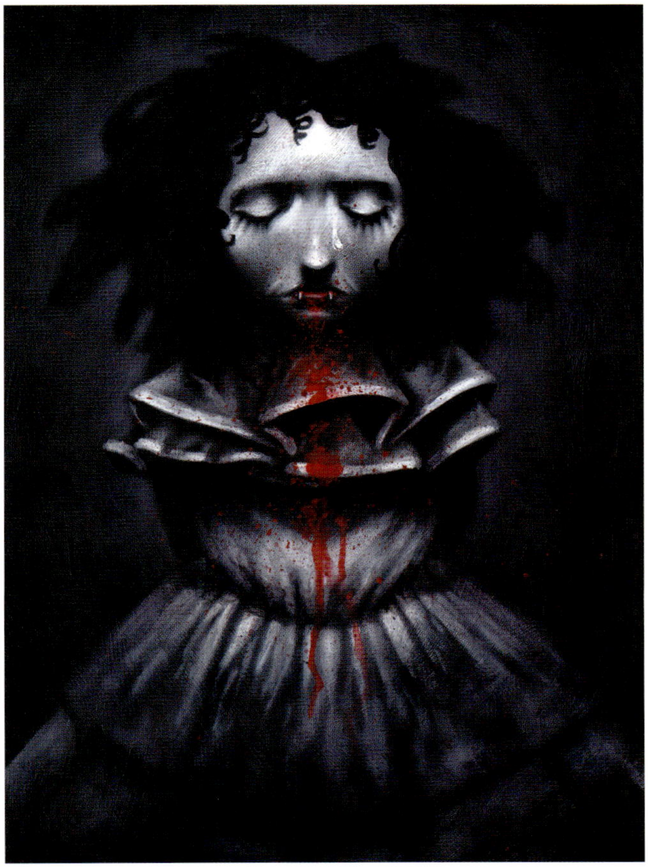

5

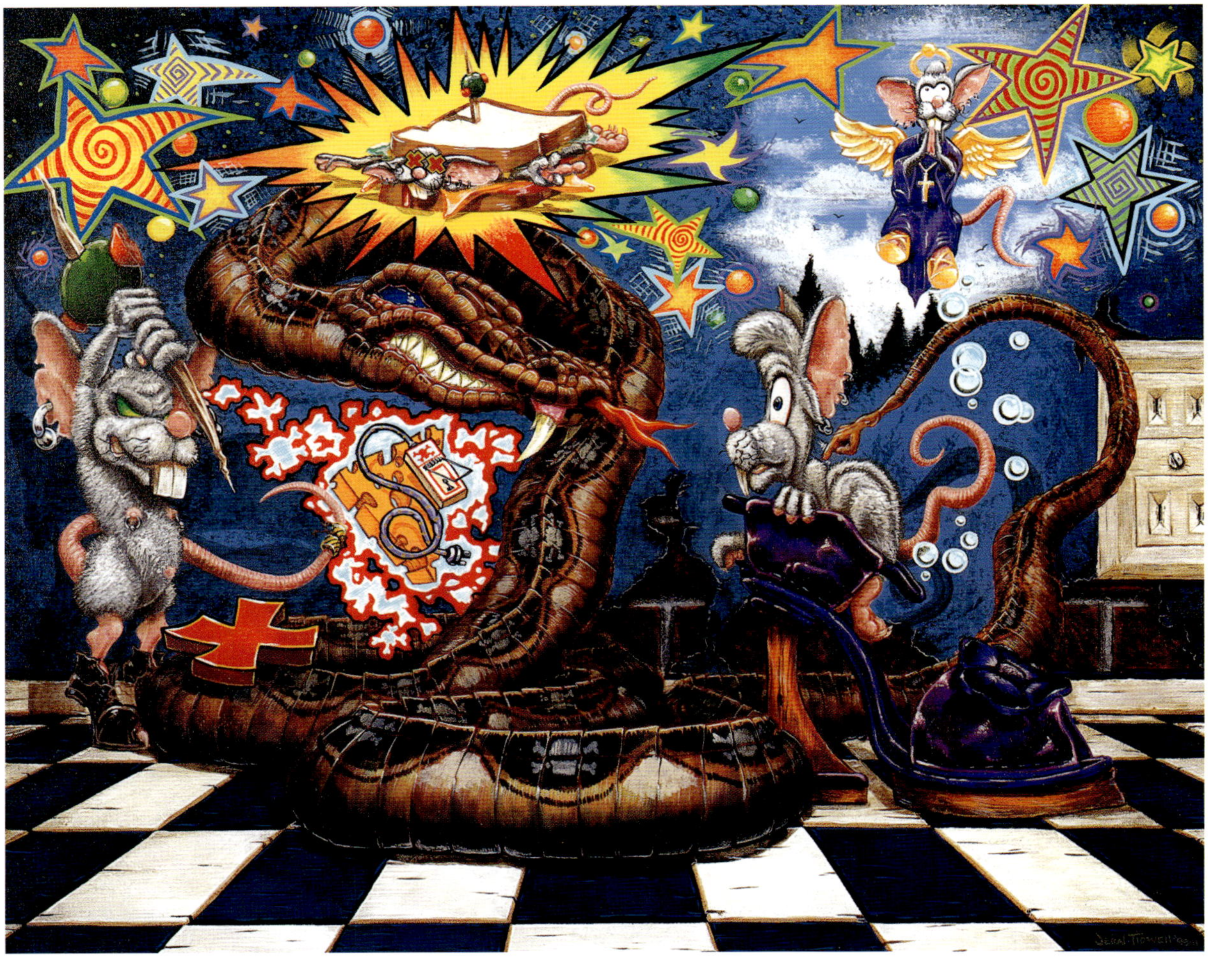

unpublished

1
artist: JEFFREY JONES
medium: Oil

2
artist: EDWARD MILLER
title: Avalon Heights
medium: Acrylic

3
artist: BRAD R. KUNKLE
title: Wish
medium: Oil
size: 24"x32"

4
artist: JEFFREY JONES
medium: Oil

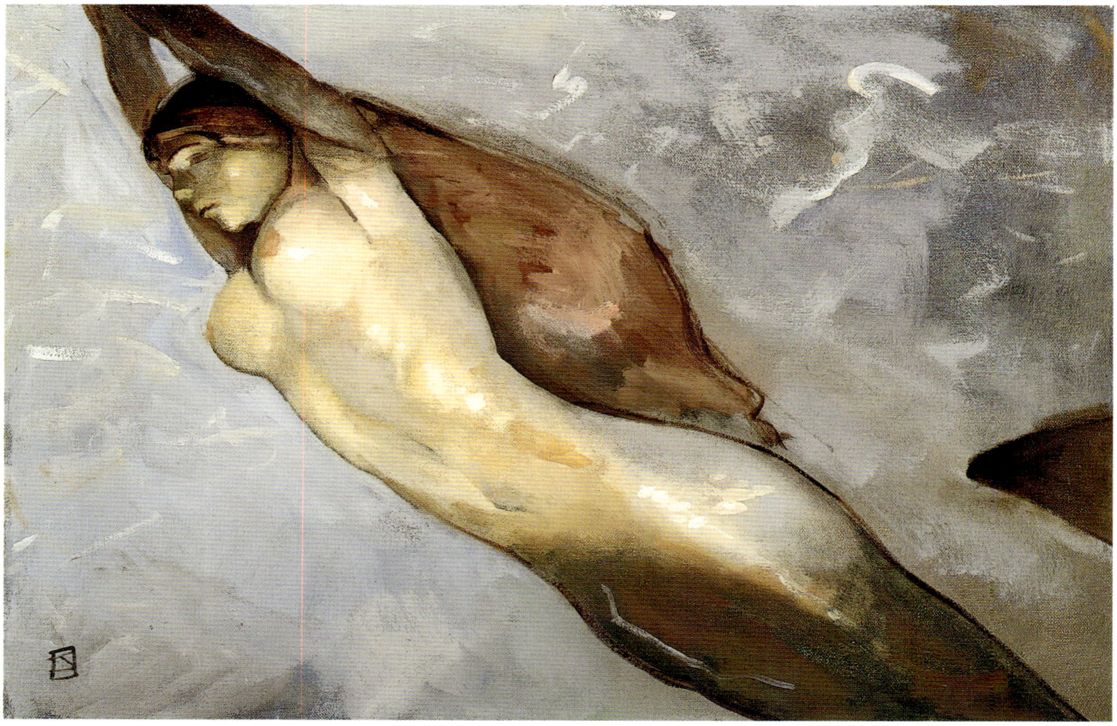

1

2

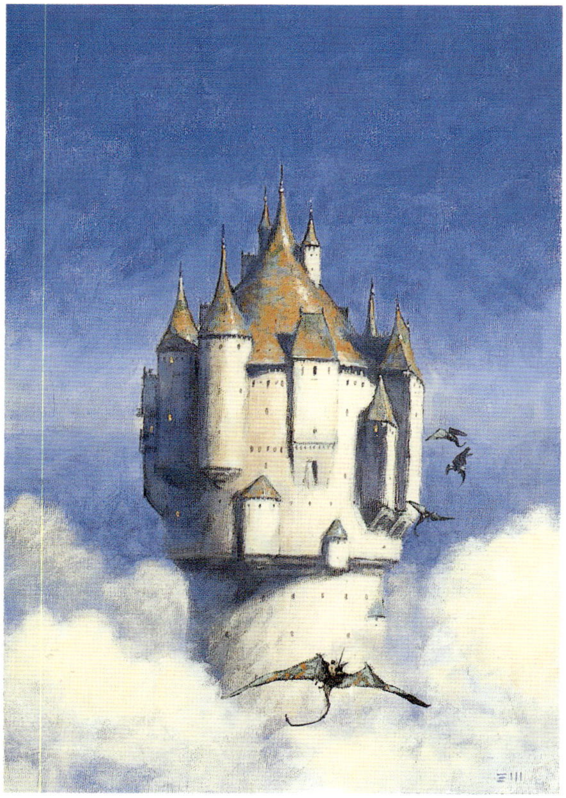

3

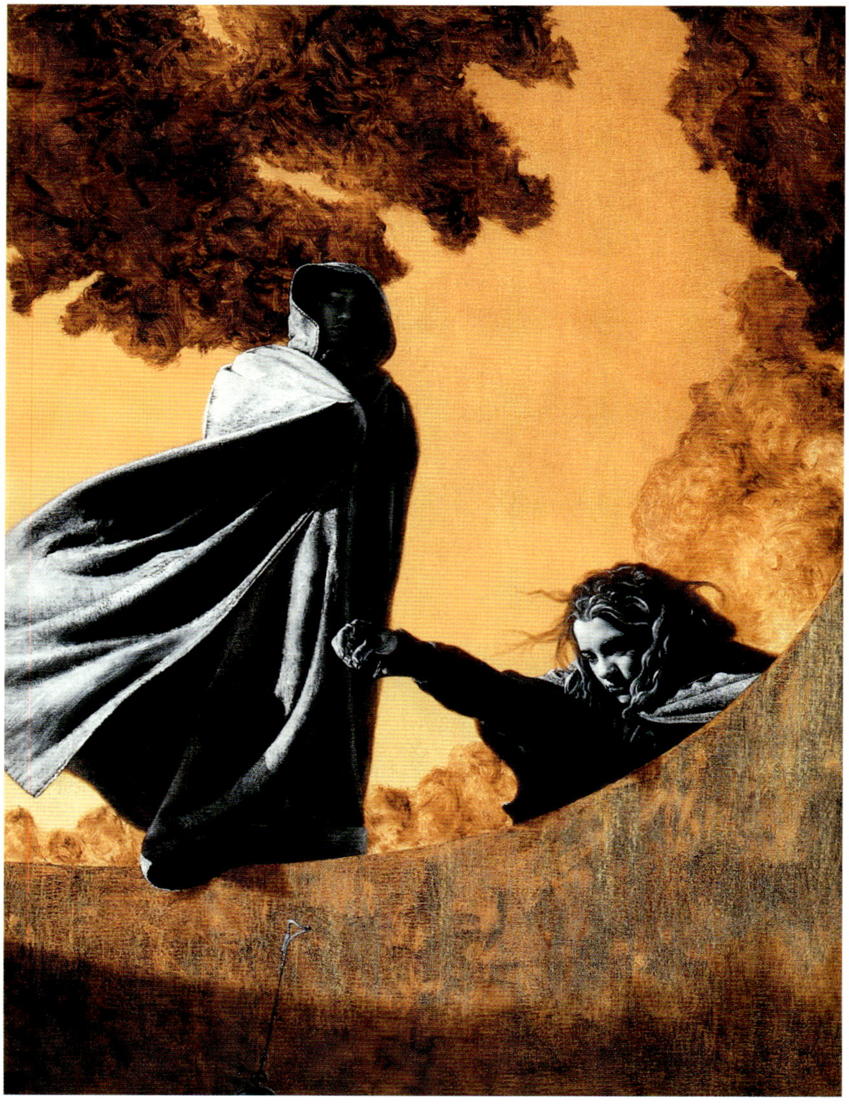

4

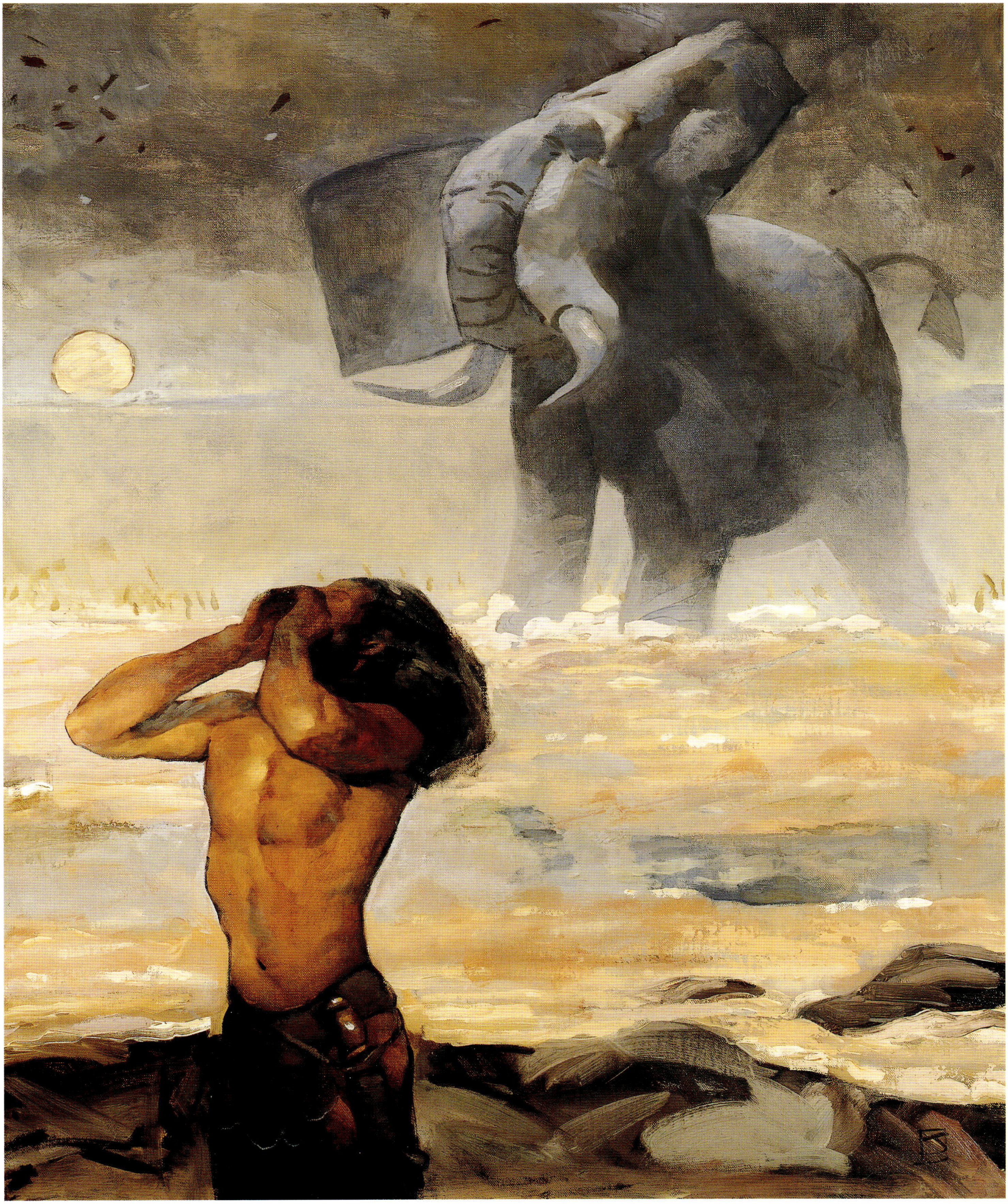

1
artist: SCOTT GRIMANDO
designer: Scott Grimando
client: Grim Studios
title: Sand Gunner
medium: Digital
size: 11"x8 1/2"

2
artist: DAVID HO
art director: David Ho
title: The Way
medium: Mixed/digital
size: 30"x40"

3
artist: JON FOSTER
art director: Jon Foster
title: Blue Bolt
medium: Oil
size: 20"x30"

4
artist: JON FOSTER
art director: Jon Foster
title: Crowbot
medium: Oil
size: 24"x40"

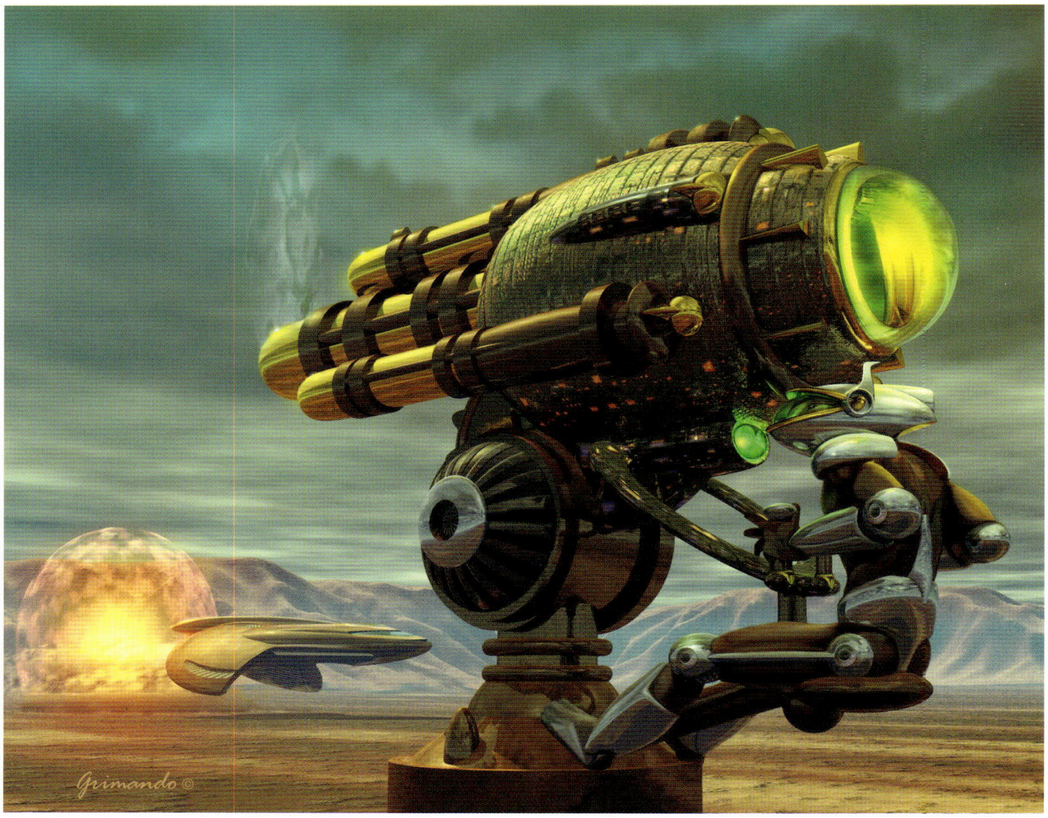

1

2

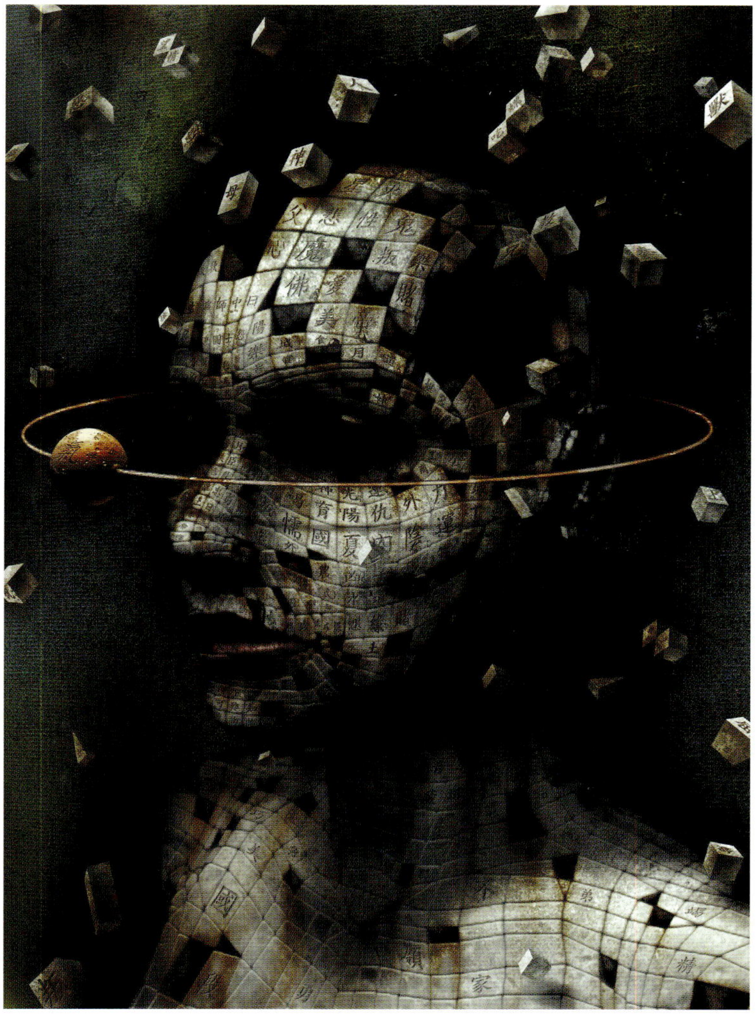

3

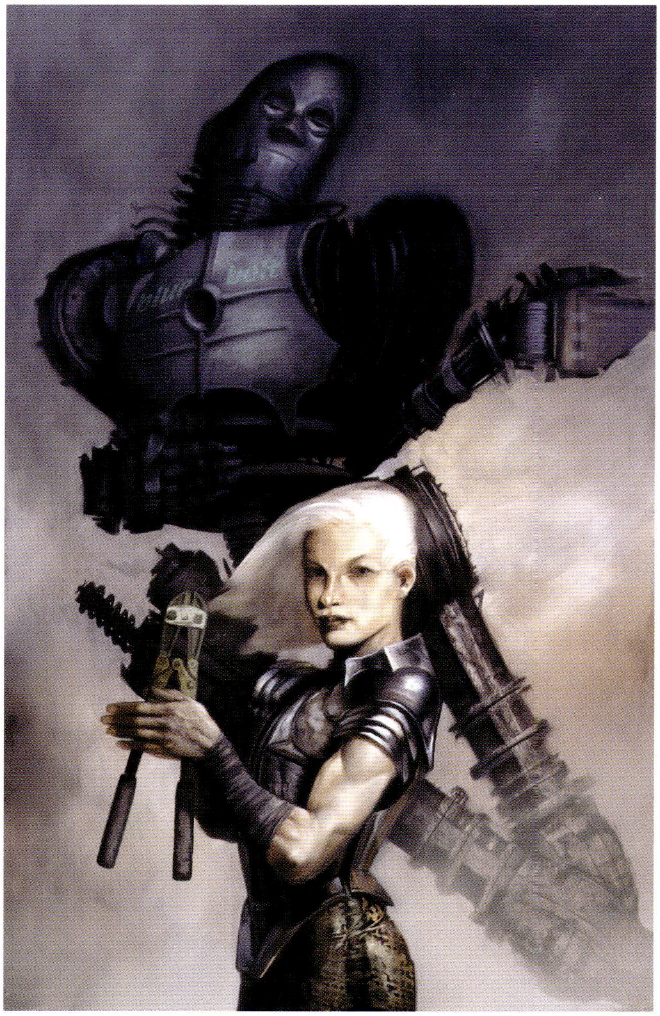

4

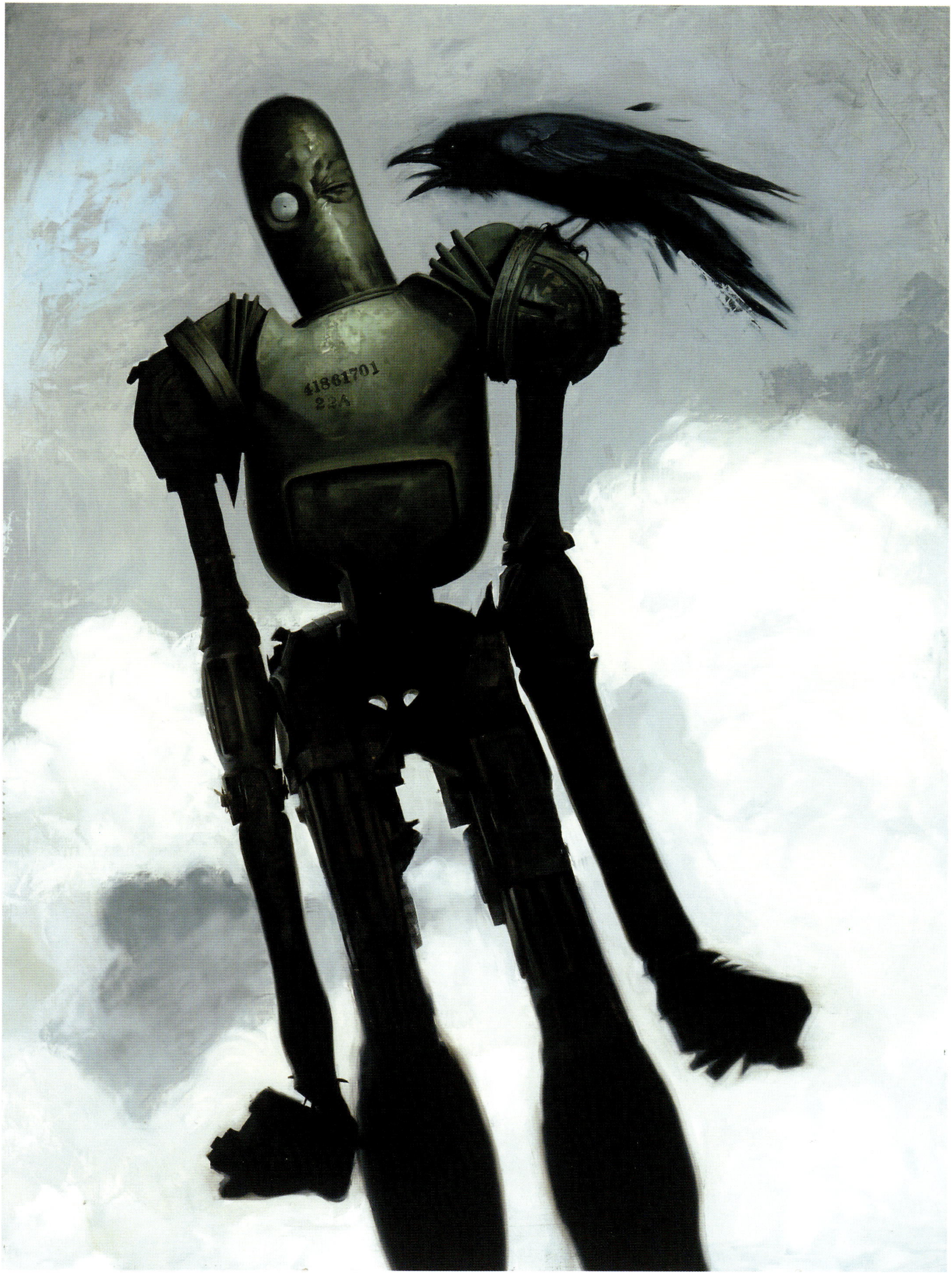

1
artist: JOHN JUDE PALENCAR
title: Bird Shrine
medium: Acrylic
size: 12"x12"

2
artist: PETAR MESELDZIJA
art director: Jan-Willem Lodder
client: Verkerke Reprodukties
title: The Lord of the Rings: Shadow Comes
medium: Oil
size: 21 1/4"x31 1/2"

3
artist: MARC FISHMAN
client: Rose & Harald Kinney
title: La Belle elam Sans Meri
medium: Oil
size: 30"x40"

4
artist: PETAR MESELDZIJA
art director: Jan-Willem Lodder
client: Verkerke Reprodukties
title: The Lord of the Rings: Gandalf
medium: Oil
size: 19 1/2"x27 1/2"

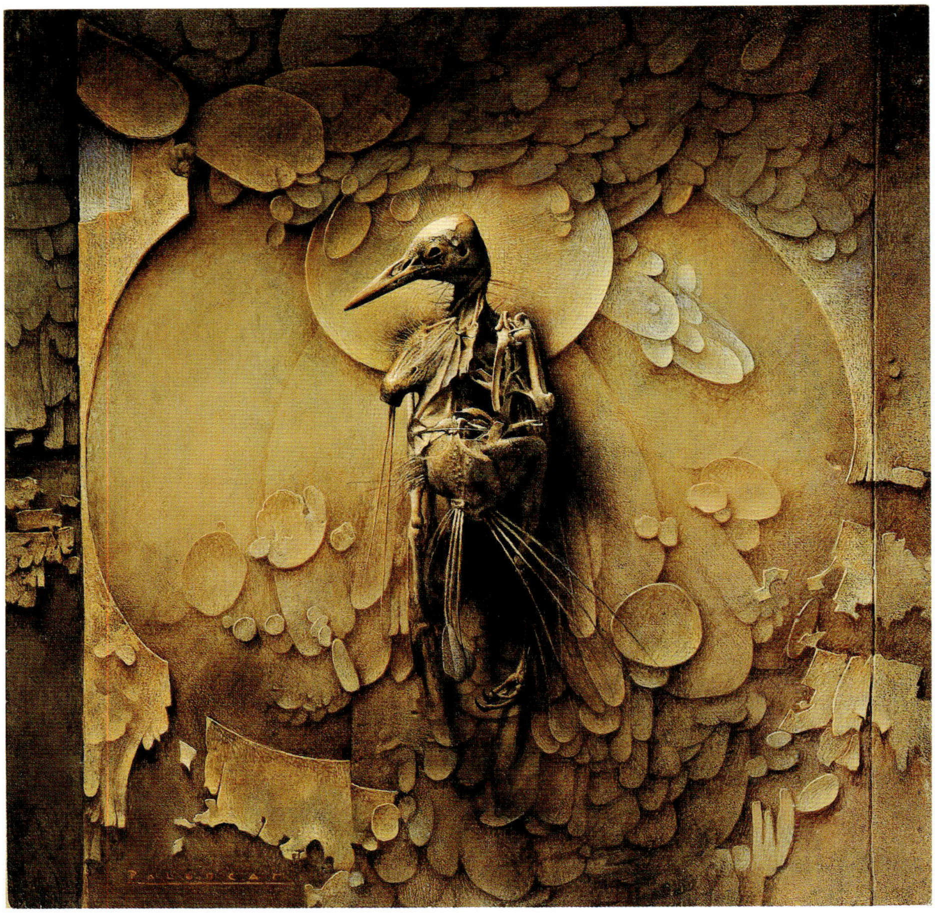

1

2

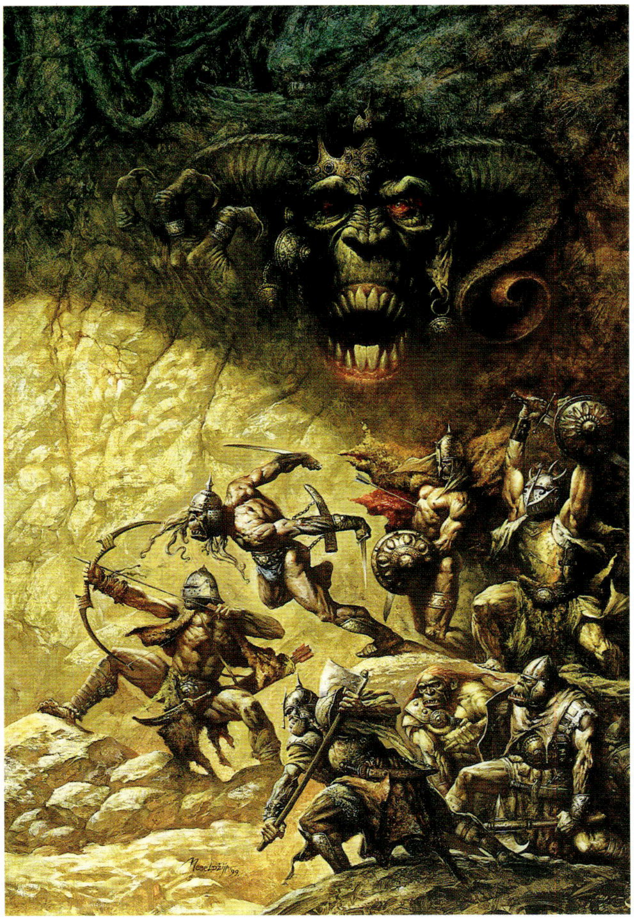

3

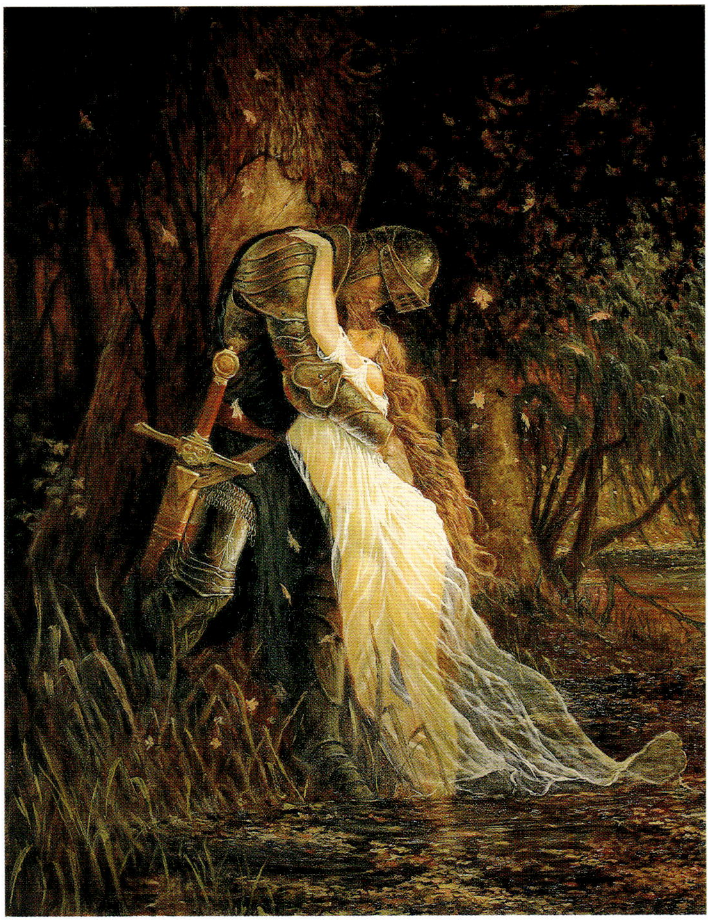

4

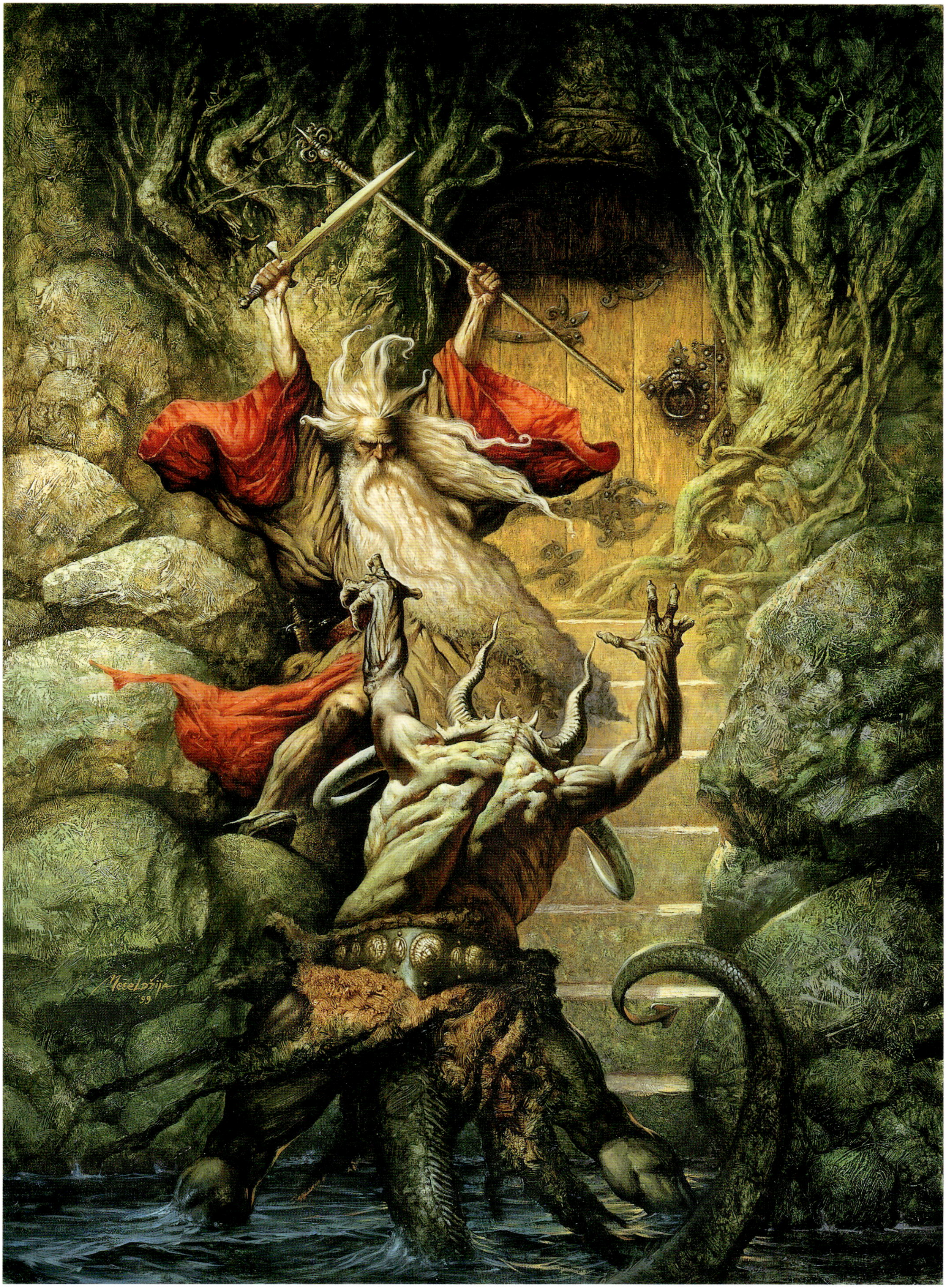

1
artist: LORI KOEFOED
art director: Lori Koefoed
title: Hel's Domain
medium: Oil
size: 11"x16"

2
artist: CHRISTOPHER SCALF
title: Siren's Warning
medium: Acrylic
size: 15"x20"

3
artist: JENNIFER EMMETT WEYLAND
title: Queen of Malachite
medium: Oil
size: 16"x20"

4
artist: CAROL HEYER
title: Guardian at the Gate
medium: Acrylic
size: 30"x40"

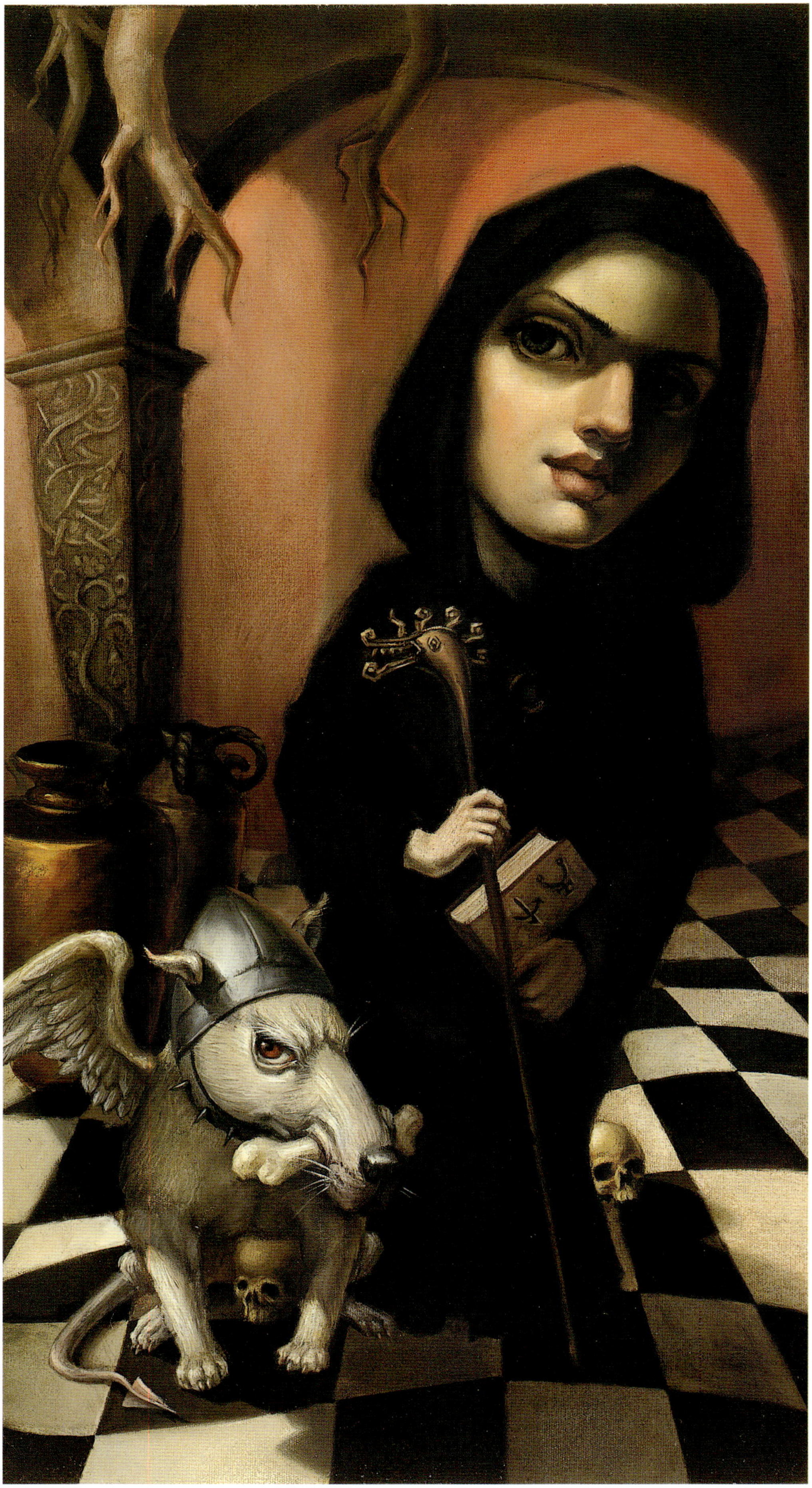

1

2

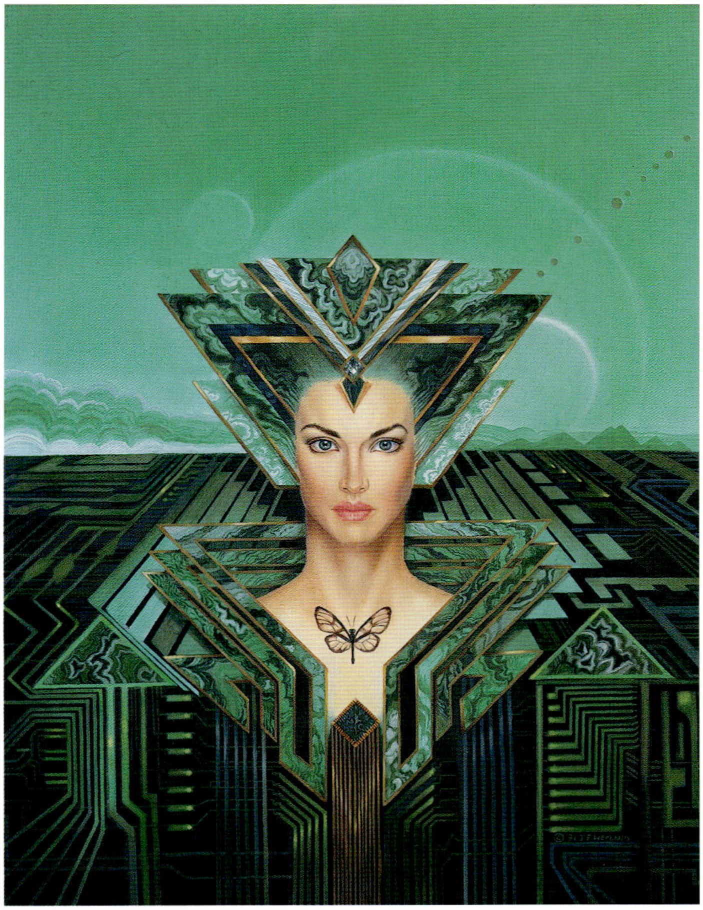

3

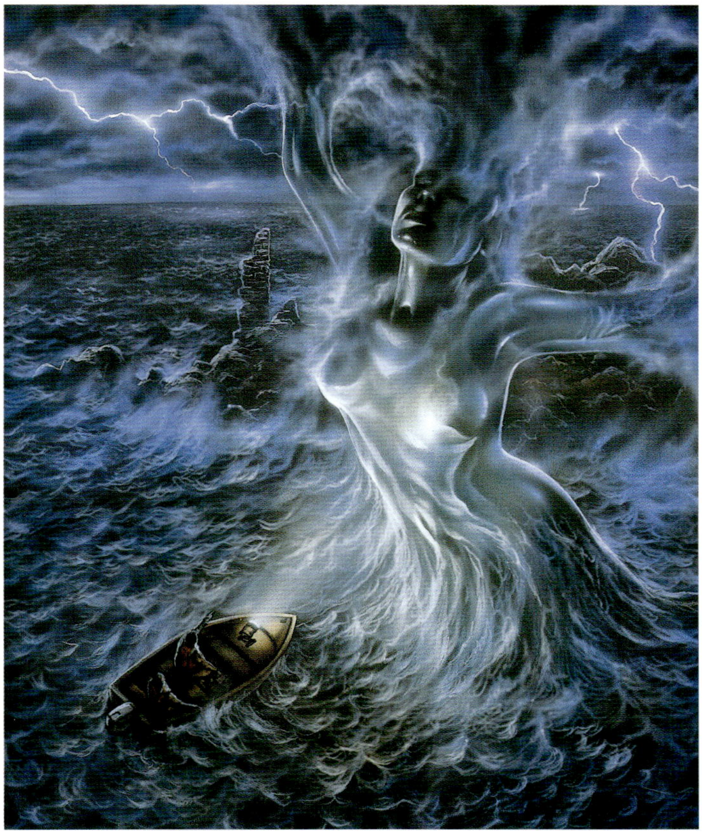

4

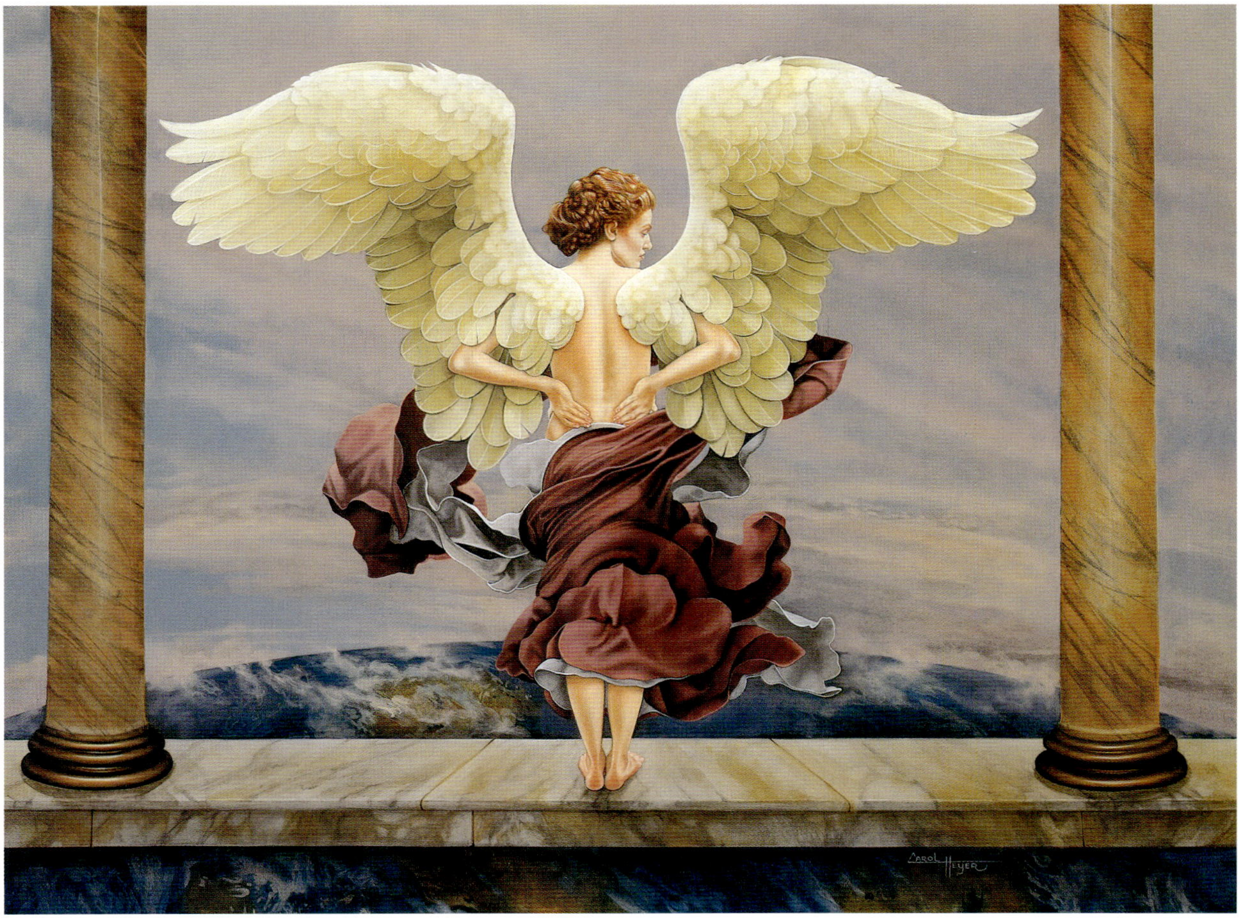

unpublished

1
artist: RON WOODALL
art director: Ron Woodall
title: Keep Off
medium: Photo/digital
size: 10"x8"

2
artist: KYLE ANDERSON
title: Bioremm
medium: Digital
size: 7 1/2"x10"

3
artist: MIKE BOHATCH
title: Gates of Vision
medium: Mixed/digital
size: 6"x9"

4
artist: STEPHAN MARTINIERE
title: Horol
medium: Mixed

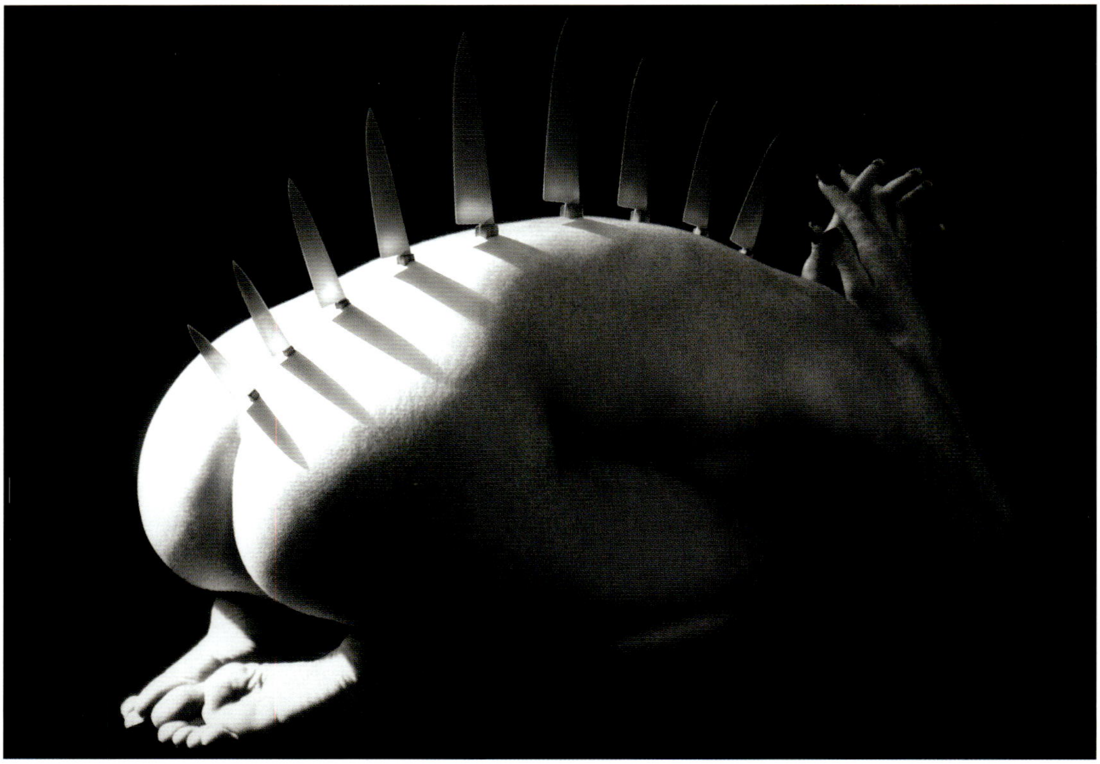

1

2

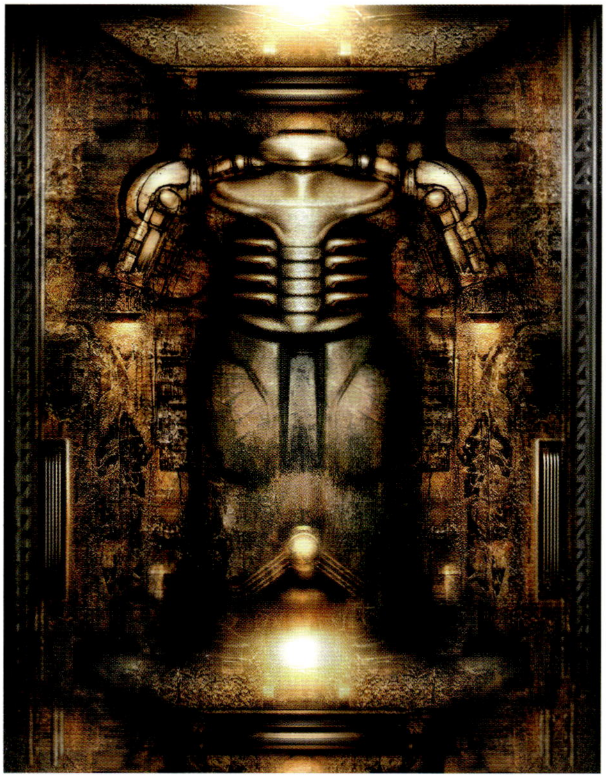

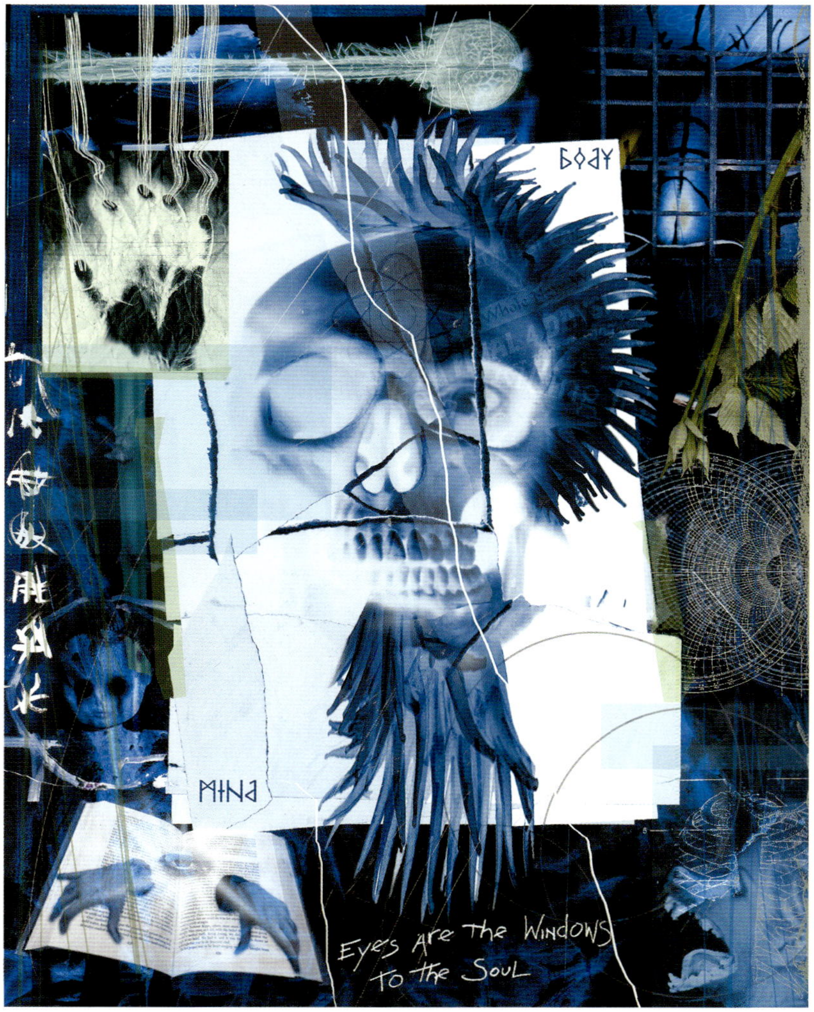

3

4

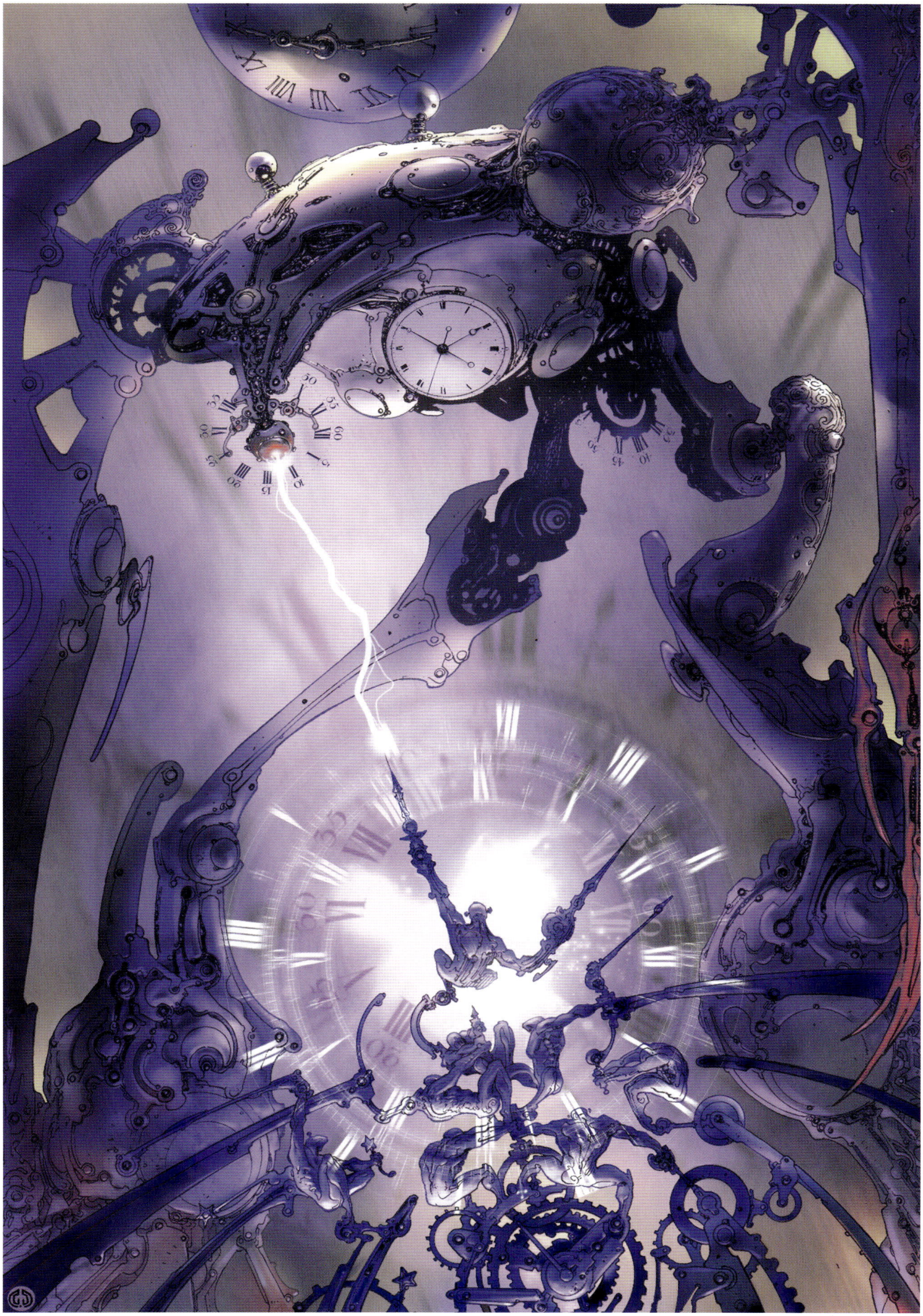

1
artist: SHANE JOHNSON
art director: Glen Grant
client: Chickenskin Press
title: Inugami
medium: Ink/digital
size: 5 1/2"x9"

2
artist: CATHY WILKINS
title: Atropos
medium: Digital

3
artist: CHRIS TREVAS
title: Chance Encounter
medium: Acrylic
size: 18"x8"

4
artist: EDWARD BINKLEY
title: The Ticketeer
medium: Digital
size: 22"x9"

5
artist: EDWARD BINKLEY
title: Come Closer
medium: Digital
size: 22"x9"

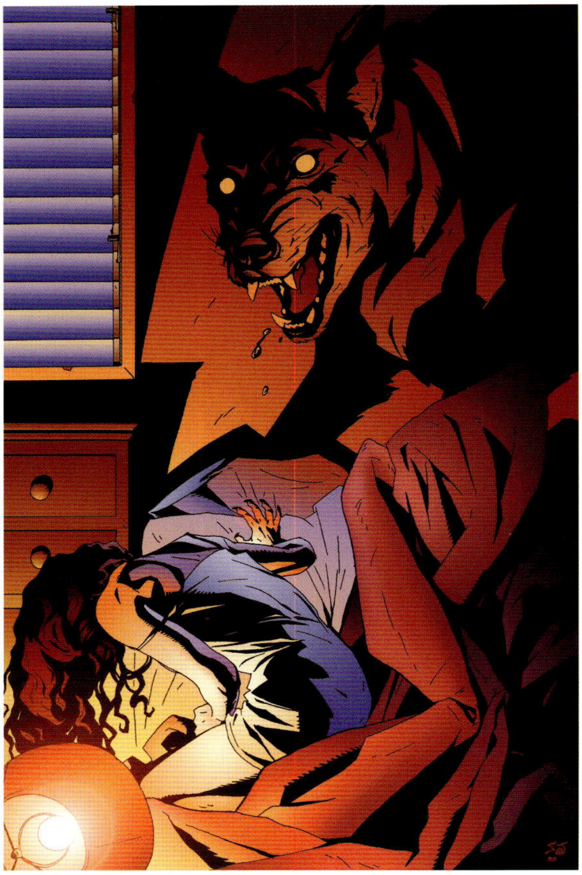

1

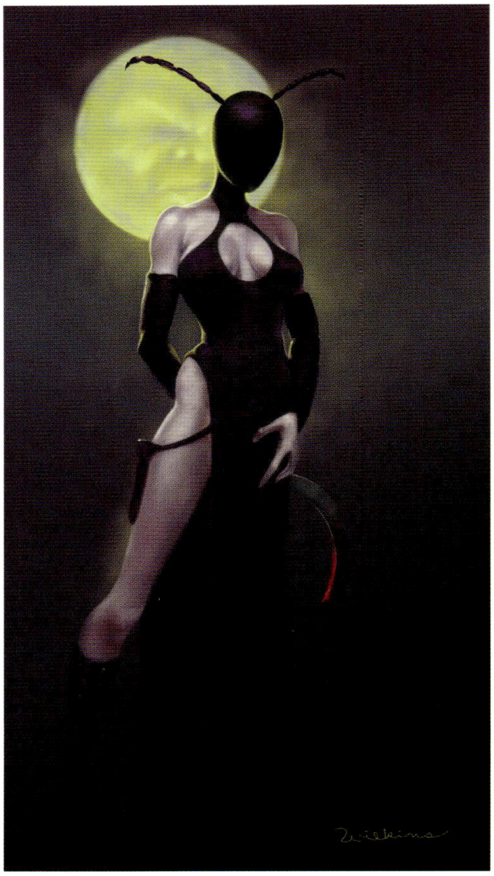

2

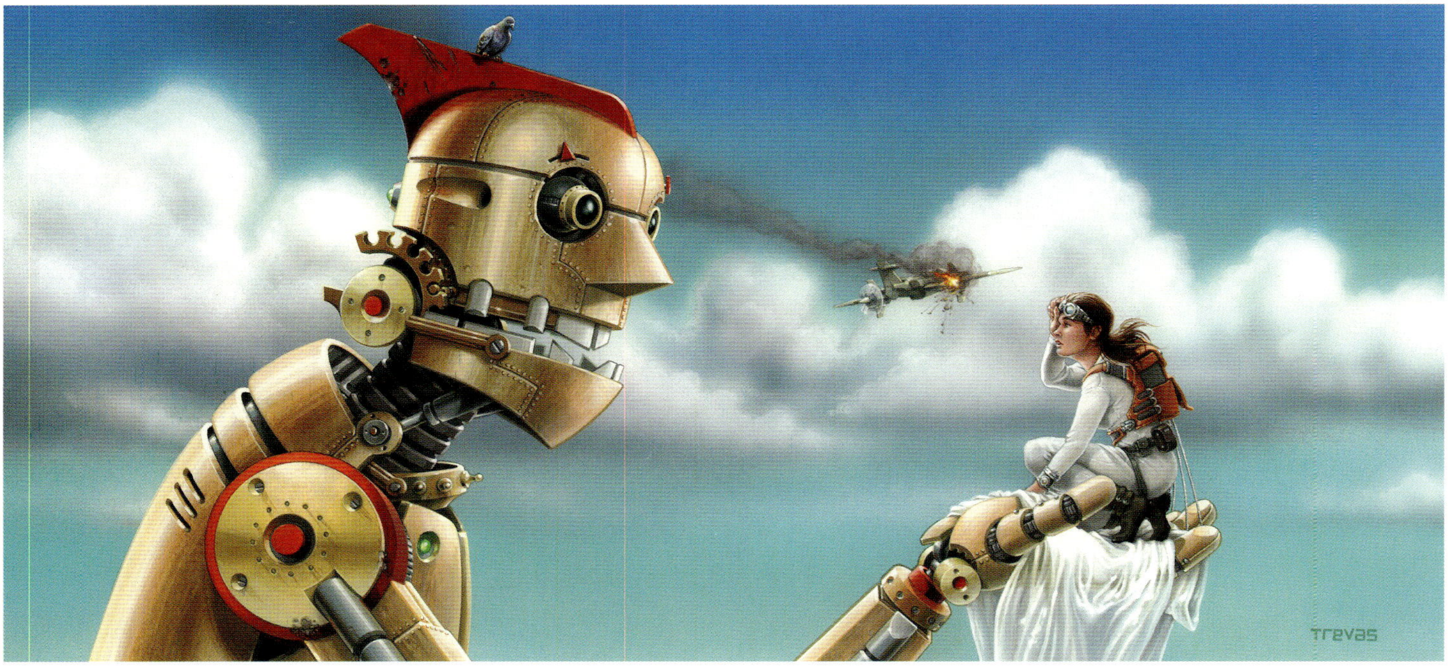

3

6
artist: ALAN POLLACK
art director: Irene Gallo
client: Tor Books
title: Plague
medium: Oil
size: 20 1/2"x7 1/2"

4
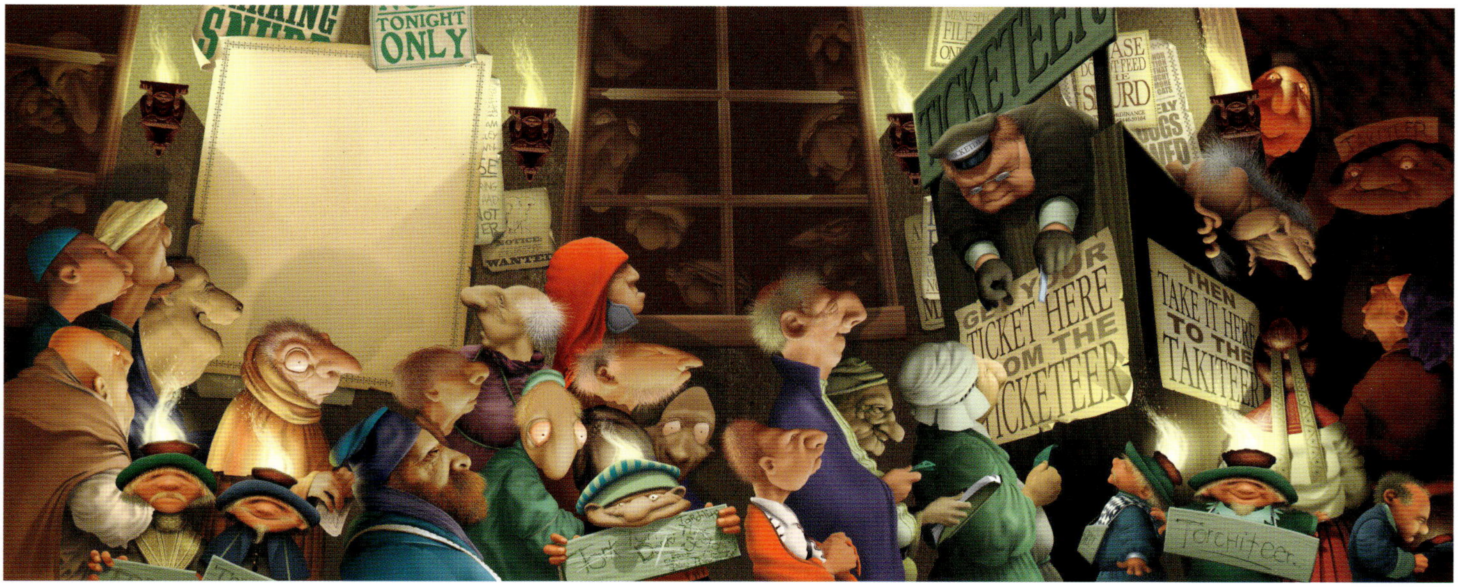
TONIGHT ONLY
TICKETEER
TICKET HERE
TICKETEER
THEN TAKE IT HERE TO THE TAKITEER
Torchiteer

5
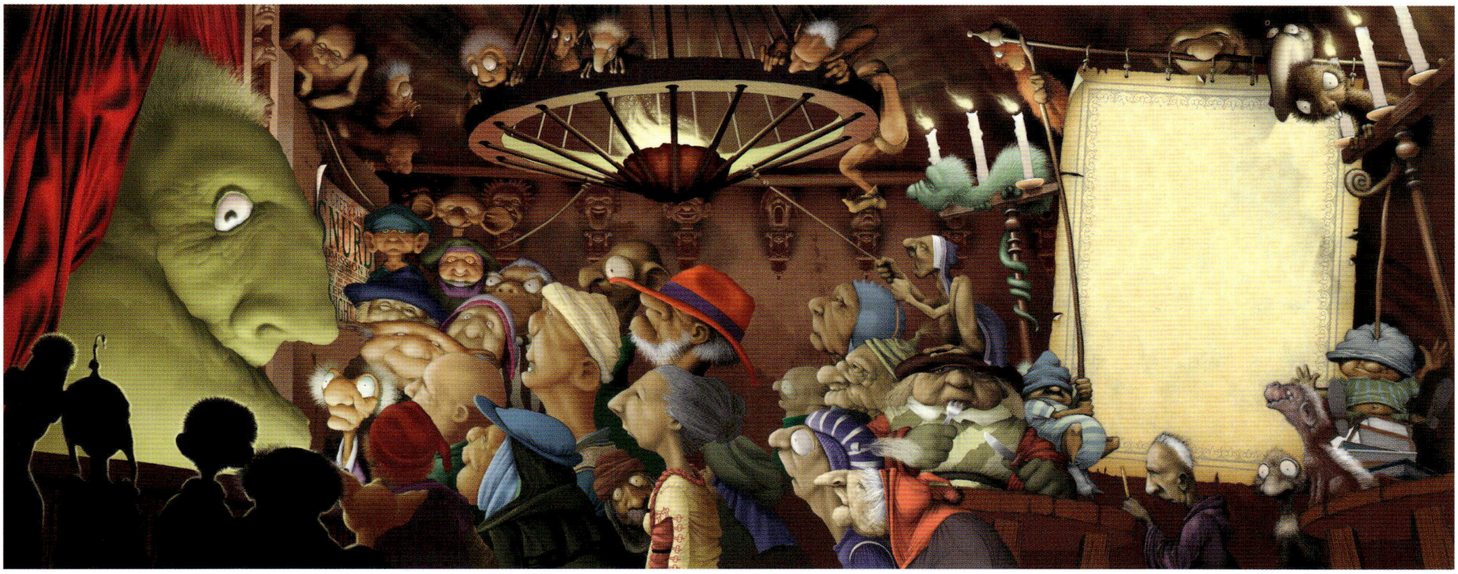

6
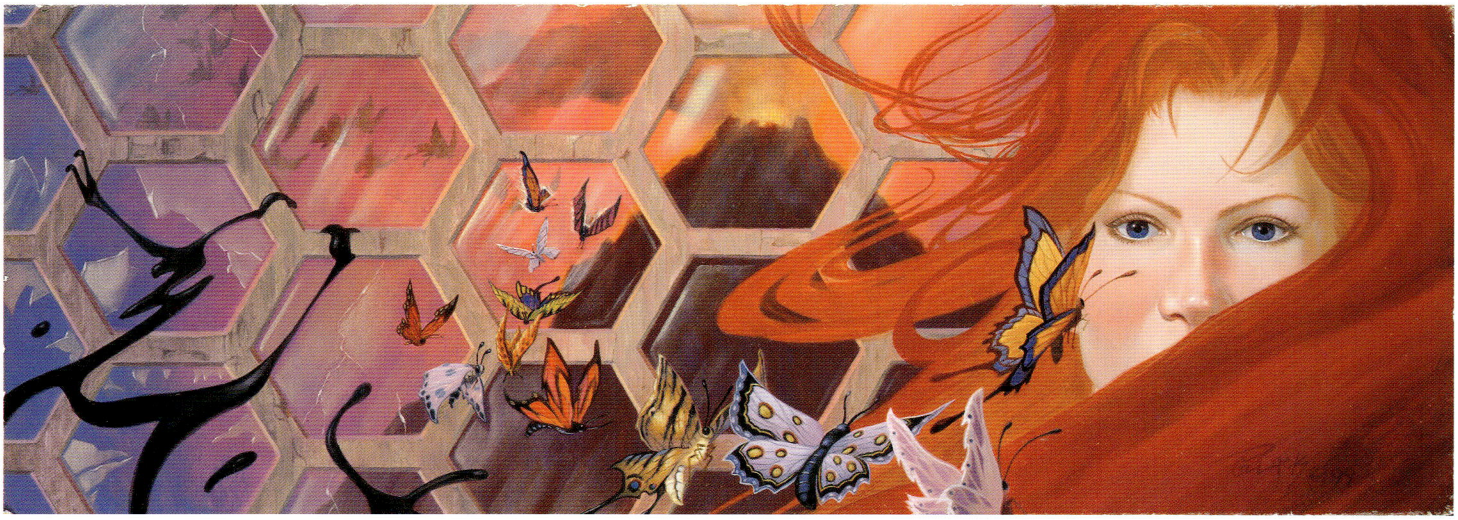

1
artist: MARC FISHMAN
title: Hercules and The Hydra
medium: Oil
size: 48"x66"

2
artist: MARC FISHMAN
title: Gabriel's Lament
medium: Oil
size: 42"x56"

3
artist: CHARLES KEEGAN
title: Silver Shield
medium: Oil
size: 16"x20"

4
artist: ZOOK
title: The Forbidden
medium: Oil
size: 25"x12"

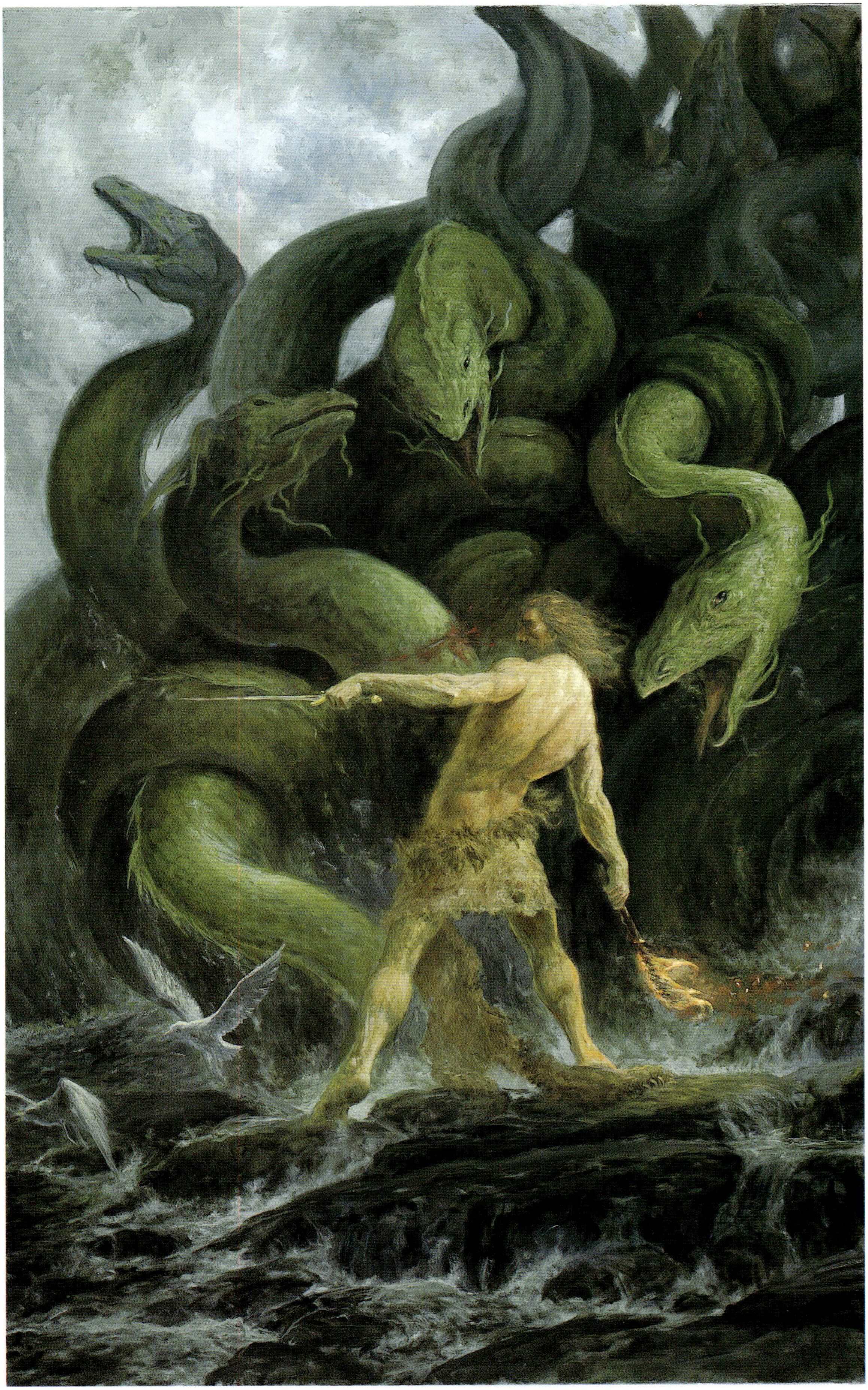

1

2

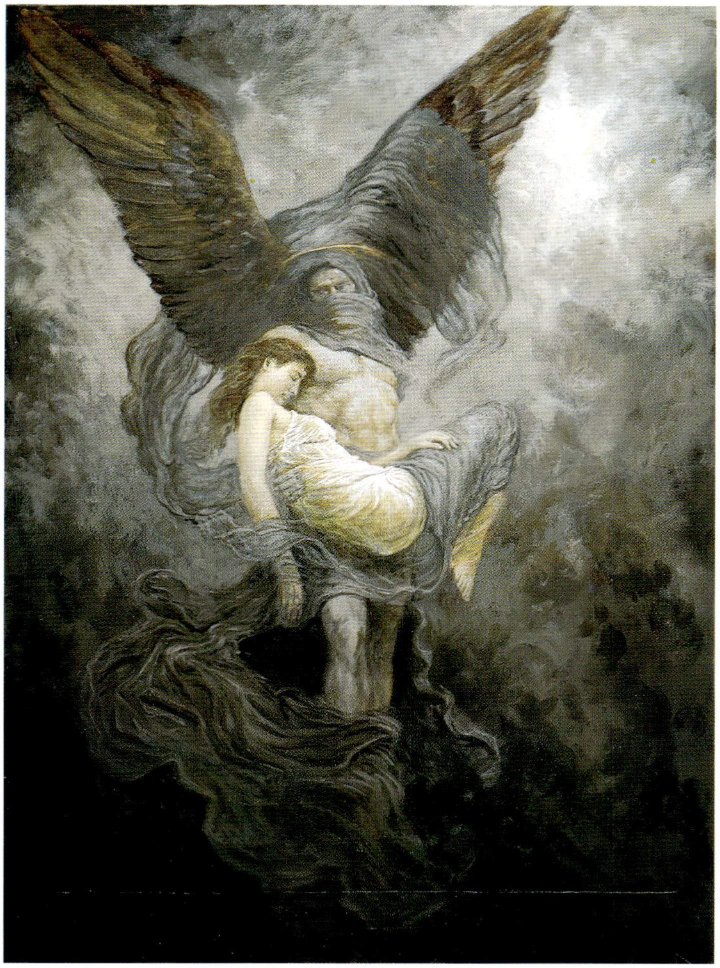

3

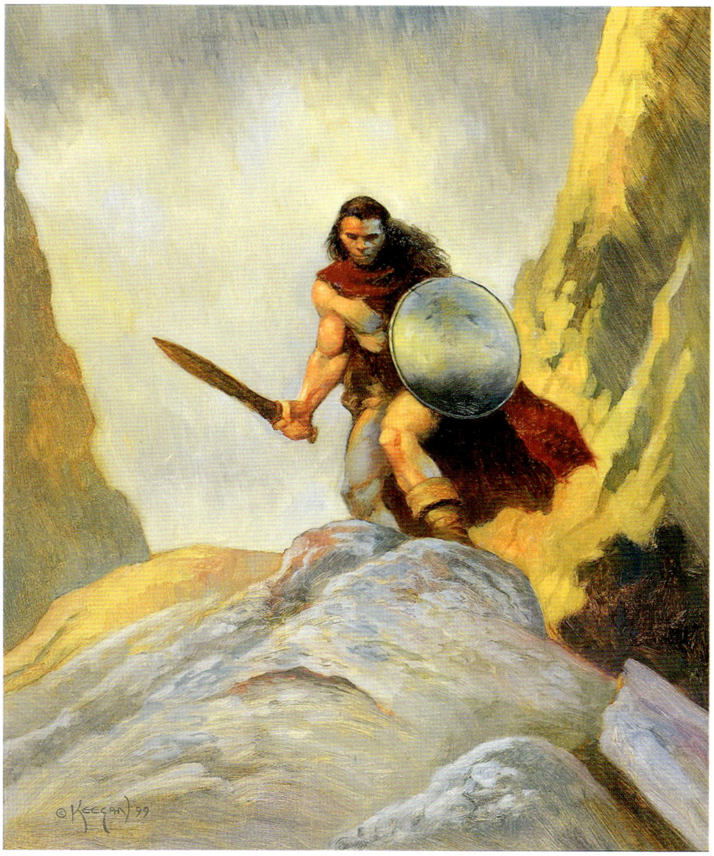

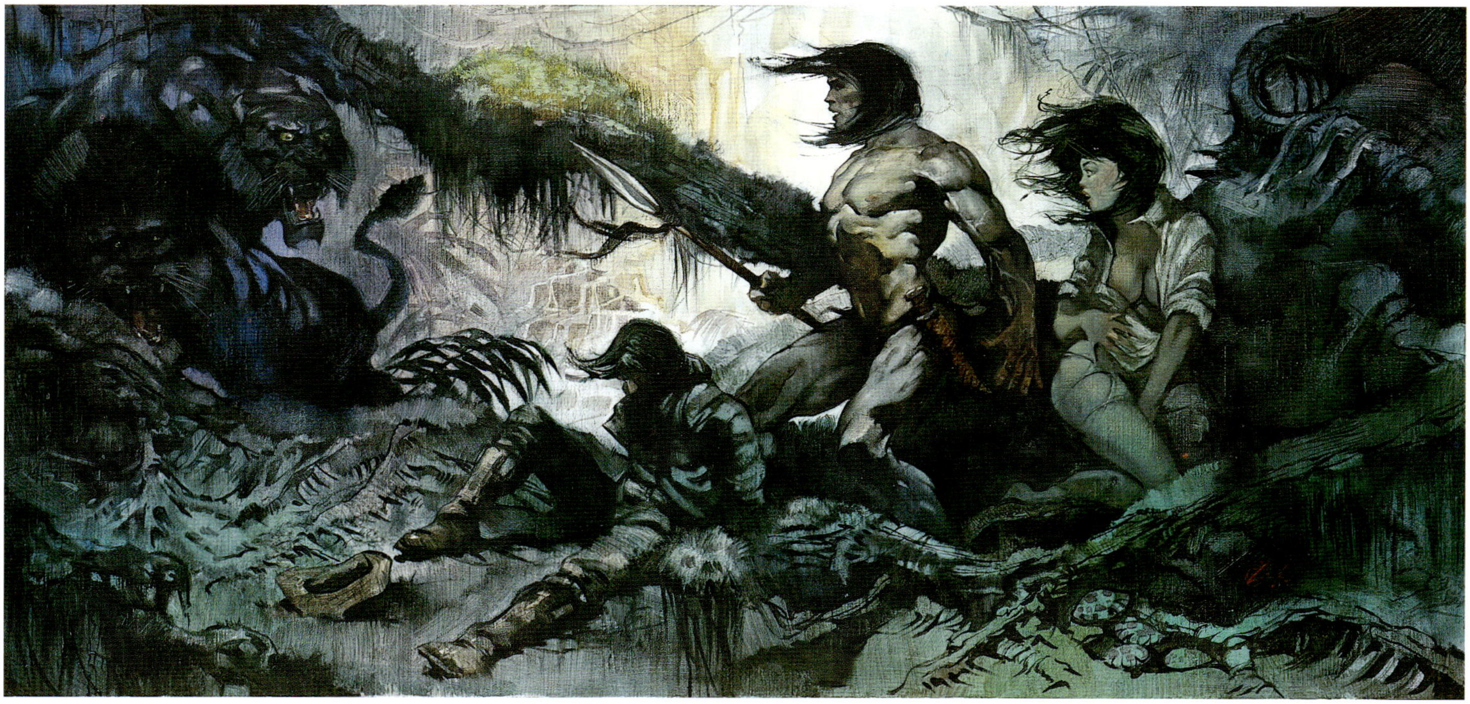

4

1
artist: O.B. SOLINSKY
art director: Marvin Mattelson
designer: O.B. Solinsky
client: Re-Evolution Exhibition
title: Cloned Slavery
medium: Oil
size: 9 3/4"x10 1/4"

2
artist: JOHN POUND
title: The Martyrdom od St. Valentine
medium: Digital
size: 6"x8 1/4"

3
artist: DAVE SEELEY
title: Turtle
medium: Photo/digital

4
artist: DAVE SEELEY
title: Tinkerbot
medium: Photo/digital

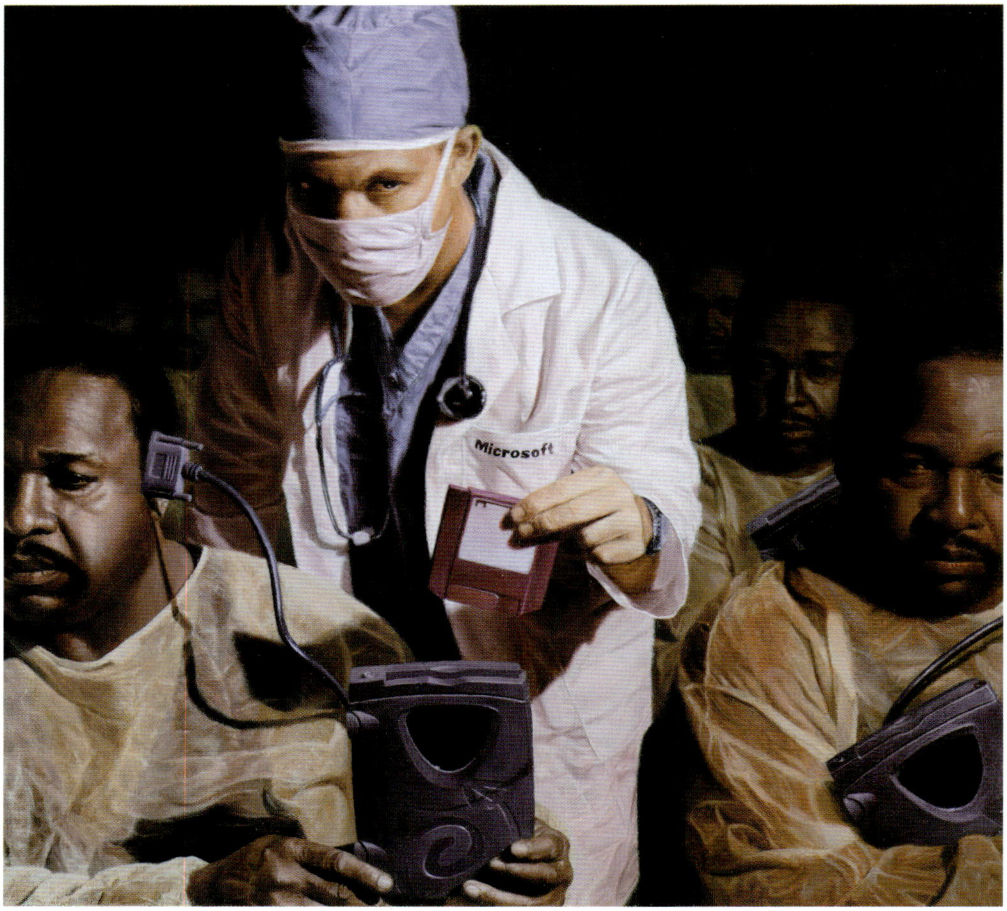

1

2

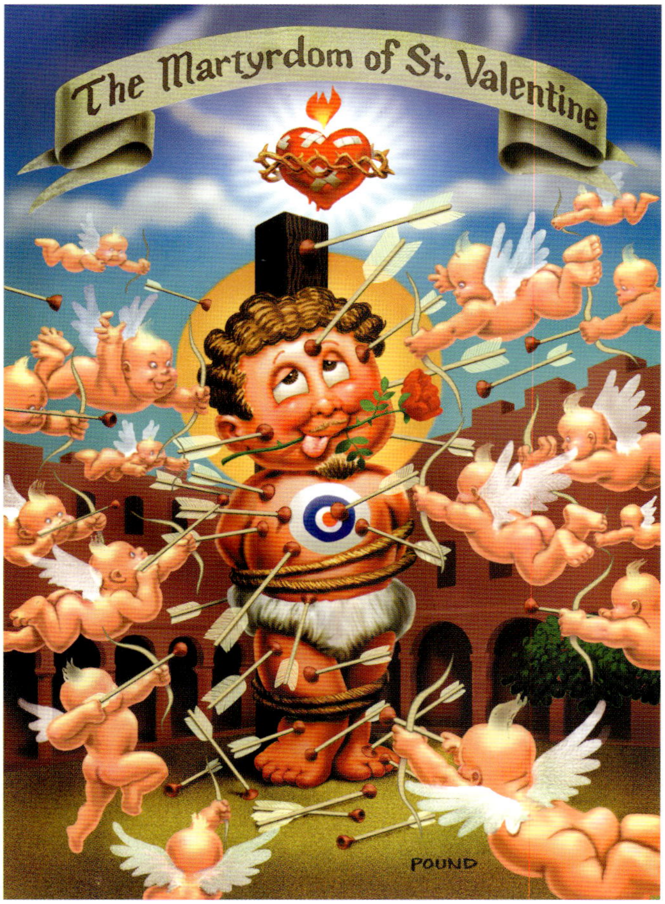

3

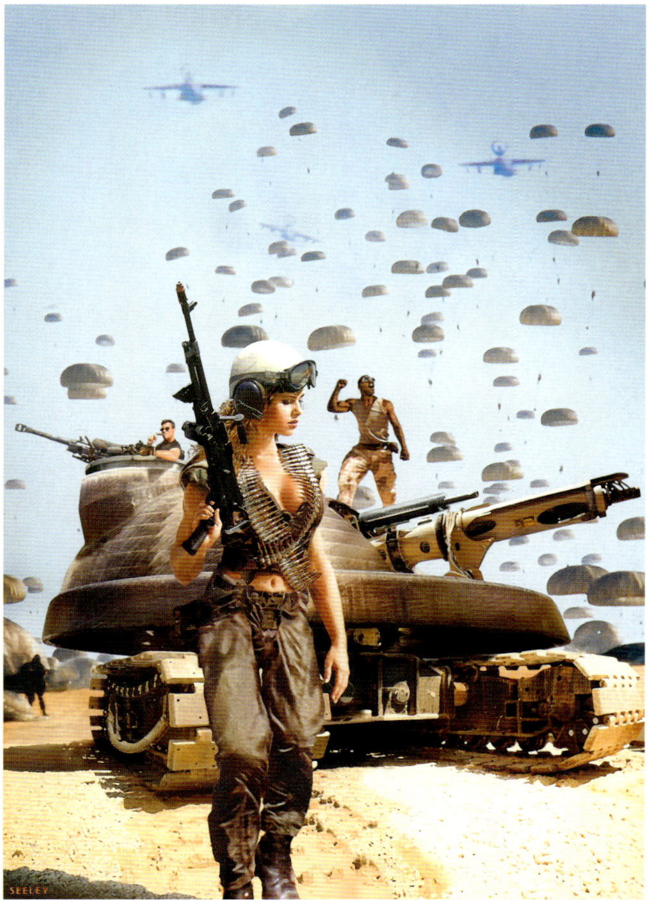

4

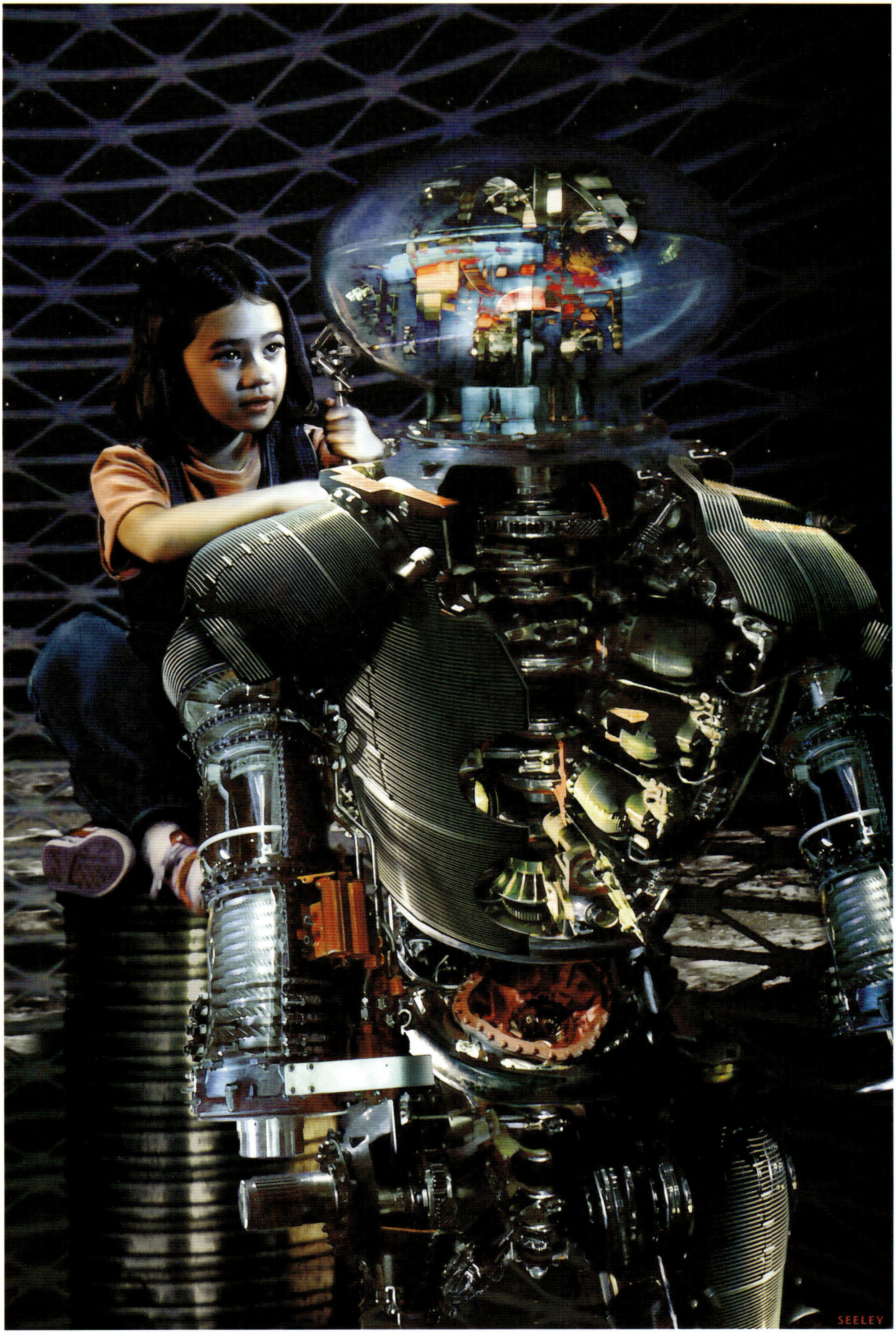

1
artist: NILSON
title: Nocturnals/Bot 18
medium: Oil/acrylic
size: 50cmx20cm

2
artist: RAY LAGO
art director: Madeleine Robins
client: Classics Illustrated/Acclaim
title: Food of the Gods
medium: Watercolor
size: 9"x12 1/2"

3
artist: NICK CHOLES
title: Bullgod
medium: Oil
size: 20"x30"

4
artist: NILSON
medium: Mixed
size: 30cmx20cm

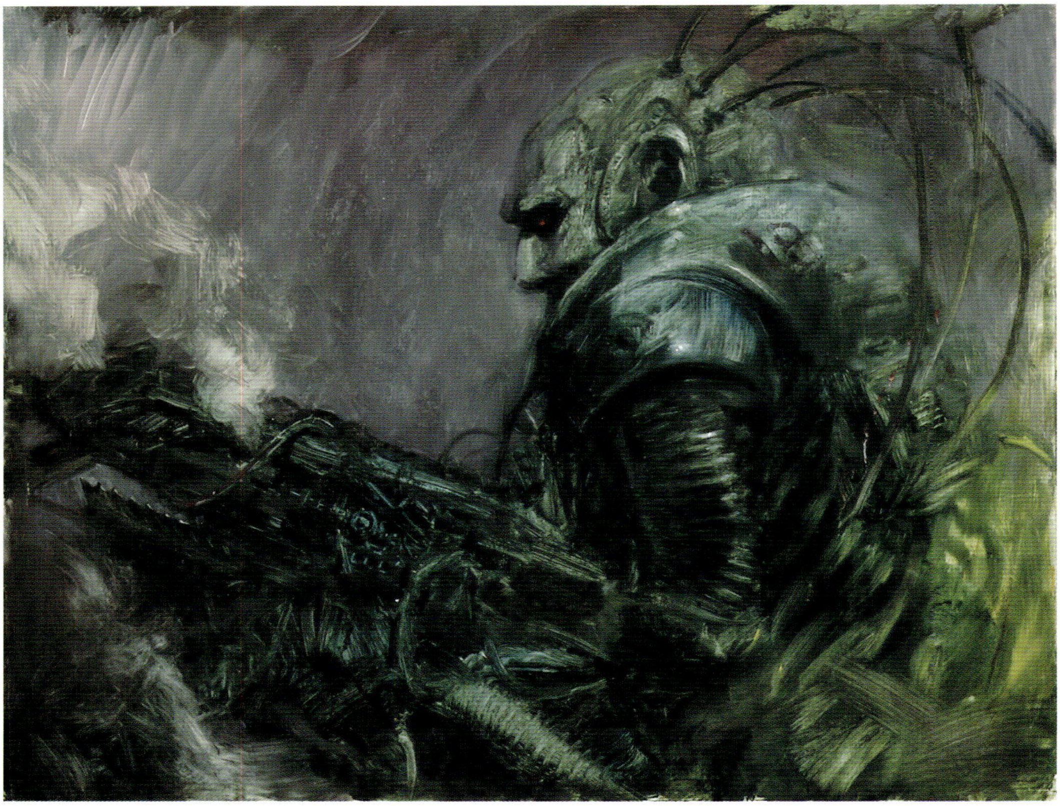

1

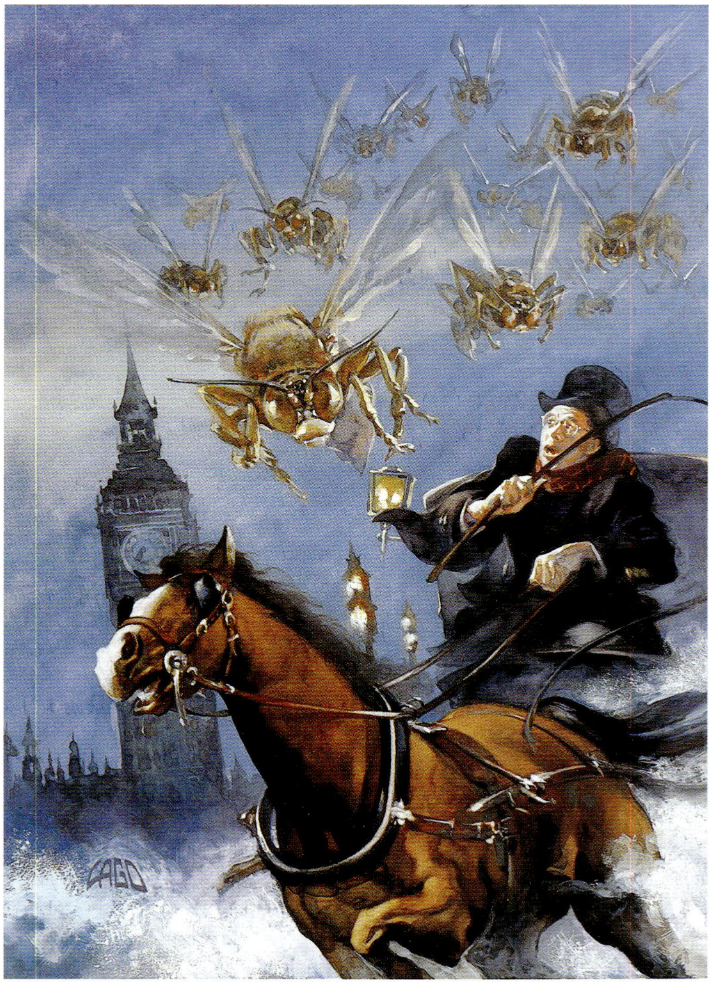

2

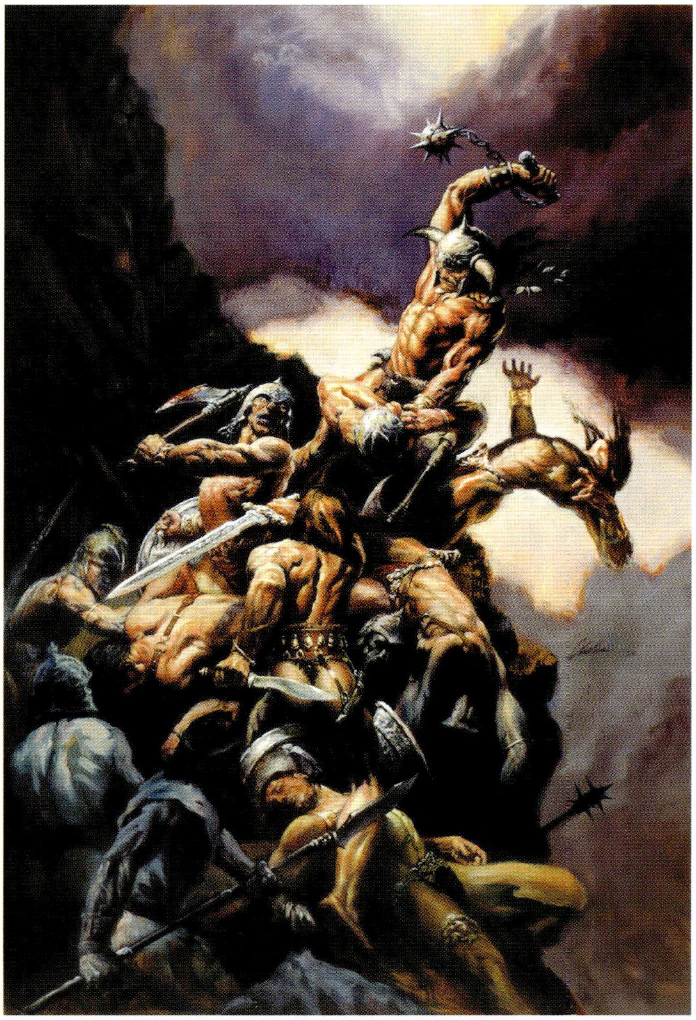

3

4

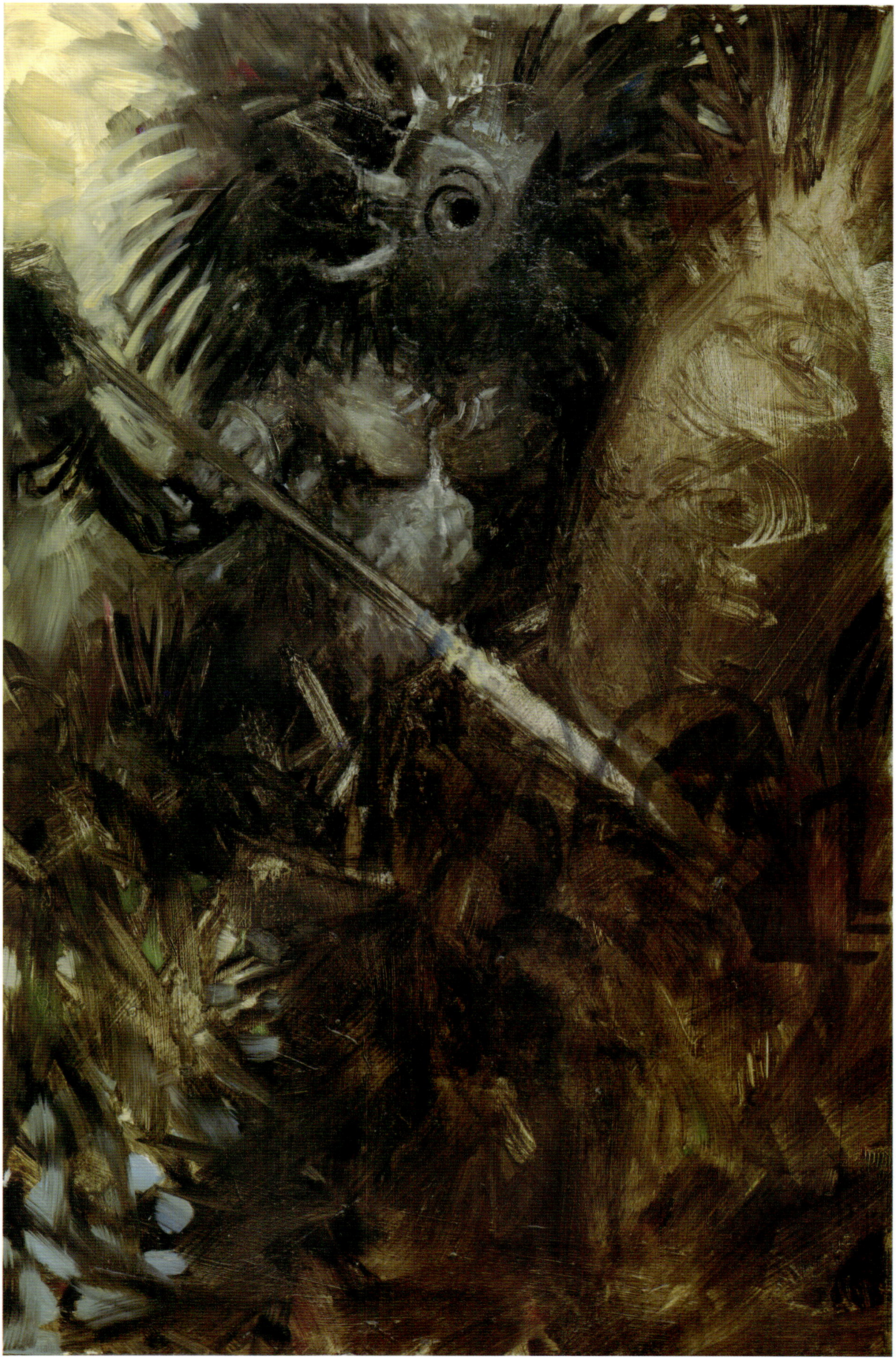

1
artist: SCOTT EVERETT BURTON
title: From Ancients Echoes
Nature Immortal
medium: Acrylic/pencil
size: 20"x20"

2
artist: BOB EGGLETON
art director: Bob Eggleton
title: Retro-Rocket
medium: Acrylic
size: 30"x8"

3
artist: JOHN C. BERKEY
art director: John C. Berkey
designer: John C. Berkey
client: John C. Berkey
title: Clowns Waltz
medium: Acrylic
size: 25"x15"

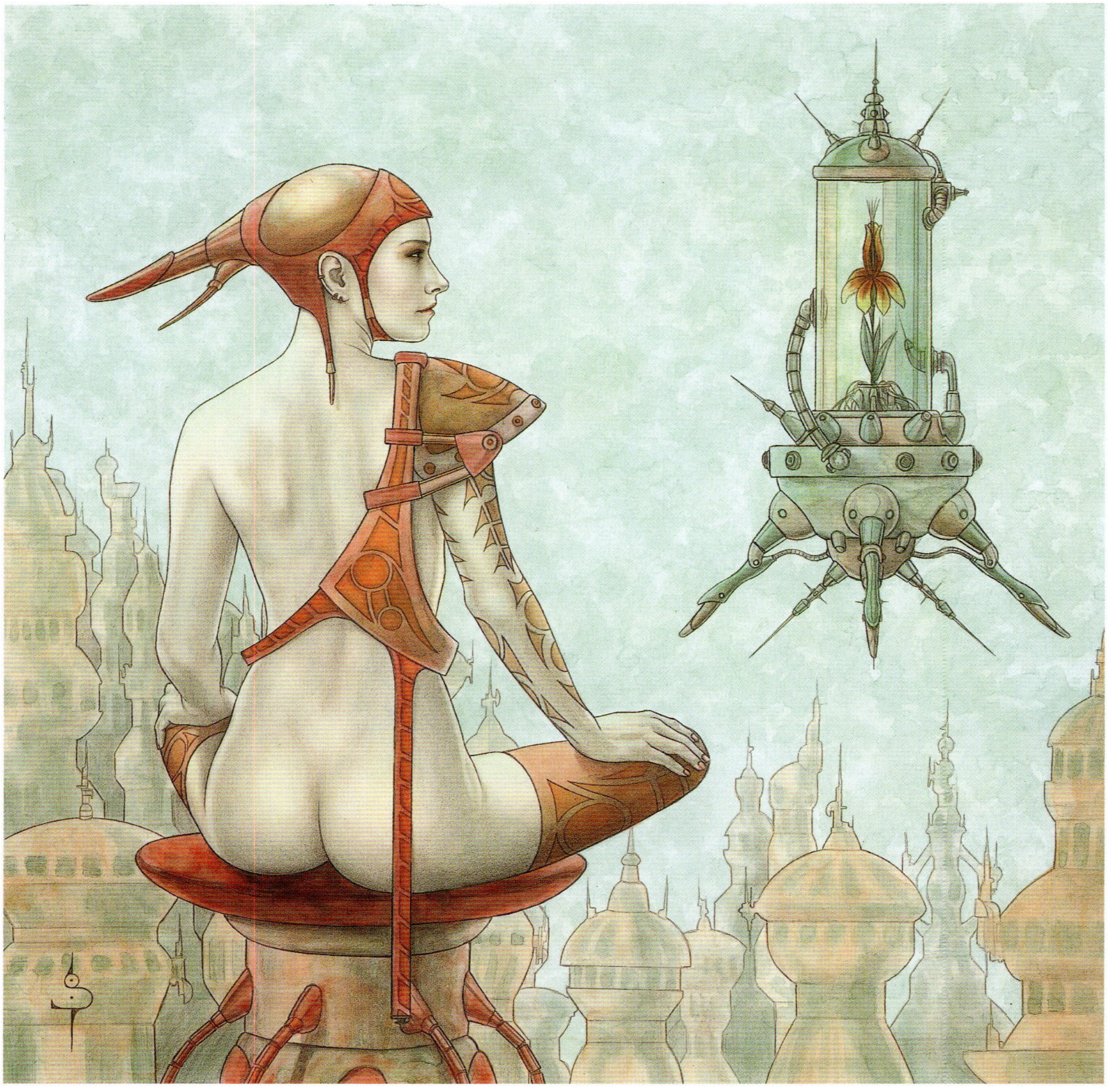

1

2

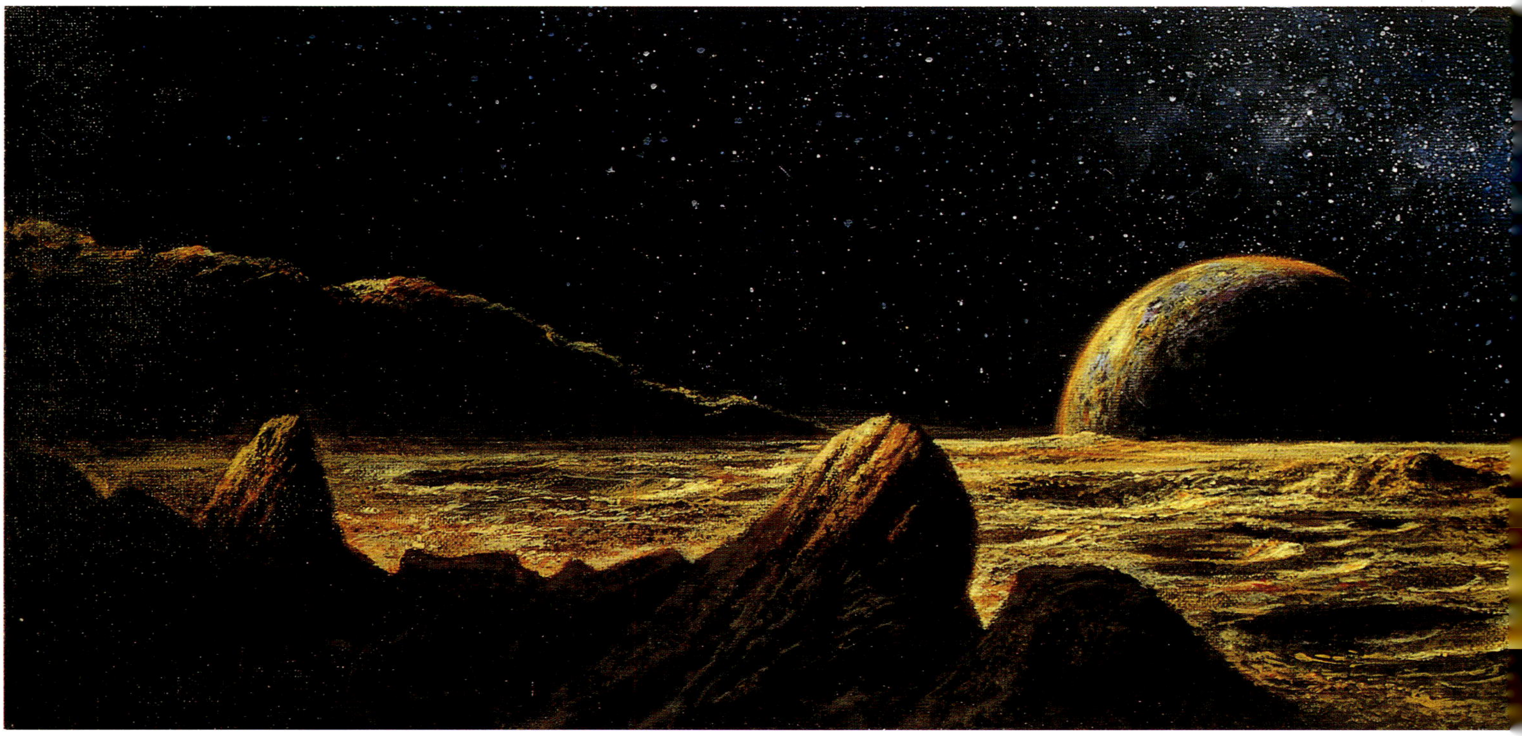

3

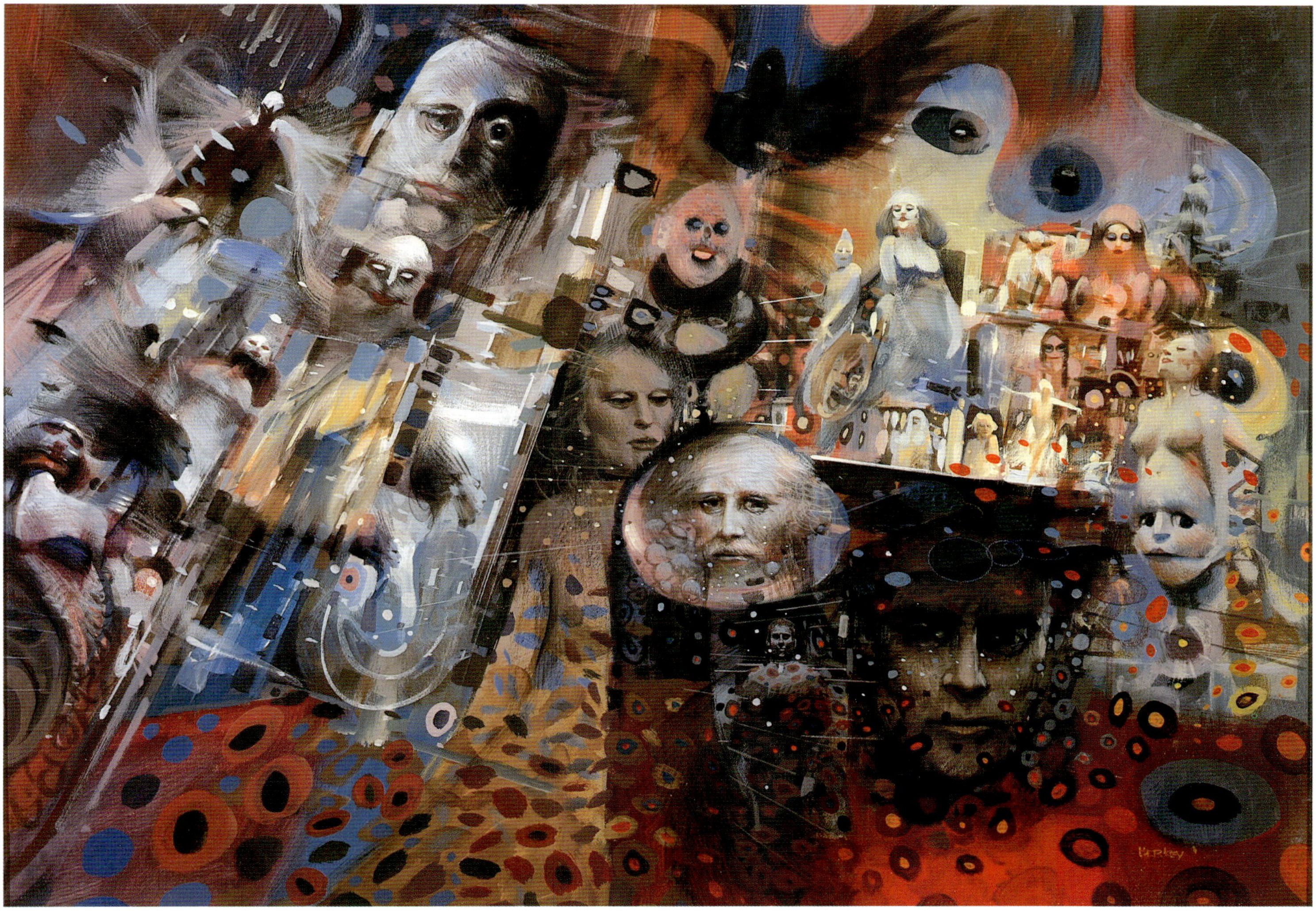

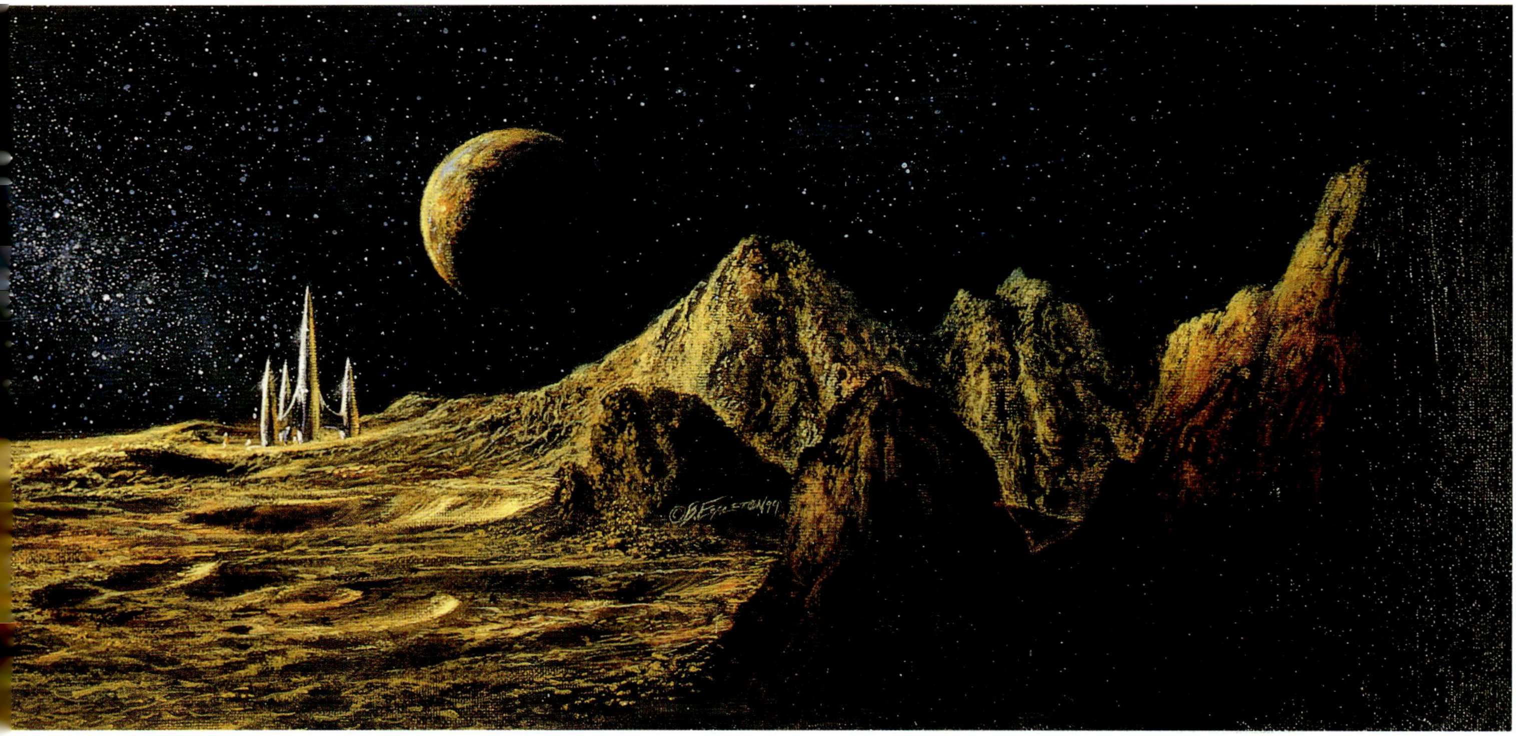

unpublished

1
artist: JASON NOBRIGA
title: Wizard
medium: Oil
size: 9"x12"

2
artist: DAVID CHOE
medium: Mixed
size: 8 1/2"x11"

3
artist: JOHN C. BERKEY
art director: John C. Berkey
designer: John C. Berkey
client: John C. Berkey
title: Norseman's Yesterday
medium: Acrylic
size: 26"x18"

4
artist: OMAR RAYYAN
title: Pear Meditations 1
medium: Watercolor
size: 8"x10"

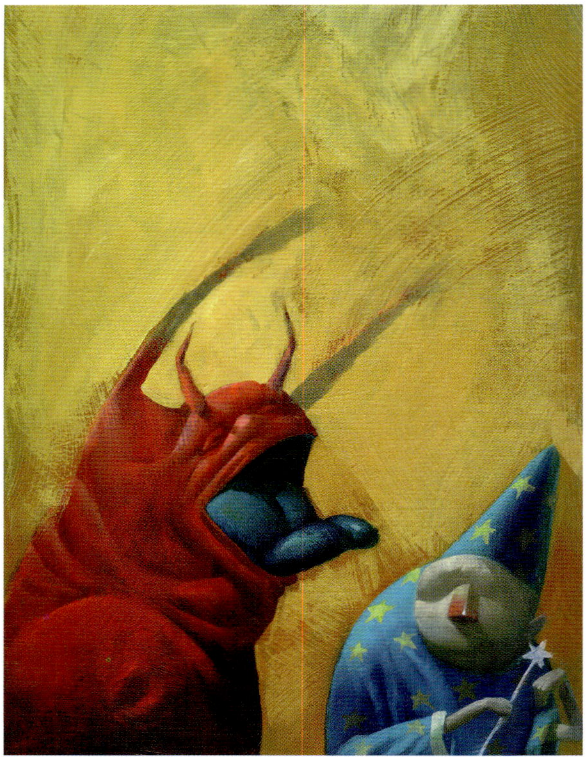

1

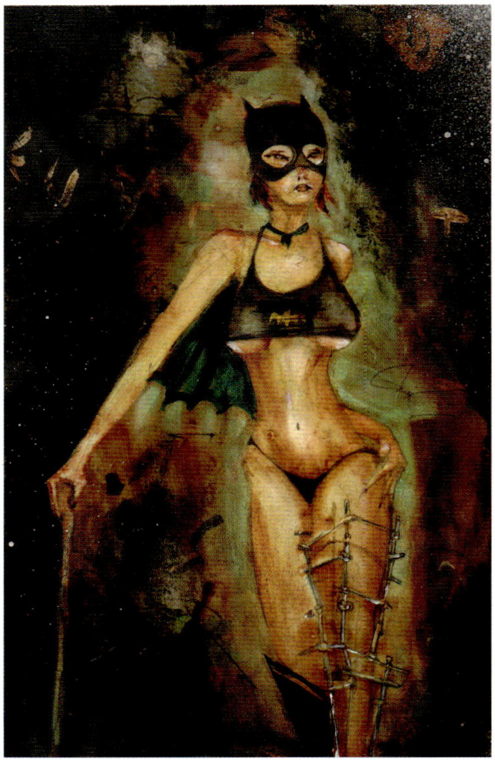

2

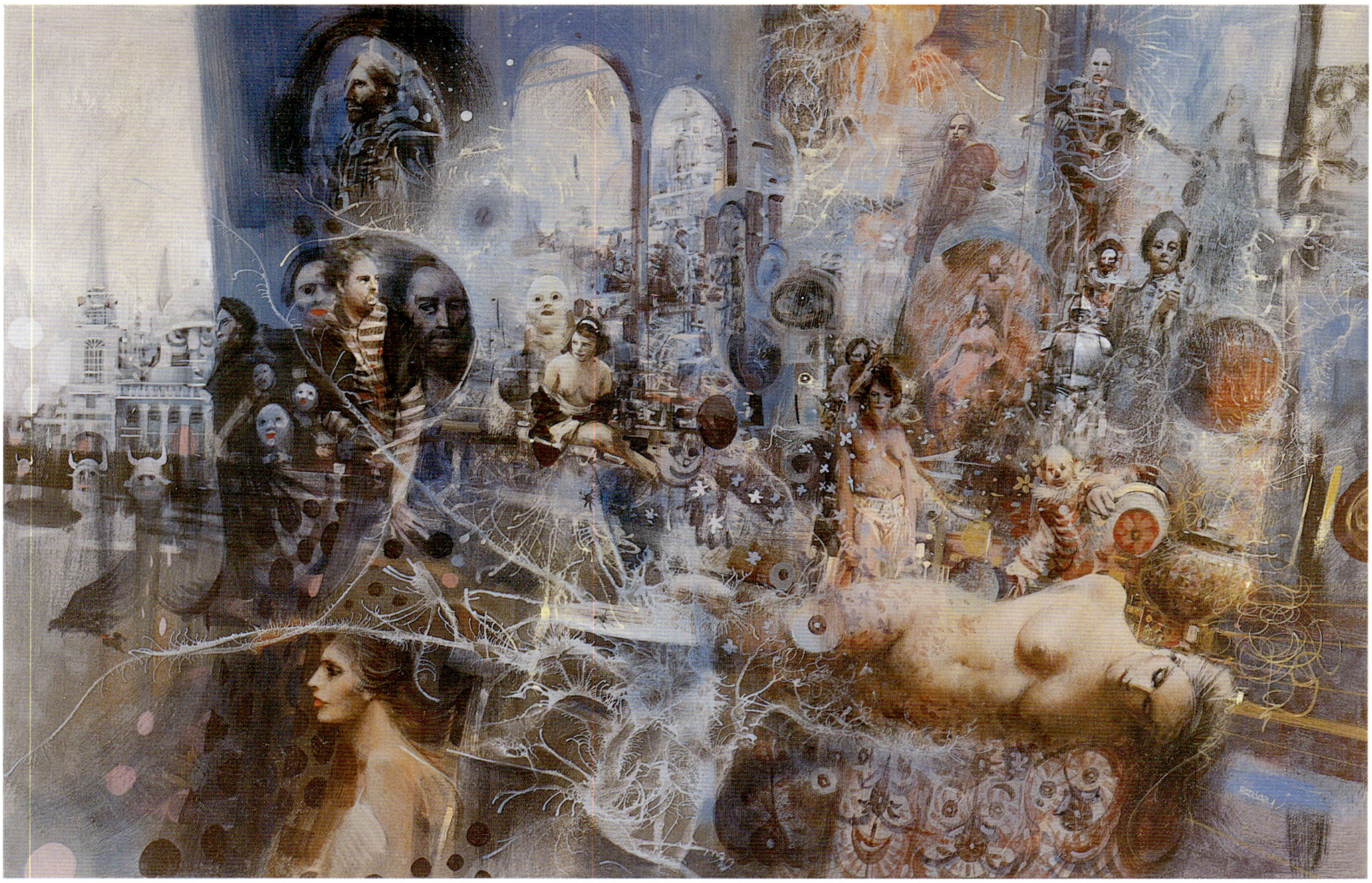

3

4

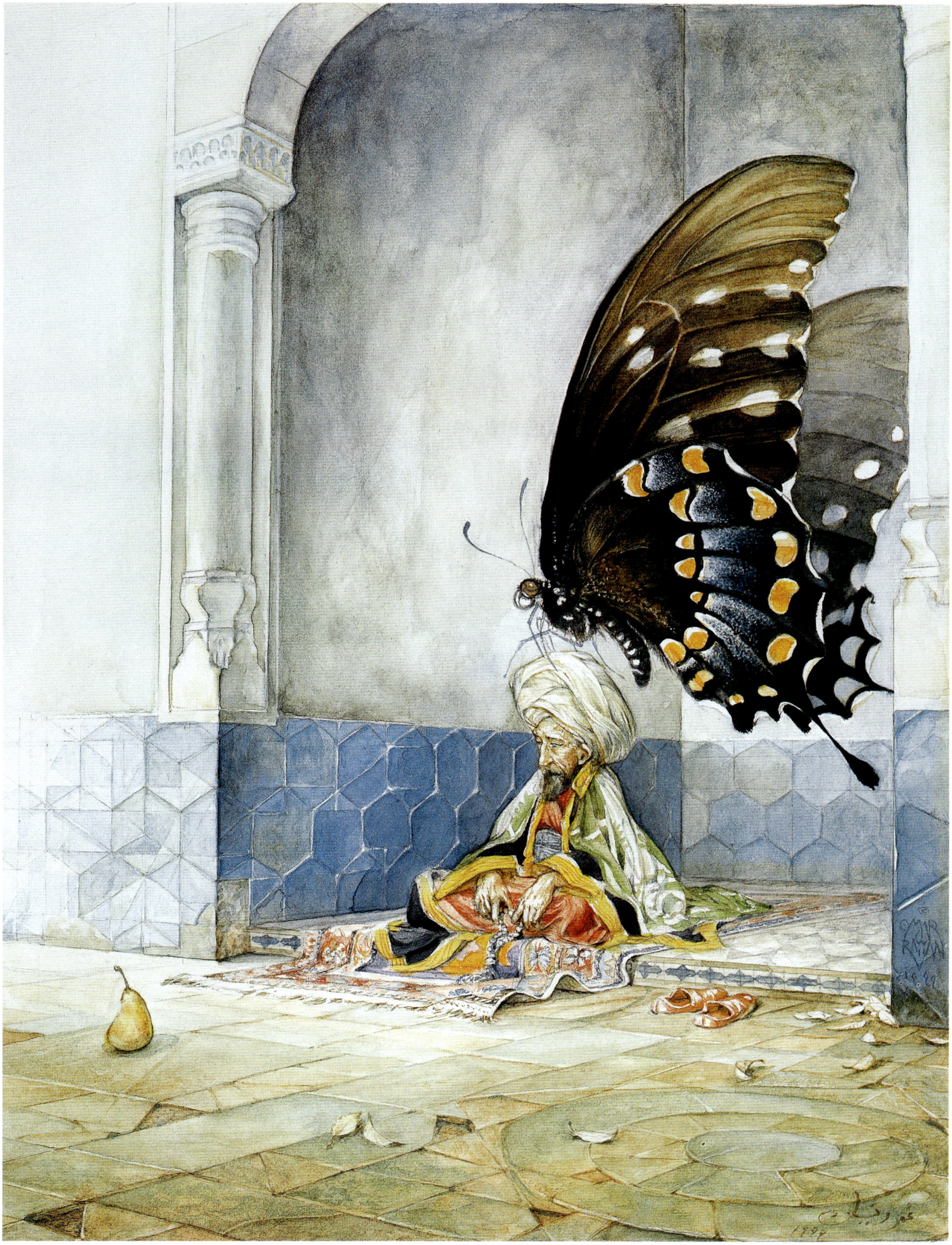

1
artist: NORIAKI KANEKO
art director: Noriaki Kaneko
client: Inertia Pictures
title: Genera-Zane
medium: 3-D CGI

2
artist: TANNER GOLDBECK
medium: Mixed
title: RACECAR MOTHER
size: 35"x32"

3
artist: CHUCK LUKACS
title: Ganesha
medium: Woodcut
size: 5"x9"

4
artist: KURT MITCHELL
title: Millennial Breakfast
medium: Digital
size: 10"x8"

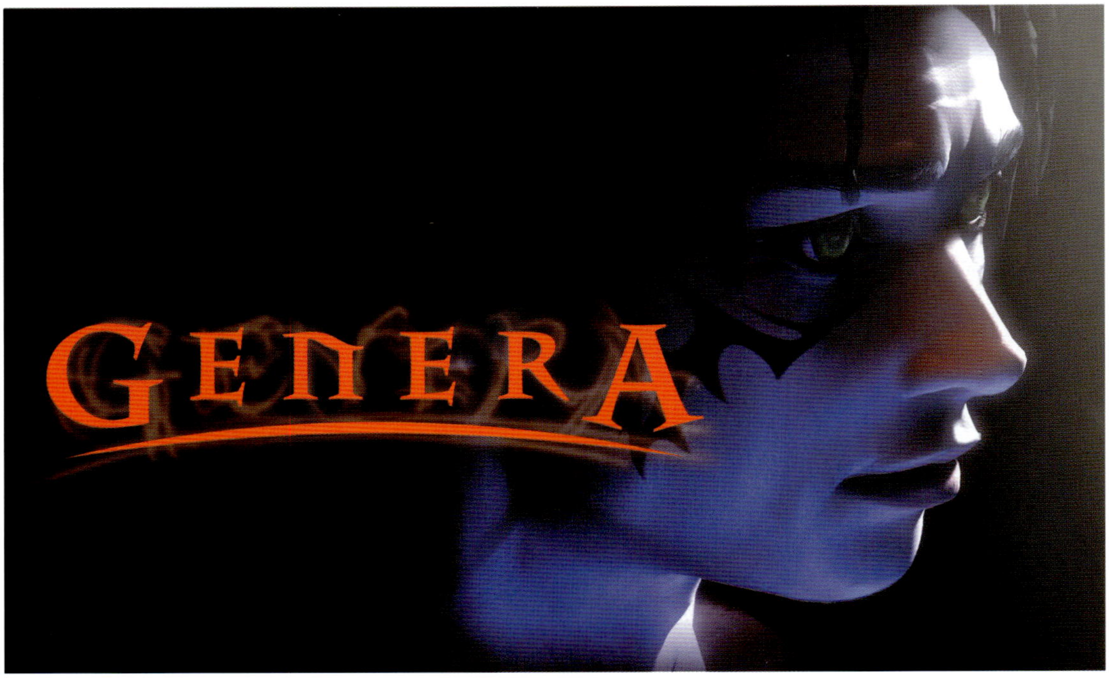

1

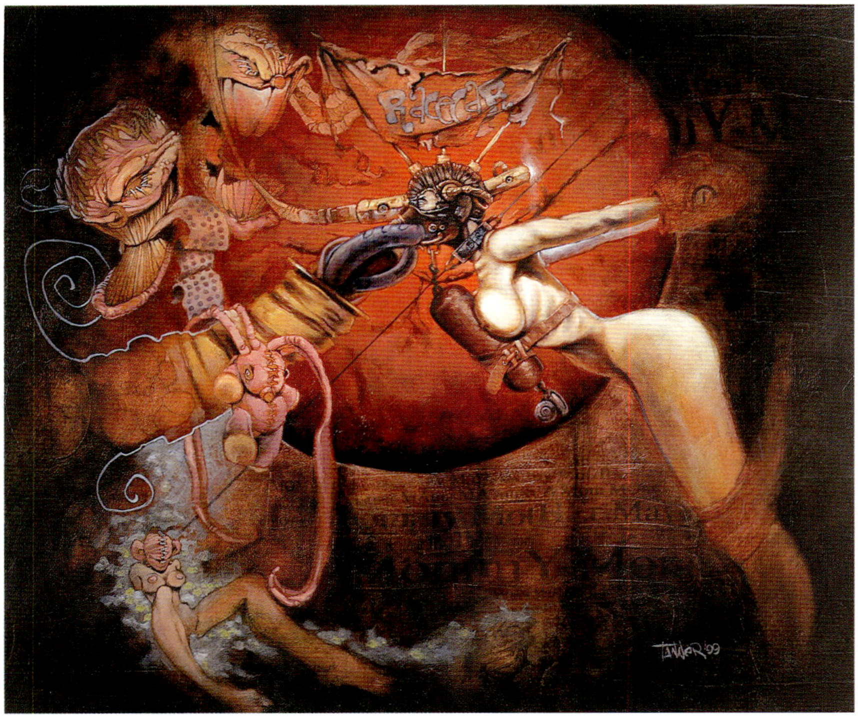

2

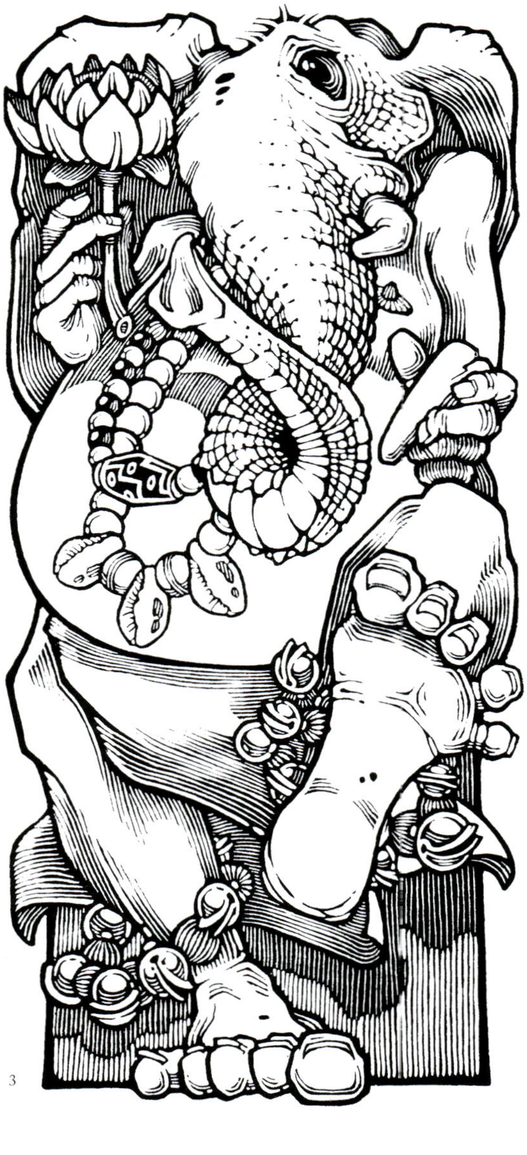

3

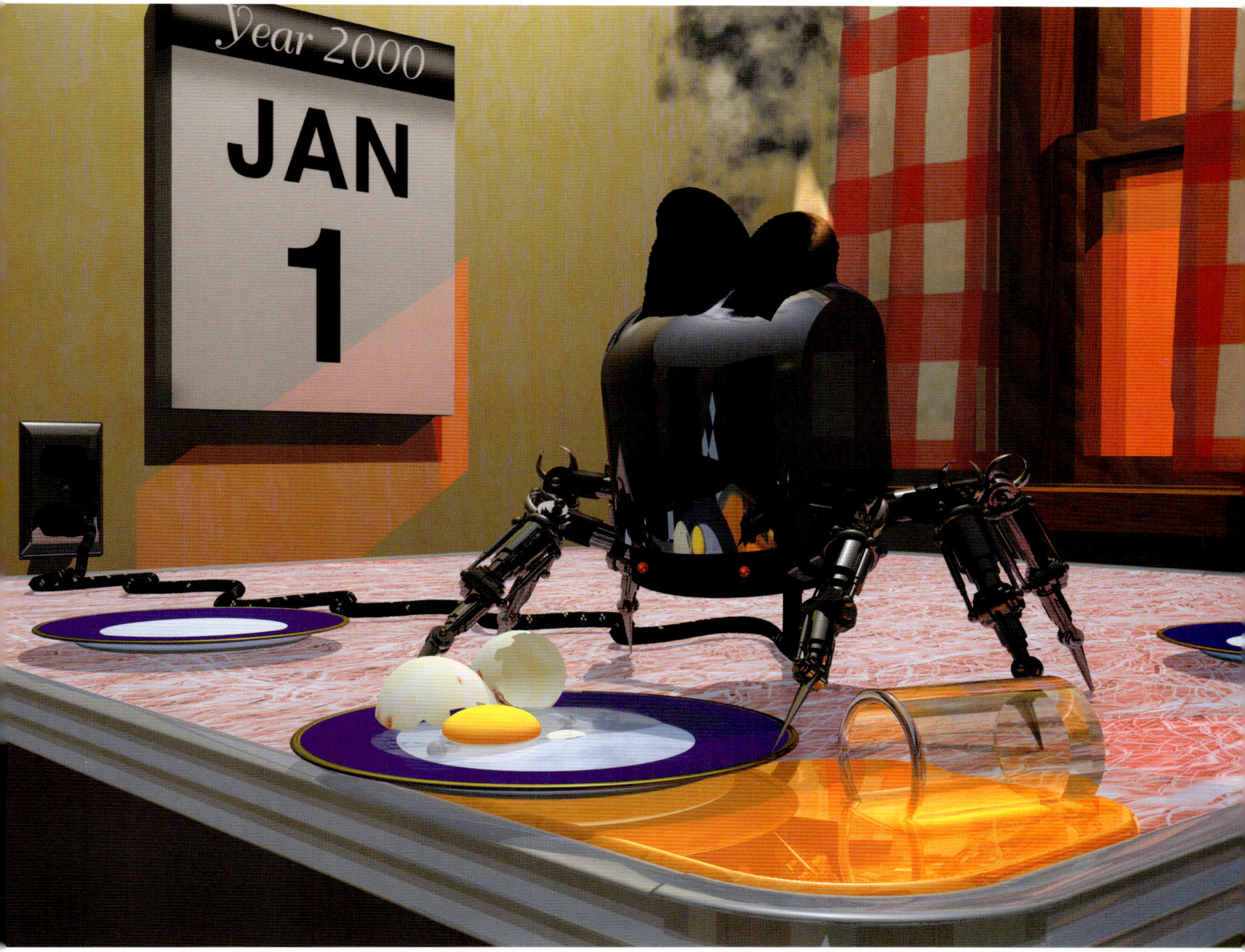

4

1
artist: GEORGE KLAUBA
client: Ann Nathan Gallery
title: Colossus
medium: Acrylic
size: 20"x24 1/2"

2
artist: LORI KOEFOED
art director: Lori Koefoed
title: Freya's Temptation
medium: Oil
size: 10"x10"

3
artist: LORI KOEFOED
art director: Lori Koefoed
title: Hyndla's Magic Horn of Mead
medium: Oil
size: 13 1/2"x13 1/2"

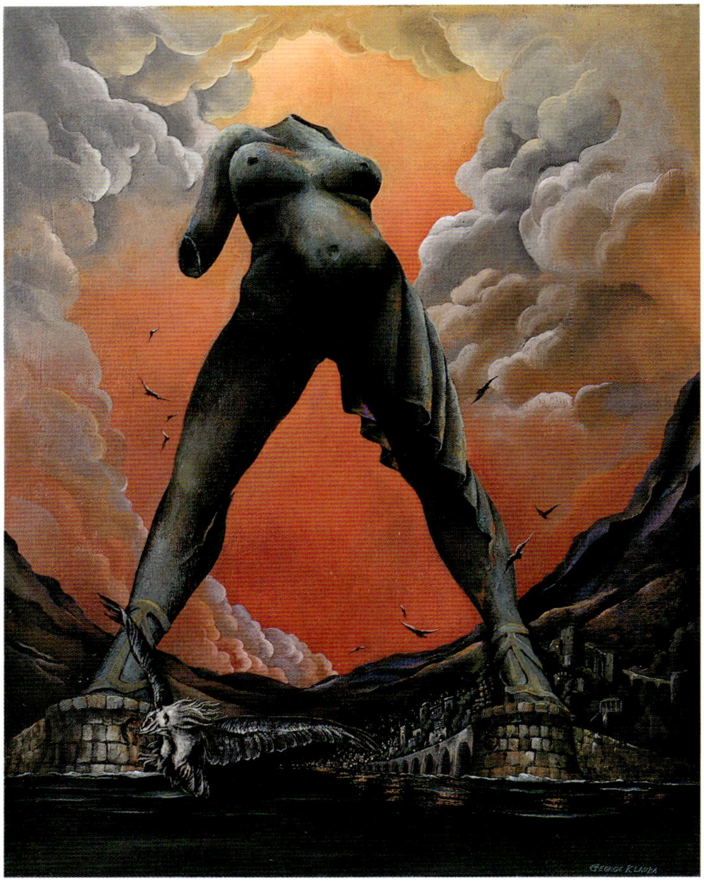

1

2

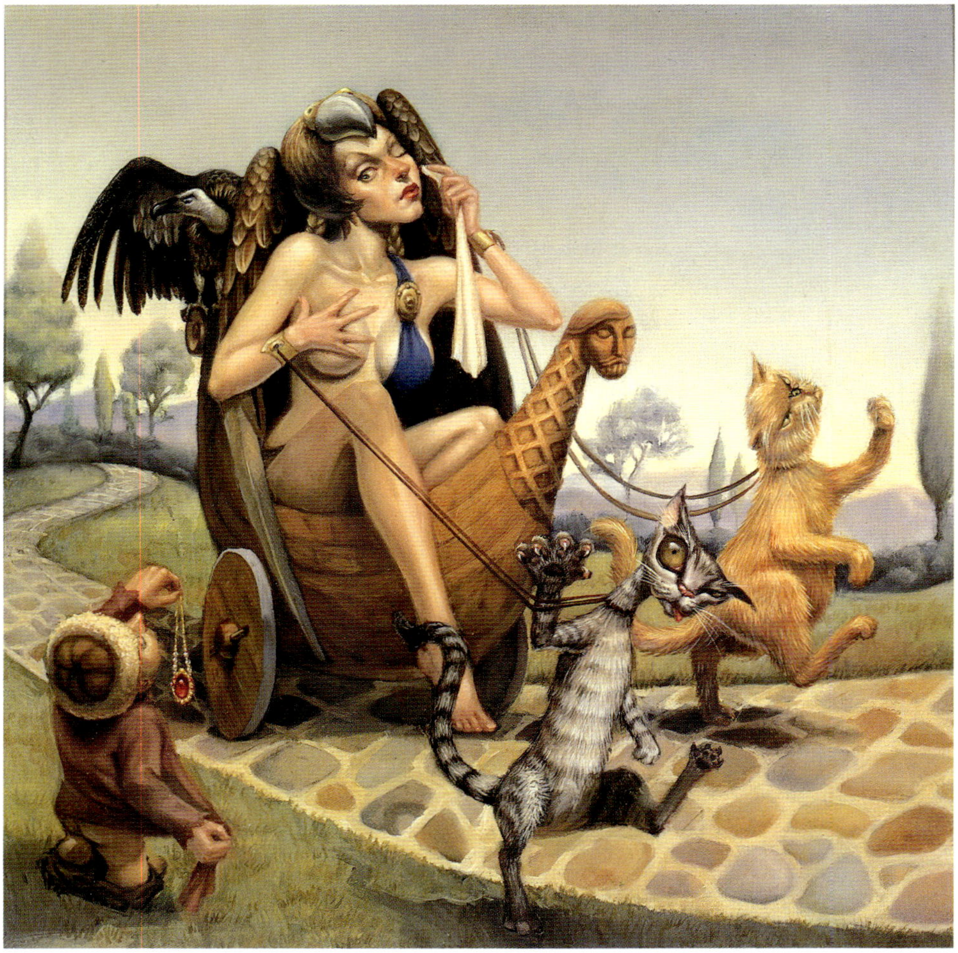

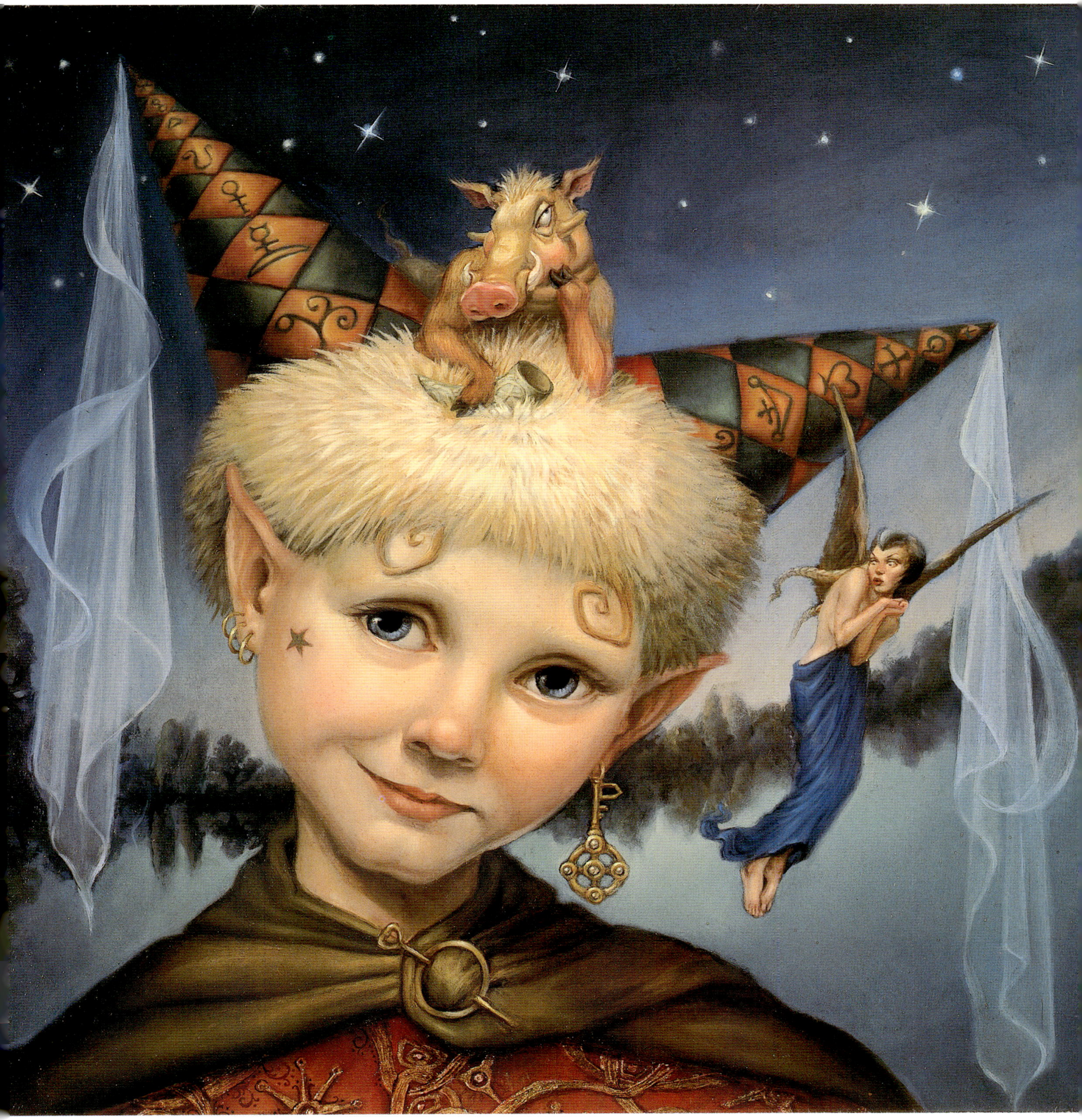

3

1
artist: DAREN BADER
client: Angel Studios
title: T-Rex
medium: Acrylic
size: 27 1/2"x17"

2
artist: PAUL BONNER
art director: Paul Bonner
title: Camarasaurs & Ceratosaurs
medium: Watercolor
size: 372mmx507mm

3
artist: STEPHEN HICKMAN
art director: Stephen Hickman
title: Moon Shadows
medium: Oil
size: 24" diameter

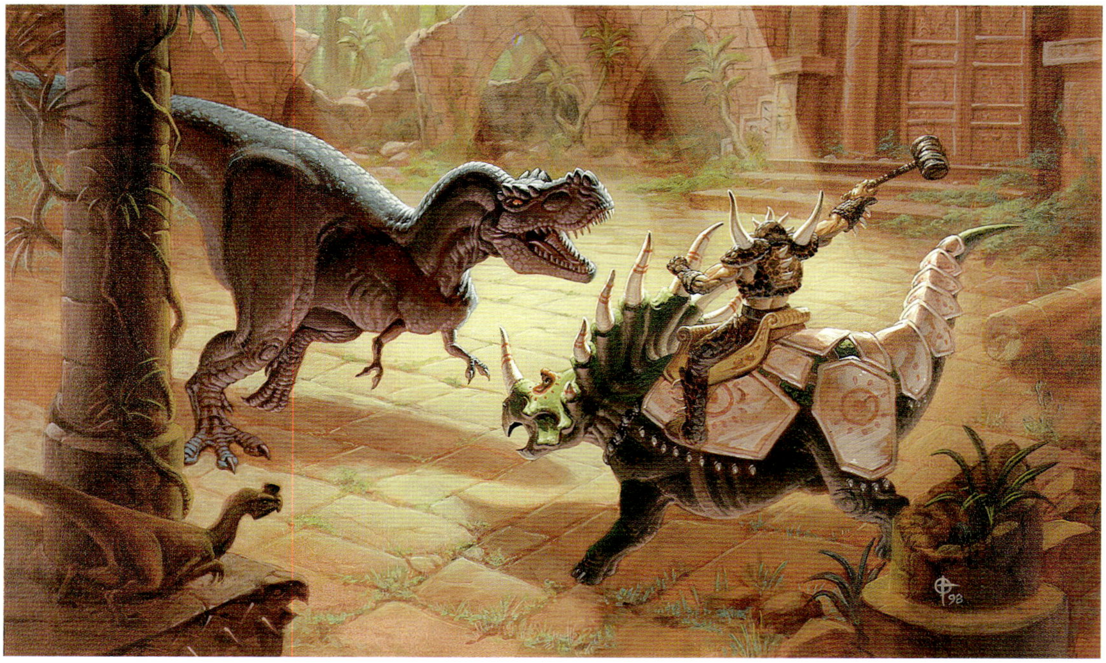

1

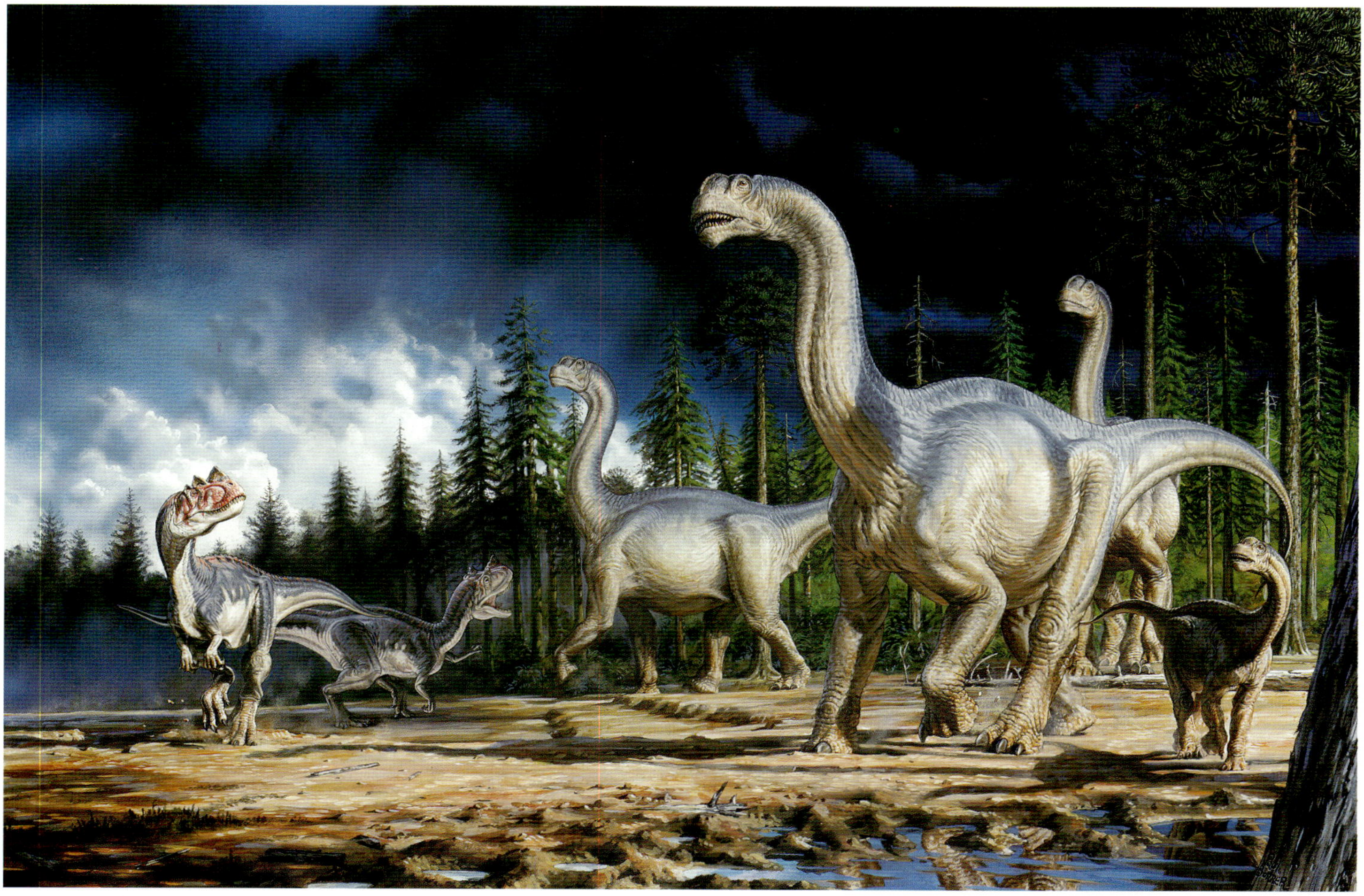

2

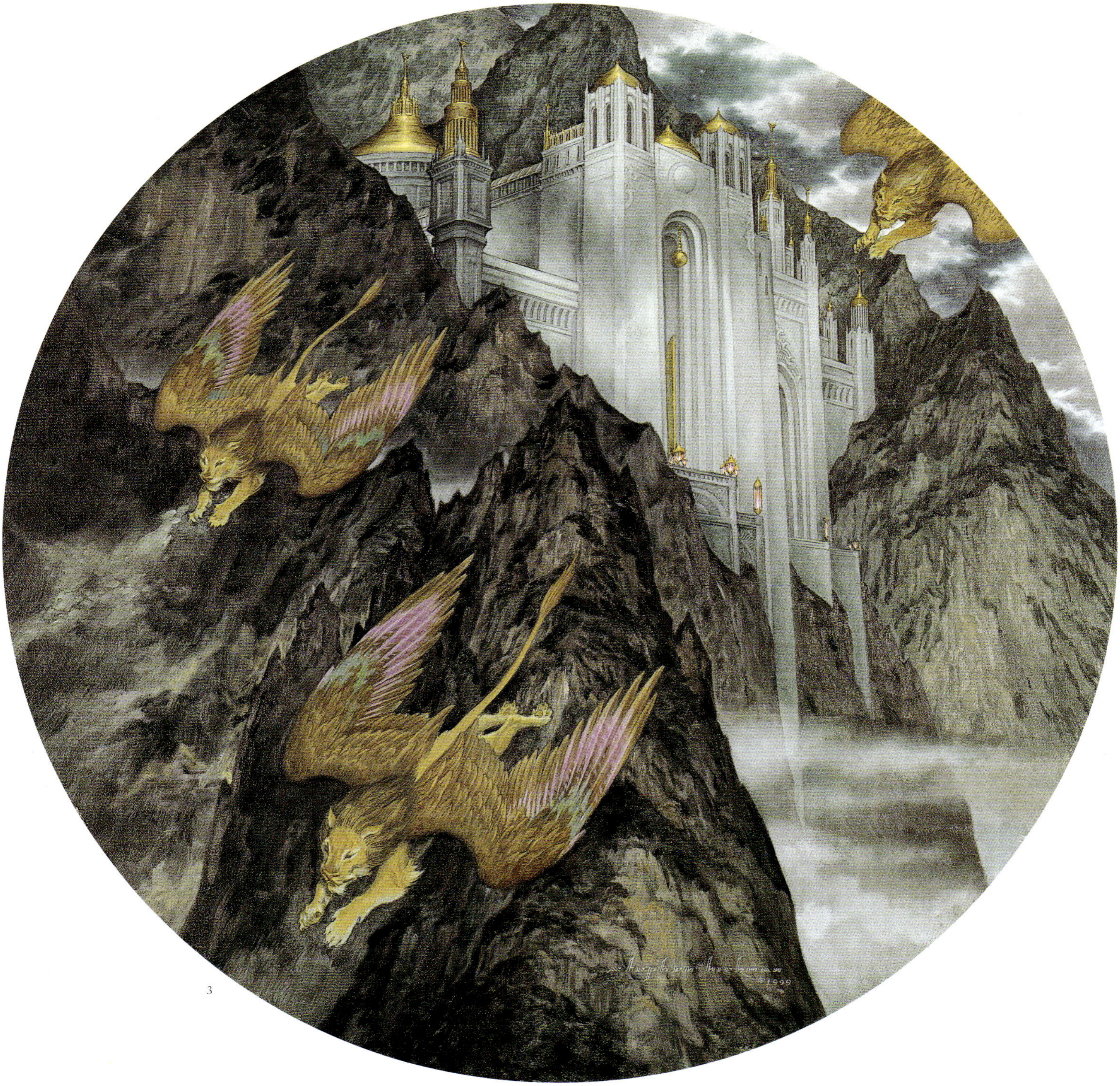

3

1
artist: JOHN HARRIS
title: Fire: Cleaning the Ducts
medium: Oil
size: 42"x30"

2
artist: KIM COGAN
art director: William Maughn
client: Academy of Arts Gallery
title: Garden of Delight & Sin
medium: Oil/acrylic
size: 40"x30"

3
artist: ERIC BOWMAN
title: Stock Nazis
medium: Oil
size: 10 1/2"x14"

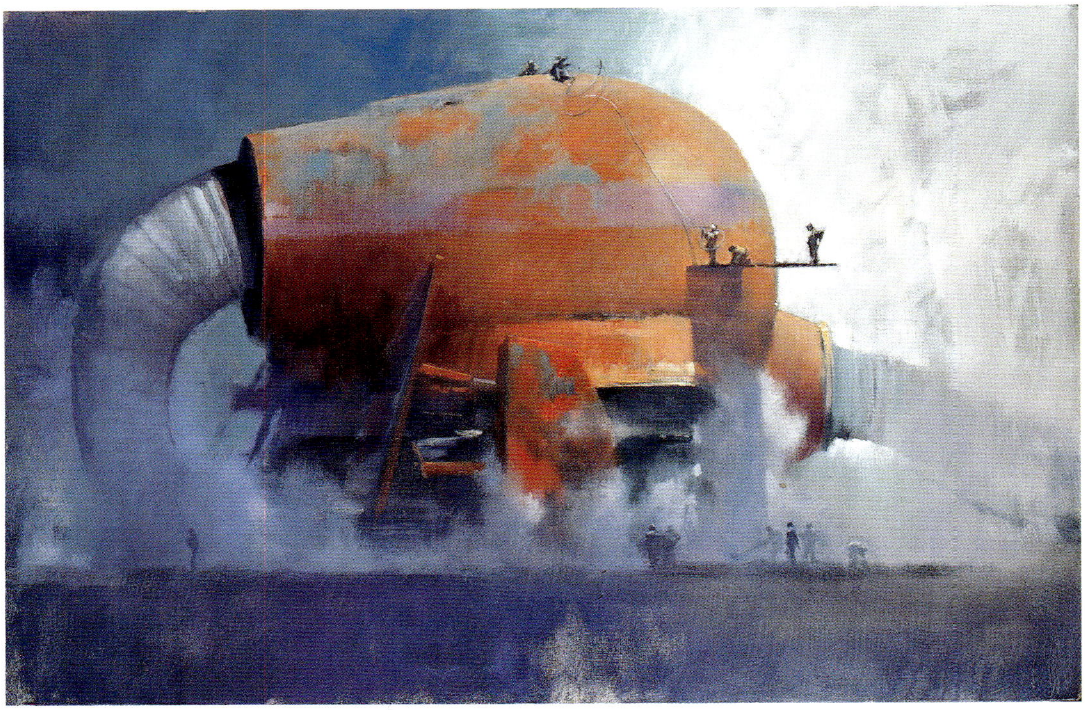

1

2

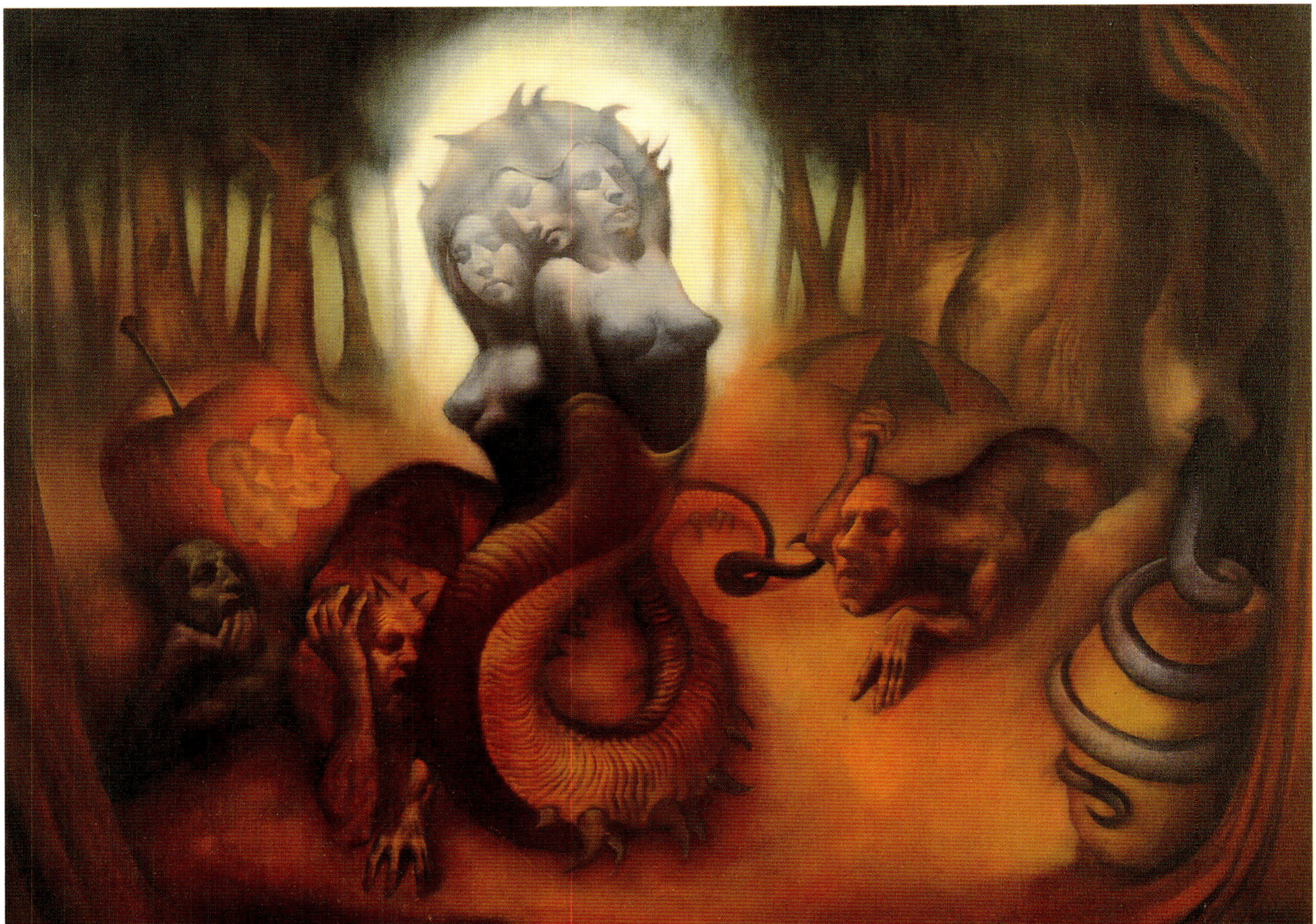

3

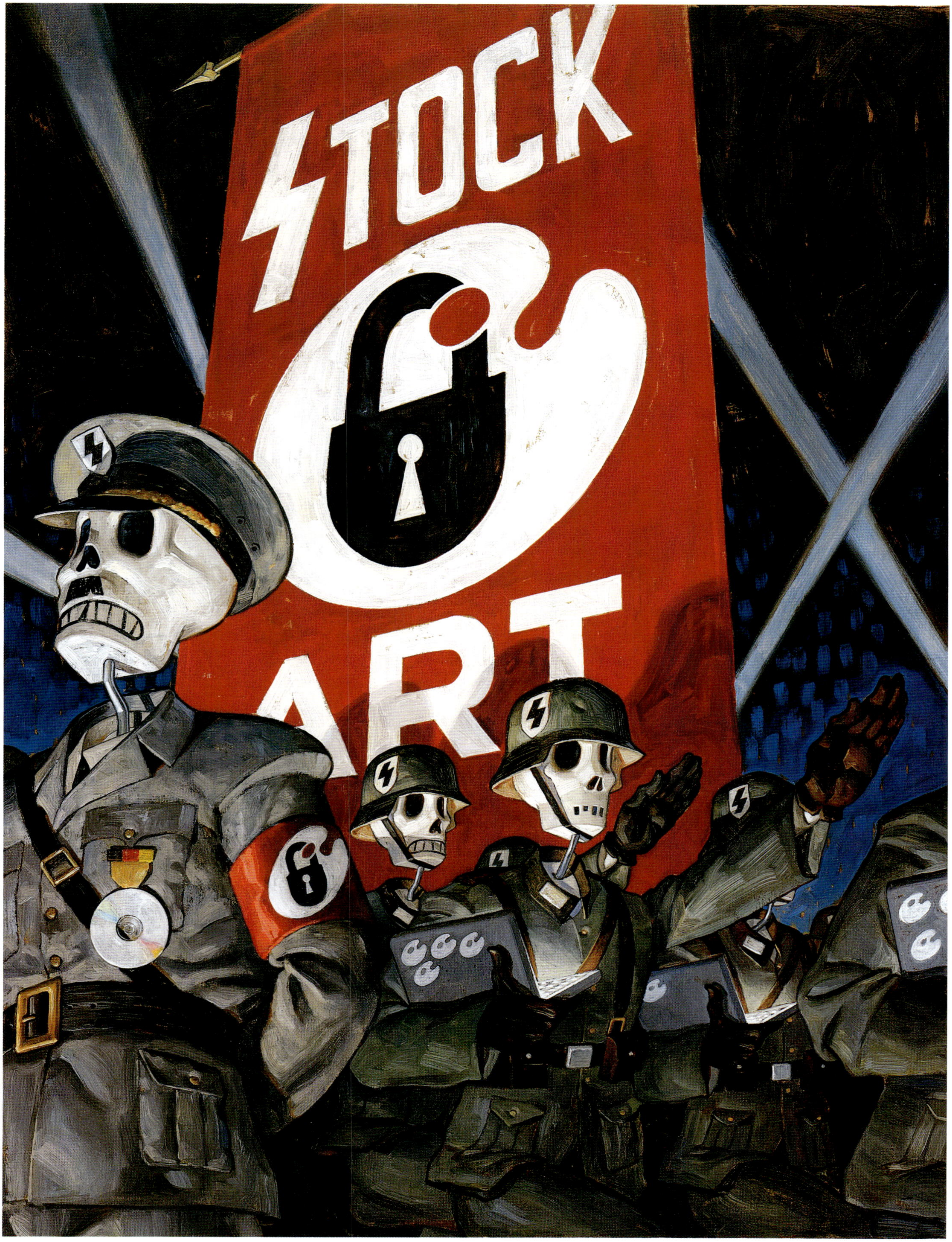

Spectrum 7
artist index

A

Rob Alexander 38
46451 McKenzie Hwy.
Vida, OR 97488
541-896-0283
em: rob@robalexander.com

Henry Alvarez 93
c/o Wolf's Head Productions, Inc.
1540 W. Gaylord
Long Beach, CA 90012-1233
310-337-7911

Darrel Anderson 128
5360 Seven Oaks Dr.
Colorado Springs, CO 80919
719-535-0407
em: darrel@braid.com

Kyle Anderson 174
6000Shepherd Mtn. Cove/Apt. 1912
Austin, TX 78730
512-418-8243
em: kyle@kyleanderson.com

Thom Ang 42, 117
c/o Allen Spiegel Fine Arts
221 Lobos Ave.
Pacific Grove, CA 93950
408-372-4672
em: asfa@redshift.com

Patrick Arrasmith 87
309 6th St./#3
Brooklyn, NY 11215
718-499-4101

B

Darin Bader 192
625 Poinsettia Park N
Encinitas, CA 92024
760-632-1618
em: daren@angel.com

Istvan Banyai 116

Wes Benscoter 105, 108
5532 Ridgeview Dr
Harrisburg, PA 17112
717-545-7221 [fax]
wes@wesbenscoter.com

Doug Beekman 76
P.O. Box 573
Putney, VT 05346

John C. Berkey 43, 185, 186
5940 Christmas Lake Rd.
Excelsior, MN 55331
612-474-3042

Rick Berry 38, 135, 141
93 Warren St.
Arlington, MA 02174
781-648-6375
em: berry@braid.com

Edward Binkley 48, 177
110 Green Lake Pass
Madison, WI 53705
608-238-3980
em: binkpix@tds.net

Laurel Blechman 82, 83
818-785-7904
[fax] 818-908-9382

Neil Blevins 20
em: neil@soulburn3d.com

Richard Bober 155
c/o Jill Bauman
162-19 65th Ave.
Fresh Meadows, NY 11365
718-886-5616

Mike Bohatch 174
10642-A Merriman Rd.
Cupertino, CA 95014
408-252-8138
em: mike@eyesofchaos.com

Michel Bohbot 139
3823 Harrison St.
Oakland, CA 94611
510-547-0667
em: michelb@jps.net

Peter Bollinger 17
c/o Shannon Associates
327 E. 89th St./Box 3E
New York, NY 10128

Paul Bonner 146, 161, 192
Tegnestuen F3
Storekongensgade 110 F3
1705 Copenhagen •K • Denmark
33120031

David Bowers 40, 41, 56, 156
206 Arrowhead Ln.
Eighty-Four, PA 15330
724-942-3274
em: david.m.bowers@att.net

Eric Bowman 138, 195
7405 SW 154th Place
Beaverton, OR 97007
503-644-1016
em: ebowmanart@aol.com

Tim Bradstreet 76

Jacques Bredy 110
60 Union St.
Newark, NJ 07105
973-274-9280
em: jbredy@aol.com

Brom 23, 60
2916-218th Ave. SE
Issaquah, WA 98029
425-427-8934
em: morb@home.com

Tim Holter Bruckner 98, 99
256 125th St.
Amery, WI 54001
715-268-7291
em: artfarm@win.bright.net

Jim Burns 36
c/o Alan Lynch
11 King's Ridge Rd.
Long Valley, NJ 07853
908-813-8718

Scott Everett Burton 184
1245 Del Rey Ave.
Pasadena, CA 91107
626-345-9159
em: sbuniverse@tcsn.net

C

Ciruelo Cabral 44, 45
PO Box 57
08870 Sitges
Barcelona, Spain
34-938946761
em: ciruelo@dac-editions.com

Greg Call 18, 19
403 Chestnut Drive
Kalispell, MT 59901
406-257-0683
em: callart@digisys.net

Oscar Chichoni 47, 110
c/o Alan Lynch
11 King's Ridge Rd.
Long Valley, NJ 07853
908-813-8718

David Choe 186
665 S. Highland Ave.
Los Angeles, CA 90036
213-626-7553
em: imageecho@aol.com

Nick Choles 182
3733 N. Bell Ave.
Chicago, IL 60618
773-404-8883

James C. Christensen 97, 156

Kim Cogan 194
1100 Masonic Ave., No. 1
San Francisco, CA 94117
415-863-6235
em: kcogan9@hotmail.com

Ray-Mel Cornelius 144
1526 Elmwood Blvd.
Dallas, TX 75224
214-946-9405
em: rmbc@earthlink.net

Greg Couch 122

Kinuko Y. Craft 26, 34
83 Litchfield Rd.
Norwalk, CT 06058
860-542-5018
www.fsartists.com

Mark Crilley 84, 86
c/o Sirius Entertainment
264 E Blackwell St
Dover, NJ 07801
973-328-1455

James Cukr 146
11361 S. Deer Creek Rd.
Littleton, CO 80127
303-697-8862
em: james@cukr7.com

D

Stephen Daniele 149
3816 S. Lamar Blvd./Apt. 1502
Austin, TX 78704
512-447-6787
em: me@stephendaniele.com

Peter deSève 32, 114, 115
25 Park Place
Brooklyn NY 11217
718-398-8099
em: deseve@quicklink.com

Brian Despain 136
111 Thorndike St./Apt. 1
Cambridge, MA 02141
617-491-8390
em: fantomjack@aol.com

Joseph DeVito 102, 114
11 Shady Hill Dr.
Chalfont, PA 18914
215-822-3002
em: jdevito4@aol.com

David DeVries 106
67 Benson Dr.
Wayne, NJ 07470
973-696-3782
em: turbobonn@aol.com

Tony Diterlizzi 69
190 Garfield Place #4B
Brooklyn, NY 11215
718-768-8044
www.diterlizzi.com

Dave Dorman 147
P.O. Box 15.
Shalimar, FL 32579
850-609-0197
em: webmaster@dormanart.com

Allen G. Douglas 162
309 6th St. #3
Brooklyn, NY 11215
718-499-4101

Andrej Dugin & Olga Dugina 58, 59
Weser Strasse 34
Stuttgart, Germany 70376
0711/591158

E

Les Edwards 30
c/o Alan Lynch
11 Kings Ridge Rd.
Long Valley, NJ 07853
908-813-8718
908-813-0076[fax]

Tommy Lee Edwards 64
c/o Allen Spiegel Fine Arts
221 Lobos Ave.
Pacific Grove, CA 93950
408-372-4672
em: asfa@redshift.com

Bob Eggleton 149, 184, 185
P.O. Box 5692
Providence, RI 02903
401-738-6281
em: zillabob@ids.net

Mark Elliott 32, 53
960-2 South Anson Rd.
Stanfordville, NY 12573
845-868-7383

Larry Elmore 60
1314 Sunbeam Rd.
Leitchfield, KY 42754
270-259-5878
em: larry@larryelmore.com

Tristan Elwell 109
41 Main St.
Dobbs Ferry, NY 10522
914-674-9235

F

Jeff Faerber 108
221 23rd St./Apt. 3R
Brooklyn, NY 11232
718-499-7207
em: jfaerber@hotmail.com

Fernando Favila 100
c/o Wolf's Head Productions, Inc.
1540 W. Gaylord
Long Beach, CA 90012-1233
310-337-7911

Marc Fishman 170, 178, 179
14440 Dickens St. #305
Sherman Oaks, CA 91423
818-783-6307

Jon Foster 50, 127, 141, 168, 169
231 Nayatt Rd.
Barrington, RI 02806
401-245-8438
em: buzzworks@earthlink.net

Gary Freeman 16
1344 Echo Creek St.
Henderson, NV 89052
702-435-8542

Charles Frizzell 140
P.O. Box 738
Salida. CO 81201
em: frizzell@chaffee.net

G

Marc Gabbana 140
2453 Olive Rd.
Windsor, ONT
Canada N8T 3N4
519-948-2418
em: mgabbana@mnsi.net

Chris Gall 136
4421 N. Camino Del Santo
Tucson, AZ 85718
520-299-4454
em: chris@chrisgall.com

Donato Giancola 22, 50, 51, 52, 118, 119
397 Pacific St
Brooklyn, NY 11217
718-797-2438
www.donatoart.com

Gary Gianni 38, 39, 80
2540 W Pensacola
Chicago, IL 60618
773-267-4345
em: ggiann@enteract

Yvonne Gilbert 67
c/o Alan Lynch
11 King's Ridge Rd.
Long Valley, NJ 07853
908-813-8718

Gnemo 63
c/o Tom Kidd
59 Cross Brook Rd.
New Milford, CT 06776
em: gnemo@spellcaster.com

Tanner Goldbeck 188
P.O. Box 39
Summerland, CA 93067
805-565-3181
em: racecar@silcom.com

Douglas Gray 142
54 Esplanade Rd.
Scarborough•N•Yorks
England 7011 2AU
+44 (0) 1723 360312

Scott Grimando 168
6-Fifth Ave.
Westbury, NY 11590
http//home.earthlink.net/~stgrimm

James Gurney 34
P.O. Box 693
Rhinebeck, NY 12572
www.dinotopia.com

Scott Gustafson 33, 152, 153
4045 N. Kostner Ave
Chicago, IL 60641
773-725-8338
em: gustafsn@enteract.com

H

Brian Haberlin
28411 Rancho de Linda
Laguna Niguel, CA 92677
949-425-9622
em: bjhaber@aol.com

Joel Haffner 162
204 14th St. #14
Brooklyn, NY 11215
718-832-3168

Phil Hale 70, 76, 78
16 Anton St..
London, UK E8 2AD

Joel Harlow 92
5713 Chicofee Ave.
Encino, CA 91316-1306
818-342-5892
em: joelhca@earthlink.net

John Harris 194
c/o Alan Lynch
11 King's Ridge Rd
Long Valley, NJ 07853
908-813-8718

Mark Harrison 46
Flat 3/13 Palmeira Ave.
Hove, E. Sussex, UK BN3 3GA
01273 739 286
em: ms.harrison@virgin.net

Daniel L. Hawkins 96
30017 Post Oak Rd.
Tollhouse, CA 93667
559-855-4975

Richard Hescox 156, 163
P.O. Box 338
Hobart, WA 98025
richh@premier1.net

Jody Hewgill 104

Carol Heyer 173
925 E. Ave. De Los Arboles
Thousand Oaks, CA 91360
805-492-3683
em: cheyer@gte.net

Stephen Hickman 92, 193
10 Elm Street
Red Hook, NY 12571
914-758-3930
em: shickman@ulster.net

David Ho 27, 48, 159, 168
3586 Dickenson Common
Fremont, CA 94538

Jack Hood 101
c/o Wolf's Head Productions, Inc.
1540 W. Gaylord
Long Beach, CA 90012-1233
310-337-7911

Brian Horton 74, 150
c/o Allen Spiegel Fine Arts
221 Lobos Ave.
Pacific Grove, CA 93950
408-372-4672
em: asfa@redshift.com

John Howe 132, 133
c/o Alan Lynch Rep.
11 King's Ridge Rd.
Long Valley, NJ 07853
908-813-8718

Mike Huddleston 86
4112 Genessee/Second Floor
Kansas City, MO 64111
816-561-0829
em: mhuddl@hotmail.com

Adam Hughes 75
6500 McDonough Dr./D-1
Norcross, GA 30093
em: ah@gaijinstudios.com

J

Nicholas Jainschigg 111
80 King St
Warren, RI 02885
401-245-2954
em: nickej@earthlink.net

H.P. Jansen 112
Heersh.11
53111 Bonn, Germany
0228-637230

Bruce Jensen 36, 37
3939 47th St.
Sunnyside, NY 11104
718-482-9125

Shane Johnson 176
P.O. Box 801
Beavercreek, OR 97004
503-632-7387
em: shanej@internetcds.com

Jeffrey Jones 166, 167
P.O. Box 166
Bearsville, NY 12409
www.jeffreyjones.com

Joe Jusko 81
35 Highland Rd/ #4404
Pittsburgh, PA 15102
412-833-7528

K

Michael Wm. Kaluta 71

Noriaki Kaneko 20, 188
c/o Inertia Pictures, Inc.
1503 Franklin St.
Santa Monica, CA 90404

Charles Keegan 179
P.O. Box 2532
Forest Park, GA 30297
404-366-1490
em: charles@keeganprints.com

Tom Kidd 54
59 Cross Brook Rd.
New Milford, CT 06776
860-355-1781
em: tomkidd@spellcaster.com

Douglas Klauba 138
9741 S. Hamlin Ave.
Evergreen Park, IL 60805
708-229-2507
www.douglasklauba.com

George Klauba 190
5247 N. Bernard
Chicago, IL 60625
773-583-3808

Lori Koefoed 172, 190, 191
338 Mira Mar Ave.
Long Beach, CA 90814
562-433-6122
www.lorikoefoed.com

Michael Koelsch 55
c/o Shannon Associates
327 E. 89th St./Box 3E
New York, NY 10128

Joseph Page Kovach 136
6733 Lower Brook Way
New Albany, OH 43054
614-939-1130
em: josephpagekovach@aol.com

Joseph Kresoja 164
1243 5th Ave. 162N #4
Seattle, WA 98109
206-285-4858

Brad Kunkle 166
314 Held St.
Lehighton, PA 18235
610-377-1254

Anita Kunz 106, 107
218 Ontario St.
Toronto, ONT
Canada M5A 2V5
416-364-3846
em: akinz@globalseri.net

L

Andy Lackow 134
7004 Boulevard East/Apt. 29-C
Guttenberg, NJ 07093
201-868-9585
em: andylackow@aol.com

Ray Lago 182
P.O. Box 36
Jersey City, NJ 07303
201-659-3905

Jean-Marc Laroche 96
16 rue Alexandre Dumas
78160 Marly le Roi—France
00-33-1-39-16-16-58
www.jmlaroche.com

Steven Lawrence 98
21416 Chase St. #1
Canoga Park, CA 91304
818-701-6839

Jody A. Lee 40
90 Longview Ave.
White Plains, NY 10605
914-686-5834

Joseph Michael Linsner 80, 85
c/o Sirius Entertainment
264 E Blackwell St
Dover, NJ 07801
973-328-1455

Todd Lockwood 62
20523 125th St. CT E
Bonney Lake, WA 98390
253-826-2265
em: lockwood@wizards.com

Jerry LoFaro 146
58 Gulf Rd
Henniker, NH 03242
603-428-6135

Greg Loudon 60
1804 Pine Rd.
Homewood, IL 60430
708-799-4339
em: g101062@aol.com

Travis Louie 145
18 Echo Valley Rd
Red Hook, NY 12571
845-758-9460
em: louieart@webjogger.net

Chuck Lukacs 188
1883 W. 13 Mile #22
Madison Hts., MI 48071
248-583-3324
em: earthnwd@mich.com

Carl Lundgren 142
P.O. Box 825
Lecanto, FL 34460
800-795-9272
em: lundgren@hitter.net

Howard Lyon 32
3134 East McKellips Rd. #87
Mesa, AZ 85213
480-981-7907
em: conte@home.com

M

Larry MacDougall 150
846 Highway #8
Stoney Creek, ONT
Canada L8E 5J3
905-643-7231

Corey Macourek 134
6233 S. 153rd St.
Seattle, WA 98188
206-244-9511
em: cmacourek@aol.com

Don Maitz 124
5824 Bee Ridge Rd./Box #106
Sarasota, Fl 34233
fax: 941-925-3494

Gregory Manchess 68, 154
13358 SW Gallop Ct.
Beaverton, OR 97008
503-590-5447

Stephan Martiniere 175
10500 Missouri Bar Rd.
Nevada City, CA 95959
530-478-0911

Stanley Martucci/Cheryl Griesbach 50, 142
34 Twinlight Terr.
Highlands, NJ 07732
732-291-5945

Sharon Matsumoto 90
c/o Tom Ang: The Winter House
766 N. Mentor Ave.
Pasadena, CA 91104

Tony Mauro 149
13791/2 Vienna Way
Venice, CA 90291
310-314-3669
em: tmauro@loop.com

Peter Max 106

Dave McKean 15, 24, 64, 120
c/o Allen Spiegel Fine Arts
221 Lobos Ave.
Pacific Grove, CA 93950
408-372-4672

Syd Mead 119

Petar Meseldzija 170, 171
Kogerwatering 49
1541XB Koog A/D Zaan
Netherlands
+31-75-6708649

Edward Miller 166
c/o Alan Lynch
11 King's Ridge Rd.
Long Valley, NJ 07853
908-813-8718

Kurt Mitchell 189
3004 W. 66th St.
Chicago, IL 60629
773-476-4429

Christopher Moeller 125, 152
210 Parkside Ave
Pittsburg, PA 15228
412-531-3629
em: moeller@aol.com

John Monteleone 154
138 Cleveland Ave.
Rockville Centre, NY 11570
516-594-9297

Chris Moore 42, 62
c/o Worlds of Wonder
P.O. Box 814
McLean, VA 22101
703-847-4251
em: chrismoore@illust.demon.co.uk

Clayburn Moore 94, 95
c/o Moore Creations
3038 SE Loop 820
Fort Worth, TX 76140
817-568-2620

Michel Morgenstern 128
429 East 73rd St.
New York, NY 10021
212-861-7391

John J Muth 66, 151
c/o Allen Spiegel Fine Arts
221 Lobos Ave.
Pacific Grove, CA 93950
408-372-4672

N

Vince Natale 28
P.O. Box 1353
Woodstock, NY 12498
914-679-0354

James Nelson 30
2011 W. Byron #2
Chicago, IL 60618
773-868-0803
em: mothman@sprintmail.com

Greg Newbold 28
1231 E. 6600 S.
Salt Lake City, UT 84121
801-268-2209
www.gregnewbold.com

Cliff Nielsen 64, 65
c/o Shannon Associates
327 E. 89th St./Box 3E
New York, NY 10128

Terese Nielsen 24, 57, 132
6049 Kauffman Ave.
Temple City, CA 91780
626-451-0454
em: tnielsen@flashcom.net

Nilson 182, 183
c/o Hamm
Fluegelstrasse 13
40227 Dusseldrorf, Germany
+49 211-78-86-28-7

Jason Nobriga 186
1212 8th Ave. #8
Honolulu, HI 96816
808-381-9913
em: jasonnob@lava.net

Lawrence Northey 96
9580 Kirkmond CR
Richmond, BC
Canada V7E 1M8
604-275-9594
www.homestead.com/robotart/pageone.html

O

Oddworld Inhabitants 21, 134
869 Monterey St.
San Luis Obispo, CA 93401

Eni Oken 66
11800 Goshen Ave. #302
Los Angeles, CA 90049
310-268-1006
em: eni@oken3d.com

Rafal Olbinski 14, 157
192 E. 35th St.
New York, NY 10016
212-532-4328

Glen Orbik 80, 82, 83
818-785-7904
818-908-9382 [fax]

P

Michael D. Page 161
1401 Dixwell Ave.
Hamden, CT 06514
203-281-6350

John Jude Palencar 48, 49, 108, 112, 113, 170
6763 Middlebrook Blvd.
Middleburg Hts., OH 44074
216-676-8839
em: jjp@apk.net

William Paquet 98, 103
127 Wall St
Belvidere, NJ 07823
908-475-3440

Paolo Parente 148
Via Trivulzio 30
Milano, Italy 20146
+39 02-404-9383
em: paoloparente@iol.it

Keith Parkinson 148
1681 W. Geranium Pl.
Oro Valley, AZ 85737
520-229-1621
em: keithparkinson@earthlink.net

Shawn Alan Peters 165
8439 Gardens Dr. #39-8
Sarasota, FL 34243
941-358-0364

Jeff Peterson 100
402 Oakland Ave.
Council Bluffs, IA 51503
712-325-1769

Stephen John Phillips 82
3 Hardy Court
Towson, MD 21204
410-583-6880

John Picacio 30
334 E. Craig Pl.
San Antonio, TX 78212
210-734-7671
em: picacio@texas.net

Drew Piece 74

Alan Pollack 177
20 Yard Ave
Freehold, NJ 07728
732-294-0456
em: alanpollack@studios.net

Greg Polutanovich 91, 100
22332 Paraguay Dr.
Saugus, CA 91350
661-296-4674

RK Post 134, 143
19205 78th St. E
Bonney Lake, WA 98390
253-862-8013
em: postrk@aol.com

John Pound 180
P.O. Box 6174
Eureka, CA 95502
707-444-8170
em: jpound@poundart.com

R

Ravenwood 78
c/o Sell, Inc.
333 N. Michigan Ave,/Rm. 800
Chicago, IL 60601

Omar Rayyan 124, 160, 187
P.O. Box 958
West Tisbury, MA 02575
508-693-5909
em: rayyan@tiac.net

Owen Richardson 137, 141
325 North 200 West
Salt Lake City, UT 84103
801-575-6147

Luis Royo 52
c/o Alan Lynch
11 King's Ridge Rd.
Long Valley, NJ 07853
908-813-8718

Steve Rude 38, 89
PO Box 660583
Arcadia, CA 91066-0583

Gary Ruddell 40
875 Las Ovejas Ave.
San Rafael, CA 94903
415-479-1016

Robh Ruppel 25
1639 Broadview
Glendale, CA 91208
818-249-9341
em: ruppel@earthlink.net

S

Dominick Saponaro 165
1626 South St. Apt. 3
Philadelphia, PA 19146
215-546-3199
em: dwsap@aol.com

Marc Sasso 120
27 General Heath Ave.
North White Plains, NY 10603
914-949-1949
em: blkmetal1@aol.com

Christopher Scalf 173
248-366-3066
em: chrisgs@netzero.com

Peter Scanlon 36
6 Cedar Lane
Closter, NJ 07624
201-750-0732

Don Seegmiller 22
1665 N. Main St.
Orem, Utah 84057
801-224-6635
em: don@saffire.com

David Seeley 120, 180, 181
102 South St./#4
Boston, MA 02111
617-423-3195
em: seeley@javanet.com

Christopher Shy 78
c/o Sirius Entertainment
264 E Blackwell St
Dover, NJ 07801
973-328-1455

Gregory S. Smith 92
4215 La Junta Drive
Claremont, CA 91711
909-596-1490

John K. Snyder III 84
1620 Argonne Pl. NW
Washington DC 20009-5901
202-265-0469

Joy Snyder 94
209 Sanora Blvd.
Sanford, FL 32773
407-322-4055

O.B. Solinsky 180
82-17 Grenfell St.
Kew Gardens, NY 11415
718-847-9169

Greg Spalenka 126
21303 San Miguel St
Woodland Hills, CA 91364
818-992-5828
em: greg@apalenka.com

Ron Spears 144
23306 SE 209th Pl.
Maple Valley, WA 98038
425-413-1184
em: ronspears@sprynet.com

Matt Stawicki 52
2503 Cratchett Rd.
Wilmington, DE 19808
302-993-0683

Jim Steranko 77

Dave Stevens 130

William Stout 74, 130, 131
1468 Loma Vista St.
Pasadena, CA 91104
626-798-6490
em: wmstout@bbs-la.com

Stu Suchit 114
117 Jayne Ave.
Port Jefferson, NY 11777
631-928-6775
em: stusuchit@aol.com

Jon Sullivan 44
c/o Alan Lynch
11 King's Ridge Rd.
Long Valley, NJ 07853
908-813-8718

Michael Sutfin 132
720 South Cross
Sycamore, IL 60178

Greg Swearingen 121
18900 Detroit Ext. #208
Cleveland, OH 44107-3255
216-226-7462

T

Jean Pierre Targete 28, 29
PO. Box 960955
Miami, FL 33296-0955
305-752-8545
em: jptargete@aol.com

Miles Teves 56
22243 Cass Ave.
Woodland Hills, CA 91364
818-883-2028
em: miles@milesteves.com

Jill Thompson 84, 88
c/o Sirius Entertainment
264 E Blackwell St
Dover, NJ 07801
973-328-1455

Jeral Tidwell 165
P.O. Box 4561
Louisville, KY 40204
502-454-9956
em: artboy@humantree.com

Chris Trevas 176
6010 Runnymeade Dr.
Canton, MI 48187
734-455-5882

Ezra Tucker 24
P.O. Box 1611
Monument, CO 80132
719-487-0648

Bleu Turrell 22
857 SE Stratford Ct.
Bend, OR 97702
541-617-1362
em: azulart@aol.com

V

John Van Fleet 61, 79
c/o Allen Spiegel Fine Arts
221 Lobos Ave.
Pacific Grove, CA 93950
408-372-4672

Ben Verkaaik 16
c/o David Bartels
3284 Ivanhoe Ave.
St. Louis, MO 63139
314-781-4350

Roxana Villa 112
P.O. Box 260485
Encino, CA 92426
818-906-3355

Jose Villarrubia 82
701 Cathedral St./Apt. 61
Baltimore, MD 21201
410-685-4890

W

James Warhola 118
56 Walkers Hill Rd.
Tivoli, NY 12583
914-757-3123

Ken Westphal 144
9208 Roe Ave.
Prairie Village, KS 66207
913-381-8399
em: ken@kenwestphal.com

Jennifer Emmett Weyland 173
RR8 Box 104
Cynthiana, KY 41031
606-234-4705
em: guiniver@setel.com

Michael Whelan 35, 158
P.O. Box 88
Brookfield, CT 06804
203-792-8089
em: whelanart@aol.com

Cathy Wilkins 176
fax: 302-993-0684

Bradley Williams 130
862 Holroyd Dr.
Ogden, UT 84403
801-479-8055
em: brad123@gateway.net

Kent Williams 72, 73, 116
c/o Allen Spiegel Fine Arts
221 Lobos Ave.
Pacific Grove, CA 93950
408-372-4672

Slawek Wojtowicz 20
33 Bissett Place
Metuchen, NJ 08840
732-548-1143
em: slawcio@interstat.net

Corey Wolfe 154
18612 NE Risto Rd.
Battle Ground, WA 98604
360-687-0699
www.coreywolfe.com

Thomas Christian Wolfe 110
c/o The Masterworks
P.O. Box 1221
Kilauea, HI 96754
808-828-0333
www.mythmaker.org

Ashley Wood 88, 129
660 Ocean Blvd.
Shell Beach, CA 93449
805-556-0738
em: ash@woodhaus.com

Christopher Wood 164
4540 S. Rural Rd. #P-4
Tempe, AZ 85282
602-775-6416
em: bigchris@cinematix.com

Ryan Wood 18
649 N. 650 West
American Fork, UT 84003
801-772-0958
em: ryemelog@juno.com

Ron Woodall 174
3160 Kerner Blvd.
San Rafael, CA 94901
em: woodall@ilm.com

Bill Wray 86
510 E. Laurel Ave.
Sierra Madre, CA 91024
626-836-5931

Y

Judy York 46
13 Buckingham Lane
Gaylordsville, CT 06755
860-354-1459
em: judy@mohawk.net

Paul Youll 31
c/o Alan Lynch
11 Kings Ridge Rd.
Long Valley, NJ 07853
908-813-8718
908-813-0076[fax]

Stephen Youll 62
296 Pegasus Rd.
Piscataway, NJ 08854
732-985-0086

Z

John Zeleznik 54, 56
25876 The Old Road/PMB #315
Stevenson Ranch, CA 91381
661-799-9987

Zook 179
577 Silver Berry Place
Encinitas, CA 92024
760-753-5378
em: jwatts@dellnet.com

Mark Zug 52, 122, 123

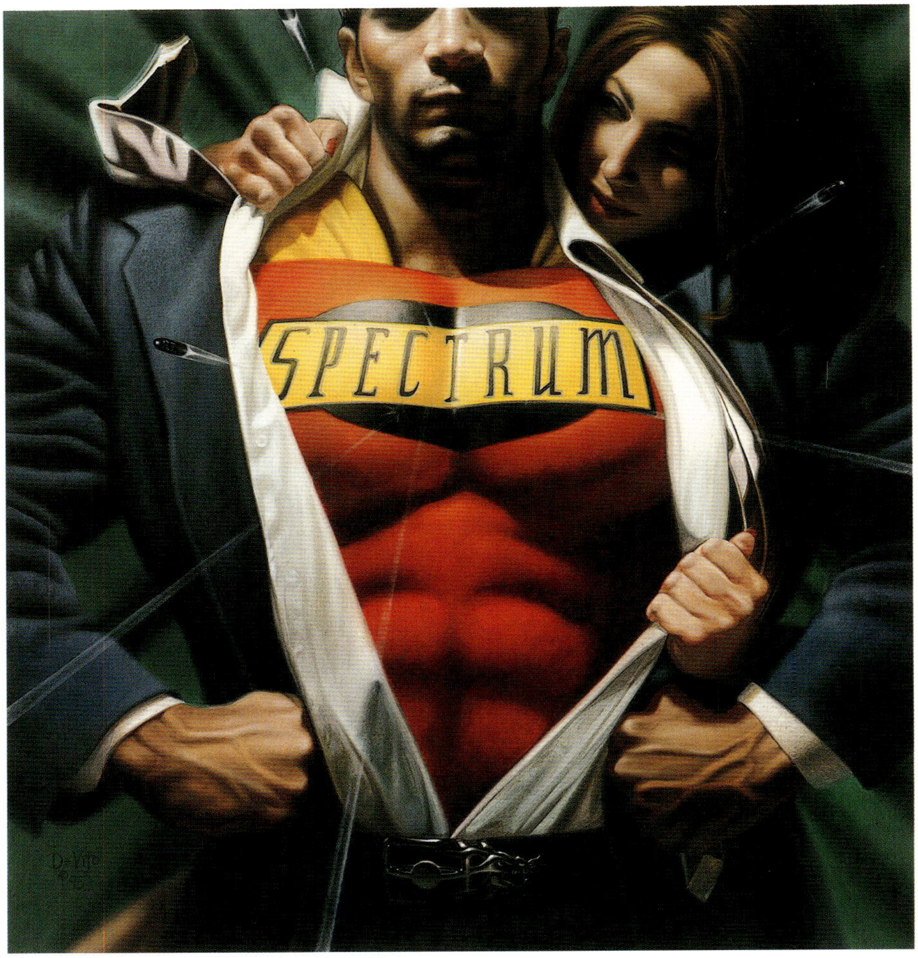

PAINTING BY JOSEPH DeVITO

This book was set in the Adobe version of the Caslon.
Spectrum 7 was designed on both a Macintosh G4
and a 7200Power PC.

Book design and typography by ***Arnie Fenner.***
Art direction and editing by ***Cathy Fenner*** and ***Arnie Fenner.***

Printed in Hong Kong.

ARTISTS, ART DIRECTORS AND PUBLISHERS INTERESTED IN RECEIVING ENTRY INFORMATION FOR THE NEXT SPECTRUM COMPETITION should send their name and address to:

Spectrum Design
P.O. Box 4422
Overland Park, KS
66204-0422

Call For Entries posters (which contain complete rules, fees, and forms for participation) are mailed out in Sept./Oct. each year.

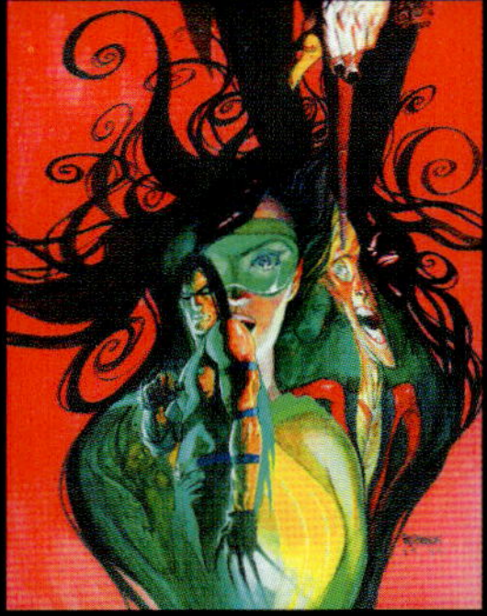
Andrew Robinson

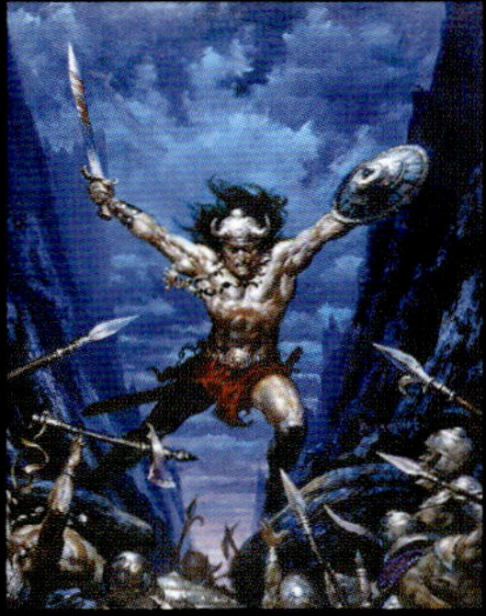
Doug Beekman

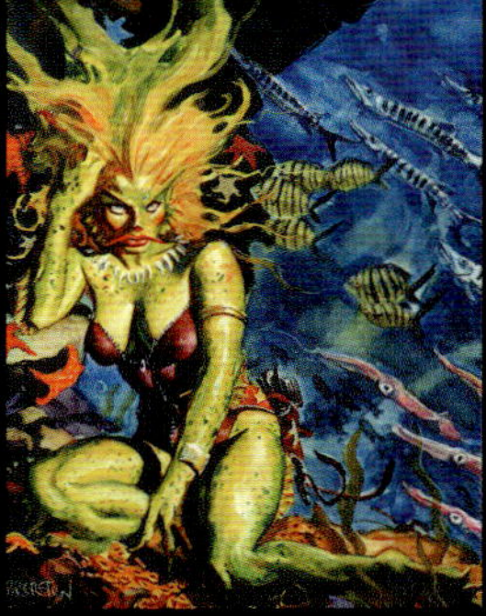
Dan Brereton

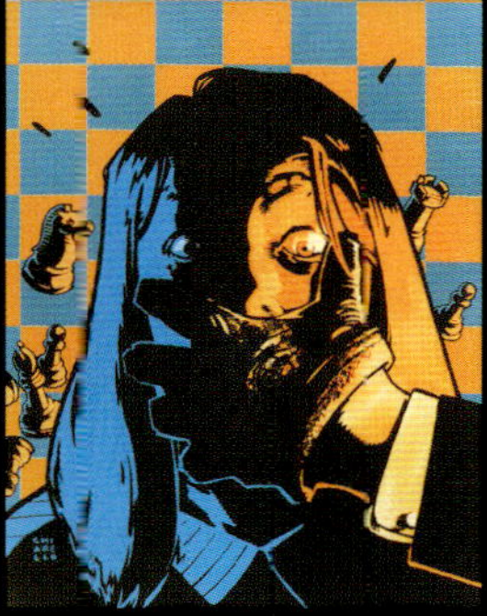
Mark Chiarello

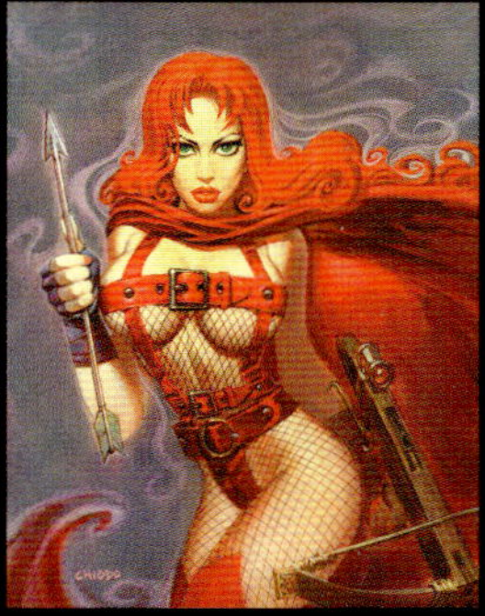
Joe Chiodo

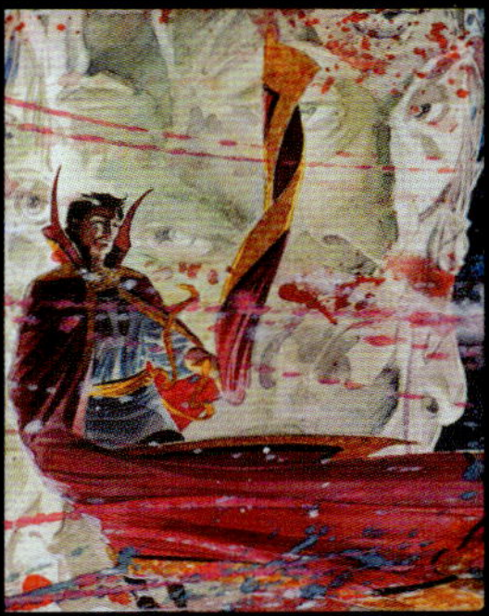
Dan Green

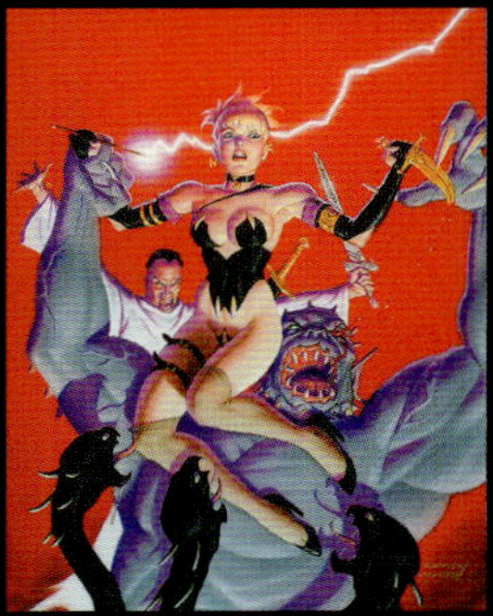
Fastner & Larson

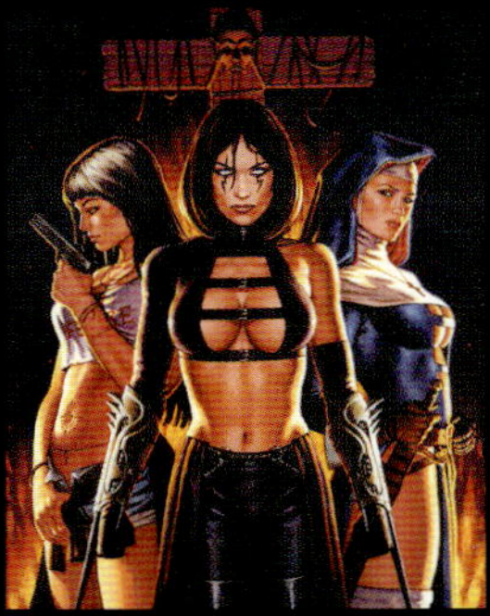
Dorian Cleavinger

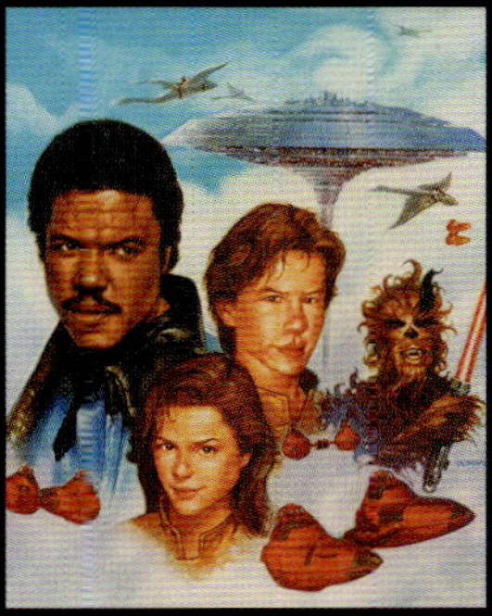
Dave Dorman

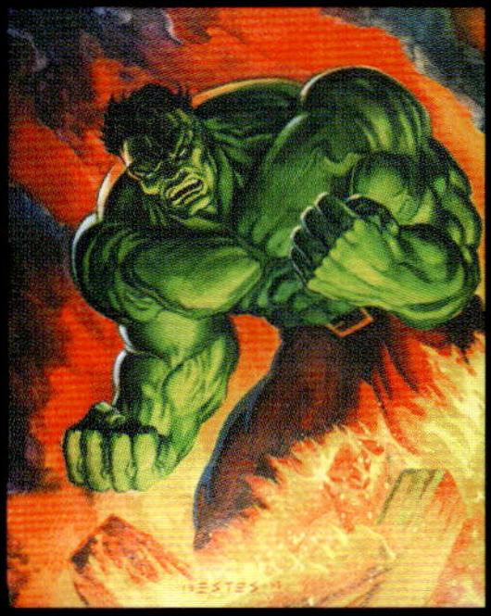
John Estes

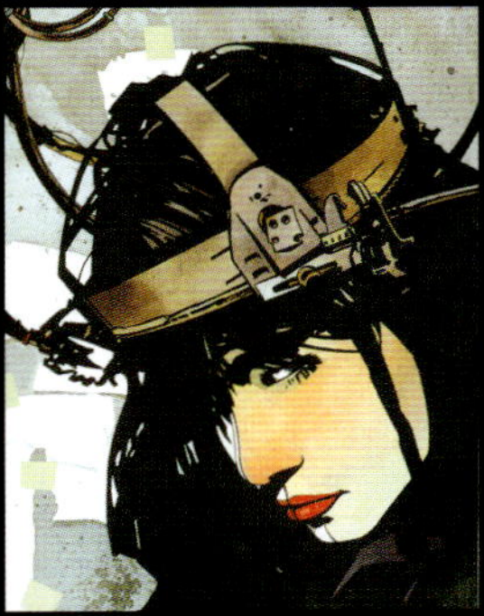
John Van Fleet

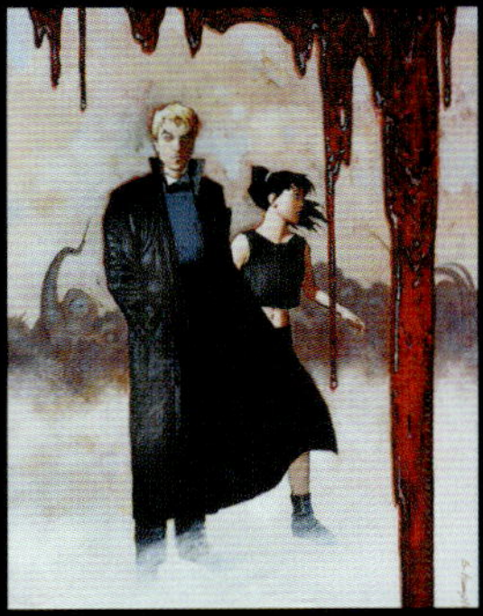
Scott Hampton

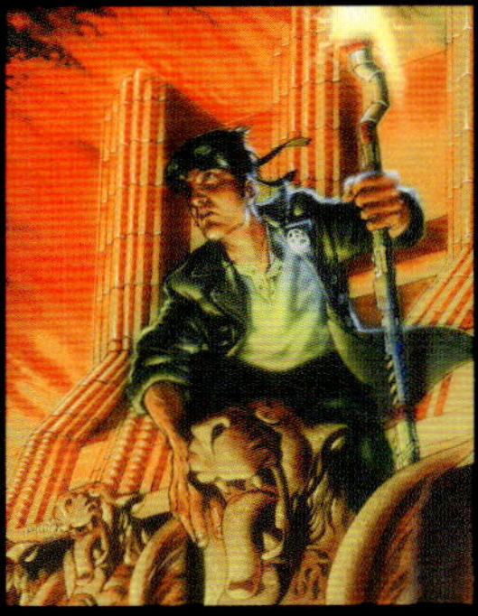
Tony Harris

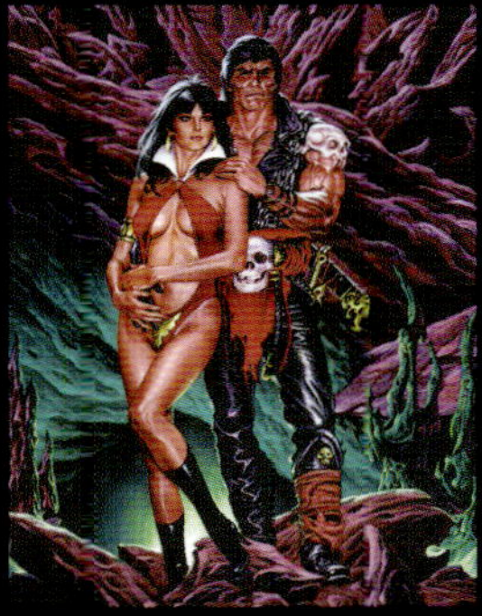
Joe Jusko

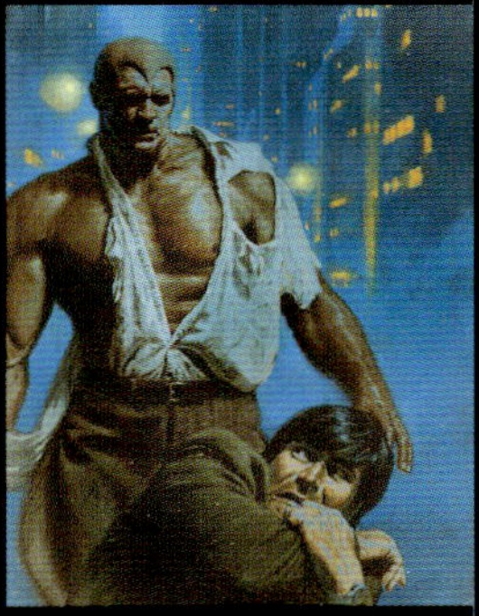
Bob Larkin

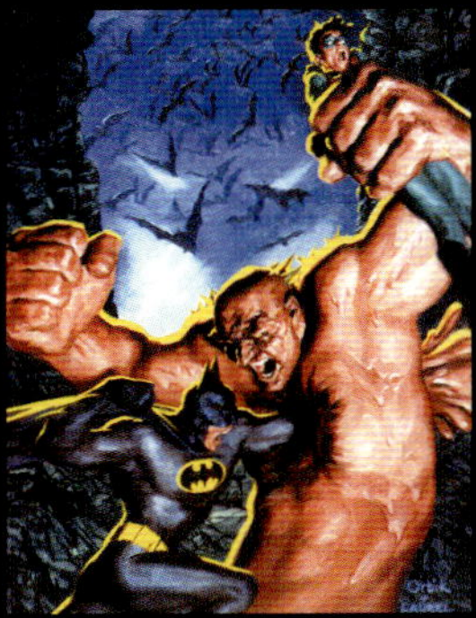
G. Orbik & L. Blechman

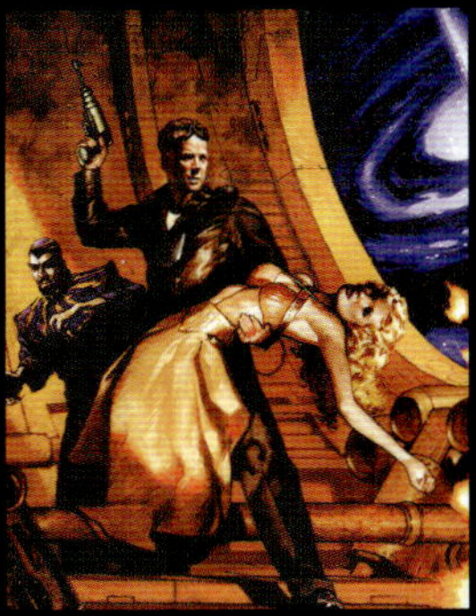
Chris Moeller

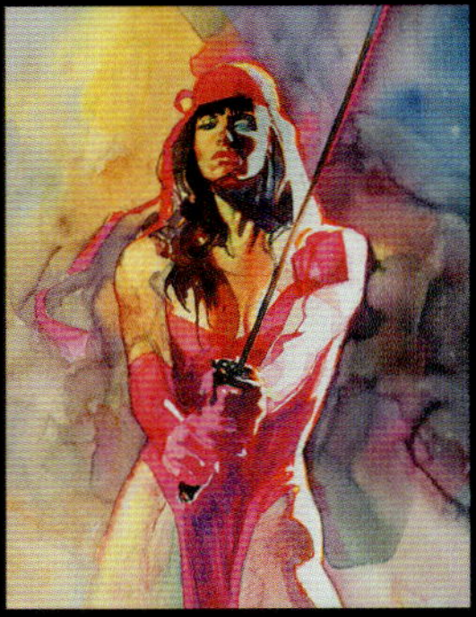
Bill Sienkiewicz

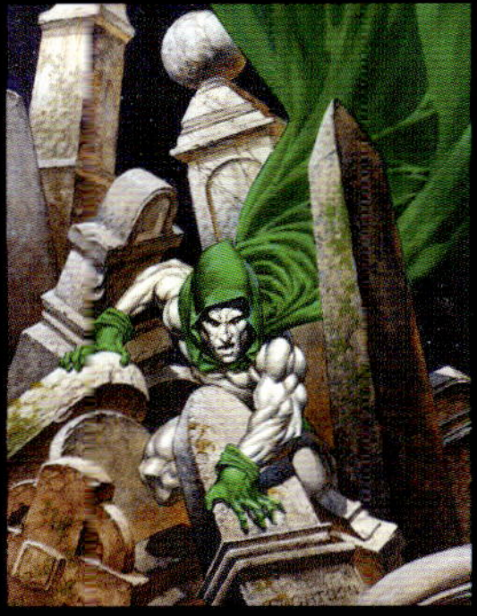
Bernie Wrightson

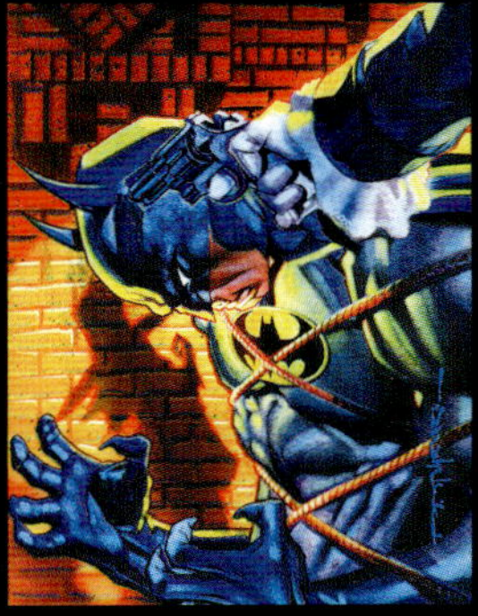
Brian Stelfreeze

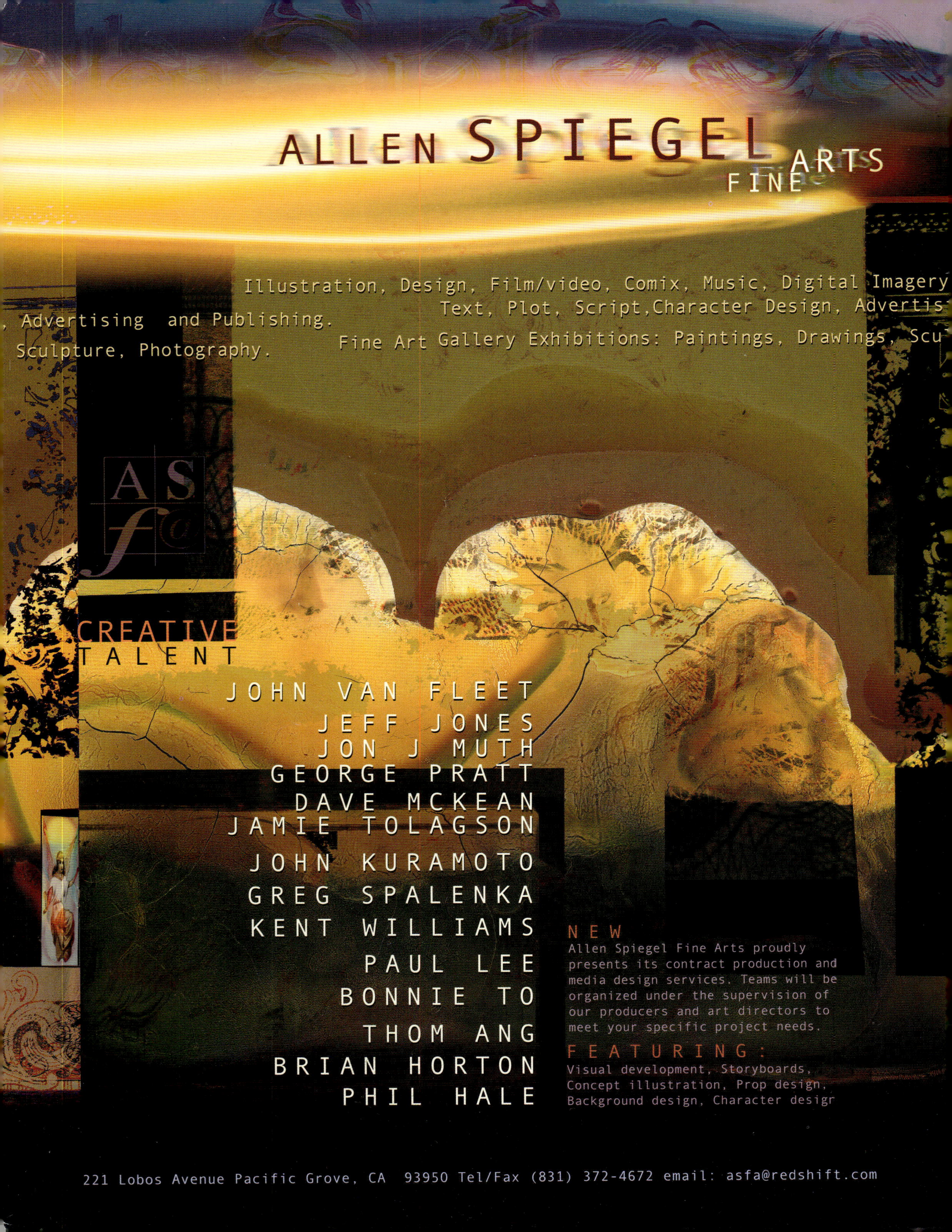
ALLEN SPIEGEL FINE ARTS
Illustration, Design, Film/video, Comix, Music, Digital Imagery
Text, Plot, Script, Character Design, Advertis
, Advertising and Publishing.
Sculpture, Photography.
Fine Art Gallery Exhibitions: Paintings, Drawings, Scu
ASfa
CREATIVE TALENT
JOHN VAN FLEET
JEFF JONES
JON J MUTH
GEORGE PRATT
DAVE MCKEAN
JAMIE TOLAGSON
JOHN KURAMOTO
GREG SPALENKA
KENT WILLIAMS
PAUL LEE
BONNIE TO
THOM ANG
BRIAN HORTON
PHIL HALE
NEW
Allen Spiegel Fine Arts proudly presents its contract production and media design services. Teams will be organized under the supervision of our producers and art directors to meet your specific project needs.
FEATURING:
Visual development, Storyboards, Concept illustration, Prop design, Background design, Character desigr
221 Lobos Avenue Pacific Grove, CA 93950 Tel/Fax (831) 372-4672 email: asfa@redshift.com